THE
SENATE
WATERGATE
REPORT

THE
SENATE
WATERGATE
REPORT

ABRIDGED

THE FINAL REPORT OF THE SENATE SELECT COMMITTEE
ON PRESIDENTIAL CAMPAIGN ACTIVITIES
(The Ervin Committee)

Introduction by
DANIEL SCHORR

CARROLL & GRAF PUBLISHERS
NEW YORK

THE SENATE WATERGATE REPORT
Abridged

Carroll & Graf Publishers
An Imprint of Avalon Publishing Group Inc.
245 West 17th Street
11th Floor
New York, NY 10011

AVALON
publishing group incorporated

The special contents of this edition are copyright © 1974 by
Herman Graf Associates, Inc.

Introduction copyright © 1974 by Daniel Schorr

First Carroll & Graf edition 2005

Library of Congress Cataloging-in-Publication Data is available.

ISBN-13: 978-0-78671-709-5
ISBN-10: 0-7867-1709-2

Printed in the United States of America
Distributed by Publishers Group West

Contents

*These, plus the individual views of Senator Weicker (pp. 643 ff. in this edition), comprise Chapter XI of the Report as released by the Committee.

*This chapter appears as Chapter VIII in the Report as printed by the Government Printing Office.

PUBLISHER'S NOTE

The Senate Watergate Report—or the Final Report of the Senate Senate Select Committee on Presidential Campaign Activities, as it was more formally known—was first published in a two-volume edition for bookstores in the summer of 1974. The Ervin Committee Report, as it was also known—named after its Chairman, Samuel J. Ervin, Jr., the senator from North Carolina—was published by Herman Graf Associates in association with Dell Books. For purposes of brevity, the 2005 edition of the work includes only Volume One, omitting the second volume's analysis of corporate contributions to the 1972 presidential campaign, and the use of computer technology in the Senate Committee's investigation. All of the contents, including Daniel Schorr's introduction, have been reproduced as they first appeared in the original edition.

THE
SENATE
WATERGATE
REPORT

INTRODUCTION

by Daniel Schorr

Let's go back on the wings of memory to recall some of those catchy lines that kept millions glued to daytime television.

MAURICE STANS: "Give me back my good name!"

JOHN DEAN: "A cancer growing on the Presidency."

JOHN EHRLICHMAN: "Twisting slowly, slowly in the wind."

PATRICK GRAY: "I carried out my orders and I destroyed them."

GORDON STRACHAN: "My advice would be to stay away!"

They ring so nostalgically now, like hit songs of the Nineteen Thirties. It is hard to imagine, so much has happened since, that it was the Summer of 1973 when the scene in the Senate Caucus Room dominated the living room and the cocktail lounge. Endless it seemed then, this drama of the Senate Select Committee on Presidential Campaign Activities, as it was known to almost nobody, or the Watergate Committee, as it was known to almost everybody. But now it shrinks into a brief interlude, and a prelude to greater events to follow on other stages.

The Watergate Committee's televised heyday, which left some shaking their heads and other shaking their fists, but sensitizing a nation to Watergate, represented just thirty-seven days of hearings, from May 17 to August 7. Then the Committee recessed, to return for sixteen more days of hearings, September 24 to November 15, by then losing public attention to the other dramas which the Senate investigation had helped to generate.

By the Fall a Special Prosecutor, Archibald Cox of Harvard, was circling the wagons drawn around the White House, getting fired, being replaced by Leon Jaworski of Texas, who would resume the siege. The House of Representatives, reacting mainly to the "Saturday Night Massacre" of Cox, along with the Justice Department's two top men, Elliot Richardson and William Ruckelshaus, was moving to mount an impeachment investigation.

The Watergate Committee found itself being brushed into the background. Some witnesses, facing indictment, became unavailable. Former Presidential Special Counsel Charles Colson, so eager to testify before the August recess, now took refuge behind the Fifth Amendment. Concern over pending indictments and trials forced postponement of hearings after November, and postponement finally turned into curtains for the public hearings. The Senate committee was looking for legislative remedies for Watergate, but the demand for surgery took precedence.

Senator Howard Baker's oft-repeated question, "What did the President know and when did he know it?" was less a question now for Caucus Room rhetoric when it had become a question in the Grand Inquest of the Nation.

So, the Watergate Committee, having helped to open the floodgate, was swept aside by the torrent. The television cameras shifted from the Caucus Room, like Omar's moving finger, to the next dramas. The Ervin Committee felt the sting of neglect, of defied subpenas and unimpressed judges.

No more the nation's gaze focussed on the Seven Senators, supported by pedantic-sounding Counsel Sam Dash and burly counter-thrusting Minority Counsel Fred Thompson, co-starring with the stellar cast of witnesses! No more those Senators playing their separate roles—Chairman Sam Ervin, the Bible-quoting "country lawyer"; Vice-Chairman Howard Baker, the mellifluous straddler; Herman Talmadge, the hard-bitten cross-examiner; Daniel K. Inouye, the soft-spoken rapier artist; Joseph M. Montoya, the earnest plodder; Edward J. Gurney, the angry defender, and Lowell P. Weicker, Jr., the avenging angel! In composite, the instrument of a unanimous Senate when the Senate could still be unanimous in demanding to know the great unknown of Watergate.

A cruel fate for the Committee which had, aided only by part of the news media, first dinned the magnitude of Watergate into a resistant public consciousness!

Cruel fate! The Committee could not even get what it had unearthed—the Presidential tapes. They had been discovered, by inspired staff interrogation of former White House Aide Alexander Butterfield in executive session. They eventually went to the Grand Jury, to the House Judiciary Committee, to the Mitchell-Stans trial jury in New York, to the lawyers in the Ralph Nader milk-price suit. But the courts denied access for the Ervin Committee. In October, 1973, as part of a plan to isolate Prosecutor Cox, President Nixon offered Senators Ervin and Baker transcripts to be prepared by Senator John Stennis. But that plan quickly collapsed. So, Moses-like, the Watergate Committee led other investigators to the Promised Land of Presidential tapes, and never got to enjoy them. But, by opening up this Comstock Lode for other prospectors, the Committee changed the course of history.

The tapes—the decisive evidence which put the White House thereafter on the defensive, wrestling with prosecutors, resisting subpenas, explaining mysterious gaps, releasing selected transcripts—would be enough to earn the Watergate Committee its place in history. But there was more. It is debatable whether the re-invigorated prosecution and the impeachment inquiry would have happened at all had the Senate investigation not turned illegality, corruption and impropriety in high places into a national issue. It is hard to remember, looking now at the gashed investigative landscape, how hard it was to cut the first furrow. Now that we know so much, we can hardly recollect how it was when we knew so little.

Remember how it was at the end of the first Watergate trial in January, 1973, when the book was closed with seven men adjudged guilty on the strength of a prosecution theory of an enclosed conspiracy, led by H. Gordon Liddy, using misappropriated campaign funds to go off on an adventure of his own?

Chief Judge John J. Sirica of the Federal District Court was frank to say that the trial he had conducted had failed to get to the bottom of the case, and that he looked to Congress to succeed where he had failed.

"Everybody knows," said Judge Sirica on February 2, "there's going to be a Congressional investigation in this case. I would hope, frankly, not only as a judge, but as a citizen of a great country and one of millions of Americans who are looking for certain answers—I would hope that the Senate committee is granted power by Congress by a broad enough resolution to get to the bottom of what happened in this case."

There were, we now know, other forces of disintegration at work within the cover-up. Those whose silence had been induced were becoming increasingly restive about money and about the prospects for clemency. James McCord, burning with resentment about the higher-ups still free while he faced rotting in prison, was preparing to shake the scotch-taped structure with his "J'accuse!" letter to Judge Sirica.

But something more was needed, and if a conspiracy within the Executive could not be breached by the Judiciary, perhaps it could be breached by the Legislative branch.

Quietly, within days after the Watergate break-in on June 17, 1972, the staff of Senator Edward Kennedy's Judiciary Subcommittee on Administrative Practice and Procedure had started its own investigation. It issued subpenas to tie down witnesses and prevent further shredding of files. And, in a "routine" activities report to the Judiciary Committee on January 22, 1973, it said that there appeared to be "a wide range of espionage and sabotage activities" during the Presidential campaign, warranting a "comprehensive inquiry," which would require "the calling of various Executive Branch and White House personnel."

·The Senate Democrats were impressed. But Senator Kennedy, scarred by Chappaquidick and a potential Presidential contender, could hardly lead such an investigation. It would have to be, the Democratic Caucus concluded, a special committee of respected lawyers without known Presidential ambitions (which one or two would acquire only after national exposure).

The prospect of a Senate investigation hung like a specter over the Oval Office. From tapes and testimony we have now learned how it dominated tortured White House strategy sessions, which explored avenues of escape like hiding behind Executive privilege, the Fifth Amendment, a bogus John Dean "report," a Warren-type special commission, or even, as a last resort, the Grand Jury.

Long before there was an Ervin Committee, the White House, having successfully contained the first Watergate prosecution and blocked an inquiry by the House Banking Committee, began to view the Senate as the looming threat.

In December, 1972, Dean testified, the White House was already sounding out Senator Henry M. Jackson about the prospects for a Senate investigation. (He didn't know.) In January, when Majority Leader Mike Mansfield proposed holding hearings, the White House tried to steer them towards Senator James Eastland's Judiciary Committee, regarded as the friendliest possible forum. On February 5, Senator Ervin introduced Resolution 60—unanimously adopted two days later—to create a Select Committee. Dean said the White House then became actively alarmed that "we were fast moving into an uncontrollable, if not hostile forum."

Hectic consultations culminated in a high-level strategy session on February 9 and 10 at La Costa Hotel and H. R. Haldeman's villa at San Clemente. According to Dean, a strategy was laid down as follows, "The White House will take a public posture of full cooperation, but privately will attempt to restrain the investigation and make it as difficult as possible to get information and witnesses."

Increasingly haunted by fear of the oncoming probe, the men in the White House thrashed around to implement that strategy, their labors documented in the incomplete Presidential tape transcripts.

On February 28, the President discussed with Dean such options as preparing a statement for the Committee, but refusing to testify; trying to get the hearings into executive session, away from public view, as much as possible; trying to get Chairman Ervin to enforce courtroom rules of evidence. The President: "We can try to get some pieces out to try to get a little pressure on him to perform that way, to make it look partisan when he doesn't . . . This will be a model of Congressional hearing that will disappoint the (adjective deleted) press. No hearsay! No innuendo! No leaks!"

"It is important," said Mr. Nixon, "in the sense that all this business is a battle, and they are going to wage the battle."

On March 13, the President talked with Dean of refusing to let him, H. R. Haldeman, John Ehrlichman or Charles Colson testify. The President: "We will cooperate with the Committee under the rules I have laid down in my statement on executive privilege . . . We said we will furnish information, but we are not going to be called to testify . . . My feeling is that I better hit it now rather than just let it build up where we are afraid of these questions and everybody, etc."

And, later in that conversation: "When will the Ervin thing be hitting the fan? Most any day? . . . Well, it must be a big show. Public hearings I wouldn't think, though. I know from experience, my guess is that I think they could get through in about three weeks of those, and then I think it would begin to peter out somewhat . . . Our members of the committee should at least say, 'Let's get it over with, and go through five-day sessions, etc.' "

On March 17, Mr. Nixon expressed concern to Dean that the Ervin Committee would go into the break-in on Daniel Ellsberg's psychiatrist. The President: "I can't see that getting into, into this hearing . . . It's irrelevant . . . That's the point. That's where—that's where—where Ervin's rules of relevancy (unintelligible) . . ."

On March 21, the climactic meeting in the Oval Office with Dean and Haldeman, the alarm so great that the President was ready to propose a Grand Jury inquiry to forestall the Senate investigation. The President: "Is there some way that we can get our story before a Grand Jury? . . . I want everybody in the White House called, and that gives you a reason not to have to go before the Ervin and Baker committee. It puts it into executive session, in a sense . . . You can say, 'I don't remember.' You can say, 'I can't recall. I can't give any answer to that that I can recall.' . . . Suppose we have a Grand Jury thing. What would that do to the Ervin Committee? Would it go right ahead?" Discouragingly,

Dean replied, "Probably, probably."

Mr. Nixon grasped for another straw. "How about a special prosecutor? We could use (Henry) Peterson, or use another one."

The President explored another possibility—a Dean "report." The President: "You could say that 'now that the hearings are going on, I can now give a report that we can put out.' . . . The fact that cover-up—I am not sure. Maybe I am wrong. The fact that the President says, 'I have shown Ervin. Remember, we had nobody there.' I think that something has to go first. We need to put something out . . .And then I offer the Ervin Committee report this way. I say, 'Dear Senator Ervin: Here is the report before your hearings. You have this report and, as I have said previously, any questions that are not answered here, you can call the White House staff member. And they will be directed to answer any questions on an informal basis (inaudible)." Haldeman commented, "Yeah." The idea didn't seem to fly. At the close of the meeting Mr. Nixon reflected, "What the hell does one disclose that isn't going to blow something?"

But next day, March 22, they were back seeking ways of thwarting the Senate investigation. Mr. Nixon said he had heard from Senator Baker that "he did not think Ervin would accept the written interrogatories and that they would probably go to subpena." So, they talked of making White House witnesses available under negotiated conditions. The President brooded, "This thing could go on for a hell of a long time." They talked of trying to lure the Senate committee into a time-consuming court test of executive privilege. They talked of naming a special Presidential commission. Ehrlichman: "You can call Ervin down. You can tell him the plans and explain why you're doing it, that justice is not being carried out now, there's finger-pointing and a lot of problems. And you ask him to hold his hearings in abeyance until the panel serves its purpose."

But painfully they seemed to realize that nothing might work and that the principals might, after all, end up before the Senate committee. President Nixon, in a passage deleted from the White House transcript and supplied by the House Judiciary Committee, gave orders to John Mitchell: "I don't give a ——— what happens. I want you to (unintelligible) stonewall it, plead the Fifth Amendment (unintelligible) else, if it'll (unintelligible). That's the big point . . . The whole theory has been containment, as you know, John."

By April 14 the President was exploring with Haldeman and Ehrlichman whether the indictment of Mitchell and Jeb Magruder would serve to stave off the Ervin hearings.

The President: "I think Ervin's best bet is to suspend as soon as these indictments are announced. If he were smart, that's what he'd do, and then just let this thing (unintelligible), and then come around afterwards and punch up places that they missed. Just go around the battlefield and get the Croix de Guerre."

There was more—much more—talk reflecting obsession with the Senate investigation, mostly in terms of what its impact on the public might be. There was a detailed discussion of whether the hearings, if they could not be kept private, could be kept off television, or at least off evening television.

On April 16, the transcripts show, President Nixon was still trying to get the hearings postponed, finding new opportunity in the word he had just gotten from Attorney General Richard Kleindienst that Jeb Magruder had confessed and the prosecutors were closing in. The President told Assistant Attorney General Henry Peterson, "You've got to tell Senator Ervin that his continued investigation will jeopardize the rights of the defendants and also will jeopardize the possibilities of prosecution."

But Senator Ervin stood firm, and the President retreated. Next day, announcing unspecified "major developments" in the Watergate case, the President stated on television that "all members of the White House staff will appear voluntarily when asked by the Ervin Committee." But with two reservations, or desperate hopes—"in executive session, if appropriate," and "executive privilege is expressly reserved and may be asserted during the course of the questioning as to any questions."

One month later, on May 17, the hearings opened in the cavernous Senate Caucus Room, whose panelled walls held the echoes of earlier historic confrontations like Army-McCarthy and the Kefauver crime hearings. But the Caucus Room had never been the scene for an issue so large. As Senator Ervin defined it in his opening statement, what this was about was "the very undergirding of our democracy . . . the right to vote in a free election . . . a black cloud of distrust over our entire society."

In the way that it only does for great moments in history, television dropped everything to focus collectively on "gavel-to-gavel" coverage. In the coming weeks, America sat through two billion viewing hours—an average of thirty hours per household—of Watergate hearings—many of them avidly, some of them resentfully, wondering where the scheduled soap operas had gone. But, for some of those the Watergate hearings, with a tearful Strachan, a mocking

Ehrlichman, a stonewalling Mitchell, became a soap opera itself. And, in the end, having drifted to rotating coverage, selective coverage and then no coverage, the networks were surprised to learn that their aggregate audience during the hearings was greater than it would have been with normal programming.

Beyond the public impact, another heritage was left to the prosecutors, the impeachers and history in the record of the hearings, packed into thirteen green-covered volumes. On that record Haldeman was indicted three times and Mitchell once for perjury—Mitchell for having testified that he had not heard of the Gemstone wiretap files when he met with campaign aides two days after the Watergate break-in, Haldeman for having testified of his ignorance of hush money, of the President's rejection of the idea of paying further money for silence, and of not knowing about Jeb Magruder's perjury.

In that record also was a spate of exhibits—once-secret documents, many of which John Dean had taken with him from the White House. There were documents that revealed Ehrlichman as having approved, "if not traceable," a covert attempt to get Daniel Ellsberg's psychiatric file. There was Charles Colson's memo warning that the President might be implicated in the ITT affair. The treasure trove of documents became vital raw material for the Special Prosecutor and for the House impeachment inquiry. Counsel Dash says that perhaps ninety per cent of the information of the House Committee came from the Senate Committee.

The fifty-three days of hearings were not the end of the Senate investigation. In anticipation of resumed hearings, and even when it had become clear that they would not be resumed, the staff pressed on, behind closed doors, with its investigation of such matters as the mysterious $100,000 transaction between Howard Hughes and the President's friend, Charles "Bebe" Rebozo; the link bewteen the dairy producers' $2,000,000 campaign pledge and Administration concessions such as the 1971 milk subsidy increase; the "Responsiveness Program" for funneling Government contracts, grants and jobs where they would do the most good for the Nixon campaign. All this also went to those investigating the President and those investigating his subordinates.

History may one day record how much the Senate Watergate Committee, even after being relegated to the back seat, did to help those in the drivers' seats.

Another impact of the Committee's work came from news leaks. Periodically there appeared eye-popping stories from anonymous sources. Herbert Kalmbach had testified that

Rebozo had told him of giving Hughes money to President Nixon's brothers and to his secretary, Rose Mary Woods. Dairy Lobbyist Jake Jacobsen was saying he had given $15,000 to former Secretary of the Treasury John Connally in cash. The campaign managers for Senator Hubert Humphrey and Rep. Wilbur Mills were taking the Fifth Amendment and refusing to explain how some campaign money was handled. "We didn't invent the leak," says Senator Baker, "but we raised it to its highest art form."

Committee Counsel Sam Dash deplored the leaks, and said he was sure his staff was not responsible for them. The leaks seldom occurred before the staff reports were distributed to the seven senators on the committee. Without defending—or, for that matter, criticizing—the widespread leaks, perhaps it will appear, in retrospect, that they were an inevitable part of the unprecedented process of disclosure. Early in the game Senator Ervin said that it was "more important that the American people get the truth than that a few people go to jail." Leaks were certaintly not the most orderly way of providing the truth; for those hurt by them, they were an outrageous way. But the leaks seemed unstoppable, as though the cover-up constipation had produced a reaction in a disclosure diarrhea.

But leaking time is over, for the final report is here. Its preparation was the third important phase of the Senate inquiry, following the hearings and the post-hearings investigation. It was the phase which, for this reporter, produced one of the greatest surprises. For it has turned out to be a much more unified, integrated and bi-partisan product than could have been anticipated.

The early appearance of bi-partisanship had seemed to have long since dissolved under the strain of contentious issues. The majority staff drafted a report that produced indignation on the minority side and the threat that it would be challenged by dissenting reports. But, in the end, the committee was seized with a renewed spirit of bi-partisanship In round-the-clock negotiation against an oft-postponed deadline, the draft underwent a metamorphosis of softening, balancing and harmonization.

Ironically, it was just about the time that the House Judiciary Committee was falling into partisan squabbles that the aging Watergate parents re-united in a semblance of mellowing harmony. After all the storm and stress that attended the seventeen-month travail of the Senate Select Committee, nothing seemed to become it more than the manner of its expiring.

It is all there now in the report—some things we have

known, but not so fully, and some things we have not known. There are also broad legislative proposals, which, to the extent that they are not already on their way to enactment, will probably go the way of most investigative recommendations—onto the shelf. The answer to Watergate, indeed, may not lie in new statutes. For Watergate, some believe, was not so much a failure of law as a failure of men using their positions to subvert law and the Constitution. So, while laws may need to be changed, that appears to have a lower priority than the issue now being dealt with in the courts and in the impeachment process—the officials who may need to be changed. But, in that process, the Senate investigation has played its part, as in 1924, when a Federal Grand Jury handed up indictments in the Teapot Dome scandal only after Congressional hearings.

There are many lessons to be drawn from this exhaustive report of an exhausted committee. Permit one weary Watergate wallower to stress one theme that seems to be subtly interwoven through the fabric of the pages that follow.

If one stands back, one sees now that June 17, 1972, when the plain-clothes police found the burglar-wiretappers in the office of the Democratic National Committee, was not the beginning or the end of the affair, but just the time that something much larger broke to the surface and thereby got a name—Watergate.

Oddly, the break-in itself remains still partly an unsolved mystery. Some of the planners and participants say they are still not sure why it was ordered. Certainly the Cuban-Americans—called "jackasses" by President Nixon for their pains—must now know that the mission was not meant to uncover Castro financing of Senator McGovern.

More likely, it has been suggested, a primary motive was to try to get something on Democratic National Chairman Lawrence O'Brien, apparently out of fear among President Nixon's people that he might have something on *them*. O'Brien had worked for Howard Hughes, and might therefore know about the Hughes-Rebozo transaction, and about how Hughes lieutenants had used the President's brother, Donald. So there was fear of Larry O'Brien.

It was fear that seemed the dominant theme, along with the unrestrained use of power prompted by that fear.

Watergate had to be covered up, partly out of fear that its exposure would hurt the President's re-election prospects, but more importantly, according to John Mitchell, out of fear that the previous "White House horrors" would come to light.

Those horrors—wiretapping, surveillance, break-ins,

planned smears—had in turn been prompted by earlier fears—fear of Daniel Ellsberg, fear of Senators Kennedy and Muskie, fear of anyone who could conceivably stand in the way of a massive re-election victory.

There was fear of exposure of millions of dollars in secret money, which had been amassed in fear that there would never be quite enough to insure triumph at the polls.

Many of the fears appear now to have been self-generated. O'Brien apparently did not know any dire things. Mr. Nixon's re-election, as former Campaign Chairman Clark McGregor has observed, was never really in doubt since the Summer of 1971.

One can only speculate on the source of that pervasive fear. Perhaps it was that Mr. Nixon had too often lost, or come close to losing, to face the next contest with equanimity. A lesson could have been learned from a previous occupant of the White House, Franklin D. Roosevelt, that "there is nothing to fear but fear itself."

But to be able to apply that lesson would have required inner resources of confidence, some confidence about the working of democracy without manipulation, some perception of the outside world in terms other than "enemies," and some restraint about the uses of entrusted power.

Because these attributes were lacking, there were, instead, self-defeating schemes, overkill, paranoia. There was Watergate.

THE FINAL REPORT
OF THE

SELECT COMMITTEE
ON
PRESIDENTIAL
CAMPAIGN ACTIVITIES

PURSUANT TO
S. RES. 60, FEBRUARY 7, 1973

A resolution to establish a Select Committee
of the Senate to investigate and study illegal
or improper campaign activities in the
Presidential election of 1972

JUNE 1974

MEMBERS OF THE
SELECT COMMITTEE ON PRESIDENTIAL CAMPAIGN ACTIVITIES

Senator Sam J. Ervin, Jr., North Carolina,
Chairman

Senator Howard H. Baker, Jr., Tennessee,
Vice-Chairman

Senator Herman E. Talmadge, Georgia

Senator Daniel K. Inouye, Hawaii

Senator Joseph M. Montoya, New Mexico

Senator Edward J. Gurney, Florida

Senator Lowell P. Weicker, Jr., Connecticut

3

ADMINISTRATIVE STAFF

Carolyn M. Andrade, *Administrative Assistant*

Laura Matz,* *Administrative Assistant*

Carolyn E. Cohen, *Office Manager*

SUBCOMMITTEE ON SEPARATION OF POWERS PERSONNEL
(On loan to Select Committee)

Walker F. Nolan, Jr.,* *Counsel*

J. L. Pecore,* *Assistant Counsel*

This edition omits the names of many members of the various staffs that produced the Committee's Report. Their names are to be found in the Government Printing Office edition.

* Indicates that the person was not with the Select Committee at the time of the filing of this report but had during the life of the Committee been a member of he staff.

4

PREFACE

This report represents the culmination of one and a half years' work of the Senate Select Committee on Presidential Campaign Activities. Our mandate was Senate Resolution 60, adopted on February 7, 1973 by a Senate vote of 77-0, which directed the Select Committee to make one of the most comprehensive investigations in the history of Congress. Although the task given to the Committee appeared in the beginning to be hardly possible to fully accomplish, I am pleased to report at the end of our work that the Committee did, in fact, successfully complete the mission given it by S. Res. 60.

It is a matter of special satisfaction and pride to me that our committee assumed its responsibility initially in a bipartisan manner, and despite all the pressures inherent in such a highly politically charged investigation, ended its work in a bipartisan manner. This report is a unanimous report of the full Committee.

I wish to express my deep appreciation and gratitude for the untiring and dedicated contributions and support of all the members of the Committee. Without their sacrifice, valuable advice and whole-hearted participation our task would not have been so fully accomplished.

I wish to expecially express my gratitude and admiration for the remarkably splendid and professional job done by the Committee's Chief Counsel, Sam Dash. His was the responsibility to plan and supervise the investigation, the presentation of witnesses at our hearings and the preparation of the report. Our hearings and report are a tribute to his excellent fulfillment of this responsibility.

The staff who worked under Professor Dash's supervision were exceptionally able and talented young men and women. They were given a herculean task and proved equal to the challenge. The Committee is indebted to them for their tireless and inspired efforts, involving, through most of the Committee's existence, late evening hours, seven days a week. Special recognition should be given to Assistant Chief Counsel, David Dorsen, James Hamilton and Terry Lenzner. The bipartisan constructive effort and cooperation of Minority Counsel Fred Thompson and his staff helped the Committee to complete its work with one unanimously approved report.

A Select Committee, such as ours, created by the Senate for a special function, appears briefly on the Nation's scene, does its work and disappears. It is my firm belief that the bright light this Committee has shed on the matter given it to study illuminated the American public's understanding and consciousness of the Watergate affair and will not quickly fade.

SAM J. ERVIN, JR.
Chairman

SENATOR SAM J. ERVIN, JR.
Chairman

Since the Senate Select Committee on Presidential Campaign Activities is filing with the Senate its final report concerning the investigation that body authorized and directed it to make, I deem it appropriate to state as succinctly as possible some of my personal observations respecting the tragic events known collectively as the Watergate, which disgraced the presidential election of 1972.

In doing this, I ask and endeavor to answer these questions: What was Watergate? Why was Watergate? Is there an antidote which will prevent future Watergates? If so, what is that antidote?

Before attempting to answer these questions, I wish to make these things plain:

1. I am not undertaking to usurp and exercise the power of impeachment, which the Constitution confers upon the House of Representatives alone. As a consequence, nothing I say should be construed as an expression of an opinion in respect to the question of whether or not President Nixon is impeachable in connection with the Watergate or any other matter.

2. Inasmuch as its Committee on the Judiciary is now studying whether or not it ought to recommend to the House the impeachment of the President, I shall also refrain from making any comment on the question of whether or not the President has performed in an acceptable manner his paramount constitutional obligation "to take care that the laws be faithfully executed."

3. Watergate was not invented by enemies of the Nixon Administration or even by the news media. On the contrary, Watergate was perpetrated upon America by White House and political aides, whom President Nixon himself had entrusted with the management of his campaign for reelection to the Presidency, a campaign which was divorced to a marked degree from the campaigns of other Republicans who sought election to public office in 1972. I note at this point without elaboration that these White House and political aides were virtually without experience in either government or politics apart from their association with President Nixon.

4. Life had not subjected these White House and political aides to the disadvantaged conditions which are glibly cited

7

as the causes of wrongdoing. On the contrary, fortune had smiled upon them. They came from substantial homes, possessed extraordinary talents, had had unusual educational opportunities, and occupied high social positions.

5. Watergate was unprecedented in the political annals of America in respect to the scope and intensity of its unethical and illegal actions. To be sure, there had been previous milder political scandals in America history. That fact does not excuse Watergate. Murder and stealing have occurred in every generation since earth began, but that fact has not made murder meritorious or larceny legal.

What Was Watergate?

President Nixon entrusted the management of his campaign for reelection and his campaign finances to the Committee for the Reelection of the President, which was headed by former Attorney General John N. Mitchell, and the Finance Committee to Reelect the President, which was headed by former Secretary of Commerce, Maurice Stans. Since the two committees occupied offices in the same office building in Washington and worked in close conjunction, it seems proper to call them for ease of expression the Nixon Reelection Committees.

Watergate was a conglomerate of various illegal and unethical activities in which various officers and employees of the Nixon Reelection Committees and various White House aides of President Nixon participated in varying ways and degrees to accomplish these successive objectives:

1. To destroy insofar as the presidential election of 1972 was concerned the integrity of the process by which the President of the United States is nominated and elected.

2. To hide from law enforcement officers, prosecutors, grand jurors, courts, the news media, and the American people the identities and wrongdoing of those officers and employees of the Nixon Reelection Committees, and those White House aides who had undertaken to destroy the integrity of the process by which the President of the United States is nominated and elected.

To accomplish the first of these objectives, the participating officers and employees of the Reelection Committees and the participating White House aides of President Nixon engaged in one or more of these things:

1. They exacted enormous contributions—usually in cash—from corporate executives by impliedly implanting in their minds the impressions that the making of the con-

tributions was necessary to insure that the corporations would receive governmental favors, or avoid governmental disfavors while President Nixon remained in the White House. A substantial portion of the contributions were made out of corporate funds in violation of a law enacted by Congress a generation ago.

2. They hid substantial parts of these contributions in cash in safes and secret deposits to conceal their sources and the identities of those who had made them.

3. They disbursed substantial portions of these hidden contributions in a surreptitious manner to finance the bugging and the burglary of the offices of the Democratic National Committee in the Watergate complex in Washington for the purpose of obtaining political intelligence; and to sabotage by dirty tricks, espionage and scurrilous and false libels and slanders the campaigns and the reputations of honorable men, whose only offenses were that they sought the nomination of the Democratic Party for President and the opportunity to run against President Nixon for that office in the presidential election of 1972.

4. They deemed the departments and agencies of the Federal Government to be the political playthings of the Nixon Administration rather than impartial instruments for serving the people, and undertook to induce them to channel federal contracts, grants, and loans to areas, groups, or individuals so as to promote the reelection of the President rather than to further the welfare of the people.

5. They branded as enemies of the President individuals and members of the news media who dissented from the President's policies and opposed his reelection, and conspired to urge the Department of Justice, the Federal Bureau of Investigation, the Internal Revenue Service, and the Federal Communications Commission to pervert the use of their legal powers to harass them for so doing.

6. They borrowed from the Central Intelligence Agency disguises which E. Howard Hunt used in political espionage operations, and photographic equipment which White House employees known as the "Plumbers" and their hired confederates used in connection with burglarizing the office of a psychiatrist which they believed contained information concerning Daniel Ellsberg which the White House was anxious to secure.

7. They assigned to E. Howard Hunt, who was at the time a White House consultant occupying an office in the Executive Office Building, the gruesome task of falsifying State Department documents which they contemplated using in their altered state to discredit the Democratic Party by

9

defaming the memory of former President John Fitzgerald Kennedy, who as the hapless victim of an assassin's bullet had been sleeping in the tongueless silence of the dreamless dust for nine years.

8. They used campaign funds to hire saboteurs to forge and disseminate false and scurrilous libels of honorable men running for the Democratic presidential nomination in Democratic Party primaries.

During the darkness of the early morning of June 17, 1972, James W. McCord, the security chief of the John Mitchell Committee, and four residents of Miami, Florida, were arrested by Washington police while they were burglarizing the offices of the Democratic National Committee in the Watergate complex to obtain political intelligence. At the same time, the four residents of Miami had in their possession more than fifty $100 bills which were subsequently shown to be a part of campaign contributions made to the Nixon Reelection Committees.

On September 15, 1972, these five burglars, E. Howard Hunt, and Gordon Liddy, General Counsel of the Stans Committee, were indicted by the grand jury on charges arising out of the bugging and burglary of the Watergate.

They were placed on trial upon these charges before Judge John Sirica, and a petit jury in the United States District Court for the District of Columbia in January, 1973. At that time, Hunt and the four residents of Miami pleaded guilty, and McCord and Liddy were found guilty by the petit jury. None of them took the witness stand during the trial.

The arrest of McCord and the four residents of Miami created consternation in the Nixon Reelection Committees and the White House. Thereupon, various officers and employees of the Nixon Reelection Committees and various White House aides undertook to conceal from law enforcement officers, prosecutors, grand jurors, courts, the news media, and the American people the identities and activities of those officers and employees of the Nixon Reelection Committees and those White House aides who had participated in any way in the Watergate affair.

Various officers and employees of the Nixon Reelection Committees and various White House aides engaged in one or more of these acts to make the concealment effective and thus obstruct the due administration of justice:

1. They destroyed the records of the Nixon Reelection Committees antedating the bugging and the burglary.

2. They induced the Acting Director of the F.B.I., who was a Nixon appointee, to destroy the State Department

documents which E. Howard Hunt had been falsifying.

3. They obtained from the Acting Director of the F.B.I. copies of scores of interviews conducted by F. B. I. agents in connection with their investigation of the bugging and the burglary, and were enabled thereby to coach their confederates to give false and misleading statements to the F. B. I.

4. They sought to persuade the F. B. I. to refrain from investigating the sources of the campaign funds which were used to finance the bugging and the burglary.

5. They intimidated employees of the Nixon Reelection Committees and employees of the White House by having their lawyers present when these employees were being questioned by agents of the F. B. I., and thus deterred these employees from making full disclosures to the F. B. I.

6. They lied to agents of the F. B. I., prosecutors, and grand jurors who undertook to investigate the bugging and the burglary, and to Judge Sirica and the petit jurors who tried the seven original Watergate defendants in January, 1973.

7. They persuaded the Department of Justice and the prosecutors to take out-of-court statements from Maurice Stans, President Nixon's chief campaign fund raiser, and Charles Colson, Egil Krogh, and David Young, White House aides, and Charles Colson's secretary, instead of requiring them to testify before the grand jury investigating the bugging and the burglary in conformity with the established procedures governing such matters, and thus denied the grand jurors the opportunity to question them.

8. They persuaded the Department of Justice and the prosecutors to refrain from asking Donald Segretti, their chief hired saboteur, any questions involving Herbert W. Kalmbach, the President's personal attorney, who was known by them to have paid Segretti for "dirty tricks" he perpetrated upon honorable men seeking the Democratic presidential nomination, and who was subsequently identified before the Senate Select Committee as one who played a major role in the secret delivery of "hush money" to the seven original Watergate defendants.

9. They made cash payments totaling hundreds of thousands of dollars out of campaign funds in surreptitious ways to the seven original Watergate defendants as "hush money" to buy their silence and keep them from revealing their knowledge of the identities of the officers and employees of the Nixon Reelection Committees and the White House aides who had participated in the Watergate.

10. They gave assurances to some of the original seven

defendants that they would receive presidential clemency
after serving short portions of their sentences if they refrained
from divulging the identities and activities of the officers
and employees of the Nixon Reelection Committees and the
White House aides who had participated in the Watergate
affair.

11. They made arrangements by which the attorneys
who represented the seven original Watergate defendants
received their fees in cash from moneys which had been
collected to finance President Nixon's reelection campaign.

12. The induced the Department of Justice and the
prosecutors of the seven original Watergate defendants to
assure the news media and the general public that there
was no evidence that any persons other than the seven
original Watergate defendants were implicated in any way
in any Watergate related crimes.

13. They inspired massive efforts on the part of segments
of the news media friendly to the administration to persuade
the American people that most of the members of the Select
Committee named by the Senate to investigate the Watergate
were biased and irresponsible men motivated solely by
desires to exploit the matters they investigated for personal
or partisan advantage, and that the allegations in the press
that presidential aides had been involved in the Watergate
were venomous machinations of a hostile and unreliable
press bent on destroying the country's confidence in a great
and good President.

One shudders to think that the Watergate conspiracies
might have been effectively concealed and their most dramatic
episode might have been dismissed as a "third-rate" burglary
conceived and committed solely by the seven original Watergate defendants had it not been for the courage and penetrating understanding of Judge Sirica, the thoroughness of
the investigative reporting of Carl Bernstein, Bob Woodward,
and other representatives of a free press, the labors of the
Senate Select Committee and its excellent staff, and the
dedication and diligence of Special Prosecutors Archibald
Cox and Leon Jaworski and their associates.

Why Was Watergate?

Unlike the men who were responsible for Teapot Dome,
the presidential aides who perpetrated Watergate were not
seduced by the love of money, which is sometimes thought
to be the root of all evil. On the contrary, they were instigated by a lust for political power, which is at least as cor-

rupting as political power itself.

They gave their allegiance to the President and his policies. They had stood for a time near to him, and had been entrusted by him with great governmental and political power. They enjoyed exercising such power, and longed for its continuance.

They knew that the power they enjoyed would be lost and the policies to which they adhered would be frustrated if the President should be defeated.

As a consequence of these things, they believed the President's reelection to be a most worthy objective, and succumbed to an age-old temptation. They resorted to evil means to promote what they conceived to be a good end.

Their lust for political power blinded them to ethical considerations and legal requirements; to Aristotle's aphorism that the good of man must be the end of politics; and to Grover Cleveland's conviction that a public office is a public trust.

They had forgotten, if they ever knew, that the Constitution is designed to be a law for rulers and people alike at all times and under all circumstances; and that no doctrine involving more pernicious consequences to the commonweal has ever been invented by the wit of man than the notion that any of its provisions can be suspended by the President for any reason whatsoever.

On the contrary, they apparently believed that the President is above the Constitution, and has the autocratic power to suspend its provisions if he decides in his own unreviewable judgment that his action in so doing promotes his own political interests or the welfare of the nation. As one of them testified before the Senate Select Committee, they believed that the President has the autocratic power to suspend the Fourth Amendment whenever he imagines that some indefinable aspect of national security is involved.

I digress to reject this doctrine of the constitutional omnipotence of the President. As long as I have a mind to think, a tongue to speak, and a heart to love my country, I shall deny that the Constitution confers any autocratic power on the President, or authorizes him to convert George Washington's America into Gaius Caesar's Rome.

The lust for political power of the presidential aides who perpetrated Watergate on America blinded them to the laws of God as well as to the laws and ethics of man.

As a consequence, they violated the spiritual law which forbids men to do evil even when they think good will result from it, and ignored these warnings of the King James version of the Bible:

13

1. "There is nothing covered, that shall not be revealed; neither hid, that shall not be known."

2. "Be not deceived; God is not mocked: For whatsoever a man soweth, that shall he also reap."

I find corroboration for my conclusion that lust for political power produced Watergate in words uttered by the most eloquent and learned of all the Romans, Marcus Tullius Cicero, about 2100 years ago. He said:

"Most men, however, are inclined to forget justice altogether, when once the craving for military power or political honors and glory has taken possession of them. Remember the saying of Ennius, 'When crowns are at stake, no friendship is sacred, no faith shall be kept.' "

As one after another of the individuals who participated in Watergate goes to prison, we see in action an inexorable spiritual law which Rudyard Kipling phrased in this fashion in his poem about Tomlinson's Ghost:

"For the sin ye do by two and two you must pay for one by one."

As we contemplate the motives that inspired their misdeeds, we acquire a new awareness of the significance of Cardinal Wolsey's poignant lament:

"Had I but serv'd my God with half the zeal I serv'd my King, He would not in mine age have left me naked to mine enemies."

The Antidote for Future Watergates

Is there an antidote which will prevent future Watergates? If so, what is it?

The Senate Select Committee is recommending the enactment of new laws which it believes will minimize the danger of future Watergates and make more adequate and certain the punishment of those who attempt to perpetrate them upon our country.

Candor compels the confession, however, that law alone will not suffice to prevent future Watergates. In saying this, I do not disparage the essential role which law plays in the life of our nation. As one who has labored as a practicing lawyer, a judge, and a legislator all of my adult years, I venerate the law as an instrument of service to society. At the same time, however, I know the weakness of the law as well as its strength.

14

Law is not self-executing. Unfortunately, at times its execution rests in the hands of those who are faithless to it. And even when its enforcement is committed to those who revere it, law merely deters some human beings from offending, and punishes other human beings for offending. It does not make men good. This task can be performed only by ethics or religion or morality.

Since politics is the art or science of government, no man is fit to participate in politics or to seek or hold public office unless he has two characteristics.

The first of these characteristics is that he must understand and be dedicated to the true purpose of government, which is to promote the good of the people, and entertain the abiding conviction that a public office is a public trust, which must never be abused to secure private advantage.

The second characteristic is that he must possess that intellectual and moral integrity, which is the priceless ingredient in good character.

When all is said, the only sure antidote for future Watergates is understanding of fundamental principles and intellectual and moral integrity in the men and women who achieve or are entrusted with governmental or political power.

Josiah Gilbert Holland, a poet of a bygone generation, recognized this truth in a poem which he called "The Day's Demand", and which I like to call "America's Prayer". I quote his words:

"God give us men! A time like this demands
Strong minds, great hearts, true faith and ready hands;
Men whom the lust of office does not kill;
Men whom the spoils of office cannot buy;
Men who possess opinions and a will;
Men who have honor—men who will not lie;
Men who can stand before a demagogue
And damn his treacherous flatteries without winking;
Tall men, sun-crowned, who live above the fog
In public duty, and in private thinking."

INDIVIDUAL STATEMENT BY
SENATOR HOWARD H. BAKER, JR.
Vice-Chairman

I believe that the activities and inquiry of the Senate Select Committee on Presidential Campaign Activities have been, by and large, useful and appropriate. The bipartisan tone for the Committee was established by the unanimous adoption of Senate Resolution 60 by the vote of 77 to 0 on February 7, 1973. I think, with some exceptions that bipartisan attitude was preserved throughout the long and tedious proceedings. From time to time, there occurred conflicts and disagreements in the Committee, and between the respective staffs, but they usually were resolved. The final act of the Select Committee is to file its Report; and I am pleased. It is not a perfect Report. Some may say that it is without grace or style, and that is probably true; but it is the culmination of an extraordinary effort, and I am particularly gratified that the majority and minority staffs cooperated carefully in comparing their respective views and adjusting the text so that in most instances a satisfactory joint staff position was submitted to the Committee for adoption. The Report is not adjudicatory and indeed it often goes to some lengths to avoid "finding fact" in the traditional sense. This requirement was directed to the Committee staff by the Chairman in deference, I believe, to the sensitivity of litigation in process, or upcoming, and of course to the inquiry into impeachment by the House of Representatives. I commend the Chairman for that point of view.

In an historical perspective, I believe that the Committee's principal service may have been in the public ventilation of the facts and circumstances collectively assembled under the title of Watergate. The Committee's gathering and disseminating the often shocking, frequently embarrassing, and sometimes incriminating evidence and testimony before it certainly should exert a deterrent effect; and that effect may be far more important than the Committee's recommendations. I rather suspect that it may be a long while before a future President permits the occurrence of such unfortunate circumstances. If that is the case, then the Committee's laborious effort, the considerable expense, and the national frustration will have been worth the investment.

I hope so.

Recommendations

I. ESTABLISHMENT OF AN OFFICE OF PUBLIC PROSECUTOR WITHIN THE DEPARTMENT OF JUSTICE, APPOINTED BY THE PRESIDENT FOR A FIXED TERM AND SUBJECT TO SENATE CONFIRMATION.

The Committee Report recommends the creation of a judicially-appointed Permanent Public Attorney to investigate and prosecute cases in which there are conflicts of interests within the Executive Branch. This recommendation and my own evidence recognition that the Federal Government is poorly equipped for investigating and prosecuting crimes allegedly committed by high-ranking Executive Branch officials. Prior to the appointment of the Watergate Special Prosecutor, there did not exist within the Department of Justice a division solely and specifically entrusted with the authority to investigate allegations of official misconduct, cloaked with the requisite independence and statutory authority necessary for unimpeded access to government officials and documents, and I believe the investigation would have proceeded more rapidly and effectively, had such an arrangement existed.

Consequently, I agree in principle with the Committee Report's recommending the establishment of a Permanent Public Prosecutor, possessing a statutory mandate to investigate and prosecute allegations of governmental misconduct. I have great doubts, however, regarding the Constitutionality of the Committee's proposal that the Public Attorney be appointed by the representatives of the Judiciary.

The appointment of a Permanent Public Prosecutor, within the Department of Justice, for a fixed six-year term as nominated by the President and subject to Senate confirmation possesses none of the potential Constitutional infirmities presented by a judicially-appointed public prosecutor, as were discussed in the Senate debate this past fall on the Hart-Bayh Special Prosecutor Bill.

Senator Percy and I, together with Senators Brock, Cook and Young, introduced S. 2734 on November 20, 1973, that provided for the Presidential appointment of a Special Watergate Prosecutor, subject to confirmation by the Senate.

Senator Ervin on June 17, 1974, introduced S. 3652, providing for Presidential appointment of a Permanent Public Prosecutor with Senate confirmation and a fixed term of six years. I believe both of these proposals avoid the Constitutional pitfalls of the Committee's recommendation and are attractive alternatives.

17

II. ESTABLISHMENT WITHIN THE CONGRESS OF A JOINT INTELLIGENCE OVERSIGHT COMMITTEE SO AS TO PROVIDE FOR INCREASED CONGRESSIONAL MONITORING OF GOVERNMENTAL INTELLIGENCE GATHERING ACTIVITIES.

Both in the Committee Report and in other Committee documents, there is found a substantial body of evidence regarding the activities of the Central Intelligence Agency, the Federal Bureau of Investigation, the National Security Council, and other Governmental intelligence gathering and/or investigative organizations, which provides insight into the activities, as well as the abuses, of these organizations relative to the matters under the Select Committee's perusal. Testimony was presented to the Committee to the effect that there was an attempt by high-ranking White House officials to somehow "involve" the CIA in the Watergate coverup; that the FBI investigation of the Watergate matter was impeded at the very highest levels of the Bureau itself; and that under the supervision of the White House, intelligence-gathering operations, including unlawful activity, was conducted outside the purview of the Congressionally-authorized intelligence and investigative agencies. Moreover, as indicated in separate Committee documents, the CIA provided extensive logistical support to the participants in both the Fielding and Democratic National Committee break-ins and expressed a keen interest in the subsequent investigations.

The intelligence-related material before the Committee is not conclusive. It does not answer the question of what the President or other individuals knew or when they knew it, nor does it explain why the Democratic National Committee headquarters twice was the target of an illegal entry. It seems apparent, however, that Congressional committee oversight did not function effectively as a deterrent to those who may have sought to utilize governmental intelligence and investigative agencies for unlawful or unauthorized purposes.

Thus, because of the cost, the secrecy, the lack of effective supervision, the uncertainty of domestic activities, and the extreme difficulty in obtaining access to classified materials, I am of the opinion that the subject of government intelligence operations requires extensive further examination. I wish to associate myself with the recommendation in the Committee Report for closer supervision of Central Intelligence Agency activities by the appropriate Congressional oversight committees.

I would go one step further and propose that the Congress should consider the creation of a Special Joint Committee on

Intelligence Activities. I believe the highly sensitive nature of intelligence operations, the expanding scope of the intelligence gathering requirement, and the enormous cost and dedication of manpower and resources to the intelligence undertaking in the United States, fully justifies a new committee arrangement. Such a committee, not dissimilar to the Joint Committee arrangement. Such a committee, not dissimilar to the Joint Committee on Atomic Energy, could more effectively coordinate among the various intelligence investigative agencies, now subject to Congressional oversight, than can the several committees now having partial oversight responsibilities. Thus, I believe that a joint committee would present no legitimate threat to the intelligence community in terms of jeopardizing or compromising their necessary intelligence operations, and would provide greater assurance that our intelligence gathering and investigative agencies are complying with the law and are working in the best interest of the nation.

III. REFORMATION OF CONGRESSIONAL INVESTIGATORY HEARING PROCEDURES SO AS TO PROVIDE INCREASED PROTECTION FOR THE RIGHTS OF INDIVIDUALS.

Although this recommendation does not clearly fall within the province of S. Res. 60, the Select Committee hearings highlighted the fact that Congressional investigatory proceedings exhibit a determination to ferret out the facts even if the investigative process may grievously injure the protected rights of individuals who are or may become defendants in judicial proceedings. Thus, I believe that Congress should give careful attention to the codification of Rules of Legislative Hearing Procedure so as to provide the same assurance that individual Constitutional rights are not impaired by legislative hearings as the Federal rules of criminal procedure provide in criminal proceedings. I believe that such rules should provide a mechanism whereby witnesses and proposed witnesses before legislative hearings, who are or may be subject to criminal prosecution, can be identified and afforded additional procedural protections than is now the case. For instance, a "vulnerable" witness might be given the right to have counsel participate in the questioning of other witnesses presenting testimony adverse to the interests of the vulnerable witness. In addition, the Congress should study the advisability of imposing common law and/or federal evidentiary rules in certain types, if not all, legislative hearings. Finally, the Congress may wish to establish a Legislative Public Defender whose duty would be to proctor legislative hearings and investigations so as to provide for the protection of the rights of individuals.

As exemplified by the history of the Select Committee, the investigatory power of a Congressional committee is extremely broad and pervasive, and, in actuality, is restricted only by the wording of the resolution or other legislative vehicle creating the committee and the authority of the committee to investigate such matters. While litigation and Congressional discretion have provided some due process limitations upon Congressional investigations, a Congressional committee is not a jury nor a court; and common law anl statutory evidentiary rules are not applicable to committee investigations. The most obvious example is hearsay testimony, which is recited throughout the Committee Report. Moreover, through its contempt power, "use" immunity, and public pressure, a Congressional committee can in many cases indirectly overcome an individual's privilege against self-incrimination in a manner which could never occur in a court of law. As mentioned above, individuals whose conduct is being investigated, often are not afforded the opportunity to have counsel "cross examine" witnesses presenting testimony detrimental to them. Thus, while I will protect jealously the privilege and the right of Congressional committees to conduct inquiries concerning the administration of existing laws, as well as new statutes, I believe that legislation conveying the recognition of the need to protect the rights of potential defendants, the sanctity of criminal trials and the impartiality of the impeachment process can be effected without constituting a detriment to a legislative committee's fact-finding power.

IV. CAMPAIGN AND ELECTORAL REFORMS

Among the several inadequacies in our political process highlighted by Watergate, none is more glaring than the need for comprehensive campaign and electoral reform. The types of campaign abuses prevalent during the 1972 campaigns, though shocking in terms of their scope, were by no means unprecedented. The fact of the matter is, and has been, that political campaigns take place in a legal vacuum. With the possible exception of the Federal Elections Campaign Act of 1971, there has been no significant attempt by Congress to regulate political campaigns since the Corrupt Practices Act of 1925; and even that was "more loophole than law." Thus, it is not surprising that campaigns have taken on the appearance of a political free-for-all in which the distinction between illegal, unethical, anl immoral conduct is generally obscured.

The fallout from that atmosphere is cumulative and has resulted in a devastating erosion of public trust and confidence in the process by which public officials are elected. Moreover, if the country is to benefit from the experience of the past two years, it is essential that the Congress undertake fundamental reform of the electoral process—reform which includes not only campaign finance, but also various aspects of the actual election process.

The type of reform most vital, and about which the Select Committee assembled a wealth of data, was campaign finance. From a financial standpoint, the 1972 campaign for President was no different from past campaigns in that there was no effective regulation of the source, form or amount of political contributions. Although the Federal Elections Campaign Act of 1971 required more complete disclosure of contributions, the 1972 campaign was still largely funded through a system of unrestricted, large sum private financing. It was this system that permitted one individual to give two million dollars while over 200 million people gave nothing. It was this system that gave rise to the allegations that the milk producers received an increase in the support price of milk in return for the pledge of large contributions. It was this system which permitted individuals to "launder" cash through Mexico in an effort to suppress the identity of the source. And finally, it was this system which permitted the accumulation of $350,-000 in a White House safe, none of which was reported and most of which purportedly was disbursed for political espionage and alleged "hush" money. Consequently, it is not surprising that considerable support has developed within the country and the Congress for complete abandonment of this system in favor of substantial public financing. I can sympathize with that view, for public financing certainly appears pure and absolute; but it is not the answer.

Although public financing probably would solve a limited number of problems afflicting the present process, it would almost ecrtainly create an equal number of potentially greater dangers. Some of those would stem, no doubt, from the incestuous nature of the government's financing the process by which it is selected. The Responsiveness portion of the Select Committee's Report details the repeated efforts of members of the Administration to influence or abuse the various departments and agencies for purely political purposes. Would it not be possible under a system of public financing, in which an arm of the government was responsible for allocating funds, to abuse that authority on behalf of one candidate or party under the guise of bureaucratic red tape? Some would argue that it is overly cynical to make such an assumption, but perhaps it would have been cynical a few years ago to assume that an administration would try to actively utilize its broad powers to punish political adversaries. We can ill afford to overlook the possibility of such an incident in the public financing sector ten or twenty years from now.

Another serious problem with comprehensive public financing, in my judgment, is the effect it will have upon the individual's First Amendment Right of Freedom of Political Expression. I believe that right gives each citizen the right of expressing himself politically, whether by contribution, or otherwise, or conversely, refraining from such expression; and in a nation which prides itself on protecting individual rights, the option to refrain from exercising that right must be considered as vital as the right itself. I, therefore, urge that it is essential to maintain participation in our political process on a voluntary basis, while attempting to increase the opportunities and incentives to participate.

Public financing, however, provides no such choice. Rather, it states that the need to eliminate the influence of large sum contributors and special interests is so compelling that we must abandon the use of all voluntary private financing in favor of mandatory, public financing; and in the case of the latter, we have no control over which candidate receives our tax dollars, nor whether they are actually used for that purpose. In fact, taxpayers would be directly supporting candidates whom they consider repugnant.

If it were merely a question of unrestricted, private financing, or comprehensive public financing, then I would support the latter. But, there is a third, more reasonable option which would retain some continuity while avoiding some of the hazards of public financing. That option is a system of effectively regulated private financing in which the incentives for small contributions are vastly enhanced. Such a system is in essence what the Select Committee recommends. A strict limitation on the size, amount, and form of private contributions, a single campaign committee, a single campaign depository, an overall expenditure limitation, a requirement for full public disclosure before, rather than after the election, and an independent elections commission, are all necessary reforms which would impose order upon the current campaign chaos. Moreover, I would make one further recommendation which would do more to eliminate distortive influence of special interests than any other single action, and that is, to prohibit, altogether, contributions from any and all organizations. Only individuals can vote, and I believe only individuals should be permitted to contribute.

Some have argued, however, that if we eliminate the financial influence of the special interests and strictly limit the size of individual contributions, we cannot effectively fund a competitive two-party system. Indeed, without some new incentives for millions of Americans to make small contributions, such a system would clearly discourage constructive opposition and tend to bolster the inherent advantages of incumbency. Thus, I would propose a 100 percent tax credit on all contributions made in a calendar year up to $50 on an individual return and $100 on a joint return. Such a credit would enable each taxpayer to divert up to $50 of his tax money to a candidate or candidates if, and only if, he desires to do so. This approach would be entirely voluntary, thereby protecting the individual's freedom of political expression. Moreover, it would generate sufficient funds so that we might avoid having to resort to the direct appropriation of tax monies for political purposes. A realistic and effective tax incentive, combined with the aforementioned list of statutory reforms, would afford a fair, and competitive means of funding political campaigns.

I am convinced further that we cannot hope to reverse the current trend of erosion of public trust and confidence without sharply increasing public participation in the political process. In that regard, I would urge that serious consideration be given automatic registration of voters in federal elections at age 18. The history of the United States has been a history of the extension of the voting franchise. Yet, even today, a significant number of our citizens are effectively prevented from participating in elections by complex, and often archaic, registration and residency requirements. The postcard voter registration bill passed by the Senate last year was an effort to deal with this problem, but I opposed it because of my concern for the potential for mail fraud and abuse of such a system.

Several western nations have already successfully implemented a form of automatic voter registration. In the Scandinavian countries, for example, and in Switzerland, every eligible citizen is registered *ex officio* in a voting register. A list of voters is published by the elections authorities in advance of the election date. Any citizen whose name has not been included in the list then has until approximately a week before the election to correct the situation. In the United States, however, citizens still must contend with what amounts to a perpetual registration process. I fully realize that some difficulties will arise in translating automatic registration to the realities of the American experience and attempting to reconcile it with state registration procedures. Perhaps Social Security numbers could be utilized to standardize this procedure, since more than 95 percent of eligible voters are already registered with Social Security. In any event, the concept deserves consideration, in my view; and, if workable, it could provide a valuable incentive to increase citizen participation.

I would also urge major reform of our present spasmodic system of Presidential primaries. There are essentially three alternatives in this regard: a refinement of the present system requiring the 25 states who hold Presidential primaries to do so on four or five specific dates at two or three week intervals; a single national primary for each party with a subsequent run-off unless one candidate polls more than 40 percent; and a system of regional primaries also held at specific intervals, but encompassing all of the country.

Of these three proposals, I am most inclined to support the one for a system of regional primaries in which every eligible voter who desires to participate in the selection of a party nominee can do so by voting in the regional primary which includes his state. This would permit the millions of Americans who support candidates who will not receive the party nomination to express that support in a meaningful way. It would also give them a personal stake in the election and increase the likelihood of their participation in the subsequent general election campaign. Specifically, I would propose dividing the country into four geographic regions, largely along the lines of time zones so as to avoid holding a "southern" or a "New England" primary with a distinct ideological slant. I would make those regions of roughly equal population and would hold the four primaries at three week intervals beginning in early June and ending in early August. The respective primary candidates would compete for state delegates who would be won according to the proportion of vote received in each state, rather than on a winner-take-all basis. Although I am aware of the high cost involved in running in regional primaries, the basic idea is to vastly expand the public participation in the nominating process and to significantly reduce the official length of Presidential campaigns.

As it is now, the first Presidential primary normally takes place in early March with the general election eight months later, in November. But, as I see it, there is absolutely no reason why that process must take that long. It exhausts the candidates, costs exorbitant sums of money, and eventually bores a great many people. I would propose that all primaries for Federal office be held no earlier than the 1st of June and no later than the 15th of August. This would significantly shorten the official length of campaigns for Federal office and permit the Congress to work at relatively full strength for four months before most members are forced to return to their states or districts to campaign full-time for the nomination.

I also recommend that we open and close polls all across the country at a uniform time and that they be opend a full 24 hours. The arguments for this are simple and well known; but briefly stated, this is the best way I know of to prevent the harmful effects of broadcast networks projecting the outcome of elections, based on very early returns, when polls in the western states are still open. Moreover, 24 hours would maximize the individual's opportunity to vote before, after, or during work.

I further recommend that the Presidential electoral system be made more responsive and representative by the abolition of the electoral college, that 18th century vestigial remnant of Constitutional compromise. I personally favor and have always supported the direct election of the President by popular vote, but having unsuccessfully urged that move, I am willing to settle for an improvement if not a cure for this situation. I propose that Congress and the States fully debate the merits of popular vote, Congressional District vote, proportional allocation of electoral votes by states according to the popular vote, or any other electoral process calculated to eliminate what I view as the two most onerous elements of the present system. That is to say, one, the winner take all by state process, which created and perpetuated the one-party South for a century after the Civil War, and, secondly, the possibility of the selection of the President by the House of Representatives, which constitutes the most undemocratic of all of the allocation systems. Some say that the reform of the electoral college is not related to the mandate of S. Res. 60, but I disagree; I think that the sensitivity of the electoral system, the coherence of the selection process, the vitality of the two-party system, and the integrity of financial support are essential to the political prosperity of the country and are paramount in their importance to every other democratic consideration.

V. THE INSTITUTION OF THE PRESIDENCY

I believe there exists a fundamental infirmity in the relationship of the Chief Magistrate of the Nation to the two other coordinate branches of government. This development is not of recent origin—it has matured steadily since at least the beginning of the twentieth century and at an accelerated pace since the Great Depression of the 1930's. The Presidency has become splendid, and it has become increasingly isolated. Surrounded by the trappings of privilege and the sanctuary of security, both national and personal, the Presidency is indeed the most equal of all the equal branches. Its jurisdiction and the scope and sweep of its powers are enormous and broad. While it may be that gradually grafting onto the Presidency of additional powers and authorities is a natural development in the evolution of our democracy, there are certain elements of what has come to be known as a "strong" Presidency that I do not believe to be desirable.

In recent years, the President's personal staff has served as his council of advisers, and in some instances, the primary delegates of Presidential authority. This is counter to the historical concept of the Cabinet system where the President's Cabinet served as his principal advisers, in addition to being the administrators of the several departments of the government. By way of example, under Article II, Section 2, the President is empowered constitutionally to require the written opinion of the principal officer in the Executive Departments. I think that the original Cabinet system is preferable to a plethora of Presidential counselors, White House counselors, special advisers and the like. The cross-pollination that occurs in councils of individuals operating from independent bases of jurisdictional authority is distinctly preferable to the highly structured, closely supervised personal staff. Strong persons in strong positions are a significant force for good or evil; and I believe that the opportunity for good is greatly expanded and the possibility of a "Yes" man syndrome is greatly diminished in the Cabinet situation.

The under-utilization of the resources and personnel of the Department of Justice and almost complete reliance upon the White House legal staff is another recent development which I consider to be unfortunate. I believe it essential that there be one arm of the Executive Branch that is the primary legal authority and which is responsible for providing the entire Administration, including the President, with objective legal advice. I propose that the Office of Legal Counsel in the Department of Justice be formally charged with the responsibility to serve as legal counsel to the President.

I have come to believe, notwithstanding my earlier support for the ratification of the Twenty-second Amendment, that we made a mistake in limiting a President to two terms and that the Twenty-second Amendment should be repealed. I believe that the discipline of standing for re-election, or at least contemplating the possibility of standing for re-election, is a desirable one and that the nature of the Presidency is materially altered by the Constitutional limitation of two terms. I think the incumbency factor which is much vaunted and highly prized by political observers is overstated in the first instance, but that it would be diminished by the repeal of the Twenty-second Amendment. After all, incumbency is less regal if one must at least consider the possibility of standing for re-election four years hence. In short, the atmosphere engendered by the removal of political pressures from a President who has been re-elected to his second term presents, in my opinion, far grater potential for abuse of power than a situation in which an incumbent President always is presented with the opportunity to seek re-election.

As for most public issues, we have spawned our share of cliches and one of the favorites describes the Chief Magistrate as an "Imperial President"—implying isolation, arrogance, and non-responsiveness. While I may not subscribe to all the elements of that characterization, I do feel that separation of powers has become more than a Constitutional doctrine, it has become a geographic fact. Although the nature of the Presidency certainly is influenced by the individual occupant, interaction between the Executive and the Legislative departments and with the public is not only desirable but essential. I have often proposed that the President should maintain an office in the Capitol and that the President, or at least some of his principal staff should occupy that office from time to time and be available to legislators on matters of mutual interest.

Certainly the single most notable evidentiary achievement of the Select Committee was the revelation by Alexander Butterfield of the tape recording system utilized in Presidential offices in both the White House and the Executive Office Building. I am not sure I understand why the tape recording facilities were installed, but I find the practice objectionable and not in keeping with the grandeur of the Presidency. I rather suspect that recent experiences will mitigate against that practice in the future. In any event, I believe that Congress should consider carefully a prohibition of the electronic recording of conversations occuring both in rooms and on telephones, except with the express prior consent of all the participants to the conversation, or unless carefully supervised by a court of competent jurisdiction for specified statutory purposes.

VI. INCREASED NATIONAL PARTY COMMITTEE ROLE IN FEDERAL ELECTIONS

Finally, I believe Watergate might never have occurred had there been more politics instead of less in the White House. Politics is an honorable profession. It is probably a free citizen's highest secular calling. The republic could not function without the dedication of miliions of citizen politicians; and, consequently, I hope that politics as an honorable undertaking is not a casualty of Watergate. I urge that our young people, who are easily the best educated, most aware and the most participatory of any generation, involve themselves in the politics of the nation.

The two party system must flourish as a system of two broad based national parties, each able to accommodate the wide variety of viewpoints and ideas and to synthesize the majority view on any given election day. I think Presidential and Vice Presidential campaigns in particular ought to be the responsibility of the national party structure and not temporary, collateral organizations such as the Committee to Reelect the President. I take great pride in noting after these extended hearings that neither the Republican National Committee nor the Democratic National Committee were involved in campaign illegalities in any way, nor were their chairmen or principal officers. Both our parties are great parties, and they are essential to the functioning of the country.

SENATORS JOSEPH M. MONTOYA
AND DANIEL K. INOUYE

Despite the fact that there is not unanimity among the members of the Committee as to the constitutionality, advisability and practicality of providing public financing of presidential and other federal campaigns, there is a consensus in the United States Senate and among the public at large in favor of such reform of our electoral system. We count ourselves part of that consensus.

The testimony and evidence made public during our hearings document the inherent potential for abuse and corruption in any campaign financing system that is dependent upon a small number of large private contributors. Unfortunately, a cure for these abuses which would place strict limitations upon campaign contributions and expenditures would produce an equally unfair system. Such limitations have the inevitable effect of increasing the existing advantages of the major political parties and well-known individuals—i.e., incumbent officeholders—who have greater access and appeal to donors, over minor parties and unknown individuals who wish to enter the political arena.

An open, fair and honest campaign financing system must combine effective and timely public disclosure of the sources of campaign dollars, realistic limitations upon contributions and expendtures in campaigns and an efficient method for increasing citizen participation in the financing of campaigns.

In his State of the Congress Address of February 6, 1974, Majority Leader Mansfield stated, "We shall not finally come to grips with the problems (of our campaign methods) except as we are prepared to pay for the public business of elections with public funds." The Senate Committee on Rules and Administration in its favorable report on S. 3044—the Federal Election Campaign Act Amendments of 1974—which passed the Senate on April 11, 1974 by a 53 to 32 vote, stated "the election of federal officials is not a private affair. It is the foundation of our government." Senate approval of a comprehensive system of public financing of federal elections as shown in the vote for S. 3044 is but the latest in a number of successful legislative measures designed to bring public dollars into the electoral arena in order to offset the corrupting reliance on large private contributors.

For public financing of campaigns is not a new idea. In fact, it is not new law. Public financing measures are now on the books at the national level—in the form of the dollar tax check-off and tax credits and deductions for small political contributions—and in many states. The constitutionality of these measures stands unchallenged.

Congress adopted both the check-off and the tax incentive in 1971. It is important to look at the actual results since then, for critics of public financing have sometimes attempted to interpret the early response as demonstrating lack of popular support for the idea. We believe that the opposite is in fact true: in two short years the American people have shown that, given the chance, they are very willing to support this important innovation.

In 1972, the first year it was in effect, 3.1% of all tax returns filed were "checked-off," producing the first $3 to $4 million for the new Presidential Election Campaign Fund. Anyone who says this was an inauspicious beginning must be reminded that the check-off was in effect hidden on a separate tax form, was unseen by most taxpayers, and that virtually no public education was undertaken to explain the new system and how it worked.

As a result of Congressional pressure, the IRS remedied this major flaw last summer, requiring that the check-off be placed visibly on page one of the IRS form 1040 for 1973 and thereafter. In addition, after a court challenge, citizens who failed to use the check-off in 1972 were given a second chance. As a result, a special "make-up" check-off box was placed on the 1973 returns.

The response? More than 15% of the 1973 returns used the check-off designating $17,575,054 for the Presidential Fund. This 15% equals over one quarter of those who actually voted in the 1972 presidential election. The current IRS projections indicate that there will ultimately be at least $29 million in the Fund by the end of the year. And, if taxpayers continue to check-off at a rate no higher than this year, it will mean at least $64 million in the Fund in time for the 1976 Presidential election. Moreover, taxpayers are rapidly becoming aware that dollars checked-off do not mean additional taxes. Instead they represent an authorization for Congress to appropriate for the Presidential election campaign fund the amount "checked-off." Given the degree of public cynicism about all politics this spring, a 15% check-off rate may well represent the bottom rather than the top line of public support. If the number of those checking-off increases, as we are convinced it will, with greater citizen education and understanding, so will the amount of money "appropriated" by the people to promote open, honest elections. The voluntary Fund is clearly an excellent way to provide a broader system of public financing for qualified federal candidates.

Tax incentives and, if necessary, general revenues are additional and legitimate sources for public campaign funding. We do not share the concern expressed by the majority of the Committee over using Treasury funds for public elections. Tax credits and deductions are methods of public financing of campaigns that merely bypass tax collection. We are not adverse to continued or expanded use of tax incentives to aid in paying for national campaigns, and after further study the Congress may well wish to change the Internal Revenue Code to strengthen inducements for campaign contributions.

We do believe that any candidate or party which receives public funds should be required to manifest significant public support. A system of matching private contributions with public money, such as provided in S. 3044 meets this requirement. It also maintains the element of individual initiative that is so essential to the Democratic process.

We have only to look around us to see that public financing is a major new political issue, that it may become the most important new aspect of our continuing experiment in democracy. The current activity of many public officials and citizen organizations in debating methods and mechanism of public financing indicates a realization that not all, or even most, of the problems of our current election system can be solved by more criminal laws, more controls and limits on political activity.

We are faced with a need to change not just the rules but the framework within which our elections and campaigns are conducted. Public financing is no panacea itself, of course, and its staunchest advocates are the first to note that it raises its own new and different questions. What public financing *can* do, however, is move us one step closer toward that goal which we must always and continually pursue—open, fair, honest elections in which the ideas of citizens and candidates compete regardless of the size of their pocketbooks. With the energy and good faith this country brings to its biggest problems, we can devise an equitable system of public financing that will help treat an illness, evident in the Watergate tragedy, that goes to the heart of this democracy.

INDIVIDUAL STATEMENT BY
SENATOR EDWARD J. GURNEY

I am in basic agreement with the thrust of the report. However I do point out that because the bulk of the report came in during the July 4th recess of the Senate, and the last portions within hours of the deadline time of submission of these views, there has not been sufficient time to review the report thoroughly.

The investigation clearly reveals that there was a scheme and an organized effort, participated in by persons in high official places in this Administration, to obtain political intelligence by breaking and entering into Democratic National Committee Headquarters. There is, however, a dispute in the evidence as to who was responsible for putting this plan into operation and who knew about the Watergate break-in and when. This is a matter that should be determined by the judicial branch of our government. In my opinion, there has been no proof gathered by the Committee to indicate that the President of the United States participated in or approved of the planning or had advance knowledge of the break-in.

The testimony and documents presented to the Committee also clearly shows that there was a conspiracy to cover-up the Watergate break-in and that certain persons at the White House were involved in that conspiracy. In my opinion, the evidence gathered by the Committee does not indicate that the President had knowledge of the cover-up until March, 1973.

The evidence is clear as to the part played by some characters in this tragedy and unclear as to what others may have done. It was not the mission of the Special Committee, pursuant to Senate Joint Resolution 60, to place responsibility for individual criminal acts.

The Committee had an important responsibility in its efforts to uncover the salient facts surrounding the Watergate break-in and cover-up and other improper activities occuring in the 1972 election campaign. By exposing these unethical, improper and illegal political campaign practices to the American electorate, we have provided the necessary groundwork to bring about a strong demand for needed political campaign reform. As a consequence, the Senate has already enacted a far reaching campaign reform bill which is now under consideration in the House.

Despite reservations which many of us held at the outset and the possibilities of prejudicial effect upon subsequent criminal actions, I believe that the televising of the hearings served a very useful purpose. Overnight the whole country became jurors as well as spectators in the unfolding drama. The American people were permitted to observe everything which transpired—the questions and answers, the witnesses' responses, the actions and attitudes of the panel of Senators and their staffs. I think, too, that by televising our proceedings we counteracted prejudicial selectivity by the media of the material presented to the Committee.

I do believe, however, that we spent too much time on the hearings, especially on testimony from witnesses of minor importance to the investigation, and on certain matters, like the burglary of the office of Ellsberg's psychiatrist, which were not germane to our inquiry. It is obvious that, while it could not confine itself to strict evidentiary rules, the Committee did permit too much unsubstantiated evidence to enter the record. Because of the impact of the hearings upon millions of Americans, who watched their progress on television or read newspaper accounts of what was happening, I believe that we should have exercised greater discretion in handling hearsay testimony.

I was also troubled by the continual leaking of information from the Committee. It was not unusual to find that matters which transpired in executive session appeared in the headlines the next morning. Permitting highly prejudicial matters to be disclosed to the media reflected badly upon the manner in which the United States Senate conducted this important and highly sensitive investigation.

I agree emphatically that political spying should be purged from the American political scene. I consider that the Committee's exposure of the machinations involved in the Watergate affair will help to eliminate "dirty tricks" as an accepted political campaign practice. It must be emphasized that, from our own political experience and from the evidence we have received concerning this one notorious political affair, we know that this Administration or the Republican Party does not have a monopoly on "dirty tricks" or other illegal campaign activities. It should be pointed out and it is clear from the evidence that the abuses of 1972 were committed by a few misguided individuals, overambitious and overzealous in their efforts on behalf of certain candidates and causes. The wrong-doing was not the work of the Republican Party or its professional campaign staff. The vast majority of people who worked in the 1972 Presidential campaigns, Republican or Democrat, worked in honorable fashion for their candidates with no knowledge nor use of any Watergate type activities.

I have strongly supported efforts to reform the campaign laws, and the experience of the recent Presidential campaign demonstrates the need to enforce these laws consistently and strenuously. The most pervasive abuse of 1972 was careless handling of cash contributions, which should be barred from future elections. This matter was common to both political parties, but it was to a lesser extent a problem for the Democrats since the Republican Party held the White House and was heavily favored to win reelection, and so inevitably attracted more money.

I favor a simplified codification of federal and state election statutes to which the candidates and the public can readily refer. We have enough laws on the books to deal with illegal campaign practices, but we desperately need a handy guidebook for campaign staff members of candidates for public office.

I am totally opposed to the Committee's recommendation for a Public Attorney with prosecutorial powers outside of the executive branch of the government. The President of the United States must be held responsibile for the business of the executive branch, including prosecution of criminals. It is his constitutional duty—and his alone—to faithfully execute the laws of the land. I oppose the creation of a czar who could literally hound and intimidate governmental officials in the proper exercise of their responsibilities. Criticisms directed at certain officials for their handling of the Watergate investigations reflect dissatisfaction with individuals rather than with institutions. I do favor, however, the establishment of an office within the Department of Justice charged with investigating alleged campaign law violations and prosecuting wrongdoers. (See Attachment A for Legal Argument)

Finally, I must add that I was utterly appalled by the revelations of Watergate, and I deplore the performance of individuals employed by or connected with the Committee to Reelect the President which the Committee's hearings has brought to light. Of course, we cannot legislate goodness, reform mankind or alter the ethical standards of individuals. But I believe that the Select Committee's findings relative to the 1972 Presidential campaign will profoundly affect the actions and attitudes of political partisans in future campaigns. I hope that a genuine "post Watergate morality" will prevail in the political life of our country. I hope, too, that the Committee's investigations of the Watergate break-in and cover-up and the prosecutions that have been generated by our inquiry will deter future Administrations, Republican or Democrat, from indulging in illegal practices and improper conduct in their quest for victory and political power.

I wish to express my personal appreciation to my colleagues on the Committee with whom I have been fortunate to labor in this important task and to whom I have been able to express freely my views over the past sixteen months.

ATTACHMENT A

Legal Argument Against the Establishment of an Independent Public Attorney. The recommendation for a Public Attorney with prosecutorial powers outside of the executive branch is unprecedented in our constitutional history. Its unprecedented nature is a forceful reminder of the constitutional problems inherent in such a blend of the traditionally separate roles of the prosecutor and judiciary. It violates the principle of separation of powers. It is at odds with the judicial function of the federal courts as provided in Article III and it does not comport with due process.

The Constitution provides in Article II, Section 3 that the President is charged with the responsibility of insuring that the laws of the United States are faithfully executed. Thus the function of conducting legal proceedings on behalf of the United States cannot be transferred to a prosecutor who is wholly independent of the executive branch. Professor Paul Bator of the Harvard Law School has written:

> The Constitution vests executive power in the President and commands him to take "care that the laws be faithfully executed." The enforcement of the Federal criminal law is a central part of the function of executing the laws. For the Congress or anyone else to purport to create an agency wholly independent from the executive branch with power to enforce the criminal law would probably be unconstitutional. (N.Y. Times, May 5, 1973)

In *Ponzi v. Fessenden,* 258 U.S. 254, 262 (1922), the Supreme Court rules that the prosecution of offenses against the United States is an Executive function stemming from the power vested in the President by Article II of the Constitution, the discharge of which is committed to the Attorney General:

> The Attorney General is the head of the Department of Justice . . . He is the hand of the President in taking care that the laws of the United States in protection of the interests of the United States in legal proceedings and in the prosecution of offences be faithfully executed.

35

Similarly, in *Springer v. Philippine Islands,* 277 U.S. 189, 202 (1928), the Supreme Court declared that "the authority to enforce laws or to appoint the agents charged with the duty of enforcing them" are Executive functions. See also 2 Op. A. G. 482, 487-493 (1831).

In *United States v. Cox,* 342 F. 2d 167 (5th Cir.) cert. denied, 85 S. Ct. 1767 (1965), the Court of Appeals held that a United States Attorney could not be required by a court to sign an indictment initiating the prosecution of offenses against the United States. In addressing the Constitutional authority of the Executive Branch in the enforcement of criminal laws, the court reiterated the principle of *Ponzi, supra,* that "the Attorney General is the hand of the President in taking care that the laws of the United States in legal proceedings and in the prosecution of offenses, be faithfully executed." 342 F. 2d at 171. It then considered that role of the U.S. Attorney in discharging this Executive power:

> The U.S. Attorney is an Executive official of the Government, and it is as an officer of the Executive department that he exercises a discretion as to whether or not there shall be a prosecution in a particular case. It follows, as an incident of the constitutional separation of powers, that the courts are not to interfere with the free exercise of the discretionary powers of the attorneys of the United States in their control over criminal prosecutions.

Thus, the court ruled that to transfer the power which is committed to the Executive to determine whether to prosecute to another body (the grand jury) would be derogation of Article II which grants to the President all "executive power" and vests in him the responsibility to take care that the laws be faithfully executed. Similarly in *Newman v. United States,* 382 F. 2d 479 (D. C. Cir. 1967), the court held that the lower court had no authority to review decisions of the prosecutor and that "it is not the function of the judiciary to review the exercise of executive discretion" 382 F. 2d at 487. Rejecting the suggestion in a concurring opinion that "irrational" decisions might be reviewable, the court said:

> The Constitution places on the Executive the duty to see that the 'laws are faithfully executed' and the responsibility must reside with that power. (*Id.* n. 9)

The same principle applies with equal force to prohibit transfer of the power to prosecute offenses to an independent prosecutor or commission outside the executive branch.

Finally, it should also be noted that the resolution authorizing the appointment of a Special Prosecutor during the Teapot Dome scandal provides no precedent for the appointment of Public Attorney. Prior to the introduction of the resolution in that instance, President Coolidge had suggested the appointment of special counsel, B. Naggel, *Teapot Dome*, p. 92, and the language of the resolution itself recognized the authority of the President to make the appointment. S. J. Res. 54, February 8, 1924.

INTRODUCTION

This report presents the findings and recommendations of the Senate Select Committee on Presidential Campaign Activities based on its investigation of the Watergate break-in and coverup; illegal and improper campaign practices and financing and other wrong doing during the presidential campaign of 1972. Once termed "a cancer growing on the Presidency" by a principal Committee witness (3 *Hearings* 998), Watergate is one of America's most tragic happenings. This characterization of Watergate is not merely based on the fact that the Democratic National Committee headquarters at the Watergate was burglarized in the early morning hours of June 17, 1972. Rather, it is also an appraisal of the events that led to the burglary and its sordid aftermath, an aftermath characterized by corruption, fraud, and abuse of official power.

The Select Committee is acutely conscious that, at the time it presents this report, the issue of impeachment of the President on Watergate-related evidence is pending in the Judiciary Committee of the House of Representatives. The Select Committee also recognizes that there are pending indictments against numerous defendants, most of whom were witnesses before the Committee, which charge crimes that, directly or indirectly, relate to its inquiry. It thus must be stressed that the Committee's hearings were not conducted, and this report not prepared, to determine the legal guilt or innocence of any person or whether the President should be impeached. In this regard, it is important to note that the Committee, during its short lifespan, has not obtained all the information it sought or desired and thus certain of its findings are tentative, subject to reevaluation when the full facts emerge. Moreover, the Committee, in stating the facts as it sees them, has not applied the standard of proof applicable to a criminal proceeding—proof beyond a reasonable doubt. Its conclusions, therefore, must not be interpreted as a final legal judgment that any individual has violated the criminal laws.

The Committee, however, to be true to its mandate from the Senate and its Constitutional responsibilities, must present its view of the facts. The Committee's enabling resolution, S. Res. 60, 93rd Cong., 1st Sess. (Feb. 7, 1973), which was passed by a unanimous Senate, instructs the Committee to make a "complete" investigation and study "of the extent . . . to which illegal, improper, or unethical activities" occurred in the 1972 Presidential campaign and election and to determine whether new legislation is needed "to safe-guard the electoral process by which the President of the United States is chosen." S. Res. 60, §§ 1 (a) and 2. Thus the factual statements contained in this report perform two basic legislative tasks. First, they serve as a basis for the remedial legislation recommended herein which the Committee believes will assist in preserving the integrity of the electoral process not only for present day citizens but also for future generations of Americans. Second, they fulfill the historic function of the Congress to oversee the administration of executive agencies of government and to inform the public of any wrongdoing or abuses it uncovers. The criticial importance of this latter function cannot be over-emphasized. As the Supreme Court said in *Watkins v. United States*, 354 U.S. 178, 200 (1957):

> "[There is a] power of the Congress to inquire into and publicize corruption, maladministration or inefficiency in agencies of the Government. That was the only kind of activity described by Woodrow Wilson in *Congressional Government* when he wrote: 'The informing function of Congress should be preferred even to its legislative function.' *Id.*, at 303. From the earliest times in its history, the Congress has assiduously performed an 'informing function' of this nature."

And, in *United States v. Rumely,* 345 U.S. 41, 43 (1953), the Supreme Court termed the informing function "indispensable" and observed:

> " 'It is the proper duty of a representative body to look diligently into every affair of government and to talk much about what it sees. It is meant to be the eyes and the voice, and to embody the wisdom and will of its constituents. Unless Congress have and use every means of acquainting itself with the acts and the disposition of the administrative agents of the government the country must be helpless to learn how it is being served; and unless Congress both scrutinize these things and sift them by every form of discussion, the country must remain in embarrassing, crippling ignorance of the very affairs which it is most important that it should understand and direct. The informing function of Congress should be preferred even to its legislative function.' Wilson, *Congressional Government,* 303."

It is in part to fulfill this historic "informing function" that the Committee reveals to the public the detailed facts contained in this report.

Before turning to a recitation of the facts as the Committee sees them, certain general observations based on the evidence before the Committee are appropriate. The Watergate affair reflects an alarming indifference displayed by some in high public office or position to concepts of morality and public responsibility and trust. Indeed, the conduct of many Watergate participants seems grounded on the belief that the ends justified the means, that the laws could be flaunted to maintain the present Administration in office. Unfortunately, the attitude that the law can be bent where expediency dictates was not confined to a few government and campaign officials. The testimony respecting the campaign-funding practices of some of the nation's largest and most respectable corporations furnishes clear examples of the subjugation of legal and ethical standards to pragmatic considerations. Hopefully, after the flood of Watergate revelations the country has witnessed, the public can now expect, at least for some years to come, a higher standard of conduct from its public officials and its business and professional leaders. Also, it is hopeful that the Watergate exposures have created what former Vice President Agnew has called a "post-Watergate morality" where respect for law and morality is paramount.

In approaching its task of recommending remedial legislation, the Committee is mindful that revelations of past scandals have often failed to produce meaningful reform. Too frequently there is a tendency to overreact in the wake of a particular scandal and burden the penal code with ill-considered laws directed to the specific—perhaps aberrational—conduct exposed. This proliferation of criminal laws has tended to over-complicate the penal code and, consequently, to impair the effectiveness of its administration. Moreover, legislation is, at best, a blunt weapon to combat immorality.

While this report does make certain specific recommendations for new criminal legislation or for strengthening existing criminal laws, the Committee has been careful to recommend only where the need is clear. Its major legislative recommendations relate to the creation of new institutions necessary to safeguard the electoral process, to provide the requisite checks against the abuse of executive power and to ensure the prompt and just enforcement of laws that already exist. Surely one of the most penetrating lessons of Watergate is that campaign practices must be effectively supervised and enforcement of the criminal laws vigorously pursued against all offenders—even those of high estate—if our free institutions are to survive.

41

The Committee's mandate was broad and its time to meet it brief. Nonetheless, the Committee believes that, through its efforts and those of others, the basic facts of the Watergate scandal have been exposed to public view and, as a result, the American people have been re-awakened to the task democracy imposes upon them—steadfast vigilance of the conduct of the public officials they choose to lead them. This public awareness, in turn, has provided the atmosphere necessary to support other essential governmental responses to Watergate such as the work of the Special Prosecutor and the activities of the House Judiciary Committee on impeachment. Because the nation is now alert, because the processes of justice are now functioning and because the time is ripe for passage of new laws to safeguard the electoral process, the Committee is hopeful that despite the excesses of Watergate, the nation will return to its democratic ideals established almost 200 years ago.

1. The Committee and Its Staff

As noted, the United States Senate created the Senate Select Committee on Presidential Campaign Activities on February 7, 1973 by unanimous adoption of S. Res. 60. The seven Committee members appointed by the Senate leadership to answer the mandate of S. Res. 60 were Sam J. Ervin, Jr. (D-N.C.), Chairman; Howard H. Baker, Jr. (R-Tenn.), Vice Chairman; Herman E. Talmadge (D-Ga.); Daniel K. Inouye (D-Hawaii); Joseph M. Montoya (D-N. Mex.); Edward J. Gurney (R-Fla.); and Lowell P. Weicker, Jr. (R-Conn.).

Like the Select Committee formed to investigate the "Teapot Dome" scandals nearly a half century ago, the Senate "Watergate" Committee, as it was quickly renamed by the news media, was born in the crisis of a serious loss of confidence by the public in its national government. At the time the Committee was established, the trial of the Watergate burglars had been recently completed with the conviction of the seven defendants, all but two of whom had pleaded guilty. The trial was prosecuted on the theory that G. Gordon Liddy, former FBI agent and counsel for the Finance Committee to Re-elect the President,* had masterminded the break-in of the Democratic National Committee headquarters and that no higher campaign or White House officials were involved. Chief Judge John Sirica, the presiding judge, never accepted this theory. His repeated questions to witnesses and the prosecution staff indicated his disbelief that criminal involvement stopped at Liddy. Courageous investigative reporters raised

* Hereinafter often referred to as FCRP.

similar doubts in news stories and columns. The smell of coverup was in the air. S. Res. 60, passed after the Watergate trial concluded, evinces the Senate's belief that the Department of Justice could not be trusted fully to investigate and uncover the true story of Watergate. But no substantial indication of the magnitude of the Watergate affair had yet emerged.

The Senate Select Committee was given the broadest mandate to investigate completely not only the break-in of the DNC headquarters and any subsequent coverup but also all other illegal, improper or unethical conduct occurring during the Presidential campaign of 1972, including political espionage and campaign financing practices. All the investigative powers at the Senate's disposal were given the Committee. Thus the Committee had the power of subpena, the power to grant limited or "use" immunity to witnesses to obtain their testimony* and the power to enforce the Committee's subpenas by initiating contempt procedures.

On February 21, 1973, at its first organizational meeting, the Committee, on the recommendation of Chairman Ervin, unanimously appointed Professor Samuel Dash as Chief Counsel and Staff Director for the Committee. Professor Dash had formerly been District Attorney in Philadelphia, an active trial lawyer and Chairman of the Section of Criminal Law of the American Bar Association. At the time of his appointment, Mr. Dash was Professor of Law and Director of the Institute of Criminal Law and Procedure of Georgetown University Law Center. Shortly afterwards, Vice-Chairman Baker, acting under the provisions of S. Res. 60, appointed as Minority Counsel Mr. Fred Thompson, a trial lawyer and former Assistant United States Attorney in Nashville, Tennessee.

During the month of March, the Chief Counsel selected as Deputy Chief Counsel Mr. Rufus Edmisten, who also served as Chief Counsel of the Senate Subcommittee on Separation of Powers, and his Assistant Chief Counsel for the three areas of the investigation—Watergate break-in and coverup, campaign practices and campaign financing. David M. Dorsen was assigned supervision of the campaign financing phase, including investigation of the milk fund affairs. Mr. Dorsen was specially aided in the milk fund investigation by Assistant Counsel Alan S. Weitz. Mr. Terry Lenzner took charge of the campaign practices phase and also headed the investigation into the Hughes/Rebozo matter. Serving as Mr.

---

* To grant "use" immunity is to ensure a witness that his testimony, or the fruits of his testimony, will not be used against him directly or indirectly in any subsequent criminal procedure. *See* 18 U.S.C. § 6002-6005.

Lenzner's principal aides in those investigations were Assistant Counsel Marc Lackritz and investigator Scott Armstrong. Mr. James Hamilton was assigned responsibility for the Watergate break-in and coverup phase; because of the rapid change in events, Messrs. Dorsen and Lenzner also spent considerable time on this phase. Mr. Hamilton, with the aid of Assistant Counsel Ronald D. Rotunda and Special Counsel Richard B. Stewart and a number of expert consultants,* was also responsible for most of the Committee's litigation efforts, including the preparation of the pleadings and briefs in its suit against the President, and, with Mr. Dorsen, supervised the investigation into the so-called Responsiveness Program. Both Mr. Dorsen and Mr. Lenzner had been Assistant United States Attorneys in the Southern District of New York, and Mr. Hamilton was a trial attorney with the Washington law firm of Covington and Burling.

Mr. Carmine Bellino, former FBI agent and a veteran of numerous important Congressional investigations, was appointed Chief Investigator. Professor Arthur Miller of George Washington Law School was named Chief Consultant to the staff. Minority Counsel Fred Thompson appointed as his chief assistant and investigator Donald Sanders, a former FBI agent and Chief Counsel and Staff Director to the House Internal Security Committee.

Appointment of other lawyers, investigators, secretarial personnel and research assistants followed over the next several months bringing the staff to a peak strength of approximately ninety persons by August of 1973.

2. Investigative Procedures

On March 21, 1973, while the Committee staff was still in its formative stages, James McCord, one of the convicted Watergate defendants, began the unraveling of the Watergate story by transmitting a sealed letter to Judge Sirica. On the morning of March 23, which had been set by Judge Sirica for the sentencing of the Watergate defendants, Judge Sirica in open Court unsealed the letter and read aloud McCord's first accusations of perjury at the trial and coverup.

At 1:00 p.m. the same day, Mr. McCord, through his attorney, called the Select Committee's Chief Counsel and offered to give information to the Committee. The Chief Counsel met with Mr. McCord and his counsel that afternoon and the following day, and Mr. McCord testified before an exe-

---

* Professor Arthur S. Miller, Professor Jerome A. Barron, Professor Donald S. Burris, Professor Sherman Cohn and Eugene Gressman. The Committee is particularly grateful to Professor Stewart who devoted many hours of his considerable talents to the Committee's litigation efforts.

cutive session of the full Committee early the following week. McCord's revelations to the Committee were the first indication that former Attorney General John Mitchell, Counsel to the President John W. Dean, III and Deputy Director of the Committee for the Re-election of the President* Jeb Stuart Magruder had participated in the planning and discussion with G. Gordon Liddy respecting a large-scale covert intelligence operation that ultimately resulted in the Watergate break-in.

Although McCord had been a participant in the break-in, he had obtained information about the planning meetings and the later payments of "hush" money to purchase silence through discussions with Liddy and others. Thus, the involvement of higher officials in Watergate activities could not be fully proved through McCord's testimony, since it was largely hearsay. Although a Senate investigating committee may receive hearsay testimony, the Select Committee decided, because of its desire to limit unfounded rumor and speculation, to employ a higher standard of proof for the establishment of crucial facts. It was thus decided that McCord's testimony would not be presented in public session unless it could be corroborated by other evidence.

Accordingly, the staff began an intensive investigation. Secretaries to key officials at CRP, the White House and the Department of Justice, as well as other staff personnel, were questioned and their records subpenaed and examined. Gradually, corroboration for McCord's story emerged. A secretary's diary was uncovered which showed meetings in Mr. Mitchell's Justice Department office on January 27 and February 4, 1972, attended by Messrs. Mitchell, Dean, Magruder and Liddy. A CRP staff member remembered Liddy's agitated search for an easel in the CRP offices on the morning of January 27. (McCord had told the Committee that, according to Liddy, Liddy had that day made a show and tell presentation respecting his intelligence plan in the Attorney General's office using large cards on an easel.) A secretary recalled seeing Liddy with several large white cards wrapped in brown paper in the CRP office prior to the January 27 meeting. The former FCRP treasurer, Hugh Sloan, informed the Committee of Magruder's effort to suborn his perjury before the Grand Jury. Sloan also gave evidence as to the large amounts of cash paid to Liddy with Mr. Mitchell's approval for purposes concerning which Sloan said Maurice Stans told him "I do not want to know and you don't want to know." (2 *Hearings* 539)

As hundreds of details were collected, it became clear that the Committee could corroborate with circumstantial evidence

* Hereinafter often referred to as CRP.

much of McCord's hearsay testimony. More importantly, in April certain of the principals involved—Mr. Magruder and Mr. Dean—signified their willingness to testify before the Committee.

A. USE OF IMMUNITY POWERS

It was then that the use of immunity powers granted the Committee became important. Magruder and Dean were being questioned by the United States Attorneys in preparation for their grand jury testimony. They were targets for indictment and could not be expected to cooperate with the Committee without a grant of "use" immunity. The Committee voted immunity for these witnesses and others and thus secured the direct testimony of persons who had participated in criminal acts.

The staff, most of whom had been employed in April, had uncovered by the middle of May, much of the evidence it was to present during the Watergate phase of the hearings, a result obtained by around-the-clock efforts. Also, the members of the Committee held frequent Executive Committee meetings to receive staff progress reports, legal opinions and to vote use of subpena and immunity powers to assist the staff in obtaining the facts. In exercising its immunity power, the Committee weighed carefully the determinative question whether the testimony to be gained was vital to the Committee's investigation or would reveal the significant involvement of persons of greater rank. The Committee did not seek an immunity order for any witness who could not meet these tests and would only provide information as to his own involvement in the Watergate affair.

In April, the Committee announced that public hearings would begin May 17, 1973 on the Watergate and coverup phase of the investigation. While this provided only short lead time, the Committee was deeply conscious of public concern about the true parameters of the Watergate matter. It thus believed public hearings should start as promptly as possible. The Committee opened its hearings on May 17, 1973, and maintained its hearing schedule, which increased from three to five days a week, without interruption (except for two brief recesses) until August 7, 1973. Thirty-seven witnesses testified during this period, hundreds of exhibits and documents were introduced into the record and over three thousand pages of testimony were transcribed. The Committee's hearings on the Watergate break-in and coverup phase constituted the longest uninterrupted Congressional hearings in the history of the Congress.

B. "SATELLITE" CHARTS ON KEY WITNESSES

While many techniques to gain evidence were used, one investigative strategy in particular was responsible for some of the staff's most significant results, including the discovery of the White House taping system. In regard to each major witness, the Chief Counsel assigned a team of lawyers and investigators to collect as much evidence as possible respecting this witness from secondary sources. To accomplish this most efficiently, each team prepared what the staff came to call a "satellite" chart for every major witness. Plotted on the chart would be the name and position of every person who had a significant contact with the witness during relevant time periods and who had been in a position to receive pertinent information and records. One principal witness alone had sixty satellites on his chart. Each satellite witness was interviewed by the staff and his or her records subpenaed and examined. The now famous ITT memorandum from Charles Colson to H.R. Haldeman was obtained from a satellite on Mr. Colson's chart. (Exhibit 121, 8 *Hearings* 3372-76) And Mr. Butterfield, who revealed the White House taping system, was interviewed simply because he was a satellite on Mr. Haldeman's chart.

After John Dean informed the Committee that he suspected that the President had taped a conversation between them in the Oval Office on April 15, 1973, some potentially knowledgeable witnesses were asked whether the President did, in fact, tape conversations. When Deputy Minority Counsel Donald Sanders asked Mr. Butterfield whether he knew of any facts supporting Dean's intimation that conversations in the President's office were tape recorded, Butterfield responded by informing the Committee of the White House taping system. Then, in response to an earlier question by investigator Scott Armstrong, Butterfield stated that the reconstruction of the President's conversations wih John Dean, which had been given to the Committee by Special Counsel to the President J. Fred Buzhardt, must have been prepared by use of the tapes of those meetings.

C. COMPUTER OPERATIONS

Another important investigative tool was the computer of the Library of Congress whose capabilities were offered the Committee shortly after its formation. The Committee accepted this offer and developed a computer staff to utilize this facility. To the Committee's knowledge, this was the first time a Congressional investigating committee employed a computer for the storage of information for investigative and analytical purposes.* Almost all of the Committee's investigative files and records were stored on computer tapes including documentary records, witness interviews, executive sessions, public sessions, depositions in related civil cases, the transcript of the first Watergate trial and certain newspaper clippings for the period from June 17, 1972 through the investigative phase. Computer printouts on individual witnesses permitted the staff to retrieve all available information respecting a given witness. Thus discrepancies in testimony could easily be spotted and relevant documents identified for use in examination. The computer also proved a valuable tool for preparation of the Committee's final report.

On the basis of its experience, the Committee recommends the use of computer technology in future Congressional investigations. It also notes that the computer staff has assisted the Special Prosecutor and the House Judiciary Committee with a complete duplicate of its computer tape, and that Committee's impeachment inquiry thus has at its disposal the Select Committee's complete computer input.

D. OTHER INVESTIGATIVE PROCEDURES

The Committee employed a variety of procedures for obtaining facts. Witnesses were usually interviewed informally and not under oath. Hundreds of witnesses were interviewed either in the Committee offices in the New Senate Office Building or at various places throughout the country. In cases where the witness was testifying under a grant of immunity or it was otherwise important to have his or her testimony under oath, the witness was examined in executive session. Oaths for executive sessions were administered by a member of the Committee and verbatim transcriptions of testimony prepared.

Thousands of documents, records and other tangible evidentiary materials were subpenaed by the Committee, examined by the staff and the Committee and stored in secure files. The Committee's investigation was aided by the fact that the staffs of the White House and the CRP frequently recorded their activities in documentary form. It appeared to be the practice of the officials involved to circulate duplicate copies of various memoranda throughout the White House and CRP and the files of CRP were filled with duplicate copies of memoranda written by top White House officials. After the 1972 election, CRP delivered its files to the National Archives. When the Select Committee learned this had occurred, a subpena for these files was issued and, over a period of months, staff investigators examined a vast collection of documents stored at the Archives. A great number of "confidential/eyes

* A report on the computer technology used appears in Chapter X (Vol. 2).

only" memoranda thus became available for the Committee's inspection. A significant number of the memoranda revealed during the public hearings and/or embodied in this final report came from this source.

3. The Public Hearings

The character of the Committee's hearings resulted from considerable planning and a basic philosophy. The Committee, aware of the gravity of the national scandal it was investigating and the fact that its activities would be highly publicized, was determined to present dignified, objective hearings. It recognized that the ultimate impact of its work depended upon obtaining and keeping public confidence.

In part for these reasons, the Committee resisted calling certain so-called "big name" witnesses at the beginning of its hearings. The Committee and staff wished to present a careful presentation of the evidence, establishing a foundation for the later testimony that implicated high government and campaign officials. Early witnesses of lesser stature that enabled the public to understand the context in which the Watergate affair unfolded were essential. The Chief Counsel and staff recommended this "building block" approach to the Committee and the Committee unanimously adopted it.

The Committee followed a practice not typical of many Congressional hearings. It refrained from calling a witness in public session that it knew would refuse to testify on the assertion of the Fifth Amendment privilege against self-incrimination. When a witness in executive session claimed this Constitutional right and declined to answer the Committee's queries, the matter ended and the witness was not required to assert his privilege in public session. This policy was instituted upon the recommendation of the Chief Counsel, with which the Committee agreed, on the belief that no legislative purpose would be served by public exhibitions of witnesses who claimed their privilege.

The Committee believed it was important that its public hearings be televised. Live television coverage occurred during the first phase of the Committee's hearings covering the Watergate break-in and the coverup.

Public Television carried, through its evening gavel-to-gavel coverage, most of the Committee's public hearings.

The Committee's interest in televised hearings was not to obtain publicity for publicity's sake. The facts which the Committee produced dealt with the very integrity of the electoral process; they were facts, the Committee believed, the public had a right to know. Most citizens are not able personally to attend the working sessions of their government. Although thousands of people spent short periods in the Caucus Room during the hearings, these visitors represented only a small percentage of the electorate. Thus, it was desirable that every citizen be able to view the hearings, if not in the Caucus Room, then in his home or place of business. The ability to read about the hearings in the printed media was not sufficient. The full import of the hearings could onyl be achieved by observing the witnesses and hearing their testimony.

It was for this reason that the Committee opposed the efforts in federal court of Special Prosecutor Cox to proscribe television and radio coverage of the testimony of Magruder and Dean. The Special Prosecutor's expressed concern was that public hearings might prejudice future criminal trials. It was the Committee's position that they would not, but, even if they did, it was more important in this period of crisis and national concern that the full facts be promptly made known. The public should not have to wait a year or more until the Watergate trials were over to know the scope of the corruption in its government.

The court agreed with the Committee's position and refused to interfere with the Committee's public hearings. The Committee believes that its position has proven correct and that its public hearings awakened the public to the specific perils posed by the Watergate affair to the integrity of the electoral process and our democratic form of government.

Perhaps proof of the impact of the Committee's hearings is found in the unprecedented public response to the firing of Special Prosecutor Cox on October 20, 1973. On that weekend alone, a half million telegrams came to the Congress. Hundreds of thousands of telegrams flowed in during the following days. The overwhelming sentiment of these telegrams was in opposition to the President's action. It is doubtful that public sentiment would have been so aroused by the President's action had the public not been sensitized to the issues involved through the Committee's hearings.

The Committee wishes to note that it has received no evidence suggesting any complicity in wrongdoing on the part of the Republican National Committee or the Democratic National Committee or its principal officers during the Presidential Campaign of 1972.*

* During the time covered by this investigation, the Chairman of the Republican National Committee was Senator Robert Dole and the Chairman of the Democratic National Committee was Lawrence F. O'Brien.

CHAPTER I

THE WATERGATE BREAK-IN
AND COVERUP

The Watergate drama is still unfolding.* Because all the facts
are not yet in, because all the Watergate criminal trials and
the impeachment proceeding are not concluded, and because
the President has refused to produce to the Select Committee many crucial tape recordings and other evidence, this
report—although it is the Committee's final report—is limited
by these factors. And this report is limited in another way.
Because of the massive amount of evidence now available as
to Watergate developed in the Committee's hearings and
elsewhere, it is impossible in a document of reasonable length
to deal with every fact or every version of the facts. The
Committee, therefore, in preparing this report, has exercised
its judgment as to what facts are important and which versions of disputed facts should be included. Others may disagree with our account, but it is the Committee's mandate
under Sen. Res. 60 to present the Watergate affair to the
public as it sees it.

1. The Watergate Break-in and Its Prelude

In the early morning hours of June 17, 1972, James Mc-
Cord, Bernard L. Barker, Frank Sturgis, Eugenio Martinez
and Virgilio Gonzales illegally entered the sixth floor headquarters of the Democratic National Committee in the Watergate Office Building. (1 *Hearings* 128) Nearby, in a room
in the Watergate Hotel, Howard Hunt and G. Gordon Liddy,
the supervisors of this burglary operation, stood by keeping
in walkie-talkie communication with Alfred Baldwin who
served as a lookout across the street from the Watergate complex in the Howard Johnson Motor Lodge. (1 *Hearings* 158,
402; 9 *Hearings* 3688; Hunt Executive Session, Sept. 10,
1973, pp. 37-8) The mission was ill-fated. Within a short
time after the break-in, a Washington Metropolitan Police
Department plainclothes unit in an unmarked car responded
to a call to assist a guard at the Watergate Office Building.
(1 *Hearings* 96) The guard, Frank Wills, had become suspicious when, for the second time that night, he found masking tape on the edge of a door in the garage leading to
the office building. (Wills Interview, May 22, 1973, pp. 2-3)

* This report was prepared prior to the public release of any evidence or
materials by the Judiciary Committee of the House of Representatives.

The tape had been placed to hold back the locking mechanism, permitting the door to be opened without a key. (1 *Hearings* 98) Earlier that night, Wills had removed tape from the same door thinking it had been inadvertantly left by a building engineer. (Wills Interview, May 22, 1973, pp. 1-2)

The plainclothes unit, under the direction of Sergeant Paul Leeper (1 *Hearings* 95), entered the Watergate Office Building stairwell through the garage door and ascended to the eighth floor. The policemen worked their way down to the sixth floor level and entered that floor through the stairwell door which they found unlocked by the same masking tape technique employed on the garage door. (1 *Hearings* 103-104)

Alfred Baldwin, across the street at the Howard Johnson Motor Lodge, at first took no interest in the unmarked car which parked in front of the Watergate Office Building and in the casually dressed individuals who entered the building. (1 *Hearings* 403) That a plainclothes police squad in an unmarked car answered the police dispatcher's call was fortuitous. The call initially went out to a marked police car but that vehicle was on its way to a gasoline station. The dispatcher thus repeated the call for any tactical unit in the vicinity of the Watergate. (1 *Hearings* 96) Had the marked police car answered the call and had uniformed policemen entered the office building, Baldwin would have immediately taken notice and alerted the burglars who might have escaped. The true nature of the break-in might not have been discovered and there might have been no need for the massive coverup that followed which, when exposed, became the most serious political scandal in the nation's history.

Baldwin did not become alarmed until he noticed lights go on in the building—first on the eighth floor, then on the sixth—and saw two casually dressed individuals emerge on the sixth floor terrace of the DNC headquarters, one holding a pistol. Then he radioed Hunt and Liddy and asked "are our people in suits or are they dressed casually?" When the answer came back, "Our people are dressed in suits. Why?" Baldwin replied "You have some trouble because there are some individuals around here who are dressed casually and have got their gun out." Within minutes, Sergeant Leeper and his unit discovered the five burglars and arrested them. (1 *Hearings* 404) Hunt and Liddy, however, escaped unnoticed from the Watergate Hotel. Baldwin was told by Hunt to leave the Motor Lodge, which he promptly did. (1 *Hearings* 405)

Subsequently Hunt and Liddy were indicted with the five

men apprehended in the DNC headquarters (*United States v. Liddy, et al.,* Indictment of September 15, 1972) and Baldwin became a principal government witness against his former co-conspirators. All defendants initially pleaded not guilty. But, as the trial opened in early January, 1973, Hunt, Barker, Sturgis, Martinez, and Gonzales changed their pleas to guilty. (Watergate Trial Transcript, pp. 106-129 and 357-423; January 11, 15, 1973) The remaining defendants—McCord and Liddy—were found guilty (Watergate Trial Transcript, p. 2247) after a trial that left a number of questions which disturbed the Trial Judge, Congress and the American people. The crimes of wiretapping, burglary and conspiracy had been proved. But, why had these crimes been committed? Who sponsored them? What were the motivations? Was the break-in, as the White House immediately claimed, merely a "third-rate burglary"?

This report attempts to put this crime in focus. We discuss below the background and planning that led to the break-in as well as other activities by the burglary team now uncovered. We then deal with the extensive coverup that followed the apprehension of the burglars.

A. THE BACKGROUND OF WATERGATE

The Watergate break-in cannot be understood unless viewed in the context of similar White House activities. The evidence presented below shows that, from the early days of the present Administration, the power of the President was viewed by some in the White House as almost without limit. Especially if national or internal security was invoked, even criminal laws were considered subordinate to presidential decision or strategy. The manifestations of this philosophy that preceded the Watergate break-in are now discussed.

1. The Huston Plan. The earliest evidence that this concept of Presidential power existed is found in a 1970 top secret document entitled *Operational Restraints on Intelligence Collection* (Exhibit 35, 3 *Hearings* 1062, 1319) and the various memoranda from Tom Charles Huston to H. R. Haldeman which were first revealed by John Dean. (Exhibits 36-40, 42, 3 *Hearings* 1062, 1324-33, 1338) In preparation for his testimony before the Select Committee, Dean placed these papers, some of which bore the highest security classification, in the custody of Chief Judge John Sirica of the United States District Court for the District of Columbia. This step was taken by Dean, on the advice of counsel, to avoid violation of any presidential directive or federal laws prohibiting release of government documents affecting national security. After due consideration, Judge Sirica released one copy of these papers to the Department of Justice and one copy to the Select Committee, pursuant to its motion (*United States v. John Doe, et al.*, Misc. No. 77-73, May 14, 1973)

The Committee, with the aid of various intelligence agencies, reviewed these documents. While the Committee sealed a few items therein which could involve national security considerations, it concluded that these papers, for the most part, dealt primarily with domestic affairs and were unrelated to national security matters. (3 *Hearings* 1060, 1062) The papers, as sanitized by the Committee, were entered into the Committee's record during Dean's testimony. (Exhib-it 35-41, 3 *Hearings* 1062, 1319-1337)

These papers and the President's own statement of May 22, 1973, disclose that the President approved the use of illegal wiretapping, illegal break-ins and illegal mail covers for domestic intelligence purposes. The President was fully advised of the illegality of these intelligence-gathering techniques prior to approving them. In the top secret document entitled *Operational Restraints on Intelligence Collection,* the recommendation for surreptitious entries (break-ins) contained the following statement under the heading "Rationale":

"Use of this technique is clearly illegal. It amounts to burglary. It is also highly risky and could result in great embarrassment if exposed. However, it is also the most fruitful tool and can produce the type of intelligence which cannot be obtained in any other fashion." (Exhibit 35, 3 *Hearings* 1321)

On July 14, 1970, Haldeman sent a top secret memorandum to Huston, notifying him of the President's approval of the use of burglaries, illegal wiretaps and illegal mail covers for domestic intelligence. In the memorandum, Haldeman stated:

"The recommendations you have proposed as a result of the review, have been approved by the President. He does not, however, want to follow the procedure you outlined on page 4 of your memorandum regarding implementation. He would prefer that *the thing simply be put into motion* on the basis of this approval. The formal official memorandum should, of course, be prepared and that should be the device by which to carry it out . . ." (Exhibit 36, 3 *Hearings* 1324) (emphasis added)

It appears that the next day, July 15, 1970, Huston prepared a decision memorandum, based on the President's approval, for distribution to the federal intelligence agencies involved in the plan—the FBI, the CIA, the National Security Agency and the Defense Intelligence Agency. (New York *Times*, June 7, 1973, p. 36) In his May 22, 1973, public statement, the President reported that the decision memorandum was circulated to the agencies involved on July 23, 1970. However, the decision memorandum is dated July 15, 1970, indicating that it was forwarded to the agencies on that day or shortly thereafter. (New York *Times,* June 7, 1973)

Huston's recommendations were opposed by J. Edgar Hoover, Director of the FBI. (3 *Hearings* 916) Hoover had served as the chairman of a group comprised of the heads of the Federal Intelligence agencies formed to study the problems of intelligence-gathering and cooperation among the various intelligence agencies. (Presidential Press Statement May 22, 1973) In his public statement of May 22, 1973, President Nixon stated:

> "After reconsideration, however, prompted by the opposition of Director Hoover, the agencies were notified five days later, on July 28, that the approval had been rescinded."

Haldeman's testimony is to the same effect (7 *Hearings* 2874). Dean, however, testified that he was not aware of any recision of approval for the plan (3 *Hearings* 1066) and there apparently is no written record of a recision of July 28 or any other date. There is, however, clear evidence that, after receipt of the decision memorandum of July 15, 1970, Mr. Hoover did present strong objections concerning the plan to Attorney General Mitchell. (3 *Hearings* 916; 4 *Hearings* 1603)

Huston was concerned that Hoover's objections would interfere with the plan's implementation. On August 5, 1970, eight days *after* the President states he ordered recision, Huston sent Haldeman a lengthy top secret memorandum on the subject, *"Domestic Intelligence,"* which strongly attacked Hoover's objections and made a number of recommendations concerning a forthcoming meeting regarding the plan among Haldeman, the Attorney General and Hoover. (Exhibit 37, 3 *Hearings* 1325-1329) Illustrative of the fact that the plan was still quite alive, but imperiled by Hoover, is the following language in this memorandum:

> "At some point, Hoover has to be told who is President. He has become totally unreasonable and his conduct is

detrimental to our domestic intelligence operations . . . It is important to remember that the entire intelligence community knows that the President made a positive decision to go ahead and Hoover has now succeeded in forcing a review. If he gets his way, it is going to look like he is more powerful than the President. He had his say in the footnotes and RN decided against him. That should close the matter and I can't understand why the AG is a party in reopening it. All of us are going to look damned silly in the eyes of Helms, Gayler, Bennett, and the military chiefs if Hoover can unilaterally reverse a Presidential decision based on a report that many people worked their asses off to prepare and which, on the merits, was a first-rate, objective job." (Exhibit 37, 3 *Hearings* 1326)

It should be noted that this memorandum indicates that the NSA, DIA, CIA and the military services basically supported the Huston recommendations.

Two days later, on August 7, 1970, Huston sent a brief, confidential memorandum to Haldeman urging that Haldeman "meet with the Attorney General and secure his support for the President's decision, that the Director (Hoover) be informed that the decision will stand, and that all intelligence agencies are to proceed to implement them at once." (Exhibit 38, 3 *Hearings* 1330) Huston noted that: "Mr. Hoover has departed for the West Coast to vacation for three weeks. If you wait until his return to clear up the problems surrounding our Domestic Intelligence operations, we will be into the new school year without any preparations." (id.) Later, on September 18, 1970 (almost two months after the President claims the plan was rescinded), Dean sent a top secret memorandum to the Attorney General suggesting certain procedures to *commence our domestic intelligence operation as quickly as possible.*" (emphasis added) This memorandum specifically called for the creation of an Inter-Agency Domestic Intelligence Unit which had been an integral part of the Huston plan. Dean's memorandum to the Attorney General observed that Hoover was strongly opposed to the creation of such a unit and that it was important "to bring the FBI fully on board." Far from indicating that the President's approval of Huston's recommendation to remove restraints on illegal intelligence-gathering had been withdrawn, Dean, in his memorandum, suggested to the Attorney General:

"I believe we agreed that it would be inappropriate to

56

have any blanket removal of restrictions; rather, the most appropriate procedure would be to decide on the type of intelligence we need, based on an assessment of the recommendations of this unit, and then proceed to *remove the restraints as necessary to obtain such intelligence.*" (Exhibit 41, 3 *Hearings* 1335) (emphasis added)

Dean's memorandum indicated that the creation of the Inter-Agency Domestic Intelligence Unit would go forward and provided recommendations for the choosing of a Unit Director to serve as a "righthand man" to the Attorney General and for the selection of representatives from the various intelligence agencies who would serve on it. Dean closed his memorandum with the suggestion that the Attorney General call weekly meetings to monitor problems as they emerged and "to make certain that we are *moving this program into implementation as quickly as possible.*" (Exhibit 41, 3 *Hearings* 1337) (emphasis added) Recognizing that Hoover was still a problem, Dean added a note to the bottom of his memorandum, stating, "Bob Haldeman has suggested to me that if you would like him to join you in a meeting with Hoover he will be happy to do so." (Exhibit 41, 3 *Hearings* 1337)

Hoover, however, never did come completely "on board" and the plan for an Inter-Agency Domestic Intelligence Unit was never implemented. A clue to the fate of the Huston plan is provided by the edited, unauthenticated submission of Recorded Presidential Conversations to the Judiciary Committee of the House of Representatives by President Richard Nixon, April 30, 1974, where the following passage appears:

D . . . what Bill Sullivan's desire in life is, is to set up a domestic national security intelligence system, a White House program. He says we are deficient. He says we have never been efficient, because Hoover lost his guts several years ago. If you recall he and Tom Huston worked on it. Tom Huston had your instructions to go out and do it and the whole thing just crumbled.

P (inaudible) (Edited Presidential Conversations, pp. 123-124)

Dean testified that the plan for the creation of an Inter-Agency Domestic Intelligence Unit was the product of White House fear of demonstrations and dissent. (3 *Hearings* 916) Haldeman denied that such an atmosphere of fear existed in the White House. (7 *Hearings* 2874) In his statement before the Committee, Haldeman gave as the reason for

White House interest in improving intelligence-gathering operations the "critical proportions" of the domestic security problem in 1970 as illustrated by "a wave of bombings and explosions, rioting and violence, demonstrations, arson, gun battles and other disruptive activities across the country— on college campuses primarily—but also in other areas." (7 *Hearings* 2874) On this issue, Ehrlichman's testimony corroborates Haldeman's. (6 *Hearings* 2512-13)

The Huston recommendations themselves refer to "a major threat to the internal security" (Exhibit 35, 3 *Hearings* 1319) and an expression of the belief that "the potential for even greater violence is present and we have a positive obligation to take every step within our power to prevent it (Exhibit 37, 3 *Hearings* 1327) . . . for surely drastic violence and disorder threaten the very fabric of our society." (Id. at 1328)

The Committee notes that the evidence presented to Senator McClellan's Permanent Subcommittee on Investigations of the Senate Committee on Government Operations in hearings beginning in July, 1970 indicates that, in the several years preceding the hearings, there were significant increases in illegal acts of violence directed against government facilities and a disturbing number of such acts directed against law enforcement officials. *(See generally, 24 Hearings Before the Permanent Subcommittee on Investigations, tr. at 5313 et seq.)*

Dean testified, however, that the White House concern was directed not only toward violent demonstrations, but also to peaceful demonstrations and dissent. As an illustration he said:

". . . [D]uring the late winter of 1971 . . . the President happened to look out of the windows of the residence of the White House and saw a lone man with a large 10-foot sign stretched out in front of Lafayette Park. Mr. Higby called me to his office to tell me of the President's displeasure with the sign in the park and told me that Mr. Haldeman said the sign had to come down. When I came out of Mr. Higby's office, I ran into Mr. Dwight Chapin who said that he was going to get some 'thugs' to remove that man from Lafayette Park. He said it would take him a few hours to get them, but they could do the job." (3 *Hearings* 917)

2. *The Enemies List.* The White House apparent concern over dissent and opposition is reflected in an organized effort to compile a constantly updated list of the Administration's "enemies." The basic rationale for maintenance of the enemies list is specified in an August 16, 1971 memorandum

prepared by Dean for Haldeman, Ehrlichman and others. (4 *Hearings* 1349-50) It reads in relevant part:

> *"Dealing with our Political Enemies*
> "This memorandum addresses the matter of how we can maximize the fact of our incumbency in dealing with persons known to be active in their opposition to our Administration. *Stated a bit more bluntly—how can we use the available federal machinery to screw our political enemies.*
>
> * * *
>
> "In brief, the system would work as follows:
> "—Key members of the staff (e.g., Colson, Dent, Flanigan, Buchanan) should be requested to inform us as to who they feel we should be giving a hard time.
> —The project coordinator should then determine what sorts of dealings these individuals have with the federal government and *how we can best screw them (e. g., grant availability, federal contracts, litigation, prosecution, etc.).*
> —The project coordinator then should have access to and the full support of the top officials of the agency or department in proceeding to deal with the individual.
>
> * * *
>
> "As a next step, I would recommend that we develop a small list of names—not more than ten—as *our targets for concentration.* Request that Lyn [Nofziger] 'do a job' on them and if he finds he is getting cut off by a department or agency, that he inform us and we evaluate what is necessary to proceed. . . ." (Exhibit 48, 4 *Hearings* 1689-90) (emphasis added)

Dean's advice to limit the list to not more than ten was not followed. Even before this memorandum, George T. Bell circulated to Dean, Jerry Warren and Van Shumway a sizeable "list of opponents" that "would be useful from time to time." (Exhibit 49, Memorandum of June 24, 1971; 4 *Hearings* 1693) The list contained such comments next to various names as: "A scandal would be most helpful here;" "Positive results would stick a pin in Jackson's white hat;" "Has known weakness for white females;" "A real media enemy." (*Id.* at 1695-96) On September 9, 1971, Colson sent the same list to Dean, with blue check marks next to the "enemies" who were "top priority." Colson concluded: ". . . I think you will find this a pretty good list. Right on!" (Exhibit 49, 4 *Hearings* 1692) Other exhibits indicate that the list was constantly updated and expanded to include businessmen, actors and actresses, labor leaders, reporters, Senators and Representatives, civil rights leaders, McGovern aides, leaders of peace organizations, general "anti-Nixon" people, Democratic contributors and others. (Exhibits 50-65, 4 *Hearings* 1693-1753)

Dean testified that the plan to penalize Administration enemies was considered important to Haldeman, Ehrlichman and others. (4 *Hearings* 1527) Strachan testified that he believed that the Enemies List "was in existence when I arrived at the White House in [August 1970] . . [T]he list was maintained by Colson's office . . ." (Strachan Executive Session, July 12, 1973, p. 15)

White House efforts to use the federal bureaucracy to punish its supposed enemies are further reflected in Committee Exhibits 44 and 65. (4 *Hearings* 1682, 1753) Exhibit 44 (4 *Hearings* 1682) is a memorandum and briefing paper prepared for Haldeman for a meeting with the head of the Internal Revenue Service which came from John Dean's White House file entitled "Opponents List and Enemies Project." (4 *Hearings* 1349) The memorandum is undated and not marked other than its heading: *"To accomplish:* Make IRS politically responsive." (4 *Hearings* 1682) Attached to this memorandum is an *"I.R.S. Talking Paper"* that concludes with the following:

"[Johnnie] Walters [of the I.R.S.] must be made to know that discreet political actions and investigations on behalf of the Administration are a firm requirement and responsibility on his part.
"We should have direct access to Walters for action in the sensitive areas and should not have to clear them with Treasury.
"Dean should have access and assurance that Walters will get the job done—properly!" (4 *Hearings* 1684)

Dean recalled that, after an article was published in *Newsday* on Charles ("Bebe") Rebozo, one of the President's closest friends, Dean was told that the "authors of that article should have some problems." (3 *Hearings* 1072) Dean discussed this with John Caulfield, who had friends in the I.R.S. (Dean was reluctant to discuss it with Walters). Dean recalls that the I.R.S. did audit the newsman involved. *(Id.)*

It appears other "enemies" were also subjected to I.R.S. investigation and audit. During the September 15, 1972 meeting with the President, "Dean reported on IRS investigation of Larry O'Brien," according to information Fred Buzhardt, Special Counsl to the President, provided to Minority Counsel.

(Exhibit 70A 4 *Hearings* 1796) * In a memorandum of June 12, 1972 to Dean, Colson wrote that there should be an IRS audit of a union official whom "you should know is an all out enemy, a McGovernite, ardently anti-Nixon . . . Please let me know if this one can be started on at once and if there is an informer's fee, let me know. There is a good cause at which it can be donated." (Exhibit 45, 4 *Hearings* 1686)

In Dean's meeting with the President on September 15, 1972, the President, Dean and Haldeman discussed retaliation against Administration "enemies," according to a purported transcript of this meeting prepared by the House Judiciary Committee published in the Washington *Post* on May 17, 1974, at pp. A 26-8. This transcript indicates the President may have known of the enemies list. Haldeman, at the beginning of this meeting, referred to the fact that Colson "has gone through, you know, has worked on the list, and Dean's working the, the thing through IRS and, uh, in some cases, I think . . ." and the President allegedly replied: "Yeah." Other relevant excerpts from this September 15th meeting based on the Judiciary Committee's purported transcript appear below with emphasis added:

(Unintelligible words)

H   John (Dean), he is one of the quiet guys that gets a lot done. That was a good move, too, bring Dean in. But its—

P   Yeah.

H   It—. He'll never, he'll never gain any ground for us. He's just not that kind of guy. But, he's the kind that enables other people to gain ground while he's making sure that you don't fall through the holes.

P   Oh. You mean—

H   Between times, *he's doing, he's moving ruthlessly on the investigation of McGovern people, Kennedy stuff, . . and all that too.* I just don't know how much progress he's making, 'cause I—

P   The problem is that's kind of hard to find.

H   Chuck, Chuck has gone through, *you know, has worked on the list,* and Dean's working the, the thing *through IRS* and, uh, in some cases, I think, some other (unintelligible) things. He's—He turned out to be tougher than I thought he would, which is what—

P   Yeah.

* * *

---

* Dean's reference to the use of the IRS to attack "enemies" is supported by a recent federal court decision in which the Court found that in the plaintiff's case White House corrupt influence of the IRS was not only attempted but was successful. *Center for Corporate Responsibility v. Schultz,* F. Supp. 00 (D.D.C., Dec. 11, 1973) (C.A. No. 846-73)

P   Well, just remember all the trouble they made us on this. *We'll have a chance to get back at them one day.* How are you doing on your other investigations? Your— How does this (unintelligible).

D   I'm just about the end of the, uh—

H   What's happened on the bug?

P   Hard, hard to find—on the what?

H   The bug.

* · * · *

P   Perhaps the Bureau ought to go over—

H   *The Bureau ought to go into Edward Bennett Williams and let's start questioning that son-of-a-bitch.* Keep him tied up for a couple of weeks.

P   *Yeah, I hope they do.* They—The Bureau better get over pretty quick and get that red box. We want it cleared up—(unintelligible)

D   That's exactly the way I, I gave it to Gray, I uh,—

* · * · *

D   On this case. Uh, there is some bitterness between for example, the Finance Committee and the Political Committee. They feel that they're taking all the heat, and, and, uh, all the people upstairs are bad people and they're not being recognized.

P   Ridiculous.

D   It is—I mean—

P   They're all in it together.

D   That's right.

P   *They should just, uh, just behave and, and, recognize this, this is again, this is war.* We're getting a few shots and it'll be over, and we'll give them a few shots, and it'll be over. Don't worry. (Unintelligible), and I wouldn't want to be on the other side right now. Would you? *I wouldn't want to be in Edward Bennett Williams', Williams' position after this election.*

D   No. No.

P   *None of these bastards.*

D   He, uh, he's done some rather unethical things that have come to light already, which he, again, Richey has brought to our attention.

P   Yeah?

D   He went down—

H   Keep a log on all that—

D   Oh, we are, indeed, we are.

P   Yeah.

H   Because afterwards that is a guy,

P   We're going to—

H   That is a guy we've got to ruin.

D   He had, he had an ex parte—

P   You want to remember, too, he's an attorney for *The Washington Post*.

D   I'm well aware of that.

P   *I think we are going to fix the son-of-a-bitch. Believe me. We are going to. We've got to, because he's a bad man.*

D   Absolutely.

P   He misbehaved very badly in the Hoffa matter. Our—some pretty bad conduct, there, too, but go ahead.

D   Well, that's uh, along the line, uh, one of the things I've tried to do, is just keep notes on a lot of the people who are emerging as—

P   That's right.

D   as less than our friends.

P   Great!

D   Because this is going to be over someday and they're—We shouldn't forget the way some of them have treated us.

P   I want the most—I want the most comprehensive notes on all those who tried to do us in. Because they didn't have to do it.

D   That's right.

P   They didn't have to do it. I mean, if the thing a had been clo—uh, they had a very close election everybody on the other side would understand this game. But now they are doing this quite deliberately and they are asking for it and they are going to get it. And this, this, we—we have not used the power in this first four years, as you know.

D   That's right.

P   We have never used it. *We haven't used the Bureau and we haven't used the Justice Department, but things are going to change now.* And they're going to change, and, and they're going to get it right.

D   That's an exciting prospect.

P   It's got to be done. It's the only thing to do.

*   *   *

D   Well, there has been some extensive clipping by the counsel in this case, and I've gone through some of these clippings and it's just phenomenal the, uh,

P   Yeah.

D   the amount of coverage this case is getting. They may never get a fair trial, may never get a fair—I mean they'll never get a jury that can convict them or pull it together. And *The Post,* as you know, has got a, a, a real large team that they've assigned to do nothing but this, sh—, this case. Couldn't believe they put Maury Stans' story about his libel suit, which was just playing so heavily on the networks last night, and in the evening news, they put it way back on about page 8 of *The Post.*

P   Sure.

D   and didn't even cover it as a—in total.

P   I expect that, that's all right. We've (unintelligible)

H   *The Post* (unintelligible)—

P   *It's going to have its problems—*

H   (Unintelligible)

D   (Unintelligible) The networks are good with Maury coming back 3 days in a row and (unintelligible)

P   That's right. The main, main thing is *The Post is is going to have damnable, damnable problems out of this one. They have a television station.*

D   That's right, they do.

P   Does that come up too? The point is, when does it come up?

D   I don't know. But the practice of non-licensees filing on top of licensees has certainly gotten more,

P   That's right.

D   more active in the, this area.

P   And it's going to be God damn active here.

D   (Laughter) (Silence)

P   *Well, the game has to be played awfully rough.* I don't know, well now, you, you'll follow through with who will over there? Who—Timmons, or a Ford, or a (unintelligible) there are a number of Republicans.

3. *The Plumbers.* In June 1971, the leak of the Pentagon Papers prompted the President to create a special investigations unit (later known as the Plumbers) inside the White House under the direction of Egil Krogh. (6 *Hearings* 2603) Krogh, in turn, was directly supervised by John Ehrlichman. (6 *Hearings* 2529) Krogh was soon joined by David Young and in July the unit, staffing up for a broader role, added G. Gordon Liddy and E. Howard Hunt, both known to the White House as persons with investigative experience. (6 *Hearings* 2531) Liddy was a former FBI agent (Hunt Executive Session, Sept. 14, 1973, p. 423), Hunt, a former CIA agent. (9 *Hearings* 3662)

The Strategic Arms Limitation Treaty negotiations were compromised by the leak of sensitive documents at the time this unit was being formed (July 23, 1971). This problem was included within the Plumbers' mission. (6 *Hearings* 2604) Two subsequent leaks were likewise added to the purview of the unit's activities: The India/USSR leak (Tad Szulc article of August 13, 1971), and the India/PAK leak (Jack Anderson article of December 16, 1971). (David Young Memorandum, December 11, 1973 at p. 2.) According to Ehrlichman, it was felt that White House supervision of the leak-finding unit would "stimulate the various departments and agencies to do a better job controlling leaks and the theft or other exposure of national security secrets from within their departments." (6 *Hearings* 2529)

This special investigations unit planned and carried out the burglary of the office of Dr. Daniel Ellsberg's psychiatrist, Dr. Fielding (6 *Hearings* 2578, 2644-2645, 9 *Hearings* 3663). While this burglary is discussed more fully elsewhere in this report,* it is relevant here as reflective of the White House attitude towards illegal intelligence-gathering. Moreover, the activities of the Plumbers are closely related to the Watergate break-in because both operations were under the supervision of Hunt and Liddy (1 *Hearings* 158; 9 *Hearings* 3663), and both employed as burglars certain Cuban-Americans recruited by Hunt. (1 *Hearings* 357; Barker Executive Session, May 11, 1973, pp. 160-65). Two of the Hunt recruits participated in both burglaries. (9 *Hearings* 3711-3712) Also, fear of revelations of the Ellsberg break-in contributed significantly to the massive coverup following the Watergate break-in.

The Committee record demonstrates that Krogh and Young, as directors of the Plumbers, recommended to Ehrlichman a covert operation to obtain Ellsberg's psychiatric records which were in the custody of Ellsberg's psychiatrist, Dr. Fielding. Krogh pled guilty on November 30, 1973 to a federal charge based on his role in that affair. (Watergate Special Prosecutor Force Annual Report, May 25, 1974.) On the question whether Krogh and Young were acting with the approval of Ehrlichman, the Select Committee received considerable evidence. On August 11, 1971, Young and Krogh sent a memorandum to Ehrlichman which included the following report and recommendation:

"We have received the CIA preliminary psychology study (copy attached at Tab A) which I must say I am disappointed in and consider very superficial. We will meet tomorrow with the head psychiatrist, Mr. Bernard Malloy, to impress upon him the detail and depth that we expect. We will also make available to him some

* See Chapter II on Campaign Practices, p. 180.

of the other information we have received from the FBI on Ellsberg. In this connection we would recommend that a covert operation be undertaken to examine all the medical files still held by Ellsberg's psychoanalyst covering the two-year period in which he was undergoing analysis." (Exhibit 90, 6 *Hearings* 2644-45)

Beneath this recommendation were the words "Approve" and "Disapprove," each followed by a blank space. The handwritten letter "E" was placed in the blank space after the word "Approve" and beneath it, also in handwriting, was the message "if done under your assurance that it is not traceable." (Exhibit 90, 6 *Hearings* 2546, 2644-45) Ehrlichman testified that the letter "E" and the handwriting beneath it are his. (6 *Hearings* 2546)

Ehrlichman testified that he did not approve or have knowledge of the break-in in advance and that his understanding of the term "covert operation" did not include a break-in. (6 *Hearings* 2547, 2578-79) And, in the edited Presidential transcripts for a March 27, 1973 meeting, (p. 330) Ehrlichman, in reference to this break-in, is quoted as saying, "Well, sir, I didn't know. I didn't know what this crowd was up to until afterwards."

However, the Committee notes that the August 11 memorandum called for a "covert operation" to obtain medical files *still held by Ellsberg's psychoanalyst.*

Other documentary evidence on this question is also very relevant. Thus, in a memorandum dated August 26, 1971, from Young to Ehrlichman, concerning a plan to disparage Ellsberg by feeding selected information to a Congressional investigation, a footnote makes the following point:

"In connection with issue (9) [relating to changing Ellsberg's image] it is important to point out that with the recent article on Ellsberg's lawyer, Boudin, we have already started on a negative press image for Ellsberg. *If the present Hunt/Liddy Project #1 is successful, it will be absolutely essential to have an overall game plan developed for its use in conjunction with the Congressional investigation.* In this connection, I believe that the point of Buchanan's memorandum on attacking Ellsberg through the press should be borne in mind; namely, that the situation being attacked is too big to be undermined by planted leaks among the friendly press.

"If there is to be any damaging of Ellsberg's image and those associated with him, it will therefore be necessary to fold in the press planting with the Congressional investigation. I mentioned these points to Colson earlier this week, and his reply was that we should just leave it to him and he would take care of getting the information out. I believe, however, that in order to orchestrate this whole operation we have to be aware of precisely what Colson wants to do.

"*Recommendation:* That you sign the memorandum to Colson asking him to draw up a game plan (Tab A)." (Exhibit 91, 6 *Hearings* 2650) (Emphasis added)

"Tab A" was a memorandum from Ehrlichman to Charles Colson, dated August 27, 1971, (which was only several days prior to the Ellsberg break-in), on the subject, "Hunt/Liddy Special Project #1." The brief memorandum from Ehrlichman to Colson stated:

"On the assumption that the proposed undertaking by Hunt and Liddy would be carried out and would be successful, I would appreciate receiving from you by next Wednesday a game plan as to how and when you believe the materials should be used." (Exhibit 91, 6 *Hearings* 2651)

The only Hunt/Liddy special project under consideration when these memoranda were written was the "covert operation" to obtain Ellsberg's medical records, and thus, the only materials to be received if the project were successful would be those medical records.

It appears from these memoranda and Hunt's later testimony before the Committee (9 *Hearings* 3666), that a primary strategy of the Plumbers was seeking information to fuel a campaign to damage Ellsberg's image. This political motivation is highlighted in Young's August 26 memorandum to Ehrlichman by a bracketed note connecting Democratic Party leadership with the Ellsberg matter, which states:

"I am sending you a separate Hunt to Colson memorandum which attempts to select the politically damaging material involving the Democratic hierarchy. I personally believe a good deal more material could be developed along these lines. To begin with, we have Conein, Lansdale, Harkins, and Nolting who could possibly be called to testify." (Exhibit 91, 6 *Hearings* 2649)

See also the July 28, 1971 memorandum from Hunt to Colson in which Hunt states:

"I am proposing a skeletal operations plan aimed at building a file on Ellsberg that will contain all available

67

overt, covert and derogatory information. This basic tool is essential in determining how to destroy his public image and credibility." (Exhibit 150, 9 *Hearings* 3886)

In his testimony before the Committee, Hunt denied that the primary reason for the break-in was to destroy Ellsberg's public image, but he did admit that certain material expected to be obtained from Dr. Fielding's files might have been useful in discrediting Ellsberg. (9 *Hearings* 3674)

David Young has insisted to Committee staff that the thrust of the entire psychiatric study of Ellsberg was to determine whether Ellsberg was the kind of person capable of manipulation or whether he was acting alone. (David Young Memorandum, *supra,* p. 6) In this regard it should be noted that in the same memorandum of August 26, referred to above, Young informed Ehrlichman:

> "It may well be that although Ellsberg is guilty of the crimes with which he is charged, he did not in fact turn the papers over to the New York Times. The Defense Department's analysis of the printed material may even show that Ellsberg did not have some of the papers which the New York Times printed.
>
> "Furthermore, the whole distribution network may be the work of still another and even larger network." (Exhibit 91, 6 *Hearings* 2646)

Krogh, in his statement after sentencing, disavowed any continuing belief that the Fielding operation was justified by national security. Judge Gerhard Gesell, the trial judge for the Ellsberg break-in case, also has rejected national security as a defense in that matter. (Order of May 24, 1974) The edited transcripts of Presidential conversations submitted to the House Judiciary Committee suggest that the "national security" defense for the Ellsberg break-in may well have been an afterthought contrived to provide protection for those involved. (*e.g.* Edited Presidential Conversations 158, 190-191, 220-22) *See also, Id.* at 336:

E (If Hunt talks) I would put the national security tent over the whole operation.
P I sure would.

Also, on June 3, 1974, Charles W. Colson pled guilty to a charge of obstructing justice by engaging in a scheme to prepare and obtain derogatory information about Daniel Ellsberg and leaking such information to certain newspapers for the purpose of publicly discrediting Ellsberg. Colson admitted he engaged in this conduct to prejudice Ellsberg in the criminal case against Ellsberg relating to the Pentagon Papers incident being prosecuted by the federal government. Colson had agreed with Hunt's recommendation that Ellsberg's psychiatrist's records be obtained—a recommendation that led to the burglary of Dr. Fielding's office by the Plumbers.

The evidence before the Committee demonstrates that, in July-August 1971, the CIA provided technical assistance to Howard Hunt that, among other uses, was instrumental in the break-in of Dr. Fielding's office. This assistance was made available after then Deputy Director General Robert E. Cushman received a request for aid from the White House and met with Hunt on July 22, 1971. According to Cushman, CIA assistance to Hunt was terminated when Hunt's demands became so extravagant that Cushman refused to meet them.

Cushman testified before the Committee that in July 1971 he received a call from Ehrlichman asking for assistance for Hunt. (8 *Hearings* 3292, 3296) Cushman has further testified that Ehrlichman "stated that Howard Hunt was a bona fide employee, a consultant on security matters, and that Hunt would come to see me and request assistance which Mr. Ehrlichman requested that I give." (Senate Appropriations Subcommittee on Defense, Testimony of General Robert Cushman on May 11, 1973, p. 148) Ehrlichman has denied any recollection of this call. He has also said that "any call to the CIA is the kind of call that I usually have little or no difficulty in remembering." (Senate Appropriations Subcommittee on Defense, Opening Statement of John Ehrlichman on May 31, 1973; *reprinted in* New York *Times,* June 1, 1973, p. 16) *

CIA records, however, show that it was Ehrlichman who made the July 1971 telephone call. The minutes of a meeting of top CIA officials held several days after the telephone call show that Cushman reported that it was made by Ehrlichman. (8 *Hearings* 3292) A transcript of the Cushman-Hunt meeting on July 22, 1971, indicates that Ehrlichman placed this call. (Exhibit 124, 8 *Hearings* 3385)

* * *

Also, the CIA has provided the Committee with a recently discovered transcript of the Ehrlichman to Cushman phone call prepared by Cushman's secretary. The transcript clearly

---

* Colson supports Cushman's version of the story. Colson testified on June 19, 1973 before the Senate Appropriations Subcommittee on Defense that Ehrlichman knew Hunt would be seeking CIA assistance. (Senate Appropriations Subcommittee on Defense, Testimony of Charles Colson on June 19, 1973, pp. 451-52, 496-97, 506-07)

shows that Ehrlichman made the call seeking assistance for Hunt and invoked the President's name in order to procure this aid. The transcript of this conversation follows:

Telephone Call to General Cushman from John Ehrlichman—7 July 1971

Mr. Ehrlichman: I want to alert you that an old acquaintance, Howard Hunt, has been asked by the President to do some special consultant work on security problems. He may be contacting you sometime in the future for some assistance. I wanted you to know that he was in fact doing some things for the President. He is a long-time acquaintance with the people here. He may want some help on computer runs and other things. You should consider he has pretty much carte blanche. (Ehrlichman-Cushman tape transcriptions provided by the CIA as part of the Committee's files.)

NOTE: After the above conversation, General Cushman called Mrs. Osborn to alert him.

There is additional evidence regarding this telephone call that is instructive. On December 16, 1972, after the Department of Justice began its investigation of the Fielding matter, Cushman called Ehrlichman and stated that he was uncertain who called him in early July 1971 about Hunt.* Ehrlichman told this to Dean who requested that Ehrlichman ask Cushman to put this in writing. (Senate Appropriations Subcommittee on Defense, Testimony of John Ehrlichman on May 30, 1973, pp. 333-34) But Cushman, on January 8, 1973, sent a memorandum on the Hunt matter to Ehrlichman stating that the early July telephone call was probably made by Ehrlichman, Colson or Dean. (8 *Hearings* 3295-96; Exhibit 125, 8 *Hearings* 3390) Ehrlichman immediately called Cushman to complain about the inclusion of his name. (8 *Hearings* 3296) Cushman, therefore, sent Ehrlichman another memorandum regarding Hunt dated January 10, 1973, which stated that he could not recall who in the White House had called him. This memorandum was later given to Assistant United States Attorney Silbert. (*See* Exhibit 126, 8 *Hearings* 3391) The two memoranda were written before Cushman refreshed his recollection by examining CIA logs and documents prior to his testimony before the Select Committee.

In late August 1971, after Hunt's demands became excessive, Cushman called Ehrlichman to complain. (8 *Hearings* 3294; Senate Appropriations Subcommittee on Defense, Testimony of General Cushman on May 11, 1973, pp. 150-

---

* Cushman's recollection was later refreshed by reference to the CIA minutes noted above. (8 *Hearings* 3296)

51) Ehrlichman said he then asked Cushman what Hunt's assignment was and Cushman said he did not know. According to Ehrlichman, he (Ehrlichman) then said that he would take responsibility for terminating the CIA's assistance to Hunt and if there were any "squawks or kickbacks from anyone in the White House to simply refer them to me." (Senate Appropriations Subcommittee on Defense, Testimony of John Ehrlichman on May 30, 1973, p. 239) Shortly after this telephone call, CIA assistance to Hunt was terminated.

4. *Project Sandwedge*. The Committee to Re-elect the President was gearing up for its own political intelligence-gathering program around the same time as the Ellsberg break-in. In September 1971, John Dean asked Jeb Stuart Magruder to join him for lunch with Jack Caulfield. (2 *Hearings* 786) Caulfield, a White House investigator who had conducted numerous political investigations, some with Tony Ulasewicz (6 *Hearings* 2268), wanted to sell Magruder his political intelligence plan, "Project Sandwedge," for use by CRP. (2 *Hearings* 786) Magruder had been organizing the campaign effort since May 1971, having received this assignment from Mitchell and Haldeman. (2 *Hearings* 784) In essence, the Sandwedge plan proposed a private corporation operating like a Republican "Intertel"* to serve the President's campaign. (3 *Hearings* 924) In addition to normal investigative activities, the Sandwedge plan also included the use of bag men and other covert intelligence-gathering operations. (3 *Hearings* 925)

Project Sandwedge had been proposed to the White House by Caulfield in the spring of 1971 (3 *Hearings* 924) but not favorably received by Mitchell and Ehrlichman. (3 *Hearings* 925) After the initial luncheon meeting between Magruder and Caulfield, the plan was again put to Mitchell—this time for use by CRP—but he again rejected it. (4 *Hearings* 1605)

5. *The Hiring of G. Gordon Liddy by the Campaign Committee*. With Sandwedge rebuffed, Magruder and Gordon Strachan of Haldeman's staff asked Dean to find a lawyer to serve as CRP General Counsel who could also direct an intelligence-gathering program. (3 *Hearings* 927) Dean and Magruder had, on previous occasions, discussed the need for such a program with Attorney General Mitchell. (2 *Hearings* 786) ** The man Dean recruited was G. Gordon Liddy (3

* Intertel is a private international detective agency.
** Mitchell, however, testified that the first time he recalled discussing an intelligence capacity for CRP was on November 24, 1971, in a meeting with Dean and Liddy. (4 *Hearings* 1608)

Hearings 927-8), who moved from the Special Investigations Unit in the White House to CRP. (2 *Hearings* 810; 3 *Hearings* 927-8) Magruder testified that, when Dean sent Liddy to the Committee to Re-elect the President in 1971, he (Magruder) was unaware of Liddy's activities for the Plumbers, particularly his participation in the break-in of Dr. Fielding's office. (2 *Hearings* 786)

Dean had first asked Krogh whether David Young would be available for the special CRP assignment. Krogh said no, but suggested Liddy (3 *Hearings* 927) with the caveat that Ehrlichman must approve of the transfer; subsequently, Krogh informed Dean that Ehrlichman did approve. Dean then called Mitchell to tell him that Krogh, with Ehrlichman's sanction, had recommended Liddy and to arrange for Mitchell to meet Liddy. (3 *Hearings* 927-28) Ehrlichman, however, denied in a Committee staff interview that he approved Liddy's assignment to the CRP and has stated that he first learned of Liddy's CRP employment after the Watergate break-in. (Ehrlichman Interview, May 4, 1973, p. 8) The record shows that Mitchell (still the Attorney General) interviewed Liddy on November 24, 1971 (3 *Hearings* 928; 4 *Hearings* 1608), and approved Liddy for his position with CRP. (5 *Hearings* 1924)

B. THE COMMITTEE FOR THE RE-ELECTION OF THE PRESIDENT AND ITS RELATION TO THE WHITE HOUSE

Before relating the evidence as to the planning of CRP's political intelligence-gathering program that ultimately resulted in the Watergate break-in, it is important briefly to identify its close relationship with, if not domination by, the White House. The evidence accumulated by the Select Committee demonstrates that CRP was a White House product, answerable to top White House leadership. It appears that H. R. Haldeman, the President's Chief of Staff, was principally responsible for organizing CRP, and John Mitchell has stated that Haldeman was the moving force. (4 *Hearing* 1606-7)

In May 1971, Jeb Magruder, then a Haldeman staff assistant, was released from his White House position and assigned the task of building the re-election committee. (2 *Hearings* 784) With Magruder on this assignment were Harry S. Flemming, Hugh W. Sloan, Jr., Herbert Porter, Robert Odle and Dr. Robert Marik. All but Marik were former White House aides. (1 *Hearings* 10)

Magruder cleared all recruitment of White House personnel for the Committee with Haldeman. (3 *Hearings* 3023)

Though Attorney General Mitchell also passed on the appointment of persons to important re-election committee positions (1 *Hearings* 14; 4 *Hearings* 1606), in a meeting with the President on April 15, 1973, Kleindienst characterized Mitchell's role in the formulation of CRP as that of "a puppet." (Edited Presidential Conversations, p. 741) The evidence, however, shows that Mitchell assumed a political managerial role with the re-election effort as early as the spring of 1971, a year before he left his position as Attorney General. (2 *Hearings* 785; 4 *Hearings* 1606) It was understood, even at that early time, that Mitchell would take full charge of the campaign when it went into high gear. (2 *Hearings* 785) Thus, Mitchell received memoranda for his information and approval from CRP as early as May, 1971. (1 *Hearings* 18, 40-41)

The campaign organization eventually evolved into two entities: (1) the Committee for the Re-election of the President, which had the responsibility for political activity, and (2) the Finance Committee for the Re-election of the President, the organ responsible for campaign fundraising and disbursement. (1 *Hearings* 12)* Approximately thirty-five White House aides left their positions to assume key or lower level positions at CRP or FCRP. (1 *Hearings* 10, 437-47) A comparison of the CRP organization chart (Exhibit 7, 1 *Hearings* 19) and the White House organization chart for the period 1971-1972 (Exhibit 9, 1 *Hearings* 77), shows that most important positions in the campaign organizations were held by former White House aides.

Magruder was the caretaker director of the campaign political arm from May 1971 until March 1972 when Mitchell took over the duties of Campaign Director. (1 *Hearings* 12-13; 2 *Hearings* 784) To keep Haldeman informed daily of CRP operations, Gordon Strachan, a Haldeman staff assistant, was designated as the liaison between Haldeman and Magruder. (8 *Hearings* 3024) On a regular basis, Magruder provided Strachan with reports of CRP activities and decision memoranda requiring Haldeman's approval. (2 *Hearings* 785; 8 *Hearings* 3023)

Moreover, Robert Odle, CRP Administrative Assistant under Magruder, testified that CRP memoranda went to the White House in such significant numbers that there was a sample memorandum in the Staff Manual showing the prescribed form for a memorandum from a CRP staffer to Haldeman or other White House personnel. (1 *Hearings* 58; Ex-

---

* Several days prior to April 7, 1972, the effective date of the new campaign fund reporting law, this entity was renamed the Finance Committee to Re-elect the President.

hibit 4, 1 *Hearings* 454)* Magruder also sent a flow of memoranda to Mitchell for his reaction or approval. (1 *Hearings* 18, 40-1; 4 *Hearings* 1607) Examples of memoranda to Mitchell while he was still Attorney General are Exhibits 74 and 75. (4 *Hearings* 1810-11) Mitchell's campaign activity began as early as May 1971. (2 *Hearings* 785; 4 *Hearings* 1606, 1653-53) Prior to his appearance before the Select Committee, Mitchell testified in March 1972 before the Senate Judiciary Committee that he had "[n]o re-election campaign responsibilities" before his resignation as Attorney General. (Hearings before the Committee on the Judiciary of the United States Senate on the Nomination of Richard G. Kleindienst to be Attorney General, 92d Cong., 2d Sess., Part 2, p. 633)

The two divisions of the campaign organization were ultimately headed by two Cabinet Members—Mitchell became Director of CRP (1 *Hearings* 12) and Secretary of Commerce Maurice Stans retired to head FCRP. (1 *Hearings* 13) Mr. Stans testified before the Committee that, as FCRP Director, he raised approximately $60 million for the campaign. These funds were disbursed on the basis of decisions made by a budget committee consisting of key officials of CRP and FCRP. (1 *Hearings* 12) These decisions were at times reviewed by Haldeman.

After the November election, FCRP had a substantial surplus, much of which was apparently used to defend itself in lawsuits and to pay legal fees of former CRP and FCRP officials involved in various Watergate-related legal matters. (Washington *Post*, March 30, 1974, p. A6) As the Select Committee files its final report, approximately $3.5 million in FCRP surplus is still held by the Campaign Liquidation Trust.

On the basis of this evidence, the Committee finds that the Committee for the Re-election of the President and the Finance Committee to Re-elect the President were, in the main, White House-staffed and White House-controlled political organizations. It finds that they were initially conceived and created with the purpose of assuring White House control over the campaign funds raised by FCRP and the campaign strategies planned and implemented by CRP.

C. THE PLANNING OF "GEMSTONE"

From the time G. Gordon Liddy was appointed CRP General Counsel in December 1971 (2 *Hearings* 786), his prin-

* Moreover, Haldeman testified that there were "twice weekly meetings in Mr. Ehrlichman's office with the campaign committee people and senior White House people." (8 *Hearings* 3023)

cipal efforts were devoted to developing, advocating and implementing a comprehensive political intelligence-gathering program for CRP under the code name "Gemstone." (1 *Hearings* 126-27; 2 *Hearings* 786-87; 9 *Hearings* 3751) The Select Committee's knowledge of Liddy's activities comes from sources other than Liddy, himself, since he refused to testify, although instructed to do so by the Committee upon the conference, pursuant to court order, of "use" immunity. (Liddy Executive Session, June 4, 1973) Liddy's role in the Gemstone plan was detailed to the Committee through the testimonies of James McCord, Jeb Stuart Magruder, John Dean, John Mitchell and E. Howard Hunt. Although it is not clear from the testimony who originated the Gemstone concept, there is no dispute that it was Liddy who, with the aid of Hunt and McCord, formulated the plan and presented it for approval to Dean and Magruder.

1. The Meeting of January 27, 1972. The first Gemstone plan was presented to Attorney General Mitchell by Liddy at a meeting in Mitchell's Justice Department office on January 27, 1972. Magruder and Dean were also in attendance. The plan was a Liddy, Hunt and McCord composite. McCord's input was the budget for the equipment needed to implement the electronic surveillance aspects of the plan. (1 *Hearings* 127-28) Hunt, still employed at the White House, aided Liddy in formulating the plans for other intelligence gathering operations. (9 *Hearings* 3663)

The testimony of Mitchell, Dean and Magruder as to this meeting is fairly consistent concerning the nature of Liddy's presentation and the general contents of the plan. Liddy illustrated his presentation with six large posters on an easel, each one portraying a specific coded component of the overall plan. The plan called for: (1) the use of mugging squads and kidnapping teams to deal with leaders of anti-Nixon demonstrations; (2) prostitutes stationed on a yacht, wired for sound, anchored offshore from Miami Beach during the Democratic Convention; (3) electronic surveillance and break-ins at various targets not yet identified at the time of the meeting. The budget for the plan was $1 million. (2 *Hearings* 787-788; 3 *Hearings* 929; 4 *Hearings* 1610)

Liddy's plan was not approved at the meeting. Dean testified that he was surprised at Liddy's plan and had not known of its contents prior to the meeting. (4 *Hearings* 1442) He testified that Mitchell was likewise amazed and told Liddy to revise the plan, focusing on the problem of demonstrations. (3 *Hearings* 930) Magruder and Dean also indicated to Liddy that the project must be redone. (2 *Hearings* 789)

According to Dean, Mitchell told him privately that Liddy's proposal was out of the question. (3 *Hearings* 930)

Mitchell testified that at the January 27 meeting he told Liddy to "take the stuff out and burn it." (5 *Hearings* 1816) However, Hunt testified that Liddy reported that the plan had been turned down because it was too expensive and that he (Liddy) had been instructed to redraft it. (9 *Hearings* 3734, 3767) McCord confirms this testimony. (1 *Hearings* 145)

Despite these reactions of record by those who listened to Liddy's plan on January 27, the fact remains that such a plan was presented in the office of the Attorney General of the United States and that Liddy, after the meeting, still held his position as CRP General Counsel and continued to have the responsibility of developing an intelligence-gathering plan.

Magruder testified that he reported the details of this meeting to Strachan in accordance with his custom of keeping Strachan advised on important matters so he (Strachan) could report to Haldeman. (2 *Hearings* 789) Strachan, however, claimed that Magruder mentioned nothing to him regarding a CRP intelligence plan until after March 30, 1972. (6 *Hearings* 2440-41)

2. *The February 4, 1972 Meeting.* On February 4, 1972, the same group again met in the Attorney General's office and listened to Liddy present a watered-down version of his intelligence plan. This time the plan called only for surreptitious photography and electronic surveillance. (2 *Hearings* 789) The budget for the new plan had been "stripped down" to $500,000. (2 *Hearings* 825) According to Magruder, Mitchell actually discussed possible targets for the new plan including the Democratic National Committee headquarters in Washington and at the Convention, and the headquarters of the Democratic nominee. Also according to Magruder, Mitchell suggested as additional targets DNC chairman Larry O'Brien and Las Vegas publisher Hank Greenspun, who allegedly had explosive material damaging to Senator Muskie in his office safe. (2 *Hearings* 790-791)

Liddy's proposal, according to Magruder, was not approved at the February 4 meeting, but postponed for consideration at a later time. (2 *Hearings* 791) Dean testified that, after arriving late for this meeting, he advised Liddy that such discussions should not go on in front of the Attorney General of the United States.* After the meeting, Dean testified, he told Liddy that he would never again

---

* In his March 21, 1973, meeting with the President, Dean gave the President this same account. (Edited Presidential Conversations, pp. 175-176).

discuss the matter with him and that, if Liddy's plan were approved, he did not want to know about it. (3 *Hearings* 930) Mitchell testified that he and Dean were still aghast at Liddy's proposal. (4 *Hearings* 1612)

Liddy apparently left the meeting believing that the basics of his plan were unobjectionable but that his budget was still too high. (9 *Hearings* 3767-3768)

Moreover, McCord testified that Liddy said Dean had stated to Liddy that a method would have to be devised to ensure Mitchell's deniability regarding the operation, including the means by which the money would be disbursed. (McCord DNC Deposition, April 30, 1973, pp. 70-71; McCord Executive Session, March 28, 1973, pp. 12-15) Magruder also testified that a discussion concerning the Attorney General's deniability took place at the February 4 meeting. (Magruder Executive Session, June 12, 1973, pp. 79-80) Dean testified that Liddy may have misunderstood his statements concerning the impropriety of discussing the plan in front of the Attorney General and believed that Dean's only concern was with Mitchell's deniability, not with the appropriateness of the plan. (3 *Hearings* 1023)

Magruder testified that once again after the meeting he reported the event to Strachan so Haldeman could be informed. (2 *Hearings* 824-25) This time, Magruder testified, he sent Strachan the documents Liddy had presented at the meeting, including budget sheets (2 *Hearings* 825) and told Strachan by telephone the general content of the meeting, including the specific proposed targets for the intelligence operation. (2 *Hearings* 825) Strachan, according to Magruder, told him that any decision made by Mitchell regarding the bugging proposal was acceptable to the White House. (2 *Hearings* 839) But Strachan, during his testimony, denied receiving this information from Magruder after the February 4 meeting, and claimed he had no knowledge of the Liddy plan until after March 30, 1972. (6 *Hearings* 2451-52) (*But see* Edited Presidential Conversations, p. 146)

Dean testified that, following this meeting, he met with Haldeman and told him about the meeting and the Liddy plan was incredible, unnecessary and unwise and that the White House should have nothing to do with it. Haldeman, according to Dean, agreed and instructed him to have no further dealings on the matter. (3 *Hearings* 930)

Thus, according to both Magruder's and Dean's testimony, Haldeman knew about the Liddy intelligence plan after the February 4 meeting. Haldeman testified that he has no recollection of Dean's telling him about the February 4 meeting but was willing to accept Dean's version of this conversation. (8 *Hearings* 3035) But, on March 27, 1973, Haldeman admitted to the President that he had this meeting with Dean, during which Dean warned Haldeman about Liddy's plan and recommended that it be dropped. (Edited Presidential Conversations, pp. 323-24) Moreover, Dean informed the President of his conversation with Haldeman, telling the President, "Bob and I have gone over that after the fact and he recalls my coming to the office and telling him about this crazy scheme that was being cooked up." (*Id.* at p. 962)

While Dean felt the plan had been disapproved, Magruder did not leave the February 4 meeting with that view since, as subsequent developements show, he continued to work with Liddy on modifying the plan and on March 30, 1972, presented it himself a third time to Mitchell in Key Biscayne, Florida.

After the February 4 meeting, Liddy continued to serve as General Counsel for CRP.

3. The Colson Phone Call. There is evidence that Liddy believed he needed additional White House assistance to get his intelligence plan approved. After the February 4 meeting, and before his meeting with Mitchell in Key Biscayne on March 30, Magruder, according to his testimony, received a call from Charles Colson, Special Counsel to the President, who told him to "get on the stick and get the Liddy project approved so we can get the information from O'Brien." (2 *Hearings* 835) Hunt testified that, after the February 4 meeting, Liddy requested an introduction to Colson and that he brought Liddy to Colson's office. Hunt said he sat in the rear of the office while Liddy and Colson conversed. Colson made some phone calls during the conversation. (9 *Hearings* 3683-84)

Colson did not testify under oath before the Committee but asserted his Fifth Amendment privilege after he was informed he was a target of the Grand Jury. However, Colson had earlier submitted to a staff interview. There Colson admitted that Liddy and Hunt told him they could not get anyone to listen to them and that he therefore called Magruder to ask him to hear their plan. (Colson Interview, May 3, 1973, pp. 2-3) Colson summarized this meeting with Liddy and Hunt in a June 20, 1972 memorandum. Colson said Hunt and Liddy told him about elaborate proposals for security activities which they could not get approved. Colson said he called Magruder and urged resolution of the Hunt-Liddy proposal. He stated in the memorandum that he declined Hunt's offer to apprise him of the details because

78

it was "not necessary [and] it was of no concern to me."
Hunt, however, testified that he did not offer to provide
details to Colson. (Hunt Executive Session, July 25, 1973,
pp. 99-110)

In his public testimony, Hunt testified that when they left
Colson's office, after Colson had made the phone calls, Liddy
told Hunt, "I think I may have done us some good." (9
Hearings 3684) Hunt also testified that it was not necessary
in the March meeting to give Colson details about the Liddy
plan. He stated that in January, 1972, he had informed
Colson that he would be working on a special project with
Liddy that would require him to use the same Cuban-
Americans he had employed in the Ellsberg break-in and
that Colson indicated he was aware of the comprehensive
covert intelligence plan which Liddy had in preparation
and which had the approval of the White House. (9 Hearings 3674-80) Hunt testified, however, that Colson was not
specifically aware that the DNC headquarters would be a
target of the Gemstone plan. (9 Hearings 3722)*

Another witness to the Colson call to Magruder apparently
was Fred LaRue. Magruder testified that LaRue was in
the room with him when he received the call (2 Hearings
794), and Mitchell testified that LaRue told him that he
was present when Colson called. (5 Hearings 1929) La-
Rue, however, could not recall being present. (6 Hearings
2284)

Magruder's description of Colson's call, especially the reference to a need to "get the information from O'Brien" (2
Hearings 793), provides some evidence that Colson was doing more than simply being helpful to Liddy and Hunt.
Dean told the President in the Oval Office on March 21,
1973, that he thought Colson's call to Magruder "helped
get the thing off the dime." At the same time Dean also
told the President that Strachan, on Haldeman's behalf, was
pushing Magruder for intelligence information and that Magruder "took that as a signal to probably go to Mitchell and
to say, 'They are pushing us like crazy for this from the
White House.'" (Edited Presidential Conversations, pp. 178-
179)

4. *The March 30, 1972 Meeting.* The third and final time
Liddy's intelligence plan was presented to Mitchell was on
March 30 in Key Biscayne, Florida. Magruder testified that
he had a large number of accumulated matters, including the

---

* In earlier executive sessions, Hunt had not provided this information, but
testified to it for the first time in the executive session of September 20,
1973, pp. 467-73, and at his appearance before the Committee in public
hearing. (See 9 Hearings 3681-83)

Liddy plan, to submit to Mitchell for his approval. By this time, the plan's budget had been reduced to $250,000. (2 *Hearings* 794) Prior to traveling to Florida, Magruder testified, he sent a copy of a memorandum on the pared down Liddy plan to Strachan for communication to Haldeman. Magruder said this was in accordance with his practice to send key papers for discussion with Mitchell to Haldeman so that Haldeman could comment prior to his (Magruder's) meetings with Mitchell. (2 *Hearings* 794) Strachan, however, denied receiving an advance copy of this memorandum. (6 *Hearings* 2452)

Magruder testified that the Liddy memorandum was the last item discussed in his meeting with Mitchell in Key Biscayne, and that, although no one was enthusiastic after discussing its pros and cons, Mitchell approved the project. (2 *Hearings* 794) Magruder testified that the approved quarter of a million dollar project called for an initial entry into the Democratic National Committee headquarters in Washington and, at a further date, if funds were available, entries into the headquarters of the Democratic Presidential contenders in Washington and at the Convention in Miami. (2 *Hearings* 795)

Mitchell, however, denied approving the Liddy plan. He said that he told Magruder "we don't need this, I'm tired of hearing it, let's not discuss it any further." (4 *Hearings* 1613-14) LaRue, who was present with Mitchell and Magruder during the discussion of the various proposals Magruder presented to Mitchell, testified that, when Mitchell asked him (LaRue) what he thought of Liddy's plan, he replied it was not worth the risk and Mitchell said, "Well this is not something we will have to decide on at this meeting." (6 *Hearings* 2281)

In a March 27, 1973 meeting between the President, Haldeman and Ehrlichman, Haldeman reported on information CRP lawyer Paul O'Brien had received from Magruder:

> "[T]he final step [in approving the Watergate break-in plan] was when Gordon Strachan called Magruder and said Haldeman told him to get this going. 'The President wants it done and there is to be no more arguing about it.' This, meaning the intelligence activity, the Liddy program. Magruder told Mitchell this, that Strachan had told him to get it going on Haldeman's orders on the President's orders and Mitchell signed off on it. He said, 'OK, if they say to do it, go ahead.'" (Edited Presidential Conversations, p. 321)

(Magruder did not give information of this nature to the

Select Committee in either public or executive session.) In addition, during an April 14 1973 meeting between the President, Haldeman and Ehrlichman, Ehrlichman stated that Magruder told him that Mitchell orally approved Liddy's third proposal, but that the approval was reluctant and that they (Mitchell and Magruder) felt "bull-dozed" into it by Colson. (Edited Presidential Conversations, p. 585)

5. *Financing the Operation.* When Magruder returned to Washington the following day, April 1, he took certain actions that indicated his belief that the plan was approved. He told Robert Reisner, his administrative assistant, that Liddy's project had been approved and asked him to notify Liddy. He called Strachan, telling him the project was approved, and informed Hugh Sloan, FCRP Treasurer, that Liddy was authorized to draw $250,000 during the campaign and would probably initially need a sizable amount. (2 *Hearings* 795)

Liddy quickly requested $83,000 from Sloan. (2 *Hearings* 539) Sloan testified that he first checked Liddy's request with Magruder, who told him that it was in order and to comply. Sloan became concerned because the quarter million dollar budget was to come from cash funds kept in a safe in his office that represented cash received prior to April 7, 1972, the effective date of the new Campaign Fund Reporting Law. Since $83,000 was "totally out of line of anything we had ever done before," Sloan took the matter up with Stans, Director of FCRP. Stans told Sloan he would check with Mitchell. After meeting with Mitchell, Stans confirmed that Magruder had authority to make this kind of decision and that Sloan should pay the funds to Liddy. Responding to Sloan's concern about the purpose of such a payment, Stans, according to Sloan, said "I do not want to know and you don't want to know." (2 *Hearings* 539) Although Stans disputed the context in which Sloan placed the remark he agreed that it was "the substance of what was said." (2 *Hearings* 727) Mitchell, however, testified that he only told Stans that Magruder had authority to pay money to Liddy and that there was no mention of substantial funds. (5 *Hearings* 1616-1617) Stans' meeting with Mitchell to clear the cash payment occurred only a few days after the March 30 meeting in Key Biscayne among Mitchell, Magruder and LaRue.

6. *Transmittal of Information to Strachan.* Magruder testified that he "completely apprised" Strachan of the Liddy quarter-million dollar plan, including the fact that its first target

was the Watergate DNC headquarters. (2 *Hearings* 826) In his March 13, 1973 meeting with the President, Dean told the President that Strachan had prior knowledge of the Watergate burglary. Nixon immediately concluded: "Well, then, he probably told Bob. He may not have." (Edited Presidential Conversations, p. 146) Dean assured the President Strachan would not testify against Haldeman: "He was judicious in what he relayed, but Strachan is as tough as nails. He can go in and stonewall, and say, 'I don't know anything about what you are talking about.' He has already done it twice you know, in interviews." *(Ibid.)*

Strachan testified that Magruder told him only that a "sophisticated political intelligence gathering system had been approved with a budget of $300,000." (6 *Hearings* 2441) Strachan stated that he prepared political action memorandum #18* for Haldeman that relayed this information. Strachan said that, when the memorandum was returned for filing, Haldeman had checked the item concerning this matter, indicating that he had read it. (6 *Hearings* 2453) Haldeman, however, claimed he did not recall seeing such an item. (8 *Hearings* 3036)

Four days after the March 30 meeting in Key Biscayne, Haldeman and Mitchell met. Strachan testified he prepared a talking paper for Haldeman for the meeting that included a section respecting CRP's $300,000 intelligence plan. (6 *Hearings* 2454) Haldeman testified he does not recall directing Strachan to prepare this talking paper; nor did he recall seeing such a document. Haldeman and Mitchell both testified that a CRP intelligence plan was not discussed at the April 4 meeting. Haldeman testified that his meeting with Mitchell on April 4, 1972 was in connection with a meeting with the President and Mitchell which "covered the ITT-Kleindienst hearings and a review of Mitchell's plans for assigning campaign responsibilities. They [his notes] indicate no discussion of intelligence." (7 *Hearings* 2881; *e.g.* Exhibit 121, 8 *Hearings* 3372)

Also in April, according to Strachan, Haldeman called him into his office and told him to inform Liddy to transfer whatever intelligence capability Liddy had for Muskie to McGovern. Haldeman, Strachan said, had a "particular interest in discovering what the connection between McGovern and Senator Kennedy was." (6 *Hearings* 2455) Strachan said he made a note of the instruction, called Liddy to his office and literally read the statement to him. (6 *Hearings* 2455)

---

* The transcript of Strachan's testimony at this point refers to memorandum #8, a typographical error that should read #18. (*See e.g.*, 6 *Hearings* 2459)

D. EVENTS LEADING TO THE BREAK-IN

1. The McGovern Headquarters Attempts. In addition to the DNC offices at Watergate and propitious targets at the Miami Convention, the Watergate conspirators hoped to bug Senator George McGovern's Washington campaign headquarters. (1 *Hearings* 185) This target appears consistent with the instruction Liddy received from Haldeman through Strachan in April "to transfer whatever capability he had from Muskie to McGovern," although bugging was not specifically mentioned in that instruction. McCord said he was involved in several attempts to bug McGovern's headquarters. (McCord DNC Deposition, April 30, 1973, p. 157)

On May 15, McCord and Tom Gregory, a student Hunt had hired to infiltrate the McGovern campaign, walked through the McGovern headquarters in order to acquaint McCord with the office layout. (1 *Hearings* 164) Later, on the evening of May 26, McCord and Baldwin drove to the McGovern headquarters and, through the use of walkie-talkies, rendezvoused with another car occupied by Hunt, Liddy and others. The group had planned to break into the McGovern headquarters that evening but, because of Gregory's absence and the continued presence of a man standing in front of the headquarters, the mission was cancelled. (Baldwin Interview, March 30, 1973, p. 7) The Watergate conspirators also unsuccessfully attempted to bug the McGovern headquarters on May 28. McCord had hoped that the offices of Frank Mankiewicz and Gary Hart would be vacant so that bugging devices could be installed. (McCord DNC Deposition, April 30, 1973, pp. 157-58) But the mission this time was aborted because persons were working late inside the headquarters, and Gregory, who had been instructed by Hunt to stay outside and report when they left, was asked by a policeman to leave the area. (Watergate Trial Transcript, pp. 37-39, 488-90)

2. The First Watergate Break-In. Liddy and Hunt then turned to the main target of the "Gemstone" plan—the Democratic National Committee Headquarters in the Watergate Office Building. They planned the break-in for the Memorial Day weekend. Hunt alerted his Cuban-American contact in Miami, Bernard Barker, to be prepared to bring a trained burglary team to Washington. Barker, who had performed this same type of mission for Hunt in the Ellsberg break-in, had also served under Hunt in the Bay of Pigs operation. He was a refugee from his native Cuba and considered himself a patriot committed to the mission of freeing Cuba from Castro.

The Cuban-Americans he recruited for Hunt's projects were cut from the same cloth. The motivations of Barker and his crew were clearly stated by Barker: ". . . E. Howard Hunt, under the name of Eduardo, represents to the Cuban people their liberation. I cannot deny my services in the way that it was proposed to me on a matter of national security, knowing that with my training, I had personnel available for this type of operation. I could not deny this request at the time." (1 *Hearings* 365)

On May 10 or 12, McCord and Hunt reconnoitered the Watergate Office Building by walking through it in the early evening after work and, again, around 9:00 or 10:00 p.m. (Hunt Executive Session, December 17, 1973, pp. 17-19) On May 17, Martinez purchased six one-way tickets to Washington, from Miami, for Frank Carter (alias for Barker), J. Granada (alias for Reynaldo Pico), Joseph di Alberto (alias for Sturgis), Raoul Godey (alias for Gonzales), Jose Piedra (alias for De Diego), and G. Valdes (alias for Martinez). (Gray Confirmation Hearings, Feb. 28, 1973, p. 51) On May 22, the Miamians registered at the Manger-Hamilton Hotel in Washington and, on May 26, moved to the Watergate Hotel, where they stayed until May 30. (*Ibid.*)

Barker testified that he met with Hunt at the Manger-Hamilton Hotel shortly after his arrival in Washington, and Hunt explained to him the general nature of the mission. Barker, however, did not relay the nature of the assignment of his team until just before entry into the DNC headquarters. (1 *Hearings* 377) At that time, the different tasks of the participants were discussed. (McCord DNC Deposition, April 30, 1973, pp. 106-108)

By the early morning hours of May 28, the Watergate conspirators, after two frustrated attempts, completed their first break-in of the DNC (1 *Hearings* 156) The entry was made late on May 27 when Gonzales picked the lock of the ground floor door of the Watergate Office Building. (Sturgis Executive Session, May 15, 1973, p. 430) The burglary team then went to the 6th floor offices of the DNC headquarters. McCord placed electronic bugging devices in the form of miniature transmitters in the telephones of DNC Chairman Larry O'Brien and another official, Spencer Oliver (1 *Hearings* 156-157), and Barker and his team photographed papers from DNC files. (Barker Executive Session, May 11, 1973, pp. 165-7; 1 *Hearings* 358)

3. *The Fruits of the First Break-in.* After the DNC telephones were tapped, Alfred Baldwin, a former FBI agent recruited by McCord, monitored intercepted telephone conversations

from a room in the Howard Johnson Motor Lodge across the street from the Watergate Office Building. (1 *Hearings* 401) He typed the conversations almost verbatim and gave the logs to McCord. (1 *Hearings* 409-410) McCord gave the logs to Liddy who had several retyped by his secretary, Sally Harmony. Liddy told McCord he wanted them in final form before his discussions with Mitchell and other recipients of the logs. (1 *Hearings* 233)

The Gemstone project had its own stationery with the word, "Gemstone" printed in large letters at the top. (Exhibit 16, 2 *Hearings* 464, 877) Sally Harmony testified that she used Gemstone stationery when she retyped the telephone logs. (2 *Hearings* 467) Harmony also said she saw a stack of 8″ by 10″ photographs of documents from the DNC headquarters held by fingers in rubber gloves. (2 *Hearings* 462)

Ms. Harmony testified that she began to type certain general intelligence memoranda for Liddy in April that led her to believe that CRP had infiltrated the headquarters of McGovern and Muskie. (2 *Hearings* 482-483) In keeping with the spy motif that characterized Liddy's operations, code names referring to information sources were used in the intelligence memoranda. The three code names she could recall were Ruby 1, Ruby 2, and Crystal. (2 *Hearings* 462)*

Magruder testified that, after Liddy's project was approved, he did not hear from Liddy until after May 27, when Liddy reported the DNC break-in and installation of the telephone tapping devices. (2 *Hearings* 796-99) Magruder said that he reported the May 27 entry to Strachan, but, at that time, gave Strachan no further details. (2 *Hearings* 826)

After the May 27 DNC break-in, Magruder received from Liddy two installments of documents embodying the fruits of the break-in. The installments included summaries of phone conversations on Gemstone stationery and photographs of documents. (2 *Hearings* 796-97) Magruder testified that he showed these Gemstone materials to Mitchell in a regular 8:30 morning meeting with him in his office in either CRP headquarters or his law firm, which was located in the same building. (2 *Hearings* 797)

According to Magruder's testimony, Mitchell found the documents of no use and called Liddy to his office and told him that the materials he received "were not satisfactory and it was not worth the money that he had been paid for it." (2 *Hearings* 797) Magruder said Liddy explained there was a technical problem with one wiretap and that one had

* These "sources" are discussed in more detail in Chapter IV of this report. [Chapter V in this edition.]

been improperly placed. Liddy said he would correct these matters and hopefully obtain useful information. (2 *Hearings* 797)

Mitchell denied receiving any of the Gemstone material or informing Liddy that he was unhappy with the intelligence information. In fact, Mitchell testified that he did not see nor talk with Liddy between February 4, 1972, and June 15, 1972. (4 *Hearings* 1620)

However, Magruder's administrative assistant, Robert Reisner, testified that several weeks prior to June 17, 1972, Magruder handed him materials on stationery bearing the letterhead "Gemstone" for the purpose of preparing a file for Mr. Mitchell for a meeting between Mitchell and Magruder. (2 *Hearings* 494) Reisner also testified that, on another occasion, he saw the Gemstone stationery and envelopes and "photographs or what appeared to be photographs with the stationery." (2 *Hearings* 495) Mr. Reisner identified Committee Exhibits 16 and 18 which were copies of Gemstone stationery and the envelope for Gemstone materials as being the same type of stationery and envelopes he saw in Magruder's office and which he used to prepare Mr. Mitchell's file. (2 *Hearings* 493-97) The Gemstone envelopes bore the words "Sensitive Material" in large red capital letters and the words "handle as code word material" in smaller letters. In the lower left-hand corner of the envelope were printed the abbreviated words, "Ex Dis." followed by "No Dism." These abbreviations apparently stood for "Executive Distribution" and "No Dissemination." Also, at the bottom of the Gemstone stationery were the printed words, "Warning, this information is for intelligence purposes only. Exploitation may compromise source and terminate flow of information." (Exhibit 2, 1 *Hearings* 450)

Magruder also testified that he showed the Gemstone documents he received from Liddy to Strachan. He said that, because of their sensitive nature, he had Strachan view them in Magruder's office. He and Strachan, Magruder said, agreed there was no substance to the documents. (2 *Hearings* 797-98)

Strachan denied that Magruder showed him wiretap reports of Gemstone documents and said that he never heard the term "Gemstone" prior to June 17, 1972. (6 *Hearings* 2451) Haldeman also stated in a staff interview that Strachan never reported to him that he had seen the Gemstone file. (Haldeman Interview, June 14, 1973, p. 3)

4. Factors Leading to the Second Break-in. The second Watergate break-in was apparently made to correct the difficulty experienced with the wiretap device on Mr. O'Brien's telephone. Dean testified that on June 19, 1972, two days after the June 17 break-in, he met with Liddy who told him that the men arrested in the DNC were his men. (3 *Hearings* 933) When Dean asked Liddy why he had been in the DNC, he told Dean that "Magruder had pushed him into it. He told me that he had not wanted to do it, but Magruder had complained about the fact that they were not getting good information from a bug that had been placed in the DNC earlier. He then explained something about the steel structure of the Watergate Office Building that was inhibiting transmission of the bug and that they had gone into the building to correct this problem." (3 *Hearings* 933) Dean later gave this same account to President Nixon on March 21, 1973. (Edited Presidential Conversations, pp. 180-181) Ehrlichman, during a meeting with the President and Haldeman on April 14, 1973, said that Magruder told him that the second DNC break-in was "Liddy's own notion" and that "neither Mitchell nor Magruder knew that another break-in was contemplated."

Ehrlichman said Magruder told him that Liddy had met with Mitchell and, referencing the difficulties experienced, had only said "Mr. Mitchell, I'll take care of it." (Edited Presidential Conversation, p. 587) McCord testified that Liddy had told him a second break-in was necessary because Mitchell wanted a second photographic operation and that, in addition, "as long as that team was going in that Mr. Mitchell wanted . . . Mr. Liddy to check . . . the malfunctioning of the second device that was put in . . . and see what the problem was because it was one of two things—either a malfunction of the equipment or the fact that the installation of the device was in a room which was surrounded by four walls. In other words, it was shielded and he wanted this corrected and another device installed." (1 *Hearings* 157)

It appears, therefore, that the second DNC break-in in the early morning hours of June 17 was carried out with a sense of urgency by Liddy and without the planning engaged in for the first successful break-in. The urgency of the second break-in is emphasized by the fact that the burglars decided to proceed with the operation even though McCord found that the tape placed on the garage door leading to the stairwell had been removed, making it necessary to pick the lock again. The risk of discovery was obvious to all the break-in team, yet, after hurried consultation with Liddy in the Watergate Hotel, the decision was made to continue.

A second piece of tape was placed on the basement garage door, the action that was the burglars' undoing. For it was the Watergate guard, Frank Wills, who had found the first piece of tape and removed it, thinking that one of the engineers of the building had put it on the door. When he made his rounds again and saw the door retaped, he telephoned the police. (Wills DNC Deposition, March 9, 1973, pp. 19-20, 24-25)

Within minutes, Sergeant Leeper's plainclothes squad had arrived at the Watergate Office Building, searched the stairwell and entered the sixth floor offices of the Democratic National Committee headquarters. When Officer Barrett discovered the burglars and yelled, "Hold it! Come out!," the break-in team was apprehended in the midst of setting up photographic equipment. The next afternoon, Leeper obtained search warrants for the rooms which the burglars had occupied. (1 *Hearings* 107) There police found $4,200 in $100 bills, all with serial numbers in sequence, more electronic equipment, sets of blue surgical gloves, and a small notebook with the name, E. Howard Hunt, in it. (1 *Hearings* 107-108)

The burglary was over, but the Watergate scandal had just begun.

2. The Coverup

The news of the break-in at the DNC that reached the public in the newspapers on June 17 and 18 provided little hint of involvement of high campaign and Administration officials. For many months the facts set forth above regarding the planning and implementation of the Gemstone plan were hidden from public view. This is because on June 17, just hours after the burglars were arrested, a massive coverup was begun to conceal the true facts from the nation. This coverup eventually encompassed destruction and secretion of documents, obstruction of official investigations, subornation of perjury and offers of money and executive clemency to the Watergate defendants to secure silence.

That there was a coverup of some form can no longer be seriously disputed since four of its participants—John Dean, Jeb Magruder, Fred LaRue, and Bart Porter—have pleaded guilty to crimes related to it. Dean, Magruder and LaRue have admitted involvement in a conspiracy to obstruct justice, the basis of which was their participation in coverup activities, and Porter has confessed to making false statements to the FBI to hide the true Watergate facts.

A. WHITE HOUSE AND CRP ACTIVITY—FIRST THREE DAYS AFTER THE BREAK-IN

On the morning of June 17, Liddy called Magruder in Los

Angeles and informed him that five men, including McCord, had been apprehended in the DNC headquarters. Magruder, who was on a campaign trip with Mitchell, Fred LaRue, Robert Mardian and Bart Porter, repeated Liddy's report to LaRue, who relayed it to Mitchell. (2 *Hearings* 798; 6 *Hearings* 2284-85). Magruder testified that, later in the day, Mitchell told Mardian to have Liddy speak to Kleindienst concerning the possibility of releasing McCord. (2 *Hearings* 798) Mardian denied this, but LaRue said that Mitchell asked someone—probably Mardian or Magruder—to tell Liddy to contact Kleindienst, who in turn was to contact Police Chief Jerry Wilson, for details. (6 *Hearings* 2285, 2330, 2353)

In any event, in the late morning hours of Saturday, June 17, Liddy accompanied by CRP Staffer Powell Moore, went to the Burning Tree Country Club near Washington to ask Kleindienst to arrange the release of the five Watergate burglars. (6 *Hearings* 2353) Kleindienst, who had received word of the break-in from Henry Petersen at eight a.m., telephoned Petersen in Liddy's presence and ordered that the Watergate Five receive no special treatment. Kleindienst testified that he then told Liddy to leave the premises. (6 *Hearings* 2353; 9 *Hearings* 3561-62, 3613)

That afternoon the scene of activity shifted to CRP headquarters. Liddy, rushing by Hugh Sloan, commented tersely: "My boys got caught last night; I made a mistake; I used someone from here which I told them I would never do; I'm afraid I'm going to lose my job." (2 *Hearings* 542) Robert Odle later observed Liddy shredding a pile of documents about "a foot high." (1 *Hearings* 44)

In a telephone conversation later in the day, Magruder, still in California, directed Odle and Robert Reisner to take certain sensitive CRP files home over the weekend. In particular, Magruder asked them to remove the blue file containing Gemstone papers from the office. Reisner put the Gemstone blue folder file in Odle's briefcase for Odle to remove. (1 *Hearings* 45-49; 2 *Hearings* 495-496, 799)

Meanwhile the FBI investigation of the Watergate incident had begun. FBI agents first became aware of Hunt's involvement during the afternoon of June 17, when, in the course of searching the two hotel rooms previously occupied by the arrested men, they discovered address books with White House telephone numbers used by Hunt and Liddy. The FBI interviewed Hunt on the evening of June 17, but he revealed little. On that same evening, the FBI contacted Alexander Butterfield of the White House Staff to determine Hunt's precise affiliation with the White House and to inform the White House that Hunt was possibly involved in the Watergate break-in. (Gray Confirmation Hearings, pp. 52, 114, 128)

After the disclosure of McCord's association with CRP appeared in the newspapers on June 18, Mitchell issued a statement from Los Angeles: "McCord and the other four men arrested in Democratic headquarters Saturday were not operating either in our behalf or with our consent in the alleged bugging attempt." He commented further that there "is no place in our campaign or in the electoral process for this type of activity and we will not permit it or condone it." (Washington *Post*, June 19, 1972, pp. A 1, A 6)

In a telephone conversation on June 18, Magruder informed Haldeman, then in Key Biscayne with the President, of the break-in and McCord's involvement. (3 *Hearings* 3039) Haldeman responded by asking Magruder to "get back to Washington immediately . . . [and] talk with Mr. Dean and Mr. Strachan and Mr. Sloan and others on Monday to try to find out what actually had happened and whose money it was and so on." (2 *Hearings* 799, 815) Haldeman confirms the phone call, but he said the conversation concerned a review of a press release on the break-in. (8 *Hearings* 3039)

The next day, June 19, Ronald Ziegler, also in Key Biscayne, announced that the White House was not conducting an inquiry into the Watergate incident. (3 *Hearings* 955) He declined to comment on what he termed a "third-rate burglary attempt." (Washington *Post*, June 20, 1972, A 1) On June 20, the press reported that Hunt's name had been found in the address books of Barker and Martinez. (Washington *Post*, June 20, 1972, p A 1) After first identifying Hunt as a consultant to Colson, the White House later denied he worked for Colson.

The coverup began to take form in a number of meetings held on June 19. Probably the most significant was an evening meeting in Mitchell's apartment attended by Mitchell, Magruder, LaRue, Mardian, and Dean. (2 *Hearings* 799-800; 3 *Hearings* 933-35; 4 *Hearings* 1622; 5 *Hearings* 1877; 6 *Hearings* 2286) Earlier in the day, Odle had returned various files, including the Gemstone files, to Magruder. (1 *Hearings* 67; 2 *Hearings* 507)* Magruder, according to his testimony, asked the others present at the meeting what he should do with these sensitive files. LaRue testified that Mitchell replied that it might be a good idea if Magruder had a fire in his house. Magruder similarly testified that those at the meeting concluded that the Gemstone file should be de-

---

* On June 18, Reisner had shredded what he assumed were copies of some papers in the files which Odle had taken home. (2 *Hearings* 507)

stroyed imediately. (2 *Hearings* 800) Mitchell testified that there was no reference to a Gemstone file at the meeting and that he did not suggest the destruction of any papers. (4 *Hearings* 1622; 5 *Hearings* 1877; *but see* 6 *Hearings* 2285-86) * Dean did not remember whether destruction of files was mentioned. (3 *Hearings* 935) Mardian testified that there was no discussion of destruction of "Gemstone files or Sensitive files" while he was at the meeting. (6 *Hearings* 2256-2257)

Dean testified that he participated in a number of other Watergate-related meetings and conversations on June 19. In the morning, Ehrlichman told Dean to discover what he could about the Watergate incident and, specifically, to explore Colson's involvement. Dean immediately informed Ehrlichman of a conversation he had just had with Magruder, who had stated that "this was all Liddy's fault." Dean later talked with Colson who suggested that they should meet with Ehrlichman as soon as possible and expressed concern over the contents of Hunt's safe.

Shortly before noon, Dean and Liddy met. Liddy told Dean that the men arrested in the break-in were "his men" and that "Magruder had pushed him into doing it." (3 *Hearings* 933) Dean testified that, shortly after his meeting with Liddy, Strachan came to Dean's office and reported that, at Haldeman's direction, he had removed and destroyed damaging materials from Haldeman's files over the weekend. (3 *Hearings* 933-934) Strachan later confirmed this in testimony before the Committee. (6 *Hearings* 2442, 2490) Haldeman testified he did not recall giving Strachan such instructions. (8 *Hearings* 3038)

Dean met with Ehrlichman twice during the afternoon of June 19. In the first meeting, Dean testified, he told Ehrlichman everything he had learned from Liddy, and Ehrlichman requested that Dean keep him advised of the results of his inquiries. Dean testified he also told Ehrlichman at this time about the earlier meetings he attended in Mitchell's office in late January and early February and his subsequent conversation with Haldeman where he expressed concern over the proposed Liddy plan. (3 *Hearings* 934) Ehrlichman testified he had no recollection of receiving such a report from Dean at that time. (7 *Hearings* 2823) According to the edited Presidential tapes, Ehrlichman also told this to the President. (Edited Presidential Conversations, pp. 1022, 1179-80)

Colson was present at the second meeting, during which,

---

* Mitchell was indicted by the Watergate Grand Jury for perjury for this testimony. (Indictment of March 1, 1974, at pp. 23-24.)

91

Dean testified, Ehrlichman instructed him to call Liddy and advise Liddy to tell Hunt to leave the country. Dean said he did this "without even thinking," but later called Liddy back to retract the instruction after he and Colson convinced Ehrlichman that such a course would be unwise. (3 *Hearings* 934) Ehrlichman, however, testified that he gave Dean no orders to instruct Liddy to tell Hunt to leave the country. (7 *Hearings* 2718-20, 2830) And, the edited Presidential transcripts (pp. 1022, 1179-80) indicate that Ehrlichman told the President that he gave no such instruction.

Colson raised, at this meeting, the matter of Hunt's safe and suggested—with Ehrlichman's concurrence—that Dean take custody of its contents. Bruce Kehrli, the White House staff secretary, entered the meeting and was instructed by Ehrlichman to have the safe opened in Dean's presence. (3 *Hearings* 934-35; 7 *Hearings* 2822) The safe was opened that evening, after Dean had departed, by Kehrli with Fred Fielding, Dean's assistant, in attendance. Kehrli knew that the contents of the safe were to be delivered to Dean. (3 *Hearings* 935) Colson's concern about Hunt's safe apparently derived from a comment Hunt had made to Colson's secretary, Joan Hall, earlier in the day. Before leaving the White House for the last time, Hunt stopped by Colson's office and said to Hall, "I just want you to know that that safe is loaded." (9 *Hearings* 3689)

On June 19 (or possibly June 20), Dean also met with Kleindienst and Henry Petersen in Kleindienst's office. (3 *Hearings* 934; 9 *Hearings* 3563, 3613-14) Kleindienst testified, and Petersen agreed, that the purpose of the meeting was "to inform [Dean] as counsel to the President that the Department of Justice and the FBI would be compelled and would immediately launch a full-scale intensive, thorough investigation . . ." (9 *Hearings* 3563, 3613-14) Dean also testified he told Kleindienst earlier in the meeting, before Petersen arrived, that he was "very concerned that this matter could lead directly to the President," and that if the investigation led into the White House he suspected that the chances of re-electing the President would be severely damaged." (3 *Hearings* 936) Dean also testified he informed Petersen, after Kleindienst left, that he had no idea where "this thing" might end but he did not think the White House could stand a wide-open investigation. Dean said Petersen gave him "the impression . . . that he realized the problems of a wide-open investigation of the White House in an election year." (3 *Hearings* 937) Petersen recalls only some discussion about a general probe of the White House in an election year. He gave assurances there would be no fishing expedition. (9 *Hearings* 3614)

B. THE DISPOSITION OF THE CONTENTS OF HUNT'S SAFE

Dean testified that, in mid-morning on June 20, GSA representatives brought him several cartons containing the contents of Hunt's safe and, in the afternoon, he and Fielding examined these materials. In addition to electronic equipment in a briefcase, Dean discovered numerous memoranda to Colson regarding the Plumbers, a psychological study of Ellsberg, various materials relating to the Pentagon Papers, a number of classified State Department cables, and a forged cable implicating the Kennedy Administration in the assassination of South Vietnamese President Diem. Dean called David Young, who agreed to store the caassified cables in his office. (3 *Hearings* 937-38; 7 *Hearings* 2826; 9 *Hearings* 3513-14)

Subsequently, Dean testified, he met with Ehrlichman and described for him the contents of the safe. According to Dean's testimony, Ehrlichman instructed Dean to shred the documents and to "deep six" the briefcase containing the electronic equipment. Dean said that when he asked Ehrlichman what he meant by "deep six," Ehrlichman explained, "Well, when you cross over the bridge on your way home, just toss the briefcase into the river." (3 *Hearings* 938) Fred Fielding has testified that Dean told him that Ehrlichman instructed Dean to "deep six" the briefcases. (Fielding DNC Deposition, May 15, 1973, pp. 39-40) Ehrlichman has denied giving such instructions. (7 *Hearings* 2825, 2719) Ehrlichman also denied to the President that he (Ehrlichman) had given a "deep six" instruction. (Edited Presidential Conversations, pp. 935 and 1179)

Dean testified he did not follow Ehrlichman's order. (3 *Hearings* 938, 948-949) However, in January 1973, Dean, in fact, did destroy the Hunt notebooks which had been in the safe.* He did not volunteer this information to the Special Prosecutor until after he had pleaded guilty to a conspiracy to obstruct justice charge. Furthermore, he did not volunteer this information when he testified publicly or privately before this Committee.

Dean testified that, on June 25 or 26, he went to Ehrlichman to argue that, because there were many witnesses to the removal of the various items from the safe, it would be too dangerous to destroy 'them. He suggested that the material be turned over to the FBI and that sensitive

* Testimony of Dean in *United States v. Hunt, et al.*, Crim. No. 2827-72, Transcript of November 5, 1973, at 4.

documents be given directly to Patrick Gray, its Acting Director. (3 *Hearings* 948) By following this procedure, Dean said, he would be able to testify under oath that to the best of his knowledge "everything found in the safe had been turned over to the FBI."

Dean retrieved the State Department cables from Young and, on June 26 or 27, gave FBI agents all the materials from the safe except the two envelopes containing politically sensitive materials and the Hunt notebooks. Dean told Ehrlichman what he had done on June 28 (apparently not mentioning the Hunt notebooks). Ehrlichman informed Dean that he was meeting with Gray later that day and that Dean should attend and bring the politically sensitive documents. (3 *Hearings* 948; 6 *Hearings* 2614)

Dean testified that, when Gray met with Dean and Ehrlichman in Ehrlichman's office, Dean told Gray that the Hunt materials had been turned over to the FBI agents with the exception of two envelopes which he did not believe related to Watergate in any way. But, Dean testified, he told Gray "if they should leak out they would be political dynamite in an election year and thus should never be made public." (3 *Hearings* 948-949) Dean gave the envelopes to Gray. (3 *Hearings* 948-49; 6 *Hearings* 2614-15)

Gray testified that Dean said that these files were "political dynamite," and "clearly should not see the light of day." He testified that, although Ehrlichman and Dean did not expressly instruct him to destroy the files, "the implication of the substance of some of their remarks was that these two files were to be destroyed and I interpreted this to be an order from the counsel to the President of the United States issued in the presence of one of the two top assistants to the President of the United States." (9 *Hearings* 3467) Ehrlichman has denied that anyone instructed Gray that the documents in the envelope should never see the light of day. (6 *Hearings* 2614-15) However Gray, in December 1972, burned the documents at his home in Connecticut. (9 *Hearings* 3468)

C. WHITE HOUSE CONCERN OVER THE MEXICAN AND DAHLBERG CHECKS

On the morning of June 21, 1972, Ehrlichman called Gray to inform him that Dean would be handling the Watergate inquiry for the White House and that he should deal directly with Dean on Watergate matters. (9 *Hearings* 3450) Dean and Gray met on the 21st and again on the 22nd. During these meetings Gray informed Dean that the FBI, in the course of investigating the $100 bills found on the burglars and in their hotel rooms, had discovered that four Mexican checks totaling $89,000 and a check for $25,000 from Kenneth Dahlberg, which were originally contributed to the President's campaign, had been deposited in Bernard Barker's bank account in Miami. (2 *Hearings* 577; 3 *Hearings* 942-43; 9 *Hearings* 3451)

Dean testified that, about the same time, Mitchell and Stans asked him to attempt to prevent disclosure of the Dahlberg check, which might prove embarrassing for Dwayne Andreas, the campaign contributor behind the check. Dean testified he went to see Gray on June 22 at the request of Haldeman and Ehrlichman to discuss the Dahlberg and Mexican checks. (3 *Hearings* 942-943; 9 *Hearings* 3450-3451) Dean was informed that the checks had reached Barker's account after Sloan turned the checks over to Liddy for cashing. Liddy had used Barker for this purpose. (3 *Hearings* 942) The serial numbers on the $100 bills obtained from the burglars demonstrated that this was money Barker gave Liddy when he cashed the Mexican and Dahlberg checks. (2 *Hearings* 577)

D. WHITE HOUSE USE OF THE CIA TO RESTRICT THE FBI WATERGATE INVESTIGATION

On June 22, Helms and Gray conversed by telephone. According to Gray, Helms, during that conversation, assured Gray that the CIA had nothing to do with the Watergate break-in. (9 *Hearings* 3451) Haldeman testified that the next day, acting at President Nixon's direction after meeting with him, Haldeman and Ehrlichman called CIA Director Helms and Deputy Director Walters to the White House for a meeting. (7 *Hearings* 2884) At this session, according to Helms and Walters, Haldeman asked if there were any CIA connection with the Watergate break-in. Helms replied there was none. Haldeman, however, suggested that an FBI investigation in Mexico might uncover CIA operations or assets. Helms replied that no FBI investigation of Watergate would jeopardize any CIA operations. Nevertheless, Haldeman and Ehrlichman directed Walters to meet with Gray and tell him that any further investigation into Mexico could endanger CIA assets there. (8 *Hearings* 3238-3239; 9 *Hearings* 3404-3405)

Ehrlichman contends the meeting's only conclusion was that Walters and Gray "would sit down together and talk through what the problem might be." (6 *Hearings* 2557) Haldeman does not recall that the question of the Mexican money was raised at the meeting with Helms and Walters or with the President earlier in the day. (8 *Hearings* 3042)

But Haldeman testified that he did request Walters to meet with Gray to assure that the FBI investigation would not expose "earlier national security or CIA activities." (7 *Hearings* 2884) Ehrlichman, however, recalled the President's concern about "the Mexican money or the Florida bank or whatever . . ." (6 *Hearings* 2563)

Walters and Gray met later in the afternoon. Walters told Gray he had just talked with "senior staff members" at the White House and then related the White House concern about the investigation into the Mexican money. Gray assured Walters that he would abide by the general agency agreement that the CIA and the FBI would not expose each other's sources. (9 *Hearings* 3407, 3452-3453). A memorandum which Walters prepared on this meeting indicates that Gray was concerned with how to "low key" the Watergate investigation (Exhibit 129, 9 *Hearings* 3815), but Gray testified he did not mean to imply "that the FBI investigation would be other than aggressive and thorough" and only wanted to "pursue this investigation without compromising CIA assets and resources." (9 *Hearings* 3452-3453)

After the meeting between Walters and Gray, Gray telephoned Dean, who urged that the FBI not conduct any interviews that would expose CIA sources. Gray agreed to postpone temporarily the interview of Manuel Ogarrio, whose name appeared on the four Mexican checks deposited in Barker's account. (9 *Hearings* 3453-3454)

Meanwhile, General Walters, after discussions at the CIA had concluded that the ongoing FBI investigation could not jeopardize any CIA sources or activities in Mexico. (9 *Hearings* 3408) On June 28, Walters was called by Dean regarding the matters Haldeman and Ehrlichman had earlier discussed with Walters at the White House. Walters testified that he checked on Dean with Ehrlichman, who 'told him it was appropriate to discuss these items with Dean because "he is in charge of the whole matter." (9 *Hearings* 3408)

Walters met with Dean on June 26. He testified and Dean confirmed, that Dean pressed him about the possibility of CIA involvement in the Watergate break-in and that he emphasized to Dean that there was no CIA connection. He said he told Dean:

"Mr. Dean, any attempt to involve the Agency in the stifling of this affair would be a disaster. It would destroy the credibility of the Agency with the Congress, with the Nation. It would be a grave disservice to the President. I will not be a party to it and I am prepared to resign before I do anything that would implicate the Agency in this matter." (9 *Hearings* 3409)

Walters testified that the following morning, June 27, he again received a telephone call from Dean asking him to come to Dean's office. He said Dean told him that "some of his suspects were wobbling and might talk" and that Dean again asked if he had discovered any CIA involvement in the matter. Walters testified that, when he replied there was none, Dean asked whether there was any way the CIA could meet the bail or pay the salaries of the defendants while they were in jail. Walters said that he informed Dean there was no way the Agency could involve itself in this. (9 *Hearings* 3410) Dean testified that he first heard discussion concerning payments to the defendants at a meeting on June 23 or 24 with Mardian, Mitchell and LaRue where Mardian told the group "the CIA could take care of this entire matter if they wished." (3 *Hearings* 945-946).

Walters testified that, on June 28, Dean called him again, asking him to come to his office. Dean then told Walters that a scheduled meeting between Helms and Gray had been cancelled and that Ehrlichman wanted Gray to deal with Walters instead. Dean asked whether Walters could assist to limit the FBI investigation to the five defendants. Walters said he had no authority in this matter and told Dean that the CIA could becomed involved only at the President's direction. (9 *Hearings* 3411-3412) Dean confirmed this testimony. (3 *Hearings* 947-48)

Dean testified that his meetings with Walters were at Ehrlichman's express request. Dean said Ehrlichman told him to deal with Walters because he was a good friend of the White House, that the White House had installed him as Deputy Director so it would have influence over the CIA. (3 *Hearings* 946)

On the evening of July 5, Gray telephoned Walters and said that he would pursue the investigation in Mexico unless Helms or Walters wrote a letter stating that the investigation would uncover CIA assets or activities. (9 *Hearings* 3413, 3457) The next morning, Walters met with Gray. Walters testified "I told Mr. Gray right at the outset that I could not tell and, even less, could I give him a letter saying that the pursuit of the FBI's investigation would in any way jeopardize CIA activities in Mexico." (9 *Hearings* 3948) It was at this meeting, Gray testified, that he first suspected that someone might be trying to interfere with his investigation. (9 *Hearings* 3523)

After Walters left Gray's office, Gray called MacGregor in

San Clemente and expressed the opinion that "people on the White House staff are careless and indifferent in their use of the CIA and FBI." (9 *Hearings* 3462) Gray asked MacGregor to inform President Nixon of his problem. Thirty-seven minutes later the President telephoned Gray. [*Id.*] Gray testified that he said to the President:

> "Mr. President, there is something that I want to speak to you about.
> "Dick Walters and I feel that people on your staff are trying to mortally wound you by using the CIA and FBI and by confusing the question of CIA interest in, or not in, people the FBI wishes to interview." (*Id.*)

Gray testified that after a "slight pause," the President said:

> "Pat, you just continue to conduct your aggressive and thorough investigation." (9 *Hearings* 3462)

Gray testified he believed his message to the President was "adequate to put him on notice that the members of the White House staff were using the FBI and the CIA." (9 *Hearings* 3498). However, in his May 22, 1973, statement, the President maintained that, despite his July 6 conversation with Gray, he was not aware of "efforts to limit the investigation or to conceal possible involvement of members of the Administration and the campaign committee." (Presidential Press Statement, May 22, 1973) The President did not ask Gray what people on the staff were trying to use the CIA and FBI; he did not indicate that the charges were serious or that he would suspend or fire those involved. Gray testified:

> "Frankly, I expected the President to ask me some questions and for two weeks thereafter, I think it was on the 12th and again, the 28th, I asked General Walters if the President had called him. And when I heard nothing, you know, I began to feel that General Walters and I were alarmists . . ." (9 *Hearings* 3498)

In his May 22, 1973 statement, the President admitted directing Haldeman and Ehrlichman to take steps to restrict the FBI Watergate investigation purportedly on the basis of an incorrect suspicion that the CIA, in some way, was involved. The President also conceded in his May 22 statement that he had directed Haldeman and Ehrlichman to restrict the FBI Watergate investigation to prevent the exposure of the activities of the Plumbers. As is shown later in this report, the payoffs and promises made to Howard Hunt ap-

98

pear to have been largely motivated from a fear of Hunt's revelation of his activities for the Plumbers.

E. MARDIAN/LaRUE/LIDDY MEETING

On June 20 or 21, 1972, Liddy, Mardian and LaRue met in LaRue's apartment to allow Liddy to give a firsthand report of the Watergate operation. (6 *Hearings* 2286-2287, 2357) Liddy told Mardian and LaRue that he had employed the five men arrested at the DNC, that he and Hunt had organized the operation, that they had occupied a room in the Watergate Hotel during the break-in and that he had shredded documents from his files that related to the break-in. (6 *Hearings* 2286-2287, 2309, 2362) Liddy assured LaRue and Mardian that the operation could not be traced to him, but that, if an investigation did implicate him, he would never reveal any information. He stated that he was even willing to be assassinated "on any street corner at any time" if LaRue and Mardian were not satisfied with his assurances. (6 *Hearings* 2288, 2362) Mardian testified (6 *Hearings* 2359) that Liddy conveyed the impression that he conducted the break-in "on the express authority of the President" and with CIA assistance. According to Mardian, Liddy said Hunt felt it was CRP's obligation to provide bail money, legal fees and family support. (6 *Hearings* 2358)

LaRue testified that Liddy did not discuss who had approved the Watergate operation, although he did mention that Magruder had been pressuring him to improve the surveillance equipment in the DNC offices. (6 *Hearings* 2288-2289, 2304) During this meeting, LaRue first became aware of financial commitments to the Watergate defendants for bail, attorneys' fees, and family support. (6 *Hearings* 2307)

On the same day, LaRue and Mardian briefed Mitchell on Liddy's report. According to Mitchell, he then learned, for the first time, of Liddy's involvement in the Watergate burglary, "the Ellsberg matter . . . the Dita Beard matter, and a few of the other little gems." (4 *Hearings* 1621-1622; *see also* 6 *Hearings* 2318, 2362-63) Referring to these other scandals as "White House horrors," Mitchell testified that, in his opinion, their exposure would have been more destructive to the re-election campaign than the Watergate break-in, and that therefore he had participated in acitivites to conceal these matters from the public during the campaign. (4 *Hearings* 1625-26)

F. PRESSURES ON HUGH SLOAN

On June 22, 1972, FCRP Treasurer Hugh Sloan and Magruder met in Magruder's office prior to Sloan's being interviewed by FBI agents late in that day. Magruder suggested the total amount Sloan had disbursed to Liddy was approximately $75,000-$80,000. When Sloan protested that the figure was far too low and that he had no intention of perjuring himself, Magruder, according to Sloan's testimony, replied, "You may have to." (2 *Hearings* 543; *see also* 2 *Hearings* 800-801)

On the same day, Sloan testified, he was questioned by La-Rue concerning a $50,000 cash contribution delivered to Sloan by Porter after April 7, 1972. Sloan confirmed that he had received this cash, which was still in his safe because Porter had never identified its source. Sloan testified that when he expressed his concerns to Mitchell, Mitchell's only response was, "When the going gets tough, the tough get going." (2 *Hearings* 544) Sloan testified that he did not understand what Mitchell meant and found his remark of no assistance. (2 *Hearings* 544, 809) Magruder confirms Sloan's recollection of Mitchell's response to Sloan's expression of concern. (2 *Hearings* 809)

The FBI interview of Sloan was confined to the identification of Alfred Baldwin and his employment at CRP. After this interview, Sloan testified, LaRue sought a briefing on the FBI's questions and emphasized to Sloan the importance of giving a low figure for "the Liddy money" because it was "very political[ly] sensitive." (2 *Hearings* 544)

Sloan was becoming very concerned and thought he should talk to top White House officials about the troublesome CRP financial transactions. He arranged an appointment with Ehrlichman on June 23. Prior to that meeting, Sloan testified, he stopped by Dwight Chapin's office, expressed his concerns, and was told by Chapin that he was only overwrought and needed a vacation. (2 *Hearings* 544-545)

Sloan testified that, when he met with Ehrlichman, he did not "point fingers." He did not mention his conversation with Magruder, but told Ehrlichman he believed that somebody "external to the campaign" should look at the cash disbursements since the entire campaign might be in danger. According to Sloan, Ehrlichman's initial response was to interpret Sloan's statement as a personal problem. Ehrlichman said he would be glad to help Sloan obtain a lawyer, but then, Sloan testified, Ehrlichman said, "Do not tell me any details; I do not want to know; my position would have to be until after the election that I would have to take executive privilege." (2 *Hearings* 545-546) Ehrlichman generally concurred in Sloan's testimony. (7 *Hearings* 2699)

On June 23, Sloan made a final report to Stans on cash disbursements of pre-April 7 contributions. This report showed cash disbursements totalling $1,777,000. Of this amount, Liddy had received $199,000. Other cash disbursements of significance were $250,000 to Kalmbach, $350,000 to Strachan, $100,000 to Porter, and $20,000 to Magruder. As of the final report to Stans, there was a balance of $81,000 in cash in the safe. (2 *Hearings* 535-540, 546, 750-751, 891)

According to Sloan, Stans, fearing a GAO audit, told Sloan to take approximately $40,000 of the remaining $81,000 home with him. (2 *Hearings* 546-547) Sloan understood that Stans would take a similar amount with him. However, Sloan said that Stans later told him he never removed the money from the office. (*Id.*) On June 23, at Herbert Kalmbach's suggestion, Sloan destroyed the cash book he had used to prepare the report for Stans. (2 *Hearings* 572) Stans later gave his $40,000 to LaRue either directly or through Mardian. Sloan gave his $40,000 to LaRue about July 5, 1972 after receiving a telephone call from LaRue asking for the money (2 *Hearings* 548, 702)

Around June 24, according to Magruder, Mitchell and Magruder requested that Stans "try to work with Mr. Sloan to see if Mr. Sloan could be more cooperative about what had happened with the money." (2 *Hearings* 809) Sloan testified that he met with Mardian and gave him a full report on the cash disbursements from the pre-April 7 contributions. Sloan recalls that, when Mardian learned about the $199,000 to Liddy, he exploded, saying, "Magruder lied to John Mitchell. He told him it was only $40,000." (2 *Hearings* 547) Mardian's account is basically consistent with Sloan's. (6 *Hearings* 2363)

On July 5, after Sloan had returned from a Bermuda vacation, Magruder asked him to have a drink at the Black Horse Tavern. During this meeting Magruder suggested that they visit United States Attorney Harold Titus. Magruder said he would tell Titus he authorized the payments to Liddy and that Sloan should merely confirm he made distributions under Magruder's instructions. However, according to Sloan, Magruder said that they had to agree on a figure. The figure mentioned this time by Magruder, $40,000-$45,000, was even lower than the $74,000 Magruder suggested earlier. Sloan testified he told Magruder he would think about the request. (2 *Hearings* 548) But when Sloan met Magruder again, on the morning of July 6, he told Magruder he would not perjure himself. Sloan said Magruder dropped the subject and never again suggested seeing Titus. According to Sloan, LaRue checked with him later that day to ascertain whether he had agreed on a figure with Magruder, but when Sloan informed LaRue what he told Magruder, LaRue discontinued the conversation. (2 *Hearings* 549)

On July 6, Sloan testified, he met with Kenneth Parkinson and Paul O'Brien, attorney for CRP, during their debriefing of Mrs. Judy Hoback, Sloan's bookkeeper, following her testimony before the grand jury. Odle was also present at the beginning of the meeting. Sloan testified that he asked everyone to leave the room except the attorneys because he wanted to talk to them alone. (2 *Hearings* 549) Sloan then gave O'Brien and Parkinson a complete accounting of the cash disbursements and also informed them of Magruder's efforts to have Sloan alter his story. Sloan testified that O'Brien and Parkinson became angry and said, "Well, we have been lied to by the people here. We have not even been able to see John Mitchell, and we are a month in this thing." (2 *Hearings* 550)

Sloan said the attorneys remarked that, with the new information they had available to them, they needed time to confront other campaign officials and suggested that Sloan leave town if he had any legitimate business reason to do so. Mr. Stans at that time was on a trip on the West Coast and the attorney suggested that Sloan join him. Stans, during his testimony, recalled that Mardian recommended that Sloan join him in California. (2 *Hearings* 776) That evening, Sloan received a telephone call from LaRue in which LaRue impressed on him tht urgency of his departure to California. LaRue suggested he take a 6:00 a.m. flight from Dulles Airport the next morning. Sloan followed this recommendation. (2 *Hearings* 550)

Sloan returned from California on July 12 and met with LaRue the next day. Sloan said LaRue began by reviewing the options open to Sloan. He suggested that Sloan might have campaign law problems and might consider taking the Fifth Amendment with regard to any testimony before the grand jury. Sloan remarked to LaRue that it appeared obvious to him that the only way for him to stay in favor with the campaign organization was either to commit perjury or plead the Fifth Amendment, but that he would do neither. He told LaRue it would probably be in the interest of all concerned if he resigned. (2 *Hearings* 550-551)

LaRue did not challenge Sloan's assessment of the situation and suggested that he talk to Stans. Sloan called Stans that evening; Stans told him not to talk on the telephone but to come to see him the following morning. When Sloan met Stans the next morning, July 14, Stans told him that he had already informed the FBI that Sloan had resigned. Although Sloan had not yet resigned, he did so immediately. (2 *Hearings* 551-552) Stans confirmed the call, stating Sloan wanted to talk about his resignation. (2 *Hearings* 778)

On the same day, Sloan retained a lawyer and on July 20, he and his attorney met with Messrs. Silbert, Glanzer and Campbell of the United States Attorney's Office and gave them a complete statement, including Sloan's account of Magruder's effort to suborn his perjury. (2 *Hearings* 552)

G. MAGRUDER AND PORTER PERJURY

Mitchell resigned his position as Campaign Director on June 30, 1972, but Magruder was retained as Deputy Director. (5 *Hearings* 1885) Dean testified that during the last ten days of June he attended a meeting in Haldeman's office where Haldeman and Ehrlichman asked Dean for his recommendation on removing Mitchell and Magruder from the re-election committee. Dean said he told them there was a real chance Magruder would be indicted and thus should be removed in a graceful way that would not jeopardize his position. (3 *Hearings* 951) Dean was therefore surprised when it was publicly announced that Mitchell was resigning but that Magruder would remain. He said it was clear to him that Magruder was the link to the White House and that he might not hold his tongue if indicted. Dean testified that he specifically warned Haldeman about this possibility. (3 *Hearings* 951-952)

Thereafter, Dean testified, Haldeman and Ehrlichman displayed a greatly increased interest in Magruder's problem. Dean testified he kept them informed on the strategy being developed to create the appearance that involvment in the break-in stopped at Liddy. Haldeman and Ehrlichman, according to Dean, frequently asked him how Magruder was progressing with the FBI investigation and his preparation for the grand jury. Dean said he also received calls concerning Magruder's status from Larry Higby, Haldeman's staff assistant. (3 *Hearings* 952) Mitchell corroborates this (4 *Hearings* 1624-1625), although Ehrlichman denies he used Dean as a liaison man to keep informed about Magruder. (7 *Hearings* 2845)

Magruder testified, and Mitchell confirmed, that he (Magruder) volunteered to develop a coverup story that would conceal his involvement and leave Liddy the top figure in the Watergate conspiracy. (2 *Hearings* 802; 4 *Hearings* 1625-1626) He said it was important that involvement be stopped at Liddy, since "if it got to me, it would go higher." (2 *Hearings* 802)

The cover-up story, Magruder testified, was developed during a series of meetings from the time of the break-in until his second grand jury appearance, most of which were in Mitchell's office. Attending the meetings were Mitchell, La-

Rue, Mardian, Dean and himself. (3 *Hearings* 951-952; 4 *Hearings* 1624) At some point prior to his second grand jury appearance on August 16, 1972, a rationale was developed to justify Liddy's expenditure of almost $200,000. Magruder testified that the story invented involved exaggerating "to the tune of $230,000" the amount of money spent on certain legitimate activities for which Liddy was responsible. (2 *Hearings* 801-802) Magruder said that Porter was willing to help on the cover-up story, "so he took care of, in effect, $100,000 and I took care of, in effect, $150,000 by indicating that Mr. Liddy had legal projects for us in the intelligence field." Magruder worked on this story with Mitchell, Dean, LaRue, and Mardian. "My primary contacts on the story were Mr. Dean and Mr. Mitchell," Magruder told the Committee. (2 *Hearings* 801-803) Dean agrees. (3 *Hearings* 952) Ehrlichman, during a meeting with the President and Haldeman on April 14, 1973, stated that Mitchell had admitted being present when Dean helped Magruder prepare false testimony for the grand jury. (Edited Presidential Conversations, p. 527)

Porter testified he agreed to join in the false coverup story when Magruder swore to him that neither Magruder nor anyone higher than Liddy in the campaign or the White House had any involvement in the Watergate break-in. Porter said Magruder told him the problem was with the amount of money spent, that Liddy was authorized to spend the money for certain dirty tricks but "nothing illegal," and that the figures could be very embarrassing to the President, Mitchell, Haldeman and others. Magruder told Porter that his name was suggested as someone whom "we can count on to help in this situation." (2 *Hearings* 635) Together they agreed that Porter would falsely tell the FBI and the grand jury that $100,000 of the money Liddy spent was for the purpose of infiltrating radical groups that could endanger the personal safety of the surrogate speakers, for whom Porter was responsible. (2 *Hearings* 636) Dean testified he informed Haldeman and Ehrlichman of Magruder's fabricated story and Porter's corroboration. (3 *Hearings* 952) Ehrlichman, however, contended that Dean did not apprise him of such information. (7 *Hearings* 2845)

LaRue testified that, during June, July and August, he attended meetings at which Magruder discussed his coverup story, which LaRue knew to be false. (6 *Hearings* 2292) LaRue said his motivation in helping prepare this fake account was a desire to do all in his power to keep secret information of the connection between the burglary and CRP. (6 *Hearings* 2340-2341) Mitchell testified that he listened to rehearsals of Magruder's story, which he knew to be perjurious. (5 *Hearings* 1865)

Prior to their appearances before the grand jury, Magruder and Porter gave the false coverup story to FBI agents. (2 *Hearings* 637, 803) When Magruder made his first grand jury appearance on July 5, 1972, he testified only as to the organization of the CRP. However, when called for his second appearance on August 16, 1972, he was aware he was a target of its investigation. The day before his grand jury appearance he was briefed by lawyers for CRP and Mr. Mardian. Ehrlichman informed the President of these activities during an April 15, 1973 meeting, stating that "apparently Mardian was able to get around and coach witnesses," he "was very heavy-handed," and asked the witnesses "to say things that weren't true." (Edited Presidential Conversations, pp. 687-688)

Magruder, before his second appearance, was interrogated for approximately two hours by Dean, and approximately one-half hour by Mitchell. (2 *Hearings* 803) Dean, fully aware of the false story Magruder was going to tell, played "devil's advocate" asking Magruder questions the prosecutor might ask. (2 *Hearings* 803, 869; 3 *Hearings* 952)

On August 16, 1972, Magruder gave the false coverup story to the grand jury. (2 *Hearings* 803) After Magruder's appearance, Dean, at Haldeman's request, called Assistant Attorney General Henry Petersen to ask how Magruder's testimony had gone. (3 *Hearings* 952) Dean testified Petersen said Magruder "had made it through by the skin of his teeth." (3 *Hearings* 952) According to Petersen, who subsequently informed the President of this call during an April 16, 1973, meeting (Edited Presidential Conversations, pp. 868-9), he later called Dean back to give him Earl Silbert's evaluation: "Magruder had been a good witness in his own behalf," but that no one believed "the story about the money." (9 *Hearings* 3651) Dean repeated Petersen's comments to Mitchell, Magruder and Haldeman. Dean testified that Haldeman was "very pleased" because the White House strategy to "stop the involvement at Liddy" was succeeding. (3 *Hearings* 952)

Magruder was called before the grand jury a third time in early September to testify concerning entries in his diary reflecting meetings in Mitchell's office on January 27 and February 4 among Liddy, Magruder, Dean and Mitchell. Magruder testified he met with Mitchell and Dean to arrive at an explanation for these diary entries. The story finally developed that the first meeting on January 27 had been cancelled and that, at the second, the participants discussed the new election law. The presence at the meeting of Liddy, counsel for CRP, and of Dean, Counsel to the President, gave some credence to this account. An initial suggestion that the diary entries be erased was abandoned when it was recognized that erasures could be discovered by the FBI. Magruder testified he gave the false story to the grand jury when he appeared. (2 *Hearings* 804)

H. PARTICIPATION OF WHITE HOUSE AND CRP PERSONNEL IN FBI INTERVIEWS

White House and CRP officials took other steps to keep abreast of and interfere with the Watergate investigation. When White House staff personnel were interviewed by FBI agents, Dean or his assistant, Fred Fielding, attended the interviews. (3 *Hearings* 940-941; Gray Confirmation Hearings, p. 653) Also, in most cases when FBI agents interviewed CRP staff persons, CRP counsel O'Brien or Parkinson were present. And, on October 12, the White House received 82 FBI investigative reports relating to Watergate. (Gray Confirmation Hearings, pp. 630, 677-678)

The interest in and preparation for the FBI interview of Kathleen Chenow, the secretary for the Plumbers, is illustrative of the concern and activity in the White House regarding the FBI's investigation. Dean testified that, when the FBI indicated its interest in Chenow, she was in London. Dean discussed the Chenow matter with Ehrlichman and suggested that someone to go London and explain to her that she should not reveal to the FBI Hunt's and Liddy's activities with the Plumbers. With Ehrlichman's approval, Fielding flew to London and brought Chenow back to Washington on first class airline accomodations paid for by the White House. Fielding and Young briefed Chenow before her FBI interview and were present when the FBI questioned her. (3 *Hearings* 941)

Moreover, special arrangements were developed to prevent top White House officials from directly testifying before the Grand Jury. Certain officials—Colson, Krogh, Young, Chapin and Strachan—were permitted to give their testimony to the prosecutors at the Department of Justice and were therefore not exposed to direct questioning by grand jurors. When Dean asked Petersen to repeat this special procedure for Maurice Stans, Petersen at first refused. (3 *Hearings* 954) Under direction from the President, Ehrlichman then complained to Petersen and Kleindienst to prevent Stans from appearing before the grand jury. (7 *Hearings* 2700-2701) Although both told Ehrlichman he could not dictate policy to the Justice Department, they agreed to make another concession for Stans and permitted his interrogation by the prosecutors with no grand jurors present. (9 *Hearings* 3564-3565, 3580, 3618-3620)

In considering the FBI interviews it is important to note that neither the FBI nor other Department of Justice personnel interviewed Robert A. Reisner, the administrative assistant to CRP Deputy Director Magruder. (2 *Hearings* 489) The first time Reisner was subpenaed by any investigative body was on or about March 30, 1973, when he was subpenaed by this Committee. (2 *Hearings* 496, 507-508) The failure to question Reisner was a crucial omission because, as Magruder later testified, the coverup might have ended months earlier if Reisner had been interrogated. (2 *Hearings* 805)

I. THE PRESIDENT'S STATEMENT OF AUGUST 29—THE SO-CALLED DEAN REPORT

On August 29, 1972, President Nixon, at a press conference, told the American people that Dean had conducted a "complete investigation" for the White House which enabled the President to declare: "I can state categorically that no one in the White House staff, no one in this Administration, presently employed, was involved in this very bizarre incident." (Washington *Post,* August 30, 1972, p. A1) The President was briefed for this press conference by Ehrlichman and Ziegler. (7 *Hearings* 2720, 2776) Dean testified before the Committee that there never was a "Dean Report," that he never made the investigation referred to by the President. (3 *Hearings* 955-956; 4 *Hearings* 1510) To the contrary, Dean testified, far from investigating, he was spending most of his time participating in the coverup on instructions from Haldeman and Ehrlichman as liaison between the White House and CRP. The Edited Presidential Conversations (at pp. 167-68) of a March 20, 1973 telephone call between the President and Dean casts further light on the President's August 29 statement. In the March 20 telephone call, the President suggested to Dean that he prepare some kind of report that would appear complete, but would be "very incomplete" which the President could use for public release and to reassure the Cabinet. Dean asked, "As we did when you, back in August, made that statement that—" and the President replied, "That's right." (Edited Presidential Conversations, pp. 167-68)

J. THE SEPTEMBER 15 MEETING BETWEEN DEAN AND THE PRESIDENT

The Grand Jury returned indictments against Liddy, Hunt, McCord, Barker, Sturgis, Martinez and Gonzales on September 15, charging a number of crimes arising out of the Watergate break-in. The coverup had worked and the indictments had stopped with Liddy. Higher CRP and White House officials were not yet exposed.

John W. Hushen, the Justice Department's Director of Public Information, declared on that day that the Department had concluded its investigation, stating: "We have absolutely no evidence to indicate that any others should be charged." (New York *Times*, September 16, 1972, p. 1) Hushen's comments were followed the next day by those of Attorney General Kleindienst, who said that the investigation by the FBI and the United States Attorney's Office had been "one of the most extensive, objective, and thorough" in many years. That same day Assistant Attorney General Petersen denied there had been a "whitewash" and cited statistics to prove the thoroughness of the investigation. (Washington *Post*, September 17, 1972)

On September 15, after the indictments were issued, the President summoned Dean to the Oval Office. (4 *Hearings* 1474-1475) Haldeman was also present. (4 *Hearings* 1475) Dean testified:

"The President told me that . . . Haldeman . . . had kept him posted on my handling of the Watergate case. The President told me I had done a good job and he appreciated how difficult a task it had been and the President was pleased that the case had stopped with Liddy . . . I told him that all that I had been able to do was to contain the case and assist in keeping it out of the White House. I also told him that there was a long way to go before this matter would end and that I certainly could make no assurances that the day would not come when this matter would start to unravel . . ." (3 *Hearings* 957-959; 4 *Hearings* 1372, 1474-1477, 1494-1495)

According to Dean, other topics discussed at the meeting included the bugging of the 1968 Nixon Campaign, the date of the criminal trial, progress in the various Watergate civil suits, press coverage of Watergate, a GAO audit, the Patman Committee's inquiry, use of the IRS to attack Administration "enemies," post-election plans to place officials responsive to the White House requirements in the IRS and other federal agencies. He said the President also asked him "to keep a good list of the press people giving us trouble, because we will make life difficult for them after the election." (3 *Hearings* 958-959; 4 *Hearings* 1477-1482) When he left the meeting, Dean said, he was "convinced" that the President was aware of the cover-up. (3 *Hearings* 959, 1028; 4 *Hearings* 1435, 1564-1567)

Haldeman gave a different version of this meeting. He denied any contemporaneous knowledge of the coverup or that he had informed the President of such activities. He testified that the President merely expressed his satisfaction as to Dean's investigative work which had shown no involvement of White House personnel in the break-in. Haldeman confirmed that the 1968 bugging of the Nixon campaign was discussed along with the civil suit, the GAO audit, the Patman Committee investigation, and use of the IRS. (7 *Hearings* 2888-2889)

Alexander Butterfield's testimony before the Committee revealed that there is a complete tape recording of what was said by the participants to the September 15 meeting. (5 *Hearings* 2073-2091) This fact was corroborated by Haldeman who informed the Committee that he had in fact listened to the tape. (7 *Hearings* 2894) The Committee on July 17, 1973, requested the President to provide the Committee with the tape recording of this meeting, among others. (5 *Hearings* 2178-2179) When the President refused on July 23, 1973, the Committee issued a subpena to the President for this and other tape recordings. (6 *Hearings* 2478-2479) The President on July 25, 1973, refused to comply with this subpena (7 *Hearings* 2657), and the matter was taken to court. (See Chapter IX [in Vol. 2].)

The Select Committee has now received—along with the American public—an edited, unauthenticated partial transcription of the tape recording of this conversation (and others) prepared by the White House. These transcripts are not conclusive proof as to the contents of these conversations. They contain a number of deletions, and portions of the taped conversation are alleged to be inaudible or unintelligible. Also transcripts cannot provide voice tone and inflections which at times are crucial for understanding the meaning of speakers' words. Moreover, the Presidential version of the September 15 meeting differs in significant respects from that purportedly prepared by the House Judiciary Committee, which has a copy of the actual recording. (*See* Washington *Post*, May 12, 1974, pp. A26-28) At least, however, the transcripts are useful as a White House version of what occurred and thus—with the caveat that it is not the best evidence available—it has been utilized by the Committee in the preparation of this report.

The transcript of the September 15 meeting supports many aspects of Dean's testimony. Thus the transcript begins with the President's greeting Dean: "You had quite a day today didn't you. You got Watergate on the way didn't you?" Dean replied, "We tried,"* and then, in answer to Haldeman's question "How did it all end up?" answered "Ah, I think we can say well at this point." (Edited Presidential Conversations, p. 55) Shortly thereafter the following colloquy occurred:

> D   Three months ago I would have had trouble predicting there would be a day when this would be forgotten but I think I can say that 54 days from now nothing is going to come crashing down to our surprise.
> P   That what?
> D   Nothing is going to come crashing down to our surprise.
> P   Oh well, this is a can of worms as you know a lot of this stuff that went on. And the people who worked this way are awfully embarrassed. *But the way you have handled all this seems to me has been very skillful putting your fingers in the leaks that have sprung here and sprung there.*** (*Id* at 62)

                                    * * *

> D   Well as I see it, *the only problems we may have are the human ones* and I will keep a close watch on that.
> P   Union?
> D   Human.
> H   Human frailties.
> D   People get annoyed—some fingerpointing—false accusations—
> P   You mean on this case?
> D   On this case. There is some bitterness between the Finance Committee and the Political Committee—they feel they are taking all the heat and all the people upstairs are bad people—not being recognized.
> P   *We are all in it together. This is a war. We take a few shots and it will be over. We will give them a few shots and it will be over. Don't worry. I wouldn't want to be on the other side right now. Would you?* (*Id.* at 64) (emphasis added)

The transcript also records significant discussion relating to possible hearings proposed by Congressman Wright Pat-

* The purported House version also has Dean responding, "Quite a three months."
** The purported House version reads, ". . . but the way you, you've handled it, it seems to me, has been very skillful, because you—putting your fingers in the dike every time that leaks have sprung here and sprung there."

man, Chairman of the House Banking and Currency Committee:

D [The Patman Committee] is the last forum where we have the least problem right now. Kennedy has already said he may call hearings of the Administrative Practices subcommittee. As these committees spin out oracles we used to get busy on each one. I stopped doing that about two months ago.* We just take one thing at a time.

P You really can't sit and worry about it all the time. The worst may happen but it may not. *So you just try to button it up as well as you can and hope for the best, and remember basically the damn business is unfortunatly trying to cut our losses.***

D Certainly that is right and certainly it has had no effect on you. That's the good thing.

H No, it has been kept away from the White House and of course completely from the President. The only tie to the White House is the Colson effort they keep trying to pull in.

D And, of course, the two White House people of lower level—indicted—one consultant and one member of the Domestic Staff. That is not very much of a tie.

H That's right. (Edited Presidential Conversations, pp. 69-70) (emphasis added)

The edited transcript does not contain a statement by Dean, as he testified, that "all that I had been able to do was to contain the case and assist in keeping it out of the White House" and that "there was a long way to go before this matter would end and . . . I certainly could make no assurances that the day would not come when this matter would start to unravel."

Although the edited transcript also does not reflect a discussion between the President and Dean regarding the use of the IRS on Administration enemies, or any specific reference to an IRS investigation of DNC Chairman Lawrence O'Brien, the reconstruction of this meeting prepared by White House Counsel Fred Buzhardt and submitted to the Committee confirms that there was such a discussion at the September 15 meeting. (Exhibit 70A, 4 *Hearings* 1796) Moreover, the

* The purported House version reads, ". . . as this case has been all along, you spin out horribles that uh, you can conceive of, and so we just don't do that. I stopped that about, uh, two months ago."
** The House version allegedly states in part: "And remember that basically the damn business is just one of those unfortunate things, we're trying to cut our losses."

transcript indicates that the final portion of the meeting is deleted. (Edited Presidential Conversations, p. 75)

K. PAYOFFS TO WATERGATE DEFENDANTS

1. Early Payoff Discussions. As already noted, on June 20 or 21, Liddy met with LaRue and Mardian and told them of commitments made to provide bail, legal expenses and family support funds for the Watergate defendants. (6 *Hearings* 2289, 2358) Mardian said he also discussed Hunt's request to CRP for legal fees with CRP counsel Kenneth Parkinson and Paul O'Brien, and with William Bittman, Hunt's attorney. Mardian said he thought this request was blackmail and should not be paid. He said that he had no other discussions regarding payment of money to the defendants. (6 *Hearings* 2367-2368)

Dean, however, testified that Mardian suggested that the CIA assist regarding financial support for the defendants. (3 *Hearings* 945-946) This discussion concerning the CIA, Dean said, arose at a meeting among Dean, Mardian and Mitchell during which Mitchell suggested that Dean contact Ehrlichman and Haldeman to have the White House request CIA financial assistance for the defendants. (3 *Hearings* 946) Dean did meet with General Walters on June 26, June 27 and June 28 and asked Walters whether the CIA could provide financial assistance for bail, legal defense and family support. Walters answered in the negative. (3 *Hearings* 946-47)

2. The Activities of Herbert Kalmbach and Tony Ulasewicz. On June 28, Dean testified he met with Mitchell, LaRue and Mardian and informed them that the CIA would not provide financial assistance. (3 *Hearings* 949-50) According to Dean, LaRue then indicated that Stans had only limited cash— $70,000 or $80,000—and that much more would be needed. (3 *Hearings* 950) Dean testified that Mitchell asked him to obtain Haldeman's and Ehrlichman's approval to use Herbert Kalmbach to raise the necessary money. (3 *Hearings* 950) Mitchell denied being at this meeting and asking Dean to acquire Kalmbach's approval. (4 *Hearings* 1672)

Dean testified he conveyed the suggestion to Haldeman and Ehrlichman who told him to contact Kalmbach. During an April 14, 1973 meeting between the President, Ehrlichman and Haldeman, Haldeman confirmed this fact, stating: "we [Ehrlichman and Haldeman] referred him [Dean] to Kalmbach." (Edited Presidential Conversations, p. 494) As a result, Dean called Kalmbach on June 28, 1972 and told him that Haldeman, Ehrlichman and Mitchell had requested that he come to Washington as quickly as possible. (3 *Hearings* 950) Kalmbach immediately flew to Washington and met with Dean on June 29. (5 *Hearings* 2097-2098) Dean knew Kalmback did not wish to engage in further fundraising. In order to persuade Kalmbach to take this new assignment, Dean said, he told Kalmbach all he knew respecting the break-in and suggested that the scandal might involve the President himself, although he did not know this for a fact. He told Kalmbach that Haldeman, Ehrlichman and Mitchell felt it very important that he raise the money and instructed Kalmback to contact LaRue as to the amounts needed and the timing. (3 *Hearings* 950)

Kalmbach confirmed that he met with Dean on June 29 and was asked by Dean to assume the fundraising assignment. (5 *Hearings* 2098) He said Dean stressed that the assignment required absolute secrecy and indicated that, if it became known, it might jeopardize the campaign. (5 *Hearings* 2164) Kalmbach said that, in giving him this assignment, Dean indicated he spoke for others, not only for himself. He said that, although Dean did not use Haldeman's or Ehrlichman's name, he knew that Dean reported to Ehrlichman and worked for Haldeman. (5 *Hearings* 2099) And, since Dean was Counsel to the President, Kalmbach believed Dean had authority to ask him to undertake this task. (5 *Hearings* 2100)

Stans confirmed he met with Kalmbach on June 29 and gave him $75,000, after being informed that the money was needed for a special White House project. Stans said that Kalmbach stated he was asking for the money on "high authirity." (2 *Hearings* 702-703) According to both Kalmbach's and Stans' testimony, Kalmbach did not inform Stans how the money would be used. (2 *Hearings* 703; 5 *Hearings* 2100)

Kalmbach distributed the money through Tony Ulasewicz, who was hired originally by John Ehrlichman at the White House. (1 *Hearings* 288) Ulasewicz was unable to deliver the money to either Douglas Caddy or Paul O'Brien, the first two contacts Kalmbach suggested, because of their reluctance to receive funds under the conditions set by Ulasewicz. (5 *Hearings* 2103-2104) The third contact, William Bittman, Hunt's attorney, after an initial rejection, agreed to accept $25,000 in cash in a brown envelope placed on a ledge in a telephone booth in his law office building. Ulasewicz wanted to deliver the full amount received from Stans ($75,000) but Bittman only wanted his initial fee of $25,000. (6 *Hearings* 2225)

The delivery of these funds was typical of the procedure Ulasewicz used on future occasions. He placed the envelope containing the $25,000 in the telephone booth and called

113

Bittman to retrieve it. Bittman described the color of the suit he was wearing; Ulasewicz hid and watched until Bittman came out of the elevator, went to the booth, took the envelope and went back into the elevator. Ulasewicz then left the building. (6 *Hearings* 2226-2227)

After making this delivery to Bittman, Ulasewicz received a call from Kalmbach at another telephone booth. Kalmbach gave Ulasewicz a telephone number and told him to contact the "writer" or the "writer's wife," code names for Hunt and Mrs. Hunt. Ulasewicz, using his alias "Mr. Rivers," called Mrs. Hunt. He asked her what sums of money would be needed for the various defendants. Mrs. Hunt gave Ulasewicz figures for a five month period that covered salaries for Hunt, McCord and Liddy ($3,000 a month for each), family support for Barker, Sturgis, Gonzales and Martinez (totaling about $14,000) and a separate $23,000 to Barker which included "$10,000 bail, $10,000 under the table and $3,000 for other expenses." (6 *Hearings* 2234-2235) Mrs. Hunt also told Ulasewicz what would be required for legal fees. The lawyers for Hunt, McCord, Liddy and Barker were each to receive $25,-000; and an additional $10,000 in legal fees for each of the remaining three defendants, Sturgis, Gonzales and Martinez, was also required. These were only the initial requirements. The total sum Mrs. Hunt was requesting was in the vicinity of $400,000-$450,000. (6 *Hearings* 2236) This, of course, was very much above the $75,100 Ulasewicz had received from Kalmbach. Ulasewicz kept Kalmbach informed respecting his discussions with Mrs. Hunt.

Ulasewicz arranged with Mrs. Hunt the supply of $40,000 as a "down payment." (6 *Hearings* 2236) Ulasewicz placed the $40,000 for Mrs. Hunt in a locker at National Airport in Washington and telephoned her instructions to pick up the key to the locker which would be scotch-taped under the ledge in a telephone booth at the airport. The key was placed exactly five minutes before Mrs. Hunt arrived to retrieve it. Again Ulasewicz assumed a position where he could observe the telephone booth unseen. He saw Mrs. Hunt (whose clothing was known to him) go to the telephone booth, retrieve the key, open the locker and remove the money. (6 *Hearings* 2227-2231)

Kalmbach came to Washington on July 19 to meet with Dean and LaRue and receive an additional amount of money from LaRue. (5 *Hearings* 2104) According to Kalmbach the amount was $40,000; LaRue, however, estimated $20,000. (5 *Hearings* 2104; 6 *Hearings* 2291) This money came from the $81,000 which Sloan and Stans had removed from Stans' safe and given to LaRue. (2 *Hearings* 546-548) Kalmbach tetsified that he took the $40,000 to New York and gave it to Ulasewicz. (5 *Hearings* 2105)

After the July 19 meeting, Kalmbach became concerned over the clandestine nature of the funding operations, which he found distasteful. Dean, at that meeting, had asked Kalmbach to raise additional funds for the Watergate defendants and Kalmbach had determined to talk to Ehrlichman about it. (5 *Hearings* 2105) He wanted Ehrlichman's assurances as to the propriety of the assignment. Until that time he had distributed funds given him by Stans or LaRue. Now he was being asked to seek an outside contributor. (5 *Hearings* 2105-2106)

On July 26, Kalmbach travelled to Washington and met with Ehrlichman. He found Ehrlichman familiar with the fundraising assignment he had received from Dean. He explained to Ehrlichman that the secrecy of the operation and the various activities connected with it disturbed him. Kalmbach said that he remembered vividly the meeting with Ehrlichman because:

> "I looked at him and I said, 'John, I am looking right into your eyes. I know Jeanne and your family, you know Barbara and my family. You know that my family and my reputation mean everything to me and it is just absolutely necessary, John, that you tell me, first that John Dean has the authority to direct me in this assignment, and that I am to go forward on it.'" (5 *Hearings* 2106)

Kalmbach said Ehrlichman declared, "Herb, John Dean does have the authority, it is proper, and you are to go forward." (*Id.*) Ehrlichman also emphasized the need for the secrecy, stating that if the press were to learn of these activities, "they would have our heads in their laps." (5 *Hearings* 2107) This satisfied Kalmbach. He left the meeting and later obtained an additional $30,000 from LaRue which he transmitted to Ulasewicz. (5 *Hearings* 2108) Ehrlichman denied that he reassured Kalmbach but did recall a conversation where secrecy was discussed, and that Kalmbach told him "Mr. Ulasewicz was carrying money back and forth." (6 *Hearings* 2571-72)

Kalmbach said he returned to California and raised an additional $75,000 in cash from a private contributor, Thomas V. Jones, Chairman of Northrop Corporation. Mr. Jones did not know the intended use of the money, and apparently believed he was making a campaign contribution to the President. Kalmbach notified Ulasewicz to come to California and meet him in front of the Airporter Inn near Kalmbach's office in Newport Beach. Kalmbach picked Ulasewicz up in his car, they drove a distance, parked and Kalmbach gave the cash to Ulasewicz. (5 *Hearings* 2108-2109) Ulasewicz told the Committee that, while in California, he warned Kalmbach that "something here is not Kosher," that ". . . it's definitely not your ball game, Mr. Kalmbach." He told Kalmbach that, because of the increasing size of the money demands and other surrounding circumstances, it was time for both of them to get out of the project. (6 *Hearings* 2237)

Kalmbach testified that in mid-August Dean and LaRue contacted him again seeking additional funds. He decided, however, that he would not participate further in this assignment. (5 *Hearings* 2110) Kalmbach told the Committee that one factor that disturbed him and led him to quit were the newspaper stories about Watergate appearing in the press. (5 *Hearings* 2110)

On September 19, at LaRue's urgent request, Ulasewicz flew to Washington from New York and delivered the remaining funds Kalmbach had given him—$53,000 to Mrs. Hunt, $29,000 to LaRue. This terminated Ulasewicz's and Kalmbach's activities respecting the funding of the Watergate defendants. (6 *Hearings* 2237-2238)

Kalmbach testified that, after these funds were delivered by Ulasewicz to Mrs. Hunt and LaRue, he arranged a meeting with Dean and LaRue in Dean's office to reconcile with LaRue the amount of money distributed in the operation. He testified that the total amount received by him and disbursed through Ulasewicz was approximately $220,000. As soon as he had made the reconciliation with LaRue, Kalmbach destroyed his notes by shredding and burning them in Dean's office. (5 *Hearings* 211; *see also* 6 *Hearings* 2293)

LaRue took over the raising of funds and their distribution to the Watergate defendants. His contact became William Bittman, Hunt's attorney. (6 *Hearings* 2293) However, because of the rising demands for money, it was soon necessary for LaRue to find additional funds.

3. The Hunt to Colson Telephone Call. In late November 1972, Hunt called Colson to complain about the failure of the White House and CRP to meet their monetary commitments. Colson recorded the conversation and a copy of its transcript is entered in the record as Exhibit 152. (9 *Hearings* 3888-3891) In this call, Hunt, among other things, stated:

". . . there is a great deal of unease and concern on the part of 7 defendants . . . But there is a great deal of financial expense that has not been covered and what

116

we have been getting has been coming in very minor gibs and drabs and Parkinson, who has been the go-between with my attorney, doesn't seem to be very effective and we are now reaching a point of which . . . These people have really got to . . . this is a long haul thing and the stakes are very high and *I thought that you would want to know that this thing must not break apart for foolish reasons* . . .

All right, now we've set a deadline now for close of business on the 25th of November for the resolution on the liquidation of everything that is outstanding . . .

. . . *we're protecting the guys who are really responsible,* but now that's that . . . and of course that's a continuing requirement, but at the same time, this is a two-way street and as I said before, we think that now is the time when a move should be made and *surely the cheapest commodity available is money.* These lawyers have not been paid, there are large sums of money outstanding."
(emphasis added)

Colson gave a copy of the tape recording to Dean. On November 15, Dean, Ehrlichman and Haldeman met at Camp David to discuss the conversation and the increasing, threatening demands transmitted through Hunt's lawyer to Paul O'Brien. Dean testified that his instructions from Haldeman and Ehrlichman were to meet with Mitchell, play the tape, and tell him to take care of these problems. (3 *Hearings* 969-970) Dean went to New York, played the tape for Mitchell, but received no indication from Mitchell that he would take any action.

4. *The $35,000 White House Fund.* Prior to April 1972, $350,000 in cash previously kept in Sloan's safe at CRP had been sent to the White House at Haldeman's request, apparently for polling purposes. (6 *Hearings* 2442, 2461) Strachan had received the money in Sloan's office and had taken it to the White House. Haldeman had arranged for a person he trusted, not identified with the White House, to keep the funds in a private bank account. (7 *Hearings* 2879)

According to Dean's testimony: In the first week of December, Mitchell called Dean and told him that a portion of this $350,000 must be used to meet the demands by Hunt and others. Mitchell indicated that the money used would be later replaced. Mitchell asked Dean to obtain Haldeman's approval for this action. Dean conveyed Mitchell's message to Haldeman. Although both Dean and Haldeman were reluctant to use this money, they had no alternative. Haldeman

117

authorized Dean to inform Strachan to deliver the money to CRP. (3 *Hearings* 970-971; 7 *Hearings* 2879)

Strachan testified that, at first, he delivered only $40,000 of the $350,000 to LaRue. (6 *Hearings* 2463) Haldeman confirmed this delivery when, in an April 14, 1973, meeting with the President, he stated: "then they got desperate for money, and being desperate for money took back—I think that it was $40,000." (Edited Presidential Conversations, p. 531) But this delivery, Dean testified, did not satisfy the demands that "continued to be relayed by Mr. Bittman to Mr. O'Brien who, in turn, would relay them to Mr. Mitchell, Mr. LaRue, and myself. I, in turn, would tell Haldeman and Ehrlichman of the demands." (3 *Hearings* 971)

Dean testified that the demands reached the crescendo point shortly before the trial in early January. He said that O'Brien and LaRue came to his office and told him of the seriousness of the problem. Also, he said, Mitchell called him to instruct that once again he should ask Haldeman for the necessary funds. Dean said he called Haldeman, told him of Mitchell's request and recommended that they deliver the entire balance of the $350,000 to LaRue. Haldeman acquiesced, according to Dean, and said "send the entire damn bundle to them but make sure we get a receipt for $350,-000." Dean testified he called Strachan and told him to take the mony to LaRue. (3 *Hearings* 971)

In a meeting on April 14, 1973, Haldeman told the President that he had given the balance of the $350,000 to LaRue because ". . . they needed money, and we wanted to get rid of money, it seemed it was of mutual interest in working it out." (Edited Presidential Conversations, p. 531) In an April 16, 1973 meeting Haldeman told the President that his participation in payments to the defendants "[i]n my viewpoint . . . wasn't to shut them up, but that is a hard case for anybody to believe, I suppose." (Edited Presidential Conversations, p. 833)

5. *Additional Pressures by Hunt.* Severe pressure from Hunt for additional funds came after the Watergate trial and prior to his sentence.* Hunt testified that he requested his attorney, Mr. Bittman, to arrange a meeting between Hunt and O'Brien. (9 *Hearings* 3703) Hunt told O'Brien when they met that his legal fees amounted to approximately $60,000, and that he was also concerned about the future of his family and desired to have the equivalent of two years' subsistence

* This pressure for money and how to handle it was one of the topics discussed at the La Costa meeting attended by Haldeman, Ehrlichman, Dean and Richard Moore. This meeting is discussed in detail in Chapter IV [Chapter V in this edition] of this report.

available to them before his incarceration. Although Hunt testified he did not intend any threat, he told the Committee:

"And I put it to Mr. O'Brien that I had engaged as he might or might not know, in other activities, which I believed I described as seamy activities, for the White House. I do not believe that I specified them. However, I did make reference to them. The context of such references was that if anyone was to receive benefits at that time, in view of my long and loyal service, if not hazardous service, for the White House that certainly I should receive priority consideration." (9 *Hearings* 3704)

Hunt said O'Brien suggested that he send a memorandum to Colson. Hunt did not want to write a memorandum but thought he should contact Colson to explain his situation to him. (9 *Hearings* 3705)

Bittman contacted Colson's office and arranged for Colson's law partner, David Shapiro, to meet him on February 16, 1973. Hunt testified he told Shapiro substantially the same things he told O'Brien, including a reference to his "seamy activities" for the White House. Hunt was very disappointed with the meeting since Shapiro did not appear sympathetic. Hunt said he made it clear to Shapiro that he wanted the money prior to the date of his sentence so he could make "prudent distribution of that among the members of my family, my dependents, taking care of insurance premiums and that sort of thing, that it would have to be delivered to me before I was in jail." Hunt testified that on March 20 or 21, just prior to his sentence, he received $75,000 in cash. (9 *Hearings* 3706) LaRue admitted making the payment to Hunt after approval from Mitchell. (6 *Hearings* 2297-2298; 2321)

6. *The March 21 Meeting in the Oval Office.* The indictment returned against Haldeman, Ehrlichman, Colson, Mitchell, Strachan, Mardian and Parkinson alleges that the final payment to Hunt by LaRue was made on March 21, 1973, (not March 20) shortly after Dean, Haldeman and the President discussed Hunt's demands for money. According to the edited Presidential transcripts, it now appears that the conversation Dean testified he had with the President on March 13, 1973, concerning Hunt's demand, actually occurred on the morning of March 21, although in his testimony before the Committee Dean insisted that he correctly placed this conversation on March 13. (4 *Hearings* 1567) In this conversation, Dean said, he told the President:

". . . that there were money demands being made by the

119

seven convicted defendants, and that the sentencing of these individuals was not far off. It was during this conversation that Haldeman came into the office. After this brief interruption by Haldeman's coming in, but while he was still there I told the President about the fact that there was no money to pay these individuals to meet their demands. He asked me how much it would cost. I told him that I could only make an estimate that it might be as high as $1 million dollars or more. He told me that that was no problem, and he also looked over at Haldeman and repeated the same statement. He then asked me who was demanding the money and I told him it was principally coming from Hunt through his attorney . . .

The conversation then turned back to the question from the President regarding the money that was being paid to the defendants. He asked me how this was done. I told him I didn't know much about it other than the fact that the money was laundered so it could not be traced and then there were secret deliveries. I told him I was learning about things I had never known before, but the next time I would certainly be more knowledgeable . . ." (3 *Hearings* 995-996)

Dean also testified that money matters were discussed during his morning meeting with the President on March 21. (3 *Hearings* 998-1000)

The edited transcript of the March 21 meeting demonstates that Dean's recollection of this meeting in his testimony, concerning what he told the President about the hush money demands from the Watergate defendants, was in a large part accurate. The following portions of the edited transcript supplied by the President are particularly illustrative:

D   So that is it. That is the extent of the knowledge. So where are the soft spots on this? Well, first of all, there is the problem of the continued blackmail which will not only go on now, but it will go on while these people are in prison, and it will compound the obstruction of justice situation. It will cost money. It is dangerous. People around here are not pros at this sort of thing. This is the sort of thing Mafia people can do: washing money, getting clean money, and things like that. We just don't know about those things, because we are not criminals and not used to dealing in that business.

P   That's right.

D   It is a tough thing to know how to do.

P   Maybe it takes a gang to do that.

D   That's right. There is a real problem as to whether we could even do it. Plus there is a real problem in raising money. Mitchell has been working on raising some money. He is one of the ones with the most to lose. But there is no denying the fact that the White House, in Ehrlichman, Haldeman and Dean are involved in some of the early money decisions.

P   How much money do you need?

D   I would say these people are going to cost a million dollars over the next two years.

P   We could get that. On the money, if you need the money you could get it in cash. I know where it could be gotten. It is not easy, but it could be done. But the question is who the hell would handle it? Any ideas on that?

D   That's right. Well, I think that is something that Mitchell ought to be charged with.

P   I would think so too. (pp. 193-4)

* * *

P   What do you think? You don't need a million right away, but you need a million? Is that right?

D   That is right.

P   You need it in cash don't you? I am just thinking out loud here for a moment. Would you put that through the Cuban Committee.

D   No.

P   It is going to be checks, cash money, etc. How if that ever comes out, are you going to handle it? Is the Cuban Committee an obstruction of justice, if they want to help?

D   Well they have priests in it.

P   Would that give a little bit of a cover?

D   That would give some for the Cubans and possibly Hunt. Then you've got Liddy. McCord is not accepting any money. So he is not a bought man right now.

P   OK. Go ahead. (pp. 194-5)

* * *

P   Just looking at the immediate problem, don't you think you have to handle Hunt's financial situation damn soon?

D   I think that is—I talked to Mitchell about that last night and—

P   It seems to me we have to keep the cap on the bottle that much, or we don't have any options.

D   That's right.

P   Either that or it all blows right now? (pp. 196-7)

* * *

P   . . . Talking about your obstruction of justice, though, I don't see it.

D   Well, I have been a conduit for information on taking care of people out there who are guilty of crimes.

P   Oh, you mean like the blackmailers?

D   The blackmailers, Right.

P   Well, I wonder if that part of it can't be—I wonder if that doesn't—let me put it frankly: I wonder if that doesn't have to be continued? Let me put it this way: let us suppose that you get the million bucks, and you get the proper way to handle it. You could hold that side?

D   Uh, huh.

P   It would seem to me that would be worthwhile. (p. 206)

* * *

P   Another way to do it then Bob, and John realizes this, is to continue to try to cut our losses. Now we have to take a look at that course of action. First it is going to require approximately a million dollars to take care of the jackasses who are in jail. That can be arranged. That could be arranged. But you realize that after we are gone, and assuming we can expend this money, then they are going to crack and it would be an unseemly story. Frankly, all the people aren't going to care that much. (pp. 225-6)

* * *

D   They're going to stonewall it, as it now stands. Excepting Hunt. That's why his threat.

H   It's Hunt's opportunity.

P   That's why for your immediate things you have no choice but to come up with the $120,000, or whatever it is. Right?

D   That's right.

P   Would you agree that that's the prime thing that you damn well better get that done?

D   Obviously he ought to be given some signal anyway.

P   *(Expletive deleted) get it*. In a way that—who is going to talk to him? Colson? He is the one who is supposed to know him? (pp. 236-7) (emphasis added)

At this meeting and at the afternoon meeting on March 21 other alternatives to paying hush money were considered including certain public disclosures. During the afternoon meeting, with regard to public disclosures the participants perceived no viable "option" which would not precipitate revelation of the coverup. At the close of the afternoon March 21 meeting, the President, telling Dean, Haldeman and Ehrlichman he had to leave, concluded with an un-answered question:

P   What the hell does one disclose that isn't going to blow something? (Edited Presidential Conversations, p. 269)

7. *Other Relevant Presidential Meetings Concerning Pay-offs.* The following morning, on March 22, 1973, Dean met with Haldeman, Ehrlichman and Mitchell in Halde-man's office. At the beginning of this meeting, Dean said, Ehrlichman asked Mitchell whether Hunt's money prob-lem had been resolved. Dean said Mitchell replied he didn't think it was a problem. (3 *Hearings* 1001) Mitchell de-nied this discussion took place. (4 *Hearings* 1650) Ehrlich-man recalls a conversation on March 22 when Dean (not Ehrlichman) asked Mitchell, without specific reference to Hunt, "is that matter taken care of"? Mitchell's answer, Ehrlichman says, was something like "I guess so." (7 *Hear-ings* 2853)

Dean's version is also supported by the Edited Presi-dential Transcripts. The transcripts show that, in a meet-ing between the President and Dean in the Oval Office on April 16, 1973, Dean recalled that, a few days after the March 21 meeting, he met with Haldeman, Ehrlich-man and Mitchell. Dean said Ehrlichman asked him: "Well, is that problem with Hunt straightened out?" Dean said he told Ehrlichman to ask Mitchell who, in turn, replied, "I think the problem is solved." The conversation between the President and Dean continued:

P   That's all?
D   That's all he said.
P   In other words, that was done at the Mitchell level?
D   That's right.

P   But you had knowledge; Haldeman had knowledge; Ehrlichman had knowledge and I suppose I did that night. That assumes culpability on that, doesn't it? (Edited Presidential Conversations, p. 798)

Also relevant is an April 17, 1973 conversation among the President, Haldeman and Ehrlichman:

P   Well (inaudible). I suppose then we should have cut—shut it off, 'cause later on you met in your office and Mitchell said, *'That was taken care of.'*

H   The next day. Maybe I can find the date by that—

P   Yeah. And Dean was there and said, 'What about this money for Hunt?' Wasn't Dean there?

H   No, what happened was—Ehrlichman and Dean and Mitchell and I were in the office, in my office, and we were discussing other matters. And in the process of it, Mitchell said—he turned to Dean and said, 'Let me raise another point. Ah, have you taken care of the other problem—the Hunt problem?' *But we all knew instantly what he meant.* Dean kind of looked a little flustered and said, 'Well, well, no. I don't know where that is or something,' and Mitchell said, 'Well I guess it's taken care of.' And so we assumed from that that Mitchell had taken care of it, and there was no further squeak out of it so I now assume that Mitchell took care of it. (Edited Presidential Conversations, pp. 1035-1036) (emphasis added)

Just prior to the above exchange, the President recalled his discussion with Dean on March 21 about the possibility that it might require a million dollars to meet the blackmail demands from Watergate defendants. Haldeman (inaccurately) recalled to the President that he (the President) had told Dean, 'Once you start down the path with blackmail it's constant escalation.' Then Haldeman said: "They could jump and then say, 'Yes, well that was morally wrong. What you should have said is that blackmail is wrong not that it's too costly.' " (Edited Presidential Conversations, p. 1034) At the same meeting, the following colloquy took place between the President and Haldeman:

H   We left it—that we can't do anything about it anyway. We don't have any money, and it isn't a question to be directed here. This is something relates to Mitchell's problem. Ehrlichman has no problem with this thing with Hunt. And Ehrlichman said, (ex-

124

pletive removed) if you're going to get into blackmail, to hell with it.

P   Good (unintelligible) Thank God you were in there when it happened. But you remember the conversation?

H   Yes sir.

P   I didn't tell him to go get the money did I?

H   No. (*Id.* at 1033)

Some of the participants involved in the payments to defendants (Haldeman, Ehrlichman, Kalmbach) told the Committee that payments were authorized, not to buy the silence of the defendants, but solely to create a defense fund for the Watergate burglars, a fund which they said they believed was legitimate. (5 *Hearings* 2092, 2165; 6 *Hearings* 2568, 2570-72; 7 *Hearings* 2879) In an April 14, 1973 meeting between the President and Haldeman, the following colloquy took place:

H   That was the line they used around here. That we've got to have money for their legal fees and family.

P   Support. Well, I heard something about that at a much later time.

* * *

P   And, frankly, not knowing much about obstruction of justice, I thought it was perfectly proper.

* * *

P   Would it be perfectly proper?

E   The defense of the—

P   Berrigans?

E   The Chicago Seven.

P   The Chicago Seven?

H   They have a defense fund for everybody. (Edited Presidential Conversations, p. 431; *see* also p. 833)

This testimony must be viewed against the evidence presented above.

None of those who authorized or participated in the making of these payments used their own money; to the contrary they used campaign funds contributed by others who had no knowledge that their money was being employed to pay the legal fees of the Watergate defendants and to support their families. Also relevant is the clandestine nature of the payoffs which were made with the $100 bills and placed in "drops" by an unseen intermediary using a code name.

125

Even the President recognized that the payoffs smacked of coverup. In an April 27 meeting with Henry Petersen, the secret payments of money to the Watergate defendants were discussed:

> HP . . . Once you do it in a clandestine fashion, it takes on the elements—
> P Elements of a coverup.
> HP That's right, and obstruction of justice. (Edited Presidential Conversations, p. 1281)

L. REPRESENTATIONS CONCERNING EXECUTIVE CLEMENCY

Only the President of the United States can grant Executive clemency in a matter involving a federal crime. The evidence reveals that, during the latter part of 1972 and in early January, 1973, prior to the first Watergate trial, promises of Executive clemency were made to certain Watergate defendants in a further effort to maintain their silence. These promises of Executive clemency were made with the representation that they were authorized by high officials close to the President.*

Ehrlichman testified that he discussed Executive clemency with the President as early as July 1972. According to Ehrlichman, the President did not even want members of the White House staff to discuss clemency with anyone involved in the case, much less to offer it. (6 *Hearings* 2608) The President, in a statement on August 15, 1973, confirmed Ehrlichman's statement that he told Ehrlichman in July that under no circumstances could Executive clemency be considered for participants in the Watergate affair.

1. Representations to James McCord. McCord testified that, in late September or early October, 1972, Gerald Alch, his attorney, met with William Bittman who represented Hunt. After this meeting McCord said Alch told McCord that Executive clemency, financial support and rehabilitation would be made available to the Watergate defendants.

Alch denied in his testimony before the Committee that he made these assurances of executive clemency to McCord. To the contrary he testified he told McCord: "Jim, it can be Christmas, Easter and Thanksgiving all rolled into one, but in my opinion, the President would not touch this with a 10-foot pole, so do not rely on any prospect

---

* The Watergate indictment issued on March 1, 1974, alleges that, as part of a conspiracy to obstruct justice, offers of Executive clemency were made to McCord, Hunt, Magruder and Liddy. (See indictment p. 7)

of Executive clemency." (1 *Hearings* 303) McCord testified Hunt also told him that Executive clemency would be granted and "spoke in terms as though it had already been committed." (1 *Hearings* 150) McCord said these assurances from Hunt were made in late September or October while Hunt and McCord were at the court house. (1 *Hearings* 131)

McCord stated that discussions involving Executive clemency also occurred with Hunt's wife, and that, from September to December, Mrs. Hunt pressured McCord to remain silent and accept the proposal for Executive clemency, which he declined. McCord was told that similar proposals were made to Barker, Gonzales, Martinez, Sturgis and Liddy. (McCord DNC Deposition, May 1, 1973, pp. 301-302)*

More direct promises of Executive clemency came to McCord after he sent an anonymous letter on December 31 to Jack Caulfield, which dramatically warned that: "If Helms goes and if the Watergate operation is laid at the CIA's feet, where it does not belong, every tree in the forest will fall. It will be a scorched desert. The whole matter is at the precipice now. Just pass the message that if they want it to blow, they are on exactly the right course. I am sorry that you will get hurt in the fall-out." (3 *Hearings* 1235) McCord had become increasingly alarmed over what he considered efforts by his attorney and persons at CRP and the White House to have him falsely assert, as a defense to the criminal charges against him that the break-in was part of a CIA mission. (1 *Hearings* 193)

Caulfield, who believed the letter came from McCord, immediately telephoned its contents to Dean's assistant, Fred Fielding, and later gave the letter to Dean. Dean discussed the problem with Paul O'Brien. O'Brien reported the matter to Mitchell who directed O'Brien to have Caulfield determine McCord's intentions. (3 *Hearings* 974) On January 8, 1973, Dean asked O'Brien to communicate to McCord's lawyer that a friend of McCord's would contact McCord, which O'Brien did. O'Brien also told Hunt's lawyer, Bittman, about the conversation with Dean. (O'Brien Interview, May 31, 1973, p. 5) Later that day, McCord and Alch visited Bittman's office and, after Alch met with Bittman alone, Alch told McCord that he would receive a call that evening from a White House "friend." (1 *Hearings* 135 and 150)

* On March 21, Dean told the President that *"You are going to have a clemency problem with the others."* (Edited Presidential Conversations, p. 205) (Emphasis added)

The initial contact with McCord was made by Caulfield through Tony Ulasewicz, who telephoned McCord in the early morning hours of January 9, 1973, and told him to go to a nearby phone booth to receive a message. McCord complied and heard a voice, unfamiliar to him, say:

"Plead guilty. One year is a long time. You will get Executive clemency. Your family will be taken care of and when you get out, you will be rehabilitated and a job will be found for you. Don't take immunity when called before the grand jury." (1 *Hearings* 135)

After delivering the message, Ulasewicz reported McCord's apparent satisfaction to Caulfield. (1 *Hearings* 254-255)

In the meantime, according to Dean, O'Brien and Mitchell both contacted Dean and told him that since Hunt had received an assurance of Executive clemency, McCord and the others were similarly entitled. Mitchell and O'Brien felt Caulfield could most effectively carry that message to McCord. (3 *Hearings* 975) Dean testified that he called Caulfield, told him to see McCord in person, and gave him a clemency message for McCord similar to the one transmitted to Hunt through Bittman. (3 *Hearings* 975) Mitchell's testimony before the Committee indicated he knew in January 1973 that Dean asked Caulfield to talk to McCord to ascertain McCord's plans, but Mitchell does not remember contemporaneously learning that Caulfield had offered McCord clemency. (4 *Hearings* 1632)

Caulfield arranged a meeting with McCord on the George Washington Parkway in Virginia (the first of several) through another telephone call from Ulasewicz to McCord at the telephone booth near McCord's home. This meeting took place on January 12. (1 *Hearings* 137) McCord testified that Caulfield then urged him to plead guilty, receive clemency and be rehabilitated afterward. According to McCord, Caulfield said that he carried the clemency message "from the very highest levels of the White House." (1 *Hearings* 138 and 228) McCord said he was told by Caulfield that the President would be apprised of the meeting and that Caulfield said "I may have a message to you at our next meeting from the President himself." (1 *Hearings* 138)

Caulfield testified that, on January 13, Dean advised him to stress to McCord the sincerity of the clemency offer. When Caulfield asked if the offer came from the President, Dean replied it came "from the top." Caulfield said that he assumed this implied Ehrlichman speaking for the President, because Dean rarely made decisions without Ehrlichman's input. Caulfield, however never had personal discussions with the President on this matter and had no personal knowledge that the President authorized a clemency offer to McCord. (1 *Hearings* 256-257, 266, 273-274)

On January 14 Caulfield again met with McCord on the George Washington Parkway and told McCord that his efforts to develop, as a defense to the criminal charges against him, his claims of government wiretaps of certain phone calls he had made to foreign embassies would not be successful. McCord became very concerned and was assured that he would receive clemency after 10 or 11 months' imprisonment. Caulfield on this occasion told McCord:

"The President's ability to govern is at stake. Another Teapot Dome scandal is possible and the government may fall. Everybody else is on track but you, you are not following the game plan, get closer to your attorney." (1 *Hearings* 139-40, 152)

There followed two telephone conversations on January 15 and January 16, during which McCord indicated to Caulfield that he had no desire to talk to him further and suggested that, if the White House wanted to be honest, it should look into McCord's perjury charges against Magruder and his claims as to the tapping of his two embassy calls. (1 *Hearings* 140) However, a final meeting was arranged between McCord and Caulfield on the George Washington Parkway for January 25. McCord testified that, at this meeting, Caulfield repeated the offers of clemency, financial support and rehabilitation. According to McCord, Caulfield discouraged his hopes for White House action on his wiretap defense and cautioned him that, if he made public allegations against high Administration officials, the Administration would undoubtedly defend itself. McCord interpreted this as a "personal threat" to his safety, but stated his willingness to take the risk. (1 *Hearings* 140-41, 260)

Caulfield testified that, in this final meeting, he concluded that McCord was definitely going to speak out on the Watergate burglary and would probably make allegations against White House and other high officials. (1 *Hearings* 260) Caulfield said he told McCord, "Jim, I have worked with these people and I know them to be as tough-minded as you and I. When you make your statement, don't underestimate them. If I were in your shoes, I would probably be doing the same thing." (1 *Hearings* 266)

2. *Representations to Howard Hunt.* On December 8, 1972, Hunt's wife, Dorothy, died in an airplane crash in Chicago.

Three weeks later, on December 31, Hunt sent a letter to Colson that stated:

"I had understood you to say that you would be willing to see my attorney, Bill Bittman, at any time. After my wife's death, I asked him to see you, but his efforts were unavailing. And though I believe I understand the delicacy of your overt position, I nevertheless feel myself even more isolated than before. My wife's death, the imminent trial, my present mental depression, and my inability to get any relief from my present situation, all contribute to a sense of abandonment by friends on whom I had in good faith relied. I can't tell you how important it is under the circumstances, for Bill Bittman to have the opportunity to meet with you, and I trust that you will do me that favor.

"There is a limit to the endurance of any man trapped in a hostile situation and mine was reached on December 8. I do believe in God—not necessarily a Just God but in governance of a Divine Being. His Will, however, is often encacted through human hands, and human adversaries are arraigned against me." (Exhibit 153, 9 *Hearings* 3892)

Colson sent Dean a copy of the letter with note that asked, "Now what the hell do I do?" (3 *Hearings* 1053)

Dean testified that on January 2, 1973, Paul O'Brien called him and, with some urgency, requested that Dean meet with him concerning serious problems with Hunt. When Dean met with O'Brien that evening, O'Brien told Dean that Hunt wished to plead guilty but, before changing his plea, Hunt wanted White House assurance of Executive clemency. (3 *Hearings* 973-74) On January 3, Colson called Dean to say that he did not want to meet with Bittman. Dean testified he went to Ehrlichman and told him the situation. Ehrlichman according to Dean, asked Colson to meet with Bittman, which Colson did. (3 *Hearings* 973, 1053)

After meeting with Bittman that same day, Colson met with Dean and Ehrlichman in Ehrlichman's office. Dean testified that Colson was upset and said it was imperative to offer Hunt Executive clemency. Dean said Ehrlichman indicated he would speak to the President about it and directed Colson not to address the President on the subject. (3 *Hearings* 973, 1079) Ehrlichman testified that, at this meeting, he told Dean and Colson of his July 1972 conversation with the President where the President had stressed that no one in the White House was to discuss or offer clemency. (6 *Hearings* 2608-2609)

The next day, according to Dean, Ehrlichman confided to Dean that he had given Colson an affirmative answer regarding clemency for Hunt and that Colson had again met with Bittman. On January 5, Colson reported his second meeting with Bittman to Ehrlichman and Dean. Colson said he gave Bittman a "general assurance" respecting clemency, rather than a firm commitment, saying that although a year is a long time, clemency, usually comes around Christmas.* (3 *Hearings* 973-974) Dean said he expressed the feeling that the other defendants would expect the same type of arrangement and that Ehrlichman said the same assurance would apply to all. (3 *Hearings* 974 and 1079) According to Dean, Colson after the meeting told Dean he had ignored Ehrlichman's instructions and discussed clemency with the President. (3 *Hearings* 974; 4 *Hearings* 1984)

Ehrlichman confirms that on January, he met with Colson and Dean to discuss the Hunt-Bittman request for help. Erhlichman said the main purpose of the meeting was to attempt to deal with Hunt's depressed state of mind and to determine how best to aid him. But, Ehrlichman testified, he made it clear to Colson that under no circumstances could Executive clemency be offered Hunt. (7 *Hearings* 2770-2771) His version of the January 5 meeting was that Colson gave Dean and Ehrlichman "the strongest kinds of assurances that he had not made any sort of commitments." (6 *Hearings* 2610) However, Hunt did change his plea to guilty at the opening of the trial on January 10. (Watergate Trial Transcript, p. 91)

The edited presidential transcripts reveal that the following comments and recollections regarding clemency to Hunt were made at the March 21, 1973, meeting among the President, Haldeman and Dean, when Hunt had not yet been sentenced:

> D . . . Here is what is happening right now. What sort of brings matters to the (unintelligible). One, this is going to be a continual blackmail operation by Hunt and Liddy and the Cubans. No doubt about it. And McCord, who is another one involved. McCord has asked for nothing. McCord did ask to meet with somebody, with Jack Caulfield who is his old friend who had gotten him hired over there. And when Caulfield had him hired, he was a perfectly legitimate security man. And he wanted to talk about commuta-

---

* Mitchell testified that, early in 1973, he learned of meetings where Executive clemency was discussed between Hunt's lawyer and Colson. (4 *Hearings* 1632)

tion, and things like that. *And as you know Colson has talked indirectly to Hunt about commutation.* All of these things are bad, in that they are problems, they are promises, they are commitments. They are the very sort of thing that the Senate is going to be looking most for. I don't think they can find them, frankly.

P   Pretty hard.

D   Pretty hard. Damn hard. It's all cash.

P   Pretty hard I mean as far as the witnesses are concerned. (pp. 188-89) (emphasis added)

* * *

P   . . . As a matter of fact, there was a discussion with somebody about Hunt's problem on account of his wife and I said, of course commutation could be considered on the basis of his wife's death, and that is the only conversation I ever had in that light.

D   Right (p. 192)

* * *

P   . . . You have the problem with Hunt and his clemency.

D   That's right. And you are going to have a clemency problem with the others. They all are going to expect to be out and that may put you in a position that is just untenable at some point. You know, the Watergate Hearings just over, *Hunt now demanding clemency or he is going to blow.* And politically, it's impossible for you to do it. You know, after everybody—

P   That's right!

D   I am not sure that you will ever be able to deliver on the clemency. It may be just too hot.

P   *You can't do it politically until after the '74 elections, that's for sure.* Your point is that even then you couldn't do it.

D   That's right. It may further involve you in a way you should not be involved in this.

P   No—it is wrong that's for sure. (pp. 206-07) (emphasis added)

* * *

P   . . . And the second thing is, we are not going to be able to deliver on any of a clemency thing. *You know Colson has gone around on this clemency thing with Hunt and the rest?*

D   *Hunt is now talking about being out by Christmas.*

H   This year?

D   This year. He was told by O'Brien, who is my conveyor of doom back and forth, that hell, he would

132

be lucky if he were out a year from now, or after Ervin's hearings were over. He said how in the Lord's name could you be commuted that quickly? He said, 'Well, that is my commitment from Colson.'

H   By Christmas of this year?

D   Yeah.

H   See that, really, that is verbal evil. Colson is— that is your fatal flaw in Chuck. He is an operator in expediency, and he will pay at the time and where he is to accomplish whatever he is there to do. And that, and that's,—I would believe that he has made that commitment if Hunt says he has. I would believe he is capable of saying that.

P   The only thing we could do with him would be to parole him like the (unintelligible) situation. But you couldn't buy clemency. (pp. 226-27) (emphasis added)

Another relevant discussion occurred on April 14, 1973, when the President met with Haldeman and Ehrlichman. In a discussion of the possibility of Executive clemency the President said:

"It's a shame. There could be clemency in this case and at the proper time having in mind the extraordinary sentences of Magruder, etc., etc., but you know damn well it is ridiculous *to talk* about clemency. They all knew that. Colson knew that. I mean when you [Ehrlichman] talked to Colson and *he talked to me.*" (Edited Presidential Conversations, p. 544) (emphasis added)

Dean met again with the President on April 15, 1973. By this time, Dean had retained counsel, gone to the United States Attorney's Office and begun to give information about the coverup. Dean testified he was somewhat shaken when he went to the meeting because he was acting to end the coverup and knew there would be serious problems for the President. (3 *Hearings* 1015) Dean said the most interesting event of the meeting came near the very end. He said the President "got up out of his chair, went behind his chair to the corner of the Executive Office Building office and in a nearly inaudible tone said to me he was probably foolish to have discussed Hunt's clemency with Colson." (3 *Hearings* 1017) It was this conduct that led Dean to believe that this conversation was taped. As the Committee learned later, there was, indeed, a taping system in operation. However, the President has informed the United States District

Court for the District of Columbia that, unknown to the President at the time, the recorder's tape had "run out" just prior to the President's meeting with Dean and that the meeting was thus not recorded. (Watergate Tapes Hearings, October 31, 1973, p. 21) *

Subsequently, in an April 16, 1973 meeting, the President and Dean again discussed the subject of Executive clemency to Hunt:

D   All the obstruction is technical stuff that mounts up.

P   Well, you take, for example, the clemency bit. That is solely Mitchell apparently and Colson's talk with Bittman where he says he will do everything I can because as a friend.

D   No, that was with Ehrlichman.

P   Hunt?

D   That was with Ehrlichman.

P   Ehrlichman with whom?

D   Ehrlichman and Colson and I sat up there. Colson presented his story to Ehrlichman regarding it and then John gave Chuck very clear instructions on going back and telling him. "Give him the inference he's got clemency but don't give him any commitment."

P   No commitment.

D   Right.

P   That's alright. No commitment. I have a right to say here—take a fellow like Hunt or a Cuban whose wife is sick or something and give them clemency for that purpose—isn't that right?

D   That's right.

P   But John specifically said "No commitment", did he?

D   Yes.

P   And then Colson went on apparently to—

D   I don't know how Colson delivered it—

P   To Hunt's lawyer—isn't that your understanding?

D   Yes, but I don't know what he did or how—

P   Where did this business of the Christmas thing get out, John? What in the hell is that all about it? That must have been Mitchell, huh?

D   No, that was Chuck again.

P   That they would all be out by Christmas?

D   No, I think he said something to the effect

* During another April 15, 1973 meeting, before the recorder's tape "ran out," the President indicated to Ehrlichman he was aware that Hunt and Bittman could provide a link to Colson "up to his navel." (Edited Presidential Conversations, p. 672)

134

that Christmas is the time the clemency generally occurs.

    P Oh yeah. Well, I don't think that is going to hurt him. Do you?

    D No.

    P Clemency is one thing. He is a friend of Hunt's. I am just trying to put the best face on it, but if it is the wrong thing to do I have to know. (pp. 811-12)

3. Representations to Jeb Magruder. Dean testified that on August 16, 1972, Magruder, concerned over his upcoming grand jury appearance, asked him, "What happens if this whole thing comes tumbling down? Will I get Executive clemency and will my family be taken care of?" (4 *Hearings* 1444) Dean told Magruder that "I am sure you will," but Magruder did not consider that statement to be a firm offer of Executive clemency. *(Id.)*

On March 23, 1973, Chief Judge Sirica read aloud the sealed letter received from McCord. As noted, the letter charged that pressure had been exerted on the defendants to plead guilty and remain silent, that perjury had been committed during the Watergate trial and that others than those judicial had participated in the Watergate operation. McCord indicated his desire to meet with Judge Sirica and elaborate further on his assertions. He stated that he lacked confidence in presenting such information to FBI agents, the Department of Justice, or to other "government representatives." McCord, however, was willing to speak to representatives of the Select Committee.

McCord's letter caused Magruder concern regarding his previous testimony. (2 *Hearings* 806) On March 25, Magruder presented his situation to CRP lawyers and they advised him to retain counsel. *(Id.)* Magruder testified that the lawyers apparently transmitted his concern to Mitchell because, on March 27, Mitchell phoned Magruder and asked Magruder to meet with him in New York. (2 *Hearings* 806-807) Magruder flew there that day and told Mitchell his worries. As Magruder recalled it, Mitchell assured him "he would take care of things, that everything would be taken care of." According to Magruder, "everything" included a guaranteed salary and Executive clemency. (2 *Hearings* 807) Mitchell confirmed the meeting with Magruder, as well as Magruder's discussion of the potential perjury charge against him. (4 *Hearings* 1633) While Mitchell recalled offering to help Magruder "in any conceivable way," he denied promising clemency. (4 *Hearings* 1634)

Mitchell also testified that, in their March 27 meeting, Magruder requested further assurance from someone still in the White House and Mitchell suggested a meeting with Haldeman. (4 *Hearings* 1634) Magruder testified that in January, when he became concerned he might be made a scapegoat, he went to Haldeman and said, "I just want you to know that this whole Watergate situation and other activities was a concerted effort by a number of people, and so I went through a literal monologue on what had occurred." (2 *Hearings* 806) However, Haldeman testified, "At no meeting with Magruder did he raise with me a monologue as he has described." (7 *Hearings* 2887)

Dean testified that on March 28, Haldeman called him at Camp David and asked him to return to Washington to meet with Mitchell and Magruder. Although Dean resisted, Haldeman persuaded him to participate. (3 *Hearings* 1005) Dean said his meeting with Haldeman, Mitchell and Magruder concerned how Dean planned to testify, if called before an appropriate body, regarding the January 27 and February 4, 1972 meetings in Mitchell's office. Dean said he would not agree to help support the perjured testimony already given by Magruder in this regard. (3 *Hearings* 1006) Mitchell testified that, at the meeting, Haldeman offered to help Magruder as a friend, but made no other commitments. (4 *Hearings* 1634) Magruder recalled that Haldeman was careful to articulate that he "could make no commitments for the President." (2 *Hearings* 807) Because of Dean's stand and the advice of CRP lawyers, Magruder decided to retain personal counsel. (2 *Hearings* 808)

The transcript of an April 14, 1973 meeting among the President, Haldeman and Ehrlichman indicates the President's view as to how an inference of Executive clemency could be given to Magruder in return for his claiming ultimate responsibility (along with Mitchell) for the Watergate affair:

P   I would also, though I'd put a couple of things in and say, Jeb, let me just start here by telling you the President holds great affection for you and your family. I was just thinking last night, this poor kid

H   Yeah, beautiful kids.

P   Lovely wife and all the rest, it just breaks your heart. And say this, this is a very painful message for me to bring—I've been asked to give you, but I must do it and it is that: Put it right out that way. Also I would put that in so he knows I have personal affection. *That's the way the so-called clemency's got to be handled.* Do you see John?

E   I understand.

H   Do the same thing with Mitchell. (Edited Presidential Conversation 502-503) (emphasis added)*

4. Representations to G. Gordon Liddy. The edited Presidential transcript contains a reference to a purported promise by Mitchell of a pardon or clemency to Liddy. The following passage is from the April 14, 1972 meeting among the President, Haldeman and Ehrlichman:

P   He's not talking because he thinks the President doesn't want him to talk? Is that the point?

E   He's—according to them, Mitchell's given him a promise of a pardon.

P   Bittman?

E   According to Colson and Shapiro.

P   I don't know where they get that. Mitchell has promised Liddy a pardon?

E   Yes, sir. (p. 412)

On pages 485-487, the following colloquy from the same meeting appears:

P   Colson to Bittman. I guess that's the only thing we have on that—except Mitchell, apparently had said something about clemency to people.

H   To Liddy.

P   And Mitchell has never, never—Has he ever discussed clemency with you?

E   No.

P   Has he ever discussed it with you?

H   No.

P   (unintelligible) We were all here the room.

H   Well, may have said, "Look we've got to take care of this."

P   But's he's never said, "Look you're going to get a pardon from these people when this is over." Never used any such language around here, has he; John?

E   Not to me.

H   I don't think so.

P   With Dean has he?

E   Well I don't know. That's a question I can't answer.

P   Well, but Dean's never raised it. In fact, Dean

---

* *See also id.* at 439, 442, 451, 459, 501, where the need to have Magruder and Mitchell present a congruent, false story is discussed.

137

told me when he talked about Hunt. I said, John,
"where does it all lead?" I said, what's it going to
cost. You can't just continue this way. He said,
"About a million dollars." (Unintelligible) I said, John,
that's the point. (Unintelligible) Unless I could get
them up and say look fellows, it's too bad and I give
you executive clemency like tomorrow, what the hell
do you think, Dean.

P   I mean, you think, the point is, Hunt and the
Cubans are not going to sit in jail for four years and
they are not being taken care of?

H   That's the point. Now where are you going to
get the money for that?

P   That's the reason this whole thing falls apart.
It's that—It's that that astonishes me about Mitchell
and the rest.

E   Big problem.

(Material unrelated to Presidential actions deleted)

P   The word never came up, but I said, "I appreciate what you're doing." I knew it was for the
purpose of helping the poor bastards through the trial,
but you can't offer that John. You can't—or could
you? I guess you could. Attorney's fees? Could you
go a support program for these people for four years.

E   I haven't any idea. I have no idea. (*See also,*
3 *Hearings* 975; 7 *Hearings* 2801)

5. *Consideration of Clemency for Dean and Mitchell.*
Comments by the President, at an April 14 meeting with
Ehrlichman, indicated he considered Executive clemency
for Dean and Mitchell in return for Dean's and Mitchell's cooperation in the Watergate affair:

P   . . . one point, you are going to talk to Dean?

E   I am.

P   What are you going to say to him?

E   Well to get off this passing the buck business.

P   John, that's—

E   It is a little touchy and I don't know how far
I can go.

P   John, that is not going to help you. Look he
[Dean] has to look down the road to one point there
is only one man who could restore him to the ability to practice law in case things go wrong. He's got
to have that in the back of his mind.

E   Uh, huh.

P   He's got to know that will happen. You don't

tell him, but you know and I know that with him and Mitchell there isn't going to be any damn question, because they got a bad rap. (Edited Presidential Conversations, pp. 668-669)

M. ACTIVITIES RELATING TO OTHER INVESTIGATIONS AND COURT PROCEEDINGS

White House and CRP officials were also concerned that other investigations besides the grand jury proceeding might uncover the true facts relating to the Watergate break-in.

1. The Patman Hearings. On August 19, 1972, Representative Wright Patman, Chairman of the House Banking and Currency Committee, ordered his committee staff to investigate the President's campaign finances, including the checks deposited in Barker's account. By early September, White House concern over the Patman Committee's investigation had mounted. Dean testified that, from the beginning of this probe, the White House had two major fears: "First, the hearings would have resulted in more adverse pre-election publicity regarding Watergate and, second, they just might stumble into something that would start unraveling the coverup." (3 *Hearings* 953-9) *See also,* Edited Presidential Conversations, p. 67-69, which concern the meeting of September 15, 1972, among the President, Haldeman and Dean and show substantial conversation between the President and Dean as to how to deal with the problems posed by these hearings.

According to Dean, CRP Counsel Parkinson was put in touch with Congressman Garry Brown, a Committee member, to persuade Brown to help limit the scope of the Committee's hearings. On September 8, Brown sent a letter to Attorney General Kleindienst which according to Dean, Parkinson had drafted. (3 *Hearings* 959) The letter inquired as to the propriety of Stans' testimony before the Committee, scheduled for September 14, in view of pending civil and criminal suits. Congressman Brown has filed a sworn statement with the Committee denying that Parkinson drafted this letter, and Dean's knowledge, admittedly based on hearsay, has not been corroborated. (Exhibit 69, 4 *Hearings* 1791) The Committee has found no evidence that Congressman Brown committed any improprieties.

The Justice Department, according to Dean, declined at this time to recommend that Stans not be required to testify, being of the view such a suggestion would appear part of a concerted effort to block the hearings. Nonetheless, Parkinson informed the Committee that Stans would not appear in order to avoid prejudicing pending criminal investigations. (3 *Hearings* 959-960)

In the last week of September, Dean took an active role in White House efforts to hinder the work of the Patman investigation. After Patman announced, on September 25, that he would hold a vote on October 3 on issuing subpenas to witnesses, Haldeman suggested that Dean talk to John Connally about blocking the Committee's hearings. Connally, Dean said, responded that Patman's only "soft spot" was a rumor that he had not reported large contributions from lobbyists. Dean then asked Parkinson to investigate the reports filed by members of the Committee with the Clerk of the House concerning campaign contributions. Parkinson furnished such a report on September 26, which Dean said he did not use.

Dean next presuaded Henry Petersen, Chief of the Criminal Division of the Department of Justice, to write Committee members to dissuade them from issuing subpenas. (3 *Hearings* 960-962) Petersen, in an October 2 letter to the members, asked that they delay their investigation because it might jeopardize fair criminal trials. (3 *Hearings* 1194) On October 3, the Committee voted not to hold hearings. (3 *Hearings* 962)

On October 10, Patman announced that his Committee would convene in two days in another attempt to investigate the Watergate affair. Patman requested Dean, Mitchell, MacGregor and Stans to appear. (3 *Hearings* 962) Dean declined to appear, claiming Executive Privilege. The others declined on advice of counsel and Patman did not reconvene the Committee.

2. The Civil Suits. A counter-offensive was likewise mounted regarding the civil suit brought by the Democratic National Committee against CRP. Dean testified that, around September 9 or 10, both Haldeman and Colson relayed to him a request from the President that a counter-action be filed against the Democrats "as quickly as humanly possible." (3 *Hearings* 956) On September 13, CRP filed a $2,500,000 counter-suit against the DNC for abuse of process and, on September 14, Stans brought a $5 million libel suit against Lawrence O'Brien, DNC Chairman.

Dean testified that, when he met with the President on September 15, the various civil cases were discussed. Dean stated he told the President that CRP lawyers were handling both the DNC suit and one filed by Common Cause. He said Judge Ritchie had been helpful in slowing down these civil cases. The President was informed as to the status of the CRP abuse of process suit and the Stans libel action. Haldeman's testimony and the edited transcripts support Dean's testimony in this regard. (3 *Hearings* 958; 7 *Hearings* 2888-2889; Edited Presidential Conversations, pp. 60-61, 74-75) The edited transcripts, at p. 60, contain the following exchange:

D   You might be interested in some of the allocations we got. The Stans' libel action was assigned to Judge Ritchie

P   (Expletive deleted)

D   Well now that is good and bad. Judge Ritchie is not known to be one of the (inaudible) on the bench, that is considered by me. He is fairly candid in dealing with people about the question. He has made several entrees off the bench—one to Kleindienst and one to Roemer McPhee to keep Roemer abreast of what his thinking is. He told Roemer he thought Maury ought to file a libel action.

P   Did he? [*]

H   Can he deal with this concurrently with the court case?

D   Yeah. The fact that the civil case drew to a halt —that the depositions were halted he is freed.

H   It was just put off for a few days, wasn't it?

D   It did more than that—he had been talking to Silbert, one of the Assistant U.S. Attorneys down here. Silbert said, "We are going to have a hell of a time drawing these indictments because these civil depositions will be coming out and the Grand Jury has one out on this civil case but it is nothing typical." (Edited Presidential Conversations, pp. 60-61)

3. CIA Investigative Materials. According to Dean, shortly after the Select Committee was created, Ehrlichman urged him to have the CIA retrieve from the Department of Justice certain photographs which came from a CIA camera supplied Hunt that Hunt had returned to the Agency. The pictures included one of Liddy posed in front of Dr. Fielding's office which was burglarized. (3 *Hearings* 977-978) Dean said Ehrlichman wanted the photographs and accompanying documents retrieved "before the Senate investigators got a copy of the material." (3 *Hearings* 978)

* The purported House version has the President adding the comment "Good" after the above question.

Dean further testified he sought to obtain the photographs from Henry Petersen, claiming they had nothing to do with Watergate. Petersen told Dean the Justice Department had received a letter from Senator Mansfield, asking preservation of all evidentiary materials that might have any relationship to Watergate. Petersen stated he would be willing to return the materials to the CIA, if it requested such action, and leave a card in the Department's file indicating what he had done. (3 *Hearings* 978) Subsequently, General Walters of the CIA visited Dean to state that he was opposed to retrieving the material under those circumstances and the idea was dropped. (3 *Hearings* 979)

4. Other Activities Relating To The Select Committee. Evidence received by the Select Committee demonstrates considerable concern on the part of certain White House officials as to how to deal with the Select Committee, which, Dean said, was viewed as an uncontrollable, if not hostile body that presented new and possibly more dangerous problems than the criminal trials. (3 *Hearings* 980-81)

a. The La Costa Meeting. A major meeting of the White House officials to develop strategy regarding the Select Committee took place at the La Costa Resort Hotel, south of San Clemente, on February 10 and February 11. Attending the meeting were Haldeman, Ehrlichman, Dean and Richard Moore. (3 *Hearings* 982) Dean stated that the meeting at La Costa was wide-ranging, involving an evaluation of Select Committee members and the White House strategy for dealing with the Committee. (3 *Hearings* 983-984) According to Dean, the basic strategy was:

"The White House will take a public posture of full cooperation but privately will attempt to restrain the investigation and make it as difficult as possible to get information and witnesses. A behind-the-scenes media effort would be made to make the Senate inquiry appear very partisan. The ultimate goal would be to discredit the hearings and reduce their impact by attempting to show that the Democrts have engaged in the same type of activities." (3 *Hearings* 984)

Dean said a special program was planned to handle press coverage of the Senate hearings. Haldeman, he said, suggested that Pat Buchanan be used as a press watchdog. Buchanan would prepare speeches on biased press coverage, write op-ed articles, attend the hearings and be the White House spokesman to take pressure off Ronald Ziegler in his daily briefings. (3 *Hearings* 985) Moore and Haldeman, however, recollect that it was Dean who suggested this role for Buchanan. (5 *Hearings* 1941; 7 *Hearings* 2891)

Special plans were made as to CRP activities regarding the hearings. It was decided that CRP would increase its legal and public relations staff and that Paul O'Brien and Ken Parkinson would be responsible for handling CRP witnesses called to testify. (3 *Hearings* 985) Ehrlichman testified it was generally concluded that CRP, with Mitchell returning as its head, would operationally be the best entity to deal with the Select Committee hearings. (7 *Hearings* 2850)

Dean said that toward the end of the meeting on February 11, Ehrlichman raised the "bottom line" question: "Would the seven Watergate defendants remain silent through the Senate hearings?" (3 *Hearings* 985) This was important, Dean said, since their entire strategy rested on the continued silence of the Watergate defendants. Dean told Haldeman and Ehrlichman there were still demands for more money. Richard Moore, Dean said, was therefore assigned to go to New York to see Mitchell "simply [to] lay it out that it was Mitchell's responsibility to raise the necessary funds for these men." (3 *Hearings* 985-986) Moore confirmed this testimony:

> "Dean, in a sort of by-the-way reference, said he had been told by the lawyers—and I think that was the way he put it, but I cannot be precise about his language— that they may be needing some more money, and did we have any ideas? Someone said, isn't that something that John Mitchell might handle with his rich New York friends. It was suggested that since I would be meeting with Mr. Mitchell I should mention this when I saw him and I said I would." (5 *Hearings* 1941-1942)

Ehrlichman also confirms that Moore was sent to New York to see Mitchell about raising money for the Watergate defendants whose sentencing was pending. (7 *Hearings* 2850) When Moore raised the issue with Mitchell, Mitchell said— according to Moore—"get lost," or "tell them to get lost." (5 *Hearings* 2049) Mitchell confirms that he declined Moore's fundraising suggestion. He testified that the "general tenor of the subject matter" was that the money was for the "payment for the support and the legal fees of the people that were involved in the Watergate." (5 *Hearings* 1935)

Moore, Ehrlichman and Haldeman provided further confirmation and elaboration of Dean's testimony concerning the La Costa discussion. Moore testified that at this meeting the participants discussed preparation for the Select Committee

hearings, Executive privilege, a possible White House statement on Watergate in advance of the hearings, manpower
for CRP to cope with the hearings, and the pending lawsuits.
(5 *Hearings* 1940-41, 1964, 1966) Ehrlichman testified that
the La Costa meeting was called "because the President had
asked who was handling the preparation of the White House
case for the Senate Select Committee hearings, and what planning was being done, and what was the White House position
going to be on matters like executive privilege, and there
were no answers to those questions." (7 *Hearings* 2849)
Ehrlichman admitted that the La Costa group discussed steps
to affect the Select Committee's Resolution and also evaluated members of the Committee. (7 *Hearings* 2850) He
also confirmed that a strategy to block or delay the hearings
was discussed, including a proposal to seek judicial delay. (7
Hearings 2850-51) Haldeman basically concurred in Moore's
recollections of the La Costa meeting. (7 *Hearings* 2890) The
interest of the White House in affecting the outcome of the
Select Committee's hearings is further demonstrated by
numerous passages in the edited Presidential transcripts
where the President, Ehrlichman, Haldeman and Dean discussed various ways to deal with the upcoming hearings to
limit the Select Committee's effectiveness, and to "cut the
losses" of the White House. *See e.g.*, the meetings of February 28, 1973 between the President and Dean at pp. 55-76,
which is subsequently discussed.

b. Documentary and Other Evidence Indicating the White
House Strategy. In support of his testimony concerning
White House preparations for the hearings, Dean submitted
a February 9, 1973 "Eyes Only" memorandum from Haldeman to Dean emphasizing the need for a Minority Counsel to
the Ervin Committee, who was a "real tiger, not an old man
or a soft-head. . . ." Also, Haldeman indicated therein that
Dean instruct Kleindienst to order the FBI to prepare a file
on the "1968 bugging" of candidate Richard Nixon in 'preparation for a counter-offensive. (Exhibit 34-33; 3 *Hearings*
1240) Haldeman, under questioning, authenticated this memorandum. (8 *Hearings* 3203-3205)

Another memorandum supplied by Dean was from Lawrence Higby, Haldeman's assistant, to Dean, dated February 10, 1973. This document emphasized the need "to get a
thorough itemization as quickly as possible of all the disruptions that occurred in the campaign . . . for our Watergate
tactics with the Ervin Committee." (3 *Hearings* 1241)

A demonstration of the strong counter-offensive Haldeman was planning is found in a memorandum from Halde-

144

man to Dean, dated February 10, 1973:

"We need to get our people to put out the story on the foreign or Communist money that was used in support of demonstrations against the President in 1972. We should tie all 1972 demonstrations to McGovern and thus to the Democrats as part of the peace movement. "The investigation should be brought to include the peace movement which leads directly to McGovern and Teddy Kennedy. This is a good counter-offensive to be developed. . .

"We need to develop the plan on to what extent the Democrats were responsible for the demonstrations that led to violence or disruption.

"There's also the question of whether we should let out the Fort Wayne story now.*—that we ran a clean campaign compared to theirs of libel and slander such as against Rebozo, etc.

"We could let Evans and Novak put it out and then be asked about it to make the point that we knew and the President said it was not to be used under any circumstances. In any event, we have to play a very hard game on this whole thing and get our investigations going as a counter move." (3 *Hearings* 1242)

Haldeman accepted responsibility for the contents of this memorandum. (8 *Hearings* 3180)

Dean testified the White House feared the Senate hearing might force the Justice Department into further criminal investigations that would lead back to the White House. It was important, Dean said, that the President meet with Kleindienst and "bring [him] back in the family to protect the White House . . ." (3 *Hearings* 989) Dean said that the President should "solicit Kleindienst's assistance during the hearings and if anything should develop during the hearings, to not let all hell break loose in a subsequent investigation." (3 *Hearings* 989) The proposed meeting between the President and Kliendienst was to be a "stroking session." In a February 22, 1973 talking paper which Dean submitted to Haldeman for transmittal to the President the following recommendations were made respecting this proposed meeting:

"Kleindienst should be asked to remain in office until at least one full year from this date (i.e. until after the Watergate hearings have passed), because

* The Fort Wayne story involved a Democratic public official's alleged illegitimate child.

145

the hearings may well result in a request for additional action by the Department of Justice. We can't afford bitterness at Justice nor can we risk a new Attorney General being able to handle some of the potential problems.

"Kleindienst should be asked to follow the hearings closely and keep us apprised of any potential problems from a Department of Justice standpoint.

"Kleindienst should be given the feeling that he is an important member of the team and it is not merely because of these hearings that he is being asked to stay on." (Exhibit 34-36; 3 *Hearings* 1247-1248)

Kleindienst confirmed that he met with President Nixon in late February and that the President requested him to stay at his post until the investigation was over. (9 *Hearings* 3568-3569)

Several days later, on February 28, the President personally expressed to Dean his concern over the upcoming Select Committee hearings. The President stated his hope that the Committee would have one "big slambang thing for a whole week," after which "interest in the whole thing will fall off." (Edited Presidential Conversations, p. 79) Dean warned the President that:

"I think this is going to be very different. It will be hot, I think they are going to be tough. I think they are going to be gory in some regards, but I am also convinced that if everyone pulls their own oar in this thing, in all those we've got with various concerns, we can make it through these things and minimal people will be hurt. And they may even paint themselves as being such partisans. . . ." (Edited Presidential Conversations, p. 93)

The President said he hoped the Committee would "be partisan rather than for them to have a facade of fairness and all the rest." (Edited Presidential Conversations, p. 93) The February 28 meeting concluded with President Nixon telling Dean that he expected Mitchell "won't allow himself to be ruined [by Watergate]. *He will put on his big stone face* [before the Committee]. But *I hope he does* and he will." (Edited Presidential Conversations, p. 110.) (emphasis added) Dean expressed concern that the Select Committee was out to get him, a notion the President discounted. The President, however, did express a belief that the Select Committee was "after" Haldeman

146

Colson or Ehrlichman. (Edited Presidential Conversations, p. 110)

5. *Henry Petersen's Communications to the President.* The edited transcripts of presidential conversations show that Henry Petersen, Chief of the Justice Department's Criminal Division, served as a conduit for a constant flow of information from the Grand Jury and the prosecutors first to Dean and then to the President. The transcripts also demonstrate that the President kept Haldeman and Ehrlichman informed of what he learned from Petersen. Petersen's conduct raises a serious question as to whether high Department of Justice officials can effectively administer criminal justice where White House personnel, or the President himself, are the subejcts of the investigation. The conflict of interests is apparent and a Committee recommendation deals directly with this issue. (See Recommendation I)

Early in the Watergate investigation (in 1972) Petersen had kept Dean informed. Dean told Petersen during their morning March 21 meeting that Petersen had made him "totally aware" of relevant information with respect to the prosecutorial effort.

"There is no doubt that I was totally aware of what the Bureau [FBI] was doing at all times. I was totally aware of what the Grand Jury was doing. *I knew what witnesses were going to be called. I knew what they were asked, and I had to.*" (Edited Presidential Conversations, p. 185: Meeting of March 21, 1973) (emphasis added)

The President asked Dean: "Why did Petersen play the game so straight with us?" Dean replied:

"Because Petersen is a soldier. He kept me informed. *He told me when we had problems,* where we had problems and the like. He believed in you and he believes in this Administration. This Administration made him. *I don't think he had done anything improper, but he did make sure that the investigation was narrowed down to the very, very fine criminal thing which was a break for us. There is no doubt about it.*" (Edited Presidential Conversations, p. 185) (emphasis added)

Dean assured the President during this meeting that Petersen is "the only man I know . . . that really could tell us how this could be put together so that it did the max-

147

imum to carve it away with a minimum damage to individuals involved." (Edited Presidential Conversations, p. 205)

Later, in April 1972, Petersen and the President met on several occasions to discuss the progress of the Watergate investigation. At one session, Petersen assured the President that the investigation would not reach him because the Department of Justice had no jurisdiction to investigate the President:

"I've said to [U.S. Attorney Harold H.] Titus 'We have to draw the line. We have no mandate to investigate the President. We investigate Watergate.'" (Edited Presidential Conversation, p. 1259: Meeting of April 27, 1973)

He continued:

"My understanding of law is—my understanding of our responsibilities, is that if it came to that I would have to come to you and say, 'We can't do that.' The only people who have jurisdiction to do that is the House of Representatives, as far as I'm concerned." (Edited Presidential Conversations, pp. 1259-1260)

Petersen, however, at an April 17 meeting told the President that:

"Mr. President, if I thought you were trying to protect somebody, I would have walked out" (Edited Presidential Conversations, p. 1086)

Petersen's role as a conduit of secret grand jury information is illustrated by his telephone conversation of April 16, 1973, with the President (from 8:58 to 9:14 p.m.). The conversation began:

P I just want to know if there are any developments I should know about and, second, that *of course,* as you know, *anything you tell me, as I think I told you earlier, will not be passed on.*
HP I understand, Mr. President.
P *Because I know the rules of the Grand Jury.* (Edited Presidential Conversations, p. 966) (emphasis added)

Petersen then began to relate to the President secret information before the Grand Jury. He relayed to the President the factual details of the investigation, even indicating where there were gaps. Thus he told the President that Dean "got in touch with Kalmbach to arrange for money, the details of which we really don't know as yet." (*id.*, at 969)*

The next morning, April 17, from 9:47 to 9:59 a.m., the President met with Haldeman and discussed strategy for dealing with the Watergate Affair. In the course of that conversation, the President, who had been informed that the Justice Department did not know the details of Kalmbach's arrangement for money, said to Haldeman:

"Another thing, if you could get John [Ehrlichman] and yourself to sit down and do some hard thinking about what kind of strategy you are going to have with *the money. You know what I mean.*" (Edited Presidential Conversations 983) (emphasis added)

The President also told Haldeman:

"Well, be sure that Kalmbach is at least aware of this, that LaRue has talked very freely. He is a broken man. . . ." (*Id.* at 983)

Petersen had informed the President on April 16, 1973, that Dean had said that Liddy "confessed to Dean" on June 19, 1972, and that Dean then told Ehrlichman what Liddy had said. (Edited Presidential Conversations, p. 974). The next morning the President told Haldeman:

P   Dean met with Liddy on June 19th, must have been when he did it. He was in California in January but that is irrelevant. But they keep banging around and banging around. The prosecution gets out the damn stuff. Did John talk with you about it?

H   Yeh, he mentioned it. Dean did tell us that story in Ehrlichman's office last week or two weeks ago.

P   But not to go all through this.

H   I don't think so. (Edited Presidential Conversations, p. 982)

The transcript of the President-Petersen meeting of April 17 provides another example of Petersen's briefing the President on information received by the prosecutors and Grand Jury. (Edited Presidential Conversations, at p. 1060, *et seq.*) This conversation also shows that Petersen was giving the President tactical advice as to the posture the White House should strike during the investigation. During this conversation, the President told Petersen not to tell

* Earlier in the day, the President had informed Ehrlichman and Ziegler that "I've got Petersen on a short leash". (Edited Presidential Conversations 941)

149

him "anything out of the Grand Jury unless you think I need to know it. If it corroborates something or anybody here I need to know it—otherwise I don't want to know about it." (*Id.* at 1060) The President then asked: "I guess it would be legal for me to know?" and Petersen responded: "Well yes, I think it is legal for you to know." (*Id.* at 1061) Peterson left, Handeman and Ehrlichman appeared and the President proceeded then to relay to them the information obtained from Petersen. (Edited Presidential Conversations 1115 *et seq.*)

At least by April 27, Petersen's constant contact with the White House created suspicions among the Department of Justice Watergate investigators. Petersen admitted to the President on April 27:

"We had a kind of crisis of confidence night before last . . . And in effect it concerned me—whether or not they were at east with my reporting to you, and I pointed out to them that I had very specific instructions, discussed that with them before on that subject . . . As a consequent—I kind of laid into [Harold] Titus yesterday and it cleared the air a little bit, but there is a very suspicious atmosphere. They are concerned and scared . . ." (Edited Presidential Conversations, p. 1258)

N. THE BEGINNING OF THE UNRAVELING OF THE COVERUP

The coverup began publicly to unravel when McCord broke his silence on March 21, 1972 with his letter to Judge Sirica which was read in open court on March 23. It was soon learned that McCord had accused Magruder of perjury and Mitchell, Magruder and Dean of participating in planning the Watergate break-in. Even before McCord broke his silence, Magruder and Dean were concerned about the viability of the coverup. Magruder, according to his testimony, expressed his concerns to Haldeman as early as January 1973, and to Mitchell and Dean in March; Dean voiced his fears to the President on several occasions.

1. The February 28 Meeting. According to Dean, he met with the President on February 28, 1973, and, after discussion of a number of matters, informed him that he (Dean) was involved in the post-June 17 activities regarding Watergate. "I briefly described to him why I thought I had legal problems, and that I had been a conduit for many of the decisions that were made and, there-fore, could be involved in an obstruction of justice." Dean said the President did not accept his analysis, wanted no details and told him not to worry because he had no legal problems. (3 *Hearings* 992-993)

The edited Presidential transcript of this meeting does not, in significant respects, bear out Dean's recollection of this meeting. However, in Dean's meeting with the President on March 21, he did tell the President that he could go to jail for obstruction of justice since he was acting as a conduit in the payments of money to the defendants. The President discounted this possibility, as Dean has testified, on the ground that Dean was acting as a lawyer. (Edited Presidential Conversations, pp. 204-206) This conversation is quite similar to the one Dean testified took place on February 28 and it thus appears, from these unauthenticated transcripts, that Dean placed this discussion with the President on the wrong date when he testified before the Select Committee. Nonetheless, there are certain statements during the February 28th meeting that can be construed as referencing the coverup then in progress:

P I feel for those poor guys in jail, particularly for Hunt and with his wife dead.

D *Well there is every indication they are hanging in tough right now.*

P What the hell do they expect though? Do they expect clemency in a reasonable time? What would you advise on that?

D I think it is one of those things we will have to watch very closely. For example,—

P You couldn't do it, say in six months.

D No, you couldn't. This thing may become so po-litical as a result of these hearings that it is a ven-detta. This judge may go off the deep end in sentenc-ing, and make it so absurd that its clearly injustice that they have been heavily— (p. 102) (emphasis added)

* * *

D *Well I was—we have come a long road on this thing now. I had thought it was an impossible task to hold together until after the election until things started falling out, but we have made it this far* and I am convinced we are going to make it the whole road and put this thing in the funny pages of history books rather than anything serious because actually—

P It will be somewhat serious but the main thing,

151

of course is also the isolation of the President.

D Absolutely! Totally true!

P Because that, fortunately, is totally true.

D I know that sir!

P (expletive deleted) Of course, I am not dumb and I will never forget when I heard about this (adjective deleted) forced entry and bugging. I thought, what in the hell is this? What is the matter with these people? Are they crazy? I thought they were nuts! A prank! But it wasn't! It wasn't very funny. I think that our Democratic friends know that too. They know what the hell it was. They don't think we'd be involved in such. (pp. 108-9) (emphasis added)

* * *

P But I think it is very important that you have these talks with our good friend Kleindienst.

D That will be done.

P Tell him we have to get these things worked out. We have to work together on this thing. I would build him up. He is the man who can make the difference. Also point out to him what we have. (expletive deleted) Colson's got (characterization deleted), but I really, really, —this stuff here—let's forget this. But let's remember this was not done by the White House. *This was done by the Committee to Re-Elect, and Mitchell was the Chairman, correct?*

D That's correct!

P And Kleindienst owes Mitchell everything. Mitchell wanted him for Attorney General. Wanted him for Deputy, and here he is. Now, (expletive deleted) Baker's got to realize this, and that if he allows this thing to get out of hand *he is going to potentially ruin John Mitchell. He won't. Mitchell won't allow himself to be ruined. He will put on his big stone face.* But I hope he does and he will. There is no question what they are after. What the Committee is after is somebody at the White House. They would like to get Haldeman or Colson or Ehrlichman.

D *Or possibly Dean. —You know. I am a small fish.*

P *Anybody at the White House they would—but in your case I think they realize you are the lawyer and they know you didn't have a (adjective deleted) thing to do with the campaign.*

D That's right.

P That's what I think. Well, we'll see you. (pp. 109-110) (emphasis added)

152

2. The March 13 Meeting. Dean's testimony was that the money demands by Hunt and how to meet them and the promise of clemency to Hunt were discussed with the President and Haldeman at this meeting. This testimony is not supported by the edited Presidential transcripts of this meeting. It appears from that document and Haldeman's testimony (7 *Hearings* 2898) that Dean confused this morning meeting with the President on March 21—where Hunt's money demands and clemency were discussed—with the events of March 13. Nevertheless, the March 13 transcript is significant because it shows that, on that date, Dean revealed at least some of the aspects of the coverup to the President. Some illustrative passages follow:

P   Who is going to be the first witness up there?
D   Sloan
P   Unfortunate.
D   No doubt about it—
P   He's scared?
D   He's scared, he's weak. He has a compulsion to cleanse his soul by confession. We are giving him a lot of stroking. Funny thing is this fellow goes down to the Court House here before Sirica, testifies as honestly as he can testify, and Sirica looks around and called him a liar. He just said—Sloan just can't win! So Kalmbach has been dealing with Sloan. Sloan is like a child. Kalmbach has done a lot of that. The person who will have a greater problem as a result of Sloan's testimony is Kalmbach and Stans. So they are working closely with him to make sure that he settles down. (p. 138)

* * *

D   . . . *[Kalmbach] is solid.*
P   He will—how does he tell his story? He has a pretty hard row to hoe—he and Stans have.
D   *He will be good.* Herb is the kind of guy who will check, not once nor twice, on his story—not three times—but probably fifty to a hundred times. *He will go over it. He will know it. There won't be a hole in it.* Probably he will do his own Q and A. He will have people cross-examine him from ten ways. He will be ready, as Maury Stans will be ready.
P   *Mitchell is now studying, is he?*
D   He is studying. Sloan will be the worst witness. I think Magruder will be a good witness. This fellow, Bart Porter, will be a good witness. They have already been through Grand Jury. They have been through a

153

trial. They did well . . . (p. 140) (emphasis added)

* * *

D Chapin didn't know anything about the Watergate

P Don't you think so?

D Absolutely not.

P *Strachan?*

D *Yes.*

P *He knew?*

D *Yes.*

P *About the Watergate?*

D *Yes.*

P *Well, then he probably told Bob. He may not have.*

D He was judicious in what he relayed, but Strachan is as tough as nails. *He can go in and stonewall and say, "I don't know anything about what you are talking about." He has already done it twice you know, in interviews.*

P *I guess he should, shouldn't he? I suppose we can't call that justice, can we?*

D Well, it is a personal loyalty to him. He doesn't want it any other way. He didn't have to be told. He didn't have to be asked. It just is something that he found was the way he wanted to handle the situation.

P But he knew? He knew about Watergate? Strachan did?

D Yes.

P I will be damned! *Well that is the problem in Bob's case.* Not Chapin the, but Strachan. Strachan worked for him, didn't he?

D Yes. They would have one hell of a time proving that Strachan had knowledge of it, though.

P Who knew better? Magruder?

D Magruder and Liddy.

P Oh, I see. The other weak link for Bob is Magruder. He hired him et cetera.

D That applies to Mitchell, too (pp. 146-7) (emphasis added)

* * *

P Is it too late to go the hang-out road?

D Yes, I think it is. The hang-out road—

P The hang-out road (inaudible).

D It was kicked around Bob and I and—

P Ehrlichman always felt it should be hang-out.

D Well, I think I convinced him why he would not want to hang-out either. *There is a certain domino sit-*

154

uation here. If some things start going, a lot of other things are going to start going, and there can be a lot of problems if everything starts falling. So there are dangers, Mr. President. I would be less than candid if I did not tell you there are There is a reason for not everyone going up and testifying.

P   I see, Oh no, no, no! I didn't mean to have everyone go up and testify.

D   Well I mean they're just starting to hang-out and say here's our story—

P   I mean put the story out PR people, here is the story, the true story about Watergate.

D   They would never believe it . . . (Edited Presdential Conversations, pp. 150-51) (emphasis added)

3. The March 21 Meeting. On March 21, two days before McCord's letter to Judge Sirica became public, Dean met with the President to give him a report of his knowledge of the Watergate facts and to explain the implications of those facts. Dean's testimony before the Select Committee was as follows: Dean told the President that "there was a cancer growing on the Presidency and that if the cancer was not removed the President himself would be killed by it." He told the President that the cancer must be excised immediately because it was growing more deadly every day. He then gave the President a broad overview of the Watergate affair, including a description of the meetings in January and February 1972 in Mitchell's office. He told the President he did not know how the plan was approved but that he was informed that Mitchell and Haldeman (the latter through Strachan) had also received illegal wiretap information. (3 *Hearings* 998; *see also* 8 *Hearings* 3074-75) Dean informed the President of the highlights of the cover-up, including the use of Kalmbach by Ehrlichman, Haldeman and Mitchell to raise hush money to pay the Watergate defendants. He spoke of Magruder's false story before the grand jury and of his role in assisting Magruder to commit perjury. He told the President that, for the coverup to continue, it would require even more perjury and more money. (3 *Hearings* 998-1000; *see also* 8 *Hearings* 3074)

Certain portions of the edited Presidential transcripts for this meeting relating to hush money and clemency have been previously presented in this report. The following quotations provide further indication of the tenor of the conversation at that meeting.

P   Magruder is (unintelligible)

D   Yeah. Magruder is totally knowledgeable on the whole thing.

P   Yeah.

D   Alright now, we have gone through the trial. I don't know if Mitchell has perjured himself in the Grand Jury or not.

P   Who?

D   Mitchell. I don't know how much knowledge he actually had. I know that Magruder has perjured himself in the Grand Jury. I know that Porter has perjured himself in the Grand Jury.

P   Who is Porter? (unintelligible)

D   He is one of Magruder's deputies. *They set up this scenario which they ran by me. They said "How about this?" I said, "I don't know. If this is what you are going to hang on, fine."* (p. 182) (emphasis added)

* * *

D   . . . Now what has happened post June 17? *I was under pretty clear instructions not to investigate this,* but this could have been disastrous on the electorate if all hell had broken loose. *I worked on a theory of containment—*

P   *Sure.*

D   To try to hold it right where it was.

P   Right. (p 185) (emphasis added)

* * *

D   . . . Liddy said if they all got counsel instantly and said we will ride this thing out. Alright, then they started making demands. "We have to have attorneys fees. We don't have any money ourselves, and you are asking us to take this through the election." Alright so arrangements were made through Mitchell, initiating it. And I was present in discussions where these guys had to be taken care of. Their attorney fees had to be done. Kalmbach was brought in. Kalmbach raised some cash.

P   *They put that under the cover of a Cuban Committee, I suppose?*

D   Well, they had a Cuban Committee and they had —some of it was given to Hunt's lawyer, who in turn passed it out. You know, when Hunt's wife was flying to Chicago with $10,000 she was actually, I understand after the fact now, was going to pass that money to one of the Cubans—to meet him in Chicago and pass it to somebody there.

P   (unintelligible) *but I would certainly keep that cover for whatever it is worth.*

D   That's the most troublesome post-thing because (1) Bob is involved in that; (2) John is involved in that; (3) I am involved in that; (4) Mitchell is involved in that. And that is an obstruction of justice. (p. 187) (emphasis added)

Dean told the Committee that he informed the President on March 21 that he did not believe that all of the seven defendants would maintain their silence forever and that one or more would likely break rank. (3 *Hearings* 998-1000). The transcripts reveal an extended discussion of various individuals "blowing" (Edited Presidential Conversations, p. 196), and others who were "solid." (*Id.* at 192) The edited transcripts indicate that Dean told the President, "I know, sir. I can just tell from our conversation that these are things you have no knowledge of." The President replied: "You certainly can!" (Edited Presidential Conversations, p. 202) These remarks are consistent with Richard Moore's testimony. (5 *Hearings* 1945) According to the edited transcripts, the President, shortly thereafter, told Dean:

P   Let's come back to this problem. What are your feelings yourself, John? You know what they are all saying. What are your feelings about the chances?

D   *I am not confident that we can ride through this. I think there are soft spots.*

P   You used to be— (p. 203) (emphasis added)*

Dean said that in this meeting he told the President that because he did not think they could carry the coverup any further, it was important for the President to get out in front in revealing the true facts. (3 *Hearings* 1000) The edited transcript released by the President reveals the following exchange:

P   So what you really come to is what we do. Let's suppose that you and Haldeman and Ehrlichman and Mitchell say we can't hold this? What then are you going to say? What are you going to put out after it. Complete disclosure, isn't that the best way to do it?

* * *

D   One way to do it is for you to tell the Attorney General that you finally know. Really, this is the first time you are getting all the pieces together. (Edited Presidential Conversation, pp. 203-204)

---

* On the *afternoon* of March 21st, the following colloquy was transcribed:
   P Well, it is a long road isn't it? When you look back on it, as John has pointed out here, *it really has been a long road for all of you, of us.*
   H It sure is
   P *For all of us, for all of us* . . . (p. 253) (emphasis added)

But this recommendation was not followed. Dean testified that despite his full disclosures to the President, a meeting with the President, Haldeman, Ehrlichman and Mitchell the following day, March 22, focused entirely on the White House's relationship with the Select Committee, particularly in regard to the assertion of Executive privilege. The edited transcript of that meeting shows that this was the principal subject of discussion. Dean testified that he then became convinced that there would no effort to stop the coverup. (3 *Hearings* 1002)

4. *The Camp David Trip.* Dean testified that March 23, 1973, after McCord's letter was read in open Court, the President called Dean and, referring to McCord's letter, said, "Well, John, you were right in your prediction." (3 *Hearings* 1003) The President suggested that he go to Camp David to analyze the situation. According to Dean, when he arrived at Camp David, he received a telephone call from Haldeman who instructed him to write a report on everything he knew about Watergate. (3 *Hearings* 1003) While Dean indicated this was his first instruction to put his knowledge in writing, the edited transcript of the March 21st afternoon meeting indicates that the President, at that meeting, asked Dean to write a report on Watergate. (Edited Presidential Conversations, p. 283) Dean said he spent that day and the next thinking about the entire matter and concluded that the true facts must be publicly revealed because the situation would not improve, only worsen. He said he had several telephone conversations with Richard Moore, trying out ideas as to how the President could make the whole truth public. He said Moore seemed receptive but suggested he get Haldeman's reaction.

Dean spoke to Haldeman and concluded he was "intrigued but not overwhelmed" by the idea of public revelation. "It was," Dean said, "becoming increasingly clear that no one involved was willing to stand up and account for themselves." (3 *Hearings* 1003-1005) Dean, at Camp David, did write a report but decided not to give it to Haldeman or the President when he returned. (3 *Hearings* 1006)

5. *Dean's Initial Contacts with Prosecutors and the Select Committee.* On March 28, Haldeman asked Dean to return to Washington to meet with Mitchell and Magruder. Although Dean did not wish to do so Haldeman insisted. Dean testified he had the distinct impression that Haldeman was "backpedaling fast," that he was in the process of uninvolving himself even if it meant sacrificing others. (3 *Hearings* 1006)

The March 28 meeting between Dean, Mitchell and Magruder has been discussed earlier in this Report. Magruder was concerned that everyone stick to the coverup story he had given the grand jury as to the entries in Magruder's diary for the meetings in Mitchell's office on January 27 and February 4, 1972. Dean testified he refused to perpetuate this false story.

On March 30, Dean retained an attorney, and, on April 2, he and his attorney met with the United States Attorneys. Dean told them he was willing to come forward with everything he knew about the Watergate affair. (3 *Hearings* 1009) Shortly afterwards, Dean began providing information to the Select Committee under a special arrangement, approved by the Committee, whereby he would speak only with the Chief Counsel to allow him to evaluate the information Dean could provide to determine whether the Committee should offer Dean "use" immunity.

6. The Ehrlichman Investigation. As indicated above, when Dean returned from Camp David he did not submit a written report on Watergate to the President or Haldeman. Because of this, Haldeman said, the President, on March 30, ceased dealing with Dean on Watergate and transferred the White House Watergate investigation to Ehrlichman. (7 *Hearings* 2902) * It appears, however, from the edited Presidential transcripts that this account of the genesis of the Ehrlichman "investigation" was developed during an April 16, 1973 meeting among the President, Haldeman and Ehrlichman. According to the transcript, the President asked Haldeman and Ehrlichman how the "scenario worked out." Ehrlichman and Haldeman advised the President that the White House's position should be that the Watergate investigation was taken from Dean and given to Ehrlichman because Dean failed to write a report. According to this "scenario," it was Ehrlichman's report to the President that led the President to contact Kleindienst and Petersen on April 15 to inform them of his knowledge of the Watergate facts.** (Edited Presidential Conversations, pp. 820-23)

Ehrlichman, however, told the Committee he did not conduct a thorough investigation of the Watergate matter but only interviewed several White House and CRP officials including

---

* It is noteworthy that on March 28, 1973, Ehrlichman called Kleindienst and taped the telephone conversation. (Exhibit 99, 7 *Hearings* 2941-45) During this discussion, Ehrlichman told Kleindienst that according to the President's best information, "neither Dean nor Haldeman nor Colson nor anybody in the White House" had any prior knowledge of this burglary. In fact, as indicated earlier in this report, the President was told by at least March 13 that Strachan and possible Haldeman had prior knowledge.
** This episode is discussed below.

Mitchell, O'Brien and Magruder. (7 *Hearings* 2763) He testified that he gave an oral report to the President on April 14, 1973, that was based on these few interviews. (7 *Hearings* 2757) Ehrlichman testified that, after his report, the President directed him to "advise the Attorney General" of his findings. (7 *Hearings* 2758) Ehrlichman telephoned Kleindienst at 5:15 p.m. on April 14 and related to him the contents of his report to the President. (7 *Hearings* 2857) As will subsequently appear, the prosecution already possessed much of the evidence Ehrlichman offered.

7. The Attempt to Have Mitchell Take the Blame. Dean testified that his first meeting to give information to the federal prosecutors was scheduled for April 8. He said he felt obliged to tell Haldeman of his intentions and thus telephoned him that morning at San Clemente. Haldeman advised Dean against this course, saying: "Once the toothpaste is out of the tube, it's going to be very hard to get it back in." Dean ignored Haldeman's advice and met with the prosecutors that afternoon. (3 *Hearings* 1010) Magruder, also, in early April began talking with the prosecutors; his first substantive conversation with them was on April 14. (2 *Hearings* 808)

Dean, according to his testimony, then began avoiding Haldeman and Ehrlichman. He did, however, have several conversations with them between April 9 and April 14, 1973. Certain of these discussions, according to Dean, involved a strategy to persuade Mitchell to "step forward" and take the blame. (3 *Hearings* 1011) Dean's testimony that this strategy existed is corroborated by the edited transcript of the April 14 meeting among the President, Ehrlichman and Haldeman. This transcript basically portrays a discussion as to how to persuade Mitchell and Magruder, whom they evidently believed involved, to assume responsibility for the Watergate affair and proclaim that the White House was in no way involved. (*See, e.g.,* Edited Presidential Conversations, pp. 442, 443, 450-1, 459, 501) Various methods of persuasion were discussed. One was to suggest to both Mitchell and Magruder—without being specific—that clemency would be possible. The Preisdent instructed Ehrlichman to tell Mitchell and Magruder that "the President holds great affection for you and your family." He added, "That's the way the so-called clemency's got to be handled." (Edited Presidential Conversations, pp. 502-3)

The April 14 conversation also indicates discussion regarding the dismissal of Dean, who was then talking to the federal prosecutors. From the conversation, it appears that the strategy to sacrifice Mitchell was motivated by the information Ehrlichman had received that Hunt was going to testify before the grand jury. Ehrlichman reported that Colson was very concerned about Hunt's possible testimony because "once Hunt goes on, that's the ball game." The President summarized Colson's advice to the White House as "[G]et busy and nail Mitchell in a hurry." (Edited Presidential Conversations, pp. 409-410, 412) The President, Ehrlichman and Haldeman decided to appeal to Mitchell's loyalty and enlist his aid in limiting the unraveling of the coverup. The President instructed Ehrlichman and Haldeman to approach Mitchell by saying, "there's nobody that can really do it except you." The President wanted Mitchell to testify that "[n]obody in the White House is involved, etc. and so on." (Edited Presidential Conversations, p. 451)

8. *The President's April 15 Meeting with Kleindienst and Petersen.* Meanwhile, United States Attorney Titus, and Assistant United States Attorneys Silbert, Campbell and Glanzer were outlining for Henry Petersen their discoveries in the case, which were largely based on information they were obtaining from Magruder and Dean. According to Petersen, he subsequently arranged for Kleindienst to meet with these prosecutors on the evening of April 14.* An all-night session ensued and the next day, a Sunday, Petersen and Kleindienst briefed the President on the evidence they had received, which indicated a massive coverup. (9 *Hearings* 3627-28) Both Petersen and Kleindienst said the President expressed no sign to them that Dean or anyone else had already imparted such information. (9 *Hearings* 3586-3587, 3634) Petersen testified he urged the President to dismiss Haldeman and Ehrlichman because of their apparent involvement in the coverup, but not Dean, since Dean was cooperating with the prosecutors in its unraveling. (9 *Hearings* 3628-3629)

The edited transcript of an April 14 Oval Office meeting among the President, Haldeman and Ehrlichman reveals that this meeting focused in part on Dean's plans

* According to Dean's opening statement before the Committee, Silbert, Campbell and Glanzer had originally agreed with Dean's counsel to keep the information Dean was giving them confidential. But after Dean told Ehrlichman on April 14 that his attorney told him that Haldeman and Ehrlichman were targets of the grand jury, late that evening Dean's counsel called Dean and told him that the prosecutors had informed him (Dean's counsel) that "they were going to have to breach the agreement they had made regarding keeping all my conversations with them private." The reason given by the prosecutors for this change of position was that "the Attorney General had called Petersen and them and wanted a full report on everything that was going on before the grand jury and where the grand jury was headed." (3 *Hearings* 1014)

to give testimony to the prosecutors and the question of whether Dean should be dismissed. The President described one tactic supporting Dean's dismissal as follows: ". . . cut your losses and get rid of 'em. Give 'em an hor d'oeuvre and maybe they won't come back for the main course. Well, out, John Dean." (Edited Presidential Conversations, pp. 491-492)

9. *Further Meetings Between the President and Dean.* On the evening of April 15, 1973, Dean said, he met with the President to inform him of his discussions with the prosecutors. He testified he told the President his conduct was not "an act of disloyalty" but an action he believed necessary because "I felt this matter had to end." The President asked whether he had received immunity and he advised that no deal had been made. Dean stated the President instructed him not to discuss national security matters or Presidential conversations with the prosecutors. He said the President then attempted to clarify his earlier March 21 comment that it would be no problem to raise one million dollars in hush money. Dean said the President told him he had only been joking when he made that remark.

Contrary to Petersen's advice, the President decided that Dean should leave the White House but that Haldeman and Ehrlichman should stay. Dean testified that, on April 16, the President called him into the Oval Office and gave him two letters prepared for his signature, "one letter requested the acceptance of Dean's resignation, the other letter requested an indefinite leave of absence." Both letters cited "my . . . involvement in the Watergate matter" as cause for departure. Dean testified he refused to sign either letter. The President then, Dean said, requested Dean to prepare his own letter of resignation, which Dean agreed to do. (3 *Hearings* 1017-1018) However, later in the day, Dean said, he informed the President that he would not resign unless Ehrlichman and Haldeman followed suit. (3 *Hearings* 1017-1018)

The edited transcripts of these meetings confirm Dean's testimony in large part. At the first meeting, the President told Dean he would have to say something about Dean's resignation "or otherwise they will say 'What the hell, after Dean told you all of this, what did you do?' You see?" The following colloquy then took place:

P   But what is your feeling on that? See what I mean?

D   Well, I think it ought to be Dean, Ehrlichman and Haldeman.

P   Well, I thought Dean at the moment.

D   Alright

* * *

P   . . . And what I would think we would want to do is to have it in two different forms here . . . It seems to me that your form should be to request an immediate leave of absence. That would be one thing. The other, of course, would be a straight resignation.

D   Uh, huh—

P   First, what I would suggest is that you sign both . . .

* * *

D   What I would like to do is draft up for you an alternative letter putting in both options and you can just put them in the file. Short and sweet.

P   All right. Fine. I had dictated something myself. All my own. If you can give me a better form, fine. I just want to do it either way. Do you? Or do you want to prepare something?

D   I would like to prepare something. (Edited Presidential Conversations, pp. 788-91)

Later that day Dean returned with his draft:

D   I wrote: "Dear Mr. President: Inasmuch as you have informed me that John Ehrlichman and Bob Haldeman have verbally tendered their requests for immediate and indefinite leave of absence from the staff, I declare I wish also to confirm my similar request as having accepted a leave of absence from the staff." Well, I think there is a problem.

P   You don't want to go if they stay—

D   There is the problem for you of the scapegoat theory

P   You mean making use of it

D   That's right (*Id.*, p. 958)

10. *The Question of Immunity for Dean*. In the evening of April 17, 1973, President Nixon told the nation:

"I have expressed to the appropriate authorities my view that no individual holding in the past or at present, a position of major importance in the Administration should be given immunity from prosecution."

Dean testified that:

"When the President issued this statement on April 17, in which he was quite obviously trying to affect any discussions I was having with the Government regarding my testimony by inserting the phrase therein regarding 'no immunity' and combined with the fact that he had requested that I sign a virtual confession on Monday of that week, I decided that indeed I was being set up . . ." (3 *Hearings* 1020)

The edited Presidential transcripts provide some support for Dean's intimation that the President did not want him to receive immunity because of concern over his testimony. On the afternoon of April 17, the President expressed his concern over the threat Dean posed:

P I'm not ruling out kicking him (Dean) out. But you got to figure what the hell does Dean know. What kind of blackmail does he have? (Edited Presidential Conversations, p. 992)

Later that afternoon the President, observing that "Dean is the only one who can sink Haldeman or Ehrlichman," informed Haldeman and Ehrlichman that he had told Assistant Attorney General Petersen "specifically, that nobody should be granted immunity in any case." (Edited Presidential Conversations, p. 1193) He told them, "I want you to go forward at all costs to beat the damned rap. They'll have one hell of a time proving it." (Edited Presidential Conversations, p. 1197)

On April 18, Petersen testified, the President called him to inquire whether Dean had been immunized. After checking with Dean's lawyer and Mr. Silbert, Petersen assured the President that Dean had not received immunity. The President told Petersen that he had a tape of an April 15 conversation with Dean in which Dean said he had been immunized. The President offered to let Petersen hear the tape, but Petersen refused. (9 *Hearings* 3655) *

On April 19, the President met with Haldeman's and Ehrlichman's lawyers, John J. Wilson and Frank Strickler. The following passage from the edited transcript of this conversation is significant:

P Then, you got to remember Dean, as I have said, is a loose cannon.
W I know he is.
P The damnest charges you've ever heard. Some of them are unbelievable.

---

* It was this conversation that the White House said later was never recorded because the tape "ran out."

W   Yes.

P   This fellow that was sitting in here and who in the Office of the President—a very bright young guy —but he now wants to drag them down with him.

W   Yes. Oh, he's bad.

P   They must have told him what I—they—I think—have told Dean that, *"If he'll—if he can get Haldeman and Ehrlichman—he gets immunity." How on that point, do you want Petersen to give him immunity, or not?*

W   Uh—

P   Dean.

W   Well.

P   Should he?

W   Uh. Let me—as I understood, they were hung up on that right now.

P   They are.

W   Now.

P   *See, that's why—I put out a statement that no major figure should be given immunity.*

W   Let me tell you—

P   Basically, because I think it would look bad if— (unintelligible) from our standpoint . . . (Edited Presidential Conversations, pp. 1239-40) (emphasis added)

The edited transcripts also demonstrate that Secretary of State Rogers agreed with the President that it would look bad to give Dean immunity. (Edited Presidential Conversations, p. 1144)

On April 19, two days after the President's no immunity statement, Dean issued a public statement that he would not be made a "scapegoat" in the Watergate affair. (3 *Hearings* 1020) On the same day Dean made this statement, White House aide Stephen Bull was asked to investigate Dean's awareness of the White House taping system. In his testimony during the Watergate Tapes' hearings before Judge Sirica, Bull was unable to recall who instructed him to make this check. He ascertained from a White House Secret Service official that Dean did not know about the system. (Watergate Tapes Transcript, pp. 2544-2547) As former Presidential Assistant Alexander Butterfield testified, very few individuals were cognizant of the secret taping system. (5 *Hearings* 2077) On Easter Sunday, April 22, according to Dean, the President telephoned to wish him happy Easter. Dean characterized this as a "stroking" call. (3 *Hearings* 1020)

11. The President's April 30 Statement. On April 30, 1973, President Nixon addressed the American public on Watergate, declaring he accepted full "responsibility" for the abuses that had transpired. The President announced the resignations of Haldeman and Ehrlichman, "two of my closest associates in the White House" and "two of the finest public servants it has been my privilege to know." He also revealed the resignations of Kleindienst and Dean and his selection of Elliot Richardson as Kleindienst's replacement. The President stated that Dean's resignation had been requested.

The President also claimed in this address that he had begun an "intensive" new investigation into the Watergate matter on March 21. The background of this statement is found in the edited Presidential transcript of a meeting on April 17, at pp. 1121-22:

P   The next part is what I'm concerned about. "I began new inquiries," shall we say?

E   Well, I don't know

P   "I began new inquiries into this matter as a result of serious charges, which were reported publicly and privately." Should we say that?

E   Publicly, comma "which in some cases were reported publicly."

P   "Four weeks ago we," *Why don't we say, shall we set a date? That sounds a hell of a lot stronger if we set a date.*

E   All right.

P   "On March 21, I began new inquiries," Strike that. "I ordered an investigation, new inquiries throughout the government—" (emphasis added).

On May 17 the Committee opened its public hearings into the Watergate burglary and its aftermath. By August 7, 1973, when the first phase of hearings ended, the Gemstone plan, the break-in, the details of the coverup and much more had been revealed.

Recommendations

I. THE COMMITTEE RECOMMENDS THAT CONGRESS ENACT LEGISLATION TO ESTABLISH A PERMANENT OFFICE OF PUBLIC ATTORNEY WHICH WOULD HAVE JURISDICTION TO PROSECUTE CRIMINAL CASES IN WHICH THERE IS A REAL OR APPARENT CONFLICT OF INTEREST WITHIN THE EXECUTIVE BRANCH. THE PUBLIC ATTORNEY WOULD ALSO HAVE JURISDICTION TO INQUIRE INTO (WITH POWER TO GAIN ACCESS TO EXECU-

TIVE RECORDS) THE STATUS AND PROGRESS OF COMPLAINTS AND CRIMINAL CHARGES CONCERNING MATTERS PENDING IN OR INVOLVING THE CONDUCT OF FEDERAL DEPARTMENTS AND REGULATORY AGENCIES. THE PUBLIC ATTORNEY WOULD BE APPOINTED FOR A FIXED TERM (*e.g.*, 5 years), BE SUBJECT TO SENATE CONFIRMATION AND BE CHOSEN BY MEMBERS OF THE JUDICIAL BRANCH TO ENSURE HIS INDEPENDENCE FROM EXECUTIVE CONTROL OR INFLUENCE.

In each of the nation's two major scandals during the past half century, Teapot Dome and Watergate, the appointment of a special prosecutor was essential to preserve the integrity of the criminal justice system and public confidence in the rule of law. In both situations, the office was created after serious abuses had occurred.

The evidence gathered by the Select Committee indicates that unmonitored executive investigative and prosecutorial agencies may be reluctant to expose wrong-doing in the executive branch. It is thus essential that an independent Public Attorney's Office be created to investigate and prosecute where conflicts of interest in the executive branch exist. This office should be given power to inquire fully into corruption in the executive branch and have access to all records relating to such corruption. The operations of the current Special Prosecution force demonstrate the effective role such an entity can play.

The *preventative* role this Office could fulfill must be emphasized. Permanent status for this Office could help ensure responsible action by executive branch officials who have primary responsibility to administer and enforce the law. Indeed, it is reasonable to speculate that the existence of a Public Attorney's Office might have served as a deterrent against some of the wrongful acts that comprise the Watergate scandal. Because of this preventive role, it is unwise to wait until another national crisis to re-institute the Office of Special Prosecutor. It is far better to create a permanent institution now than to consider its wisdom at some future time when emotions may be high and unknown political factors at play.

The Public Attorney we recommend would not be only a "special prosecutor" but an ombudsman having power to inquire into the administration of justice in the executive branch. With the power of access to executive records, he could appropriately respond to complaints from the public, the Congress, the Courts and other public and private institutions. If he became aware of misconduct in the executive branch, he could assume the role of special prosecutor. The

167

Public Attorney should also be required to make periodic reports to Congress on the affairs of his office and the need for new legislation within his jurisdiction, a function that should be of great assistance to the relevant Congressional oversight committees.

The Attorney General should find such an Office advantageous in cases involving charges against administration officials or persons otherwise close to high executive officers, particularly where a *proper* exercise of discretion *not* to prosecute would give rise to public suspicion of coverup. Such cases could be referred by the Attorney General to the Public Attorney. The Public Attorney would also have jurisdiction to prosecute all criminal cases referred to it by the Federal Elections Commission, which is elsewhere recommended in this report.

It is not anticipated that there would be substantial jurisdictional disputes between the Justice Department and the Public Attorney. The statute establishing the Public Attorney should grant him discretionary jurisdiction in any situation where there is a reasonable basis to conclude that a conflict of interest exists. He should have exclusive jurisdiction over criminal cases referred to him by the Federal Elections Commission. As to cases where a jurisdictional dispute cannot be resolved, provision should be made for special judicial determination on an expedited basis. Deciding such jurisdictional disputes is well within the competence of the courts for the question would primarily be one of statutory interpretation.*

The present immunity statute would have to be amended to allow the independent prosecutor to grant use immunity without the consent of the Attorney General. The procedure by which the Public Attorney obtains immunity should be made similar to that applicable to congressional requests for immunity. The Attorney General would be informed of an immunity request, but he could only delay the immunity, not prevent it. Similarly, the Attorney General would inform the Public Attorney of his immunity decisions; the Public Attorney would have the power to delay, not prevent, immunity.

To guarantee true independence from the Executive Branch, the Public Attorney should be appointed for a fixed term (*e g.*, five years). He should be removable only by the appointing authority (described below) for gross improprieties. Because it is highly important that the Special

---

* When Dwayne Andreas attacked the jurisdiction of Special Prosecutor Cox to investigate a campaign violation that allegedly occurred during the 1968 election, the District Court in Minnesota promptly decided the jurisdictional issue in favor of the Special Prosecutor. See *United States v. Andreas*, 4-73-CR. 201 (D. Minn. 1973).

Prosecutor act solely in the interest of justice and not for personal benefit, he should be ineligible for appointment or election to federal office for a period of two years after his term expires or he resigns or is removed.

Crucial to the independence of the Public Attorney is the appointing authority. If the appointing authority is vested in the President or the Attorney General (who is responsible to the Preisdent), the appearance of political influence would remain even if the Public Attorney has such tenure. The argument in favor of Presidential appointment is that criminal prosecution is an executive function and there is a presumption of regularity respecting the exercise of Presidential power that should not be discarded because of the unique abuses of Watergate. But Watergate at least teaches that the abuse of power must be anticipated. The Committee's recommendation that responsibility for appointment of the Public Attorney should rest with the judicial rather than with the Executive would establish a check against future abuse of power.

The Constitution allows the vesting of the appointment power in others besides the Chief Executive. Article II, Section 2, Paragraph 2, Cl. 2, provides:

"... [T]he Congress may by Law vest the appointment of such inferior Officers, as they think proper, in the President alone, in the *Courts of Law,* or in the Heads of Departments." (emphasis added.)

The few cases interpreting this clause support a plan by which the Public Attorney is appointed by the courts of law.

The leading case is *Ex Parte Siebold,* 100 U.S. 371 (1879). Congress, pursuant to the Enforcement Acts of 1870 and 1871, vested the appointment of election supervisors in the circuit courts. The Supreme Court upheld the constitutionality of this appointment power, observing that there could be other appointments which Congress might want a court to make, such as a marshal. "The marshal is preeminently the officer of the courts . . ." *Id.* at 397. Apparently, the only limitation on the courts' appointment power is that the office involved must not be of "such incongruity [to the judicial function] as to excuse the courts from . . . performance [of the appointing function], or to render their acts void." *Id.* at 398. Since a prosecutor is more an officer of the court than a marshal or election supervisor, it is difficult to contend that the appointment of a Public Attorney is "incongruous" to the judicial function.

The District Court for the District of Columbia relied heavily on *Ex Parte Siebold* in upholding the constitutionality of a provision of the D.C. Code which required the members of the Board of Education to be appointed by the judges of that Court. *Hobson v. Hansen*, 265 F. Supp. 902 (D.D.C. 1967).* The Court read the congruity requirement of *Ex Parte Siebold* narrowly:

> "The limitation which is referred to in *Siebold* is not an affirmative requirement that the duty of the officer be related to the administration of justice. It is a negative requirement that the duty may not have 'such incongruity' with the judicial function as would void the power sought to be conferred." *Id.* at 913.

In short, given the clear congruity between the Public Attorney's tasks and the judicial function, it should be constitutional for the Congress to vest the appointment power in the judicial branch. *See also Rice v. Ames*, 180 U.S. 371 (1901) (Congress has power to authorize circuit courts to appoint commissioners to handle extradition matters); *Russell v. Thomas*, 21 Fed. Cases 12, 162 (1874) (Congress has power to authorize courts to appoint United States commissioners of insolvency); *Birch v. Steele*, 165 F. 577 (5th Cir. 1908) (Congress has power to authorize courts to appoint referees in bankruptcy).**

While it is thus constitutional to vest the appointment of a Public Attorney in the judicial branch, the question remains as to what part of the judicial branch should have this power. It would be a safer constitutional scheme if the appointing authority were in no way involved in hearing the cases to be prosecuted by the Public Attorney. If a district judge, for example, was directly responsible for appointing a Public Attorney to prosecute certain individuals before that same district judge, questions respecting an appearance of partiality and the lack of due process might be raised. In *Hobson v. Hansen*, 265 F. Supp. 902 (D.D.C. 1967), the Court recognized possible due process problems, but stated that the

> "official act of participating in the selection of Board Members does not in and of itself preclude on due process grounds the ability of the judge to decide fairly the merits of litigation challenging the validity of the performance by a Board Member of his duties as such.

* *Hobson* also relied on the plenary power of Congress to legislate for the District. Yet it seems clear that its statement on the reach of Article II, Section 2, Cl. 2, should be regarded as at least an alternative holding. See *Id.* at 911:
"[W]e could rest alone upon Article I, but Section 31-301 gains support also from Article II §2, Cl. 2, of the Constitution."
** It is of interest that in some states, *e.g.*, Connecticut, the courts generally appoint prosecutors. 51 Conn. Gen. Stats., Sec. 175. And federal courts have long appointed defense counsel for indigents.

170

If in a particular case such a challenge were made its soundness on due process grounds would depend on the circumstances bearing thereon and not on the mere fact that the judge had performed the duty reposed upon him by Congress in Section 31-101." 265 F. Supp. at 918.

The possible problems raised in *Hobson* were also discussed in *United States v. Solomon,* 216 F. Supp. 835 (S.D.N.Y. 1963). The *Solomon* court upheld the validity of 28 U.S.C. §506 (now 28 U.S.C. §546) which permitted the district court to appoint a United States Attorney when a vacancy occurs to serve until that vacancy is filled by the President. But the court emphasized that the judicial appointment was temporary, and thus stated that the "statutory scheme for the temporary appointment by the judiciary of the United States Attorney comports in all respects with due process of law." *Id.* at 843. The court was apparently concerned that, if it also had the power to remove the prosecutor it appointed, there might be a "nexus between Court and Prosecutor too close to comport with due process." Although the concerns expressed in *Solomon* were dictum, it would be the wiser course to avoid an appointment procedure which would involve active judges who might hear cases brought by a prosecutor they appointed and could remove.*

To avoid these constitutional problems and to create an Office of Public Attorney that is not only truly independent but also appears truly independent, the Congress should vest the appointment power as follows: The Chief Justice should be given the power and duty to select three retired circuit court judges who, in turn, would appoint the Public Attorney. After the Chief Justice makes the initial appointment of the three circuit court judges, the Chief Justice's responsibilities would be ended; the three retired circuit court judges—who would not sit on any cases either at trial or in an appellate capacity in which the Public Attorney's Office was involved—would make the actual appointment, which would be subject to confirmation by the Senate. The Public Attorney could be removed only by the three retired circuit court judges and only upon a finding of gross improprieties. At the end of the five year period, the Chief Justice would appoint (or reappoint) three retired circuit

* See also *Nader v. Bork,* C.A. 1954-73 (D.D.C. Nov. 14, 1973), where the court, in opposing Congressional proposals to have the courts appoint a special prosecutor for Watergate matters, stated in obvious dictum that the courts "must remain neutral. Their duties are not prosecutorial." (File Opinion at 10). We do not suggest that courts be given prosecutorial duties. As *Hobson v. Hansen,* 255 F. Supp. 902 (D.D.C. 1967) made clear, the appointing of an election supervisor is not the performance by the court of the functions of election supervisor. *Id.* at 913.

court judges and they, in turn, would choose a new Public Attorney, or reappoint the outgoing Public Attorney for one additional term only.*

Although Canon 5(g) of the Code of Judicial Conduct discourages extra-judicial appointments in controversial matters, it does permit assignments dealing with "the administration of justice." Thus, the acceptance of an appointment by a senior judge to a Public Attorney Supervisory Committee would be permissible under the canons. A senior judge accepting the appointment would not receive any additional salary because of such service.

II. THE COMMITTEE RECOMMENDS THAT, IN CONNECTION WITH ITS REVISION OF THE FEDERAL CRIMINAL CODE, CONGRESS SHOULD TREAT AS A SEPARATE FEDERAL OFFENSE, WITH SEPARATE PENALTIES, ANY FELONY DEFINED IN THE CODE (EXCEPT THOSE FELONIES THAT SPECIFICALLY RELATE TO FEDERAL ELECTIONS) THAT IS COMMITTED WITH THE PURPOSE OF INTERFERING WITH OR AFFECTING THE OUTCOME OF A FEDERAL ELECTION OR NOMINATING PROCESS.

The purpose of this proposal is primarily to establish as a separate federal crime the commission of certain traditional common law offenses such as burglary and larceny where these crimes are committed with the intent of interfering with or affecting a federal election or nominating process. To understand this proposal, it is necessary to comprehend the workings of the three main proposed revisions of the criminal code now before Congress—H.R. 10047 (the Brown Commission proposal), S. 1400 (the Administration's proposal) and S. 1 (the proposal of the staff of the Criminal Procedure Subcommittee of the Senate Judiciary Committee).

Each of these proposals would make certain traditional common law offenses, usually prosecutable only in the state courts, *federal* offenses in certain circumstances—*e.g.*, if the victim is a federal public servant or if the property that is the subject of the offense is federally owned. Each proposal defines the various common law crimes that will become federal crimes triable in federal courts in the proper circumstances. In each case the list is lengthy.

As noted, the proposal the Committee offers is to make various common law crimes federal offenses prosecutable in federal courts when the offenses are conducted with the intent to interfere with or affect a federal election. It would add another jurisdictional base for the federal courts to those

---

* Senior circuit judges, with salaries fixed for life, are, of course, totally independent from the other two branches of government.

already suggested by the existing revisions—*e.g.*, that the crime is against a federal employee. The proposal also establishes as a separate offense all other violations of federal criminal law (except those laws that specifically relate to federal elections) where the offense is committed with intent to interfere with or affect a federal election or nominating process.

The Committee feels that the amendment it proposes is needed. Under existing law, the DNC burglary and the break-in of Dr. Fielding's office could not be tried in a United States District Court under a burglary indictment. The Ellsberg break-in had to be prosecuted under the Civil Rights Act.

Adoption of the above proposal would not add redundancy to the criminal law. Rather, it would allow the prosecution of crimes in which there is a federal interest in federal courts. And it would allow the prosecutor to present an election related offense to the jury in proper perspective —that is, as an attempt to violate the integrity of a federal election or nominating process. Such a statute would carry appropriate penalties to indicate the gravity of corrupt interference with the federal electoral process (e.g., a fine up to $25,000 and/or imprisonment up to five years).

III. THE COMMITTEE RECOMMENDS THAT CONGRESS ENACT LEGISLATION MAKING IT UNLAWFUL FOR ANY EMPLOYEE IN THE EXECUTIVE OFFICE OF THE PRESIDENT, OR ASSIGNED TO THE WHITE HOUSE, DIRECTLY OR INDIRECTLY TO AUTHORIZE OR ENGAGE IN ANY INVESTIGATIVE OR INTELLIGENCE GATHERING ACTIVITY CONCERNING NATIONAL OR DOMESTIC SECURITY NOT AUTHORIZED BY CONGRESS.

The evidence received concerning the establishment, by direction of the President of a special investigative unit in the White House (the Plumbers) and the operations of the Plumbers illustrates the danger to individual rights presented by such a secret investigative activity.

By statute Congress has already established various professional investigative agencies to serve the Executive's legitimate investigative needs, *e.g.*, the CIA, the FBI, the Secret Service. These bodies are wisely restricted in their jurisdiction and authority by stringent statutory provisions and are answerable not only to the Executive but also to special oversight committees of Congress. Thus our free society is served, not controlled, by its police agencies. No President should be allowed to circumvent these agencies and erect a secret White House investigations operation such as the Plumbers not subject to statutory controls and Congressional oversight. If an agency charged with investigative efforts is deficient, the President should reform it, not create a substitute.

Under the proposed recommendation it would be a criminal offense for anyone in the White House or the Executive Office of the President to perform investigative or police functions relating to internal or national security matters, unless existing statutory law already authorizes such functions (as with the Secret Service). Similarly, it would be illegal for anyone in the Executive Office of the President or on the White House staff to employ any person to conduct such functions.*

IV. THE COMMITTEE RECOMMENDS THAT THE APPROPRIATE CONGRESSIONAL OVERSIGHT COMMITTEES SHOULD MORE CLOSELY SUPERVISE THE OPERATIONS AND INTERNAL REGULATIONS OF THE INTELLIGENCE AND LAW ENFORCEMENT "COMMUNITY". IN PARTICULAR, THESE COMMITTEES SHOULD CONTINUALLY EXAMINE THE RELATIONS BETWEEN FEDERAL LAW ENFORCEMENT AND INTELLIGENCE AGENCIES AND THE WHITE HOUSE, AND PROMPTLY DETERMINE IF ANY REVISION OF LAW IS NECESSARY RELATING TO THE JURISDICTION OR ACTIVITIES OF THESE AGENCIES.

From its beginning, the Central Intelligence Agency has been prohibited from performing police and internal security functions within the United States. Thus, 50 U.S.C. §403(d)(3) explicitly provides:

> "That the Agency shall have no police, subpoena, law enforcement powers, or internal-security functions . . ."

Notwithstanding this clear and long-standing prohibition, the Select Committee found that the White House sought and achieved CIA aid for the Plumbers and unsuccessfully sought to involve the CIA in the Watergate cover-up. These efforts on the part of the White House underline the need for constant and vigorous Congressional oversight. Committees charged with responsibility for the CIA should consider the need for hearings to determine if more explicit statutory language would be useful to restrain the CIA to its legitimate sphere of operation.

As for law enforcement agencies, testimony of the former Acting Director of the Federal Bureau of Investigation, Patrick Gray, as well as evidence received by the Committee

---

* This proposal would not restrain otherwise lawful investigations carried out for political purposes—e.g., to discover the foibles of one's political opponents.

of efforts by the White House to interfere with the IRS, indicate that similar oversight functions should be strengthened with regard to the FBI, the IRS and similar agencies.

V. THE COMMITTEE RECOMMENDS THAT CONGRESS AMEND:

(1) THE FALSE DECLARATION PROHIBITION OF 18 U.S.C. §1623 TO MAKE IT EQUALLY APPLICABLE TO CONGRESSIONAL PROCEEDINGS UNDER OATH.

(2) SECTION 1621 OF TITLE 18 TO PROVIDE THAT, ONCE THE OATH HAS BEEN PROPERLY ADMINISTERED BY A CONGRESSMAN IN A PUBLIC OR PRIVATE CONGRESSIONAL HEARING, IT IS NOT A DEFENSE TO A PERJURY CHARGE THAT SUBSEQUENTLY A QUORUM WAS ABSENT OR NO CONGRESSMAN WAS PRESENT WHEN THE ALLEGED PERJURIOUS STATEMENT WAS MADE.

(1) The false declaration prohibition of 18 U.S.C. §1623 (c) in effect provides that, to sustain a perjury conviction regarding statements made under oath to a court or grand jury, or in a civil deposition, the government must only show that two statements made under oath in any of these forums, are inconsistent.* This provision should be made equally applicable to Congressional proceedings under oath. There is no policy justification for granting proceedings in other forums a greater protection from perjury than given Congressional investigations.

(2) Under section 1621 of Title 18, as interpreted by the courts, it appears that conviction for perjury before a Congressional body will not lie in the absence of a quorum when the offending statement was made. *See Christoffel v. United States*, 338 U.S. 84 (1949) which concerned a House subcommittee and the analogous District of Columbia perjury statute, D.C. Code §22-2501. The Select Committee has found it necessary to conduct numerous executive sessions under oath where a Senator was not present for the entire hearing.

* An indictment or information for violation of this section alleging that, in any proceedings before or ancillary to any court or grand jury of the United States, the defendant under oath has knowingly made two or more declarations, which are inconsistent to the degree that one of them is necessarily false, need not specify which declaration is false if—(1) each declaration was material to the point in question, and (2) each declaration was made within the period of the statute of limitations for the offense charged under this section. In any prosecution under this section, the falsity of a declaration set forth in the indictment or information shall be established sufficient for conviction by proof that the defendant while under oath made irreconcilably contradictory declarations material to the point in question in any proceeding before or ancillary to any court or grand jury. It shall be a defense to an indictment or information made pursuant to the first sentence of this subsection that the defendant at the time he made each declaration believed the declaration was true.

To require a Senator or Congressman to be present at all times during executive sessions would stifle vigorous, far reaching investigations because there is simply not enough Congressional time available.

Section 1621 of Title 18 should thus be amended to provide that, in regard to a perjury charge relating to Congressional testimony under oath, it is not a defense that there was no quorum * or no Congressman present when the perjurious statement was made. Since the witness has been placed under oath, he is on fair notice that his testimony must be truthful. A civil litigant can depose a witness, under penalty of perjury, without a judge present and the law should not re quire that, in order to sustain a perjury charge regarding Congressional testimony, a Congressman be present. The fact that a Congressman is required to place a witness under oath should provide ample protection against possible harassment by staff investigators. *See* 2 U.S.C. §191 ("Oath to Witnesses").**

The present recommendation is not intended to require a witness to answer questions when a quorum of the Congressional committee is not present. It relates only to a witness who has been sworn when a quorum is present, and who chooses to respond to questions in the absence of a quorum.

VI. THE COMMITTEE RECOMMENDS THAT THE CONGRESS REFRAIN FROM ADOPTING PROPOSED REVISIONS OF TITLE 18 WHICH WOULD UNJUSTIFIABLY BROADEN THE PRESENT DEFENSES TO CRIMINAL CHARGES OF OFFICIAL MISTAKE OF LAW AND EXECUTION OF PUBLIC DUTY. THE COMMITTEE SUPPORTS THE PREDOMINANT RULE OF LAW ADOPTED IN THE AMERICAN LAW INSTITUTE'S MODEL PENAL CODE, THAT ANY RELIANCE ON A MISTAKE OF LAW OR SUPERIOR ORDERS MUST BE OBJECTIVELY REASONABLE TO CONSTITUTE A VALID DEFENSE.

There are several proposals before the Congress—H.R. 10047 (§§521 and 532) and S. 1 (§§303 and 1-306(b))—which would expand the present common law defense of official mistake of law and execution of public duty. Under

---

* Present Select Committee rules provide that a quorum for the purposes of taking testimony and receiving evidence is one Senator. Rule 5, Select Committee Rules of Procedure.

** If the hearing is recessed to another date, a Congressman's further presence would not be required since the witness will already be sworn, but the witness cannot be required to attend a recessed session unless the Committee issues a new subpoena. Moreover, normally a witness will not be held in contempt for failure to answer a question unless the full House of Congress votes to initiate the statutory contempt procedure found in 2 U.S.C. §194.

existing law, a public official, who can show that conduct taken in the course of his duties resulted from an *objectively reasonable* mistake of law or reliance upon superior orders, has a valid defense to a criminal charge relating to that conduct. *See Perkins on Criminal Law* (2 ed. 1969), pp. 921-2. The proposed drafts would apparently erect as a defense to a criminal charge a *subjective, good faith reliance* by a public official on an official grant of permission or interpretation of the law. Under the proposals, it appears that the defense would still lie even if the official grant of permission or interpretations of the law were oral and secret. These proposed revisions were drafted before the Select Committee's hearings, which presented substantial relevant evidence bearing on this question.

The Select Committee rejects the broadening of this defense incorporated in the proposals now before the Congress. The Committee recognizes that the proposed revisions are based on extensive studies of the present criminal law that range far beyond the scope of the Committee's own investigation. However, based on its experience, the Committee believes that the present law, as reflectd in the American Law Institute's Model Penal Code, is adequate to meet all legitimate claims of official mistake of law or public duty and should not be expanded.

VII. THE COMMITTEE RECOMMENDS THAT THE APPROPRIATE COMMITTEES OF CONGRESS STUDY AND RECONSIDER TITLE III OF THE OMNIBUS CRIME AND SAFE STREETS ACT OF 1968 FOR THE PURPOSE OF DETERMINING WHETHER THE ELECTRONIC SURVEILLANCE PROVISIONS CONTAINED IN THAT ACT REQUIRE REVISION OR AMENDMENT.

The Committee's investigation has revealed incidents of unlawful violations of privacy through electronic surveillance, some of which may have been committed directly or indirectly under federal branch auspices in whose trust Congress placed the protection of privacy under the provisions of Title III of the Safe Streets Act of 1968. The restrictions contained in that Act have proved to be inadequate to protect individuals against unjustified invasions of privacy. A thorough reevaluation of this legislation, including a factual investigation of federal wiretapping practices is necessary.

Under the 1968 Act a special Commission was to be appointed by the President five years after the effective date of the Act. The President has appointed this Commission for the purpose of evaluating the strengths and deficiencies of this legislation. However, the Committee believes that in light of the facts revealed in its investigation of a scandal in the executive branch unforeseen by the Congress when it enacted the 1968 Act, it is essential that the appropriate committees of Congress make their own investigations and evaluations of the experience under the new federal electronic eavesdropping law. It appears to be inappropriate to rely solely on a Presidential Commission which must report to the same administration under which such violations of privacy took place.

An important issue for consideration is whether national security electronic surveillance should require prior court approval. Both the Supreme Court and the Congress have left this matter unresolved. In *United States v. U. S. District Court,* 407 U.S. 297 (1972), the Court firmly rejected the Government's claim that warrantless electronic searches in domestic security cases were a reasonable exercise of Presidential power. Justice Lewis Powell's opinion for a unanimous Supreme Court concluded that "prior judicial approval is required" for domestic security surveillance. The issue arose in a case in which the Attorney General had authorized wiretaps "to gather intelligence information deemed necessary to protect the nation from attempts of domestic organizations to attack and subvert the existing structure of the Government."

The Court said that although the Fourth Amendment's requirement of a warrant before a search is not absolute, the prior judgment of an independent magistrate is the norm. "Fourth Amendment freedoms cannot be properly guaranteed if domestic security surveillances may be conducted solely within the discretion of the executive branch." Although Justice Powell carefully limited his opinion to "the domestic aspects of national security" and expressed no opinion on "the issues which may be involved with respect to activities of foreign powers or their agents," he did state (with respect to the issue of domestic security): "Nor do we believe prior judicial approval will fracture the secrecy essential to official intelligence gathering. . . . *Judges may be counted upon to be especially conscious of security requirements in national security cases.*" (emphasis added). (*But see, Laird v. Tatum,* 408 U.S. 1 (1972), in which the Supreme Court, 5-4, failed to find a "justiciable" controversy so as to permit a decision on merits of the Army's surveillance of civilian political activity.)

From the fact that the Court left unanswered the question of whether warrants are necessary with respect to foreign intelligence and in light of *Laird v. Tatum,* it is clear that Congress should address itself to the question of whether prior judicial approval should be required for *all* wiretaps and other electronic surveillance, as well as other examples of surveillance. The Select Committee so recommends. In the wiretap case, *supra,* Justice Powell suggested that "Congress may wish to consider protective standards (for foreign intelligence wiretaps) which differ from those already prescribed for specified crimes in Title III (of the 1968 Crime Control Act). Different standards may be compatible with the Fourth Amendment if they are reasonable both in relation to the legitimate need of Government for intelligence information and the protected rights of our citizens."

The Supreme Court has not ruled on the issue of foreign intelligence not involving American citizens. At least two courts of appeals, however, have held that such surveillance does not violate the Fourth Amendment. See *United States v. Brown*, 484 F.2d 418 (5th Cir. 1973); *United States v. Dellinger*, 472 F.2d 340 (7th Cir. 1972). There is no reason to prohibit the Executive from conducting such surveillance but when it is done within the United States, it is preferable that a warrant be obtained prior to the wiretap. Congress should take cognizance of Justice Powell's invitation in the wiretap case and address itself to the question.

Legislation should establish procedures permitting the courts under designated standards to authorize surveillance of foreign powers. The basic standard that could be employed is whether there is reason to believe that information of importance to the nation's security would be obtained.

To obviate possible disclosure of such activities, Congress could establish special procedures to be followed. This could be done easily and effectively by a provision that all such warrants be issued by a single judge—perhaps the Chief Judge of the United States district courts in the District of Columbia. Staff work could be performed by the Department of Justice, so that only the judge himself need see the material and the warrant. And special procedures should be established to protect the rights of American citizens who might be overheard. *In net, the need is for prior judicial approval under guidelines that will protect national security.*

There is no constitutional barrier to such legislation. The ultimate power under the Constitution is that of Congress; see *Youngstown Sheet & Tube Co. v. Sawyer*, 343 U.S. 579 (1952). As Justice White said in his concurring opinion in the wiretap case, "the United States does not claim that Congress is powerless to require warrants for surveillance which the President otherwise would not be barred by the Fourth Amendment from undertaking without a warrant." The wiretap case is a direct holding by the Supreme Court that Congress can limit the Executive's power to tap without a warrant. In a footnote to Justice White's opinion, he indicates that the Justice Department, speaking through Assistant Attorney General Robert Mardian, accepted the view that Congress did have the power.

CHAPTER II

CAMPAIGN PRACTICES

Introduction

The campaign to re-elect President Nixon in 1972 was expensive, intense and long. It began in late March 1969, soon after the President's inauguration, when John Ehrlichman, Counsel to the President, hired Jack Caulfield to gather political intelligence and derogatory information on individuals considered to be unfriendly to the new administration. Caulfield and Ehrlichman interviewed a former New York City policeman, Anthony T. Ulasewicz, in late May 1969 and hired him to conduct investigations. Ulasewicz was paid secretly by Herbert Kalmbach, the President's personal attorney, from an unused reserve of 1968 Nixon campaign funds. The establishment of an offensive intelligence-gathering capability in the White House occurred, then, before many members of the administration had even moved into their Washington offices. Other intelligence-gathering capabilities later initiated included the Plumbers, the efforts of Colson and Hunt, the activities of Donald Segretti and others, and the Gemstone conspiracy.

In the Caulfield-Ulasewicz operation, as in several other examples of campaign practices investigated by the Select Committee, serious questions are raised as to what the President knew, approved or condoned and what his ethical and legal responsibilities should be for the campaign conduct of his subordinates.

This report focuses on the presidential campaign practices that raise substantial questions of legality, propriety, or ethics and that may, in the words of S. Res. 60, ". . . indicate the necessity or desirability . . . of new congressional legislation to safeguard the electoral process by which the President of the United States is chosen." [Sec. 1 (a)]

The report is not an exhaustive compendium of every campaign practice investigated by the Select Committee. Rather, it is a selection of those incidents that raise particularly serious questions of campaign propriety and ethics that, consequently, frame most clearly questions about the advantages and disadvantages of remedial legislation.

Running through the various topics raised below are several themes that merit serious discussion by Congress, for they raise fundamental questions about how our system of free elections should be run. First, the 1972 Presidential campaign was replete with abuses of positions, power, and prerogatives, particularly by White House personnel. The political advantages held by an incumbent President are immense, and they were constantly used and abused by this administration. A corollary to the abuse of Presidential incumbency for political gain is the considerable extent to which objectionable campaign practices were conceived, encouraged, and controlled by high-level Presidential aides. This was true from the early days of the first term, when there was no campaign organization, and it continued to be so through the 1972 election.

Another important theme is the misuse of large amounts of money, especially difficult-to-trace cash that was held in secret places in the White House and elsewhere. The problem with cash in political campaigns is not, of course, unique to the campaign practices facet of the Select Committee's investigation; cash contributions and funds played key roles in virtually all aspects of the 1972 Presidential election. The misuse of cash in various campaign practices, as in other areas, demonstrates the need for strict regulation of its use in political campaigns.

Another recurring theme was the search for intelligence information on political opponents which was initiated with the hiring of Caulfield and Ulasewicz. This intelligence-gathering is central to the first part of this report: White House-inspired political activities, 1968-71. In addition to Caulfield and Ulasewicz, this part summarizes the campaign activities of E. Howard Hunt, the Plumbers and the various improper uses and attempted uses of federal agencies by White House staff members. For example, evidence shows that the White House attempted to use the Internal Revenue Service to harass persons perceived as political "enemies".

In addition, some of the public relations efforts which were initiated in the White House led to practices which were deceptive and misleading to the public.

The White House also attempted to mislead and deceive the press on numerous occasions. While legislation in this area is inadvisable, examples of White House attempts to mislead the press were quite frequent during the last month of the 1972 campaign and help to explain the attitude within the White House and some of the tactics employed to re-elect Mr. Nixon.

With the above areas as background, the second half of the report outlines what happened in the campaign itself, beginning with the strategy of the campaign to re-elect President Nixon. A basic theme of this strategy was to attack Democratic opponents and prospective opponents frequently during the primaries.

Such an "attack strategy" was a key ingredient in the 1972 Nixon campaign. Although many people contributed to this strategy, its broad outlines were best explained by White House speechwriter Patrick Buchanan, whose memoranda are summarized below in this report.

The strategy, though not improper in itself, was ultimately converted by others into gross abuses and unethical manipulations of the electoral process by persons who had little political experience, and by persons, including some with considerable political experience, who had little respect for fair play in elections. The activities of Segretti and others— and of their superiors in the White House and at the Committee to Re-Elect the President—are detailed below in this report. Their activities consisted primarily of surreptitious information-gathering and disruption of Democratic campaigns.

Finally, the report discusses allegations of unfair campaign practices directed at the President. The staff did uncover some instances of improper activity directed at President Nixon's re-election campaign. The results of these investigations, however, show no pattern of illegal, improper or unethical activities carried out or condoned by any Democratic aspirant or Democratic campaign organization.

1. WHITE HOUSE-INSPIRED POLITICAL ACTIVITIES, 1968–71

A. Caulfield and Ulasewicz

From the time Richard Nixon was inaugurated President in January 1969, the White House exhibited a strong desire for political intelligence that helped lead to the events in the campaign of 1972 which have been under investigation by the Select Committee.

Shortly after President Nixon entered the White House on January 21, 1969, the decision was made in the White House to establish an in-house investigative capability that could be used by the President's staff for obtaining sensitive political information. Jack Caulfield was chosen to perform this function. Following a distinguished career in the New York City Police Department, Caulfield was hired in May of 1968 by H. R. Haldeman to "serve in the security area," [1] during the 1968 campaign. Caulfield was responsible for securing staff

1. John J. Caulfield testimony, Select Committee Hearings, Book 1, p. 250. (May 22, 1973)

quarters and working areas of the Nixon traveling campaign in 1968.

Following the election, Caulfield was interviewed and subsequently turned down by John Mitchell for the position of Chief United States Marshall.[2] Subsequently in late March 1969, Caulfield met with John Ehrlichman, at his White House office, and Erhlichman asked if Caulfield were interested in setting up a private security entity in Washington, D.C. to provide investigative support for the White House.[3] The next day Caulfield called Ehrlichman with a counter proposal that he join the White House staff under Ehrlichman and, "besides providing liaison functions with the various law enforcement agencies, thereby be available to process any investigative requests from the White House."[4] Ehrlichman agreed, and Caulfield was placed on the White House payroll.

Caulfield told Ehrlichman that he intended to use the services of Anthony Ulasewicz, a detective with the New York City Police Department who was nearing retirement. Ehrlichman wanted to meet Ulasewicz, and so in May 1969, Ulasewicz was interviewed by Ehrlichman and Caulfield in the VIP lounge at the American Airlines Terminal of New York's La Guardia Airport. Ehrlichman explained to Ulasewicz that he wanted discreet investigations done on certain political figures.[5] During their brief conversation, Ehrlichman agreed to a one year contract for Ulasewicz at $22,000 a year plus expenses, and Ulasewicz explained that he wanted to report to only one individual and to make no written reports of any kind.

Following the meeting, Ehrlichman told Herbert Kalmbach, the President's personal attorney, to make arrangements to put Ulasewicz on the payroll. Ulasewicz was paid with surplus funds from the 1968 campaign which were held in trustee accounts by Kalmbach.

At eight o'clock A.M., Sunday, June 29, 1969, Herbert Kalmbach met Jack Caulfield and Tony Ulasewicz at the Madison Hotel in Washington, D.C. Ulasewicz told Kalmbach he would use the alias Edward T. Stanley in his work,[6] and Kalmbach agreed to send salary and expense checks to Ulasewicz's home twice a month. Samples of checks used to pay Ulasewicz are attached to this report.[7] During the next three years, Kalmbach paid more than $130,000 for the

2. *Ibid.*, p. 251.
3. *Ibid.*
4. *Ibid.*
5. See Ulasewicz interview. pp. 2-3.
6. See Kalmbach diary, 6/29/69.
7. See exhibit 000.

Caulfield-Ulasewicz operation.[8]

Ulasewicz's complete travel records are available in the files of the Committee, and a summary chronology of Ulasewicz travels is appended to this report.[9] Ulasewicz received all investigative assignments from Caulfield orally whom he contacted discreetly by calling under the pseudonym of Mr. Stanley so that no one at the White House would know his true identity.

On July 8, 1969, Ulasewicz spoke with Kalmbach by telephone and agreed to use his own American Express card for air travel and other necessary expenses. Kalmbach directed Ulasewicz to apply for a second American Express card in the name of Edward T. Stanley, and Kalmbach agreed to guarantee payment on that account. Kalmbach also agreed to obtain telephone credit cards for Ulasewicz in his real name and in the name of Edward T. Stanley,[10] thus allowing Ulasewicz to maintain his secrecy during the course of his upcoming investigations and inquiries.

At about 1:00 A.M. on Saturday, July 19, 1969, Senator Edward Kennedy was involved in an automobile accident at Chappaquiddick, Massachusetts. Later that morning, as news reports of the accident reached the public, Caulfield was directed by Ehrlichman to send Ulasewicz to the scene of the accident as soon as possible. Ulasewicz flew to Boston on the Eastern Airlines shuttle on July 19, 1969 and rented a car for the trip to Martha's Vineyard and Chappaquiddick. Ulasewicz spent four days in the area on this first visit and reported back continually to Jack Caulfield in the White House, who passed the information on to Ehrlichman and others as it was developed. Ulasewicz spent a good portion of the remaining summer and much of the fall of 1969 at Chappaquiddick, trying to dig up politically valuable information from Senator Kennedy's accident.

Caulfield also gave Ulasewicz a variety of other assignments after the summer of 1969. During the next three years, Ulasewicz travelled to 23 states gathering information on assignments from Caulfield. In 1969 and 1970, Caulfield stated that he got his directions from Ehrlichman and sometimes from other high-ranking White House officials, such as H. R. Haldeman, Lyn Nofziger, and occasionally Charles Colson.

While Ulasewicz's investigations covered a variety of politi-

8. Compiled by the Committee from subpoenaed records.
9. This chronology was based on the credit records and travel records. See Exhibit 000.
10. See memo of July 8, 1969, to file, of Herbert W. Kalmbach attached as Exhibit 000.

cal opponents of the Administration and potential threats to the President's re-election in 1972, much of his attention focused on Senator Kennedy, Senator Muskie, Larry O'Brien and columnist Jack Anderson. A list of the investigations and background checks conducted by Anthony Ulasewicz at the direction of Jack Caulfield is attached to this report.[11]

After Senator Muskie became the leading Democratic contender immediately following the 1970 Congressional elections, many of Ulasewicz's investigations were directed toward discovering valuable political information on Senator Muskie.[12]

Ulasewicz usually worked alone on the assignments he was given by Caulfield. However, in December 1971, Anthony LaRocco, a former New York City police detective was hired to assist Ulasewicz.[13]

La Rocco assisted Ulasewicz in four or five investigations in New York City from December 1971 until the third week in January 1972, when Ulasewicz informed La Rocco that the operation was terminated. La Rocco received a total of about $1500 for his work on behalf of the White House.[14]

ELECTRONIC SURVEILLANCE

There has been no evidence presented to the Senate Select Committee which indicates that either Ulasewicz or LaRocco engaged in any electronic surveillance in their assignments for the White House. However, Jack Caulfield was involved twice in the implementation and monitoring of electronic surveillance.

The first occasion was in June 1969 when Ehrlichman called Caulfield into his office and said that there was an urgent need for a national security wiretap on the telephone of columnist Joseph Kraft.[15] Caulfield said that Ehrlichman told him that he did not want to go through the FBI, since it was a sieve. Ehrlichman pressed Caulfield to place the tap on as soon as possible. Ehrlichman testified that he was sure that he discussed that tap with President Nixon.[16]

Caulfield contacted Jack Ragan, a former FBI agent and

11. See Exhibit 000. This list was compiled from interviews with Ulasewicz, Caulfield, John Dean and Tony LaRocco.
12. These investigations are listed at numbers 57 through 61 of Exhibit 000.
13. Interview with LaRocco, Sept. 21, 1973, p. 1.
14. Ibid.
15. Caulfield Ex. Session, March 16, 1974, p. 2. At the time of this wiretap, neither the Supreme Court nor any Act of Congress prohibits national security wiretaps without prior judicial authorization.
16. 6 Hearings 2535.

friend from the 1968 campaign for whom Caulfield had found a job at the Republican National Committee in 1969. Caulfield told Ragan he had a directive from Ehrlichman to place a wiretap on Kraft's phone because of a matter involving "high priority national security." [17] Ragan and Caulfield drove to Kraft's residence and concluded from observation of the neighborhood and the location of the telephone lines that it would be a very difficult tap to install. Caulfield went back to Ehrlichman and explained the serious problems they would encounter in attempting to install the tap. Caulfield testified that Ehrlichman told him that the tap had to be installed. [18]

Ragan told Caulfield he could not implement the wiretap unless he had the pairs and cable numbers of the telephone lines in the Kraft home. Caulfield agreed to obtain the information and did so by requesting it from a friend of his in the Secret Service. [19] Caulfield explained to the individual in the Secret Service that he needed the information as a matter of national security. The information was obtained for Caulfield who in turn gave it to Ragan. [20]

Ragan also asked Caulfield about acquiring appropriate credentials from the telephone company to protect himself while implementing the wiretap and to insure the discretion of the assignment. Caulfield discussed the problem with Ehrlichman, who arranged for Caulfield to speak with John Davies of the White House staff. [21]

Caulfield told Davies he needed a telephone installer's card for a job concerning a "national security matter" he had been given by Ehrlichman. [22] Caulfield had the impression that Ehrlichman and Davies had already talked about the matter. Davies did provide a telephone installer's card to Caulfield, who in turn passed the card on to Ragan.

About a week or ten days after he made his initial request to Caulfield to implement the wiretap, Ehrlichman called Caulfield and directed him to desist from implementing the wiretap because J. Edgar Hoover would take care of it. Ehrlichman testified that the wiretap in 1969 "never happened." [23] Caulfield then called Ragan to direct him not to implement the tap, but Ragan told him, "it's done." [24] Apparently Ragan and an unidentified friend of his from New

17. Caulfield Ex. Session, March 16, 1974, p. 24.
18. *Ibid.*, p. 7.
19. *Ibid.*, p. 9. Name to be submitted to Senator Ervin.
20. *Ibid.*, p. 13.
21. *Ibid.*
22. *Ibid.*, p. 14.
23. *Hearings* 2535.
24. Caulfield interview, Sept. 11, 1973, p. 3.

York had already come to Washington and installed a listening device on a telephone pole in the rear of Kraft's residence.[25] Caulfield met with Ragan at the Congressional Hotel and told him he had been directed by Ehrlichman not to place the wiretap. Ragan explained to Caulfield how he and his friend had placed the tap and gave Caulfield a tape which allegedly contained some conversation from Kraft's telephone.[26] Ragan told Caulfield that Kraft's voice was not on the tape and that the overheard conversation may have involved a maid.

Caulfield testified that he took the tape from Ragan to his office, where he ran out about 40 or 50 feet of it and destroyed it by placing it in his "burn bag." Caulfield kept the remaining tape in his office for about a month or two and then destroyed it and the reel itself by placing them in the burn bag in the White House.[27] Caulfield claimed that neither he nor Ehrlichman, nor anyone else ever listened to the tape that Ragan gave him. Ragan was paid no money for his work in placing the wiretap.[28]

Ragan, Ulasewicz, and Caulfield continued to be social friends after this incident in 1969, lunching together on numerous occasions when Ragan came to Washington. During 1969 and 1970, Ragan gave approximately eight checks to Caulfield totaling about $800. While Caulfield has no recollection of the purpose of these payments, Ragan said they were to obtain information from police departments.[29]

Finally, there is no evidence at the present which indicates that Caulfield had Ragan conduct any other electronic surveillance. Ragan did, on occasion, ask Ulasewicz if he were interested in performing jobs for Ragan, but no actual work assignments developed from these suggestions.[30]

The second occasion when Caulfield was involved in electronic surveillance came in the fall of 1970 when Ehrlichman requested Caulfield to monitor the results of the Secret Service wiretap of F. Donald Nixon. Caulfield monitored the tap for about three weeks before the project was terminated.[31] Ehrlichman refused to discuss the wiretap with the Select Committee, citing national security privilege.[32] The Secret Service at the direction of the White House counsel, would not allow agents involved to testify about the matter, claim-

25. Caulfield Ex. Session, March 16, 1974, p. 25.
26. *Ibid.*
27. *Ibid.*
28. *Ibid.*, p. 26.
29. See Ragan interview.
30. *Ibid.*, p. 29.
31. *Ibid.*, p. 31.
32. Ehrlichman interview, Jan. 10, 1974, p. 9.

ing that it fell within the "protective function" of the Secret Service and therefore was privileged.

OPERATION SANDWEDGE

As early as late 1970-early 1971, Jack Caulfield began thinking about establishing a private security organization when he left the White House. In the winter and early spring of 1971, Caulfield recalled having frequent discussions about the idea with Myles Ambrose, then Commissioner of Customs.[33] Ambrose had discussed the idea of private security business with Mike Acree, then Assistant Commissioner of the IRS. Sometime in late 1970 or early 1971, Ambrose introduced Acree to Caulfield.[34]

Caulfield told Acree that Ambrose and Caulfield were planning to open a private security firm in Washington, D.C. Acree had friends at Intertel, a private security firm in Washington, and thought that such a business might be a good means of retiring from federal service. Acree said that at no time in these early discussions did Caulfield mention anything about a "covert operation." Caulfield told Acree that Ambrose wanted to head the new organization, but that Caulfield was slowly trying to move him out of the picture.[35]

Sometime in the spring of 1971, Caulfield told John Dean he was thinking about leaving the White House staff to establish an investigative and security consulting corporation. Caulfield explained to Dean that the proposed firm could be operational by campaign time and could provide important help to the re-election campaign and to the Republican National Committee. Caulfield's basic idea was that the security firm would provide services for large corporations and that, with large fees from them, it would be able to provide free services to the 1972 re-election campaign. Dean advised Caulfield to secure the advice of an attorney because such a plan was filled with legal problems.[36]

In the meantime, Caulfield discussed his proposal seriously with Joe Woods, Mike Acree, Roger Barth, and Tony Ulasewicz. Joe Woods, the brother of Rose Mary Woods, was a friend of Caulfield's from the 1968 campaign whom Caulfield envisioned as the vice president of the new corporation who would head up the Chicago office.

33. Caulfield Executive Session, March 23, 1974, p. 7.
34. Acree interview, August 1, 1973. Acree subsequently recalled his first meeting with Caulfield occurring on March 8, 1971, at the E.O.B. (See Acree letter, June 27, 1974.)
35. *Ibid.*, p. 2.
36. Vol. 3, p. 924.

Caulfield also says he discussed the proposal with Rose Mary Woods. He explained to her that he was interested in establishing a security entity and that, if he could get funding, he would be offering a principal position to her brother.[37] Miss Woods only recalled that Caulfield came to her and explained that he wanted to set up "sort of a PR" operation with her brother based in the mid-west. She testified she was opposed to the idea because she felt her brother was more qualified to head such a corporation than was Caulfield.[38] Caulfield testified that Miss Woods had general knowledge that he could obtain information of a political nature, but that he never discussed specific details of Ulasewicz's operations with her. Caulfield said he requested Miss Woods' assistance in locating Donald A. Nixon on one occasion for Tony Ulasewicz.[39]

Miss Woods testified that she had no knowledge that Caulfield had an independent investigative capability in the White House.[40]

Caulfield also talked with Ulasewicz about forming a private security business. Ulasewicz's assignments had declined as 1971 progressed, and Caulfield had often talked with Ulasewicz about entering private business when Caulfield left the government. Caulfield envisioned Ulasewicz as head of the New York office of the new corporation, with primary responsibilities for offensive intelligence-gathering. Ulasewicz subsequently rented an apartment at 321 East 48th Street (Apartment 11-C), New York City, that could be used as an office for the private detective agency.[41]

In the late summer of 1971, Caulfield met with Acree, Barth, and Joe Woods for about two hours at his home to discuss the proposal.[42]

Following the meeting, Caulfield told Dean of the group's plans, and Dean asked Caulfield to committ the proposal to writing. Caulfield then drafted the memorandum entitled Operation "Sandwedge".[43] The document called for an of-

37. *Ibid.*
38. Rose Mary Woods Executive Session, March 22, 1974, p. 116.
39. Caulfield Executive Session, March 23, 1974, p. 17.
40. Rose Mary Woods Executive Session, March 22, 1974, p. 114.
41. See Exhibit 000. The apartment was also the place for a meeting on January 10, 1972, among Caulfield, Ulasewicz, and Gordon Liddy when Liddy checked up on Ulasewicz' financial records. (Caulfield interview, September 12, 1973, p. 5.)
42. Woods, Barth, and Acree say that the meeting occurred at Caulfield's home. Caulfield testified that the meeting occurred at the Fairfax Country Club in Virginia. (Caulfield Executive Session, March 23, 1974, p. 23.)
43. See copy of the document at Exhibit 000. Caulfield recalls that the proposal was actually drafted in June of 1971. Since there is no evidence that the proposal was circulated at the meeting at Caulfield's home in mid-summer, Caulfield probably didn't actually write it until later in the summer.

fensive intelligence gathering operation which would be clandestinely based in New York and would be able to in-infiltrate campaign organizations and headquarters with "undercover personnel." [44] The offensive capability would also include a "Black bag" capability, "surveillance of Democratic primaries, convention, meetings, etc.," and "derogatory information investigative capability, world-wide." [45]

In addition, the memorandum outlined an operating cover for the entity. The new corporation would hire itself out to large Republican corporations, whose fees would finance the clandestine and offensive capability envisioned in the memorandum. Caulfield emphasized the clandestine nature of the operation:

"The offensive involvement outlined above would be supported, *supervised* and programmed by the principals, but *completely disassociated* (separate foolproof financing) from the corporate structure and located in New York in extreme clandestine fashion." [46]

Caulfield noted in the memorandum that Ulasewicz would head the clandestine operation in New York, claiming that "his expertise in this area was considered the model for police departments throughout the nation and the results certainly proved it." [47] Woods would be in charge of the midwestern office of the new corporation, heading covert efforts and acting as liaison to retired FBI agents "for discreet investigative support" from the FBI. Mike Acree would provide "IRS information input" and other financial investigations that would help support the New York City operation. [48]

In testimony before the Select Committee, Caulfield claimed that "black bag capability" meant:

". . . the carrying of monies that might be collected in a political campaign. What I meant to propose by that was that Mr. Ulasewicz and anyone else that might be connected with such a proposed undertaking would have the capability to supervise the security of the carrying of monies which might be collected during the course of a campaign." [49]

44. *Ibid.*
45. *Ibid.*
46. *Ibid.*, p. 6.
47. *Ibid.*, p. 7.
48. *Ibid.*, p. 9. Caulfield also testified that he showed the Operation Sandwedge memo to Acree (Caulfield Executive Session, March 16, 1974, pp. 24-25). However, Acree denied that he saw a draft or copy of the Sandwedge memo. (Acree letter, June 27, 1974, p. 6.)
49. Caulfield Executive Session, March 16, 1974, p. 98.

However, earlier in his memorandum, on page two, Caulfield discussed a former FBI agent who was known as a "black bag" specialist while at the FBI. Caulfield acknowledged that the term "black bag specialist," means an individual who specialized in breaking and entering for the purpose of placing electronic surveillance.[50] In addition, Caulfield noted that the term "bag job" in the intelligence community meant a burglary for the placement of electronic surveillance.[51] Thus it appears that the capability to which Caulfield was referring in his "Sandwedge Proposal" was one of surreptitious breaking and entering for the purpose of placing electronic surveillance, quite similar in nature to the Gemstone Operation which ultimately evolved. This interpretation is further buttressed by the budgetary request for $15,000 for electronic surveillance equipment, noted on the attachment to the plan that was submitted to John Dean.[52]

In August or early September, 1971, Caulfield brought Dean a copy of the Sandwedge memorandum. Dean testified that Caulfield wanted to discuss the matter with John Ehrlichman and Attorney General Mitchell.[53] Dean recalled that the memo provided for "bag men" to carry money and engage in electronic surveillance.[54] On September 17, 1971, Caulfield wrote a follow-up memorandum to John W. Dean in which he explained how the new security corporation could handle the security needs for the 1972 campaign and the Republican National Committee.[55] In addition, Caulfield had lunch in September, 1971, with Dean and Magruder to discuss "project Sandwedge." [56]

Dean discussed the Sandwedge Proposal with Attorney General Mitchell.[57] Mitchell said he was not interested in the proposal since he felt that the principal problems of the re-election campaign related to security against potential demonstrators. In addition, Dean testified that Mitchell wanted a lawyer to handle any kind of covert operation.[58] In his own testimony, Mitchell admitted to being aware of the concept that Caulfield was proposing, but he also claimed that he had never seen a copy of the Sandwedge memorandum.[59] Mitchell did, however, talk to H. R. Haldeman about the Sandwedge operation, but said that Haldeman also

50. *Ibid.*, p. 109.
51. *Ibid.*, p. 109.
52. See Exhibit 34-9, p. 1121 of the Hearings.
53. Vol. 3, p. 924.
54. Vol. 3, p. 925.
55. See Exhibit 34-9, p. 1124 of the Hearings.
56. See Vol. 2, p. 786.
57. Vol. 3, p. 925.
58. *Ibid.*
59. Vol. 4, p. 1605.

disapproved of the operation because of "the lack of experience" of the individuals involved.[60]

Mitchell did not, however, wish to discuss the proposal with Caulfield, and so Dean kept putting Caulfield off whenever Caulfield raised the subject.

However, Caulfield also took the Sandwedge Proposal to John Ehrlichman. Ehrlichman testified that Caulfield brought him a three or four page double-spaced typewritten prospectus concerning the establishment of a private security entity.[61] Ehrlichman said he told Caulfield that he could not help him on the proposal. However, Ehrlichman mentioned Operation Sandwedge to Dean, and according to Dean, said that he would like to keep Tony Ulasewicz around during the campaign even though he did not think much of Caulfield's grand proposal. Dean testified that Ehrlichman also informed him that Mitchell and Caulfield should meet to discuss Ulasewicz's future.[62]

Because of Attorney General Mitchell's lack of enthusiasm for Caulfield's project, Dean let the matter ride and did not give Caulfield a specific "yes" or "no". However, in the fall of 1971, it was decided to switch the payments from Kalmbach to Ulasewicz to a cash basis. Therefore, Kalmbach gave Caulfield and Ulasewicz $50,000 *in cash* in the fall of 1971, which was meant to fund Ulasewicz's activities at least through the campaign of 1972.[63]

By November, 1971, Caulfield knew that his proposal was going nowhere. However, he wanted to work as a scheduling aide to Attorney General Mitchell in the upcoming campaign, and therefore asked Dean to get him an appointment with Mitchell. Caulfield met with Attorney General Mitchell on November 24, 1971, just prior to the Attorney General's meeting with G. Gordon Liddy.[64]

Prior to the meeting between Caulfield and Mitchell, Caulfield directed Ulasewicz to go to New Hampshire and investigate the primary campaign of Congressman Pete McCloskey. This effort was designed in part to gather valuable political information for the potential New Hampshire primary, as well as to show Attorney General Mitchell the capabilities of Caulfield and Ulasewicz. Ulasewicz investigated the McCloskey campaign in New Hampshire from November 18 through November 21, 1971. While in New Hampshire, he interviewed a number of campaign workers and volunteers in the organization under his usual pretext

60. Notes of 6/27/73 interview of John Mitchell.
61. Vol. 6, p. 2537.
62. Vol. 3, p. 925.
63. See Ulasewicz interview, April 30, 1974.
64. Vol. 3, p. 925.

of being a newspaper reporter.[65] Ulasewicz's report on the New Hampshire campaign was forwarded over to the Attorney General along with some follow-up reports that were written after a subsequent visit to the McCloskey campaign headquarters two weeks later.[66]

Mitchell discussed possible employment in the campaign with Caulfield at their meeting on November 24, 1971. However, Operation Sandwedge may not have been turned off at this meeting because Caulfield continued to refer to his intelligence-gathering capabilities as "Operation Sandwedge." [67] For example, in a memorandum dated December 11-12, 1971, Caulfield described "a Sandwedge-engineered penetration of McCloskey's volunteer headquarters in Washington, D.C." [68]

This refers to a visit by Ulasewicz to the McCloskey headquarters to obtain information. The memo also refers to future arrangements to infiltrate the New Hampshire McCloskey campaign.[69]

In late December, 1971, Mitchell asked Dean for a summary of Caulfield's and his agent's activities. Dean wrote Mitchell on January 12, 1972, that Caulfield had prepared a list of the activities so that Mitchell could review them in order to decide whether or not further funding would be made available for Mr. Ulasewicz.[70] Mitchell stated that this memorandum was the last discussion of Sandwedge and that the proposal was finally killed then.[71] Ulasewicz continued to be funded through cash payments after this time, but his political investigations dropped off considerably until after the break-in at the Democratic National Headquarters on June 17, 1972.

"Operation Sandwedge" as envisioned by Jack Caulfield was a significantly similar precursor to the Gemstone plan which was later implemented in the campaign of 1972. The plans calling for the creation of an offensive intelligence-gathering capability were basically what the Gemstone Plan was designed to do. The placement of infiltrators in campaigns, surveillance of the Democratic convention and meetings, the creation of a "derogatory information investigative capability," and the creation of a "black bag" capability were the very measures that the Gemstone Plan in fact carried out. Discussions of the Sandwedge proposal appear to have con-

65. See Exhibit 43-11, p. 1134 of *Hearings*.
66. See Exhibits at 3 *Hearings*, pp. 1142-1144.
67. Vol. 3, p. 926.
68. See Exhibit 43-11, p. 1145 *Hearings*.
69. *Ibid.*
70. See Exhibits 43-12, p. 1149 of the *Hearings*.
71. See notes of Mitchell interview, June 27, 1973.

tinued until at least January 12, 1972, a mere two weeks prior to the initial meeting in Attorney General Mitchell's office when the Gemstone plan was first revealed.

The relationship between the Sandwedge proposal and the Gemstone plan is suggested by Jeb Magruder's statement:

"In November 1971, it was indicated to me that the project [Sandwedge] was not going to get off the ground and consequently G. Gordon Liddy came into the picture after that."[72]

OTHER SURVEILLANCE—SENATOR EDWARD M. KENNEDY

Following his investigation of the accident at Chappaquidick, Ulasewicz kept Senator Kennedy under physical surveillance on a selected basis. In the fall of 1971, John Dean testified that he received a call from Larry Higby, who said that Haldeman wanted twenty-four hour surveillance placed on Senator Kennedy and regular reports of his activities forwarded to the White House.[73] Dean passed the request to Jack Caulfield, who emphatically stated that he thought twenty-four hour surveillance was a silly idea. Caulfield contended that it would require several men and might result in Senator Kennedy discovering he was under surveillance. In addition, the twenty-four hour surveillance could be easily misinterpreted as a threat on his life, and the police or FBI could be called in to investigate.[74]

Dean agreed with Caulfields assessment of the idea and convinced Higby that the plan was unwise.[75] As an alternative, Caulfield was directed to keep track of Senator Kennedy's activity and to pursue specific investigations that could turn up valuable political intelligence. As a result, many of the investigations listed above, conducted by Anthony Ulasewicz, were a result of this original directive from Haldeman.

Other Investigations of Senator Edward Kennedy. There were other instances of White House initiated investigations designed to discredit a potential Presidential bid by Kennedy.

In the summer of 1969, John Dean, then at the Justice Department, testified that he was instructed by Deputy Attorney General Richard Kleindienst to contact Cartha DeLoach, Deputy Director of the FBI, and "obtain from him infor-

72. See Vol. 2, p. 786.
73. Vol. 3, p. 922.
74. Caulfield Ex. Session, March 16, 1974, p. 85.
75. Vol. 3, p. 923.

mation regarding the foreign travels of Mary Jo Kopechne."[76] (Kopechne was the woman who died in the Chappaquiddick auto accident.) Kleindienst told Dean that the White House wanted this "very important information."[77] Dean obtained the information and passed it on to Caulfield at the White House.[78] Dean was not sure why he was asked to be the courier of the FBI information, but he speculated before the Select Committee that he was chosen "so that others could deny they had done so should the matter become known."[79]

In another incident in about July 1971, E. Howard Hunt, who was working part-time for the White House, discussed investigating Senator Kennedy with his employer, Robert Bennett of Mullen and Company, a Washington, D.C. public relations firm. Hunt had been asked by Colson or Bennett to investigate Senator Kennedy's activities.[80]

Hunt had asked Bennett if he knew people with information on the Kennedys, and Bennett mentioned Clifton De- Motte, a General Services Administration employee in Rhode Island who had worked in John Kennedy's 1960 campaign and was, Bennett believed, antagonistic toward the Kennedy family.[81] Although Bennett testified that he warned Hunt that DeMotte might not know anything politically useful,[82] Hunt says he also told Colson that he had been given "credible information"[83] that DeMotte was worth contacting.

Hunt says Colson asked him to interview DeMotte without disclosing Hunt's White House connection. Hunt said he would need an alias, false documents, or perhaps a physical disguise for the interview. Hunt testified that Colson was wary of approaching the FBI or the Secret Service with such a request, and so he agreed to "look into" obtaining the material from the CIA.

General Robert Cushman, formerly Deputy Director of the CIA, testified that on July 7, 1971, he received a telephone call from Ehrlichman in which Ehrlichman said, "Howard Hunt had been hired as a consultant to the White House on security matters that he would be coming to pay me a visit and could I lend him a hand."[84] Alleged notes taken by Cushman's secretary during the telephone conversation show

76. Dean testimony, Hearings 3, p. 922, June 25, 1973.
77. Dean Testimony, Hearings 3, p. 922, June 25, 1973.
78. Dean interview, July 26, 1973, p. 4.
79. *Ibid.*
80. 9 *Hearings* 3677. See also Bennett interview, July 27, 1973.
81. Robert Bennett interview, July 27, 1973.
82. *Ibid.*
83. Hunt testimony, Sel. Com. *Hearings,* 9, p. 3677, Sept. 24, 1973. Unless otherwise indicated details that follow are from Hunt's public testimony at pp. 3677-78. *Hearings* 9.
84. 8 *Hearings* 3290.

that Ehrlichman explained that Hunt was working for the President and should be given "carte blanche" by Cushman.[85] However, Cushman denies hearing any such language by Ehrlichman during their conversation.[86]

Hunt subsequently obtained the disguise materials—a driver's license, a wig, and a speech altering device after a meeting on July 22, 1971 with Cushman.[87]

Hunt testified that he then went to Rhode Island on or about July 28, 1971, and, in disguise, interviewed DeMotte.[88] Colson and Hunt decided that the information obtained in the interview was "useless." [89]

In another incident, Watergate figure Alfred Baldwin testified that he was assigned by James McCord to monitor visitors to Senator Kennedy's Senatorial office for a brief period in May of 1972. The purpose of this surveillance, Baldwin testified, was "basically to determine what groups were in the area of the Senator's office." [90]

The Plumbers

Another in-house investigative arm of the White House, "the Plumbers," conducted political, as well as national security-related investigations during its existence in 1971. This report will not attempt to detail all facets of the Plumbers' actions. Excluded, for example, are David Young's declassification program, the investigation into the SALT talk leaks, the "Radford" investigation, and responsibilities for retracing U.S. policy stands in Southeast Asia for the then ongoing peace negotiations. However, the investigation by the Plumbers of Daniel Ellsberg was reviewed by the Committee primarily because of the political implications inherent in that investigation, and its relationship to the coverup. The following facts develop the origin and motivations of the Ellsberg assignment.

On June 13, 1971, the New York *Times* published the first of a three-part series of what came to be known as "The Pentagon Papers." President Nixon viewed this breach of national security with the utmost gravity.[91] As the President

85. See notes in files of Committee.
86. Cushman Ex. Sess.
87. 000, p. 000, 8 *Hearings*, 3292.
88. *Hearings*, 9, p. 3678. De Motte however claims that Hunt was not in disguise when DeMotte was interviewed. See Int., March 30, 1974, p. 4.
89. 9 *Hearings* 3678.
90. Testimony of Alfred Baldwin, 1 *Hearings* 396.
91. Speech of President Richard M. Nixon, May 22, 1973; as quoted in "Watergate: Chronology of a Crisis," *Congressional Quarterly* (Washington, D.C., August, 1973), p. 90. According to Egil Krogh, one of the Plumbers, leaks regarding the SALT talks so upset the President that, in a meeting with Ehrlichman and Krogh, he pounded the table with his fists and said such activity had to be stopped. Krogh interview.

related in his May 22, 1973, address to the Nation:

> "Therefore during the week following the Pentagon Papers publication, I approved the creation of a special Investigative Unit within the White House—which later came to be known as the 'Plumbers'. This was a small group at the White House whose principal purpose was to stop security leaks and to investigate other sensitive security matters." [92]

The President went on to explain the choice of Daniel Ellsberg as a target of the Plumbers' investigation:

> "At about the time this unit was created, Daniel Ellsberg was identified as the person who had given the Pentagon Papers to the *New York Times*. I told Mr. Krogh that as a matter of first priority, the unit should find out all it could on his motives. Because of the extreme gravity of the situation, and not knowing then what additional national secrets Mr. Ellsberg might disclose, I did impress upon Mr. Krogh the vital importance to the national security of his assignment. I did not authorize and had no knowledge of any illegal means to be used to achieve this goal." [93]

David Young and John Ehrlichman have also testified about the seriousness of the national security leaks leading to the creation of the Plumbers.[94] Supervision of this "national security assignment of the utmost gravity" was first ordered to Pat Buchanan, a Presidential speech writer, on July 6, 1971.[95] Buchanan testified that his White House responsibilities consisted of political and public relations-related tasks—speech writing, daily news summaries, and preparation for press briefings.[96] Designation of the Ellsberg assignment to him, was, in Buchanan's own words, "a waste of my time and my abilities." [97] At about this same time, a low key group to handle domestic and intra-governmental problems with leaks was created in the White House with Fred Malek in charge.[98] Supervisory responsibilities for the Plumbers ultimately fell on Presidential assistant John D. Ehrlichman with help from Charles Colson. Ehrlichman's assistant Egil "Bud" Krogh, Jr.

---

92. *Ibid.*, p. 90.
93. *Ibid.*
94. 6 *Hearings* 2518; See David Young interview.
95. Testimony of Patrick Buchanan, Vol. 10, p. 3911. Hearings before Presidential Campaign Activities Committee of the U.S. Senate.
96. 10 *Hearings* 3904-05.
97. See Exhibit 000.
98. Buchanan not only verbally rejected the assignment but warned against the media approach in attacking Ellsberg (see footnote on Exhibit at 6 *Hearings* 2650).

and former Kissinger aide David Young were given operational responsibility for the project, which employed both E. Howard Hunt and G. Gordon Liddy.

Prior to his being hired, Hunt had a telephone conversation with Charles Colson about the Ellsberg matter. Part of that conversation was the following exchange:

C   Let me ask you this, Howard, this question. Do you think with the right resources employed that this thing could be turned into a major public case against Ellsberg and co-conspirators?

H   Yes, I do, but you've established a qualification here that I don't know whether it can be met.

C   What's that?

H   Well, with the proper resources.

C   Well, I think the resources are there.

H   Well, I would say so absolutely.

C   Then your answer would be we should go down the line to nail the guy cold?

H   Go down the line to nail the guy cold, yes . . .

C   And that at this point, the profit to us in in nailing any son of a bitch who would steal a secret document of the government and publish it or would conspire to steal . . .

H   . . . Or aid and assist in its . . .

C   And that the case now can be made on that grounds where I don't see that we could lose.

H   It has to be made on criminal grounds and . . .

C   It also has to be this case, won't be tried in the court, it will be tried in the newspapers. So it's going to take some resourceful engineering to . . .[99]

Hunt added later in the conversation, "I want to see the guy hung if it can be done to the advantage of the Administration." [100] Colson had earlier commented, ". . . we might be able to put this bastard into a helluva situation and discredit the new left." [101] With Colson's recommendation, Hunt was subsequently hired to work in The Plumbers group.

On July 9, 1971, Hunt and Colson telephoned retired CIA agent Lucien Conein. According to Hunt, Colson used the alias "Fred Charles," and they attempted to elicit from Conein derogatory information about Ellsberg's activities in Vietnam.[102] Then on July 28, 1971, Hunt wrote a memo to Charles Colson which detailed an operational plan for "neu-

99. 9 *Hearings* 3878-3879.
100. 9 *Hearings* 3879.
101. 9 *Hearings* 3878.
102. Colson and Hunt taped the conversation. *See* 9 *Hearings* 3881 (Ex. 194).

tralization of Ellsberg."[103] The objective of the memo was to determine "how to destroy his public image and credibility." [104] Hunt proposed seeking CIA assistance in performing "a covert psychological assessment/evaluation on Ellsberg." [105]

However, Egil Krogh and David Young were also concerned about Ellsberg's public image. They acknowledged the suggestion to obtain Ellsberg's psychiatric files in Hunt's "neutralization" memorandum in their August 3, 1971, memorandum to Charles Colson.[106] In the meantime, as noted earlier, Howard Hunt had received disguise material from the CIA.[107]

CIA equipment and assistance in developing a psychological profile of Ellsberg overstepped the Agency's legal bounds by being involved with domestic intelligence-gathering and internal security.

When it was determined that the initial CIA psychological profile was inadequate,[108] a "covert operation" was recommended to supplement the initial profile. This covert operation led to the break-in at Ellsberg's psychiatrist's office. Interestingly, according to Hunt, the psychiatrists's office had been pinpointed through what Hunt believed might have been FBI wiretaps made available to the Plumbers.[109] On August 11, 1971, Krogh and Young wrote to Ehrlichman,

> . . . we would recommend that a covert operation be undertaken to examine all the medical files still held by Ellsberg's psychoanalyst covering the two-year period in which he was undergoing analysis.[110]

Ehrlichman approved the recommendation with the qualification of "if done under your assurance that it is not traceable." [111]

Ehrlichman maintained, however, that he had no specific prior knowledge of the Fielding break-in. His explanation of what he envisioned as the "covert operation" offered the following alternatives:

> Now, if you are asking me whether this means that I had in my contemplation that there was going to be a

103. 9 *Hearings* 3886.
104. *Ibid.*
105. 9 *Hearings* 3886.
106. See Exhibit 000.
107. 9 *Hearings* 3675; 8 *Hearings* 3235.
108. Note point #2 of the August 11, 1971, memorandum to John D. Ehrlichman from Krogh and Young. 6 *Hearings* 2644.
109. 9 *Hearings* 3786.
110. 6 *Hearings* 2645.
111. *Ibid.*

breaking and entering, I certainly did not. I heard a remark by a member of the committee to the effect that there are only two ways that one can see a medical file, and that is either to get the doctor to violate his oath or to break or enter. Well, I know that is not so, and I imagine those of you who have been in private practice well recognize there are a lot of perfectly legal ways that medical information is leaked, if you please, and when I saw this that is the thing occurred to me, that by one way or another this information could be adduced by an investigator who was trained and who knew what he was looking for.[112]

Ehrlichman also offered a national security defense to the overall Ellsberg assignment in his testimony before the Select Committee. Ehrlichman noted that a psychiatric profile would be invaluable in determining:

. . . whether we were dealing here with a spy ring or just an individual kook, or whether we were dealing with a serious penetration of the nation's military and other secrets, in such an uncertain situation that a profile of this kind might, certainly not positively, but might add some important additional ingredients which would help to understand the dimensions of the problem.[113]

Ehrlichman, however, testified that he did not approve of an actual break-in to Dr. Fielding's offices.[114] In addition, David Young has testified that there were legitimate national security considerations for obtaining Ellsberg's psychiatric file.[115]

E. Howard Hunt, however, testified that from the beginning the Ellsberg assignment had strong political and public relations overtones. When asked what was to be done with the derogatory information about Ellsberg collected by Hunt and the other Plumbers, Hunt replied:

"My assumption was that it would be made available by Mr. Colson or someone in his confidence to selected members of the media." [116]

Ehrlichman's role in orchestrating this political use of the media emerges in his approval of the August 26, 1971, memorandum to him from David Young.[117] The last ques-

112. 6 *Hearings* 2547.
113. 6 *Hearings* 2601.
114. 6 *Hearings* 2815-2816.
115. See David Young interview.
116. Testimony of E. Howard Hunt, op. cit, p. 3666.
117. 6 *Hearings* 2646.

tion put to Ehrlichman by Young in the memorandum was: "(9) How quickly do we want to try to bring a change in Ellsberg's image?" [118] David Young, who also testified about the national security need for the psychiatric file, added:

> In connection with issue (9), it is important to point out that with the recent article on Ellsberg's lawyer, Boudin, we have already started on a negative press image for Ellsberg. If the present Hunt/Liddy Project #1 is successful, it will be absolutely essential to have an overall game plan developed for its use in conjunction with the congressional investigation. . . .
> . . . I mentioned these points to Colson earlier this week and his reply was that we should just leave it to him and he would take care of getting the information out. I believe, however, that in order to orchestrate this whole operation we have to be aware of precisely what Colson wants to do." [119]

Ehrlichman responded to this information the following day in a memorandum to Charles Colson:

> On the assumption that the proposed undertaking by Hunt and Liddy would be carried out and would be successful, I would appreciate receiving from you by next Wednesday a game plan as to how and when you believe the materials should be used. [120]

The allusion in the earlier Young memorandum to "the recent article on Ellsberg's lawyer" referred to one of Colson's attempts to discredit Ellsberg and those around him in the press. Using FBI files, Howard Hunt developed a profile on Ellsberg's attorney, Leonard Boudin. Hunt took the materials to Colson and says he told him:

> ". . . I find Boudin's name cropping constantly in these F.B.I. reports, described Boudin or his long background of associations with the extreme left, to put it mildly, and said I felt we had enough material here on him to put together an article of sorts . . . Colson and I certainly discussed it, because then the name Jerry terHorst came into play." [121]

Hunt testified that Colson gave the materials developed by Hunt to terHorst, a *Detroit News* reporter.[122] Some months later an article appeared in the *Detroit News* on the Ells-

118. 6 *Hearings* 2646.
119. 6 *Hearings* 2646.
120. 6 *Hearings* 2651.
121. Testimony of Howard Hunt, Sept. 10, 1973, Executive Session, p. 121.
122. *Id.* at 122.

berg Defense Fund and the attorneys involved, including Boudin, although terHorst denied that Hunt's information was the basis for his article.[123]

White House resources were used to develop and disseminate derogatory material concerning Ellsberg as part of a negative public relations campaign against the Administration's political opponents.

Investigation of the Brookings Institution

From its early days in office, the Nixon Administration was concerned about what President Nixon, in Patrick Buchanan's words, felt was the ". . . institutionalized power of the left concentrated in the foundations that succor the Democratic Party."[124] The Brookings Institution, an influential non-profit public policy center in Washington, D.C., was of particular interest to Buchanan and others in the Administration. In a March 3, 1970, memorandum to the President, Buchanan suggested that the Administration encourage and assist the establishment of

". . . A Republican Conservative counterpart to Brookings, which can generate the ideas Republicans can use, which can serve as a repository of conservative and Republican intellectuals, the way Brookings and others do for the Democrats."[125]

Although Buchanan envisioned no more than directing ". . . future funds away from the hostile foundations, like Brookings,"[126] other Presidential aides apparently envisioned stronger tactics.

During the summer of 1971, Jack Caulfield testified that he and Charles Colson discussed a possible "investigation" of Leslie Gelb, then at the Brookings Institution and formerly a consultant to the National Security Council. Colson, like others in the White House, was concerned about the recent leak of the Pentagon Papers, and he had read that Brookings was planning a study of Vietnam based upon "documents of a current nature."[127] According to Caulfield, Colson wanted him to burglarize the Institution to determine whether, through Gelb's former NSC associations,

123. 9 *Hearings* 3895.
124. March 3, 1970, Buchanan to President memorandum, Select Committee Hearings, Book 10, p. 4114.
125. 10 *Hearings* 4114.
126. 10 *Hearings* 4115.
127. John Dean testimony, Select Committee Hearings, Book 3, p. 920 (June 25, 1973) (Dean was relating what Caulfield told him about a conversation with Colson.)

the Institution had a copy of the papers.

Caulfield remembered his conversation with Colson as follows:

"Mr. Colson . . . called me into his office, which was a rather unusual procedure in and of itself, because I did not work for Mr. Colson; indicated he had had discussions with people he did not identify in the Presidential party out in San Clemente, and stated that there was a high priority need to obtain papers from the office of a gentleman named Leslie Gelb, who apparently worked at the Brookings Institute in Washington. And Mr. Colson indicated that he thought that I could, in some fashion, obtain those papers. And I stated to Mr. Colson, how do you propose that I obtain these papers? . . .

"In substance, the suggestion was that the fire regulations in the District of Columbia could be changed to have the F.B.I. respond [to a fire] and obtain the file in question from Mr. Leslie Gelb's office." [128]

To Caulfield, the clear implication was to fire-bomb the Institution.[129] Caulfield left Colson's office and testified that he "literally ran into the office of Mr. Dean and advised him that if he was not going to take the next plane out to San Clemente, I was." [130] Caulfield told Dean that he thought Colson's instructions were "insane." [131] Dean agreed, and he flew immediately to California to ". . . tell Ehrlichman this entire thing was insane." [132]

Dean and Ehrlichman met at San Clemente. According to Dean,[133] Ehrlichman agreed that the plan was unwise and

called Colson and told him to drop the idea. Ehrlichman remembers meeting with Dean on the subject and calling someone, but he cannot remember whom he called.[134] Dean then called Caulfield to tell him the plan had been squelched.[135]

Although Caulfield testified that Colson later told Caulfield the idea was only a joke,[136] Caulfield, Dean, and Ehlichman thought it was quite serious. In addition, Lyn Nofziger, then a White House aide—who knew Caulfield well, remem-

128. Caulfield testimony, Executive Session, March 23, 1974, pp. 41-42.
129. Ibid. p. 42.
130. Ibid.
131. Dean testimony, Select Committee Hearings, Book 3, p. 920 (June 25, 1973).
132. 3 Hearings 920.
133. Ibid.
134. 6 Hearings 2536.
135. Dean testimony, p. 920.
136. Caulfield interview, Sept. 11, 1973.

bered that, shortly after his meeting with Colson, Caulfield spoke with Nofziger about the plan and says he expressed shock that Colson would make such a suggestion.[137] Nofziger says he told Caulfield not to follow Colson's directive.[138]

Although Colson's plan was not carried out, Ulasewicz visited the Institution, at Caulfield's direction (from Dean) to determine the location of offices, security provisions, and so on.[139] This cursory surveillance was done at about the time Dean went to California to see Ehrlichman.

D. Diem Cable Incident

Another White House investigation involved an effort to tie President Kennedy to the 1963 assassination of South Vietnamese President Ngo Dinh Diem. Colson contended to Hunt that President Kennedy, a Catholic, had implicitly condoned the assassination of another Catholic head of state, Ngo Diem of Vietnam. Such a theory had some political consequences if Senator Kennedy were to have run for President in 1972. Moreover, any Democratic candidate in 1972 might have suffered diminished popularity in the Catholic voting population if such history were accepted.

Early in his employment as a White House consultant, E. Howard Hunt testified that he was instructed by Charles Colson to become the White House's "resident expert on the origins of the Vietnam War." [140] Hunt proceeded to steep himself in the history of the Vietnam War, particularly the assassination of Diem.[141] In his capacity as a White House official, Hunt interviewed some CIA sources, including retired Colonel Lucien Conein, an Indochina expert. David Young obtained access for Hunt to State Department secret cables from during the war to determine if there were any bias in the selectivity of the cables quoted in the Pentagon papers.[142]

However, Hunt testified that he had a different assignment from Charles Colson, and that Colson stressed the need to Hunt of finding documentation to show "that it was not the Nixon Administration that got us involved in Indochina in the first place." [143] Hunt succinctly characterized what Col-

137. Nofziger interview, August 29, 1973.
138. *Ibid.*
139. Ulasewicz interview, May 8, 1973. Ulasewicz says his activity was not thorough enough to be called a true "casing" as Dean characterized it in his testimony. Book 3, p. 920.
140. Testimony of E. Howard Hunt, July 25, 1973, Executive Session, p. 19.
141. *Id.* at 19.
142. See David Young interview, 000; See also 9 *Hearings* 3772.
143. Hunt Executive Session, July 25, 1973, pp. 20-21.

son wanted to show with the cables as follows:

> "I believe it was desired by Mr. Colson, or at least some of his colleagues, to demonstrate that a Catholic U.S. administration had in fact conspired in the assassination of a Catholic chief of state of another country." [144]

Hunt testified that he displayed the secret cables to Colson, explaining that they laid a strong, but inconclusive, case regarding Kennedy Administration culpability in the Diem death. Hunt noted that certain cables appeared to be missing from the group he had been given, and so there was no hard evidence linking the Kennedy Administration with the assassinations of Diem and his brother-in-law.[145]

Hunt characterized the ensuing conversation with Colson as follows:

> "Well, he [Colson] said, 'Do you think you could improve on that,' and I [Hunt] said yes. I said I would need some technical assistance. I can't do a forgery on my own that will stand up. He said: 'What would you need?' I said: 'Possibly the Secret Service could help me. I would need type faces and that sort of thing.' I said I could prepare a credible text or plausible text or set of texts myself, but then we would run up against the typewriter problem. He said, 'Well, this is too sensitive, we couldn't approach the Secret Service for that. You would have to do this all on your own. Why don't you see what you can do.' So as I have stated in other forums, I set about with a razor blade and a paste pot and in effect produced two spurious cables." [146]

Hunt testified he later returned to Colson's office with the spurious cables, where Colson told him that the cables would be made available to a journalist.[147]

In September, 1971, Colson contacted *Life* magazine investigative reporter William Lambert and mentioned to him the possible existence of the Diem cables.[148] Hunt met with Lambert in late September and showed him the forged cables but, at Colson's instructions, refused to allow Lambert to keep or photocopy them. For some time after this meeting, Lambert says he pressed Colson and Hunt for the original documents and interviewed numerous people in an attempt to confirm their authenticity. Finally, on April 28, 1973,

144. Hunt testimony, Select Committee Hearings, Book 9, p. 3672 (September 24, 1973).
145. 9 *Hearings* 3672.
146. Hunt Executive Session, Sept. 10, 1973, p. 106.
147. 9 *Hearings* 3672.
148. Interview with William Lambert, August 7, 1973.

Charles Morin, one of Colson's law partners, returned one of Lambert's calls. Lambert says that Morin told him the cable was a fake. Despite Morin's assertion, when Lambert met with Colson and his attorney the next day, Lambert said Colson denied ever seeing the forged cables and refused to confirm that some of them were forged.[149]

In addition to contacting Lambert, Hunt says that Colson also instructed him to show the entire set of cables, including the forgery, to Colonel Lucien Conein.[150] Conein at the time was preparing to participate in a television documentary on the origins of the Vietnam conflict, and it was "Colson's desire for Mr. Conein to draw the conclusion that in fact the Kennedy Administration had been responsible, implicitly responsible for the assassination of Diem."[151] Colson and Conein talked earlier on the telephone, with Hunt participating,

"... about the fact that President Kennedy, himself a Catholic, had in fact—his Administration and he implicitly had authorized the assassination of another Catholic and thus would have some impact on the Catholic vote in the subsequent election, if there should be a Kennedy involved in the election."[152]

Even if Edward Kennedy were not the Democratic candidate, Hunt said, "the fabrication was intended to alienate the Catholic vote."[153]

E. ITT and Dita Beard

Columnist Jack Anderson reported on February 29, 1972 the existence of the now-famous Dita Beard ITT memorandum, alleging that a $400,000 contribution to the Nixon campaign was tied to a favorable ruling by the Justice Department on ITT's anti-trust problems. Concern about the document within the White House led to a number of activities, including clandestine investigations.

Immediate Administration reaction to the Anderson article was two-fold: (1) A White House action group of political and press advisors was assigned to set out the Administration's public position and course of conduct in reaction to the allegations and (2) Investigations were undertaken to

149. Lambert Interview, August 7, 1973.
150. Hunt Executive Session, September 10, 1973, p. 149.
151. *Id.*
152. *Id.* at 150.
153. 9 *Hearings* 3733.

determine the origin, accuracy and authenticity of the Beard memorandum.

The White House public relations explanation of the ITT incident was extensive and will not be fully covered in this report. Nearly daily strategy meetings included Richard Moore, Charles Colson, John Dean, Bill Timmons, John Ehrlichman, Fred Fielding, and Wally Johnson. This group's responsibilities included preparing daily press briefing materials and developing a strategy for the upcoming Kleindienst confirmation hearings.

The White House investigation of the ITT affair was two-pronged. Charles Colson conducted a review of internal White House contacts, correspondence, and memoranda to determine possible culpability of various persons in any possible wrongdoing surrounding Administration-ITT interaction. This investigation led to the celebrated Colson ITT memorandum to H. R. Haldeman.[154] Secondly, Howard Hunt and personnel from some government agencies were used to investigate individuals related to the actual publication of the memo.

The Colson ITT memorandum is divided into two parts. The first section discusses briefly the on-going public relations effort to minimize the political impact of the Beard memorandum. The second portion of Colson's memorandum details the Administration involvement in the ITT anti-trust settlement and the possible relation of the settlement to a campaign contribution promise.[155] This second portion outlines the findings of Colson's internal investigations into White House misconduct in the ITT matter.

Colson's findings were significant. The documents discovered in his investigation, Colson concluded, could "undermine" or "contradict" [156] previous testimony of Administration officials. Colson determined that one document ". . . would once again contradict Mitchell's testimony and more importantly directly involve the President."[157]

The first sentence of the investigative portion of Colson's memorandum implies that an attempt to supress White House involvement had been underway for some time:

> "Certain ITT files which were not shredded *have* been turned over to the SEC; there was talk yesterday in the Committee of subpoenaing these from ITT." [158]

Further, Colson acknowledged the existence of an important

154. 8 *Hearings*, p. 3372.
155. *Ibid.*
156. 8 *Hearings*, p. 3376.
157. *Id.*
158. 8 *Hearings*, p. 3375.

document relevant to the SEC investigation but concluded: "We *believe* that all copies of this have been destroyed." [159] Colson's memorandum also summarized the extent of knowledge various Administration figures had about ITT:

> "Neither Kleindienst, Mitchell, nor Mardian know of the potential dangers. I have deliberately not told Kleindienst or Mitchell since both may be recalled as witnesses and Mardian does not understand the problem. Only Fred Fielding, myself, and Ehrlichman have fully examined all the documents and/or information that *could* yet come out." [160]

Rather than disclose to law enforcement authorities or other concerned agencies what Colson's investigation had uncovered, the White House conducted further investigations of non-White House figures involved in the ITT matter. Robert Mardian testified that shortly after the Dita Beard memorandum was published, G. Gordon Liddy told him he transported ITT lobbyist Beard away from Washington, D.C. [161] Subsequently, Colson dispatched E. Howard Hunt to Denver, Colorado, where Mrs. Beard was in a hospital, to interview her about the origin and authenticity of her memorandum. [162] White House Congressional liaison, Wallace Johnson, helped Colson and Hunt on the Dita Beard project, as Hunt explained:

> "I was referred by him [Colson] to Mr. Wallace Johnson, who was the gentleman who actually dispatched me on the mission and prepared the aide memoir from which I talked subsequently to Mrs. Beard." [163]

Money was then provided for the trip from campaign funds held by G. Gordon Liddy. [164] Following Hunt's interview with her, Mrs. Beard issued a statement claiming that the famous memo was a fraud. This statement was written by Bob Bennett, Hunt's employer at the Mullen Co. [165]

Some government agencies were also used in the White House investigation. For instance, acting FBI Director Patrick Gray transmitted a copy of the Beard memorandum to White

159. 8 *Hearings*, p. 3375.
160. 8 *Hearings*, p. 3374.
161. 6 *Hearings*, p. 2359. (Liddy told Mardian about getting Mrs. Beard out of Washington shortly after the Watergate break-in.) Hunt asserted in staff interview that from his conversations with Dita Beard, he concluded that Liddy did not transport her out of town.
162. 9 *Hearings*, pp. 3752-3753.
163. 9 *Hearings*, p. 3753.
164. Hunt Executive Session, July 26, 1973, p. 150.
165. See Bennett interview, p. 000.

House counsel John Dean.[166] The memorandum, obtained in the FBI investigation, was subsequently used by Hunt in his interview of Beard.[167]

The White House was also curious about the relationship between Mrs. Beard and a secretary for columnist Jack Anderson.[168] John Martin of the Internal Security Division (ISD) of the Department of Justice said that he interviewed various people on this subject at the request of Robert Mardian, former head of ISD, and Charles Colson.[169]

F. The Plan for an Investigation of Arthur Bremer

On May 15, 1972, Alabama Governor George C. Wallace, then a contender for the Presidency, was shot and seriously injured during a campaign speech in Maryland. E. Howard Hunt testified that Charles Colson called him into his office the morning following the assassination attempt, and told Hunt that Wallace's assailant had been identified as Arthur Bremer of Milwaukee, Wisconsin.[170]

Colson said that the press "had trampled through his (Bremer's) apartment," [171] and suggested that Hunt should go through the apartment to survey the contents. Colson explained to Hunt the purpose of the assignment as follows:

"In the past when Mr. Kennedy was assassinated, when Jack Ruby was killed, and when Martin Luther King was killed, it was all immediately blazoned as a right wing plot of some sort. We would like to know what kind of kook this guy is. What has he got up there in the way of literature? Is he a neo-Nazi?" [172]

Hunt concluded: ". . . I think that the thrust of that effort was to determine his political orientation or some motivation for what he did." [173]

When initially confronted with the assignment, Hunt says he strenuously protested and explained that the apartment was probably staked out or legally sealed by this time.[174] Hunt testified that Colson then implied that a break-in could

166. Patrick Gray interview, May 10, 1973, p. 7.
167. Hunt Executive Session, July 25, 1973, p. 59.
168. Interview of John Martin, May 1973.
169. *Ibid.*
170. Testimony of E. Howard Hunt, Ex. Sess., July 25, 1973, p. 129.
171. *Ibid.*
172. *Ibid.,* p. 130.
173. *Ibid.,* p. 133.
174. *Ibid.,* p. 130.

elude the stake-out and provide revealing information.[175]
Finally, according to Hunt, Colson cancelled the entire operation.

G. Misuse and Attempted Misuse of Government Agencies by the White House, 1969 through 1972

1. INTRODUCTION

In this section, the Committee will outline just a few of the attempts by White House personnel to use government agencies for their own political ends. Elsewhere in this report will be a fuller examination of the use of the incumbency to aid in the re-election of the President.[176]

The results of these White House attempts to misuse agencies are not always clear. In most cases, the Committee did not have either the time or the resources to investigate fully the results of these attempts to abuse governmental process. However, the Committee presents these examples because they are illustrative of the attitudes and approaches to government which prevailed in the time leading up to the campaign of 1972, and which created the environment in which the events now known as "Watergate" occurred. Furthermore, these prevailing attitudes pose a far more serious long term threat to the freedom and independence of our institutions than do any of the specific acts which were advocated or accomplished.

2. INTERNAL REVENUE SERVICE

A preferred target of the White House staff in its attempts to politicize independent agencies was the Internal Revenue Service. The Political Enemies project, White House efforts to have the IRS focus on left wing organizations, White House attempts to get IRS information for political purposes, and the White House concern with tax exemptions given to liberal foundations all attest to the serious efforts made by the White House to use an independent goverment agency for political purposes.

A. Political Enemies Project. At the same time that early organizational efforts began for the Committee to Re-Elect the President, staff people in the White House were busy

175. *Ibid.* p. 131.
176. See Chapter III on Responsiveness.

organizing the Political Enemies Project.[177] Dean testified that on August 16, 1971, at the request of H. R. Haldeman and John Ehrlichman, he prepared a memorandum entitled "Dealing with our Political Enemies." Dean is quite succinct in summarizing the purpose of his memo:

> This memorandum addresses the matter of how we can maximize the fact of our incumbency in dealing with persons known to be active in their opposition to our Administration. Stated a bit more bluntly—how we can use the available federal machinery to screw our political enemies.[178]

Dean goes on to say that he has reveiewed the question of how "to screw our political enemies" with a number of persons "possessed of expertise in the field," and he concludes that the requirements for the project are to have an individual in the White House with full access and support of the top officials of various independent agencies and departments in order to effectively deal with individuals who are giving the White House a hard time.[179]

Dean recommends that Lyn Nofziger be the project coordinator, since "he appears the most knowledgeable and most interested." [180] Dean then goes on to recommend that the White House staff develop a small list of names that could be singled out as targets for action by various departments or agencies of the government. The potential of such an operation is clearly recognized by Dean, who advised, "we can learn more about how to operate such an activity if we start small and build." [181]

In response to Dean's memorandum, Charles Colson forwarded to Dean a list of twenty enemies that had been prepared on June 24, 1971, by George Bell. In response to Dean's suggestion that the White House focus on only ten names to try out their techniques, Colson checked off eleven priority targets that he "would give top priority." [182]

Lyn Nofziger, formerly a White House staff aide, denied any involvement in the Enemies Project with John Dean or anyone else.[183]

However, Jack Caulfield's memorandum to John Dean of August 12, 1971, explicitly stated that Caulfield had asked

177. See Exhibits numbers 44 through 49, pp. 000-000.
178. See Exhibit 48, p. 1689.
179. *Ibid.*
180. *Ibid.*, p. 1690.
181. *Ibid.*
182. See Exhibit No. 49, p. 1692.
183. Interview with Nofziger, Aug. 29, 1973, p. 3.

Nofziger to come up with a candidate to assist in the Enemies Project.[184]

Nofziger stated that he was aware that Joanne Gordon was working on an enemies list in the White House while doing political research for Charles Colson. Nofziger said he saw no need for a formal "Enemies List" because anyone with political savvy would be able to name Richard Nixon's opponents with no trouble.[185]

Nofziger also felt that it was fully appropriate for the Administration to ask government agencies to review carefully the projects of individuals who were unfriendly to the Administration.[186]

Scores of lists were prepared in the White House from the spring through the late fall of 1971 of "Enemies" and "Opponents" of the Administration.[187] Most of these lists were prepared by Charles Colson's office, particularly by Joanne Gordon and George Bell. They were sent to Dean's office, since Dean had "the action on the Political Enemies Project." [188]

Dean testified that he did very little to carry out any attacks on the so-called enemies. He testified that the compiling of a list was "merely" an exercise that I had no intention to implement.[189] Dean said he was unaware if any of the specified individuals on the lists were subjected to any harm or injury, since he said the lists were "principally used by Mr. Colson and Mr. Haldeman." [190] In a September 14, 1971, memorandum to Larry Higby, Dean notes that he will "await the review" of the names on his attached list before taking any action.[191]

Charles Colson has stated publicly that these lists were compiled to insure that no opponents of the Administration would be included on the invitation lists of the White House.

H.R. Haldeman testified that the enemies list was compiled so that it could serve as an exclusion list for extending White House privileges.[192] Haldeman explained that these lists were compiled since they were "a part of carrying out the effort of the White House . . . to carry out the policies of the Administration rather than to provide a forum for the

184. *Ibid.*, p. 8.
185. See Exhibit No. 47, p. 1688 of the Hearings.
186. Nofziger Interview, August 29, 1973, p. 11; See, for example, 4 *Hearings* 1702 for material relating to Chet Huntley's Big Sky project in Montana.
187. See Dean Exhibits Nos. 44-65, pp. 1682-1754.
188. See Exhibit No. 53, p. 1701.
189. Vol. 4, p. 1529.
190. *Ibid.*
191. 4 *Hearings* 1697.
192. Book 8, pp. 3156, 3214.

expression of opposition." [193]

However, a quick glance at the memorandum headed *"Opponent Priority Activity"* [194] shows that the individuals targeted for action were destined to lose far more than their invitations to the White House. For example, under the name of Maxwell Dane is the comment "they should be hit hard starting with Dane." [195] And under the name of Mort Halperin, a former Kissinger aide whose telephone had been tapped by the Administration, the memo says that "a scandal would be most helpful here" in a reference to Common Cause where Halperin worked. [196] In light of the comments appended to the individual names on the "enemies list," it is dubious that Haldeman's characterization of "mere exclusion from White House privileges" was what he had in mind when it came to dealing with "enemies."

B. The Enemies List and the Internal Revenue Service. At the same time that the political enemies project began in the summer of 1971, John Dean testified he was asked to use the Internal Revenue Service on an increasingly frequent basis to get political information for the White House or to initiate audits on opponents of the Administration. Dean testified that he had little success in his efforts with Commissioner Johnnie Walters. [197] The objective of a briefing paper Dean prepared for Haldeman was "to make IRS politically responsive." [198] Dean catalogued the White House woes with IRS as follows:

—We have been unable to crack down on the multitude of tax exempt foundations that feed left wing political causes.
—We have been unable to obtain information in the possession of IRS regarding our political enemies.
—We have been unable to stimulate audits of persons who should be audited.
—We have been unsuccessful in placing RN supporters in the IRS bureaucracy. [199]

As part of the means for making the Internal Revenue Service politically responsive, Dean suggested that "Walters should be told that discreet political action and investigations are a firm requirement and responsibility on his part." [200]

193. 8 *Hearings* 3156.
194. 4 *Hearings* 1694.
195. *Ibid.*
196. 4 *Hearings* 1695.
197. See Exhibit No. 44, p. 1682.
198. 4 *Hearings* 1682.
199. 4 *Hearings* 1682.
200. 4 *Hearings* 1682.

In the White House reconstructed version of John Dean's meeting with President Nixon on September 15, 1972, as relayed by Fred Buzhardt to Fred Thompson, the memorandum states that "Dean reported on IRS investigation of Larry O'Brien." [201] Dean testified that at the meeting that day with the President and Bob Haldeman, the President discussed "the use of the Internal Revenue Service to attack our enemies."[202] Dean also testified that the President wanted to place individuals in the independent agencies "who would be responsive to the White House requirements." [203]

In the purported House Judiciary Committee transcript of the September 15, 1972, meeting reported by the *Washington Post*, Haldeman reported to President Nixon that John Dean was working on "the list" "through IRS." [204]

On September 11, 1972, four days prior to his meeting with President Nixon, Dean met with IRS Commissioner Johnnie Walters at Dean's office in the Executive Office Building. At this meeting, Dean turned over to Walters a list of 490 individuals, and informed Walters that John Ehrlichman had asked IRS to determine what type of information could be developed concerning those individuals.[205] At this time, according to Walters, Dean was hopeful that the Internal Revenue Service could acquire the information that was requested without creating any political problems.

Walters subsequently discussed the matter with Secretary Shultz who directed Walters to "do nothing".[206] Walters has testified that he did nothing after the meeting.

After Dean's meeting with the President, on September 15, 1972, Dean again called Commissioner Walters on September 25. On this occasion, Dean wanted to know what progress had been made in checking the list that had been provided, and Walters advised Dean against any checking, but agreed to reconsider the matter again with Secretary Shultz. The matter was never taken up again, and the list which was given to Commissioner Walters was sealed and locked in his safe in the Commissioner's office.[207]

Despite the reluctance of Commissioner Walters to involve the Internal Revenue Service in carrying out the po-

201. See volume 4, p. 1796. See also White House transcript of September 15, 1972, meeting.
202. 3 *Hearings* 958.
203. 3 *Hearings* 958.
204. See *Washington Post*, May 17, 1974, p. A26. It should be noted that the section of the discussion between the President and Dean about the O'Brien audit by IRS has been deleted from the September 15, 1972, tape turned over to the Special Prosecutor and the House Judiciary Committee.
205. See Report of the Joint Committee on Internal Revenue Taxation, December 20, 1973, p. 3.
206. *Ibid.*, p. 4.
207. *Ibid.*, p. 4.

litical demands of the White House, tax information and income tax audits were still requested by the White House staff and supplied by other IRS personnel. Many of these requests came in the summer and fall of 1971, during the same period of time that the Political Enemies Project was being started, the Sandwedge proposal being considered, and the 1972 campaign being organized.

C. Tax Information and Audits Requested of the Internal Revenue Service. In the study of the Enemies List by the Joint Committee on Internal Revenue Taxation, the staff report concluded that "in none of these cases has the staff found any evidence that the taxpayer was unfairly treated by the Internal Revenue Service because of political views or activities." [208] However, the investigation of the Senate Select Committee has disclosed a number of instances where information from the Internal Revenue Service was inappropriately provided to the White House. Dean testified that Jack Caulfield had a contact inside the Internal Revenue Service, and that it was through this contact that they were able to obtain confidential information and learn how to initiate audits whenever they wanted to do so. [209] Caulfield has testified that his main contact inside the Internal Revence Service was Vernon "Mike" Acree, formerly Assistant Commissioner for Inspection. [210]

However, Acree stated that he sent Caulfield no copies of any tax returns, never discussed initiating any specific audits other than in a general sense, and that the only information that was provided to Jack Caulfield was on "type-X-checks" —an inquiry to see whether or not an individual who was being considered for appointment by the Executive Branch had tax problems. [211]

These conflicting stories will be discussed in more detail in the context of specific cases further on in this report.

One of the means by which the White House kept abreast of IRS activity was through the sensitive case reports prepared by the IRS according to long established procedure. [212]

1. Sensitive Case Reports. The IRS maintained a list of individuals who would be considered sensitive cases—Senators, Congress people, entertainers, associates of the President, and certain citizens in high income tax brackets. Sensi-

208. See Joint Committee on Internal Revenue Taxation Report, December 20, 1973, p. 12.
209. Volume 4, p. 1535.
210. See Caulfield Interview, Sept. 11, Sept. 12, see Caulfield Executive Session, Saturday, March 23, 1974.
211. Acree Interview, Sept. 27, 1973. See also Acree letter, June 27, 1974.
212. This background is also relevant to the Hughes-Rebozo section on the IRS investigation of Rebozo.

tive case reports are filed from the field office each month on investigations concerning these individuals, and are then routed to the appropriate IRS division. The heads of each division select the more significant sensitive case reports to send on to the Assistant Commissioner of Compliance. His staff subsequently reviews these files and prepares a "cull" section which are those cases which are worthy of note by the Commissioner of the IRS—usually between 20 and 25 such cases.

Subsequently, the Commissioner of the IRS and/or one of his assistants met with the Secretary of the Treasury to determine whether any of the Sensitive Case Reports were significant enough to bring to the attention of the President. For example, cases involving the President's personal friends or large contributors were usually important to bring to the President's attention in order to avoid any embarrassment for the President and the executive branch.

When Roger Barth was assistant to the Commissioner of the IRS, he would call John Ehrlichman directly (and sometimes John Dean), and the Secretary of the Treasury would contact the President directly to bring these sensitive cases to the White House's attention. Barth stated that an average of one Sensitive Case Report per month was forwarded on.[213] Former IRS Commissioner Johnnie Walters testified that he was unaware of Barth showing or sending sensitive case reports to John Ehrlichman and that it would have been "out of the routine" at IRS.[214]

This Sensitive Case Reporting procedure was important in the case of Mr. Charles G. Rebozo, and the IRS investigation into Mr. Rebozo commencing in 1972 and 1973. This matter will be discussed more fully in another chapter of this report. However, there were other channels by which the White House requested information or tax audits from IRS.

2. Requests for Audits. A. *Newsday* Reporters. In the fall of 1971, *Newsday* completed a long investigation into the affairs of Charles "Bebe" Rebozo that was to be published in early October 1971. The prospective publication of an unfavorable article about the President's best friend caused ripples of apprehension throughout the White House. For example, on September 10, 1971, Caulfield wrote to John Dean a very detailed memo concerning his inquiry into the background and circumstances of the *Newsday* article. Caulfield noted that "a discreet look at the newspaper's publication calendar has been accomplished." [215] In the same memo-

213. See Robert Barth Interview, pp. 7-8.
214. Walters Interview, June 14, p. 19.
215. See Tab 10 of Caulfield Exhibit A, March 16, 1974.

randum Caulfield notes that "Robert Greene, leader of the investigative group, has been in both Washington and Florida within the past two weeks." [216] This information was provided to Caulfield by an FBI agent and is discussed in more detail in another section.

Dean testified that after the article about Rebozo was published, he received instructions from either Haldeman or Ehrlichman that Robert W. Greene, head of the investigative team for the article, should be audited by the IRS.[217] Caulfield testified that Dean asked him to "see how an audit might be done on Mr. Greene, how it might be done in a way that might not be illegal." [218]

In response to Dean's request, Caulfield called Mike Acree at the Internal Revenue Service to determine how audits were initiated on individuals. Acree explained to Caulfield that they were often startetd from anonymous "informants' " letters which were received by the IRS. Acree recalled that the conversation only involved a general discussion of the audit process, without specific names being mentioned.[219]

The results of Caulfield's discussion with Acree are contained in a memorandum from Caulfield to Dean.[220] The memo states that a "knowledgeable source at IRS" was contacted by Caulfield, and that the source suggested that "a priority target be established within the group with preference given to one residing in the New York area." [221] Dean then asked him to initiate the audit on Robert Greene. Caulfield said he spoke to Acree to ask him to send an anonymous letter to the Internal Revenue Service about Greene. Caulfield believes that the letter was in fact sent on Acree's direction.[222] Acree denied that he knew of any request for a specific audit on Robert Greene and also denied that any anonymous letters were sent at his direction.[223]

However, in light of Caulfield's suggestion to Dean that a "priority target be established within the group with reference given to one residing in the New York area," and in light of the fact that Robert Greene resides in New York State and had his return audited by New York State under the Federal/State Exchange Program, the question arises as to whether the audit in fact resulted from Caulfield's efforts.[224]

216. *Ibid.*
217. Vol. 3, p. 1072.
218. Caulfield Executive Session, March 23, 1974, p. 79.
219. Acree interview July 31, 1973, p. 3; See also Acree letter, June 27, 1974.
220. Vol. 4, p. 1685.
221. See Vol. 4, p. 1685.
222. See Caulfield interview, Sept. 11, 1973, p. 11.
223. Acree interview, July 31, 1973.
224. The Committee has not had access to sufficient records nor interviewed enough witnesses on this matter to reach a definite conclusion.

On another occasion, Dean asked Caulfield to initiate audits on three or four individuals. Caulfield says he brought Acree over to the White House to discuss the matter with Dean and Caulfield. Caulfield stated that Acree was quite reluctant to get involved in these audits, and that he remained evasive when specifically asked to do these projects. Caulfield testified that the matter apparently died shortly thereafter because of Acree's lack of interest.[225]

B. Harold Gibbons. On June 12, 1972, Charles Colson wrote a memorandum to John Dean requesting that Dean initiate an income tax audit on Harold G. Gibbons, a Vice President of the Teamsters Union in St. Louis.[226] Colson's motivation for wishing to start the audit is rather clear:

"Gibbons, you should know, is an all out enemy and McGovernite, ardently anti-Nixon. He is one of three labor leaders who were recently invited to Hanoi." [227]

Dean testified that he ignored this request from Colson, and that nothing was ever done to initiate such an audit.

C. Emile DeAntonio, Daniel Talbot, and New Yorker Films. Caulfield felt sufficiently confident of the White House's ability to initiate income tax audits that on at least one occasion he recommended to John Dean that a "discreet IRS audit" be done. Following the release of the film "Millhouse" a number of individuals within the White House became quite concerned about the political impact of this film showing reruns of old Nixon speeches. As a result, in the summer and early fall of 1971, Caulfield directed Anthony D. Ulasewicz to view the film and to make discreet inquiries of New Yorker Films, Inc., Daniel Talbot, the film distributor, and Emile DeAntonio, the producer of the film.

Finally, on October 15, 1971, Caulfield felt that the success of the film posed such a serious threat to the White House that he suggested to John Dean that they initiate "discreet IRS audits of New Yorker Films, Inc., DeAntonio, and Talbot." [228] Caulfield stated that if his recommendation to John Dean was agreeable, he was going to approach Mike Acree about initiating the audits. Dean, however, did not

225. See Caulfield interview, September 11, 1973, pp. 11-12; and Acree interview, July 31, 1973. Acree recalled a meeting with Dean, but had no recollection of Dean asking him to "undertake any tax audits on anyone." Acree also recalled a phone call from Caulfield in which Caulfield "inquired again as to the Internal Revenue practices involving the initiation of audits," but that nothing further came of the conversation. (Acree letter, June 27, 1974, pp. 17-18.)
226. See Exhibit No. 45, Volumee 4, p. 1686.
227. *Ibid.*
228. See Tab 18 of Caulfield Exhibit A, March 16, 1974.

agree with Caulfield's recommendations, and said no further action was taken at that time.[229]

Dean forwarded Caulfield's suggestions to his assistant, Fred F. Fielding, and Fielding reacted quite negatively to the idea of initiating a discreet IRS audit or leaking derogatory information about the film producers. Nothing in Fielding's memorandum indicated that his reaction was because such tactics would be ethically improper, but rather because "doing IRS audits just doesn't seem to be a solution that will help us." [230]

D. Larry O'Brien. There is evidence before the Select Committee that an audit of Larry O'Brien was encouraged by White House officials in the summer of 1972, and that O'Brien's tax returns were specially inspected by IRS personnel at the direction of John Ehrlichman.[231] However, this activity is more fully described in a later section of this report.[232]

E. Other Requests. John Dean testified that he was asked by several people in the White House, and particularly Rose Mary Woods, if he could "do something" about an IRS audit on Dr. Kenneth Riland, President Nixon's osteopath.[233] Dean testified that he requested that the relevant officials at Justice and IRS keep him informed on the matter after he learned of the serious allegations, but that nothing further was done.[234]

Dean also testified that he was asked to "do something" about the audits of Reverend Billy Graham and actor John Wayne:

> . . . I was told that I was to do something about these audits that were being performed on two friends of the President's. They felt they were being harassed and the like . . . finally, when I got around to checking on it, Mr. Caulfield sent me some information which I think is evidenced in the exhibit and a note went to Mr. Higby. Mr. Higby sent it in to Mr. Haldeman, and Mr. Haldeman wrote a note on the bottom, "This has already been taken care of; so obviously, things were happening that I had no idea on." [235]

Roger Barth testified that he knew of no request from

229. See p. 102 of Caulfield Exec. Session, March 23, 1974.
230. See Tab 18 of Caulfield Exhibit A, March 16, 1974.
231. See Barth Executive Session, June 6, 1974.
232. See section on Hughes-Rebozo.
233. 4 *Hearings* 1530; Dr. Riland was subsequently acquitted of tax fraud by a federal jury.
234. *Ibid.*
235. Dean subsequently stated that he was to "turn off" the audits of Rev. Graham and John Wayne (Interview, July 29, 1973, p. 19).

Rev. Graham for help from the IRS, but that Barth had brought to the attention of the Secretary of the Treasury and possibly Jack Caulfield a discrepancy in the sensitive case reports concerning how an audit on Graham was initiated.[236]

Documentary evidence received by the Select Committee shows that Jack Caulfield received typed reports from the IRS indicating that neither John Wayne nor Rev. Graham was being harassed.[237] In addition, Barth testified that he was not aware of any action taken to impede the audit on Rev. Graham [238] and there is presently no evidence before the Committee showing any action taken to impede any investigation of Mr. Wayne.

3. Requests for Taypayer Information from the IRS. Individuals working in the White House requested taxpayer information as well as actual returns from the IRS.

Early in the Administration, Clark Mollenhoff, then a staff asisstant at the White House, asked IRS if he could examine nine individual tax returns. Roger Barth testified that Mollenhoff was given access to these returns only after Commissioner Randolph Thrower received written requests on behalf of the President.[239]

After Mollenhoff left the White House, Barth noted that only individuals who worked directly for the President such as Ehrlichman, Haldeman and Dean would have access to tax returns and audit information. Barth added that other individuals on their staffs, including Jack Caulfield, also had access to the tax information.[240]

Among the requests made by Caulfield for specific taxpayer information from the IRS were the following:

1. In the fall of 1971 Larry Goldberg was being considered to head up the Jewish Citizens for the Re-election of the President. Caulfield did a background investigation of Goldberg, to determine his loyalty to the re-election campaign and his involvement in Jewish organizations. Among the information obtained by Caulfield in the course of his investigation were actual copies of pages from Goldberg's tax returns from 1968, 1969 and 1970.

Caulfield testified that he obtained this information from Mike Acree, but Acree had no recollection of providing any

236. 4 *Hearings* 1530; *See* also Tab 15 of Exhibit A, Caulfield Executive Session, March 16, 1974.
237. Barth Executive Session, June 6, 1974, pp. 118-120.
238. See Tab 15, Exhibit A, Caulfield Executive Session, March 16, 1974.
239. Barth Executive Session, June 6, 1974, p. 121.
240. Barth Executive Session, June 6, 1974, p. 18. See also the IRS opinion granting access to tax returns to White House staff acting at the direction of the President at Exhibit 000.

specific information on Goldberg.[241] Roger Barth testified that he had no specific recollection of sending that information to Caulfield, but that he "may have sent that over."[242]

2. In late September, 1971, an individual wished to donate a wine storage vault to the Western White House. John Dean asked Caulfield to check out the individual. On October 15, 1971, Caulfield wrote a memo to Dean which reflected that Caulfield had obtained access to the individual's income tax returns.[243] Because of the information contained therein, Dean noted that Kalmbach would call the individual and "tell him we are not interested" on Oct. 19, 1971.[244]

Caulfield testified that the tax information was given to him by Mike Acree, and that Acree had obtained the information from a "pretext interview" conducted by an IRS agent.[245] Acree recalled being asked about the individual by Caulfield but has no recollection of conducting, authorizing, or knowing of any "pretext-interviews" of the individual.[246]

3. Caulfield requested and received specific taxpayer information on five individuals who were seeking to involve the White House in a scheme that claimed the discovery fo the fabled "Lost Dutchman" Gold Mine in the southwest. Caulfield, at the request of Peter Flanigan, investigated these five individuals and he was given access to their Internal Revenue Service tax returns. Caulfield testified that he obtained this tax information from Mike Acree,[247] but Acree denied that he furnished Caulfield any inappropriate information and did not recall any request such as that described by Caulfield.[248]

4. In October, 1971, Caulfield was asked to do an investigation of Stuart L. Udall, former Secretary of the Interior, and the Overview Corporation of which Mr. Udall was Chairman of the Board. In a memorandum of October 8, 1971, Caulfield informed Dean that he "asked for an IRS check to support this material."[249] Caulfield testified that he meant by that comment that he could sit down and speak with Mike Acree about any tax problem that Overview Corporation or Stuart Udall may have had.[250]

Dean asked Caulfield to find out if Overview had any

241. See Tab 12 of Caulfield. Exhibit A, March 16, 1974; see also Acree interview.
242. Barth Executive Session, June 6, 1974, p. 99.
243. See Tab 20 of Caulfield Exhibit A, March 16, 1974.
244. *Ibid.*
245. Page 128, Caulfield Ex. Session, March 23, 1974.
246. See Acree letter, June 27, 1974, p. 20.
247. Caulfield Executive Session, March 16, 1974, p. 55.
248. See Acree letter, June 27, 1974.
249. See Tab 17 of Caulfield Exhibit A, March 16, 1974.
250. Caulfield Ex. Session, March 23, 1974, p. 123.

Federal contracts, and so Caulfield checked with five separate Federal agencies, including IRS, only to discover no record of any Federal contracts for any of them. The testimony of Caulfield suggests that the motivation behind discovering whether or not there were any Federal contracts given to Overview Corporation was a desire of the White House to cancel these contracts if any existed.[251]

In his Sandwedge proposal, Caulfield described Mike Acree as "a strong Nixon loyalist [who] has proved it to me personally on a number of occasions." [252] Acree's potential assignment in the Sandwedge Operation was to provide "IRS information input, financial investigations," and other Federal law enforcement liaison information.[253] Therefore, according to Caulfield, many of these requests for IRS information in the fall of 1971 were in part an effort by Caulfield to demonstrate the potential effectiveness of his organization. While some requests for IRS information were apparently legitimate, the ready access to such highly confidential information should be more effectively curbed in the future.

4. Special Service Staff. On June 18, 1969, the Permanent Subcommittee on Investigations of the Senate Committee on Government Operations heard testimony from its staff and from a former member of the Black Panther Party to the effect that the Black Panthers had never filed income tax returns and had never been audited by the Internal Revenue Service.[254] In response to some of the testimony, Senator Karl Mundt commented that it seemed that the Black Panthers "get pretty special treatment." [255] There was also testimony in these hearings from Leon Greene, IRS Deputy Assistant Commissioner of Compliance, who also testified about the tax exempt status of certain politically active groups and raised the question of whether or not they should be tax exempt.[256]

Following these hearings in the summer of 1969, on about July 1, 1969, Tom Charles Huston, Assistant to the President, telephoned Roger Barth and requested that the Internal Revenue Service begin reviewing the activities of certain activist organizations.[257] IRS also received a list of organizations from the Permanent Subcommittee on Investigations

251. *Ibid.*
252. See Exhibit 000, p. 9.
253. *Ibid.*, p. 000.
254. See hearings of Permanent Subcommittee on Investigations of the Senate Committee on Government Operations, Riots, Civil, and *Criminal Disorders*, 92nd Congress, 1st Session, p. 373 et seq.
255. *Ibid.*, p. 373.
256. See Barth Interview, p. 11.
257. *Ibid.*, p. 11. See also Vol. 3, p. 1339; memo dated August 14, 1970.

that the Committee felt the IRS should investigate. Huston noted in a later memo to H.R. Haldeman that the President had "indicated a desire for IRS to move against leftist organizations taking advantage of tax shelters" in early 1969.[258]

As a result of these various pressures, the IRS moved on July 18, 1969, to establish the Activist Organizations Committee, whose principal function was to assemble data and monitor the activities of certain organizations with reference to their compliance with IRS laws.

The Committee was established on a very secretive basis. In a memorandum of July 24, 1969, that discussed the first meeting of the Committee, it was noted:

> We do not want the news media to be alerted to what we are attempting to do or how we are operating because the disclosure of such information might embarrass the Administration or adversely affect the service operations in this area or those of other federal agencies or Congressional Committees.[259]

The memorandum also noted that initially, "a type of organization in which we are interested may be ideological, militant, subversive, radical, or other, and one of our first problems will be to define and to determine what kind of organization we are interested in." [260]

In 1970, the IRS altered the name of the group to the Special Service Group, and subsequently the name of the organization was again changed to the Special Service Staff.[261]

On August 14, 1970, Tom Charles Huston requested a progress report on the project from the Commissioner of the Internal Revenue Service, which he received more than a month later. In that report, Commissioner Thrower explained the history and purpose of the group as follows:

> . . . The function of the Special Service Group is to obtain, consolidate and disseminate any information on individuals or organizations (including major financial sponsors of the individuals or organizations) that would have tax implications under the Internal Revenue laws. . . .
>
> The sole objective of the Special Service Group is to provide a greater degree of assurance of maximum compliance with the Internal Revenue laws by those involved in extremist activities and those providing financial

258. See Exhibit No. 42, p. 1338, Vol. 3 Hearings.
259. See Memorandum dated July 24, 1969, p. 3. See Exhibit 000.
260. *Ibid.*, p. 4.
261. Joint Committee on Internal Revenue Taxation Report, Dec. 20, 1973, p. 14.

support to these activities.[262]

However, it appears from Mr. Huston's memoranda that he was not anxious to limit the activities of the Special Service Staff merely to tax matters. On September 21, 1970, Huston wrote to Haldeman that "what we cannot do in a courtrom by criminal prosecutions to curtail the activities of some of these groups, IRS could do by administrative action. Moreover, valuable intelligence-type information could be turned up by IRS as a result of their field audits."[263] Huston also noted that while he had been pressing the IRS "to move against leftist organizations taking advantage of tax shelters," his efforts had been "to no avail."[264]

By September, 1970, the Special Service Group had information "on approximately 1,025 organizations and 4,300 individuals."[265]

The existence of the Special Services staff was known to certain Congressional investigating committees, but its existence was not announced to the general public until April, 1972.[266]

In August, 1973, the Special Service staff was abolished by the Internal Revenue Service, and it was announced that financial information about tax resisters and protesters could be adequately obtained by the regular divisions of the IRS. However, the compiling of vast files and information coupled with White House intentions demonstrate the potential abuses and show the need for restraints on the use of such information.

5. Tax Exempt Foundations. As it is obvious from the memoranda of Tom Charles Huston and Patrick Buchanan, one of the major concerns of the Nixon White House from 1969 to 1972 was the opinion that liberal and "left-wing" foundations were using tax exemptions from the IRS to sustain their political activities.

The difficulties experienced by the Administration were examined in a March 1970 Buchanan memorandum to the President which discussed "how to combat the institutionalized power of the left concentrated in the foundations that succor the Democratic party."[267]

Buchanan's basic theme was that a number of the large

262. See Volume 3, pp. 1343, 1344.
263. See Exhibit No. 42, Vol. 3, p. 1338.
264. *Ibid.*, p. 1338. See also next section.
265. 3 *Hearings* 1344.
266. See Joint Committee on Internal Revenue Taxation Report, Dec. 20, 1973, p. 15.
267. Memorandum to the President from Patrick J. Buchanan dated March 3, 1970; cited at p. 4114, Vol. 10 of the Hearings.

foundations had been using their tax exempt status to build
huge reservoirs of capital to fund political or quasi-political
undertakings that were almost uniquely liberal in their direction, thereby causing a serious imbalance in the political
process. These foundations, notably the Brookings Institution
and the Ford Foundation, were, according to Buchanan,
controlled by individuals with definite liberal philosophies
—philosophies which are reflected in the public policies,
public attitudes and public undertakings sponsored by the
foundation.[268]

To remedy the problem, Buchanan proposed a number
of recommendations, including the utilization of the Internal
Revenue Service to place checks on those fundations that
were hostile to the Nixon Administration; the removal of
what Buchanan perceived as a pre-existing Democratic bias
at the Internal Revenue Service; the selective distribution
of government funds to those foundations friendly to the
Nixon administration goals; and, most importantly, the
creation of a new foundation to serve as a haven for conservative intellectuals.[269]

Buchanan also suggested that there be "a strong fellow
running the Internal Revenue Division; and an especially
friendly fellow with a friendly staff in the tax exempt office.
Am not sure we have this right now." [270],

Another of Buchanan's suggestions for curtailing the
influence of certain liberal foundations was to disburse
selectively federal grants by the Administration. "The administration should begin . . . to initiate a policy of favoritism
in all future federal grants to those institutions friendly to
us, that want work—and we should direct future funds
away from the hostile foundations, like Brookings." [271]
Buchanan suggested that the President direct a study of the
top twenty-five foundations in this country, which among
other things, would reveal "which are friendly, which are
potentially friendly, which can be co-opted to support projects
that the President supports, and which are hostile to us;
which are the arms of political adversaries." [272] Buchanan
also recommended that the President direct the Bureau of
the Budget "to come up with a listing of all federal monies
from each department that go to foundations for studies
and research." Thus, with the creation of an Administration-
oriented conservative foundation, Buchanan envisioned:

All federal contracts now going to institutions which are

268. Public Hearings Transcript, pp. 3943-3952.
269. Buchanan memorandum, 10 *Hearings* 4114.
270. 10 *Hearings* 4118.
271. 10 *Hearings* 4115.
272. 10 *Hearings* 4114.

essentially anti-administration would be shifted to this new baby and to other pro-administration foundations. Anti-administration foundations should be cut off without a dime. One good talk to the Cabinet would be all that would be required to get cooperation here—and Budget could be on notice to notify the West Wing [of the White House] if Brookings gets any more money.[273]

Other individuals in the White House also gave thought to the problem of "liberal" foundations. John Dean asked Jack Caulfield in the summer of 1971 to consider how the Administration could most effectively deal with the Ford-Foundation and the Brookings Institution in 1972.

Caulfield's solution to the problem was, similar to Buchanan, to apply pressures to have the Internal Revenue Service strictly enforce existing statutes and promulgated regulations designed to "threaten the tax exempt status enjoyed by these organizations." [274]

Caulfield also observed that:

"Commissioner Walters . . . has not yet exercised the firm leadership they expected at the time of his appointment. Additionally, there appears to be a reluctance on his part to make discreet politically oriented decisions and to effect major appointments based upon administration loyalty considerations." [275]

Much of the input for Caulfield's observations came from Roger Barth, according to Caulfield.[276] On July 20, 1971, shortly after the publication of the "Pentagon Papers" by the *New York Times,* John Dean wrote a memo to Bud Krogh which stated in part:

In your work on the Pentagon Papers and related issues you will become aware of the fact that there is a publication out of the Brookings Institute indicating that they are planning for the fall of this year a study of Vietnam based on documents of a current nature. Chuck Colson has made some efforts to determine what Brookings is up to but I don't think he has produced any solid evidence of the nature of this publication. I requested that Caulfield obtain the tax returns of the Brookings Institute to determine if there is anything that we might do by way of turning off money or dealing with prin-

273. 10 *Hearings* 4117.
274. See Tab 6 of Caulfield Exhibit A, March 16, 1974.
275. *Ibid.*
276. Caulfield Executive Session, March 23, 1974, p. 37.

cipals of the Brookings Institute to determine what they are doing and deal with anything that might be adverse to the Administration.[277]

Caulfield did other checking into tax exempt institutions at about this time for John Dean. On July 6, 1971, he reported on Potomac Associates, an organization that the White House feared would develop into another Brookings Institution. Caulfield noted that the building where Potomac Associates had offices appeared to have good security with a guard present in the lobby at all times. However, Caulfield noted that "a penetration is deemed possible if required." [278]

Caulfield was also asked to investigate the Fund for Investigative Journalism.[279] Caulfield wrote a memo to John Dean on February 17, 1972, that a "discreet inquiry" determined that the Fund for Investigative Journalism had a tax exempt status granted by the IRS in April, 1970.

In addition, Caulfield said that the fund was the financial source for financing stories of the Mylai Massacre and that it was primarily financed with "extreme left wing" money. Caulfield noted that a request for more detailed information "will be in hand on a discreet basis during the early part of next week." [280] This reference concerned the investigation conducted by Tony Ulasewicz at Caulfield's direction.[281]

The request for a tax exemption by the Center for Corporate Responsibility, a non-profit organization designed to promote corporate social responsibility through educational and research activities, was denied by the Internal Revenue Service on May 16, 1973 despite unanimous approval by the Interpretive Division of the Chief Counsel's office at IRS.[282] The opinion denying the tax exemption was written by an attorney with no prior involvement in the case at the direction of Roger Barth, then Deputy Chief Counsel.[283] Notes of the Assistant Director of the Interpretive Division found in the IRS file on the case said, *"perhaps, White House pressure."* [284] Finally, in December 11, 1973, Judge Charles Richey ordered that the Center be recognized as a tax-exempt

277. See Tab 6 of Exhibit A, Caulfield Exec. Session, March 16, 1974.
278. See Tab 4 of Exhibit A, Caulfield Exec. Session, March 16, 1974.
279. See Tab 26 of Exhibit A, Caulfield Exec. Session, March 16, 1974.
280. *Ibid.*
281. Ulasewicz interview, June 9, 1973. Ulasewicz interviewed Ronald Ridenour, the Army photographer who helped to break the story in California under a pretext name. He also interviewed others involved in breaking the story.
282. See *Center on Corporate Responsibility, Inc.* v. *Shultz et al.*, U.S. District Court for the District of Columbia, Dec. 11, 1973, p. 7 (mimeo).
283. *Ibid.*, p. 8.
284. *Ibid.*, p. 6.

organization by the Internal Revenue Service.[285]

Dean testified that on another occasion while traveling with the President, Haldeman requested Larry Higby to direct the FBI to do an investigation of CBS news correspondent Daniel Schorr. Higby, in turn, informed Hoover of the request, and Hoover proceeded with a "full field wide open investigation" that soon leaked to the press. Dean testified that as a result, Fred Malek announced that Schorr was being considered for an environmental post in the administration, and that the FBI investigation was merely a preliminary background check.[286]

H. R. Haldeman had no recollection of the purpose for ordering the FBI investigation, but in light of other activities going on in the White House at that time, the question arises as to whether there was a valid basis for requesting the FBI investigation of Mr. Schorr.

Alexander Butterfield stated that both Haldeman and Ehrlichman requested about eight FBI checks on non-appointees to the government. Among these checks were Frank Sinatra, Helen Hayes, and Daniel Schorr.[287]

3. FEDERAL BUREAU OF INVESTIGATION

Another technique of the White House staff was to obtain derogatory information about individuals from investigative agencies such as the FBI and to disseminate the information to the press by way of selective "leaks." Caulfield referred to the process of disseminating derogatory information about individuals to the media as a "Nofziger job." Caulfield testified that he meant that Lyn Nofziger, "whose talents in that area were much greater than anyone else around the White House," would make the derogatory information available to reporters to do stories on the individuals.[288] Nofziger explained that he merely provided significant political information to reporters, and that there was nothing unusual about doing his in either political campaigns or in government itself.[289]

Some examples of White House use of the FBI to obtain information on individuals for non-law enforcement purposes are related below.

In the summer of 1969, while John Dean was working

285. *Ibid.*, p. 31. The order primarily resulted from defendants' failure to comply with the court's discovery orders. (*Id.*, p. 16.)
286. 3 *Hearings* 1071.
287. See Butterfield interview, July 13, 1973.
288. See Caulfield testimony, pp. 90-91, March 23, 1974.
289. See Nofziger Interview, Aug. 13, 1973.

at the Department of Justice, he testified that he was directed by Deputy Attorney General Richard Kleindienst to call Cartha DeLoach, the Deputy Director of the FBI, and obtain from him some information for the White House relating to the foreign travels of Mary Jo Kopechne (the woman who died in the Chappaquiddick accident).[290] Dean said he called DeLoach and subsequently related the information he obtained to Jack Caulfield at the White House.[291]

In August 1971, Jack Caulfield testified that he first learned of the upcoming *Newsday* series on Bebe Rebozo from Pat Henry, an FBI agent in New York.[292] Caulfield said that Henry subsequently provided him with more information that served as the basis for Caulfield's memorandum on September 10, 1971 to John Dean.[293] In this memorandum, Caulfield claimed that there had been "a discreet look at the newspaper's publication calendar," and that there was no indication that the series of articles would appear during the month of September. There is no evidence that any formal FBI investigation was launched into the *Newsday* publication of the series on Rebozo.[294]

Finally, Caulfield testified that he obtained information from the FBI about Emile DeAntonio, the producer of the film, "Millhouse." Caulfield testified that he was asked to run a name check with the FBI on DeAntonio by John Dean, despite the fact that DeAntonio was not being considered at any time for any position within the administration.

Caulfield received a summary from the FBI of what their files contained, and noted in a memorandum to Dean that if Larry O'Brien "got behind" the "Millhouse" film, "we can, armed with the bureau's information, do a Nofziger job on DeAntonio and O'Brien."[295] Finally, the success of "Millhouse" apparently reached such proportions that Caulfield recommended to Dean the "release of DeAntonio's FBI derogatory background to friendly media."[296]

Caulfield also recommended in his memo that a discreet IRS audit be done of New Yorker Films, DeAntonio, and Daniel Talbot, the distributor of the film. Caulfield testified that Dean turned down Caulfield's suggestions, but the fact that Caulfield was able to obtain access to FBI information so easily clearly poses a serious threat to the rights of individual citizens unless carefully curtailed by legislation.

290. 3 *Hearings* 922.
291. Dean interview, July 26, 1973, p. 4.
292. Caulfield Executive Session, March 23, 1974, p. 70.
293. See Tab 10 of Caulfield Exhibit A, March 16, 1974.
294. Caulfield Executive Session, March 23, 1974, p. 73.
295. See Tab 18 of Caulfield Exhibit A, March 16, 1974.
296. See October 15, 1971 memorandum from Jack Caulfield to John Dean; *Ibid.*

4. DEPARTMENT OF JUSTICE

1. Anti-trust Policy. There were some suggestions made by Jeb Magruder and others, to use anti-trust policy to intimidate and coerce the large media conglomerates to give more favorable coverage to the Nixon administration.

In an October 17, 1969, memorandum from Magruder to Haldeman entitled the "Shotgun Versus the Rifle," Magruder discussed the problem of perceived unfair coverage of the White House by news media:

> The real problem that faces the Administration is to get this unfair coverage in such a way that we make a major impact on a basis which the networks, newspapers and Congress will react to and begin to look at things somewhat differently.[297]

Magruder suggested the Anti-Trust Division as a potentially useful agency in curbing media unfairness. He recommended that the Administration

> "utilize the anti-trust division to investigate various media relating to anti-trust violations. Even the possible threat of anti-trust action I think would be effective in changing their views in the above matter." [298]

Jack Caulfield also recommended that the anti-trust laws be used to curb the media. In a memo to John Dean on November 2, 1971, Caulfield, with the concurrence of Lyn Nofziger, recommended that anti-trust action be taken against the *Los Angeles Times,* in response to their publication of a new street edition.[299] Dean requested an opinion from his aide, David Wilson, on the proposed request, but no further action was apparently taken.[300]

On April 14, 1972, the Anti-Trust Division of the Justice Department in fact filed an anti-trust suit against the three major networks.[301] It is as yet unclear whether the articulated desires of some White House staff members expressed above had any effect on the decision to file the suit.

2. Internal Security Division. The Internal Security Division (ISD) of the Department of Justice was a repository of domestic "internal security" information.

Howard Hunt testified that Robert Mardian, former Assistant Attorney General in charge of the Internal Security Division, forwarded FBI investigative information on Daniel

297. See Exhibit 000.
298. *Ibid.*
299. See Tab 21 of Caulfield Exhibit A, March 16, 1974.
300. *Ibid.*
301. See 72-219 RJK, 72-820 RJK, 72-821 RJK; District Court for the Southern District of California.

Ellsberg to the Plumbers over in the White House.[302]

After he left the ISD, Mardian also arranged to provide CRP with intelligence information on potential demonstrations. Mardian defended this practice in his testimony as practical and proper.[303] When asked if the type of information given to CRP was also available to the public, Mardian responded:

"It was available under the guidelines to any entity that might be the subject of violent civil disorder and the appropriate people that should know of the potential so that they might arrest it." [304]

James McCord testified that the initial request for additional intelligence on demonstrators originated with Robert Odle, CRP's Director of Administration.[305] In a memorandum to then-Attorney General Mitchell, Odle outlined CRP's need for additional intelligence on potentially violent disruptions at their Washington, D.C. office or at the Republican National Convention. Mardian said that Mitchell concurred in this opinion and instructed Mardian to make the appropriate arrangements.[306]

Mardian called John Martin, Chief of the ISD Analysis and Evaluation Section, on May 11, 1972, to tell him to expect a visit from the CRP security people.[307] Subsequently, CRP security chief James McCord was directed to contact Martin to obtain the needed information.[308]

After confirming the appropriateness of the meeting with his superiors, Martin met with McCord on May 18, 1972.[309] The first meeting lasted for almost an hour, and then McCord and/or his assistant, Robert Houston, met again with Analysis and Evaluation staff on May 25, May 31, and June 2, 1972.[310]

The files of the ISD shown to McCord included domestic intelligence from the FBI and other related sources, according to McCord. McCord reviewed these FBI reports, including one which he claimed talked about a Democratic contender's finance operation:

"One such report dealt with, as I recall, a funding operation that was reported in which the McGovern committee purportedly funded a so-called barn storming

302. Hunt Executive Session, June 11, 1973, p. 74.
303. 6 *Hearings* 2398-99.
304. *Ibid.*, 2399.
305. 1 *Hearings* 178.
306. Mardian interview, June 1, 1973, p. 4.
307. See ISD records; Exhibit 000.
308. Testimony of James McCord; *op. cit.*, p. 178.
309. Martin interview; See also ISD logs.
310. See logs of Internal Security Division, Exhibit 000.

tour of several members of the Vietnam Veterans Against the War . . ." [311]

Any violence to be directed against CRP by any individuals or groups might properly be disclosed to CRP security personnel and appropriate law enforcement officials. However, the free flow of information out of the Internal Security Division to the President's re-election campaign appears to have exceeded the agency's appropriate function. John Martin said that no such "intelligence information" was provided to any Democratic candidates, because the Democrats "didn't ask for it." [312] This is ironic since the Committee has received testimony that E. Howard Hunt was planning a violent demonstration for the Democratic convention.[313]

Use of the ISD personnel to conduct interviews for the White House during the Kleindienst confirmation hearings has been documented earlier in this report.[314]

3. Parole Board. On December 30, 1971, Charles Colson received a telephone call from former United States Senator George Smathers. Smathers called Colson to request his assistance in releasing Calvin Kovens from prison prior to the May 1, 1972 date set by the Parole Board. As Smathers explained to Colson, "I really think that politically it's a very astute thing to do and it would not do anything but get, gain credit and commendation for the President. I can guarantee that. There's no backlash to this at all." [315] Colson explained to Smathers that he would get to work on it, and immediately sent a memo to John Dean saying, "the attached is much too hot for me to handle." [316] Colson explained to Dean that "in view of Smathers' decision to support the President next year, . . . we had better attend to this and not let it slip." [317]

Kovens was released from jail on January 6, 1972, and subsequently donated $30,000 in cash to the Financial Committee for the Re-election of the President.[318]

Kovens stated that his release from prison four months prior to his parole date was due solely to his health condition, and was the result of personal intervention by the warden of the facility at Egland Air Force Base.[319]

311. 1 *Hearings* 180.
312. See Martin Interview.
313. 10 *Hearings* 3983; see also *infra*.
314. See *supra*.
315. Conversation with George Smathers, December 30, 1971, p. 2. See Exhibit 000.
316. December 30, 1971 memorandum from Charles Colson to John Dean attached as Exhibit 000.
317. *Ibid.*
318. Kovens Interview, October 25, 1973.
319. Kovens Interview, October 25, 1973.

There is no evidence before the Committee that Kovens was released for political reasons or in exchange for a contribution except for the ambiguous chain for events noted above. The calls referred to above, however, indicate the willingness of White House officials to attempt to utilize supposedly independent government agencies for political purposes.

5. SECRET SERVICE

Some misuse and attempted misuse of the Secret Service has already been noted in the wiretap of F. Donald Nixon in order to avoid political embarassment for the President.[320] However, there were additional instances during the course of the 1972 campaign when White House officials either sought or used information from the Secret Service obtained during the course of their official duties in protecting the Presidential candidates.

On August 16, 1972, Steve Karalekas, an assistant in the White House, wrote to Charles Colson concerning information that he had obtained indirectly from the Secret Service.[321] The information that was passed on to Colson was that a Secret Service agent was upset because Senator McGovern had stayed at the home of an individual in Massachusetts who was allegedly a "subversive." Karalekas also wrote that the agent had promised to continue to pass along similar kinds of information.[322]

As a result of this information, Colson had Dick Howard instruct John Dean to check out the facts on the suspect individual's background. Dean asked Pete Kinsey of his office to check with the White House FBI liaison to see if there were any helpful information.[323] There is no indication that this request was ever followed up any further.

On another occasion, a "top official" at the Secret Service brought John Dean a "small intelligence printout regarding Senator McGovern." The Secret Service official left the printout for Dean and said, "I thought that this might be of interest to you." [324] Dean recalled that the printout had to do with Senator McGovern attending a fund-raising function in Philadelphia along with alleged former Communist supporters.

Dean said he took the document to Charles Colson who indicated that he was interested in the information. Dean

320. See earlier section, *supra*.
321. See Tab 30 of Caulfield Exhibit A, March 16, 1973.
322. *Ibid.*
323. *Ibid.*
324. 3 *Hearings* 1071; 923.

ᶜaid that Colson later told him that he had made arrangements to have the information published.[325]

Colson took the teletype report and had Joan Hall, his secretary, retype the information contained therein.[326] William Lambert, the same individual to whom Howard Hunt had shown the forged Diem cables, stated that he was contacted by Colson and shown a short teletype-like wire of about twelve lines in Colson's office after the Democratic Convention. He also recalled that the cable said something about a fund-raising meeting at an individual's house in Philadelphia.[327]

This political utilization by the White House of information obtained from the Secret Service during the 1972 campaign was very similar to earlier efforts by the White House to obtain information on individuals from the investigative agencies, and was an abuse of power by the White House during the 1972 campaign.

Some steps have already been taken in the Secret Service to insure that such incidents do not occur again. It is critically important to safeguard the independence of the Secret Service in order that it properly fulfill the protective function with which it is charged.

6. OTHER AGENCIES

1. Federal Communications Commission. In his October 17, 1969 memorandum to H. R. Haldeman noted above, Jeb Magruder recommended that to cope with alleged media bias, the White House

". . . begin an official monitoring system through the FCC as soon as Dean Burch is officially on board as chairman. If the monitoring system proves our point, we have the legitimate and legal rights to go to the networks, etc., and make official complaints from the FCC. This will have much more effect than a phone call from Herb Klein or Pat Buchanan." [328]

Charles W. Colson also prepared a memorandum with similar objectives for Haldeman on September 25, 1970, in which he summarized the pertinent points of his meeting with the chief executives of the three major television networks. Concluding that "they are very much afraid of us and are trying to prove they are the 'good guys'," Colson recom-

325. *Ibid.*
326. See Joan Hall interview, July 25, 1973, p. 6.
327. See Lambert interview, Aug. 13, 1973.
328. See Magruder memo, Exhibit 000, p. 2.

mended that he

"pursue with Dean Burch the possibility of an interpretive ruling by the FCC on the role of the President when he uses T.V., as soon as we have a majority. I think this point could be very favorably clarified and it would, of course, have an inhibiting impact on the networks and their professed concern with achieving balance." [329]

In the purported House Judiciary Committee transcript of the September 15, 1972 meeting published by the *Washington Post*, President Nixon discussed with Dean and Haldeman possible FCC problems for the *Washington Post* when its television and radio stations applied for license renewals:

H   The *Post* (unintelligible)—
P   It's going to have its problems—
H   (unintelligible)
D   (unintelligible) The networks are good with Maury coming back 3 days in a row and (unintelligible)
P   That's right. The main, main thing is the Post is going to have damnable, damnable problems out of this one. They have a television station
D   That's right, they do.
P   and they're going to have to get it renewed.
H   They've got a radio station, too.
P   When does that come up?
D   I don't know. But the practice of non-licensees has certainly gotten more,
P   That's right.
D   more active in the, this area.
P   And it's going to be God damn active here.
D   (Laughter) (Silence)

These examples help to demonstrate the tendency of individuals in the White House to attempt to use supposedly independent agencies to achieve political ends. The following example shows how the tendency continued into the 1972 campaign.

2. *ACTION (formerly the Peace Corps and VISTA).* Jeb Magruder wrote to Ken Reitz, director of Young Voters for the President, on November 28, 1971, that ACTION "is an agency that we should be able to use politically." Magruder recommends that a meeting be scheduled with Joseph Blatchford, ACTION's director, where it should be suggested that he:

"Do a lot of speaking on campuses and in high schools.

329. See Colson memo, Exhibit 000.

He identified well with younger people and has the kind of program they like to hear about.

We used their recruiters (who talked to 450,000 young people last year), advertising program, public relations effort, and public contact people to sell the President and the accomplishments of the Administration. We should be involved and aware of everything from the scheduled appearances of ACTION's recruiters to the format and content of its advertising." [330]

Thus, the value of governmental agencies to the incumbent running for re-election was recognized early by CRP. This use of the incumbency is discussed more fully in a later chapter of this report.[331]

II. Public Relations in the White House

A. INTRODUCTION

During its first four years, the Nixon White House initiated a wide variety of public relations efforts directed toward re-electing President Nixon in 1972. Among the more successful of these efforts were: (1) letter-writing campaigns; (2) direct-mail operations; and (3) the organization of citizens' committees in response to specific issues. While public relations activities are an integral part of politics and campaigns, some of the activities initiated in the White House resulted in some deceptive and misleading practices which are described below.

B. LETTER-WRITING

The letter-writing campaigns generated by the White House were designed to give the impression to the recipients of the letters of a broad base of support for positions advocated by President Nixon, while the letters also served as a vehicle for publicizing the Administration's positions in various matters.

On October 11, 1969, H. R. Haldeman wrote a memorandum to Jeb Magruder and ordered a program of:

"sending letters and telegrams, and making telephone calls to the senators, blasting them on their consistent opposition to the President on everything he is trying to do for the country. This program needs to be subtle and worked out well so they receive these items from their

330. See Magruder memo, Exhibit 000.
331. See Section on Use of the Incumbency, Chapter III.

home districts as well as other points around the country." [332]

This memorandum initiated the White House campaign to still criticism from moderate Republican Senators Goodell, Percy, and Mathias.

Haldeman's hand-written notes from the bottom of a memo from Magruder to Haldeman on October 14, 1969, note that this campaign against the moderate senators was being carried out with the awareness of the President. In part, Haldeman wrote:

". . . this was an order, not a question, and I was told it was being carried out and so informed the P(resident)." [333]

Haldeman apparently wanted to keep this letter-writing campaign against the dissident senators secret, for he wrote across an October 16, 1969 memorandum from Jeb Magruder, "This should be reported orally—or at least in a confidential memo." [334]

Other letter-writing campaigns with letters sent to influential senators and to the "letters to the editor" column of newspapers were initiated to support the nomination of G. Harrold Carswell to the Supreme Court and to support the President's speech announcing the invasion of Cambodia in May, 1970.

Shortly after the letters-supporting-Carswell campaign, a discreet letter-writing operation was set up at the Republican National Committee by Jeb Magruder with suggestions from Patrick Buchanan.[335] Betty Nolan was hired by the RNC in May, 1970, to direct the letter-writing campaign and during this time, Nolan reported to RNC officials and to Jeb Magruder at the White House through his aides, including Gordon Strachan and Ron Baukol.[336]

Ideas for letters came from Magruder's staff, from the RNC Office of Communications and from news stories that Nolan read. Letters were prepared, except for signatures, by Ms. Nolan and then distributed to volunteers in Washington and throughout the country who signed the letters and then sent them in as personal letters to the addressees designated by the RNC.

During the first weeks of the letter-writing program, Nolan was unable to find individuals willing to sign the ghosted

332. See Exhibit 000.
333. See Exhibit 000.
334. See Exhibit 000.
335. Magruder Interview, Oct. 1, 1973, p. 1.
336. Nolan Interview, Sept. 3 and Sept. 28, 1973, p. 3.

letters. Nolan recalled that someone (she does not recall who) suggested that false names without addresses be used on the letters. Therefore, from May, 1970 until sometime in July, 1970, some falsely signed letters were sent to the newspapers.[337] In July, 1970, Gordon Strachan became Ms. Nolan's contact on the Magruder staff, and with advice from Strachan and help from the Young Republicans, Nolan organized a network of people to sign and mail the prepared letters, thus making false signatures unnecessary.[338] Subsequent letter-writing campaigns were initiated to influence key journalists such as Katherine Graham, Eric Sevareid, and some newspapers such as the Washington *Star*.[339]

In January or February 1971, Magruder assigned responsibility for the letter-writing campaign to Ron Baukol, a White House fellow. In a memorandum to Charles Colson on April 26, 1971, Baukol described the effort as "a true undercover operation in which letters are printed as letters from private citizens. One girl . . . at the RNC . . . generates 30-35 letters per week, of which an average of two to three are printed." [340] Baukol added the program was expanding "slowly, so the security of the program will not be breached." [341]

In February, 1972, Betty Nolan began to organize the Committe to Re-elect the President's letter-writing campaign. Most of the early letters generated by the CRP focused upon the leading Democratic candidates. During the course of the campaign, about 50 letters a week were prepared and mailed to volunteers, with most of the letters in final form, needing only a signature before being mailed to newspapers.

After President Nixon announced on May 8, 1972, that the United States was going to mine Haiphong harbor and resume the bombing of North Viet Nam, the letters operation was an integral part of the massive public relations effort undertaken by the CRP to generate support for the President's policies. CRP's response to the President's announcement is outlined in a memorandum from Rob Odle to John Mitchell, dated May 9, 1972.[342] Odle noted that "Betty Nolan's letters-to-the-editor apparatus began to crank up her troops and we expect over 1200 telegrams as a result of this operation." [343]

337. Betty Nolan Interview, Sept. 28, 1973, p. 1.
338. Betty Nolan Interview, Sept. 28, 1973.
339. See Exhibit 000.
340. See Exhibit 000.
341. *Ibid.*
342. See Exhibit 000.
343. *Ibid.*, p. 3.

Gordon Liddy, then counsel to the Finance Committee to Re-elect the President, wrote to John Mitchell on May 15, 1972, that:

"Betty Nolan hit four of the senators with 195 letters. In addition, early yesterday morning she had over 70 letters sent to the New York *Times* protesting its May 10 editorial. (All other staffers were instructed at the May 11 staff meeting to write similar letters to the *Times*)." [344]

Rob Odle, former Director of Administration for CRP, testified before the Select Committee that "[t]he entire campaign aparatus that week went to work in support of what happened." [845] Issues of newspapers running polls on the President's actions were bought *en masse* by the CRP, and the poll responses were mailed in to tilt the results toward the President. In addition, a full-page advertisement was placed in the New York *Times* on May 17, 1972, by a group of citizens supporting the President's decision to mine Haiphong harbor.[346] This ad was paid for with $4,400 in cash from CRP and prepared by the November group, the advertising arm of CRP. Charles Colson admitted that he "reviewed the draft and probably made changes in it" to the G.A.O. Neither the source of funds nor the group that actually wrote the advertisement was indicated in the body of the advertisement itself, an apparent violation of 18 U.S.C. the criminal statute governing publication of political statements.[347]

Finally, as part of CRP's campaign to generate support for the President's actions, Howard Hunt called Donald Segretti in Los Angeles on May 8, 1972. Hunt said the President was about to take very decisive action in Viet Nam and asked Segretti to put together support for the President's policies to counter the expected reaction of the peace groups.[848] Segretti called his main operatives in Florida, Robert Benz and Doug Kelley [349] and instructed them to set up tables for people to sign telegrams to the White House supporting the President. Segretti sent two telegrams to the White House that contained several hundred false signatures. None of the individuals whose names were on the

344. See Exhibit 000. Liddy's memorandum also described a motorcade to support the President's action in Miami, Florida, that received heavy support in a Cuban community.
345. 1 *Hearings* 68.
346. See Exhibit 000.
347. See GAO report to Department of Justice, May 3, 1973, pp. 1-2.
348. See Segretti interview and witness summary, p. 8.
349. Segretti Witness Summary, p. 8.

telegrams had, in fact, approved of the use of his or her name.[350]

President's Interest. It is significant to note that a March 9, 1970 memorandum to Magruder from Haldeman succinctly characterized the President's interest in such activities. Haldeman asked Magruder to prepare for him:

> . . . once every two weeks a summary of the various hatchet-man operations—letter to the editors, counterattack, etc., so that I can report to the President on the activity in this regard.[351]

C. DIRECT MAILING

At the request of the White House Office of Communication, the RNC built a series of mailing lists for editors, media, governors, Congressmen and political figures which were made available to offices at the White House as well as the RNC.[352]

Beginning in mid-1970, direct mail requests were received usually from Herb Klein's office, but as the presidential campaign progressed, Charles Colson's office began ordering more direct mailings.[353] From its formation, the Committee to Re-elect the President also utilized RNC mailing facilities for the reproduction and distribution of political materials.

The primary deceptive practice found in the direct mail operation was the concealment of the true source of some of the letters and mailings that were distributed. Some letters were distributed that were printed on private or business stationery of the individuals involved, but the letters failed to acknowledge that the costs of preparation, duplication, and distribution were not borne by the individuals sending out the letter. For example, a letter from former Senator George A. Smathers endorsing President Nixon for re-election was sent out by the direct mail operation of the RNC to thousands of individuals. Written instructions to Diana Burns, the individual in charge of the direct mailing operation, directed her to change the letter in any manner necessary to alter its appearance beyond identification as coming from RNC.[354] Other examples of distribution without mention of a source were also found. A reprint of a newspaper article indicating that Representative Pete McCloskey would

350. 10 *Hearings* 3995; Segretti interview notes and witness summary, p. 9.
351. See Exhibit 000.
352. Memorandum from Herbert Klein to Harry Dent, Brice Harlow, and Lyn Nofziger, Nov. 4, 1969. (See Exhibit 10.)
353. Diana Burns interview, August 14, 1973.
354. Memo to Diana Burns, March 22, 1971, Exhibit 11.

consider backing a third party candidate was set up with mail room specifications indicating that the articles should be mailed in "plain No. 10 envelopes" with commemorative or unusual stamps to disguise the source of the mailing to top newspaper and political figures.[355] Another example of a disguised source of distribution was the reproduction of an International Brotherhood of Teamsters news service press release reporting the executive board endorsement of President Nixon for Re-election. One thousand copies of this release were mailed by the RNC in plain, hand-addressed envelopes.[356]

Such procedures to disguise the true source of these direct mailings would appear to violate the spirit, if not the letter, of the law as defined in the United States Code, Title 18, Section 612, which provides:

§ Publications or distribution of political statements.

Whoever wilfully publishes or distributes or causes to be published or distributed, or for the purpose of publishing or distributing the same knowingly deposits for mailing or delivery or causes to be deposited for mailing or delivery, or, except in cases of employees of the Postal Service in the official discharge of their duties, knowingly transports or causes to be transported in interstate commerce any card, pamphlet, circular, poster, dodger, advertisement, writing, or other statement relating to or concerning any person who has publicly declared his intention to seek the office of President, or Vice President of the United States, or Senator or Representative in, or Delegate or Resident Commissioner to Congress, in a primary, general, or special election, or convention of a political party, or has caused or permitted his intention to do so to be publicly declared, which does not contain the names of the persons, associations, committees, or corporations responsible for the publication or distribution of the same, and the names of the officers of each such association, committee, or corporation, shall be fined not more than $1,000 or imprisoned not more than one year, or both.

D. CITIZENS COMMITTEES

Another aspect of the White House public relations program was the establishment of special citizens committees to generate support for the President on specific issues. Executive directors for these committees were usually found in the

355. RNC mailroom files—instructions dated November 29, 1971.
356. See Exhibit 12.

Washington area, and financial supporters were recruited by the White House. Financial support for the citizens committees came from many prominent contributors.[357] However, the White House role in establishing and operating these citizens committees was never publicly acknowledged, Advertisements supporting the President were edited, sometimes written, and reviewed by individuals in the White House.[358]

Brief descriptions follow of some of the "citizens committees" established through White House efforts:

1. Tell It to Hanoi Committee. The "Tell It to Hanoi Committee" was organized after President Nixon's announcement of the invasion of Cambodia in May 1970. Financial support came from Jack Mulcahy, a heavy contributor to the 1970 Presidential campaign and its chairman was William J. "Pat" O'Hara, a New York attorney.

Numerous memoranda attest to the close relationship between this "independent citizens committee" and the White House. Invoices for services from the advertising agency placing the ads were forwarded to Jeb Magruder at the White House, but Magruder says they were paid for by the citizens committee and not from White House funds.[359]

In a May 5, 1970, memorandum to the President, Magruder reported that the "Tell It To Hanoi Committee" had placed advertisements in more than forty newspapers and sent more than a million pieces of mail asking for public support.[360] None of the advertisements identified the role of the White House in preparing this information.

2. Citizens Committee to Safeguard America. This group was formed to support the President's policies on the proposed anti-ballistic missile system and was responsible for placing a number of full-page newspaper advertisements supporting the ABM system. Haldeman wrote to Magruder on August 6, 1970, that President Nixon was especially pleased with the "Safeguard ad" and that whoever had written it should be complimented. A hand-written note on the bottom of the memorandum by Rob Odle says "Colson says he did it." [361]

The value to the White House of such independent citizens

357. Jeb Magruder interview, October 1, 1973.
358. *Ibid.*
359. Magruder Interview, October 1, 1973. Records of the Ayer/Jorgensen/MacDonald Agency show that on an account of $193,000, exactly $178,000 was paid to the agency by the "Tell It To Hanoi Committee." The remaining balance was covered by four checks from the Republican Campaign Committee and the Republican Finance Committee. See Exhibit 000.
360. See Exhibit 000.
361. See Exhibit 000.

committees is clear: they provided a means of persuading the populace to support administration policies without identifying the White House backing for them, and, more importantly, they created the impression that independent groups supported White House policies. Another advantage of these "independent" citizens committees was illustrated in a December 1, 1970, memorandum on political polling from Larry Higby to Herb Klein.[362] To make the White House-sponsored polls effective, Higby stated, ". . . we need other organizations that we can hang the polls on that will have credibility." [363] A list of possible "independent" groups that could be used for polling was attached to the memorandum; it included that "Tell It To Hanoi" committee and the "Committee for a Responsible Congress," both creations of the White House.

The success of the "Tell It To Hanoi Committee" and the "Committee to Safeguard America" led to the formation by the White House of "citizens committees" to attack key Senatorial candidates in the 1970 Congressional elections, In a June 17, 1970, memorandum to Jeb Magruder, Larry Higby urged the formation of citizens committees to run advertisements attacking Senate opponents of the Administration.[364]

3. *Committee for a Responsible Congress.* One such group was the "Committee for a Responsible Congress." Jeb Magruder said that a series of "negative ads" aimed at the "radical-liberals" in Congress was proposed by Charles Colson, who prepared much of the copy, and the ads were placed by the "Committee for a Responsible Congress." [365]

Carl Shipley, a Republican National Committeeman, was enlisted by White House staff as the treasurer of this committee.[366] Shipley recruited six other people to serve on the committee, giving them his word that it was a legitimate request and that he was calling at the instruction of the White House.[367] None of the committee members ever solicited or contributed any money in support of the advertisements.

Shipley said he first saw the copy for the ads that were placed at a meeting in the Executive Office Building attended by Magruder and Colson, representatives of an advertising agency, and possibly Haldeman or Ehrlichman. Neither he

362. See Exhibit 000.
363. *Ibid.*
364. See Exhibit 00.
365. Magruder Interview, October 1, 1973.
366. Shipley Interview, October 15, 1973.
367. Shipley stated that some of the people contacted refused to join the committee and he told them their refusal to participate would be communicated to the White House staff. Shipley interview, October 15, 1973.

nor any of the other committee members was ever contacted as to the content or target of the advertising.[368]

4. Committee for the Congress of '70. The Committee for the Congress of 1970 was similarly established to place a series of positive advertisements supporting Congressional candidates favorable to the Nixon Administration. Its treasurer was Alexander Lankler, the former state chairman of the Maryland Republican Party. Lankler recalled that he was called by Charles Colson and asked if he would lend his name to a series of political advertisements.[369]

Money for the advertisement was given to Lankler by the White House and forwarded by him to Ayer/Jorgensen/MacDonald, Inc., the same advertising agency that handled the "Tell It To Hanoi" account.[370] Lankler does not recall who delivered the cash to him, although he did recall that $80,000 in cash was received via Colson's authorization.[371]

Despite their lack of success in the 1970 congressional elections, the White House public relations people favored the formation of citizens committees in the 1972 presidential election. Rob Odle, discussing campaign organization in an October 29, 1971, memorandum to the Attorney General, reviewed the work of committees like "Tell It To Hanoi" and suggested other citizens committees that could be used in the 1972 campaign.[372]

Patrick Buchanan, in a March 14, 1972, memorandum to John Mitchell, also recommended that citizens committees be established to attack political opponents. Buchanan suggested the following scenario:

> . . . soon after the Democratic Convention there be established one General Committee with an odd sounding name, and other committees tailored to specific issues, i.e. 'United States Security Council,' which can then be mailed in bulk to GOP or citizens groups for distribution in target states. Chuck Colson's shop could have such, one imagines, established in a matter of hours.
>
> The specific committee should zero in on issues— depending on the Democratic candidate—where the opposition is especially vulnerable. For example, were Muskie the nominee, we would have a committee on defense of the United States, one on Space, one on Aid

368. *Ibid.*
369. Alexander Lankler interview, October 10, 1973.
370. *Ibid.*
371. *Ibid.*
372. See Exhibit 000.

Non-public schools, etc.[373]

The "Citizens Campaign" in 1972 consisted of numerous committees, ranging from the "Massachusetts Lawyers Committee for the Re-election of the President" to "Nursing Homes for Nixon-Agnew." [374] Two examples are discussed below.

5. Labor for America Committee. Charles Colson requested the formation of a dummy committee as a vehicle through which a mailing to labor could be funded.[375]

In October 1972, a registration form and statement of organization was submitted to the General Accounting Office (GAO) for the "Labor for America Committee," which stated that the Committee supported President Nixon's re-election. The committee's address was a local post office box rented by Mrs. Myles Ambrose, wife of the former Commissioner of Customs. In its filing with the GAO, the Labor Committee indicated receipt of a $4,400 contribution from the FCRP. This money was used to reprint a brochure entitled "Why Labor Can't Support George McGovern," which was a reproduction of an unsigned pamphlet circulated at the Democratic National Convention attacking McGovern's voting record on issues affecting labor.[376]

The reprinting and distribution of this pamphlet by a purportedly labor-affiliated organization enhanced the credibility of the contents. Were the same charges to have been published directly by the Committee to Re-Elect the President, the impact of the charges would have been diminished.

6. Citizens for a Liberal Alternative. There were also "Citizens Committees" which had no members at all. The "Citizens for a Liberal Alternative" was such a dummy committee.

In the late fall of 1971, Bart Porter stated that Jeb Magruder told him to contact Ken Khachigian, a White House speechwriter, about a pamphlet the White House wanted distributed.[377] Magruder instructed Porter to have the pamphlet printed and mailed to a group of leading liberals. While Ken Khachigian prepared the pamphlet in the White House, the pamphlet purported to be from the "Citizens for a Liberal Alternative." The pamphlet attacked Senator Muskie on

373. 10 *Hearings* 4216. Written in the margin of the memo are Mitchell's comments, "Good. Put Colson in charge."
374. General Accounting Office Published Record.
375. See Exhibit 000.
376. 10 *Hearings* 3934. The brochure is at 10 *Hearings* 4061. Buchanan testified that this unsigned brochure was widely distributed at the Democratic Convention by George Meany and Alexander Barkan (10 *Hearings* 3958).
377. Porter interview, Sept. 6, 1973.

a variety of issues thus appearing to come from a group of liberal Democrats. According to Khachigian, Pat Buchanan edited Khachigian's draft before it was printed in final form.[378]

Porter received the final draft from Khachigian and asked Tom Bell, a staff member of the Young Voters for the President, to have 1,000 copies printed up in 72 hours.[379] All the negatives from the pamphlet were returned to Porter because of the secrecy Porter demanded.[380] Following Magruder's direction, Porter had the pamphlet mailed to about four hundred "liberals" around the country.[381] A plan for Roger Greaves, "Sedan Chair I", to distribute some of the pamphlets [382] at a Muskie fund-raising dinner in Beverly Hills fell through when the dinner was cancelled.[383]

This bogus pamphlet also found its way to the New Hampshire primary. In February 1972, Porter instructed Roger Stone, a scheduler at CRP, to fly to New Hampshire with a copy of the pamphlet and to place it in the headquarters of Senator George McGovern. Stone left the pamphlet on a table in the McGovern headquarters in Manchester, New Hampshire, and then went to the *Manchester Union Leader*, where he produced another copy of the pamphlet for an editor there which he said he had found in McGovern headquarters. Stone said he expressed outrage to the editor that the McGovern campaign was capable of printing such trash.[384] Berl Bernhard, Senator Muskie's campaign manager, testified that the pamphlet from the Citizens for a Liberal Alternative "appeared in a number of different places in New Hampshire." [385]

Finally, Donald Segretti received 500 to 1000 copies of this same pamphlet sometime after the Florida primary, and sent them to some of his agents, who presumably distributed them.[386]

378. A copy of the pamphlet is at pp. 4055-58, Book 10, Select Committee Hearings (Exhibit 158). Patrick Buchanan's testimony on this incident is at 10 *Hearings* 3922.

379. Bart Porter interview, Sept. 6, 1973, p. 22. See also Bell interview, August 15, 1973. Bell recalls that only 500 copies of the pamphlet were ordered.

380. Bell interview, August 15, 1973.

381. Porter interview, Sept. 6, 1973, p. 22.

382. The plan was Magruder's or Khachigian's idea according to Porter. Porter interview, August 20, 1973, p. 13.

383. Roger Greaves interview, August 21, 1973.

384. Foger Stone interview, August 15, 1973.

385. 11 *Hearings* 4671; See also testimony of Frank Mankiewicz that he observed the pamphlet in New Hampshire. 12 *Hearings* 4611-4612.

386. 10 *Hearings* 3994. It should also be noted that Stewart Mott placed some advertisements from the "Committee for Honesty in Politics" in the 1972 campaign. However, Mott paid for these ads and personally signed every one of them. (Mott Executive Session, October 5, 1973.)

II. 1972 CAMPAIGN

A. Political Strategy

The poliical strategy of the Committee to Re-elect the President in early 1971 and 1972 was unambiguous: undercut Senator Muskie in the Democratic primaries, divide the Democratic Party so that it could not unite after the convention, and assist where possible in getting the weakest Democratic candidate nominated. The absence of a serious fight for re-nomination gave the CRP and the White House the luxury of focusing their political efforts during this period on potential Democratic opponents rather than serious primary contenders within their own party. In the meantime, the various Democratic contenders had to concentrate their own political efforts on obtaining their party's nomination.

The Nixon strategy was best embodied in a series of political memoranda written by speechwriter Patrick Buchanan and his assistant, Ken Khachigian.[387] The early concern with Senator Muskie resulted from a series of public opinion polls in April, May and June of 1971, which showed Senator Muskie leading both President Nixon and Governor Wallace in a three-man race.[388] Buchanan outlined a "Muskie" strategy in a lengthy memorandum to President Nixon on March 24, 1971. Buchanan proposed creating a "Muskie Watch," "an operation working perhaps within the Republican National Committee, which may even be a publicized operation, doing constant research on Ed [Muskie] and putting out materials to interest groups, and to the press."[389]

A few months later, Buchanan wrote:

> Thus, Senator Muskie is Target A as of mid-summer for our operation. Our specific goals are (a) to produce political problems for him, right now, (b) to hopefully help defeat him in one or more of the primaries (Florida looks now to be the best early bet, California, the best later bet), and (c) finally, to visit upon him some political wounds that will not only reduce his chances for nomination—but damage him as a candidate, should he be nominated.[390]

The strategy Buchanan advocated was to force Muskie to

387. See Exhibits No. 164-194, Vol. 10, pp. 4114-4263 for a full exposition of these memoranda.
388. 11 *Hearings* 4637.
389. 10 *Hearing* 4146, 4153.
390. 10 *Hearings* 4186.

take more stands on controversial issues and to have President Nixon attack Muskie "on those issues that divide Democrats." [391] The anti-Muskie plan involved much "negative campaigning" against the Senator rather than positive campaigning on behalf of President Nixon. In addition, such a strategy would subject Muskie to the "pressures and harassments that go with being a front runner, pressures and harassments he is not getting today." [392]

In addition, Buchanan advocated concentrating on dividing the Democrats so that they would be unable to unite for the general election. In a July 2, 1971 memo, Buchanan advised:

> [We] maintain as guiding political principle that our great hope for 1972 lies in maintaining or exacerbating the deep Democratic rift between the elite, chic, New Left, intellectual avant garde, isolationist, bell-bottomed environmentalist, new priorities types on the one hand— and the hard hat, Dick Daley, Holy Name Society, ethnc, blue collar, Knights of Columbus, NYPD, Queens Democrats on the other.
>
> The liberal Democrats should be pinioned to their hippie supporters. The Humphrey Democrats should be reminded of how they were the fellows who escalated and cheered the war from its inception. [393]

This "attack strategy" of dividing the opposition was a main tenet of political faith both at the White House and the CRP throughout the 1972 campaign.

By April 12, 1972, Buchanan observed, "Our primary objective, to prevent Senator Muskie from sweeping the early primaries, locking up the convention in April, and uniting the Democratic Party behind him for the fall, has been achieved." [394] Further on, in the same memorandum, Buchanan rhetorically raised the question of "whom [do] we want to run against." [395] Buchanan's clear choice was Senator George McGovern. Later in April, Buchanan noted, "we must do as little as possible at this time to impede McGovern's rise." [396]

The above strategy, while not improper in itself, was ultimately converted by others into the dirty tricks outlined below. The various operatives and agents of the White House and the CRP also had three major objectives in the 1972

391. 10 *Hearings* 4148.
392. 10 *Hearings* 4147.
393. 10 *Hearings* 4183.
394. 10 *Hearings* 4225.
395. *Ibid.*
396. 10 *Hearings* 4235.

campaign: to weaken Senator Muskie, to divide the Democrats, and to nominate the weakest Democratic candidate.

The absence of primary opponents for President Nixon allowed his political strategists to target their efforts on the Democrats. The abundance of money in the CRP allowed the political operatives to set up a concerted effort to infiltrate and interfere with the Democratic primaries. The result was a campaign to re-elect President Nixon that was filled with illegal, improper, and unethical activity, much of which is described below.

B. Implementation of White House and CRP Strategy

1. DONALD SEGRETTI

A. Hiring. In early 1971, Gordon Strachan and Dwight Chapin, both staff aides in the White House working for H. R. Haldeman, discussed the need for a "non-Colson dirty tricks operation in the field" for the 1972 campaign.[397] Strachan said that Chapin explained that he and Buchanan had been involved in some campaign pranks such as a false mailing sent out in the New Hampshire primary,[398] but that it would be a good idea if the operation were moved from the White House in 1972,

As a result, a meeting was held in the early summer of 1971 among Chapin, Strachan, Buchanan, Khachigian and Ron Walker, head of White House advance operations, to discuss how to structure a political prankster operation in the field for the 1972 campaign. Buchanan testified that he advised the group that "it should be a small operation, and that because of 1971 . . . it ought to be under the Committee to Re-Elect the President." [399]

Strachan and Chapin agreed that Donald Segretti, an old college friend of theirs from USC, would be a good candidate for the job of pulling pranks to disrupt the Democratic presidential primary campaigns. Segretti was first contacted by Dwight Chapin in the spring of 1971 about possible employment following his release from the Army.[400] Se-

397. Strachan Interview, August 13, 1973.
398. *Ibid.,* p. 1.
399. 10 *Hearings* 000.
400. In informal interviews, Segretti noted that Strachan first called him in January, 1971, on a purely social basis, and that Chapin contacted him in April, 1971, about possible White House employment. Strachan claims that Segretti first contacted him about finding a job. See also transcript of *U.S. v. Chapin*, p. 220.

gretti at that time expressed some interest in a possible job, since both his friends worked in the White House and since he thought that the job might include exciting work.

Segretti stayed in touch with Chapin and Strachan during the next few months, and flew to Washington, D. C. to meet with them in late June, 1971.[401] Segretti met with Chapin and Strachan twice on this visit—once at dinner at Chapin's house, and again the following day at lunch. At these meetings, Strachan and Chapin explained to Segretti that his job would be to perform political pranks that would aid in the re-election of President Nixon.[402] Segretti was given $400 in cash from Gordon Strachan to cover his expenses for this trip. Strachan and Chapin also cautioned Segretti not to discuss this matter with anyone else if he were not interested. But Segretti expressed great interest in the job, since it seemed to involve exciting work, and after this meeting, he began to contact old friends about the possibility of doing some work for the Nixon campaign.

Meanwhile, Strachan and Chapin obtained Haldeman's approval for the project to insure that Segretti could be paid from left-over 1968 campaign funds. Mr. Haldeman specifically approved having a person in the field to disrupt the Democratic primary campaigns, and specifically approved the hiring of Mr. Segretti.[403] In late August, 1971, Haldeman and Strachan met with Herbert Kalmbach. Strachan testified that Haldeman directed Kalmbach to pay the salary and expenses of Segretti.[404]

Strachan then told Segretti to contact Herbert Kalmbach in Newport Beach, California, for the purpose of finalizing his employment. Segretti met Kalmbach in late August, 1971, and was offered a salary of $16,000 a year plus expenses for his activities.[405] Segretti said he was not sure if he was ·to be working for Mr. Kalmbach, Mr. Chapin, or others.[406]

401. 10 *Hearings* 3985.
402. 10 *Hearings* 3980.
403. 7 *Hearings* 2877. "I agreed that if this man wanted to take on this activity, Herbert Kalmbach should arrange for his compensation and expenses from the 1968 campaign fund surplus.

"It was my clear understanding that Segretti would act independently and on his own initiative within the broad guidelines outlined above. It was also my clear understanding that he was to engage in no illegal acts. Mr. Strachan has told me that he was so advised and that he understood that. I had no specific knowledge of Segretti's activities or the details of how or with whom he worked. I do not believe that there was anything wrong with the Segretti activity as it was conceived. I have only limited knowledge, and that acquired only lately, as to how it was actually carried out."
404. 6 *Hearings* 2502.
405. 10 *Hearings* 3980.
406. *Ibid.*

Following his meeting with Kalmbach, Segretti had lunch with Dwight Chapin not far from the Western White House in San Clemente, California. During this meeting, Chapin gave Segretti a list of cities and states on which to concentrate in the upcoming Presidential primary campaigns. Segretti said that Chapin stressed to him the secrecy of his duties, and said that his activities should be focused on fostering a split among the various Democratic candidates to prevent the Democratic Party from uniting behind one candidate after the convention.[407]

Chapin also emphasized to Segretti the importance of having media impact in Segretti's activities. For example, Segretti said Chapin suggested that he have pickets with Humphrey signs at Muskie rallies. Segretti said Chapin also suggested putting out phoney press releases.[408]

Chapin emphasized to Segretti that he should focus his efforts on Senator Edmund Muskie, the Democratic front-runner at that time.[409] Segretti said that Chapin further explained that his objective should be to give the President his best chance for re-election in November, 1972, by seriously weakening the leading Democratic candidate, Senator Edmund Muskie. If that could be accomplished, the Democrats would have a bitter fight over the nomination and would never be able to recover in time for the general election.[410]

The alternative objective of Segretti's activities was to divide the Democratic candidates among themselves to create bitterness and mistrust among the Democrats.[411]

Following this meeting with Chapin in California, Segretti began contacting old friends of his in California and elsewhere about doing political work in the upcoming campaign. After his release from the Army on September 13, 1971, Segretti received a telephone call from Dwight Chapin. Chapin informed Segretti that Strachan would no longer be involved in the operation. Chapin also explained to Segretti that they would leave messages for one another under the aliases of Don Morris (for Segretti) and Bob Duane (for Chapin.)[412] At Chapin's request, Segretti flew to Washington, D.C., and met Chapin in the dining room of the Hay-Adams.[413]

407. *Ibid.*
408. See Segretti witness summary, p. 3.
409. 10 *Hearings* 3987.
410. Segretti Witness Summary, p. 2.
411. 10 *Hearings* 4001.
412. 10 *Hearings* 3989. In fact, Chapin actually left messages for Segretti under the name of "Chapman."
413. See *U.S. v. Chapin*, p. 231 of transcript.

At that meeting, Chapin suggested to Segretti that he get both a post office box where he could receive mail from Chapin and an answering service so that he could be reached at all times. In addition, Segretti said Chapin gave him a list of the 1968 advancemen from Nixon's Presidential campaign so that Segretti could begin making contacts in the appropriate primary states. Segretti testified that Chapin stressed he should not say or do anything which would link his activities to Chapin, the White House, the Republican party, or the Committee to Re-Elect the President. Chapin also gave Segretti the name of Ward Turnquist, an old high school friend of Chapin's, as a possible contact in Southern California.[414]

Chapin directed Segretti to fly to Portland, Oregon, the following day, preceding the President's visit there, to observe a presidential advance. Segretti flew to Portland on September 24, 1971, and stayed at the Benson Hotel.[415] There he was able to familiarize himself wih the advance operation and the means used to handle demonstrators.[416]

On the morning of Sunday, September 26, Segretti met with Chapin in Segretti's room at the hotel. At that time, Chapin gave Segretti a copy of the Advanceman's Manual, and they had further general discussions about Segretti's activities.[417]

After his meeting with Chapin, Segretti returned to Los Angeles and received his first payment from Kalmbach, a check for $5,000 as an advance on his expenses, and a check for $667 for his two weeks salary.

Following the Presidential appearance in Portland, Chapin wrote Segretti a memorandum which said:

> From now on, we want to have a least one Muskie sign in among demonstrators who are demonstrating against the President. It should be MUSKIE FOR PRESIDENT and should be held in a location so that it is clearly visible.
>
> At Muskie events or events by other Democratic hopefuls, there should be a sign or two which goads them. For example, at a Muskie rally there should be a large WHY NOT A BLACK VICE PRESIDENT or perhaps WE PREFER HUMPHREY or something else that would goad him along.

414. *United States v. Chapin*, p. 233 of the transcript. See also Segretti interview, p. 3.
415. See Segretti interview and hotel records.
416. 10 *Hearings* 3990.
417. 10 *Hearings* 3990. Segretti was not certain whether he received the Advance Manual in Washington, D.C. or in Portland, Ore.; but see p. 234 of *U.S. v. Chapin*.

At Humphrey rallies there should be Muskie signs and at Kennedy rallies there should be Muskie or Humphrey signs and so on. These signs should be well placed in relationship to the press area so that a picture is easy to get.[418]

B. Activities. 1. Summary. After his meeting with Dwight Chapin at the Benson Hotel in Portland, Segretti set off across the country to recruit individuals to infiltrate and disrupt the upcoming Democratic Presidential primaries. Segretti traveled to more than sixteen states and contacted at least eighty individuals in his efforts to establish an organization that was capable of dividing the Democrats during their primaries.[419]

Segretti received $45,336 from Herbert Kalmbach in the period from September 29, 1971, until March 23, 1972.[420] Of this total Segretti had expenses of more than $22,000,[421] and almost $9,000 of these expenses went to twenty-two individuals that Segretti had contacted during his travels.[422]

418. Exhibit #200, 10 *Hearings* 4269.
419. Information gathered from review of Segretti documents and interviews with Segretti and contacts.
420.

Segretti Cash Inflow

September 29, 1971	$ 667.00	Check from Kalmbach
September 29, 1971	5,000.00	Check from Kalmbach
October 19, 1971	667.00	Check from Kalmbach
October 27, 1971	667.00	Check from Kalmbach
November 11, 1971	667.00	Check from Kalmbach
November 29, 1971	667.00	Check from Kalmbach
December 13, 1971	667.00	Check from Kalmbach
December 27, 1971	667.00	Check from Kalmbach
January 17, 1972	667.00	Check from Kalmbach
January 15, 1972	5,000.00	(Cash)
March 1, 1972	5,000.00	Cash from A. Harvey
March 23, 1972	25,000.00	Cash from Kalmbach
Total	$45,336.00	

421.

Segretti—Expenses (1971-1972)

1. Travel	$ 6,019.51
2. Telephone	2,099.56
3. Printing and Mailing	1,816.43
4. Accommodations	1,555.80
5. Meals	616.68
6. Office Expense	1,331.39
Sub-Total	$13,439.37
7. Payments to Operatives	$ 8,984.70
Total Expenses	$22,424.07

422.

Payments to Segretti Operatives

1. Benz	$2,417.00
2. Burdick	335.00
3. Collins	5.00
4. Frias	20.00
5. Garner	265.00
6. Gratz	50.00
7. Hayes	31.50

253

Segretti's objective in making contacts was to organize a network of agents in the following states: New Hampshire, Florida, Illinois, Wisconsin, Pennsylvania, Ohio, Indiana, California, New Jersey, New York and Texas. Almost all of these states had Presidential primaries in 1972, and they were listed for Segretti when he met with Chapin at San Clemente in the late summer.

2. Relationship with Chapin. During the early period of his travels, Segretti kept in fairly close contact with Dwight Chapin. For example, Segretti called Chapin thirty-three times in November, December, and January.[423] Segretti used the pseudonyms of Don Durham and Don Simmons, since Chapin had strongly suggested to him to maintain secrecy in his operation and to divorce totally the White House in his activities.

During these first few months' activities, Segretti occasionally received information and direction from Chapin. For example, Chapin informed Segretti when Senator Muskie would be in Los Angeles in November 1971, and asked him to line up some pickets for the appearance. Later on, Segretti said he was told by Chapin that Senator Muskie would be appearing at Whittier College and was asked by Chapin to provide pickets and hecklers in the crowd. A few days later, Segretti arranged for pickets outside of a San Francisco Hotel where Senators Muskie and Humphrey were appearing at a Democratic dinner.

Following Senator Muskie's appearance at Whittier College in November, 1971, Segretti received in the mail a copy of the White House news summary from Chapin which said, "Reynolds said that he [Muskie] had come prepared for conservative questions, but the Chicanos gave him no

8.	Kelly	3,436.00
9.	Martin	122.00
10.	Miller	22.00
11.	Neiley	40.00
12.	Norton	451.20
13.	O'Brien	40.00
14.	Oldman	20.00
15.	Popovich	130.00
16.	Sarhad	165.00
17.	Silva	140.00
18.	Staub	50.00
19.	Svihlik	200.00
20.	Turnquist	80.00
21.	Visney	710.00
22.	Zimmer	255.00
	Total	$8,984.70

423. 10 *Hearings* 4314.

chance and Big Ed proved that he can keep his cool." [424]
Penciled in on the side of the copy is a note from Chapin which reads:

> Note we really missed the boat on this—obviously the press now want to prove EM can keep his temper—let's prove he can't.[425]

In early November, 1971, Chapin instructed Segretti to travel to New Hampshire and begin work since it was the first primary state.

Chapin also gave Segretti the name of Allen Walker, Chairman of the New Hampshire committee to Re-Elect the President. Segretti said that Walker seemed very receptive to his ideas, and that he felt so much at ease with Walker that he gave him his true name.[426] Shortly thereafter, Segretti received a phone call from Dwight Chapin who told him to leave New Hampshire immediately. Segretti traveled to Washington and met with Chapin in Segretti's hotel room. Chapin told Segretti to stay out of New Hampshire, move on to Florida and never again to use his real name.[427]

Chapin had general knowledge of much of Segretti's activities.[428] Segretti testified that most of the literature, bumper stickers, and false letters that were distributed by Segretti were sent to Chapin's home in Washington after they were printed up. In addition, Segretti sent newspaper clippings to Chapin concerning his field activities as well as hand-written notes explaining his activities of the previous week. Chapin's reactions to Segretti's activities were always very positive and according to Segretti he has no recollection of the issue of the legality of Segretti's activities ever being discussed with Chapin.[429] Segretti specifically recalls sending Chapin the "Muskie Bussing" poster, the sex smear letter on Muskie stationery against Senators Jackson and Humphrey and the Humphrey press release about Shirley Chisholm (all discussed below).

During the months of December, January, and February, Segretti raised many doubts in the minds of people that he was recruiting. Many of these individuals—Young Republicans, College Republicans, and Young Voters for the President- relayed messages back to Bart Porter, Tom Bell, and Ken Rietz, at the CRP, who in turn sent the messages on to

424. 10 *Hearings* 4271-72.
425. *Ibid.*
426. 10 *Hearings* 3993.
427. *Ibid.*
428. See Segretti testimony, 10 *Hearings* 3979-4053; See also Segretti and Chapin testimony in *U.S. v. Chapin.*
429. Segretti Witness Summary, p. 6.

Jeb Magruder. Generally, the complaints were that there was an individual in the field who was causing serious problems for the Committee to Re-Elect the President.[430]

Such a complaint was sent from J. Tim Gratz of Madison, Wisconsin, to Carl Rove, President-elect of the College Republicans. This complaint was eventually assigned to Anthony Ulasewicz who flew out to Wisconsin to investigate this mysterious individual. Ulasewicz did not succeed in tracking down Segretti, but while he was out in Wisconsin, he received a call from Jack Caulfield who informed him that Segretti worked for CRP.[431]

Many of these complaints about Segretti were sent to Magruder, who wrote a memorandum to John Mitchell in January, 1972, entitled "Matter of Potential Embarrassment", in which he described this individual in the field and urged that the individual should be placed under the direction of G. Gordon Liddy.[432] After receiving a copy of that memorandum, H. R. Haldeman told Gordon Strachan to call Segretti to tell him to expect a call from Liddy, who would give him instructions in the future. This memorandum describing the "Matter of Potential Embarrassment" was shredded following the Watergate break-in by Strachan at Haldeman's directions, according to Strachan's testimony.[433]

Segretti was told by Dwight Chapin in either a phone call or at their meeting in Washington on January 20, 1972, that some people in Washington had been disturbed by some of the problems that Segretti had caused in New Hampshire and Wisconsin. Chapin told Segretti to expect a call from an individual who would be checking up on his activities.[434]

3. Relationship with Hunt and Liddy. In late January, 1972, Liddy told Howard Hunt that a Democrat was trying to infiltrate Republican headquarters in some of the primary states in the upcoming campaign. Liddy sent out a communique to all the state Committee to Re-Elect the President headquarters with the individual's description in an effort to find the person who was engaging in these "counter-productive" activities. Four or five days later, Liddy came back to Hunt and said that he had stepped on some toes since the individual really worked for the Committee to Re-Elect the President.[435] Shortly thereafter, Liddy told Hunt that he had been asked to evaluate Segretti's work by the people for

430. See interviews of Porter, Bell, and Rietz.
431. Ulasewicz interview, May 8, 1973.
432. 6 *Hearings* 2459.
433. *Ibid.*
434. 10 *Hearings* 3983.
435. Hunt Executive Session, May 14, 1973, p. 335.

whom Segretti was working.[436] Hunt also testified that Liddy told him that Segretti's principals wanted Hunt and Liddy to keep tabs on this individual as well as to provide assistance if it did not hazard their own operations.[437]

A few days after his conversation with Chapin, Segretti received a call in California from an "Ed Warren" (Howard Hunt), who asked to meet with Segretti as soon as possible. On February 11, 1972, Segretti traveled to Miami and on the following day two men came to Segretti's motel room to meet him. They introduced themselves as Ed Warren and George Leonard.[438]

Hunt immediately turned on the television set in Segretti's room to prevent surreptitious taping of the meeting. Segretti explained to Hunt and Liddy that his activities consisted primarily of providing pickets at appearances by opposition candidates and distributing bogus pamphlets and leaflets that could embarrass the Democrats. Hunt and Liddy advised Segretti to use false identification, but they never provided any for him. In addition, Hunt provided Segretti with the name of Jose Arriola to do Segretti's printing in the Miami area.[439] Segretti explained that he was having some difficulty in obtaining Senator Muskie's schedules, and so Hunt agreed to furnish this information to Segretti. In addition, Hunt gave Segretti his telephone number and told him to keep in touch.[440]

After this initial meeting of ten to fifteen minutes, Segretti maintained sporadic contact with Hunt. Occasionally Hunt would make suggestions to Segretti about possible activities. Some of these suggestions are listed below in the pages describing specific activities carried out by Segretti and his associates.

Segretti's last meeting with Howard Hunt was on June 9, 1972, at the Sheraton Four Ambassadors Hotel in Miami, Florida. At this meeting, Hunt suggested that Segretti put together a group of peaceful demonstrators to picket the Doral Hotel during the Democratic Convention. Hunt explained that another group of unruly demonstrators was to join in the demonstration and attempt to disrupt it, and that the bad conduct of the crowd would be blamed on Senator McGovern. However, the Watergate break-in occurred on June 17, 1972, and any plans for the convention by E. Howard Hunt were temporarily quashed.[441]

436. *Ibid.*
437. *Ibid.*, p. 336.
438. 10 *Hearings* 3983.
439. Segretti Witness Summary, p. 7.
440. *Ibid.*, p. 8.
441. 10 *Hearings* 3983.

4. Primary Activities. Segretti's most successful operation in the Democratic primaries was in Florida, where he recruited Bob Benz to head up the operation in Tampa, .and Doug Kelly to help him in Miami. Segretti paid Benz $2,417 for his activities, and sent Kelly $3,436 for his help.[442] Segretti was also fairly successful in recruiting people for the California primary. These individuals included James Robert Norton, who obtained an answering service for Segretti in East St. Louis and a number of other individuals with experience in state politics that Segretti could rely on to distribute literature and to harass appearances by Democratic candidates.

In addition, Segretti recruited Tom Visney and Charles Svihlik to create problems for the Democrats in Illinois, Indiana, and Wisconsin and Skip Zimmer and Bob Nieley for work in the Pennsylvania primary. Finally, Segretti enlisted the help of Michael Martin, Jr., for the New York primary, and Bobby Garner of Houston to provide help in Texas, if that state were to become crucial.[443]

The following account is a summary of the kinds of activities in which Segretti and his associates engaged during the 1972 campaign.

(a). Infiltrators. *Florida.* One of the objectives that Chapin outlined to Segretti for his operation was to place infiltrators in Democratic primary campaigns to gather information and to create division among the Democratic candidates. When Robert Benz met Segretti for the first time, he was told "to obtain hecklers, pickets, and also to get people to infiltrate into the campaigns, to gather information," and that Segretti would provide money to pay these people.[444]

Benz immediately recruited Peg Griffin, a secretary in Tampa active in Republican politics, and asked her to infiltrate the Muskie Campaign. Benz testified that he told the Muskie people that "she was a Republican, that she did not care for the President's policies, and that she was now a backer of Senator Muskie." [445] Benz paid Ms. Griffin $75 a month to infiltrate the campaign. In exchange, Griffin provided Benz with campaign literature, information about the campaign strategy, stationery from Senator Muskie's campaign, names of the campaign staff and precinct captains for Senator Muskie, and some names of financial contributors. Benz testified that he in turn sent all of the information that he received from Ms. Griffin to Segretti's post office box in

442. Witness Summary of Segretti, p. 5.
443. See Segretti Witness Summary, payments to Segretti operatives.
444. 11 *Hearings* 4404.
445. 11 *Hearings* 4405.

Los Angeles.

Much of the information that Griffin was able to provide from the Muskie campaign headquarters was subsequently used to further many of the disruptive acts that were perpetrated in the Florida campaign. Griffin was also quite successful at disrupting the campaign on her own. For example, in early January, 1972, she learned of a secret $1000-a-plate fund-raising dinner for Senator Muskie following a public reception, and added this information on as the last two lines of a press release from the Muskie campaign. The dinner was subsequently cancelled by Senator Muskie because of the publicity it received.[446]

Benz testified he also recruited Eselene Frohlich to infiltrate the Jackson campaign in Florida.[447] Frohlich provided Benz with the same kind of information from Senator Jackson's campaign that Peg Griffin gathered from Muskie's. This information proved to be most valuable in conducting Benz's "field activities." [448]

Benz attempted to recruit individuals to infiltrate the Humphrey and Wallace campaigns as well, but was unsuccessful in these efforts. Benz later traveled to Pennsylvania to recruit individuals to infiltrate the primary campaigns there, but he was not as successful as he had been in Florida.[449]

Segretti was also under the impression that Doug Kelly in Miami had two infiltrators into the Muskie campaign.[450] However, Kelly consistently testified that he had no infiltrators or informants in any campaigns in Miami.[451]

California. Segretti was also successful in recruiting infiltrators for the California primary. In the Los Angeles area, Segretti talked to Turnquist; Chapin's friend from high school, who in turn contacted Pat O'Brien and recruited him to work in the Muskie campaign in Los Angeles and report back any political intelligence. O'Brien was hired in December, 1971, and worked part-time through April, 1972, in the Muskie campaign.

In San Francisco, Mike Silva was recruited by Bob Norton to obtain campaign intelligence from the Muskie headquarters and be a contact in San Francisco for Segretti. Silva told Segretti that he had placed two infiltrators in the Muskie campaign in late February, 1972. Silva stated in an interview, however, that he did not actually place infiltrators in the

446. See Benz Executive Session, October 2, 1973, pp. 17-18; See also 10 *Hearings* 3982.
447. 11 *Hearings* 4405.
448. 11 *Hearings* 4407.
449. Vol. 11, p. 4413.
450. See Vol. 10, p. 4334 in Segretti accounts.
451. See, for example, Kelly Executive Session, October 2, 1973, p. 22.

campaign, but merely gathered campaign literature from a political science course at San Francisco State University and forwarded the material on to Segretti at his post office box in Los Angeles.[452]

New York. In New York, Segretti hired Michael Martin, Jr., to infiltrate the Humphrey campaign and report any intelligence information that he gathered. Martin apparently was such a successful infiltrator that he was offered a position as director of the northern New York campaign for Humphrey, but Segretti said that Martin turned down the position so he could stay in New York City and continue reporting to Segretti.[453]

Texas. In Texas, Segretti paid Bobby Garner of Houston $265, some of which was to go to an infiltrator in the Muskie campaign in Texas. This infiltrator was to work during the months of February, March, and April, to gather intelligence and mail it back to Segretti's post office box in Los Angeles.

The success of the Segretti operation in infiltrating primary campaigns also contributed to the success of their other efforts to disrupt and harass Democratic candidates.

(b) Surveillance. In his meeting with Dwight Chapin in early November, 1971, Segretti learned that Senator Muskie would be visiting the Los Angeles area about November 6. Segretti testified that Chapin instructed him to secure some pickets for Muskie's appearances there and to learn the logistics of Senator Muskie's traveling party.

Segretti said he called Jess Burdick, an ex-CID agent who worked as a private detective in the Los Angeles area, and hired him to tail Senator Muskie during his trip to Los Angeles. Burdick followed Muskie for the weekend, and reported back to Segretti information such as the license numbers of the vehicles used by the Muskie campaign. When Burdick charged Segretti $325 for his services, Segretti thought the price was steep for the information that was provided, and therefore did not use Burdick after the one occasion in November.[454]

Physical surveillance of Senator Muskie also occurred in the Florida primary when Robert Benz had his agents tail Senators Muskie and Jackson when they were in the Tampa area.[455]

(c) Disruptions. A. Distribution of False and Misleading Literature. One of the most successful tactics for disrupting

452. See Silva interview, Aug. 30, 1973. Segretti was clearly under the impression that Silva had two informants in the Muskie campaign. See 10 *Hearings* 4332.
453. Segretti Witness Summary, p. 12.
454. 10 *Hearings* 3981.
455. See Benz Witness Summary.

the Democratic primary campaigns used by Segretti and his operatives was the distribution of false and misleading literature. Instances of this particular campaign abuse occurred in nearly every primary state. Nowhere in any of this literature was it noted that the literature was financed by funds from the Committee to Re-Elect the President.

Pre-primary. After Segretti was informed by Dwight Chapin that Senator Muskie was appearing at Whittier College in November, 1971 he had a number of hand-outs with "hard questions" printed up which he handed out to students at the Whittier rally.[456] Someone in the crowd asked Muskie about his views on abortion, one of the questions on Segretti's hand-out. In the White House news summary of the event that Chapin sent Segretti, Chapin noted that Segretti's question had been asked.[457]

Florida. False and misleading literature was most widely distributed in the Florida primary. The following list is a catalog of the various abuses in this area perpetrated in Florida by Segretti and his operatives.

1) About three hundred red day-glow posters were distributed throughout the state which said, "Help Muskie in Bussing [sic] More Children Now." The poster was signed by the "Mothers Backing Muskie Committee," a nonexistent committee, and the intent of the poster was to identify Senator Muskie with a strong pro-busing position, a very unpopular issue in Florida. Most of these posters were distributed by Mr. Benz, Mr. Segretti and Mr. Kelly in the Tampa and Miami areas of Florida.[458]

2) About a thousand four-by-six inch cards were printed up and distributed at a Tampa rally for Governor George Wallace by Robert Benz and his agents. The cards read, "If You Liked Hitler, You'll Just Love Wallace." On the other side of the card, it stated "A Vote For Wallace Is A Wasted Vote. On March 14, cast your vote for Senator Edmund Muskie." [459] There was no indication on the cards that they were financed by Nixon campaign funds. The clear intent of the literature was to drive a wedge between the Wallace and Muskie campaigns.

3) On February 25, 1972, a letter was sent on copied Muskie campaign stationery to the campaign manager of the Florida Jackson campaign and to syndicated columnists which stated that Senator Muskie's campaign was using government typewriters as well as government employees

456. See exhibit no. 201, 10 *Hearings* 4270.
457. See exhibit no. 202, 10 *Hearings* 4272.
458. 10 *Hearings* 4267, 3982.
459. 11 *Hearings* 4410; see also exhibit #214, 11 *Hearings* 4292.

drawing government salaries.[460] This letter was sent to Jackson campaign headquarters in Tampa and in Washington, D.C., and copies of the letter were also sent to local media. The facts on which the letter was based were totally fabricated by Segretti, and Doug Kelly and Bob Benz arranged for the distribution of the letter on copied stationery Peg Griffin provided from the Muskie campaign.[461]

4) Similarly, in March, 1972, Segretti sent Benz a counterfeit letter on Muskie stationery containing allegations of sexual improprieties involving Democratic Presidential candidates Jackson and Humphrey. Segrettti instructed Benz to have twenty to forty copies of the letter printed on Senator Muskie's stationery (which Segretti enclosed) and distributed.[462] Benz gave the material to George Hearing, a local recruit of Benz's, who duplicated the letter on Muskie stationery and mailed the letter to supporters of Senator Jackson. Hearing's list of Jackson supporters was given to him by Benz who had obtained the information from Eselene Frohlich, the infiltrator in Senator Jackson's campaign.[463]

This phony, scurrilous letter on Muskie stationery against Senators Jackson and Humphrey won praise for Segretti from Chapin. On learning that the cost of the reproduction of the letter was only $20.00, Segretti testified that Chapin told him that for that small sum, he had obtained ten to twenty thousand dollars worth of benefit for the President's re-election campaign.[464]

In May, 1973, indictments concerning this incident were brought by the U.S. Attorney's office in Tampa. At that time, Robert Benz was given immunity and was not prosecuted, while George Hearing was prosecuted and convicted on one count of violating 18 U.S.C. 612, the law prohibiting distribution of unsigned political literature. Similarly, Donald Segretti was indicted for a number of violations of 18 U.S.C. 612.

Mr. Hearing, the individual who mailed the letter, was sentenced to one year in prison. Mr. Segretti, the originator of the scheme, was sentenced to six months in prison after pleading guilty to three counts [465] in Federal District Court in Washington, D.C. Robert Benz, the individual who recruited Hearing and Frohlich, and who directed Hearing to mail the letter, was neither indicted nor convicted of any

460. 10 *Hearings* 4279.
461. 10 *Hearings* 3982; 11 *Hearings* 4381; 11 *Hearings* 4411.
462. 11 *Hearings* 4411; 10 *Hearings* 3997.
463. 10 *Hearings* 4280.
464. 10 *Hearings* 3997.
465. The three counts consisted of two violations of 18 U.S.C. 612 and one count of conspiracy, 18 U.S.C. 371.

crimes.

5) A number of pamphlets advertising a free lunch at Muskie's campaign headquarters were distributed in Miami by Doug Kelly.[466] The pamphlets also advertised free liquor and a chance to meet Senator Muskie and his wife. These pamphlets were distributed all over Miami, and a small pile of them was left at the Lindsay headquarters. The morning before the lunch was to occur, Kelly called Muskie headquarters and said that the Lindsay campaign was responsible for the false invitations.[467] The dual objectives of the literature were thus to disrupt the Muskie campaign and to drive a wedge between Lindsay and Muskie.[468]

6) Another invitiation to a Muskie campaign meeting in Miami was obtained from the Muskie campaign by Segretti and Kelly. A line was added to the invitation which stated "Free Food and Alcoholic Beverages Provided", and these were distributed in the Miami area.[469]

7) Some press releases were written on Muskie stationery in Miami by Doug Kelly, Segretti's main contact in the area. Kelly recalled sending out three or four bogus press releases, most of which sought to misrepresent the position of Senator Muskie on issues such as Israel and busing, and to draw attention to the position of Senator Humphrey.[470] These releases were yet another tactic for carrying out the strategy of "Dividing the Democrats".

8) Kelly testified that he also distributed flyers announcing a speech by former Secretary of the Interior Udall that had been cancelled by the Young Democrats. The flyers resulted in some disruption, Kelly testified, since the speech had to be rescheduled after the flyers appeared.[471]

9) Flyers were passed out in Miami by Doug Kelly that appeared to be from Mayor Lindsay which attacked Senator Muskie's stand on Israel. These flyers noted that Senator Muskie felt that Israel should be treated the same way as Cuba, thus antagonizing both Jewish and Cuban-American voters. Many of these flyers were distributed in Miami Beach, by being placed under windshield wipers of cars that were parked at synagogues.[472]

10) Other examples of false literature passed out in the Florida primary by Segretti and his contacts are found in the

466. 11 *Hearings* 4380.
467. 11 *Hearings* 4380. In addition, a number of people showed up at Muskie headquarters in response to the bogus invitations. (Tim Smith Interview)
468. 11 *Hearings* 4380.
469. See Segretti Interview, p. 10.
470. 11 *Hearings* 4381.
471. Kelly Executive Session, Oct. 2, 1973.
472. 11 *Hearings* 4392.

exhibits introduced during the Segretti testimony.[473]

Wisconsin. Similar kinds of false and misleading literature were distributed in the Wisconsin primary by Segretti and his agents.

Segretti and Benz drove to Milwaukee, Wisconsin at the end of March, 1972, to pull pranks before the April 4 primary. There they distributed a false invitation for a free lunch with Senator Humphrey on April Fool's Day at which free drinks would be given away, and guests would have the opportunity to meet Senator Humphrey, Lorne Green and Mrs. Martin Luther King.[474] The invitation was intended to disrupt the Humphrey campaign much as Segretti had done to Muskie in Florida. Benz also stated that he and Segretti called the local newspapers to inform them that the invitations had been printed by Muskie supporters.[475]

Numerous bumper stickers with derogatory sexual slogans about Senator Muskie were put up and distributed by Segretti and Benz in Wisconsin.[476] They were intended to embarrass Senator Muskie and to help drive down his vote total in Wisconsin. The bumper stickers were again unidentified as to their source.

Illinois. Much of the same material that was distributed in Wisconsin was also distributed in Illinois by Tom Visney, Segretti's main recruit there. In addition, Segretti sent Visney copies of the pamphlet from the "Citizens for a Liberal Alternative," the non-existent citizens' committee discussed earlier.[477] This pamphlet, written in the White House and printed by CRP, was intended to divide the Democrats among themselves.

District of Columbia. On about April 13, 1972, Segretti testified he flew to Washington at the suggestion of E. Howard Hunt to organize disruptive activities at a Muskie fund-raiser scheduled for April 17, 1972. Doug Kelly, who also flew up for the occasion, and Segretti distributed literature which described the fund-raising dinner and requested pickets outside the dinner to "protest the fat cats." [478]

California. By the time of the California primary, the main Democratic contenders were Senator McGovern and Senator Humphrey. Most of the false and misleading literature distributed by Segretti and his contacts in California attacked one of the Democratic candidates and attri-

473. See 10 *Hearings* 4276-77.
474. See exhibit #210, 10 *Hearings* 4285.
475. See Benz interview (witness summary), Oct. 2, 1973, p. 3.
476. Copies of these bumper stickers are in the Committee's files. They referred solely to Senator Muskie.
477. See p. 118 earlier; see also Segretti witness summary (interview) p. 7.
478. 10 *Hearings* 3984.

buted the attack to another candidate, thus attempting to further divide the Democrats and make it more difficult for them to re-group following their convention.

Months before the primary, Segretti reprinted a newspaper advertisement by Stewart Mott and the "Committee for Honesty in Politics" which abhorred "The Secret Money in Presidential Politics". At the bottom of the reprint Segretti added the note, "The committee will look for your names as part of Muskie's fat cats! They better be there!" [479]

This doctored reprint was distributed to individuals entering a fund-raiser for Senator Muskie in Los Angeles by Segretti's agents in the area.[480]

As the primary approached, the literature written and distributed by Segretti and his contacts became much more vicious. Some examples follow:

1) Segretti sent out a statement on Humphrey press release stationery for immediate release which said that Representative Shirley Chisholm had been committed to a private home for the mentally ill from February, 1951, until April, 1952. The "release" went on to describe in the most vicious and scurrilous terms the "alleged behavior" that Representative Chisholm demonstrated at that time. At the bottom of the fake press release were the initials HHH. This release was mailed out to ten or fifteen California newspapers.[481] Segretti testified that he sent the release to Dwight Chapin, who "laughed for a period of time" about the bogus release.[482]

2) Two other false press releases on Hubert Humphrey stationery were mailed out to the newspapers by Segretti. One release stated that former President Lyndon Johnson favored Humphrey as the Democratic nominee, and the other one misrepresented Humphrey's position on one of the initiatives on the California ballot in 1972.[483] Most of the bogus candidates' stationery that was used by Segretti to pull his so-called "pranks" was printed for him by Jose Arriola in Miami, the printer whose name Segretti received from Howard Hunt.[484]

3) Segretti also had bumper stickers printed and distributed throughout California which said: "Humphrey: he started the war, don't give him another chance." More than 1000 of these bumper stickers were printed, most of which were distributed in California. The bumper stickers were

479. See exhibit No. 209, 10 *Hearings* 4284.
480. 10 *Hearings* 4005.
481. 10 *Hearings* 4004; See also p. 327 of transcript of *U.S. v. Chapin.*
482. 10 *Hearings* 4004.
483. 10 *Hearings* 4004.
484. 10 *Hearings* 4000.

signed by the "Democrats for a Peace Candidate," another non-existent group which was created by Segretti.[485]

4) In addition, using as a model the pamphlet from the "Citizens for a Liberal Alternative" that had been drafted by Ken Khachigian and Pat Buchanan in the White House, Segretti had 3,000 pamphlets printed up with a picture of Senator Humphrey holding a large fish and the caption, "Humphrey: a fishy smell for the White House?"[486] The objective of the pamphlet was to have the Humphrey people blame McGovern for this scurrilous and fictitious piece of literature. These pamphlets were distributed in San Francisco, Los Angeles, and in Orange County.

5) Segretti was also responsible for preparing and mailing a letter over the forged signature of Barbara Barron, the campaign coordinator of Senator McCarthy's California campaign, to McCarthy delegates and Chisholm supporters urging them to shift their support to Senator Humphrey.[487] The letter was printed on "McCarthy '72" stationery, and many of the people who received the mailing have always believed that Barbara Barron was responsible for the letter. In fact, Barbara Barron had absolutely nothing to do with the mailing since it was solely a product of Segretti's fertile imagination.

6) Segretti also sent letters on "Yorty for President" stationery to local newspapers such as the Los Angeles *Free Press*. These letters claimed that the forged letters from Barbara Barron to the McCarthy delegates and Chisholm supporters were the responsibility of the Yorty campaign.[488]

The Los Angeles Free Press ran the story that the forged letters had in fact come from the Yorty for President Committee. Thus, the forged letters, and the subsequent fake letter claiming responsibility for the initial forgeries were quite successful in sowing dissension among the California Democrats.

According to Frank Mankiewicz, these examples of false literature distributed in the campaign had a serious impact on the Democratic candidates themselves. He testified,

> We [the McGovern campaign and the Humphrey campaign] were no longer opponents; we had become enemies, and I think largely as a result of this activity.[489]

In addition, Senator Muskie and his staff blamed the false and scurrilous literature on both Senator McGovern and his

485. See exhibit 216, 10 *Hearings* 4295.
486. See exhibit 219, 10 *Hearings* 4299.
487. See exhibit 217, 10 *Hearings* 4296.
488. See exhibit 220, p. 4301.
489. 11 *Hearings* 4614.

supporters as well as Senator Humphrey's campaign.[490] The false literature exacerbated the normal differences among the candidates and helped to create a deeply divided Democratic Party at the close of the Presidential primaries.

B. False Advertising. Another deceptive practice engaged in by Segretti and his agents was the placement of false and misleading advertising for or against Democratic candidates on the radio and in local newspapers.

Florida. 1) In Miami, Doug Kelly placed an ad on a local radio station which said that Senator Muskie believed in the right of self-determination for all people, and therefore, supported the Castro government in Cuba. The ad was ostensibly purchased by the Muskie campaign organization, and was designed by Kelly to alienate the Cuban voters from Senator Muskie.[491]

2) A similar ad was placed in the local Cuban-American newspaper *Replica*, which stated that Muskie believed that the United States should not interfere with the Castro government of Cuba.[492] Again, the ad purported to be from Senator Muskie's campaign, and was designed to alienate Cuban-American supporters.

3) A number of classified ads were placed in various Miami newspapers which drew attention to Muskie's statement that he did not think the American people were ready for a black vice presidential candidate.[493]

While these small ads could hardly influence very many voters, the ads could create some division and bad feelings among the Democrats after the primary was over if Senator Muskie's campaign thought the ads were placed by other Democratic contenders.

Illinois. In Chicago, Tom Visney placed an anti-Muskie ad in the newspaper as well as on some of the radio stations.[494] These ads supported Senator McCarthy's candidacy, and stated that Senator Muskie had neither the emotional stability nor the experience to hold the office of the Presidency. In none of these ads was it stated that they had been paid for and created by agents of the White House.

Democratic Convention. In May or June, Segretti and Doug Kelly ordered an airplane to fly over the Democratic convention with a trailer which stated, "Peace, Pot, Promiscuity. Vote McGovern." Kelly was not sure if in fact the plane flew over the convention.[495] Someone later

490. 11 *Hearings* 4659, 4663-64.
491. 11 *Hearings* 4379.
492. *Ibid.*
493. *See* Exhibit 204, p. 4271.
494. Segretti Witness Summary, p. 11.
495. Vol. 11, p. 4384.

told him that they had seen a plane with a weird message flying over the Democratic convention.[496]

C. Pickets. One of the main tenets of advice given to Segretti by Dwight Chapin was to have pickets appear at campaign appearances by other Democratic candidates in order to take advantage of the media coverage of the event.[497] Therefore, much of Segretti's activity involved organizing pickets at the appearances of the Democratic primary contenders.

Even prior to the primaries, in early November, 1971, Segretti paid a friend of his from Turlock, California, to arrange for a group of pickets with signs saying, "Kennedy for President" to appear in front of a San Francisco hotel where both Senators Muskie and Humphrey were appearing at a Democratic dinner.[498]

Segretti also attempted to arrange for pickets to appear at an appearance by Senator Muskie at Whittier College that same month.[499] Unknown to Segretti, Roger Greaves (Sedan Chair I) had also been directed by Bart Porter and Jeb Magruder to have pickets present with anti-Muskie signs. The appearance must have been an important one, since Segretti was given the same direction by Dwight Chapin at the White House.

Florida. Segretti's most successful picketing operation was run by Robert Benz in the Tampa area during the Florida primary campaign. Benz recruited Kip Edwards, Al Reese, George Hearing, and an individual identified only as "Duke" to organize pickets against Senators Muskie and Jackson in the Tampa area. The logistics of the picketing were greatly aided by the information being provided to Benz by Frohlich from the Jackson campaign and Griffin from the Muskie campaign.

Many of these picketing activities were successful in getting media coverage and in provoking dissension among the Democratic candidates. These activities included:

1) Benz learned that Senator Jackson was to appear for the opening of his Tampa headquarters in January, 1972. As a result, he hired a Mr. Yancy and Kip Edwards to stand across the street from the headquarters with signs saying, "Believe in Muskie." [500] Segretti was present to observe this particular demonstration, as were some news photographers who took a picture of Senator Jackson walking across the street to offer the two picketers a glass of orange juice. This

496. *Ibid.*
497. *See page 254 above.*
498. 10 *Hearings* 3981.
499. *Ibid.*
500. 11 *Hearings* 4409.

photograph was reprinted widely in Florida newspapers.[501]

2) Benz also received the schedule of the Muskie campaign train as it traveled down through Florida. He arranged for pickets to appear at the Winter Haven stop with signs saying "Wallace Country." George Hearing, Kip Edwards, and the individual known as "Duke" showed up to picket this appearance. Benz believed that "Duke" was a member of the Nazi party and was told that he was a former SS officer in Hitler's storm troopers.[502]

In addition, Benz and Hearing discussed the possibility of disrupting Senator Muskie's train schedule by furnishing false information to his headquarters as well as to the public.[503]

3) Benz also arranged for pickets to appear at another Muskie appearance at the University of Southern Florida. There they distributed derogatory newspaper reprints concerning Muskie.[504]

4) Benz organized a number of other pickets at Muskie appearances in Tampa. On one occasion, he arranged for the picketing of a Muskie rally by blacks carrying "radically related placards" which criticized Muskie's statements about not having a black Vice Presidential candidate.[505]

5) On one occasion, Doug Kelly gave a female college student from the University of Florida twenty dollars in cash to run naked in front of Muskie's hotel in Gainesville, screaming, "Senator Muskie, I love you." [506] Kelly testified that the incident was reported in the Gainesville papers.

6) Senator Muskie had a press conference in Miami at the Four Ambassadors Hotel shortly before the Florida primary. Kelly recruited some Cubans to picket the press conference with signs saying, "Muskie go home," and "We want a free Cuba." [507]

In addition, Kelly gave the picketers Humphrey buttons to wear. One of Senator Muskie's aides asked Kelly about the identity of the picketers. Kelly explained to him "confidentially" that the picketers were really working for Senator Jackson.[508]

This example is a good case of how political "pranks" can be used both to identify a candidate with a controversial issue and to foster dissension among the Democratic candidates

501. *Ibid.*
502. 11 *Hearings* 4426.
503. 11 *Hearings* 4409. Some false ads about the train's schedule were published, but there is no evidence at present linking those to Benz or Segretti.
504. 11 *Hearings* 4410.
505. 11 *Hearings* 4408.
506. 11 *Hearings* 4399.
507. 11 *Hearings* 4382.
508. 11 *Hearings* 4383.

themselves.

California. In California, Segretti contacted many people to picket fundraising dinners by Democratic candidates as well as distribute false literature. For example, Segretti hired an individual named Jim Popovich, who told Segretti that he would put together a "flying squad" of about ten individuals who would be available to picket any local appearances by Senator Muskie. Segretti thought the idea a good one and paid Popovich about $130 before discovering that Popovich was not producing as many pickets for these appearances as he had claimed.[509]

Pennsylvania. In Pennsylvania, Segretti recruited Skip Zimmer and Bob Nieley to pass out literature at Muskie campaign appearances and to organize pickets for Muskie rallies.[510] Zimmer sent Segretti clippings from local newspapers after Muskie's appearances where Muskie was heckled and picketed to verify that the activity occurred.[511]

Exhibits in the Committee record indicate that Zimmer recruited people to stand at Muskie rallies with signs saying such things as "M-U-S-K-I-E spells Loser" and "HHH is the Man." Posters also drew attention to Muskie's pro-busing stand and pointed out that he allegedly sent his children to private schools.[512] As Zimmer described these efforts in a note to Segretti, "Though press was disappointing . . . we did grandly piss off his staff and rattle him considerably."[513]

Segretti also stated that Zimmer allegedly arranged for pickets to appear at Muskie rallies and pose with signs saying, "Gays for Muskie."[514]

Hecklers were also organized by Zimmer and Nieley during the Pennsylvania primary according to Segretti.[515] Some hecklers appeared at one Humphrey speech in Philadelphia. Following the heckling Segretti said that Zimmer called Humphrey headquarters to tell them that Muskie had hired the hecklers for $100 apiece.[516]

As noted earlier, Segretti also had Robert Benz fly to Pittsburgh to recruit agents to picket Muskie's campaign appearances. Benz was not as successful there as he had been in Tampa.[517]

509. *See* Segretti witness summary; breakdown of payments to operatives.
510. 10 *Hearings* 3998.
511. *See* Exhibit 212. 10 *Hearings* 4289.
512. 10 *Hearings* 4291.
513. 10 *Hearings* 4292.
514. *See* Segretti witness summary, p. 12.
515. Nieley denies having done this. Nieley testified that he merely collected literature and sent it on to Segretti. (Nieley interview)
516. Segretti witness summary, p. 12.
517. Benz witness summary, p. 3.

Planned Convention Activity. As discussed earlier,[518] Segretti's recruiting of pickets for campaign appearances of Democratic candidates was supposed to reach its high point at the Democratic convention in Miami during July, 1972. Howard Hunt directed Segretti to set up a demonstration which would subsequently become violent and would be blamed on the McGovern campaign. The Watergate break-in, however, put an end to these plans.

4. Other Disruptions. *A. False Orders For Food, Flowers, and Beverages.* On primary day in Florida, Segretti and Kelly placed orders on behalf of the Muskie campaign for flowers, chicken, pizzas, and about $300-$400 of liquor.[519]

Three weeks later, on the day of the Wisconsin primary, Segretti and Benz again ordered flowers, chicken and pizzas to be sent to Senator Muskie's hotel room. and also ordered two limousines to be sent to Senator Muskie's hotel for the use of the Senator. These false orders disrupted Senator Muskie's schedule considerably.[520]

Finally, two weeks later at a Muskie fund-raising dinner in Washington, D.C., Segretti and Kelly again made numerous false orders to disrupt the dinner. Kelly and Segretti ordered flowers, liquor, pizzas and other items for the banquet, charging them to the Muskie campaign committee. In addition, Kelly and Segretti invited six African ambassadors and their guests to attend the Muskie fund-raising dinner and made arrangements for them to be picked up by limousines which were to be charged to Senator Muskie's campaign.

These activities disrupted this last major fund-raising effort by Senator Muskie by diverting staff attention and resources, especially when Segretti and Kelly kept calling the limousine drivers to return to the Muskie dinner in order to be paid by the campaign. The net effect of their activities was to create a very embarrassing situation for the Muskie organization.

B. Stink Bombs. On at least three separate occasions in the Florida primary, "stink bombs" were used to disrupt or harass the Muskie campaign.

The "stink bomb" was first concocted by a chemist friend of Doug Kelly. The name of the chemical substance which he produced was "butyl percaptain," a foul-smelling substance which was not physically harmful but was very noxious.[521]

Shortly before the Florida primary, Senator Muskie had a campaign picnic scheduled in the Miami area. Kelly and Segretti took the chemical substance, put it in a coke bottle, and sealed it with wax. The bottle was taken to the picnic

518. See above. p. 267.
519. 11 *Hearings* 4382.
520. Benz witness summary, p. 3.
521. 11 *Hearings* 4382.

by Kelly and Segretti, and dropped on the ground, releasing the chemical substance to foul the air. After the stink bomb had been dropped, Kelly said that "everybody thought that the food was bad. So it kind of made the picnic a bad affair." [522]

Following the Muskie picnic, Segretti traveled north to Tampa with three vials of butyl percaptain. Segretti gave these vials to Bob Benz, with the instructions that they should be placed in Senator Muskie's headquarters.

One of the vials was taken to a Muskie campaign picnic in the Tampa area and emptied at the grounds there.[523] The other two vials were given to George Hearing by Benz with instructions to place them in the two Tampa headquarters of Senator Muskie on the evening before the primary. According to Benz, Hearing placed one of the "stink bombs" in the offices housing the telephone bank operation of Senator Muskie, and the other in the Tampa Muskie Headquarters. Benz said that Hearing told him that at one location the material was dropped through a "hole in the window," and at the other location the window was open and the "stink bomb" was tossed in.[524] Segretti testified that he was told by Benz that a screen was pried open and a window lifted in order to place the "stink bomb" in the Muskie campaign headquarters.[525]

The placing of these stink bombs in the Muskie campaign headquarters on the evening prior to the Florida primary disrupted, confused, and unnecessarily interfered with a campaign for the office of the Presidency.

5. Other disruptions. 1. A few days before the Florida primary Senator Muskie held a press conference at the Four Ambassadors Hotel. Doug Kelly walked into the Muskie press conference with a long overcoat on, and dropped two white mice with blue ribbons on their tails which said, "Muskie is a Rat Fink." Kelly also released a small finch which went flying around the room of the press conference and caused a great deal of commotion and disruption to Senator Muskie's press conference.[526]

2. Kelly also had advance notice of Muskie's schedule in Florida. As a result, Kelly would often call the individuals who were on Senator Muskie's schedule and change the hour of the appointment to some other time, or even cancel the appointment. Needless to say, this tactic greatly disconcerted

522. Ibid.
523. 11 Hearings 4412.
524. Ibid.
525. 10 Hearings 3398.
526. 11 Hearings 4382.

both Senator Muskie and the press.[527]

3. Both Kelly and Benz made a practice of placing other Democratic candidates' stickers on the posters and literature of other Democrats. This practice was designed to foster division and bad feelings among the Democratic candidates.

4. Kelly also attempted to tie up the phone banks of the Muskie campaign on the day of the Florida primary. He did this by dialing the telephone numbers of the Muskie phone bank operation from pay telephones. Kelly would then leave the telephone off the hook as soon as the call was answered at the Muskie campaign. He woud then leave the phone booth and place an "out of order" sign on the outside to insure that the line would be tied up all day.[528] The method didn't work because of the automatic cut-off from the phone company, but the idea was certainly an outrageous though ingenious means of disrupting a campaign.

C. Segretti Cover-Up. Segretti was first contacted by the FBI shortly after the Watergate break-in, when his name and phone number showed up on Howard Hunt's telephone records. Segretti immediately called Dwight Chapin at the White House to request his assistance in getting legal counsel. Chapin told Segretti to return to Washington, D.C., immediately, after consulting with Gordon Strachan at the White House.[529] Meanwhile, Strachan called John Dean and explained that the FBI had called a friend of his named Donald Segretti, and wanted to interview him in connection with the break-in at the DNC.[530]

Strachan requested that Dean meet with Segretti. A meeting was arranged for the morning of Saturday, June 24, 1972, among Segretti, Strachan, and Dean [531] in the lobby of the Mayflower Hotel. Following a short discussion of Segretti's general activities, Dean told Segretti to come to Dean's office in the White House the following day for more detailed discussion.[532]

Segretti went to the Executive Office Building the next day, and outlined in detail to Dean his relationship with E. Howard Hunt.[533] Dean told Segretti not to worry about the upcoming interview since the FBI had picked his name up on Hunt's phone records. In addition, Dean instructed Segretti not to divulge the names of Chapin, Strachan, or Kalmbach to

527. 11 *Hearings* 4383.
528. 11 *Hearings* 4382.
529. Segretti Witness Summary, p. 14.
530. 3 *Hearings* 962.
531. Segretti Witness Summary, p. 14; 3 *Hearings* 962.
532. Segretti Witness Summary, p. 14; 3 *Hearings* 963.
533. 3 *Hearings* 963.

the FBI unless the FBI felt "it was absolutely necessary to have the names." [534]

Segretti left Washington and returned to California where he was interviewed by the FBI agents. The interview focused on Segretti's contacts with E. Howard Hunt, and he was not forced to divulge any of the names about which he had been concerned.[535] Segretti telephoned John Dean after the interview to tell him that he had not been forced to reveal any of the sensitive names.

In August, 1972, Segretti was notified that he was being subpoenaed to appear before the grand jury investigating the Watergate break-in in Washington. Because of his concern about testifying before the grand jury, Segretti tried to contact his friends at the White House as well as local legal counsel.

Segretti finally reached Dwight Chapin at the Republican Convention. Chapin called Dean, who was also at the convention, to explain that Segretti was quite concerned about being called before the federal grand jury.[536] Dean said that he would be happy to meet with Segretti in Florida, since it was impossible for him to go to Washington at that time.

After Dean talked to Chapin, he called Assistant Attorney General Henry Petersen at the Department of Justice and explained the sensitive problem that was confronting Segretti. Dean said he told Petersen that Segretti had no involvement in the Watergate incident, but that he met with Hunt in connection with some campaign activities that he had been performing for the White House. Dean testified he also explained to Petersen that Segretti was being paid by Herb Kalmbach, and that he had been recruited by Chapin and Strachan. Dean said he stressed that if these facts were revealed they would be quite embarrassing and would cause political problems during the last weeks of the election. According to Dean, Petersen replied that he understood the problem and would see what he could do.[537] Dean later spoke to Petersen again, and Dean testified that Petersen explained that he did not believe it would be necessary for the prosecutors to get into the specific areas of concern to Dean when Segretti appeared.

Petersen recalls that the question of going into the "dirty tricks" of Segretti was also raised by Earl Silbert, who said that there did not appear to be a violation of the Corrupt Practices Act. The question was raised again by Charley Bowles, head of the accounting and fraud section of the FBI,

534. 3 *Hearings* 963; Segretti Witness Summary, p. 14.
535. Segretti Witness Summary, p. 14.
536. 3 *Hearings* 963.
537. 3 *Hearings* 964.

who asked Petersen if there was any violation of federal election law by Segretti. Petersen replied that he knew of none.[538]

Petersen directed Silbert not to probe the relationships between Segretti and Kalmbach, Chapin, and Strachan because he "didn't want him getting into the relationships between the President and his lawyer or the fact that the President's lawyer might be involved in somewhat, I thought, illegitimate campaign activities on behalf of the President." [539]

Segretti flew to Florida a few days prior to his appearance before the grand jury. He met with John Dean briefly on the Saturday morning preceeding the opening of the Republican National Convention.[540] Dean explained to Segretti that he did not believe the government was particularly interested in pursuing the names of Strachan, Chapin, and Kalmbach in connection with Segretti's activities, and that he doubted that Segretti would be asked any questions in these areas. Dean advised Segretti, however, that if he were asked any questions about his "dirty tricks" activities, he should answer every question truthfully, and if pressed, Dean advised Segretti to lay out the "whole ball of wax." [541] Segretti recalled that Dean was most concerned about Kalmbach's name being brought up, but that Dean mentioned that he might be able to put certain parameters on the grand jury examination through Henry Petersen.[542]

Segretti then traveled to Washington for his grand jury appearance. Prior to testifying, Segretti was interviewed by Earl Silbert and Don Campbell in the U.S. Attorney's Office. During the interview, he recalled that he was asked if he were getting paid by a "Mr. K." [543] However, once Segretti went before the grand jury, Segretti testified that Silbert did not get into that area of questioning. Segretti testified that a woman juror finally asked him who was paying him, and that he then testified that he was paid by Kalmbach and was hired by Chapin and Strachan.

Earl Silbert has filed an affidavit with the Committee denying that the original Watergate prosecutors limited their questioning of Segretti in order to conceal the involvement of Chapin, Strachan and Kalmbach. Silbert said that since Segretti's last payment was in March, 1972, prior to the effective date of the Federal Election Campaign Act of 1971, "it foreclosed the possibility of a violation of this

538. 9 *Hearings* 3620.
539. 9 *Hearings* 3621.
540. 3 *Hearings* 964.
541. 3 *Hearings* 964; Segretti Witness Summary, p. 15.
542. Segretti Witness Summary, p. 15.
543. *Ibid.*

act." [544] Silbert also denied that he or Donald Campbell ever referred to Herbert Kalmbach as "Mr. K".[545] In his affidavit, Silbert explained more fully his questioning of Segretti:

> Because none of his non-Watergate activity appeared to involve criminal violations and because the grand jury was investigating only Watergate, we did not examine Mr. Segretti at length about his political spying activities before the grand jury. However, we immediately requested the FBI to interview Messrs. Chapin and Strachan of the White House staff, who Mr. Segretti had informed us had recruited him, and Mr. Kalmbach in California. The reports of these interviews were sent to the Special Election Law Unit in the Department of Justice. The *possible* inference drawn by some that we did not explore Mr. Segretti's spying activities before the grand jury because we wanted to conceal any involvement of Messrs. Kalmbach, Chapin, and Strachan is nonsense. . . . We did not because it did not relate to the break-in and the bugging.[546]

Following his grand jury testimony Segretti called John Dean to explain that the names had been revealed by questioning from one of the grand jurors.[547] Following his grand jury appearance, the FBI scheduled interviews with Chapin, Strachan, and Kalmbach. Dean had responsibility for preparing both Chapin and Strachan for their FBI interviews. Dean recalled that Strachan stated on one occasion, in the presence of Richard Moore and Dean that he would perjure himself to prevent Haldeman from becoming involved in the matter.[548] Strachan testified that the discussion with Moore and Dean concerned a reply to a press story in which Strachan offered to take responsibility for approving the hiring of Donald Segretti instead of Mr. Haldeman.[549]

After his grand jury appearance, Segretti's next contact concerning his activities in the re-election campaign was in the middle of September when he was contacted by Carl Bernstein and later, by Robert Meyers of the *Washington Post* who called to ask about his activities. After receiving these calls, Segretti contacted Larry Young again for legal advice and also telephoned Dwight Chapin. Both Chapin

544. See Silbert affidavit.
545. *Ibid.*
546. *Ibid.*
547. 3 *Hearings* 964; Segretti Witness Summary, p. 15.
548. 3 *Hearings* 964.
549. 6 *Hearings* 2488.

and Dean advised Segretti to keep a low profile, and Dean asked Segretti to call and check in periodically.[550]

On October 10, 1972, the *Washington Post* published the first allegations that Donald Segretti had organized a massive campaign of "political spying and sabotage conducted on behalf of President Nixon's re-election and directed by officials at the White House and the Committee for the Re-election of the President." [551] Segretti recalls being called by John Dean prior to the publication of the article, when Dean told Segretti of the forthcoming article. Dean said he was in Florida and that he was going to fly to Washington to meet Segretti as soon as possible to discuss the allegations in the article.[552]

Segretti immediately flew to Washington, D.C., and called Fred Fielding, Dean's assistant, after checking in at a motel near the airport.[553] Segretti was subsequently directed by Dean or Fielding to leave the motel, since he was registered under his real name, and to take a taxi to within a block of the Executive Office Building where Fielding met him to take him into the Executive Office Building.[554]

Segretti testified that he did not sign in on the entrance logs to the Executive Office Building, since Fielding explained to the guard that "this was the individual who lost his wallet," or something similar.[555] Segretti met with Fielding and Dean for about an hour, and they discussed the allegations contained in the *Washington Post* article. Dean read the article to Segretti line by line and they discussed the truth or falsity of each of the charges.[556] At the end of the meeting there was a brief discussion about Segretti writing a statement to be released publicly on the following day. After the meeting, Segretti said that Dean and Fielding drove him to a motel near Crystal City where he registered under an assumed name.

Segretti wrote out a brief statement the following morning for possible release by the White House.[557] Segretti testified that Fielding came by his motel room at about 10 a.m. with a statement prepared by people in the White House that denied most of the allegations in the *Post*. Segretti said he read over Fielding's statement and made some corrections on it, since Fielding indicated they were under some time

550. Segretti Witness Summary, p. 15.
551. *Washington Post*, October 10, 1972, p. A-1, Column 1.
552. 10 *Hearings* 4034.
553. See Segretti Interview notes, August 24, 1973.
554. 10 *Hearings* 4035.
555. *Ibid.*
556. 10 *Hearings* 4042.
557. 10 *Hearings* 4043.

pressure to get the statement out.

Later on that same day, Segretti was contacted again by Dean who explained that the media people in the White House had decided that the story would die by itself and that there should be no further statement made by the White House at that time.[558]

Segretti's proposed press statement was discussed in a meeting at Dwight Chapin's office that day attended by Ron Ziegler, John Ehrlichman, Dwight Chapin, John Dean, Gordon Strachan, and later by Fielding after he had received a draft copy of Segretti's proposed press statement. At that meeting it was decided that Segretti should not issue his statement.[559] Following the meeting, Dean testified that Ehrlichman directed him to advise Segretti to go *incognito* and hide from the press to avoid further stories until after the election.[560]

When Dean talked to Segretti later that afternoon, Dean mentioned how "nice the Greek Islands were at that time of the year." [561] There was also some discussion about how Segretti should travel back to the west coast. Segretti recalled that Dean told him that it would be a great idea to take a train across the country.[562] Segretti, following Dean's suggestion, then took trains from Washington, D.C. to Philadelphia, from Philadelphia to Chicago, from Chicago to Houston, and from Houston to Nevada. During his travels, Segretti would periodically check in with Dean to learn the latest developments and revelations emerging from the White House and the campaign.[563] Sometime during this same period, Segretti also called Doug Kelly and Robert Benz, his two major operatives in Florida, to inform them of his real identity so that they would be prepared for the coming publicity.[564]

Following the election Dean was asked by Haldeman and Ehrlichman to meet with Segretti to determine the extent of the involvement that Chapin and Strachan had with him.[565] Soon thereafter Dean met with Segretti in Palm Springs, California, at the El Doriado Hotel, where Segretti had been staying for the week prior to the election.[566]

Dean taped his interview with Segretti, with the understanding that the material was privileged and would never

558. *Ibid.*
559. 3 *Hearings* 965; see also 6 *Hearings* 2488.
560. 3 *Hearings* 965.
561. 10 *Hearngs* 4043.
562. Segretti Witness Summary, p. 16.
563. Segretti Witness Summary, p. 16; 3 *Hearings* 965.
564. Segretti Witness Summary, p. 16.
565. 3 *Hearings* 965.
566. *Ibid.*

be released.[567] Segretti later claimed that the tape should not be disclosed because it was privileged by the attorney-client relationship.[568] However, the Committee directed Segretti to answer questions concerning his conversations with John Dean since the facts did not support a *bona fide* "attorney-client privilege." [569]

Dean testified that his visit to Palm Springs was interrupted by a request on November 11 from Tod Hullin that Dean go to Florida to meet with Ehrlichman and Haldeman, who were there with the President, to report on Dean's interview with Segretti.[570]

Dean flew to Florida immediately, and met with Haldeman and Ehrlichman on about November 12th. At that meeting, Dean played the tape of the interview that he had with Segretti. While Dean was discussing the matter with Ehrlichman and Haldeman, Dean recalled that President Nixon requested that Haldeman meet with him in his office. Dean recalled that Haldeman sent a message back to the President that he was meeting with John Dean and that he would be over shortly to report to the President on the results of his meeting.[571]

On about November 15, 1972, Dean testified that he met with Haldeman and Ehrlichman at Camp David. During the first part of the meeting the subject of Chapin remaining at the White House arose. Dean said he learned at that time that the President had decided that Chapin would have to leave the White House staff as a result of the information that had been given to Haldeman and Ehrlichman in Florida.[572]

Other officials in the White House, including Richard Moore, felt that the President should merely issue a letter of censure to Chapin and leave the matter alone. Dean raised this suggestion with Haldeman and Ehrlichman, but Ehrlichman felt it was not possible to raise the matter again with the President.[573] Dean then was given the task of telling Chapin that he had to leave the White House.[574]

Meanwhile, Dean was directed by Ehrlichman to get a job for Segretti, and so he relayed this request to Herb Kalmbach.[575] Kalmbach apparently found a job for Segretti which paid about $30,000 a year at the Holiday Inn in

567. 3 *Hearings* 966.
568. Segretti Witness Summary, p. 16.
569. 10 *Hearings* 4042.
570. 3 *Hearings* 966.
571. *Ibid.*
572. *Ibid.*
573. *Ibid.*
574. John Dean Interview, September 10, 1973, p. 8.
575. *Ibid.*, p. 4.

Montego Bay, Jamaica, in a legal-public relations capacity.[576] Segretti said he was quite interested by the prospect of this high paying job, but testified that since his mother was sick, and since he received a subpoena from the Senate Judiciary Subcommittee on Administrative Practices and Procedures at about this same time, he decided not to take the job.[577] Dean also discovered that the owner of the Holiday Inn where Segretti was going to work was a friend of President Nixon, and so Dean said he instructed Segretti not to take the job.[578]

At about this same time, Dean spoke with Paul O'Brien, counsel for CRP, about possible West Coast counsel for Segretti. O'Brien recommended Gordon Hampton, an old friend of his from Los Angeles.[579]

Segretti met with Hampton and wrote out in longhand all the details of his activities during the previous year. Hampton subsequently gave this statement, as well as Segretti's phone bills, address cards and account book to Paul O'Brien to transmit to John Dean on December 8, 1972.[580] Hampton said he sent this material to Dean even though Dean had never requested it because he felt that Dean was acting as co-counsel on the case.[581] These materials were subsequently turned over to the Select Committee by John Dean pursuant to a subpoena *duces tecum*.

After Segretti was subpoenaed by the Senate Subcommittee on Administrative Practices and Procedures, he retained John Pollock, a Los Angeles trial attorney.[582] Pollock said that Hampton told him that Pollock's name had been "submitted to or screened by or approved by the White House." [583] During the period that Hampton and Pollock represented Segretti, O'Brien kept in touch with them and reported all of their activities to John Dean.[584] There is no evidence that Hampton or Pollock received any direction from third parties on how to represent their client, Donald Segretti.

D. *White House Press Response.* On October 10, 1972, the *Washington Post* published the first allegation that the Watergate bugging incident stemmed "from a massive cam-

576. Segretti Witness Summary, p. 17.
577. *Ibid.*
578. Interview with John Dean, September 10, 1973, p. 4.
579. O'Brien interview, September 1973, p. 2.
580. Hampton interview, September 1, 1973, p. 4.
581. *Ibid.*, p. 6.
582. Pollock interview, August 28, .1973, p. 2.
583. *Ibid.*, p. 3; Hampton denied that he ever told Pollock that he had been cleared by anyone in the White House (Hampton interview).
584. Interviews with Dean, O'Brien, Hampton and Pollock.

paign of political spying and sabotage conducted on behalf of President Nixon's re-election and directed by officials at the White House and the Committee for the Re-Election of the President." [585] In addition, the *Post* alleged that Donald Segretti traveled around the country recruiting agents to sabotage opposing campaigns and to gather intelligence information on opponents. These relevations by the *Washington Post* initiated a concerted and organized effort by the White House and the Committee to Re-Elect the President to deceive, mislead, and misinform both the public and the press as to the activities of Donald Segretti and his agents.

First, as described above, Segretti was immediately called back to Washington, and then instructed to "lay low" until after the election in November. In the daily press briefing at the White House on October 10, following the publication of the story about Segretti in the *Washington Post*, White House press secretary Ron Ziegler refused to provide any details or further information at all to press inquiries concerning the Segretti matter and other information revealed by the *Washington Post*.[586]

On October 13, 1972, the White House press office was contacted by Bob Woodward and Carl Bernstein of the *Washington Post* who said that they would report on Sunday that Dwight Chapin was a White House contact for Donald Segretti, that Segretti was paid a $20,000 annual salary from a "trust account in a lawyer's name . . . a high-placed friend of the President", that Segretti received some assignments from E. Howard Hunt, and that Segretti reported frequently to Chapin on the progress of the sabotage activities. Despite the fact that Segretti had flown to Washington, D.C. on October 10, to explain exactly what he had done, and despite the knowledge of Strachan and Chapin about the details of Segretti's hiring, the White House issued the following statement:

STATEMENT BY DWIGHT CHAPIN

As the *Washington Post* reporter has described it, the story is based entirely on hearsay and is fundamentally inaccurate.

For example, I do not know, have never met, seen, or talked to E. Howard Hunt. I have known Donald Segretti since college days but I did not meet with him in Florida as the story suggests and I certainly have never discussed with him any phase of the grand jury proceedings in the Watergate case.

585. *Washington Post,* October 10, 1972, p. A 1.
586. *Ibid.*

Beyond that I don't propose to have any further comment.[587]

After the story was published on Sunday, October 15, 1972, a meeting was held in the Roosevelt Room of the White House among Ehrlichman, Ziegler, Buchanan, Richard Moore, Dwight Chapin, and John Dean. The purpose of this meeting was to prepare Ziegler for his press briefing the following day with reference to the Segretti stories in the paper. A secretary was present during the meeting and recorded much of the hypothetical questioning and answering of Mr. Ziegler by those present.[588]

The instructions given to Ziegler on October 15, 1972, and throughout the rest of the Presidential campaign were for the purpose of withholding information from the public about Segretti's activities so that the President's chances for re-election would not be affected. Ziegler's basic response was, "Gentlemen, I have nothing to add to what Chapin has already said on the subject." [589] Judging from what Chapin had already said on the subject, Ziegler's response to such press inquiries was hardly forthcoming.

Notes from the October 15, meeting indicate that it was known that Herbert Kalmbach paid Segretti for his expenses and salary during his employment.[590] And yet when the White House was informed by the *Washington Post* on October 15, 1972, that a story stating that Kalmbach had authorized payments to Donald Segretti would appear the following day, the White House had no comment.[591]

At the 8:15 a.m. meeting in the White House, on Monday, October 16, 1972, it was decided that Ron Ziegler, RNC Chairman Robert Dole, and Clark MacGregor should all make statements attacking the *Post's* stories of the previous days. Ziegler characterized the charges in the *Washington Post* as "malicious," and stated that he would neither discuss nor deny the charges because to do so would "dignify" them.[592]

During the day, MacGregor was advised that both Ziegler and Dole had made strong statements, and so he thought there was no longer a need for him to make a statement. However, MacGregor testified that John Ehrlichman called him and asked him to read a statement that had been prepared.[593] MacGregor testified that he did not know the author

587. 3 *Hearings* 1209.
588. See 3 *Hearings* 1200 for a copy of the notes.
589. 3 *Hearings* 1202.
590. 3 *Hearings* 1200.
591. *Washington Post*, October 16, 1972, p. A 1.
592. *New York Times*, October 17, 1972, p. 28.
593. 12 *Hearings* 4093.

of the statement, and that he opposed merely reading the statement to the press and then refusing to answer any questions. MacGregor also testified that he had no knowledge that the CRP or the White House were supporting any type of political espionage. However, MacGregor had talked to Dwight Chapin prior to his press conference on October 16, and had been informed that Segretti had been hired by Chapin to perform pranks during the campaign.[594] Nevertheless, MacGregor read the prepared statement on the afternoon of October 16, 1972, which said, in part:

> Using innuendo, third-person hearsay, unsubstantiated charges, anonymous sources, huge scare headlines —the *Post* has maliciously sought to give the appearance of a direct connection between the White House and the Watergate—a charge which the *Post* knows —and half a dozen investigations have found—to be false.
> The hallmark of the *Post's* campaign is hypocrisy —and its celebrated 'double standard' is today visible for all to see. . . .
> It is said that this is a dirty campaign, but all the dirt is being thrown by only one side. The mud slinging, the name calling, the unsubstantiated charges, the innunendoes, the guilt by association, the character assassination, the second-hand hearsay are all tactics exclusively employed by the McGovernites and their apologists. President Nixon will remain on the high road, discussing issues of real concern to the American people in a fair, forthright, and hard-hitting manner. . . .[595]

On October 25, 1972, the *Washington Post* reported that H. R. Haldeman was one of five individuals who had authority to approve payments from a secret cash fund during the 1972 campaign. While this article did not relate specifically to Segretti, it was published in the same time frame as the earlier Segretti articles. Again, the White House issued only a terse statement to the *Post* which said, "your inquiry is based on misinformation because the reference to Bob Haldeman is untrue." Neither Haldeman nor Gerald L. Warren, Deputy White House Press Secretary, would elaborate any further on the story.[596] Once again, Ron Ziegler labeled the story "untrue" and accused the *Washington Post* of "shabby journalism" and "a blatant effort at character assassination." Clark MacGregor joined Ron Ziegler in issu-

594. 12 *Hearings* 4905.
595. 12 *Hearings* 5019-20.
596. *Washington Post*, October 25, 1972, p. A 1.

283

ing a flat, official denial of the *Washington Post* story.[597] Subsequent testimony before this Committee revealed that Haldeman authorized the hiring of Segretti and authorized payments from the cash fund kept by Herbert W. Kalmbach.[598]

On November 1, Dwight Chapin drafted a proposed statement to be released by the White House which briefly related some details of the hiring of Segretti. Four days later, Chapin drafted a memorandum for John Dean which was marked "eyes only". This memo was entitled "Chronology of Activity", and outlined for Dean some of the facts concerning Segretti's hiring by Chapin and Strachan. The purpose of the operation, according to Chapin was that:

"We were after information as to the schedules of candidates, people who could infiltrate headquarters, could ask embarrassing questions and could organize counter demonstrations to those we expected our opposition to come forth with during the campaign." [599]

The memo also noted that in January or February, 1972, after Gordon Liddy reported to Gordon Strachan that there was an unidentified agent in the field who was causing some problems for the CRP, "Strachan checked two people (and   ) and then Don was advised to report to Liddy."[600] The two individuals whose names were left blank were Haldeman and Mitchell.

Following the election, Dean testified that Haldeman asked him to write a report for public release that would include full disclosure of the Segretti matter.[601] Taking the information provided by Chapin, Segretti, and others, Dean drafted a series of carefully worded affidavits for each individual whose name had been mentioned by the press in relation to political sabotage and espionage activities. Based on the affidavits, Dean with the help of Richard Moore, wrote a summary draft report and attached the affidavits. This report was forwarded on to Haldeman on December 5, 1974.[602]

Haldeman gave the report to Ehrlichman, who made some penciled changes, and then forwarded it to Ron Ziegler. On December 13, a meeting was held in Ziegler's office among Ziegler, Haldeman, Dean and Moore to discuss whether or not to release the information.

597. *New York Times,* October 26, 1972, p. 32.
598. 7 *Hearings* 2877.
599. Exhibit number 31, *U.S. v. Chapin.*
600. *Ibid.*
601. 3 *Hearings* 967.
602. See exhibit 34-25, 3 *Hearings* 1210.

Richard Moore, John Dean, and Dwight Chapin all testified that Chapin had been in favor from the start of releasing a brief statement whereby Chapin would accept responsibility for the hiring of Segretti and would apologize for having done so. However, at the meeting on December 13, Dean's proposed releases were discussed, and in the words of Richard Moore, "John Dean's memos just raised more questions than they asked (sic). It was not a complete statement, it wouldn't have been a proper one to put out and I think I probably said . . . it wasn't justified and it was just shelved." [603] Dean recalled that nothing was resolved at the meeting and that it was the consensus of the group that the White House should continue to do nothing on the "general theory that no one would be arrested for what they didn't say." [604]

2. OTHER INTELLIGENCE-GATHERING AND DISRUPTION

Although the activities of Segretti and his associates were the most widespread of the White House and CRP sponsored covert campaign activities, there were other significant inappropriate activities during the 1972 campaign. They are summarized below.

A. Ruby I. As noted elsewhere in this report,[605] Senator Muskie was considered the leading Democratic contender and a potentially significant threat to President Nixon's re-election until his setbacks in the Spring 1972 primaries. Trying to obtain information on his campaign activities was a high priority of those planning the re-election campaign. An early example of a covert operation aimed at Muskie was the "Ruby I" project, which involved planting someone in the Muskie campaign.

The plan was developed by Jeb Magruder, with the help of Ken Rietz, beginning in August 1971.[606] Magruder asked Rietz if he could arrange to plant someone in the Muskie campaign who would be responsible for obtaining as much information concerning the campaign as possible, including

603. 5 *Hearings* 2032.
604. 3 *Hearings* 967.
605. *See* section on Campaign Strategy, *supra.*
606. Rietz interview, Sept. 19, 1973. The idea of planting someone in the Muskie campaign was first suggested, according to Magruder, by either Mitchell, Haldeman, or Magruder. Magruder interview, Oct. 1, 1973, p. 10. Mitchell denied making such a suggestion but admitted receiving information from a plant in Muskie headquarters. Mitchell interview, June 27, 1973. Haldeman has denied any knowledge of such a political operation. DNC Deposition, May 22, 1973, pp. 21-22.

intraoffice memos, speeches, travel schedules, press releases and position papers. According to Rietz, Magruder assured him that such an operation was legal. Rietz told Magruder that he would confer with a friend on establishing a workable plan.[607]

After this conversation with Magruder, Rietz contacted John Buckley, who was director of the inspection division at the Office of Economic Opportunity (OEO) and asked Buckley to help him place a volunteer in the Muskie headquarters who would channel information to CRP. Buckley agreed to help.[608]

In late September 1971, Buckley told Rietz that he had drawn up a plan, inspired by a newspaper column telling of a free taxi ride offered to Senator Humphrey,[609] to have a cab driver offer his services to the Muskie organization. Buckley told Rietz he had already secured a cab driver for the job, and Rietz approved the plan.[610]

Buckley had selected Elmer Wyatt, an old acquaintance of his, for the job. Buckley instructed Wyatt to go to Muskie headquarters and offer his services as a volunteer. Wyatt understood that he would be paid, although he and Buckley did not talk finances at their first meeting. Rietz said that Magruder later approved payment of $1000 per month.[611] Wyatt went to the Muskie headquarters where he first worked as a volunteer doing errands such as picking up dry cleaning and mailing campaign literature to other Muskie offices. Eventually, however, Wyatt was asked to deliver inter-office mail between Muskie's Senate Office and his campaign headquarters. Wyatt kept Buckley informed on his progress as a Muskie volunteer,[612] and Buckley in turn reported to Rietz that Wyatt was established as a volunteer at the Muskie headquarters.

From September 1971 until April 1972, Buckley worked with Wyatt in obtaining and photographing confidential documents from the Muskie campaign during the time Buckley was working at OEO. In the early stages, Wyatt would call Buckley before leaving to deliver documents either to or from Muskie's Senate Office. Wyatt would then pick up Buckley on a specified corner and, while riding in Wyatt's cab, Buckley would review and photograph pertinent documents. When this operation was completed, the material was delivered to the Muskie campaign headquarters or Senate Office. This

607. Rietz interview. September 19, 1973.
608. 11 *Hearings* 4438.
609. *Washington Star*. Morris Siegal column, September 27, 1971.
610. 11 *Hearings* 4439.
611. Rietz interview. September 19. 1973.
612. Elmer Wyatt Interview. September 28, 1973, p. 1

procedure of taking pictures in the backseat was unsatisfactory for Buckley, and so he rented office space at 1026 17th St. N.W. in Washington. Buckley also purchased new equipment which was more effective in photographing documents.[613] Wyatt obtained press releases, itineraries, internal memoranda, drafts of speeches and position papers, and brought them regularly to Buckley's rented office to be photographed by Buckley during his lunch hour. Buckley testified that no mail was ever opened.[614]

After developing the film, Buckley turned it over to Rietz during meetings on various corners of Pennsylvania Avenue.[615] Rietz in turn gave the film to Magruder.[616]

In November 1971, Magruder gave Herbert Porter some developed 35 mm film and a viewer and asked him to review the film without offering any explanation of its origin. Porter stated that Magruder occasionally asked him for the film and viewer to show them to Mitchell. Porter recalled that later Rietz brought the film directly to Porter at Magruder's instructions. Porter's job was to review the film and bring anything of interest to Magruder's attention.[617]

Rietz told Porter that he and Magruder had an individual at Muskie headquarters who was giving the material to Rietz.[618] Porter reviewed the film in his office. On occasion, Martha Duncan, his secretary, typed transcripts based upon the photographed documents for forwarding to Magruder. At Magruder's request Porter testified he also sent copies of the transcripts to Strachan.[619]

In December 1971, Porter sent a transcript of one of the filmed documents from Muskie headquarters to Magruder. It was a staff memorandum from Muskie's campaign manager suggesting that Muskie, as Chairman of a Subcommittee on Government Operations, could get good coverage if he held tax hearings in California at the taxpayers' expense. Magruder asked Porter to have the transcript retyped on plain bond stationery and sent to Evans and Novak. Porter did so. Evans and Novak printed it, and the hearings were never held.[620]

On another occasion, Porter told Magruder he had a 20-page speech that Muskie was planning to deliver against the nomination of William Rehnquist to the Supreme Court. According to Porter Magruder told him to have a transcript

613. 11 *Hearings* 4441-4443.
614. 11 *Hearings* 4443.
615. *Ibid.*
616. Rietz Interview, September 19, 1973.
617. Porter Interview, September 6, 1973, p. 19.
618. *Ibid.*
619. 2 *Hearings* 670.
620. 2 *Hearings* 669-670. See also Exhibit 00. For other examples of copied information, see 11 *Hearings* 4889.

typed from the filmed document because Mitchell wanted to see it.[621] The floor plan of Muskie's headquarters was also obtained through this political intelligence operation.[622]

In December 1971, Gordon Liddy began working at the Committee to Re-Elect the President, and so Magruder instructed Porter to give the film and viewer to Liddy.[623] At about the same time Howard Hunt took over Rietz's job of obtaining film from Buckley. At Liddy's request,[624] Hunt met Buckley on various corners of Pennsylvania Avenue as Rietz had done previously. During these brief meetings, Hunt used the alias Ed Warren, and Buckley used the alias Jack Kent. Throughout their association Hunt never knew Buckley's real name.

Although Hunt was then employed by the Robert R. Mullen Company, he was also working closely with Gordon Liddy, who was responsible for the political intelligence-gathering capabilities at CRP.[625] The code name "Ruby I" evolved as part of the overall "Gemstone" plan, and was used primarily by Liddy and Hunt when referring to Wyatt. They also referred to John Buckley, alias Jack Kent, as "Fat Jack." [626]

Hunt met with Buckley approximately twelve to fifteen times. Buckley turned over film to Hunt, who then gave it over to Liddy. Hunt also gave Buckley plain envelopes containing cash on occasion to cover Buckley's expenses. This procedure continued until April 1972, when it was decided that Muskie was no longer a viable candidate and the operation was terminated.[627]

The Ruby I operation, as Hunt and Liddy referred to it, lasted approximately eight months and cost about $8,000. Buckley testified that he and Wyatt did not participate in any other political intelligence operations for the CRP.[628]

B. *Sedan Chair I.* The genesis of Sedan Chair, according to Bart Porter, was Jeb Magruder's concern with the favorable publicity the Democrats received during past campaigns from the humor generated by Democratic prankster Dick Tuck and those like him who were making Republicans the objects of their pranks.[629] In an effort to get similar headlines, Magruder instructed Porter to obtain advance schedules for

621. *Ibid.*, p. 670.
622. Rietz Interview, September 19, 1973.
623. Porter Interview, August 20, 1973, p. 20.
624. Hunt Executive Session, June 12, 1973, pp. 208-09.
625. 2 *Hearings* 792.
626. Hunt Executive Session, June 12, 1973, p. 209.
627. 9 *Hearings* 3761.
628. 11 *Hearings* 4445.
629. Interview of Herbert L. Porter, April 2, 1973.

leading Democratic contenders as part of a plan to carry out disruptive activities.[630]

The first operation arranged by Porter involved a Muskie visit to Chicago. An unidentified associate of Porter's organized a crowd carrying Nixon signs to meet Muskie at the Chicago airport, a move that generated some news in the local papers. Similar events took place in Cincinnati and Columbus, Ohio, and in cities in New Jersey. According to Porter the efforts were unsuccessful, eliciting in the media little favorable Republican publicity.[631]

Occasionally Porter paid his field operatives small amounts of money, which he received from Hank Buchannon, the accountant at CRP. In the early stages, he stated that he never distributed more than one or two hundred dollars to any individual.[632]

In conjunction with these efforts, Porter went to Ron Walker, then the President's chief "advance man," and asked Walker if he had any associates who might be proficient at "dirty tricks." [633] Walker recommended Roger Greaves, a friend of his, and shortly thereafter Greaves, Porter and Magruder met in California. Following the meeting Greaves was retained and given the code name "Sedan Chair," a reference to an old Marine Corps operation that Porter remembered.[634]

It was Porter's understanding that Magruder wanted someone to follow or precede Democratic candidates and cause general harassment. For example, Porter said that Magruder envisioned an individual who would rob motorcades of automobile keys, schedule fake meetings, or steal shoes of the opposition workers that were left in hotel halls to be polished.[635] Greaves was told that he would be reimbursed for expenses and that Porter would be the CRP contact. He was told that if successful in early forays he would be hired on a long-term basis.[636]

Greaves' recollection of the meeting with Porter and Magruder is that Magruder wanted someone to filter stories to the media, to gather information from the opposition, and to cause harassment. Magruder, according to Greaves, stressed the need for performing his tasks covertly. Greaves said he was told by Porter that he should terminate the job he then had and that cover employment would be arranged

630. Ibid.
631. Ibid.
632. Ibid.
633. Interview of Herbert L. Porter, Aug. 20, 1973.
634. Interview of Herbert L. Porter, April 2, 1973.
635. Ibid.
636. Interview of Herbert L. Porter, Aug. 20, 1973.

with a large corporation, which would pay Greaves' salary for work performed at Porter's direction.[637] According to Porter, Greaves at first expressed reservations about taking the job, but agreed with Magruder's suggestion that he perform some pranks in California on a trial basis.[638]

A November 17, 1971, confidential memo from Porter to Magruder concerning the operation reads as follows:

> Things went well in Los Angeles with our friend. I would like the "green light" to proceed with the second part of the plan. This will involve finding him a "suitable" home.
>
> He is ready, willing, and *most* able. Any ideas? [639]

Porter stated that the "suitable" home, referred to above, was finding a corporation to pay Greaves' salary while he covertly worked for CRP.[640] In addition, the date of the memo above indicates that it was written after some of Greaves' early successful activities described below.

Shortly after the meeting in California Greaves received a call from Porter, who relayed Muskie's schedule and instructed Greaves to arrange for pickets at a Muskie appearance. Blacks and "hippies" were preferred as pickets by Porter according to Greaves. Porter asked Greaves to place Nixon signs at the airport arrival of Senator Muskie and to place anti-Muskie signs at a dinner at which the candidate was scheduled to speak. On another occasion, Porter said that Magruder told him to have Greaves place some signs at the Muskie rally at Whittier College and perhaps get media coverage. This rally was the same occasion when Chapin instructed Segretti to arrange for pickets.[641]

According to Porter, money was sent to Greaves on three occasions.[642] On the first occasion, Greaves claimed he needed $300 immediately for pickets who were to appear at the Muskie appearance at Whittier College.[643] The second instance occurred when either Magruder or Ken Khachigian asked Porter to send Greaves 25 copies of the anti-Muskie pamphlet ostensibly put out by the "Citizens for a Liberal Alternative " [644] A Muskie fund-raising dinner was planned in Beverly Hills, and Khachigian or Magruder thought it would be humorous to place a copy of the pamphlet in each

637. Interview of Roger Greaves, Aug. 21, 1973.
638. *Ibid.*
639. See Exhibit 00.
640. Porter Interview, Aug. 20, 1973..
641. See p. 268 above.
642. Porter interview, Aug. 20, 1973.
643. *Ibid.*
644. See pp. 245ff., *supra,* for a fuller discussion of the "Citizens for a Liberal Alternative."

of the menus, according to Porter.[645] However, because the dinner never occurred (Senator Muskie was apparently ill), this stunt was sidetracked.[646] The third time Porter forwarded money to Greaves was in January 1972, when Greaves finally decided to join the re-election campaign as a political prankster.[647]

Porter testified that Magruder told him he needed someone to work full-time on political pranks in January, 1972. It was Porter's impression that Magruder was under pressure to make immediate arrangements for someone to go on to New Hampshire and then to Florida to perform pranks and familiarize himself with the Muskie campaign.[648]

Porter contacted Greaves and instructed him to use his imagination in performing political pranks that would get good coverage in New Hampshire.[649] A salary of $2,000 per month was agreed upon. Before Greaves commenced his activities, he had his picture taken by Porter. This was done at the request of Gordon Liddy, who explained to Porter that some of his underlings would be doing some rough work in New Hamphsire and he wanted to avoid injuring Greaves.[650]

By all accounts, Greaves' performance in New Hampshire was a dismal failure. Greaves often did nothing more than visit bars and listen to conversations about the Muskie Campaign.[651] Porter has testified that Greaves said he arranged calls to voters in the middle of the night with the caller falsely stating that they were "Harlemites for Muskie" requesting the voter's support for Muskie. In his interview with the Select Committee staff, Greaves flatly denied any involvement in this episode.[652]

Greaves spent some time in New Hampshire and then went to Florida where he again was supposed to organize activities disruptive to Muskie's campaign. Greaves stayed in Florida only a few days before returning to California.[653] The next time Porter heard from Greaves was when Greaves called and said he had returned to California and was resigning for personal reasons.[654]

C. *Sedan Chair II*. Following Greaves' departure, Magruder

645. Porter interview, August 20, 1973.
646. *Ibid.*
647. *Ibid.*
648. Interview of Herbert L. Porter, April 2, 1973.
649. Interview of Herbert L. Porter, Aug. 20, 1973.
650. *Ibid.*
651. Interview of Herbert L. Porter, Aug. 20, 1973; See also Greaves interview, Aug. 21, 1973.
652. Greaves interview, Aug. 21, 1973.
653. *Ibid.*
654. Interview of Herbert L. Porter, April 21, 1973.

told Porter he needed another operative in the field to gather information about various Democratic candidates. Magruder said he was directed to place another individual in the opposition campaign by John Mitchell.[655] Magruder stated that this person was to provide information only and was not to engage in any disruptive activities.[656] Porter instructed Roger Stone to make arrangements for someone who would work "in two or three of the primary campaigns as kind of an eyes and ears . . ."[657]

Roger Stone's recollection of the original Sedan Chair II conflicts with the testimony of Magruder and Porter. Stone recalled discussing the need with Porter for an individual who would perform political pranks as well as gather useful information concerning opposition campaigns.[658] Stone recalled discussing the need for a "clever field man" with Morton Blackwell, who recommended Michael W. McMinoway of Louisville, Kentucky.[659]

After introductory telephone conversations with McMinoway, Stone flew to Louisville, and using the assumed name of Jason Rainer, Stone explained to McMinoway that he was being recruited: to "work in the Presidential primary states and track and infiltrate the Democratic organizations . . ."[660] The two agreed that McMinoway would receive $1500 a month for his services[661] and that after "Rainer" designated which Democratic organizations were to be infiltrated, the "actual operation procedures" would be left up to McMinoway.[662] At this first meeting and throughout McMinoway's tenure, efforts were made to conceal CRP's involvement in the undertaking. Stone told McMinoway only that "he was working for a group of concerned citizens that were interested in the outcome of the 1972 Presidential election."[663] McMinoway was supplied with a post office box in Washington to which he was to send information, thereby avoiding any contact with CRP or its officials.[664] McMinoway was subsequently given instructions by Stone, who said he re-

655. Magruder interview, Aug. 18, 1973, p. 6.
656. Magruder interview, Oct. 1, 1973, p. 9.
657. 2 *Hearings* 659; interview of H. L. Porter Aug. 20, 1973, p. 23.
658. Staff interview of Roger Stone, Aug. 15, 1973.
659. *Ibid.* See also 11 *Hearings* 4478. See also Blackwell interview, Sept. 9, 1973.
660. 11 *Hearings* 4478.
661. McMinoway received periodic payments from Stone beginning on March 17, 1972 continuing through July 8, 1972. These payments, according to McMinoway, amounted to $5808.10. 11 *Hearings* 4479. (Exhibit 238)
662. 11 *Hearings* 4480.
663. *Ibid.* About one month after he began, McMinoway, reflecting upon the nature of his activities, concluded that he was working for the Republican party.
664. *Ibid.*

ceived them from Porter, who said he obtained them from Magruder.[665] Magruder received some instructions from John Mitchell.[666]

In his testimony before the Select Committee, McMinoway described how he infiltrated a Democratic candidate's campaign: "The usual procedure was to start off as a volunteer worker in the particular organization from which I wished to gather information." [667] Hard work and seemingly helpful efforts on behalf of a particular candidate advanced McMinoway in the organization. "My objective," McMinoway testified, "was to work within an organization, to gain their confidence and to therefore be able to be in a position where I could personally observe and find out the information that I felt important to the organization and its structure." [668] Occasionally McMinoway worked simultaneously for two or three Democratic candidates.[669] After obtaining relevant information from the campaign organizations, McMinoway called Stone or transmitted the materials to Stone via the Washington post office box.[670]

Stone in turn passed the information he received on to Bart Porter.[671] Porter gave the information to Magruder and Bob Reisner, his assistant, in the form of memos typed on blank paper beginning "a confidential source reports." [672] Magruder said that he sent this information on to John Mitchell and to Gordon Strachan for H.R. Haldeman.[673] Finally, Strachan testified that he included information from Sedan Chair II in his "political matters" memoranda for H.R. Haldeman. He specifically recalled including the report on the Pennsylvania Humphrey campaign discussed below.[674]

In addition to this information-gathering function, McMinoway occasionally engaged in disruptive activities which affected particular Democratic campaigns.

McMinoway's first assignment from Stone and the chain of command above him was to go to Wisconsin in March, 1972, and infiltrate the Muskie headquarters. Stone instructed McMinoway to obtain information about Muskie staff members, campaign finances, schedules of events and any other useful information. McMinoway's diary corrobo-

665. Porter interview, Aug. 20, 1973; Stone interview, Aug. 15, 1973.
666. Magruder interview, August 18, 1973, p. 6.
667. 11 *Hearings* 4481.
668. 11 *Hearings* 4507.
669. 11 *Hearings* 4483.
670. At first McMinoway testified he would call Stone every other day; later in the operation McMinoway testified he spoke with Stone "several times a day." 11 *Hearings* 4482.
671. Stone interview, Aug. 15, 1973, p. 6.
672. Porter interview, Aug. 20, 1973, p. 16.
673. Magruder interview, Aug. 18, 1973, p. 2.
674. 6 *Hearings* 2441.

rated his success in gathering information in Wisconsin.[675]

Other activities of McMinoway in Wisconsin were intended to disrupt Democratic candidates. On March 28, 1972, instead of supervising the distribution of Muskie literature, his diary shows that McMinoway talked his group of workers into drinking beer.[676] On March 30th, he visited the Humphrey headquarters and gave them a schedule of events of the Muskie campaign.[677] On March 25th, while still ostensibly a Muskie worker, McMinoway visited McGovern's headquarters and talked to a worker there about possible disruptions of a Muskie television interview.[678] Finally, on March 31, the diary shows that he "went down to headquarters and diverted some election day precinct materials."

Following the Wisconsin primary, Stone, acting on orders from Porter, told McMinoway to infiltrate the Pennsylvania Humphrey campaign. Using an alias, McMinoway presented himself as a volunteer and was welcomed to the campaign. He routinely began sending relevant information about the campaign to Washington.[679]

The Humphrey campaign also asked McMinoway to help supervise their phone bank operations. In this capacity, he "promptly put people on calling and duplicating cards that had been done by the day shift." [680] In addition, he rearranged names to be called so that the night shift would make the same calls as the day shift.[681] The impact of this action was noted in his diary: "Repetition of calls is starting to aggravate the volunteer block captains. The captains are getting called two or three times and it is beginning to bother them. Some captains have already quit because of the repeated calls." [682]

At one point McMinoway wrote in his diary that he hired people of "low calibre qualifications" to work the phone banks.[683] On another occasion, he rearranged stacks of names to be called so that prepared messages to be read by the caller were directed to the wrong group.[684] Calls for black voters were substituted for calls to union members and vice versa. On still another occasion, McMinoway falsely told volunteers who were scheduled to work the phone banks

675. 11 *Hearings* 4483.
676. 11 *Hearings* 4484.
677. *Ibid.*
678. 11 *Hearings* 4486.
679. 11 *Hearings* 4487.
680. 11 *Hearings* 4487-88.
681. *Ibid.*
682. *Ibid.*
683. *Ibid.*
684. 11 *Hearings* 4489.

that they would not be needed that particular day.[685] Mc-
Minoway testified that his phone bank activities caused considerable disruption to the Humphrey campaign,[686] because,
as he wrote in his diary, "Humphrey is spending one-third
of his budget on the phone bank and literature packets that
the block captains will distribute." [687]

As in Wisconsin, McMinoway's "loyalties" were not confined to the Democratic candidate he had volunteered to
assist. In an April 22, 1972, entry in his diary, he shows he
called people from the Humphrey headquarters and urged
them to vote for Senator Jackson.[688]

McMinoway testified that he impressed the Humphrey
people with his willingness to work. Toward the end of the
Pennsylvania campaign, McMinoway testified that a national
coordinator asked him to work at the Humphrey Los Angeles headquarters in the California primary. In his diary,
McMinoway quoted from an alleged letter that the national
coordinator prepared to introduce him in California. The letter said McMinoway was "an avid Humphrey supporter that
could be trusted in any project." [689]

McMinoway was then assigned by Stone and his superiors
to go to California and infiltrate both the McGovern and
Humphrey campaigns.[690] This assignment came after the mid-
April, 1972, meeting when Gordon Strachan testified that
H.R. Haldeman told him to tell G. Gordon Liddy "to transfer whatever capability he had from Muskie to McGovern." [691] McMinoway testified that he engaged in the same
activities in California as he had in prior primaries, and that
he reported by telephone to Stone daily.

McMinoway testified that he learned of the Watergate
break-in after the California primary, while awaiting his next
assignment. McMinoway said he immediately called Stone,
only to learn that his number had been disconnected that
same morning. About two days later, McMinoway said that
Stone called him and asked that he continue his activities,
explaining that Stone had taken no part in any illegal actions.[692] McMinoway said he remained unconvinced, but that
he agreed to go to Washington to meet with Stone's supervisor to receive reassurances of the propriety of his under-

685. 11 *Hearings* 4491.
686. 11 *Hearings* 4488.
687. 11 *Hearings* 4709.
688. 11 *Hearings* 4488.
689. 11 *Hearings* 4490.
690. 11 *Hearings* 4492.
691. 6 *Hearings* 2455.
692. 11 *Hearings* 4494. Stone said that McMinoway was in Washington before the break-in, and never expressed any concern about the break-in.
(Stone interview)

taking. In Washington, McMinoway testified he received a phone call in his hotel room: ". . . The man identified himself merely as Mr. M., just for the matter of having something, a reference, for me to contact, and he reassured me that the organization I was working with was not involved in illegal activities and quite strenuously passed on to me the fact that they were not, in fact, connected with the people that were apprehended." [693]

This mysterious caller was Bart Porter, who stated that he had discussions with McMinoway after the June 17th break-in. Porter had no recollection of any discussion about the break-in, recalling that the conversation focused on a possible increase in salary for Sedan Chair II.[694]

McMinoway testified that after this conversation he volunteered for work at McGovern's national headquarters in Washington, where he worked closely with McGovern's administrative staff.[695] As he explained, "by this time I had become a familiar face." [696]

At the Democratic National Convention, McMinoway claimed to achieve new successes in his efforts to infiltrate the opposition. The first five days there he said were used to "amass information on where different delegations were staying, where different hotels were, the locations, and so forth." [697] Thereafter McMinoway served as a member of the security staff in McGovern's headquarters at the Doral Hotel, a position which, he testified, occasionally allowed him access to otherwise private areas. As he explained in his diary, McMinoway said he was a guard on the "penthouse" floor where McGovern was staying. McMinoway also wrote in his diary that he had access to all of McGovern's convention operations rooms and that he met "all of the big time McGovern staff." [698] McMinoway wrote that he watched television with Senator McGovern on the night of the vote on the challenge to the California delegation, and added, "It is amazing how easy it would be to be right in the midst of all the operations and planning and yet be an enemy." [699]

Many of McMinoway's particular claims about his work at the Democratic convention are contradicted by sworn affidavits and testimony in the public Committee record.[700]

693. 11 *Hearings* 4495.
694. Porter interview, Aug. 20, 1973, p. 25.
695. 11 *Hearings* 4496.
696. 11 *Hearings* 4497.
697. 11 *Hearings* 4497.
698. Exhibit No. 237, 11 *Hearings* 4717.
699. *Ibid.*
700. See, for example, sworn letter of Senator McGovern, 11 *Hearings* 4743; testimony of Frank Mankiewicz, 11 *Hearings* 4616; affidavit of Thomas P. Southwick, 11 *Hearings* 4893; affidavit of Anthony Barash, 12 *Hearings* 5267.

However, there is no question that McMinoway was able to secure a position as a volunteer security guard of the McGovern floors while working directly for the Committee to Re-Elect the President.[701]

D. Ruby II. In February 1972, Howard Hunt hired Thomas Gregory, a student at Brigham Young University, to infiltrate the Muskie campaign.[702] Hunt met Gregory through Robert Fletcher, the nephew of Robert Bennett, Hunt's employer at the Mullen Company.[703]

Using the alias Ed Warren, Hunt called Gregory in Utah and asked him to come to Washington for an expense-paid job interview. About a week later Hunt and Gregory met at the Park Central Hotel in Washington, where Hunt explained that he wanted information from the Muskie campaign, including schedules, internal memoranda, and general observations of the campaign. Gregory was to work as a volunteer for Muskie, report to Hunt once a week, and receive $175 a week for his services. Gregory accepted the offer.[704]

The next day Gregory began working as a volunteer at the Muskie campaign headquarters, where he was placed in the foreign affairs section under Anthony Lake.[705] His job consisted of photocopying, picking up schedules and other random chores. Gregory did not photocopy any material for Hunt, but he did type reports based upon documents he read or conversations he overheard.[706]

Hunt and Gregory met weekly in a drugstore at 17th and K Street, N.W., in Washington, D.C. During these brief meetings, Gregory gave Hunt typed reports on the week's activities; when Hunt was not available, Gregory gave this material to Robert Fletcher to pass on to Hunt.

All information that Hunt received from Gregory was turned over to Gordon Liddy, including the memoranda that Hunt typed which summarized Gregory's oral reports. Hunt did not retain any copies of this material.[707]

Gordon Strachan testified that in mid-April, 1972, Haldeman told him to contact G. Gordon Liddy to tell him to transfer his "capability" from Muskie to McGovern "with particular interest in discovering what the connection between

701. See Barash Affidavit, *Ibid.*
702. 11 *Hearings* 4636.
703. Gregory Interview, September 1, 1973, p. 1.
704. *Ibid.*, p. 2.
705. Berl Bernhard testified that Lake was under electronic surveillance by the Administration while he was working for the Muskie campaign. (11 *Hearings* 4665)
706. Gregory Interview, p. 3.
707. Hunt Executive Session, June 12, 1973, p. 206.

McGovern and Senator Kennedy was." [708] Strachan also testified that he assumed "finally, there was going to be one unified system" of intelligence-gathering under Liddy after this conversation. [709]

At about this same time, Hunt asked Gregory to transfer to the McGovern campaign as a volunteer, which he did. Gregory's responsibilities remained the same as in the Muskie campaign, with one significant addition: he was now to prepare and assist Hunt and Liddy in their plans to place electronic surveillance on McGovern headquarters. [710]

Gregory gave Hunt a floor plan and office description of the McGovern headquarters at Hunt's request. Hunt then introduced Gregory to James McCord, in late April or early May 1972. In a meeting at the Roger Smith Hotel, Washington D.C., Hunt and McCord told Gregory they were planning to place a "bug" in the McGovern Headquarters and would need assistance. [711]

In late May 1972, Gregory took McCord through the McGovern headquarters to familiarize McCord with the physical layout. On a second occasion (May 27, 1972) Gregory again took McCord through the McGovern headquarters; on that visit McCord unsuccessfully attempted to plant a bug in Frank Mankewicz's office. [712]

Sometime in late May-early June 1972 Gregory met Gordon Liddy for the first time, during an automobile ride in which Hunt drove Liddy and Gregory around the McGovern headquarters while Liddy told Gregory that he, too, was interested in getting into the McGovern offices.

Hunt, Liddy, McCord, and Gregory met at a Washington hotel to discuss breaking into McGovern headquarters to copy documents and to go over a physical layout of offices and the location of alarm systems. [713]

By early June, Gregory had serious questions about the propriety of his activities which he discussed with his uncle, Robert Bennett. On or about June 15 or 16, 1972, Gregory met with Hunt to tell him that he no longer wished to continue with his work. [714] After terminating his employment with Hunt, Gregory also contacted the McGovern headquarters to discontinue his volunteer work. Gregory received approximately $3,400 for his services. [715]

Bart Porter recalled that Colson wanted to send someone

708. 6 *Hearings* 2455.
709. 6 *Hearings* 2470.
710. 9 *Hearings* 3685.
711. Gregory Interview, September 1, 1973, p. 4.
712. McCord DNC Deposition, April 3, 1973, pp. 155-59.
713. Gregory Interview, September 1, 1973, p. 4.
714. *Ibid.*
715. *Ibid.*

to New Hampshire to make a contribution to the campaign of Rep. Pete McCloskey on behalf of some radical group.[716] Porter testified that he gave Roger Stone $200 to travel to New Hampshire to make a cash contribution to the McCloskey campaign.[717] Jeb Magruder stated that on one occasion Charles Colson suggested that CRP send an individual wearing a "gay lib" button to a McGovern meeting.[718]

Roger Stone stated that Porter suggested that he travel to New Hampshire and contribute money to McCloskey from the Gay Liberation Front.[719] Stone said he persuaded Porter to make the contribution instead from the Young Socialist Alliance.

A few days later, Porter called Stone back to his office and gave him $200 in cash to travel and for the $135 contribution. Stone said he converted the $135 into small bills and coins to convey the image of a donation from many small contributors.

Stone said he went to New Hampshire and delivered the contribution to a McCloskey campaign worker in a store front. Stone received a receipt for the contribution from the campaign worker showing the source of the contribution as the "Young Socialist Alliance." [720]

After he returned to Washington, Stone said he met with Porter and they drafted an anonymous letter to the *Manchester Union Leader* and enclosed a photocopy of the receipt.[721] The bogus contribution was staged and subsequently attempted to be leaked to discredit the McCloskey campaign with the New Hampshire voters.[722]

E. Theodore Brill. Jeb Magruder testified that another incident initiated by Charles Colson was the infiltration of the peace vigil conducted by a group of Quakers in front of the White House. The group of Quakers gathered daily in front of the White House to protest the Administration's Vietnam policy. Magruder said Colson told him that there "should be someone finding out what the peace groups in front of the White House were doing.[723] Magruder asked Ken Rietz, head of the Young Voters for the President, to find someone to get Colson the information. Rietz, whose experience in intelligence-gathering began with the placement of "Ruby I," [724]

716. Porter interview, August 20, 1973, p. 10.
717. 2 *Hearings* 658.
718. Magruder interview, August 18, 1973, p. 4.
719. Stone interview, August 15, 1973, p. 2.
720. Stone interview, Aug. 15, 1973, p. 3.
721. *Ibid.*
722. *Ibid.*
723. Magruder interview, Aug. 18, 1973, pp. 3-4.
724. See p. 285, *supra.*

delegated the assignment to his assistant, George Gorton.

Gorton contacted Roger Stone and asked Stone if he knew a local Young Republican who "needed a summer job." [725] Stone suggested Ted Brill, a former chairman of George Washington University's Young Republican organization. Gorton asked Brill to come to CRP headquarters where he told him that the job consisted of infiltrating monitoring the Quaker vigil "as a first assignment." [726] Brill's assignment was to determine the future intentions of this group, particularly its plans for the Republican Convention in Miami. Brill periodically visited the vigil, sometimes wearing a McGovern campaign button, and talked with the protestors during the next six weeks.[727] He reported orally to Gorton six or seven times and received about $675 for his efforts. Brill was terminated the week following the Watergate break-in.

Throughout the Gorton-Brill contacts, the possibility of further assignments was discussed, including infiltrating dissident groups at the Republican Convention. Brill testified that after news of the Watergate break-in he received no further assignments.[728]

Magruder stated that the information from Brill went back to Ken Rietz and then to Richard Howard in Colson's office.[729]

F. Chapman's Friend. Chapman's Friend was a code name used by two reporters who were hired by Murray Chotiner, a veteran of many Nixon campaigns, to travel with opposition campaigns posing as newspaper reporters, and to monitor the activities of these opposition candidates during the 1972 campaign.[730] Chotiner said the operation was approved by John Mitchell but was handled directly by Chotiner.[731]

The first Chapman's Friend, Seymour K. Freidin, worked from March to November 1971, and from May until the end of August, 1972. covering as many candidates as possible.[732] Freidin was not reporting for any newspaper at the time, and received his sole source of income from Chotiner. Chotiner said he told Freiden to observe everything he could while traveling with various campaigns and to report the information back to Chotiner. Freiden identified himself as a working journalist to gain access to the Democratic campaigns. He phoned his reports to Chotiner or Chotiner's sec-

725. Stone interview, Aug. 15, 1973, p. 8.
726. Brill interview, Sept. 8, 1973, pp. 2-3.
727. *Ibid.*
728. *Ibid.*
729. Magruder interview, Aug. 18, 1973, p. 4.
730. Chotiner interview, Aug. 9, 1973.
731. Chotiner interview, Aug. 17, 1973.
732. GAO Report, Dec. 18, 1973.

retary. The reports discussed crowd reactions, interviews with staff people and events that occurred both privately and publicly while on the campaign trail.[733] The reports were typed in draft form by Chotiner's secretary and edited by Chotiner, whose final versions were sent to Haldeman and Mitchell.[734] Once the Chapman's Friend Report reached Haldeman, it was again copied and sent to members of Haldeman's staff.[735] There was no indication on the Chapman's Friend Report where the information came from or who was responsible for providing it. The reports were simply labelled "Chapman's Friend Reports." Sometime in August 1973, Freidin got another assignment as a reporter and terminated his employment with Chotiner.

Chotiner then hired Lucianne C. Goldberg. Mrs. Goldberg traveled with the campaign of Senator McGovern, and also used the code name of Chapman's Friend. Mrs. Goldberg was employed by Chotiner from September 1972 through the election in November.[736]

Both Goldberg and Friedin were paid $1000 per week plus expenses with checks drawn from Chotiner's law office account. Chotiner's secretary submitted expense vouchers to FCRP for reimbursement of Chotiner's expenses.[737] On the vouchers the payee's salary was shown only as "reimbursement for survey," and related expenses were shown only as "reimbursement for survey expenses." [738]

The only people who knew the true purpose of the "survey" expenditures, according to Chotiner, were Mitchell, Magruder, and Robert Odle. Chotiner told Odle the purpose of the payments but refused to reveal the identities of the Chapman's Friends because he did not want the name of the informant disclosed before the election. Odle, however, denied any knowledge of the purpose of the expenditures made by Chotiner until sometime in June 1973, when he was informed of the purpose during questioning by the FBI.[739] Odle wrote a memorandum on September 8, 1972 to Nick Bungato, a driver at CRP, which stated:

> Once or twice a day you will get a call from Mr. Chotiner's office in the Reeves and Harrison law firm on the fifth floor of 1701, asking you to deliver envelopes directly to Mr. Haldeman's office on the first floor of the West Wing at the White House.

733. Chotiner interview, Aug. 9, 1973.
734. *Ibid.*
735. Higby interview, May 10, 1973.
736. GAO report, Dec. 18, 1973.
737. Chotiner interview, Aug. 17, 1973.
738. GAO Report, Dec. 18, 1973.
739. *Ibid.*

Please give these requests top priority since the envelopes are very important and time will always be a factor.[740]

G. *Young Voters for the President Demonstrations.* The CRP's efforts to counter or neutralize the traditionally Democratic youth vote were coordinated by the Young Voters for the President. (YVP) Memoranda indicate that Ken Rietz, head of YVP, was directed by Jeb Magruder to organize demonstrations against the McGovern-Shriver campaign with the advice of Ed Failor, Special Assistant at CRP.[741]

Rallies organized in the spring of 1972 were initially in support of the President's announcement on May 8, 1972, of the mining of Haiphong Harbor. Rietz organized a pro-Nixon vigil at the white House [742] and organized "pro-RN demonstrations where needed." [743]

After Senator McGovern was nominated at the Democratic convention, Magruder directed Ed Failor to take responsibility for setting up "McGovern-Shriver Confontations." [744] Ken Rietz reported to Failor weekly on the success of the YVP in organizing demonstrations against the President.[745] Failor himself reported to Magruder about his own efforts to disrupt the McGovern campaign:

... I have personally endeavored to create an encounter between Shriver and a bussing opponent on the bussing issue for today in Las Vegas. Anti-bussing people will be used in this encounter and no Republicans will be surfaced.[746]

In Rietz's report on the activities of the week of September 22, 1972, he cited daily orchestrated demonstrations by Young Voters for the President at McGovern and Shriver campaign stops. Rietz explained that good media coverage resulted from these efforts:

... Reporter Bruce Morton concluded that it was not a very good stop [for McGovern]. We are told an AP wire story reported the presence of young Nixon supporters.[747]

740. See Exhibit 00. Also, there were apparently discussions in the McGovern campaign about sending a similar individual on the Agnew campaign plane. However, these plans were vetoed by Senator McGovern.
741. See Exhibit 00.
742. See Exhibit 00; Memo from Liddy to Mitchell, May 15, 1972.
743. See Exhibit 00; Memo from Odle to Mitchell, May 9, 1972.
744. See Exhibit 00.
745. An example is attached at Exhibit 00; other examples are found in Committee files.
746. See Exhibit 00.
747. See Exhibit 00.

Rietz also reported that the demonstrations "upset" candidate McGovern in Milwaukee. Finally, these demonstrations apparently forced cancellation of some of McGovern's planned activities. Failor wrote to Magruder:

We have learned the McGovern organization and/or the Secret Service has reacted to our activities. The San Gennaro Festival in Greenwich Village, New York, Saturday night was originally planned as a walking tour of a few blocks by McGovern. However, as a result of the events in Flushing, New York, on Thursday, September 21st [organized by YVP], the street walk was cancelled and McGovern spoke in an area that was barricaded off.[748]

H. Use of Advance People. On July 28, 1971, Pat Buchanan wrote a memorandum to Attorney General Mitchell which suggested the following activity for the 1972 campaign:

Special Projects. We would like to utilize Ron Walker's resources where possible to handle some close-in operations, pickets and the like, when candidates visit various cities. The candidate normally brings with him his own media; he attracts local media; and we would like to be able to "piggy back" on that media—with our own operations, anti-candidate. This requires support activities from some source; Ron has an operation in place; and they will need approval—either general or specific —for these covert operations.[749]

Ron Walker headed the White House advancemen, who were used to set up the logistics for Presidential visits. Thus, Buchanan suggested that they be used for "anti-candidate," "covert operations" against the Democratic candidates. Buchanan testified that this idea was rejected.[750]

However, Ron Walker testified about other questionable tactics sometimes used by advance men to counteract protesting signs at Presidential appearances. Walker said that groups with pro-Nixon signs on sheets would be organized by advancemen prior to the appearance. At the first sign of any protest, the group would be moved to a curbside to place their signs between the President's motorcade and the protesting observers.[751]

Walker also testified that it was the advance operation's policy to insure that "undesirables" did not show up at Presidential rallies. One technique used to keep out "un-

748. *Ibid.*
749. 10 *Hearings* 4190.
750. 10 *Hearings* 3931.
751. Walker interview, Aug. 15, 1973, p. 5.

desirables" was the "fake ticket routine," in which the advance man would ask for the ticket of an individual and then declare it a "fake" and escort the individual from the rally.[752] Walker said this technique was used in Charlotte, North Carolina, on Billy Graham Day to cope with potential protesters who were planning to show up for the President's appearance.

Walker also stated that there were other recommendations for coping with demonstrators. One idea that was discussed was that the advance operation should have ready a pick up truck with cowboys in it, and, if there were any trouble at an appearance, they would release the cowboys and "let things happen." [753] Walker said he recalled Haldeman discussing such tactics but that such tactics never actually occurred.[754]

I. Vote Siphoning Schemes. Vote siphoning is essentially a direct interference by one political campaign in the affairs of another party or campaign for the purpose of weakening or eliminating an opposition candidate.

In 1972, the Committee to Re-elect the President (CRP) secretly financed efforts to take votes away from Senator Muskie in the New Hampshire and Illinois primaries and secretly supported an effort in California to drive the registration of the American Independent Party (AIP) below the required minimum so that AIP would not qualify for a spot on the ballot in the general election.

The New Hampshire Primary. The effort to take votes away from Senator Muskie in New Hampshire was initiated by Charles Colson, according to Magruder, who told him that the project had been approved by both Haldeman and the President.[755] Magruder cleared the project (at a cost of $8,000–$10,000) with John Mitchell and also spoke to Haldeman about it.[756] Colson, or someone in his office, according to Magruder, drafted a letter supporting a write-in campaign for Senator Kennedy, whose name was not on the ballot. The draft was taken by someone in Colson's office to Robin Ficker, a Democratic politician in Montgomery County, Maryland who had been running a Kennedy-for-President headquarters since July 1971.[757]

Ficker said that in February 1972 someone, who identified himself in a telephone conversation as Mike Abram-

752. Walker interview, Aug. 15, 1973, p. 6.
753. *Ibid.*
754. *Ibid.*
755. Jeb Magruder Interviews, August 18, 1973, p. 3; and October 1, 1973, p. 11.
756. *Ibid.*, p. 11.
757. Magruder said the individual who took the letter to Ficker worked in Colson's office, but this person has not been identified.

son, asked him to sign a letter calling for a Kennedy write-in campaign. The letter was brought to Ficker's home by a "Bill Robinson," who said he was with a law firm in Washington, D.C.[758]

Ficker signed the letter because he agreed with its contents. He was later told that between 150,000 and 180,000 copies of the letter were mailed to New Hampshire residents whose names appeared on the CRP mailing list of Democrats.[759]

Ficker also went to New Hampshire, shortly before the primary, and campaigned for Kennedy for four of five days. At Abramson's suggestion, he placed one advertisement in the *Manchester Union Leader*, credited to the United Democrats for Kennedy, which he signed and paid for himself.[760]

Ficker never saw Mike Abramson and never knew where he could be reached. Ficker believed that he worked with Kennedy aides in coordinating the Kennedy write-in campaign in New Hampshire.[761]

The write-in campaign for Senator Kennedy was totally financed by the Committee to Re-Elect the President, yet that information was never disclosed either to Mr. Ficker or to the public during the campaign.

Patrick Buchanan, a Presidential speechwriter and campaign strategist, testified that, although not acquainted with the Ficker letter, he knew about Ficker's write-in campaign.[762] Asked about the propriety of the letter, Buchanan responded that it was "a borderline case," with regard to unethical campaign practices.[763] Buchanan had advocated a form of vote siphoning in an October 5, 1971, memorandum to Mitchell and Haldeman:

> 3) *Fourth Party Candidacies.* Top-level consideration should be given to ways and means to promote, assist and fund a Fourth Party candidacy of the Left Democrats and/or the Black Democrats. There is nothing that can so advance the President's chances for re-election—not a trip to China, not four-and-a-half percent employment—as a realistic black Presidential campaign.[764]

758. Robin Ficker interview, p. 1.
759. Magruder interview, October 1, 1973. For a copy of the letter, *see* 10 *Hearings* 4266. (Exhibit 197)
760. Ficker interview, p. 2. The write-in effort was not successful. Senator Kennedy received only 735 (0.9%) of the Democratic votes in the primary. *Congressional Quarterly*, March 11, 1972, p. 539.
761. *Ibid.*, p. 2.
762. 10 *Hearings* 3968.
763. *Ibid.*
764. 10 *Hearings* 4201 (excerpted from Exhibit No. 179, which begins at p. 4197).

The absence of a requirement that the true sponsors of such efforts to aid opposition party candidates be disclosed may mislead the public into thinking that there is more support for such candidates than in fact there is.

The Illinois Primary. The Committee to Re-Elect the President apparently also directed some money to the Illinois primary campaign of Senator Eugene McCarthy, hoping that McCarthy would take votes away from the other candidate on the ballot, Senator Muskie.[765] Once again, financial support of an opponent of Senator Muskie was not disclosed to the public.

American Independent Party Effort in California. The American Independent Party (AIP) was founded by supporters of George Wallace's Presidential aspirations. The attempted vote siphoning aimed at AIP was limited in scope and unsuccessful, but it nonetheless provides an insight into the tactics supported by CRP to assure President Nixon's re-election.

Under California law,[766] a political party, as of January 1 of an election year, must have registered voters exceeding one-fifteenth of one per cent of the total voter registration in the state to qualify for the ballot in a primary election. The plan was to convince enough of the approximately 140,000 registered AIP voters to re-register in another party before January 1, 1972, to drop AIP registration below the one-fifteenth of one per cent figure.

The re-registration plan was conceived in early 1971 by Robert J. Walters, a California businessman and sometime Wallace supporter who had become disenchanted with the AIP after the 1968 Presidential election.[767] Walters was upset because the AIP was drawing votes away from conservative candidates of the two major parties.

It was Walters' understanding that voters who had changed addresses since the 1970 election without notifying county authorities could be purged from the list of registered voters if proof of the address changes were presented to the officials. Walters planned to send a mass mailing to registered AIP voters, receive from the Post Office those letters undeliverable because of address changes, and then forward them to county election officials for purging. Walters also planned to enlist a large group of people who would personally contact AIP voters and urge them to re-register. Walters mailed re-registration literature under the heading of the "Committee Against Forced Busing" urging AIP members to fight

765. Gordon Strachan interview, August 13, 1973, p. 8, and John Mitchell interview, June 27, 1973.
766. Cal. Election Code, Sec. 6430.
767. Walters interview, August 31, 1973.

306

against busing by joining one of the major parties.

In the summer of 1971 Walters began writing letters to numerous conservative groups asking for support. Walters also wrote a letter to CRP in Washington. In late September 1971, an unidentified man called Walters from New York City, said he worked for a group doing public relations work for President Nixon's re-election effort, and told Walters that he would be contacted by someone else regarding the re-registration drive.

About mid-September, according to Walters, a man called him from a Los Angeles hotel and identified himself as Mr. Magruder from "out-of-town." He said that he and Jeb Magruder met and discussed Walters' re-registration plan. Magruder remembered meeting with Walters and discussing the plan.[768]

While Walters waited for a follow-up call to the meeting with Magruder, an initial mailing went out, largely funded by Willis Carto of the Liberty Lobby.[769] About October 1 Walters hired a friend, Glenn Parker, to assist in the drive.

In the meantime, Magruder received John Mitchell's approval for spending $10,000 [770] and discussed the plan with Lyn Nofziger,[771] a Californian with many years of political experience who was then at the RNC. Nofziger called Jack Lindsey, a Los Angeles businessman whom he knew. Nofziger mentioned Walters' plan to Lindsey and Lindsey agreed to monitor the project and pay the expenses.[772] Nofziger then arranged to send Lindsey $10,000 in cash that he obtained from Hugh Sloan.[773]

Lindsey called Walters to arrange a meeting to discuss funding without indicating the source of the money. Walters briefed Lindsey on the results of the mass mailing and door-to-door visits during several occasions in the late fall of 1971. Lindsey forwarded Walters' written reports on the drive to Nofziger,[774] who said he mailed them to Magruder without reading them.[775] Lindsey paid Walters' expenses plus $150 per week salary. After the re-registration drive folded in late 1971, Lindsey still held $1,000 of the $10,000, which he said he donated in his name to a Los Angeles fund-

768. Magruder interview, October 1, 1973.
769. Walters interview, August 31, 1973.
770. Magruder interviews, August 18, and October 1, 1973.
771. Nofziger interview, August 29, 1973. Unless otherwise noted, the Nofziger-Magruder discussions that follow are from Nofziger's recollection. Magruder had little recollection.
772. Nofziger interview; Lindsey interview.
773. Nofziger interview; Craig Mauer interview, August 14, 1973; See also 2 Hearings 541.
774. Lindsey interview; Nofziger interview.
775. Nofziger interview.

raising dinner for President Nixon.

The re-registration effort itself never got off the ground despite the $10,000 CRP contribution. Many county officials refused to "purge" voters who had moved.[776] In addition, the personal canvassing effort faltered from the beginning and ended up involving members of the American Nazi Party.

Walters was never able to recruit volunteers or paid canvassers in numbers sufficient to assure more than a minimal canvassing effort. His assistant, Glenn Parker, knew that Joseph Tomassi, then head of the regional Nazi Party, needed money for mortgage payments on the party headquarters.[777] Parker hired Tomassi and some of his associates who contacted AIP members on the re-registration drive without identifying themselves as Nazi Party members. Documents show that Tommassi received some $1,200 of money originally from CRP for his efforts. The re-registration drive was a complete failure numerically, according to all participants.

J. Unsigned Literature. In addition to the incidents cited above of unsigned literature printed and distributed by CRP agents prior to the break-in at the DNC,[778] there was a suggestion made by the White House after the break-in that unidentified literature should be prepared and distributed by the CRP. Richard Howard, Charles Colson's administrative assistant, wrote in a memo to Ed Failor on June 28, 1972:

> An idea that has come from very high sources is that a booklet or small brochure be prepared (with no identification as to who prepared it) on the "McGovern Platform." All the issues should be listed such as labor, national defense, amnesty, pot, poverty. abortion, etc. Under each issue should be the worst possible quote, statement, or reported position by McGovern regarding the issue.
>
> Some of his bland or non controversial issues should also be included. After the booklet is completed. a large distribution should be made to opinion leaders.[779]

There is presently no evidence before the Committee to indicate whether this suggestion was implemented.

3. IMPACT ON DEMOCRATIC CAMPAIGNS

It is difficult, if not impossible, to assess accurately the impact

776. *See, e.g.,* Exhibit 00.
777. Parker interview.
778. See pp. 260ff., above.
779. See Exhibit 00.

of the activities described above on the 1972 Presidential Campaign.

Donald Segretti testified that one of the tactical objectives outlined for him by Dwight Chapin was "to foster a split between the Democratic hopefuls." [780] In addition, much of the other disruptive activity described above appears to have been intended to "divide the Democrats," in the words of Pat Buchanan.[781] Both Berl Bernhard, Senator Muskie's campaign manager, and Frank Mankiewicz, Senator McGovern's campaign director, testified that the activities described above were successful in dividing the Democratic candidates among themselves.

Bernhard testified that the "dirty tricks" emanating from the White House and CRP "generated suspicion and animosity between the staffs of the Democratic contenders." [782] Mankiewicz testified that the objective of the "dirty tricks" was:

> . . . to create within the Democratic Party such a strong sense of resentment among the candidates and their followers as to make unity of the party impossible once a nominee was selected. At that, the effort seems to have been most successful.[783]

Though no witness could testify that the outcome of the general election would have been any different if the "dirty tricks" discussed above had not occurred, these activities helped to leave the Democratic Party bitterly divided at the close of the Presidential primaries.[784] Frank Mankiewicz noted that "what was created by the sabotage effort was an unparalleled atmosphere of rancor and discord within the Democratic Party." [785]

Senator Muskie was widely acknowledged throughout 1971 as the Democratic frontrunner and most formidable political opponent for President Nixon. As Patrick Buchanan wrote Attorney General Mitchell on July 28, 1971:

> The clear and present danger is that Senator Muskie, the favorite in the early primaries, will promenade through the primaries, come into the convention with a clear majority and enormous momentum for November. That would be bad news for us.[786]

780. 10 *Hearings* 3980.
781. 10 *Hearings* 4197 (Exhibit No. 179).
782. 11 *Hearings* 4667.
783. 11 *Hearings* 4603.
784. *See, for example,* testimony of Frank Mankiewicz at 11 *Hearings* 4603, where he states that "any reuniting of factions—normally the course in a Democratic campaign after the primaries—became far more difficult."
785. 11 *Hearings* 4604.
786. 10 *Hearings* 4186.

As a result of this concern, almost all of the activities described above—Segretti and agents, Ruby I, Ruby II, Sedan Chair, Sedan Chair II, and others—initially focused their attention on Senator Muskie. After the early primaries, Senator Muskie's campaign declined, and he withdrew from active campaigning following the Pennsylvania primary. On April 12, 1972, Buchanan and Khachigian wrote to Haldeman and Mitchell,

> Our primary objective, to prevent Senator Muskie from sweeping the early primaries, locking up the convention in April, and uniting the Democratic Party behind him for the fall, has been achieved.[787]

Berl Bernhard testified that Senator Muskie's decline was attributable to a lack of adequate financing, a proliferation of Democratic primaries, the polarization of the Democratic party, and the problems of a "centrist" candidate.[788] However, Bernhard also testified that the "dirty tricks"

> . . . took a toll in the form of diverting our resources, changing our schedules, altering our political approaches, and being thrown on the defensive.[789]

Finally, both Mankiewicz and Bernhard testified that the activities described above were not "politics as usual" for either Democrats or Republicans.[790]

Apart from the activities noted above that were directly linked to President Nixon's re-election campaign, the campaigns of Democratic contenders encountered many other instances of disruptive or deceptive behavior. For example, the well-known "Canuck Letter" was published by the *Manchester Union Leader* on February 24, 1972, less than two weeks before the New Hampshire primary.[791] The letter, allegedly from a "Paul Morrison" of Deerfield Beach, Florida, claimed that Senator Muskie had laughed at an aide's use of the racist slur "Canuck." [792] Senator Muskie issued an absolute denial of the charges on a flatbed truck outside the offices of *The Union Leader* and denounced its editor, William Loeb. The Committee was unable to discover the individuals responsible for this "dirty trick." [793] Senator Muskie also responded emotionally to an article about his wife re-

787. 10 *Hearings* 4226.
788. 11 *Hearings* 4652.
789. 11 *Hearings* 4667.
790. 11 *Hearings* 4306; 4655.
791. 10 *Hearings* 4265 (Exhibit No. 196).
792. The letter actually said "Cannocks."
793. Ken Clawson, named in some accounts as the writer of the letter, denied having anything to do with the letter in an interview (August 14, 1973).

printed in *The Union Leader,* which was subsequently reported by the media as the Muskie "crying" incident.[794]

The other instances or allegations of improper activities directed at Democratic candidates that were *not* linked to any other Presidential campaign are contained in the Committee files and are not detailed in this report.[795]

C. Improper Activities Directed Against President Nixon's Re-Election Campaign

Testimony before the Committee indicates that the 1972 re-election campaign of President Nixon was subjected to some improper, unethical or illegal activities perpetrated by persons individually or in combination with others. Some of these actvities took the form of violent acts if destruction against local campaign offices. The Select Committee condemns all acts of violence by individauls against the campaign of any political candidate. Other improper activities directed at President Nixon's campaign included demonstrations which may have prevented citizens from exercising their rights to assemble freely, and a few examples of scurrilous literature directed against the President.

It should also be noted that except for a few isolated examples noted below, there is presently no evidence indicating that these improper activities were directly or indirectly related to the campaign of any Democratic candidate.

1. DEMONSTRATIONS

Affidavits in the Committee record describe in detail some of the violent demonstrations directed against the Nixon re-election campaign.[796] The most significant of these demonstrations are described below.

In Boston, a demonstration at an appearance of Mrs. Nixon resulted in some personal injuries to bystanders and extensive property damage (e.g. smashing of windshields, the slashing of tires, and the burning of an automobile). The "Nixon Campaign Car" suffered much damage and "(expletive deleted) Nixon" was scratched in the paint all over the car.[797]

In Tulsa, Oklahoma, demonstrators chanted slogans during

794. See, e.g. *New York Times,* February 27, 1972, p. 54; and *Time,* March 13, 1972, p. 20.
795. See, for example, letters from John McEvoy and Robert Strauss and interviews with former McGovern campaign workers.
796. 12 *Hearings* 5007-5018; Exhibits 246-260.
797. 12 *Hearings* 5110-5115; 12 *Hearings* 5116-5118; 12 *Hearings* 4996-5007.

a campaign speech by President Nixon in an attempt to disrupt the President's rally.[798] Testimony from the Tulsa CRP youth coordinator alleged that the demonstration had been organized by the local McGovern campaign college co-ordinator.[799]

The Committee also received testimony that demonstrators in Fresno, California, some of whom carried McGovern campaign signs, shouted down potential Republican speakers with obscenities and abusive language.[800]

In Tampa, Florida, testimony indicates that a group of demonstrators shouted in unison and heckled a speech by then Vice-President Agnew.[801] In Chicago, Illinois, Agnew's appearance was "continually disturbed by large groups of unruly demonstrators." [802]

An appearance by President Nixon in Atlanta, Georgia, provoked a demonstration by about 75 individuals. The demonstrators apparently engaged in shouting obscenities and their "pushing and shoving" caused some observers to be concerned "for the President's safety." [803]

In Maine, the campaign appearance of then Vice-President Agnew was met by a large crowd of demonstrators protesting against the war. Testimony before the Committee indicated that some individuals threw cans and plastic bags filled with tomato juice at Republican delegates and at Vice-President Agnew.[804]

In New York City, the Nixon re-election campaign offices were harrassed by demonstrators who dumped cockroaches in the offices and threw paint on volunteer Nixon·workers at a storefront.[805] In Columbus, Ohio, testimony indicated that an appearance by then Vice-President Agnew was met by a large demonstration in which demonstrators threw rocks and other objects at both guests and police, one of which struck Agnew's car's rear window "directly behind where the Vice-President was seated." [806]

The Committee also received testimony indicating that high level McGovern campaign personnel participated in the organization of a demonstration at the campaign appearance of President Nixon at the Century Plaza Hotel in Los Angeles on September 27, 1972.

Fred Taugher, the Southern California campaign co-

798. 12 *Hearings* 5165-72.
799. 12 *Hearings* 5171-72.
800. 12 *Hearings* 5051-5054, 4947-4963.
801. 12 *Hearings* 5074.
802. 12 *Hearings* 5082-83.
803. 12 *Hearings* 5076-81.
804. 12 *Hearings* 5084-5094.
805. 12 *Hearings* 5151-5152.
806. 12 *Hearings* 5153-5158.

ordinator for McGovern, testified that at a meeting between himself, Rich Stearns, the McGovern Western campaign coordinator, and two other McGovern workers, it was decided that the McGovern phone banks in the Los Angeles headquarters "would be available to the sponsors of the demonstration" in order to call individuals "to encourge them to attend the demonstration." [807] Stearns testified that he was aware of planning for the demonstration and that he had no objections to McGovern staffers attending the demonstration, but that he recalled no requests to the campaign to provide any assistance for the demonstration.[808]

Taugher testified that the McGovern phone banks were used on two successive nights by demonstration organizers, and that leaflets announcing the demonstration were distributed in about half of the McGovern storefronts in the Los Angeles area.[809] Use of the phone banks was terminated, Taugher testified, because they were needed to organize a rally for Senator McGovern the following week.

In response to inquiries from the press about the use of the phone banks, McGovern press spokesman Fred Epstein told reporters, "I don't know who allowed them to use the phones or who told them to stop. . . It probably was some overzealous person in the campaign." [810] Taugher testified that the press statement left "the wrong impression." [811]

About 3000 individuals demonstrated aginst the President at Century Plaza,[812] but the demonstration was peaceful by all accounts.[813] The use of the resources of a political campaign, however, to organize a large demonstration against an opponent raises some questions of propriety.

H. R. Haldeman, John Ehrlichman and Rob Odle all testified that the frequency and intensity of demonstrations in the 1972 campaign were a cause of major concern both within the White House and within the Committee to Re-Elect the President.[814] Finally, the Committee received both testimony and extensive documentation describing some of the violent demonstrations which occurred in Miami Beach, Florida, during the Republican convention week, August 19-24, 1972. Congressman Tim Lee Carter testified before the

807. 11 *Hearings* 4539.
808. 11 *Hearings* 4571.
809. 11 *Hearings* 4540-41.
810. 11 *Hearings* 4549.
811. 11 *Hearings* 4550.
812. 11 *Hearings* 4558.
813. 11 *Hearings* 4559. Pat Buchanan, however, testified that this demonstration was a "near violent [demonstration] denying the President of the United States a right to speak." (10 *Hearings* 3942) Lt. Hickman testified that the demonstration did not deny the President that right to speak. (11 *Hearings* 4560).
814. See 6 *Hearings* 2502; 7 *Hearings* 2874-2876; 12 *Hearings* 5188-5192.

Committee and outlined some instances of physical violence to which he and his wife were subjected while attending the Republican convention.[815] Congressman Carter also testified about a number if personal injuries and property damage that he observed while attending the Republican National Convention.[816]

The Committee also received in evidence the "Chronological Log of Events" prepared by the Miami Beach Police Department, which recites the number of incidents of violence which were perpetrated on delegates and their families by demonstrators in Miami.[817] These incidents included, for example, the pelting of delegates with eggs and rocks, slashing tires, attempts to set buses filled with delegates on fire, stuffing potatoes in exhaust pipes, smashing windows; throwing ignited papier mache bombs into the convention compound, tear gas grenades thrown by demonstrators, shots fired at police officers, and demonstrators marching on Convention Hall attired with helmets, gas masks, and night sticks.[818] As a result of these tactics, more than 1,200 arrests were made in two days during the convention week.[819]

A delegate from South Carolina described in a letter to the Committee that the entire South Carolina delegation to the convention had stones thrown at them as they boarded their bus to proceed to the Miami Convention Hall on the last evening of the convention.[820] In addition, the South Carolina delegate described the slashing of the bus' tires, the destruction of the gas lines of the bus by the demonstrators, and the physical abuse to which the delegates were subjected:

. . . we were pushed and shoved, struck by eggs, stones, and fists and spit on, we found ourselves separated into twos and threes. They tore clothing and screamed obscenities. The slogans many of them chanted called for either ending the war in Viet Nam or dumping President Nixon. In the confusion my wife and I were temporarily separated. I finally was able to rescue her from a doorway where she was trapped by the mob. Her dress had been torn and she was hysterical. . . .[821]

From the evidence in the Committee's records, it appears that most of the demonstrators in Miami Beach during the Republican Convention were part of demonstrations against

815. 12 *Hearings* 4986-4996.
816. *Ibid.*
817. 12 *Hearings* 5219-5257.
818. *Ibid.*
819. For full expostion of the events, see 12 *Hearings* 5196-5264.
820. 12 *Hearings* 5262.
821. 12 *Hearings* 5263.

the war.[822] Any act of violence directed at participants in the political process has no place in the American political system.

It should be noted here that the Select Committee received letter on June 8, 1973, from John H. Davitt, Chief of the Internal Security Section of the Criminal Division of the Department of Justice which stated that neither the I.S.D. files nor the Federal Bureau of Investigation had any information which linked any Democratic candidate in the 1972 campaign to any criminal acts or any conspiracies to commit unlawful or disruptive acts.[823]

2. CAMPAIGN VIOLENCE AND HARASSMENT

Another problem in the 1972 Presidential campaign was the violence directed against CRP and Republican campaign offices in various cities. In Phoenix, Arizona, the CRP headquarters building was gutted by fire resulting from arsonists splashing some five gallons of gasoline throughout the headquarters.[824]

The affidavit of George Willeford, Jr., described a fire set in the State Republican headquarters offices in Austin, Texas in the Spring of 1972.[825] Other affidavits describe attempted arson against CRP headquarters in Albuquerque and New Hampshire.[826] Further affidavits describe gunshots being fired into campaign headquarters of the CRP in Massachusetts and in Pennsylvania.[827] In Springfield, Mass., the room into which the shot was fired was full of people but no one was injured.[828]

Other acts of destruction directed against the 1972 campaign to re-elect President Nixon included the smashing of plate glass windows,[829] the spraying of vulgar anti-Nixon signs on buildings and windows [830] and alleged break-ins to the campaign headquarters where campaign property was destroyed.[831]

822. 12 *Hearings* 5198.
823. 8 *Hearings* 3321.
824. 12 *Hearings* 5034-5047.
825. 12 *Hearings* 5176.
826. See 12 *Hearings* 5143-5146; 5127-5142.
827. See 12 *Hearings* 5116-5119; 5173.
828. 12 *Hearings* 5117.
829. 12 *Hearings* 5097-5101.
830. 12 *Hearings* 5147-5150.
831. See, e.g. affidavit of Chester Oman stating that motor oil was poured on Nixon campaign literature, 12 *Hearings* 5125-26; affidavit of Ella Jacques stating that Dayton CRP headquarters were broken into and McGovern signs printed on the walls, 12 *Hearings* 5163; and affidavit of Toni Greenwood stating that the Washington, D.C. Democrats for Nixon headquarters was occupied by 75-100 demonstrators and campaign literature destroyed and pro-McGovern literature left in its place. 12 *Hearings* 5185-87.

3. SCURRILOUS CAMPAIGN LITERATURE

President Nixon's re-election campaign was also subjected to some improper and distasteful literature. For example, pamphlets and brochures appeared in the campaign which ranged from cartoons depicting President Nixon with fangs dropping bombs on people to posters with crude sexual puns.[832] Other examples of literature directed against the President's campaign efforts, usually by anti-war groups, may be found in the Committee record.[833]

A piece of inappropriate campaign literature which bears mention was the unimaginative piece distributed in California which said "Nixon is treyf," and which went on to state:

> Thanks to modern technology Nixon brings the ovens to the people rather than the people to the ovens.[834]

In addition, Michael Heller testified that he observed this pamphlet both in the McGovern Fairfax headquarters in Los Angeles in September 1972, as well as being distributed in the streets by McGovern campaign workers.[835]

Paul Brindze, head of three West Side Los Angeles offices for McGovern, testified that he directed a young volunteer in the McGovern offices to mimeograph 3000 copies of the pamphlet "Nixon is Treyf." [836] Brindze also testified that at the suggestion of the southern California McGovern coordinator, the McGovern campaign decided to place the blame for the distribution of this pamphlet on the 16-year old volunteer who had merely mimeographed the pamphlet at the direction of campaign superiors. As a result, the 16-year old volunteer was terminated, and Paul Brindze remained in his capacity as the Director of one of the McGovern campaign local Los Angeles offices.[837]

III. RECOMMENDATIONS

The recommendations which follow are an effort by the Select Committee to help prevent the recurrence of improper, unethical and illegal activities that took place in the 1972 campaign. Of central importance to these recommendations is the creation of an independent Federal Elections Com-

832. 12 *Hearings* 5081, 5198, 5130, 5217.
833. 12 *Hearings* 5022, 5024, 5081, 5216-17.
834. 12 *Hearings* 5022-24. The flyer also promoted an upcoming demonstration against the President. Note that "treyf" is a Yiddish term meaning "not kosher." The area in Los Angeles where the pamphlet was distributed was primarily Jewish.
835. 12 *Hearings* 4967.
836. 12 *Hearings* 4977.
837. 12 *Hearings* 4981-4985.

mission, similar to the proposal in S. 3044 already passed by the Senate, with full enforcement and subpoena powers to monitor and enforce the election laws. This proposal is discussed more fully elsewhere in this report.[838]

1. THE COMMITTEE RECOMMENDS THAT CONGRESS ENACT CRIMINAL LEGISLATION TO PROHIBIT ANYONE FROM OBTAINING EMPLOYMENT, VOLUNTARY OR PAID, IN A CAMPAIGN OF AN INDIVIDUAL SEEKING NOMINATION OR ELECTION TO ANY FEDERAL OFFICE BY FALSE PRETENSES, MISREPRESENTATIONS, OR OTHER FRAUDULENT MEANS FOR THE PURPOSE OF INTERFERING WITH, SPYING ON, OR OBSTRUCTING ANY CAMPAIGN ACTIVITIES OF SUCH CANDIDATE. FURTHERMORE, SUCH LEGISLATION SHOULD MAKE IT UNLAWFUL FOR ANYONE TO DIRECT, INSTRUCT, OR PAY ANYONE TO JOIN ANY SUCH CAMPAIGN BY SUCH MEANS OR FOR SUCH PURPOSES AS ARE OUTLINED ABOVE.
Discussion. New legislation is needed to prevent the infiltration of Presidential and federal campaigns. The activities of Donald Segretti, Robert Benz, Michael McMinoway, Elmer Wyatt, Tom Gregory, and others are abundant documentation of the numerous infiltration efforts in the 1972 campaign.

The dangers of this infiltration range from the confusion and suspicion resulting from leaked information to the opponents or newspapers to more systematic disruption and sabotage of the opposition campaign.

Infiltration occurred in the 1972 campaign which ranged from placing a false name on a mailing list of the Democratic National Party to the systematic infiltration of Michael McMinoway in the various Democratic primary campaigns.

It is essential for a campaign or organization to have free and open discussion, without fear that one of the conversants is a spy from the oposition. Every campaign requires some maintenance of confidentiality: sensitive matters must be examined; personalities discussed; and confidential policy must be deliberated. One of the purposes of the legislation outlined above is to free political campaigns systematically back to the opposition campaign.

The proposed legislation would not ban a "Chapman's friend" or a reporting arrangement where the reporter does not actually join another campaign. While this practice may not be ethically pure, this legislation is aimed at ridding campaigns of the unhealthy deception of actual infiltrators. Where

838. See Chapter III, Recommendations.

the individual does not actually work himself into the confidences of an alien campaign, the potential harm to the campaign is diminished even though deception still exists.

2. THE COMMITTEE RECOMMENDS THAT CONGRESS ENACT LEGISLATION TO MAKE IT UNLAWFUL TO REQUEST OR KNOWINGLY TO DISBURSE OR MAKE AVAILABLE CAMPAIGN FUNDS FOR THE PURPOSE OF PROMOTING OR FINANCING VIOLATIONS OF FEDERAL ELECTION LAWS.

This recommendation is an effort to deter individuals with control over campaign funds from blindly and automatically providing money for campaign activties whenever they are so instructed. For example, Herb Kalmbach, the custodian of left-over 1968 campaign funds, funded Tony Ulasewicz's activities for nearly three years as well as the travels and illegal activities of Donald Segretti. A statute such as the one outlined above would force people with control over campaign funds to inquire more fully about the expenditures that were requested, since they would be held criminally liable for funds spent for illegal purposes.

In addition, this recommendation seeks to deter individuals working in political campaigns from requesting campaign funds in order to promote illegal activites during federal campaigns. Such a statute as is recommended above would be an effective deterrent to many activities like those occuring in the 1972 campaign.

3. THE COMMITTEE RECOMMENDS THAT CONGRESS ENACT NEW LEGISLATION WHICH PROHIBITS THE THEFT, UNAUTHORIZED COPYING, OR THE TAKING BY FALSE PRETENSES OF CAMPAIGN MATERIALS, DOCUMENTS, OR PAPERS NOT AVAILABLE FOR PUBLIC DISSEMINATION BELONGING TO OR IN THE CUSTODY OF A CANDIDATE FOR FEDERAL OFFICE OR HIS AIDES.

Discussion. The evidence of Donald Segretti, Robert Benz, Doug Kelley, Jack Buckley, Elmer Wyatt, Michael McMinoway, Tom Gregory, and Howard Hunt clearly establish the need for a larceny statute which can be used to prevent such unauthorized takings in a federal election. Present "larceny by false pretense" statutes in most states require the object that is taken to be "a thing of value." Since papers are generally not thought to have value in the sense that the term is used in the existing statute, a new federal election larceny statute is necessary to prosecute such violations.

4. THE COMMITTEE RECOMMENDS THAT CONGRESS SHOULD MAKE IT UNLAWFUL FOR ANY INDIVIDUAL TO FRAUDULENTLY MISREPRESENT BY TELEPHONE OR IN PERSON THAT HE IS REPRESENTING A CANDIDATE FOR FEDERAL OFFICE FOR THE PURPOSE OF INTERFERING WITH THE ELECTION.

Present federal criminal legislation, 18 U.S.C. §612, requires that campaign literature disclose the names of individuals and organizations responsible for its publication and distribution.[839] However, there were numerous cases of false, deceptive and misleading literature published and distributed in the 1972 campagn by fraudulent or non-existent sponsors. The existence of this literature in the 1972 campaign demonstrates the need for better publication and more rigorous enforcement of the existing federal laws in this area. The proposed new independent Federal Elections Commission would be the appropriate institution to accomplish these objectives of better publicity and more rigorous enforcement. It is important to eliminate this form of deception from federal campaigns since voters have the right to know whether the pamphlet they receive, the advertisement they read, or the expression of support they observe represent the *bona fide* views of his fellow citizens. Manipulation of voters' views through misrepresentation has no place in the democratic process.

Similarly, late night calls to voters of a state from a non-existent group purporting to support a particular candidate also have no place in the electoral process. Thus, this recommendation seeks to deter other kinds of misrepresentation in political campaigns not presently covered by existing legislation. Fraudulent door-to-door canvassing and fraudulent phone calls to voters "on behalf" of a candidate are the kinds of misrepresentation that have no place in federal

839. Section 612 reads: Whoever willfully publishes or distributes or causes to be published or distributed, or for the purpose of publishing or distributing the same, knowingly deposits for mailing or delivery or causes to be deposited for mailing or delivery, or, except in cases of employees of the Postal Service in the official discharge of their duties, knowingly transports or causes to be transported in interstate commerce any card, pamphlet, circular, poster, dodger, advertisement, writing, or other statement relating to or concerning any person who has publicly declared his intention to seek the office of President, or Vice President of the United States, or Senator or Representative in, or Delegate or Resident Commissioner to Congress, in a primary, general, or special election, or convention of a political party, or has caused or permitted his intention to do so to be publicly declared which does not contain the names of the persons, associations, committees, or corporations responsible for the publication or distribution of the same, and the names of the officers of each such associaton, committee, or corporation, shall be fined not more than $1,000 or imprisoned not more than one year, or both.

campaigns. This recomemndation is an effort to help deter such behavior.

SUMMARY

The improper and unethical activities that occurred in the 1972 campaign will not be eliminated merely by new legislation. Although law seeks both to shape and reflect the moral and ethical values of individuals, new laws cannot fully substitute for such individual values. Therefore the political process and government itself must attract individuals of the highest moral and ethical standards if the improper activities that occurred in the 1972 Presidential campaign are to be eliminated completely in the future.

USE OF THE INCUMBENCY-RESPONSIVENESS PROGRAM

I. Introduction and Overview

A significant aspect of the Select Committee's investigation was its inquiry into the Administration's programs to use the powers of incumbency to re-elect the President. Documents obtained by the Committee indicate that this effort—which had as its main vehicle a White House devised plan known as the Responsiveness Program—was an organized endeavor "to politicize" the executive branch to ensure that the Administration remained in power.

The scope of this effort was broad and its potential impact considerable. It included, for example, plans to redirect federal monies to specific Administration supporters and to target groups and geographic areas to benefit the campaign. It entailed instructions to shape legal and regulatory action to enhance campaign goals. It comprised plans to utilize government employment procedures for election benefit.

Not only were such plans laid, they were, in part, consummated, although Departmental and Agency resistance to campaign pressures limited the success of these endeavors. Particularly in regard to the expenditure of federal monies concerning certain minority and constituent groups were there flagrant abuses of proper governmental procedures. Some of these abuses appear to stem from the improper involvement of campaign officials in governmental decision making.

Several federal civil and criminal laws appear applicable to the conduct described in this Chapter. In fact, a question exists whether the planning and implementation of the Responsiveness plan rises to the level of a conspiracy to interfere with the lawful functioning of government, conduct prosecutable under 18 U.S.C. §371 as a conspiracy to defraud the United States, as that term has been interpreted by the Supreme Court.*

The evidence presented below is not exhaustive. While the staff has interviewed over 150 witnesses and reviewed thousands of documents respecting these matters, it has not been able, because of time and staffing limitations, comprehensively to cover all possible areas of investigation. This is

* See Section VIII below.

particularly the case since the Responsiveness Program was intended to pervade the entire executive branch—including regional offices.

The Select Committee believes, however, that the account presented below is a fair and accurate statement of the parameters of the Responsiveness Program, certain actions taken under its aegis, and other related conduct. It makes this assertion with confidence because much of the evidence obtained respecting these matters is documentary. The account below consists largely of excerpts from the plethora of documents uncovered by staff investigators. The principal documents are appended to this report as are certain relevant executive session transcripts.

The Committee's report on these activities concludes with certain legislative recommendations designed to restrain future misuse of federal resources for political purposes.

II. Early Manifestations of Administration's Interest in Using the Incumbency to Affect the Re-Election Effort

Throughout 1971, members of the Administration and the campaign team (which began to form in May, 1971) displayed a studied interest in using the resources of the federal government to enhance the President's re-election chances. John Dean, testifying in Executive Session before the Committee on June 16, 1973 (p. 38), expressed the concern relayed to him by H. R. Haldeman as to the activities of the White House staff.

It was probably in summer of 1971, to the best of my recollection, that Mr. Haldeman began discussion with me what my office should and could be doing during the campaign. He told me that all the officers in the White House were having discussions and were being told the President's wish was to take maximum advantage of the incumbency; and the White House would reshift itself from the current duties to focus very much on the re-election of the President.

The testimonies of Messrs. Haldeman and Ehrlichman during Committee interviews on January 31, 1974, and February 8, 1974, respectively, also indicate that the President was interested in using the resources of the federal government to best advantage in the re-election campaign. (Haldeman, 4; Ehrlichman 76-7, 79-82). The testimony of Patrick Buchanan, discussed in Chapter II of this Report, provides another account of the Administration's early interest in utilizing the incumbency for campaign purposes (e.g., *Hearings* 3940-41).

This early interest is revealed not only by testimony of witnesses before the Committee, but also in numerous documents prepared in 1971. A sampling of such documents follows.

1. On January 12, 1971, Jeb Magruder, then a White House staffer, submitted a "Confidential/Eyes Only" memorandum to Attorney General Mitchell regarding political activities in the White House in 1970 (Ex. 1). The memorandum concluded with the following paragraph under the heading "Resource Development":

> Our Administration has not made effective political use of the resources of the Federal Government, the RNC, the White House, and outside groups and corporations. In developing the structure for the campaign, proper use of these resources should be of primary concern at the outset of the planning.

2. Magruder, apparently at the Attorney General's request, began an examination of the utilization of federal resources by others in presidential campaigns. On April 14, 1971, he wrote a "Confidential" memorandum to Dean (Ex. 2), which began:

> It has been requested that we determine what use Presidents Eisenhower and Johnson and Vice President Humphrey made of resources available in the Federal Government for campaign purposes.

Dean's assistance in this project was requested.

Less than a month later, on May 6, Magruder reported his interim findings to Mitchell in a "Confidential" memorandum entitled "Utilization of Government Resources by General Eisenhower, President Johnson and Vice President Humphrey" (Ex. 3). His conclusion as to President Eisenhower's campaign was:

> "During the actual campaign no use was made of the White House or the Federal Government to specifically work on the campaign other than the normal support activities given General Eisenhower through his position as President."

Magruder, however, concluded that employment of federal resources by President Johnson and Vice President Humphrey was more extensive.

323

"Under Johnson it has been indicated that he made considerable use of the White House staff and individuals in the departments to work on the campaign. At the present time, I have not been able to get any specific information but, hopefully, will have more concise information in the near future.

"Before the convention, Humphrey used many people on his Vice Presidential staff, as well as individuals who were employed by the Cabinet Committees he was in charge of, to work specifically on the campaign. Many individuals remained on the government payroll after the convention and continued to work exclusively on the campaign. As an example, the individual who headed up his veterans activity was employed by the Veterans Administration and remained with the VA throughout the campaign. Some use was also made of the research facilities at the Census Bureau."

Because this Committee's mandate is limited to an examination of the 1972 campaign, no effort has been made to substantiate or refute Magruder's allegations.

Magruder ended his memorandum to Mitchell on a cautionary note:

"One reason why both Johnson and Humphrey had an easier time than we would have in this situation is that the control of Congress was under the Democrats and my information is that it was difficult for the Republicans to make much of this issue on the Hill. On the other hand, if we used these resources in the same way Johnson and Humphrey did, with the control of the Congress in the hands of the Democrats, they could make this an issue.

From a public relations standpoint, it would seem best to restrict the use of government employees to:
1. direct assistance for the President, and
2. to help develop strategy.

They should not get involved in the day-to-day campaign functions."

3. Magruder, however, on May 17, 1971, sent Gordon Strachan, a White House staffer working for Haldeman, a "Confidential" memorandum on "political" use of the "White House computer" (Ex. 4). And, on June 14, 1971, he forwarded to William Horton* a June 3, 1971, "Confidential—

* Horton worked for Frederick V. Malek at the White House. Malek, a former Special Assistant to the President, was responsible for the creation of the Responsiveness Program, as subsequently discussed.

Eyes Only" memorandum to Magruder from William Timmons of the White House staff which read:

"As you know, Preston Martin is head of the Federal Home Loan Bank Board. He is a California-Nixon Republican and is a little put out that nobody has sought his political advice.

"Apparently, he has given a great deal of thought to, and designed, a sound economical plan to use federal resources (projects, contracts, etc.) for advantage in 1972. He has graphs, maps, flow charts, etc., to show how available money can be directed into the areas where it would do the most good. Very scientific, I'm told.

"While I have not talked to Preston, I think it would be valuable for you to chat with him about his plan." (See Ex. 5).

The memorandum to Horton, which was also designated "Confidential/Eyes Only," suggested that Horton see Martin and "plug this into your project." The nature of Mr. Horton's "project" is discussed in detail below (item 6, this section). Mr. Martin has stated to the Committee that he never devised a plan to use federal resources for political advantage and the Committee has not uncovered additional evidence that establishes the contrary.

4. The concern respecting use of federal resources to affect the election is reflected in communications among other White House and campaign staffers. Two "Confidential/Eyes Only" memoranda from Peter Millspaugh, a White House political aide to Harry Dent, to Harry Flemming of the campaign staff, dated May 12 and June 23, 1971, are instructive (Ex. 6 and 7). The memoranda indicate that certain White House and departmental personnel were meeting to consider the use of government "resources"—particularly government "patronage"—in the campaign. The May 12 memorandum states:

". . . A consensus emerged that the range of federal resources must be inventoried and analyzed with perhaps the federal grants area broken out for priority treatment because of the immediate benefits and some budget cycle timing considerations. Additionally, the matter of a delivery system which would put these resources at our disposal on a timely basis was considered to be imperative."

Attached to the June 23, 1971 memorandum is a document listing the "Basic Types of Patronage" that could be

325

employed for campaign purposes. This document is quoted in full text:

"THE BASIC TYPES OF PATRONAGE

1) *Jobs* (full-time, part-time, retainers, consultantships, etc.)

2) *Revenue*

—Contracts (Federal Government as purchaser—GSA)

—Grants (do-good programs—EDA, Model Cities, NSF research, etc.)

—Subsidies (needy industries—airlines, etc.)

—Bank Deposits (all Federal accounts)

—Social Need Program (direct benefit to citizen, i.e., Social Security, welfare, etc.)

—Public Works Projects

3) *Execution of Federal Law* (resides mainly in Department of Justice whose interpretive power touches every vested interest).

4) *Information and Public Relations Capacity* (a professional (?) public relations office in each department and agency constitutes an enormous public information apparatus).

5) *Travel* (domestic transportation can be provided by law, foreign travel, international conferences, etc. are available)."

5. On October 26, 1971, Harry Dent of the White House staff sent a "Confidential" memorandum to Mitchell and Haldeman reporting on a recent meeting with a group of Southern Blacks. (Ex. 8). In a paragraph that presaged later Administration activity, Dent wrote:

"Grant recipients are by and large Democrat-oriented groups, said the conferees. I have already been in touch with Phil Sanchez and some Southern black leaders about channeling money to groups whose loyalties lie elsewhere. I have also delayed the promotion of the Southeastern OEO man to the #3 spot in OEO until he demonstrates proof-positive that he is rechanneling money from Democrats to RN blacks."*

6. A significant document that reflects Administration interest in 1971 in employing federal resources is a June 23, 1971, "Confidential" "Discussion Draft" entitled "Communicating Presidential Involvement in Federal Government Programs" (Malek Exhibit 8) prepared by William Horton of Fred Malek's staff. This document is also important because

* Mr. Dent's comments on this document are found at Exhibit 8.

326

it appears to be a forerunner of the Responsiveness Program concept discussed in the next section of this Chapter. Horton prepared this paper under the supervision of Malek who had received a request from Haldeman to consider how the grant making process could be used to the President's advantage. (Malek, 24-5)

The memorandum's initial paragraph recommends that:

". . . [The] President's direct control over awarding selected grants should be strengthened to ensure that political circumstances can be considered, if appropriate, in making awards."

It then states:

"To ensure politically sensitive grant applications receive appropriate consideration, two basic steps must be carried out: (1) determine which grants are politically sensitive and (2) ensure these grants receive positive consideration from OMB and the Departments."

Under the heading "Determination of Politically Sensitive Grants," Horton wrote:

"This step should be accomplished in a manner which minimizes the risk of unfavorable publicity and falsely raised expectations. Therefore the possibilities of surveying all pending grant applications or soliciting the opinion of Congressional and local Nixon supporters were rejected.

". . . Identification should rely on routine contacts with various White House and campaign officials. For example, supportive Senators and Congressmen usually inform the Congressional Relations staff of pending grants which are politically important to them. State and local representatives contact various White House officials in a similar manner. All these inputs should be passed along to Gifford * for consideration by the grant coordination group. Based on past experience, the most politically important grant applications are usually brought to the attention of White House or campaign officials. However, especially important localities where no appropriate grants seem to be in process will be checked in the grant initiation process covered below.

"This identification process will generate more grants than could be or should be given special consideration.

* The Mr. Gifford referred to is William Gifford, then of the Office of Management and Budget, who served as a clearing house for requests and information on federal grants.

327

Consequently, priorities must be set."

The memorandum then sets forth a procedure to insure that "the most recent political information and campaign priorities were considered in selecting 'must' grants." Under the heading "Initiating Grants," Horton stated:

"In addition to designating 'must' grants from pending applications there may be occasions in which political circumstances require a grant be generated for a locality. Once such a locality is identified by the campaign organization, the coordinating group would decide what kind of grant would best meet the needs and available program resources. A campaign representative would then inform the appropriate local official what to submit. When submitted, it, of course, would be designated a 'must.'
"Gifford must rely on the Departments to follow through on 'must' grants under their jurisdiction. To accomplish this, a network of Departmental coordinators should be established. These individuals must have two prime qualities: . . . loyalty to the President and sufficient authority to ensure 'must' grants are approved and Departmental announcements of all grants conform to the guidelines discussed subsequently."

The memorandum continues:

". . . Gifford must be flexible on pushing a 'must' grant in case it turns out to be substantively irresponsible or an obvious waste of government funds relative to other pending grants. In such cases, Gifford should weigh the substantive drawbacks and risk of adverse publicity against the expected political benefits, consulting with others as needed. He should then make a final decision on whether the grant is to be approved. Also, in order to minimize the risk of embarrassment to the President, the volume of grants designated 'musts' in any one Department should be limited. Gifford should make these judgments on a month-to-month basis, drawing, naturally, from the grant coordinating group and the Departmental contacts."

It may be a fair reading of the last-quoted passage that Mr. Horton is recommending that, in some cases, grants that are "substantively irresponsible or an obvious waste of government funds relative to other pending grants" should be made if the political reward is sufficiently great. Both Mr. Horton

328

and Mr. Malek disagree with this interpretation. See Malek Executive Session, April 8, 1974, at p. 45 (hereinafter referred to as Malek 000).

The Horton memorandum apparently was transmitted to Messrs. Mitchell, Haldeman, Magruder, Gifford, Millspaugh, and Flemming, among others. Malek has insisted that this document was nothing more than a "Discussion Draft" (as the first page of the document indicates) and "was not acted upon as outlined here." (Malek 30) Malek does not recall that he criticized Horton for the ideas therein presented. He does not recall that disapproval of this document was expressed to him by its various recipients. (Malek 51) To the contrary, the memoranda of transmittal for this document found at Exhibit 8 generally indicate approval of and interest in the program Horton advocated. Moreover, as will become clear in the next section, many of the specifics Horton posited were incorporated into the "Responsiveness Program," a plan largely devised by Horton under Malek's direct supervision.

III. The "Responsiveness Program"—The Administration's Basic Plan to Employ Federal Resources To Affect the 1972 Presidential Election

1. THE GENERAL PLAN

The responsibility for developing an overall strategy respecting the use of federal resources for re-election purposes was given by Haldeman to Fred Malek, as Mr. Malek has testified in Committee interview. On March 17, 1972, Malek submitted to Haldeman a document entitled "Increasing The Responsiveness of The Executive Branch." (Malek Ex. 4) The document, which was initially drafted by William Horton and designated "Extremely Sensitive—Confidential," constituted Malek's broad-view conception as to how the federal bureaucracy could be put to work for the President's re-election. His plan subsequently received Haldeman's approval. (Malek 25, Haldeman 00)

This memorandum gives a clear picture of the scope of the plan, demonstrating that the proposal was to shape diverse types of Administration activities to meet re-election needs. For example, election requirements were to be taken into account in: The letting of government grants, contracts, and loans; the bringing and prosecution of legal and regulatory action; the making of Administration personnel decisions; the determination of the issues and programs to be ᵉtressed by the Administration; the communicating of Administration activities to the voting public.

The use of federal funds for re-election purposes received particular attention. Under the heading, "Present efforts tap only a fraction of the total potential," the document says:

"The Department of Commerce provides a good example. To date Gifford has made some 35 requests. Most of these involved expediting the normal grant reviewing process and securing the release of information. Approximately a dozen of these requests resulted in favorable grant decisions (*which otherwise would not have been made*) involving roughly $1 million. Politically these actions have been most beneficial.

"Nevertheless, in spite of this achievement, the potential is much greater. In the Commerce Department, for example, there is nearly $700 million in funds remaining in this fiscal year and over $700 million in next fiscal year which could be *redirected* in some manner. The major areas of potential for fiscal year 1973 are: Economic Development Administration, $275 million; Regional Action Planning Commissions, $40 million; Minority Business Enterprises, $38 million; National Oceanographic and Atmospheric Administration, $100 million; and the Maritime Administration, $230 million. Even if only 5% of this amount can be *rechanneled* to impact more directly on *target groups or geographic areas,* it would be a substantial increase over the current efforts.

"To capitalize upon such opportunities, the Department must initiate action themselves. This would entail each Department developing a program by which it would *systematically but discreetly seek out opportunities for improving services to target groups and geographic areas* and then ensure that appropriate action is taken." (emphasis added)*

The document continues:

". . .[A]s originally envisioned in establishing Gifford's grantsmanship operation, direction to the Departments on politically sensitive operating matters should be centralized in order to utilize this resource most effectively in serving *target groups and geographic areas and to reduce the possibility of adverse publicity.*" (emphasis added)

But the program involved much more than the use of

* See further, Malek, 78-9.

federal monies. Under the heading "Guidelines," Malek stated:

"As a first step, the Departments should be given clear guidelines covering the political priorities, the types of operating decisions which are to be included in the program, and the procedures for planning and tracking progress.

"The political priorities would be spelled out in terms of key States and major voting bloc groups upon which Departmental action could have an impact. The Departments would be updated as needed, as the political priorities evolve.

"Next, the types of activities covered under this program would be discussed. The major ones, of course, are positive decisions (e.g., project grants, contracts, loans, subsidies, procurement and construction projects), and negative actions(e.g., taking legal or regulatory action against a group or governmental body, major cutbacks in programs, and relocation of Department operations).

* * *

"Also, under this program, the Departments would be expected to cultivate the leaders of organized groups which are affected by the Department to gain their support of their groups for the President's re-election. Similarly, the Departments would be expected to take discreet and subtle steps to gain employee support of the President's re-election."

Particularly important to the present study is the clear prescription in this document that "legal or regulatory action" should be shaped to benefit the campaign effort. In this regard, the memorandum quoted in the previous section that referred to legal actions by the Department of Justice as a form of "patronage" to be utilized for campaign purposes should be recalled.

The document recommended that the Departments be given certain responsibilities to implement the Responsiveness plan.

"Each Department should be required to develop a plan to ensure operating decisions reflect the priorities to the greatest extent possible. The plans would outline what amount of discretionary resources in each area identified above will be allocated to priority areas and groups along with a timetable and responsible individual. Also included would be steps planned for strengthening control over the relevant operating decisions, the announcement process, and the public relations improvements. Finally, the plan would cover actions for cultivating organized groups and for gaining the support of Departmental employees."

Various White House and OMB staffers were assigned responsibilities. For example:

". . . Gifford would work with Fred Malek and his staff in establishing and supervising the Departmental programs. Gifford would be the principal contact for operating matters with the Departments, communicating to the Departments the political priorities as well as the 'must' operating decisions. Also, he would participate in presenting the guidelines discussed earlier to the Departmental contacts, reviewing the Departmental plans, and evaluating progress reports."

Mr. Gifford, however, has represented to the Select Committee that he played no significant part in either the planning or the implementation of the Responsiveness Program. He did remark that he generally advised Cabinet officers to make expenditures in areas where it would be of value to the President. Mr. Horton has stated that Mr. Gifford was involved in implementing the concepts in the March 17 memorandum.

The Responsiveness Program was to be kept secret with efforts taken to ensure that the President and the White House were not connected with it. Under the heading "Possible Drawbacks," the March 17 memorandum states:

"The most significant drawback of the program is, of course, the risk of adverse publicity. Naturally, steps would be taken (1) to ensure that information about the program itself and the Departmental plans would not be leaked and (2) keep the President and the White House disassociated with the program in the event of a leak.

"First, written communications would be kept to a minimum. There would be no written communications from the White House to the Departments—all information about the program would be transmitted verbally. The only written material submitted by the Departments to the White House would be the plans. These would be in a brief outline format and only two copies would be permitted—one for the White House and one for the Departmental contact. Progress reports would be verbal.

"Second, the documents prepared would not indicate White House involvement in any way. Also, oral and written communications concerning the program within the Department would be structured to give the impression that the program was initiated by the Department Head without the knowledge of the White House." See further, Malek, 72-3.

The memorandum concludes with the statement that the Departments "must be given a clear understanding [that] the program [has] the President's full backing." However, Malek has testified that he did not know if the program did, in fact, have the President's "full backing." (Malek 26) Mr. Haldeman has stated that he does not recall discussing the specifics of the program with the President. (Haldeman 13).

Malek's concept of the Responsiveness Program is also contained in other documents that are appended to this Report as Exhibits:

(1) A December 23, 1971, "Confidential" memorandum from Malek to Haldeman entitled "Redirecting the White House Staff to Support the President's Re-Election." (Malek Ex. 5)

(2) Another "Confidential" memorandum of the same date and similar title from Malek to Ken Cole of Ehrlichman's staff. (Malek Ex. 5)

(3) A "Confidential" memorandum from Malek to Haldeman dated January 28, 1972, entitled "My Role in Support of Re-election". (Malek Ex. 1)

(4) An undated "Confidential Eyes Only" memorandum (the text indicates it was written in January or February 1972) from Malek to Haldeman entitled "Organizing For And Implementing New Responsibilities". A number of comments in Haldeman's handwriting are found on this document. Attached to this memorandum is a "Confidential" organization chart setting forth Malek's role in the campaign which he has confirmed as accurate in most essential particulars. See Malek 11. (Malek Ex. 3)

(5) A "Confidential" memorandum dated February 16, 1972 to Mitchell and Haldeman from Malek entitled "Meeting To Discuss My Role". (Malek Ex. 2) (The meeting referred to was with Ehrlichman and George Schultz).

(6) An April 28, 1972, document entitled "John Mitchell Briefing On Responsiveness" designated "Draft-Confidential". This document was prepared by Frank Herringer, another Malek staffer. (Malek Ex. 7)

(7) An undated memorandum containing Malek's handwrit-

ing entitled "Administration Efforts In Support Of The Re-
election" prepared in May, 1972, and used for briefing
White House Constituent Group Project Managers and CRP
Voting Bloc Directors. (Malek Ex. 15)

These documents need not be discussed in detail, but several comments are in order. First, the memoranda indicate
that the Responsiveness Program was viewed as a potentially
significant part of the re-election effort as the following quotations indicate: "*Department Responsiveness*: This is potentially one of the most productive activities we will undertake." (See Item (4) above, Malek Ex. 3) "Potentially, one
of our most significant advantages over the opposition is incumbency—if it is used properly." (See Item (6) above,
Malek Ex. 7) Haldeman, during the staff interview previously
referenced, stated that he was "serious" about sensitizing the
bureaucracy to political considerations. (Haldeman 4; see
also Ehrlichman interview at 72, 76)

Second, these documents demonstrate that the goal of the
Responsiveness Program was "to politicize" the executive
branch. Thus Malek, in discussing his potential campaign role,
suggested that someone was needed to "[t]ake the lead in the
program *to politicize* Departments and Agencies" and to
"supervise the patronage operation and closely monitor the
grantsmanship project to ensure *maximum and unrelenting
efforts*" (See Item (3) above, Malek Ex. 1) (emphasis added). A fuller statement of this concept is contained in the
December 23, 1971, "Confidential" memorandum from Malek to Haldeman. (See Item (1) above, Malek Ex. 5) After
noting that a basic campaign objective was to "politicize"
the bureaucracy, Malek, under the rubric "Politicizing the
Executive Branch," wrote:

"As you have pointed out, the President's unique asset
in the forthcoming campaign is his control of the Executive Branch. The White House must ensure that the
President is able to capitalize fully upon this asset.
"As you know, we have already initiated programs to
derive greater political benefit from grants, communications, and personnel. Also, as discussed above, we will
soon be establishing firm White House control over the
handling of key issues and constituent groups. These
White House directed efforts will control the key Executive Branch operations having the highest potential political payoff. In addition, we should take action to ensure that the day-to-day Departmental operations are
conducted as much as possible to support the President's re-election. Since it is impossible for the White

House to directly control day-to-day activities, we must establish management procedures to ensure that the Departments systematically identify opportunities and utilize resources for maximum political benefit."

To illustrate potential activity by Departments and Agencies, Malek stated:

"For instance, GSA might undertake the following:
—Emphasize building construction in key States, cities, and counties.
—Expedite disposal of property for parks and schools in key States.
—Emphasize fuel programs in ecology-minded areas of key States.
—Emphasize minority procurement in those States and areas where there is a real opportunity to win some of the Black vote."

And he noted that:

"Politicizing the regions, which we have discussed, would be a natural by-product of this program, since the regions would carry the major burden of implementing these politically helpful actions."*

Malek, however, had reservations about referring to his plan as a "politicizing" operation. In the same memorandum, he suggested:

"Naturally, carrying out this program, even if done discreetly, will represent a substantial risk. Trying to pressure 'non-political' civil servants to partisanly support the President's re-election would become quickly publicized and undoubtedly backfire. Consequently, the strategy should be to work through the top and medium-level political appointees who exercise control over most of the Departmental decisions and actions.
Also, to minimize any direct links to the President, there should be no directions on this project in writing, and most of the initiative should come from the Department Heads themselves. (In fact, as this concept is refined further, I proposed we stop calling it 'politicizing the Executive Branch,' and instead call it something like strengthening the Government's responsiveness.)"

This last suggestion was eventually followed and the con-
* See further, Malek, 79.

cept became known as The Responsiveness Program. Mr. Malek's testimony as to this document are found at Malek 33.

Mr. Malek has described the Responsiveness Program as more benign than these documents suggest. According to Malek, its main thrust was to insure that the Departments and Agencies, taking all factors into account, serviced deserving groups and then properly communicated their good works to the voting public. (e.g., Malek, 41, 104-5, 149-50) His account, however, should be compared with the description of the program in public testimony of William Marumoto, a White House aide connected with the Responsiveness Program: *

SENATOR TALMADGE What was the responsiveness group?

MR. MARUMOTO As I explained this morning, this was a group of four or five gentlemen who initially were under the leadership of Mr. Malek and later under the leadership of Dan Kingsley, who were responsible to and working with various special interest groups under Mr. Colson's operation as well as our personnel operation to make sure that the various departments and agencies were responsive to requests that went to them from the White House on personnel matters, publicity, public relations, and grants and contracts.

T Simplified, it was a group to take maximum political advantage of public dollars that were awarded in the form of public grants and contracts, was it not?

MAR A system to facilitate some of our requests.

T "Facilitate"—what do you mean by that?

MAR Try to get through the bureaucratic red tape.

T In other words, my statement is correct. It was to maximize the advantage of the American taxpayers' dollars in a political effort, was it not?

MAR Yes. (13 *Hearings,* 5318-19)

2. THE PLAN AS CONCEIVED WITH PARTICULAR REFERENCE TO MINORITY GROUPS

As discussed in Section V, there was much activity of the Responsiveness ilk in connection with minority-oriented federal programs. Because of this—and because of the considerable detail in which they were set out in written form —it is useful to discuss separately the specific plans to use the incumbency that were formulated to appeal to Spanish-speaking and Black constituents.

* See Section 1 below.

A. Spanish-Speaking Plans. The basic strategy for using federal resources for campaign purposes regarding Spanish-speaking voters was outlined in a "Confidential" document entitled *"The Campaign To Re-Elect The President. The Plan To Capture The Spanish Speaking Vote"*, (Ex. 10) prepared in early 1972 by Alex Armendariz, head of the Spanish-speaking Voters Division at CRP. Under the heading "Implementation Tools", Armendariz wrote:

> *"Use the incumbency to the greatest extent possible* to stroke this community over the next several months through appointments, grants, program development, accelerated program implementation, and publicity of the President's record through the departments and agencies." (emphasis in original)

And on p. 13 he noted:

> "The purpose of the White House Spanish Speaking Constituent Group Task Force is to mobilize the resources of the Executive Branch in support of the campaign effort. This task force is responsible . . . for obtaining Spanish-speaking personnel appointments, grants and other program initiatives. . . ."

Tab G of this document, entitled "Capitalizing On The Incumbency", is particularly important and is set forth in full text:

> "Substantial assistance to the Spanish speaking campaign can be provided through use of the control of the Executive Branch. Through this control, we can fill in any gaps in the President's record and generate favorable publicity for the campaign persuasion [sic] effort. In addition, a number of Spanish speaking programs are sources of political information.
> "Bill Marumoto is responsible for submitting a plan to capitalize on the incumbency by May 1. The elements of this plan will be directed to achieving the following end results.
> (1) To develop specific ideas for using grants, personnel appointments and programs to fill out any gaps in the President's record, e.g., appoint a Mexican American to a regulatory commission.
> (2) To set up organizational procedures and contacts with the appropriate White House Staff members and the Executive Branch for accomplishing the above steps.
> (3) To provide the campaign team with up to date

337

information on all programs directed at the Spanish
speaking community.

(4) To use the Departments and Agencies public information offices to publicize favorable Administration
activities in behalf of the Spanish speaking.

(5) To ensure that those Federally subsidized programs which serve as havens for opposition political operatives are closely supervised so that they are devoting
all their energies toward solving the problems of the
Spanish speaking poor (particularly in September and
October)." (*See* Ex. 262-1, 13 *Hearings* 5532)

Mr. Marumoto has testified that he prepared and submitted the plan referred to in the above document. (13
Hearings 5279) The Select Committee, however, has not
obtained a copy of this plan. However, the detailed account
in Section V.1. of this Chapter of the actual conduct that
occurred regarding the Spanish-speaking community presents
a comprehensive view of the type of activities encompassed
by the above outline.

B. Black Plans. The overall plans to use the incumbency to
achieve Black support in the 1972 campaign appear in several documents. The earliest is a "Confidential," "Final" document, dated March 15, 1972, and entitled "Campaign Plan—
A Strategy For the Development of The Black Vote in 1972."
(Ex. 11) Significant for present purposes is a paragraph that
appears at pp. 23-4, under the heading "Use of Administration Resources":

To augment organizational efforts it is proposed to
make use of Administration resources to provide visible
support of deserving projects. With team members working closely to monitor economic and social programs a
selective funding approach will furnish encouragement
incentives for Black individuals, firms and organizations
whose support will have a multiplier effect on Black vote
support for the President. This will call for working with
OMBE, SBA, Department of Labor, OEO, HUD, HEW
and the Justice Department. What we do economically
will be a vital key politically.

The "team" referenced in this paragraph is identified at p. 21
of this exhibit:

In order to assure maximum coordination from the
out-set a team approach to implementation of strategy
and execution of the plan of action will be used. The

338

team coordinating efforts will include Robert Brown, Special Assistant to the President; Stan Scott, White House Communications Staff Member; Ed Sexton, RNC; Samuel Jackson, Assistant Secretary of HUD (representing the Council of Black appointees); and Paul R. Jones, Black Vote Division Executive Director. It is anticipated that this group will meet regularly on a weekly basis and inter-act daily as needed.

This memorandum concludes (at p. 24):

In support of staff efforts it is proposed that emphasis be placed on closer control of grants, loans, contracts and appointments—especially from socially-oriented Departments and agencies. What the Administration does economically is key. The major issues of concern to the rank and file Black voter are those which have an economic base. They are concerned about those things that affect day to day livelihood and well-being.

Testimony taken by the Select Committee establishes that this document was probably the composite product of several contributors, among whom were Paul Jones of CRP and Robert Brown of the White House. (Jones 132-134)

The use of Administration resources in the Black area was spelled out in greater detail in a "Confidential" June 15, 1972, memorandum from John Clarke to Malek entitled "Black Vote Field Plan". (Malek Ex. 23) At pp. 5-6 of this document, the following passage appears:

SPECIAL ACTIVITIES
Grants and Government Resources

At the present time, Bob Brown and his staff are handling the grants activity. To date, they have identified all Blacks who are receiving, or have received, money from this Administration. These recipients are being utilized as a source of campaign contributions and volunteers and as a vehicle for getting our appointees invited to various Black events as speakers and participants. They also form an excellent group of visible Blacks and they are being used to reach the voters in their areas of influence. [*]

In addition to the above results, Bob and his staff are actively seeking out other projects that could be funded to the benefit of the campaign. They are specifically looking for projects that will impact heavily on

* Mr. Brown in executive session denied that he utilized Black recipients of federal funding as a source of campaign contributions. (Brown, pp. 46-9)

Blacks due to voter appeal and Black involvement. To date, they have been very successful. In this area, a local Black building contractor (Jack Crawford) has developed a program for identifying potential projects, getting them funded through Bob's office and, in return, obtaining a strong vote commitment for the President from the recipient. This plan is being actively pursued at present. Another specific project that is underway is the identification of all remaining grant and loan monies with a view to carefully allocating those funds to projects which will impact most heavily on black voters. [*]

Finally, Bob and his staff are working closely with Dan Kingsley to identify various advisory boards and commissions and job openings which can be filled by visible Blacks.

Even with the accomplishments so far, more work needs to be done in this area and plans are currently being drawn to more effectively develop and coordinate this activity.

The "Crawford Plan" mentioned above is attached as Ex. 12. The plan, at p. 2, states:

In order to obtain endorsements from . . . local Black leaders who will in all probability be at least nominal Democrats, some inducements will need to be offered. The inducements could be federal financial from the normal grant-in-aid programs administered by HEW, HUD, OEO, DOL, SBA, EDA, OMBE, and USDA. "The [recommended] locally based national representative (assisted by Black representatives of the various federal agencies) will be able to offer federal aid grant assistance to those leaders who are willing to endorse the President or at least make positive statements concerning the higher level of assistance currently being enjoyed by his institution under this administration.

In addition, Crawford recommended (pp. 3-4) that:

There should be a White House representative who can facilitate assure [sic] the delivery of federal grant-in-aid funds to leaders who endorse the President and the Administration's efforts to improve the lot of Blacks. This liaison man is charged with coordination of the

* Brown also denied seeking out projects that could be funded for the benefit of the campaign. (Brown 47). Mr. Crawford, in executive session, testified that, while he had developed the program referred to above, he was not "actively pursuing" it at the time of this memorandum. (Crawford 40-2)

federal agency personnell [sic] who are in turn charged with determining assistance needed by the institution!

During his executive session, Mr. Malek testified that he did not recall receiving or seeing a copy of the "Crawford Plan". However, as Ex. 12 demonstrates, the plan was sent on June 26, 1972, to Malek by Robert Mardian, a CRP official who is a former Assistant Attorney General for the Internal Security Division, with the suggestion that he and Malek meet with Crawford to discuss the matter.

Of the same date is a memorandum from Malek to John Mitchell entitled "Black Vote Campaign Plan." (Malek Ex. 24) Under the heading "Intensify Efforts To Utilize Government Grants and Loans" are the following paragraphs:

> I feel that our strongest selling point with Black voters is the economic assistance this Administration has provided to Blacks. To fully capitalize on this, we have to do a better job of publicizing the grants already given and of identifying new projects for which we will receive maximum impact.
>
> The major portion of the responsibility for this activity falls on the White House aide of the Black team. Bob Brown and his staff have identified all Blacks who are receiving, or have received, money from this Administration. These recipients will be utilized as a source of campaign contributions and volunteers, and as a group of highly visible Blacks to be used to reach the voters in their areas of influence.
>
>   *   *   *
>
> Effective allocation of new grants requires close co-ordination between the White House and the Campaign team. As a first step, I have asked Bob Brown to identify all major sources of grant and loan monies which could be allocated to Blacks. Then, Jones and Sexton, working through their field organization, will be responsible for finding recipients in key cities who will be supportive of the re-election effort.
>
>   *   *   *
>
> I believe that by strengthening our field organization and making better use of grants and loans, we can overcome of the problems of the Black Vote Division, and make some inroads on Black voters in November. I will keep you apprised of progress.

Malek testified he was not certain that this document was actually read or approved by him or forwarded to Mitchell; however, he did not deny sending it to Mitchell. He stated

341

that normally memoranda would not be sent to the Campaign Director over his name unless he had read and approved them. The Committee, subsequent to Mr. Malek's testimony, discovered another copy of this document in Clark MacGregor's CRP files that was initialed by Mr. Malek. (Ex. 13) Malek did not recall Mitchell's expressing disapprobation of the plans set forth in this memorandum. (Malek 142, 150-1, 157-60)

IV. Communication of the Responsiveness Concept to Government and Campaign Officials

The significance with which the Responsiveness Program was perceived is evidenced by the efforts taken to inform key government and campaign officials of the workings of the program. The most important of these briefings are now discussed.

1. The various Malek documents referenced in the previous section suggest that key White House and OMB staffers such as Ehrlichman, Shultz, and Ken Cole were made aware of Responsiveness concepts. Haldeman was particularly of the mind that Ehrlichman and Shultz should be informed about, and approve of, the Responsiveness plan. In his handwritten comments on the memorandum to him from Malek (Malek Ex. 3), he stated, in the margin by Malek's paragraph on "Department Responsiveness," that "Prob here is essential support of E & S—q. whether they really fully understand & agree to this whole deal. E esp is the key to dealing w/depts. & must be on board 100%." However, in an interview with the Committee's staff on February 8, 1974, Mr. Ehrlichman stated he had little knowledge of the Responsiveness Program. (Ehrlichman 72). Mr. Shultz, in a staff interview, likewise asserted only passing familiarity of Responsiveness activities. Mr. Shultz did state that he saw one memorandum written by Malek concerning the Responsiveness Program, decided it was a "horrible idea," and transmitted this view to Mr. Haldeman.

2. Shortly after the program was approved, key Departmental and Agency personnel were briefed on its precepts. In a "Confidential Eyes Only" memorandum entitled "Responsiveness Program—Progress Report" attached to a June 7, 1972, memorandum from Malek to Haldeman (Malek Ex. 16), Malek stated:

> Thus far, the program is on schedule. I have now reviewed the program with each Cabinet Officer (except Rogers) and with the heads of the key Agencies (AC-

TION, EPA, OEO, SBA, GSA, and VA). In each session the following was covered:
—Emphasized need to make re-election support the top priority and the need to respond to requests in this regard
—Discussed which States, counties, and voting blocs are considered key and should be targeted by them.
—Had them name a top official who would be the political contact for this program (generally the Under Secretary)
—Asked them to educate loyal appointees (including Regional Directors) as to priorities and expectations, thus forming a political network in each Department
—Asked them to review all their resources and develop a plan for maximizing impact of these resources in key areas
—Indicated particular areas in their Departments that require special attention
—Established my office as the channel of communications with the campaign and stressed that we would work solely through Bill Gifford on grant requests.

In line with this last point, two members of my staff (Stan Anderson and Rob Davison) have been relieved of other responsibilities to concentrate on this. They have now held follow-up meetings with the Secretary's designee in most Departments to discuss the program in more detail and begin development of the Department Action Plans. These sessions will be completed in the next few weeks. In addition, I have held follow-up meetings with the top political appointees and with the Regional Directors in several Departments. I will hold additional meetings of this sort over the next few weeks.

Mr. Malek testified before the Select Committee that, in his briefings with Department and Agency chiefs, he employed color-coded maps that depicted target groups and geographic areas where government resources should be concentrated for campaign purposes. (Malek 76) Listings of various government officials contacted respecting the Responsiveness Program by Malek and his associates are found at Ex. 13.

Malek also provided Haldeman with his assessment of the success of his briefings.

The response to date has been fairly good, particularly at the second echelon. The reaction of some in the Cabinet (e.g., Romney and Hodgson) was that they were,

343

of course, already considering political ramifications and there is little more that can be done. Our approach here is to concentrate on the Under Secretary and other Presidential appointees, where the job gets done anyhow. Others, such as Volpe, Peterson, and Butz, have been quite receptive and should be real assets to the program.

3. John Mitchell and other key aides at CRP were briefed. (See Malek Exs. 7 and 15.) The briefing memorandum prepared for the Mitchell Session (Malek Ex. 7) indicates that Mitchell was informed in detail of the informational meetings held with the Department and Agency heads. Malek testified that this briefing paper "probably clearly represents" his discussion with Mitchell. (Malek 79-80)

4. Stanton Anderson and Frank Herringer briefed the White House Constituent Group Project Managers and the CRP Voting Bloc Diectors on the various facets of the Administration's plans "to take advantage of the incumbency to the maximum degree possible" during a meeting at Camp David on May 25, 26, 1972. The doocuments collected (See Malek Ex. 14-15) reflect the nature of that meeting and its participants. This meeting is of particular importance because it was attended by key aides in the Spanish-speaking, Black and Old Age areas where there was considerable Responsiveness-type activity.

The briefing paper used at this meeting has been previously referenced. (See Section III.1., *supra*) It parallels other documents already discussed with several significant additions. The participants were apparently asked to "be alert to opportunities to utilize the resources of the incumbency to improve our position with your constituent group." It appears that they were instructed to attempt "to come up with a list of ten or so persons from your groups that you would like to see placed" in a government position for campaign purposes by the White House Personnel Office. This group was also apparently told that:

"In a one-shot effort, all major grants and construction decisions for next fiscal year (72-73) were reviewed prior to the finalization of the budget to ensure that to the extent possible they impacted on politically beneficial areas." (See Malek Ex. 15; see also Malek, 49, 60, 62, 83.)

5. Finally, certain State Chairmen of the Committee to Re-Elect the President from "first and second key priority

states" received a briefing on the Responsiveness Program. (Malek Ex. 13 reflects the suggestion for and approval of such a briefing. See Malek's handwritten comments.) The major purpose underlying this briefing was to encourage politically oriented requests for government action from these campaign officials. (See further, Malek, 36)

V. Results of the Responsiveness Program and Other Related Activities *

1. ACTIVITIES RESPECTING THE SPANISH-SPEAKING

The portion of the Responsiveness Program presented in public testimony involved activities in the Spanish-speaking community. On November 7, 1973, William Marumoto, former staff assistant to the President, testified concerning the wide-ranging attempts on the part of certain White House and campaign officials to divert federal resources to organizations and individuals in the Spanish-speaking community to assist the re-election effort.** His testimony, and other evidence in the Select Committee's possession, appear to demonstrate a concerted effort to reward certain Administration friends and penalize its opponents.

Marumoto's testimony prompted the following statement by Senator Montoya:

"[I]n view of the motive that permeates the planning and blueprint of this mission and the testimony of the witness, I feel very much obligated to comment on the incredible insult that the Administration has perpetrated on the Spanish-speaking people of this country by this blatant attempt to buy the Spanish-speaking voters. They are not for sale in this country. There was a concerted effort to try to convince them that there was money in the trough if they just lined up, and the Spanish-speaking people of this country are not that kind of voter." (13 Hearings 5308)

According to the 1970 census, there were then more than

* This section includes descriptions of certain activities that were not the direct result of the Responsivness Program, but that are related in character to those actually conducted under its banner.
** Marumoto's testimony gives substance to the conclusion reached in a November 14, 1972, final "Campaign Report" from Alex Armendariz of CRP to Bob Marik that:
  "The incumbancy [sic] was utilized to the greatest advantage as possible through appointments, grants, accelerated program implementation, and publicity of Administration programs through the Federal department and agencies." (See Exhibit 14, p. 4)

ten million Spanish-speaking citizens in this country. The plan to capitalize on the incumbency with respect to this community was an attempt to gain support, votes, and contributions regarding a constituency that had been "heavily Democratic in the past." (See Ex. 10) The Administration concentrated its efforts in this regard on such states as Florida, Texas and California where the greatest number of Spanish-speaking citizens reside. The major activities discovered by the Committee are now discussed.

A. *Organization of Spanish-speaking Effort.* The leaders of the Spanish-speaking effort during the 1972 Presidential campaign included officials at the White House, the Cabinet Committee on Opportunities for the Spanish-Speaking People (an independent office in the executive branch more fully described below), and the Committee to Re-elect the President. For clarity, the major figures involved are identified:

William Marumoto, former Staff Assistant to the President, was involved at the White House in a wide range of activities, including recruiting for federal employment (particularly from the minorities), assisting Spanish-speaking firms and organizations in obtaining federal funds, and public relations for Spanish-speaking efforts and activities.

Antonio F. Rodriguez was Marumoto's assistant in the White House after September 1971. In the period from January to September of 1971, Rodriguez was the Chairman of the Cabinet Committee on Opportunities for Spanish-speaking People.

Henry Ramirez became Chairman of the Cabinet Committee in September, 1971.

Carlos Conde, an assistant during 1972 to White House Communications Director Herbert Klein, was involved in the campaign's media plan to reach Spanish-speaking people.

Alex Armendariz headed the CRP Spanish-speaking Voters Division.

Benjamin Fernandez was the Chairman of the National Hispanic Finance Committee, an arm of the Finance Committee to Re-elect the President (FCRP).

According to Marumoto, the above named individuals—with the exception of Fernandez—constituted the Spanish-speaking task force. The task force, officially known as the "White House Spanish-speaking Constituent Group Task Force," was, according to Marumoto, an "informal arrangement," which met every Monday afternoon during the campaign. (13 *Hearings* 5277). While the exact lines of authority concerning these individuals is not clear, it is clear that all of them were heavily involved in attempts to use the incumbency to gain Spanish-speaking support. Furthermore, organizational charts prepared separately by Marumoto and Armendariz show the Cabinet Committee, the White House Spanish-speaking unit and the Hispanic division of CRP as part of one over-all campaign structure, although on Marumoto's chart he has Armendariz reporting to him while the converse is true on the chart prepared by Armendariz.

B. Activities Involving the Dispensing of Federal Funds. There is substantial evidence that, respecting the Spanish-speaking area, political elements in the Administration and campaign committee sought and achieved control over the awarding of certain governmental grants and contracts.* When questioned by Dash concerning an OEO grant to a Spanish-speaking firm in California, Marumoto testified:

> DASH Now, what was the role of Alex Armendariz from the Committee To Re-elect the President, which was the political branch of the CRP for the campaign, in meeting with Mr. Blacher of OEO and discussing your grant of $200,000? Why was he there?
> MARUMOTO He was involved in terms of signing off on any grants.
> D When you say "signing off," did that mean he would have to agree?
> M Approve, yes.
> D He would have to approve?
> M Yes. (13 *Hearings* 5281)

Subsequently, Marumoto, while stating that Armendariz "didn't have [legal]authority, of course, to sign off," testified that Armendariz "had a say" or "input" in the grant-making process. He then added:

> D They expected him to sign off on it and generally if he didn't sign off on it, it wasn't granted.
> M Generally speaking, yes.
> D Therefore, it would be fair to say that a very strong outside political influence was introduced in the grant-making process of the various agencies.
> M Yes. (13 *Hearings* 5322)

Armendariz denied involvement in government grants and disclaimed the power to sign-off on federal awards, stating,

* White House and campaign committee memoranda reveal political input as to $60 million in grants considered or actually awarded by the Administration regarding the Spanish-speaking community.

"I never engaged in specific discussion on any particular grant or contractor of any sorts." (Armendariz, p. 65). When asked about references to his name in reports indicating he was influencing grants, he said the references "worried" him and that he frequently objected to White House staffers Frank Herringer and Jerry Jones about their inclusion. (Armendariz, pp. 103-05).

Documents obtained by the Select Committee contain numerous indications that the campaign team was interjecting political considerations into the grant-making process. For example, a March 17, 1972, White House memorandum from Marumoto to Colson, entitled "Weekly Report for Brown Mafia, Week of March 13-17, 1972"* reads:

"Alex Armendariz, Tony Rodriguez and I met with representatives of Harry Dent's, Clark McGregor's (sic) and Bob Brown's offices with the grant officials of OEO to discuss ways of improving coordination and more effective means of getting political impact in the grant-making process. Discussion pointed out the tremendous need for a centralized computer capability for all Departments and Agencies whereby one could obtain data regarding grants to any congressional district, and/or organization." (Ex. No. 262-8, 13 *Hearings* 5543)*

To cite another example, on March 24, 1972, Marumoto wrote an "Administrative-Confidential" memorandum to Colson (copy to Malek) that stated:

"Attended a meeting called by John Evans regarding minority business enterprise. Asked that Armendariz and Rodriguez also be invited. Discussed were recipients of grants for FY 1972 as well as those being considered for additional grants for FY 1972." (Ex. No. 262-9, 13 *Hearings* 5547)

In a staff interview, Evans, then staff assistant in the Office of Domestic Council, described his role as a "liaison with the Departments and Agencies" who was mostly concerned with policy rather than specifics. He did note that he received input from Marumoto and Armendariz, among others, and acknowledged that political considerations played a role in the awarding of grants. He said that, for example, if a recom-

* The term "Brown Mafia" was discontinued following the March 24 report after Malek wrote Marumoto, "Please drop Brown Mafia title—it would look bad if it ever got out." See Ex. No. 262-8, 13 *Hearings* 5543.
* The Select Committee has received no evidence that such computer capability was actually developed.

mendation concerning an OMBE grant was made by Marumoto, the application was favored or an explanation given why it was not. The message went out, "Do something with it." Evans stated that, while he did not favor funding an unqualified group, he would rely in part on the "team's" recommendations and tend to favor qualified groups who supported the Administration over those who did not. Although he was approached by Armendariz, Marumoto and Ramirez with suggestions that political contributors be funded, Evans was not involved with specific grants where that occurred.

Another illustration of the input of political influence in the grant-making process is found in an "Administrative-Confidential" White House memorandum from Marumoto to Colson and Malek dated May 12, 1972, which reads:

"Rodriguez and I met, along with representatives from Bob Brown's office and 1701, Under-Secretary Lynn and John Jenkins, Director of OMBE, re funding proposals to Spanish-Speaking and black groups. This is about the third such meeting we've had to either approve or disapprove funding proposals from OMBE. We are generating some new proposals from the Spanish-speaking in key states."

(1) Specific Activities to Help Administration Friends. Numerous memoranda obtained by the Committee demonstrate that the Spanish-speaking "team" devoted considerable effort to helping Administration friends seeking federal monies. For example, in an "Administrative-Confidential" report to Colson and Malek, Marumoto declared:

"Rodriguez met with Carlos Villarreal, Administrator of UMTA [Urban Mass Transit Administration], to talk about setting aside specific monies for some of our Republican Spanish Speaking contractors." (Ex. No. 262-16, 13 *Hearings* 5578)

Another example of interest in aiding Spanish-speaking friends is found in an April 7, 1972, White House memorandum from Marumoto to Colson and Malek which stated:

"In the grants area, Rodriguez and I are working on the following: Reviewing with John Evans, Bob Brown and Wally Henley proposals and grants at OMBE to make sure that the *right people* are being considered and receiving grants from OMBE." (Ex. No. 262-11, 13 *Hearings* 5557) (emphasis added)

In several cases, the Committee attempted to ascertain the circumstances regarding the awarding of particular grants and contracts to the President's supporters. The results of these investigations follow.

(a) *J. A. Reyes and Associates.* The beneficiary of a number of grants was Joseph A. Reyes. Mr. Reyes was active in the President's re-election effort, particularly regarding fundraising. In fact, Reyes was Chairman of the District of Columbia, Maryland and Virginia section of the National Hispanic Finance Committee (NHFC), which was an authorized arm of FCRP formed in 1972 to solicit campaign contributions from Spanish-speaking citizens.

Reyes and his company, J. A. Reyes and Associates, were the subjects of several White House "Weekly Activity Reports," forwarded by Marumoto to Colson and Malek. One such "Administrative-Confidential" report, dated May 5, 1972, states:

> "In the grants area, the following transpired: Department of Transportation: working with UMTA re a $70,000 grant to J. A. Reyes Associates of Washington, D.C. He is the Chairman of the D.C., Maryland and Virginia section of the National Hispanic Finance Committee." (Ex. No. 262-15, 13 *Hearings* 5572) *

Reyes, in a staff interview, stated that he had been in the consulting business for approximately ten years, and that most of his business arose from the section 8 (a) program of the Small Business Administration Act. (The purpose of this act is to assist in the expansion and development of small business concerns owned and controlled by eligible disadvantaged persons.) During 1971, Mr. Reyes' firm grossed between $400,000 and $500,000; in 1972, his firm's business doubled to $1 million, all of which was under the 8 (a) program. According to Reyes, he received seven or eight contracts and one grant in that year. One such contract was a $200,000 sole source, non-competitive agreement with OEO awarded in July, 1972. Although acknowledging conversations with Marumoto and Rodriguez, Reyes denied knowledge of any efforts by them on his behalf regarding this contract.

In a Committee interview, Arnold Baker, former National Project Manager of Field Operations, Migrant Labor Division, OEO, stated that the J. A. Reyes contract with OEO was for an evaluation of and assistance to the Emergency Food and

See also Ex. No. 262-16, 13 *Hearings* 5576 which is discussed above. Reyes was one of "our Republican SS contractors" referred to in that exhibit.

350

Medical Services Program and that the contract was given without showing a need for this evaluation as required by OEO regulations. Baker said that sufficient data and expertise regarding this program had been developed through prior evaluations and it was the unanimous opinion of officials in the unit responsible for evaluation of the Reyes proposal that a study was not necessary. Over their objections, the contract was awarded.

Baker believes that the award was based solely on political motivations. He stated that the Project Division had decided not to fund Reyes' proposal but, when Peter Mirelez, Director of the Migrant Division, OEO, received word of this decision, he reversed it. According to Baker, sometime after the contract was awarded it was cancelled due to substandard work. However, Baker reported that it was reinstated by James Griffith, Director of the Migrant and Indian Division of OEO. Baker stated that this contract was "rammed down the throats" of department officials, including himself.

The Select Committee also interviewed Dan Cox, a Manpower Specialist with the Migrant Division, Department of Labor, who formerly was the Contract Application Specialist with the Migrant Division of OEO responsible for evaluating the Reyes contract. Cox agreed with Baker that the contract to evaluate the Emergency Food and Medical Services Program was not warranted. It was also Cox's belief that J. A. Reyes Associates was not qualified to make the evaluation. In addition, Cox stated that he was told by Peter Mirelez that that contract was a "political payoff."

Mirelez, in an interview, defended the need for the Reyes contract. Mirelez acknowledged that some of his subordinates had questioned the qualifications of J. A. Reyes Associates as well as to the efficacy of its proposal, but Mirelez insisted that his decision was not the result of political influence. Mirelez denied he told Cox that the contract was a "political payoff."

In another interview, James Griffith, now Acting OEO Deputy Assistant Director for Operations, denied any political influence in grant or contract processes at OEO. He did recall, however, certain rumors as to the lack of necessity for the J. A. Reyes contract, but could not remember specifics. Griffith also related that a telegram was sent from the Office of Program Review to Reyes cancelling the contract. Griffith felt this action was not programmatically justified, and thus became involved in reinstating the contract.

(b) *Ultra-Systems, Inc.* Another effort to aid an Admin-

351

istration supporter is revealed in an "Administrative-Confidential" White House Weekly Activity Report, dated May 19, 1972, from Marumoto to Colson and Malek:

> "Rodriguez is assisting Ultrasystems, Inc., of Long Beach, California with a $200,000 grant from OMBE. This organization strongly supports the Administration." (Ex. No. 262-17, 13 *Hearings* 5581)

As in the case of J. A. Reyes and Associates, Ultra-Systems, Inc. had strong ties with the National Hispanic Finance Committee. Fernando Oaxaca, Vice President of Ultra-Systems, was the NHFC National Treasurer.

The proposed OMBE grant to Ultra-Systems, Inc. was also the subject of a White House memorandum dated August 8, 1972, from former White House staffer Nathan Bayer to Armendariz and Rodriguez.

> "I spoke with John Jenkins this afternoon concerning the current status of your priority OMBE proposals. "In the case of AMEX Civil Systems* and Ultra Systems, Inc., John expects to have Requests for Information in their hands by the first of next week. I strongly advise you to encourage them to complete the RFIs as quickly as possible and return them to Jenkins. He assures me that even in the absence of their completion, he will have the investigation and security clearance begun and the audit begun." (Ex. No. 262-41, 13 *Hearings* 5652)

In a staff interview, Oaxaca denied that there was any *quid pro quo* involved in the above grant, which was awarded in October 1972. Oaxaca stated that he had applied to OMBE for federal funding in early spring of 1972. When nothing materialized, he asked Rodriguez, a long-time friend, if Rodriquez knew anyone at OMBE to whom Rodriguez could make an "inquiry" on his behalf.*

* The owner of Amex Civil Systems, M. Caldera, was a close associate of both Rodriguez and Marumoto. Rodriguez has maintained a business relationship with Caldera since leaving the White House.

* Oaxaca was also associated with the Spanish-Speaking Business Alliance of Los Angeles, which was the subject of a July 26, 1972, CRP memorandum from Armendariz to Bayer, on the subject of "OMBE Proposals" (13 *Hearings* 5633):

> We have received the list of proposed grants to be funded listed in your July 24th memo. Two of those listed that appear to be not funded at this point are highly recommended by this office.
> Spanish-Speaking Business Alliance, Los Angeles
> Amex Civil Systems, Lawndale, California

Armendariz testified he knew Oaxaca "to be a reputable person" but, when asked whether he knew Oaxaca was National Treasurer of the National Hispanic Finance Committee, stated that he was "not sure" and that he "may not have known [it] at that time." (Armendariz, p. 92)

(2) *Action Against Persons Not Supportive of the Administration.* There is evidence that qualified firms that failed to share the Administration's political goals and declined to participate in the President's re-election effort were penalized in their efforts to secure government funding.

References to "unfriendly" or pro-Democratic companies and individuals appeared with some frequency in Marumoto's Weekly Reports and in other White House and CRP documents. An "Administrative-Confidential" Weekly Report to Colson and Malek reads:

"Rodriguez working with Nate Bayer of the Domestic Affairs Council re identifying SS groups who have applied for federal grants at DOL (Department of Labor) who are unfriendly toward the Administration." (Ex. No. 262-28, 13 *Hearings* 5615)

Bayer and Armendariz have both denied to the Select Committee that cutting off contractors and grantees not supportive of the Administration was Administration policy. But there is evidence that attempts to excise unfriendly recipients of federal funds actually were made. Moreover, both Marumoto and Rodriguez have admitted that they felt persons opposing the Administration should not receive government grants.

(a) *Development Associates (Leveo Sanchez).* One of the most instructive cases involved Leveo Sanchez, the head of Development Associates, Inc., a Washington-based consulting firm. An "Administrative-Confidential" memorandum of July 19, 1972 from Marumoto to Rob Davison of the White House staff notes that Sanchez' firm has been funded for $1 to $2 million "by our Administration." After referring to Sanchez' association with Sargent Shriver and Frank Mankiewicz, the memorandum records that Sanchez' company had recently received over $900,000 in government contracts and was under consideration at DOL and HUD for additional contracts totaling $100,000. The memorandum continues:

"This is a classic example of a firm, not necessarily on our team, which is making a comfortable living off of us. These are grants that we're aware of which indicates [sic] they may have a few others.
"I would recommend if it's not too late, we stop the proposals at DOL, and HUD." (Ex. No. 262-36, 13 Hearings 5635)

Copies of this memorandum went to Armendariz and Rodriguez.

Five days later, on July 24, 1971, Armendariz wrote a "Confidential" memorandum to Davison with copies to Marumoto and Rodriguez, which stated:

"We have inquired about Development Associates and have learned of their close ties with the DNC and Cesar Chavez. We fully concur with Bill Marumoto's memo of July 19." (Ex. No. 262-36, 13 Hearings 5635-36)

The background of these memoranda is informative. According to Sanchez, in the spring of 1972 he was solicited for a campaign contribution by Joseph Reyes, Chairman of the Washington, Maryland, and Virginia Chapter of the National Hispanic Finance Committee. (As discussed above, Reyes was the beneficiary of certain grants and contracts as to which Marumoto intervened.) Reyes, Sanchez says, told him he was expected to make a $1,000 contribution to the President's re-election effort. Sanchez declined.

On July 17, 1972, at the invitation of Marumoto, Sanchez attended a White House luncheon with Marumoto and David Wimer, now Deputy Special Assistant to the President and formerly the Special Assistant to the Assistant Secretary of Labor for Administration and Management. Sanchez related that during the lunch Marumoto told him that "they" had been very good to his firm and that he was about to be awarded a $400,000 contract from the Department of Labor. Sanchez said that Marumoto then stated that Sanchez and Development Associates would be expected to show their appreciation in a substantial manner in regard to the President's re-election effort. Sanchez stated he informed Marumoto and Wimer he knew he would not receive the $400,-000 Labor contract and that Development Associates had previously received contracts because of its proficiency. Sanchez said he rejected the request to support the re-election effort and that Marumoto and Wimer then "implied" possible adverse consequences.

When questioned concerning his meeting with Sanchez, Marumoto testified:

DASH Can you, to the best of your recollection, tell the Committee what it was that you discussed with Mr. Sanchez at that meeting?
MARUMOTO If I recall, the other party that was involved in that meeting at the time was David Wimer, who was Under Secretary Silberman's aide in the Department of Labor, who had the responsibility on the

other side—on the Department side—on this responsiveness program. He and I had lunch in the White House staff dining room and discussed generally a number of things pertaining to Mr. Sanchez' operation.

D   Who initiated the meeting?

M   I believe I did, sir.

D   . . . I ask you very specifically whether or not you were making this recommendation as you show in your memorandum because you felt that this was a contractor 'who was living off of us,' and was not supporting the administration and you were recommending he be cut off for that reason. Your testimony, as I recall it, was that was the reason that you wrote the memorandum.

M   That is correct. (Hearings 5319)

Marumoto denied that there was any discussion during the luncheon concerning contributions and did not recall any exchange regarding the Labor contract. He stated he was not aware of an effort to solicit contributions from Sanchez at any time. But his testimony continued:

D   That was shortly after—just 2 days after that meeting that you wrote this memorandum?

M   Right.

D   Is there any relationship between this memorandum written 2 days after that meeting and the meeting?

M   I am sure there must have been.

D   If you are sure there must have been, can you recall what that relationship may have been or must have been?

M   I guess it was our impression—not impression, but our decision, that it appeared, from sources outside of our meeting, that he was not going to support the administration so this was a recommendation that we made. (13 Hearings 5320)

David Wimer stated in a staff interview that no discussions of campaign contributions, re-election support or government grants or contracts took place during the luncheon. Wimer further stated that he was not expecting Sanchez' presence and does not know why he was there. According to Wimer, he has never acted to inflence a decision on grants, contracts or loans for Sanchez or his firm.

Sanchez, however, did experience adverse Administration action. On September 25, 1972, Sanchez' company was "graduated" from the SBA 8(a) program. (13 Hearings 5685) This graduation, which the SBA was "pleased" to effect and for which Development Associates was "congratulated," actually meant that Development Associates could no longer qualify for preferred status under the provisions of Section 8(a) and had to compete generally with other non-disadvantaged contractors. Not only does the "graduation" from the 8(a) program adversely affect future grants, but a "graduated" company loses all previously awarded grants at the close of the fiscal year in which its eligibility ceases. In other words, "graduation" can have a devastating impact.

Marumoto acknowledged there was a "political input" on the Sanchez decision. He could not recall any other Spanish-speaking "graduates" from the 8(a) program. (13 Hearings 5292).

Subsequent to Development Associates' "graduation", efforts to reinstate the company in the 8(a) program were made by Dan Trevino, its Vice President, who also served on the Texas Spanish-speaking Committee to Re-elect the President. Trevino contacted Carlos Conde, a friend of his, to arrange for Trevino to meet with Henry Ramirez on this matter.

Trevino met with Ramirez in Washington shortly after the election. At this meeting, according to Trevino, Ramirez stated that Development Associates had been generally uncooperativve in the re-election effort. Ramirez, Trevino said, gave as examples of an uncooperative attitude Sanchez' refusal to provide campaign printing at Development Associates' expense and his failure to make a campaign contribution. Ramirez told Trevino that Development Associates lost its 8(a) certification because of this attitude.* When Trevino pointed out that he had been active in the President's re-election effort, Ramirez suggested that Trevino would have no difficulty obtaining Section 8(a) contracts if he divorced himself from Sanchez. Ramirez then suggested that Trevino see Rodriguez.

The meeting between Rodriguez and Trevino, as described by Trevino, was quite similar to his meeting with Ramirez. Sanchez was pictured as uncooperative during the campaign and close to Shriver and Mankiewicz. Rodriguez indicated that the decision to remove Development Associates from the 8(a) program was not directed against Trevino and that he would try to help Trevino in some manner.

Trevino then turned to Peter Mirilez, Director of the Mi-

* In a staff interview, Sanchez confirmed he had been asked to do some printing but stated that the request was in very general terms and that, as with the request for a contribuion, he refused. Sanchez advised the Select Committee that Trevino contemporaneously related the above events to him.

grant Division of OEO, with whom Development Associates had a contract to service migrant workers. Mirilez told Trevino that OEO was satisfied with Development Associates' work on this contract but that he was getting pressure from the White House to discontinue it. Following this conversation, Trevino returned to Houston to await word concerning the result of his efforts.

In January, 1973, not having heard from Rodriguez, Trevino had Conde arrange another appointment with him, this one attended by Sanchez as well as Trevino. There, Rodriguez informed Trevino and Sanchez that an OEO migrant contract in which they were interested was slated to go to Amex, a West Coast firm, but that Rodriguez would try to assist in Development Associates' reinstatement as a SBA 8(a) contractor, despite Sanchez' lack of cooperation.

The following month, the problem was still not resolved. According to Trevino, he again contacted Conde to arrange a meeting with Marumoto. At this meeting, Trevino said, he began to summarize the problems facing Development Associates, but Marumoto cut him short, indicating that he (Marumoto) was well aware of the situation. Trevino said Marumoto stated that re-certification was being worked on and that Rodriguez would be in contact with Trevino. Sanchez, however, has advised the Select Committee staff that Development Associates was never reinstated in the 8(a) program.

Armendariz, testifying in Executive Session, denied any involvement in penalizing Sanchez. It will be recalled that Armendariz had written Davison that "we fully concur" with Marumoto's memorandum to Davison of July 19 which recommended that Sanchez' proposals at DOL and HUD be stopped. When questioned concerning his memorandum, Armendariz stated that when he said "we fully concur" with Marumoto's memorandum, he meant he concurred only with the description of Sanchez as having close ties with Democritic leaders and the Democratic party. Armendariz, who received all of Marumoto's White House memoranda, testified that taking action against companies unfriendly to the Administration "is just completely contrary to my ethics in politics." (Armendariz, p. 95)

(B) Activities Respecting Other Nonsupportive Companies. Another instance where a nonsupportive group received attention is illustrated by a May 26, 1972, "Administrative-Confidential" White House memorandum from Marumoto to Colson and Malek.

"Expressed concern to OEO re a $3 million grant to the

357

Mexican American Unity Council only to find there are some legal hang-ups to try to cut them off. They promised to at least monitor the group." (Ex. No. 262-19, 13 Hearings 5584)

Marumoto testified in public session:

D   What was the opposition to the Mexican-American Unity Council?
M   I think this was a situation where they had received a grant from OEO and before someone realized that they had a group that weren't necessarily supportive of the administration and there was some inquiry of trying to unfund them. Upon checking with their general counsel we found that it could not be done.
D   Was there any question as to their qualification?
M   I don't recall, sir.
D   So the effort to unfund them, really, was based on your learning that they were nonsupportive?
M   Yes, sir. (13 Hearings 5285)

Still another example of the Administration's attitude toward unfriendly companies is found in a "Confidential" White House memorandum dated March 2, 1972 from Marumoto to James Lynn then the Under Secretary of Commerce, now Secretary of HUD:

"In line with our recent discussion regarding NEDA [National Economic Development Agency] and our comments of 'the tail wagging the dog,' I am attaching an editorial written by a NEDA employee opposing the appointment of Cip Guerra as Deputy Director of OMBE.

"This is the latest example of the unwillingness to cooperate in a 'spirit of cooperation' with the Administration. I think before Commerce signs off on their $2 million grant, you should sit down with Frank Viega and explain the facts of life.

"I would appreciate being kept abreast of this highly important matter." (Ex. No. 262-5, 13 Hearings 5535)

NEDA was founded by Benjamin Fernandez around 1969 with the purpose of assisting Spanish-speaking businessmen. Frank Viega (former President of NEDA), in a staff interview, stated that he did, in fact, meet with James Lynn in 1972 and that Lynn informed him that the White House would like NEDA to help the President. Lynn allegedly indicated that the White House "knew who their friends were."

Also present at this meeting was Alfred R. Villalobos, former NEDA Executive Vice President and Chief Executive Officer,* who, in a staff interview, indicated that Lynn had stressed cooperation with the Administration. Villalobos further stated that, from late 1971 until October 1972, he received numerous requests from Marumoto and Armendariz to perform services in relation to the re-election effort. According to Villalobos, considerable pressure was applied concerning the continuation of NEDA's federal grants and contracts. In fact, according to Villalobos, he resigned his NEDA post in October 1972 so that NEDA would not have difficulty renewing its Commerce Department grant.*

(3) "Neutralization" of Potential Opponents. There is evidence that the Spanish-speaking re-election "team" acted to convince potential opponents of the President's re-election effort that they were in line for a substantial government funding, when, in fact, there was no intention to make such an award. The subject of one such effort was the Southwest Council of LaRaza, a Spanish-speaking group based in Tucson, Arizona. A June 9, 1972 "Administrative-Confidential" White House memorandum from Marumoto to Colson and Malek states:

"Rodriguez working to obtain $30,000 for the Southwest Council of LaRaza for a conference next month. This is the group we want to neutralize." (Ex. No. 262-24, 13 Hearings 5601)

Apparently, this $30,000 grant was made as a showing of good faith by the Administration. On June 23, 1972, a White House memorandum notes that the $30,000 grant had been obtained from DOL and that Rodriguez was still working with the Southwest Council of LaRaza. (Ex. No. 262-28, 13 Hearings 5614)

One June 29, 1972, David L. Wimer, Special Assistant to the Assistant Secretary of Labor for Administration and Management, wrote Richard Wise, an assistant to the Under-Secretary of Labor:

"In seeking to create in key States an appropriate

* According to Fernandez, who was Chairman of the National Hispanic Finance Committee during the 1972 campaign, he was removed as President by Villalobos in a "coup d'etat." Fernandez has denied any knowledge of the facts set forth in the March 2 memorandum. (13 *Hearings* 5400-5401)
** Villalobos became a consultant to NEDA after leaving its employ. According to his successor, Arthur Negrete, Marumoto at a later date called him and said the White House wanted Villalobos fired. In fact, there was a defect in the procedure by which Villalobos was appointed and his consulting contract was terminated.

atmosphere for the re-election of the President, OASA has taken initial steps as follows:

1. *Obtainment* of $30,000 grant from Manpower Administration to support National Conference of Southwest Council of LaRaza. This is a beginning effort to de-politicize this grass roots group representing a minimum of seven States. Conference to be held in Washington, D.C. last part of July." (Ex. 15)

On the face of things, more substantial government grants were in store for the Southwest Council of LaRaza. On August 18, 1972, Marumoto noted in a report to Colson and Malek that he and Rob Davison were working to obtain funding of a $6 million HUD proposal submitted by the Southwest Council. (Ex. No. 262-45, 13 Hearings 5668). In addition the Southwest Council was being considered for OMBE grant. (Ex. No. 262-41, 13 Hearings 5652) The council did, in fact, appear well qualified. On August 8, 1972 Nathan Bayer wrote Marumoto and Armendariz:

"I spoke with John Jenkins this afternoon concerning the current status of your priority OMBE proposals. . . .
"In the case of the Southwest Council of LaRaza John met with them this morning and spoke with them for about two hours. John is very impressed with this group and says that he would have no difficulty in funding them. He awaits your signal on this matter." (Ex. No. 262-41, 13 Hearings 5652)

The signal never came. In fact, the evidence suggests that there was no intention to grant the Southwest Council of LaRaza $6 million or anywhere near that sum. Rather, it appears that the Spanish-speaking team intended to neutralize this potentially hostile group by holding out the promise of substantial federal funding. The following is from Marumoto's public testimony:

D Now, were you aware of an organization called the Southwest Council of LaRaza?
M Yes, sir.
D Did you engage in any discussions with them concerning any grants?
M Yes.
D Could you tell us what discussions you had with them?
M The Southwest Council of LaRaza is an active Democratic group that I believe was founded in Arizona and now is expanded into the Southwest states.

D   Were they supportive of the Administration?

M   Well, in some discussion that some of our people had from the campaign staff as well as our staff, there was some discussion about them supporting the President. They, in turn, said they would, provided they could get some Federal contracts.

D   Did you discuss any particular Federal contracts with them?

M   I believe there were some discussions—I had only one meeting with them, if you recall, and the others picked up on it. I think what finally happened was that the Committee to Re-elect, the Spanish-speaking division, recommended a strategy for working with them that they be funded for $30,000 for a national conference they wanted to hold.

D   What were they actually looking for—what kind of grant?

M   I believe they were looking for either two or three grants at maybe two or three different departments or agencies.

D   That amounted to approximately how much?

M   I am sure of six figures, I do not know.

D   Sums about $400,000? [sic]

M   It could be more, I do not know the exact figure.

D   What was being offered to them at that time or suggested was $30,000 for a conference?

M   Right, with consideration for assistance in a few months.

D   Mr. Marumoto, do you recall discussions we had yesterday, concerning this particular organization and your statement to us, that at no time did you believe they were going to get any grant, but that you were in a sense engaging with them in what has been known as a stroking session?

M   We were neutralizing them.

D   You were neutralizing them?

M   Yes, sir.

D   And by holding them at bay, not giving them a grant, but discussing the possibility of a $30,000 conference grant, this sort of at least held them away from being an opponent if they were not going to be supportive?

M   That is right. (13 Hearings 5320-21)

(4) Malek's Comments on Grant Making Activity as to Spanish-speaking Constituents. Fred Malek was questioned

concerning the grant and contract activities just described. He testified that, "I do not believe I knew they (Marumoto and Armendariz) were participating in the review of minority business enterprise grants." (Malek, p. 113) When confronted with copies of the numerous documents sent to him describing such activity, Malek stated that he is not certain he read the memoranda. He added that he was occupied on many matters and that reading an activity report, which did not require action on his part, had low priority. He said that, if he had read the passages in question, he would have interpreted them as evidencing cooperation with Spanish-speaking groups "to help them develop the skills with which to apply for grants . . . on a substantive basis." (Malek, pp. 118-19) Malek also stated that, in his opinion, it was improper for campaign officials to have "sign off" powers respecting government grants and contracts (Malek, p. 121). He said it was inappropriate to deny funding to responsible organizations simply because they were not supportive of the Administration. (Malek, pp. 126-27)

C. Cabinet Committee on Opportunities for Spanish-Speaking People and the Media Effort. (1) The Cabinet Committee. The Cabinet Committee, during 1972, was composed of eleven members chosen from the President's Cabinet and high level non-Cabinet posts. It had a staff of thirty-five, mostly of Spanish-American descent. As described in a fact sheet, apparently prepared by that Committee:

"The Cabinet Committee on Opportunities for Spanish-Speaking People is primarily a vehicle for carrying out the President's Program for Spanish-Speaking Americans. Signed into law on December 30, 1969 by President Nixon, the Committee is to assure that federal programs are reaching all Spanish-Speaking people, provide technical assistance and identify new programs which will benefit Spanish-speaking communities. An independent office in the Executive Branch of the government, the Cabinet Committee is responsible to Congress through the President."

While there was some ambiguity in 1972 whether the Chairman of the Committee—Henry Ramirez during the 1972 campaign—was subject to the provisions of the Hatch Act,* the balance of the staff clearly was. Nonetheless, there

* The fact sheet just referenced declares that the chairman was exempt from the provisions of the Hatch Act. A Congressional Committee with oversight responsibility in regard to the Cabinet Committee has recently concluded otherwise. See Report, Committee on Governmnt Operations, House of Representatives, September 25, 1973.

is evidence that the Cabinet Committee's staff became directly involved in the 1972 campaign. For example, a document prepared by Armendariz contains the following statement:

"The Cabinet Committee on Opportunities for Spanish-Speaking will provide research and staff support to the White House Task Force for all phases of the campaign effort. In addition, its Chairman, Henry Ramirez, should be a powerful recruiter of Spanish-speaking support." (Armendariz Ex. No. 2, p. 24)

Whether this document, addressed to Robert Marik who was in charge of planning and research at CRP, reached higher officials in the campaign or government is not known. However, an unsigned "Confidential" memorandum entitled "Interest Group Reports" on the stationery of the Committee for the Re-election of the President, dated December 16, 1971, and addressed to Attorney General Mitchell,* stated:

"The [Spanish-speaking] report makes detailed recommendations for highly-visual social and economic development projects and for publicizing the same. It suggests heavy exploitation of the Cabinet Committee on Opportunity for Spanish-speaking Peoples which is now closely allied with Colson's shop and Bill Marumoto on political and public relations questions." (Ex. No. 362-3, 14 Hearings 5534)

On January 4, 1972, Jeb Magruder sent a memorandum to Attorney General Mitchell that declared:

"Central to all our efforts [in the Spanish-speaking area] should be full politization of the Cabinet Committee, now on an $800,000 budget and going up to $1.3 million in July. The group now works through Finch, and Colson has begun assisting on the political and P.R. side. Carlos Conde, a Spanish press type, has been put on the Committee's payroll and will be working out of the White House in cultivating Spanish media, much as Stan Scott does for black media."* (Exhibit 16)

Further activity by Conde is described in an "Administrative-Confidential" Marumoto memorandum to Colson and

** Attorney General Mitchell was, at that time, a member of the Cabinet Committee.
* Carlos Conde was employed by the Cabinet Committee from February 20, 1972, to April 29, 1973, and was on detail to the White House Communications Office under Herbert Klein. It appears that the White House paid Conde's salary from July 1, 1972 until he left his position.

Malek dated July 28, 1972, that states:

"Conde completed the updating and checking for accuracy on the Administration Achievement list. The pertinent departments reviewed it, updated it and signed off on their section as being factually accurate. Sent copy to Marumoto for rapid approval by Domestic Council and then to Armendariz for insertion in Speaker's kit." (Ex. No. 262-38, 13 Hearings 5646)

(2) The Media Plan. There is evidence that the Cabinet Committee's media resources were used extensively for campaign purposes and that the Committee media operation was reorganized with the specific purpose of improving its performance in this regard. This activity is described in a memorandum from Carlos Conde to seven White House and campaign officials, including Colson, Malek, Ramirez, and Armendariz, dated May 31, 1972, and entitled, "Spanish Speaking Task Force Media Team'":

"The Campaign to Re-elect the President is to present his record and his Administration as second to none. The best way to do this is through an effective communications plan that highlights his record in all of the public sectors. The development of the best possible bilingual communications network is essential to the success of the overall plan.

"The Spanish-speaking media plan developed by this office is now underway, but it has become increasingly apparent in the past several weeks, however, that the Spanish speaking division of the Committee to Re-Elect the President will require more support than the plan originally envisioned.

". . . This situation has forced Armendariz to depend frequently on this office and on the Cabinet Committee for staff support . . . [T]he Cabinet Committee's Public Information Office, though integrated to the Spanish speaking campaign plan, has not fulfilled its function well because its staff requires broader journeyman experience." (Ex. No. 262-22, 13 Hearings 5595)

The memorandum presented two alternatives, the second of which—the one favored—was to revamp the existing media structures within the Cabinet Committee and other groups to support the campaign. Apparently the reorganization was already well under way. A memorandum from Marumoto to Colson and Malek dated April 28, 1972, stated:

"For the past two weeks Conde has been spending considerable time with the Cabinet Committee's public information Section putting a reorganization plan into effect and helping implement some projects that came from the reorganization." (Ex. No. 262-14, 13 Hearings 5569.)

On June 2, 1972, Marumoto wrote Colson and Malek that Conde was meeting with Ramirez and another official of the Cabinet Committee concerning "a revamping in personnel in order to give better support to Alex at 1701." (Ex. No. 262-21, 13 Hearings 5591).

Part of the effort to gain additional help for the campaign effort involved the use of Diana Lozano, a Cabinet Committee employee until July 12, 1972. In April and May of 1972, Lozano worked on a number of re-election media projects. (Ex. No. 262-14, 13 Hearings 5569; Ex. No. 262-19, 13 Hearings 5587). The May 31 Conde memorandum notes:

"Assisting part-time is researcher-writer Diane Lozano of the Cabinet Committee, who also does special assignments for Chairman Henry Ramirez and Alex Armendariz." (*Id.* at 5596.)

The memorandum also argues the need for a researcher-writer on Spanish-speaking topics and states that Lozano was willing to take leave of absence from the Cabinet Committee to join CRP. On his copy of the memorandum, Malek wrote: "Let her work from where she is—no way she can be added." (*Id.* at 5596). Moreover, in a memorandum to Conde dated June 5, 1972, Malek stated:

"If, however, Alex can still demonstrate the need for Miss Lozano's help, we can arrange for her to remain at the Cabinet Committee but spend part of her time supporting our activities." (*Id.* at 5593)

But two days later steps were taken to put Lozano on the staff of the Committee to Re-Elect the President where she officially started working on July 12, 1972. When questioned concerning the use of Lozano in the campaign before she joined CRP, Malek, in executive session, stated he did not know she was covered by the Hatch Act. (Malek, p. 136)

Armendariz testified in executive session that he never requested "support" from the Cabinet Committee. When shown documentary evidence (see Ex. 17) that he had asked the Cabinet Committee to send him daily news clippings and to translate certain campaign material, he stated that these matters were nothing more than requests for "information" from the Cabinet Committee. (Armendariz, pp. 120-6)

(3) Hoy. The Cabinet Committee published a minority-oriented newspaper called "Hoy," which apparently was used in the re-election effort.* There are a number of memoranda from Armendariz or Malek to Ramirez suggesting how "Hoy" could further campaign goals. An example is a memorandum from Armendariz to Ramirez dated May 11, 1972, (Ex. 18) concerning the third issue of "Hoy." The memorandum reads:

"Your committee's image should be positive and show power—not civil rights. The picture on the first page is bad news; all three individuals, non-Spanish-speaking, are minority advocates—not a positive Spanish-speaking picture in my opinion. Don't build others, just the President—*His record* with the Spanish-Speaking." (emphasis in original)

Another apparent attempt to use "Hoy" for political purposes concerned Mayor John V. Lindsay of New York, who in 1971, switched to the Democratic Party and then unsuccessfully ran for President. Attaching a May 14, 1972, newspaper article describing Lindsay's cut of funds from a bilingual education program, Armendariz, on June 7, 1972 wrote Ramirez, "How about taking a slap at Lindsay?" (Ex. 18) In response to a staff inquiry concerning this request, Ramirez stated that he complied with Armendariz' requests when he wanted to comply. He said he may have issued a release on his own initiative criticizing Lindsay as he similary issued releases criticizing other officials and agencies.

D. Other Efforts by the Spanish-Speaking Task Force to Promote the President's Re-election. (1) LaRaza Unida Matter. A significant matter uncovered by the Select Committee was an apparent effort to pay LaRaza Unida, a Texas-based Mexican-American political party, to take a neutral stand in the 1972 Presidential campaign rather than endorse the candidacy of Senator McGovern, as was anticipated. The first surfacing of this scheme appears in a pair of memoranda on CRP stationery addressed to the Attorney General, John N. Mitchell, one dated December 16, 1971, designated "Confi-

* Armendariz' Spanish-speaking campaign plan (Ex. 14, p. 11) indicates that the "CCSS newsletter" would be used in the campaign to publicize the President's record and concern for the Spanish-speaking. Ramirez, however, stated that the editor of "Hoy" worked on the McGovern campaign.

dential" and entitled "Interest Group Reports" (Ex. No. 262-
3, 13 Hearings 5533), and a similar memorandum dated
January 4, 1972, from Magruder to Mitchell (Ex. 16). These
documents concerned various interest-group reports compiled
by Bart Porter and the staff of Charles Colson. The December
16 document notes that the Porter/Colson Spanish-speaking
report "advocates consideration of undercover funding of La
Raza Unida, a splinter party, in exchange for an agreement
that LaRaza Unida runs presidential candidates in California and Texas." And the January 4 document states:

> "Perhaps the most interesting suggestion the report
> makes is that consideration be given to undercover fund-
> ing of LaRaza Unida; a left-wing Chicano political party
> in the Southwest, in exchange for agreement that LaRaza
> Unida run 1972 Presidential candidates in California
> and Texas. LaRaza Unida has done very well in several
> state and local elections in California, New Mexico,
> and Texas."

Subsequent memoranda reflect serious consideration of
activity of this type. A June 26, 1972, CRP document from
Armendariz to Malek reads:

> "Met with Jose Angel Gutierrez, LaRaza
> Unida Leader from Texas, for a 'get-acquainted' ses-
> sion; discussed LaRaza Unida's plans and the effect La
> Raza Unida Party is having on the President's campaign.
> Will continue negotiations with Gutierrez." (Ex. No. 13)

A September 8, 1972, CRP memo from Armendariz to
Malek, the subject of which is "The Raza Unida Party National Convention," states:

> "The issue of an $8,000 contribution from Muniz'
> campaign from the Republican party was brought up in
> a meeting off the convention floor. A promise was made
> to publically condemn McGovern if such a donation were
> made." (Ex. No. 262-50, 13 Hearings 5677)

Malek responded to this suggestion by writing on the top margin of the September 8 memorandum:

> "Do you think we should do this? I am doubtful—
> how could GOP contribute to a rival candidate? In ad-
> dition, it seems too cheap—Raza Unida's principles
> should be worth more than that—Fred." (Id. at 5677.)

However, the matter apparently did not die there. Less

than one week later, on September 14, 1972, Armendariz sent a "Confidential" memorandum to Colson (copy to Marumoto) which related:

"In a private meeting several weeks ago, Gutierrez approached this office for a quiet Republican contribution to La Raza Unida. A promise was made to publicly condemn McGovern if such a donation were made. This possibility is still under consideration on the grounds that an effort to maintain the neutrality of La Raza Unida is to our advantage.

"The contribution would be used for the campaign of Ramsey Muniz, Raza Unida Candidate for Governor of Texas, who won a strong endorsement from the convention. The highest-ranking Raza Unida Candidate, Muniz is an attorney and distinguished high school and college football player. He has a clean image, a professional appeal with no record of militancy and apparently has the enthusiastic support of the party.

"The dangers of such a move arouse question as to whether the end will justify the means. Such a contribution would be certain to annoy Texas Republicans as well as Connally Democrats supporting the President. Furthermore, Raza Unida may have no alternate recourse anyway, which would give us no reason for sticking our necks out. In any event, it is obvious that any contribution should not come from the Committee for the Re-election of the President, but from an independent third source." (Ex. No. 262-51, 13 Hearings 5679-5680.)

On October 30, 1972, in regard to his dealings with LaRaza Unida, Armendariz wrote Marumoto, "please be assured that so far everything went as expected." (13 Hearings 5678) Armendariz noted that LaRaza considered both parties "untrustworthy." He commented that their aim was not an endorsement of the President by LaRaza which was "unrealistic, unnecessary and unwise to expect"—but "to disassociate it from the Democratic party for which its members have voted unanimously for decades. . . . The purpose of disassociation is to elicit criticism of McGovern." A copy of this memorandum went to Malek (Ex. No. 262-50, 13 Hearings 5677-78).

Meanwhile, the Spanish-speaking team was apparently attempting to secure the neutrality of LaRaza Unida by utilizing the grant process. Involved was a $391,206 OEO grant to the Zavala County Health Association which Texas Governor

Preston Smith had vetoed on July 27, 1972. An Oct. 9, 1972, CRP memorandum (Malek Ex. 22) from Armendariz to Malek states that "it is important for political reasons" that the Administration override the veto. As Armendariz explained:

"Should the poll gap tighten in Texas, the neutrality of La Raza Unida will be important. Our studies indicate that there is 70 percent approval of Raza Unida among Mexican Americans in Texas. The fact that there are about 1 million political Mexican American voters in Texas and that Humphrey won that state in 1968 by only 38,000 votes, substantiate the possible importance of La Raza Unida neutrality in this election.
We have no way of publicly supporting this group without antagonizing Republicans and making La Raza Unida look as though they had sold out. At the same time, neither do we want to antagonize Raza Unida supporters and drive them back to their old positions as Democrat voters. The Zavala County grant provides us with an opportunity to support the party indirectly in a positive and legitimate manner. Such an action is likely to strengthen their position of neutrality which is so politically beneficial to us."

On November 2, 1972, Armendariz wrote a "Confidential" memorandum to White House aide Ken Cole, again stressing the importance of keeping LaRaza Unida neutral through election day, and explaining that LaRaza Unida would become "more conciliatory" if certain specified programs—in addition to the Zavala County grant—"could be sprung loose within the next few days." (Ex. No. 262-62, 13 Hearings 5697.)

In his November 14, 1972, campaign report, (Ex. 19), Armendariz, indicating satisfaction with the role played by LaRaza Unida, stated:

"As the Raza Unida convention endorsed no candidate for President, it was clearly to the advantage of the GOP to attempt to maintain the neutrality of this group. A Zavala County health grant became a controversial issue despite the fact that this Administration overrode the veto of Governor Smith. To placate irate Raza Unida leaders, overtures were made to assist them by expressing interest in grants of interest to them."

When questioned in executive session concerning his role in this episode, Armendariz claimed that at no time did he

369

approve payment of $8,000 to LaRaza Unida in exchange for their neutrality and that his memoranda should not be construed in this manner. He portrayed his role as only a conduit for information. Armendariz said he had no knowledge that any campaign contribution to LaRaza Unida was actually made.

(2) Reies Lopez Tijerina Matter. On August 29, 1972, Henry Ramirez sent a memorandum to Armendariz on Cabinet Committee stationery attaching a letter to Ramirez from Reies Lopez Tijerina, who was then on parole following his conviction for assaulting government officials during a demonstration in New Mexico. Ramirez' memorandum stated:

"Please see attached letter with specific reference to the third paragraph. Mr. Tijerina indicated that he would work for us in return for due considerations.
"I await your recommendations, if you want me to move on this matter." (Armendariz Ex. No. 24, p. 137.)

The Tijerina letter (dated August 14, 1972) reads in part:

"I'm very glad that I got to know you. I also want it very clear that I am very thankful for what you mentioned to me in your office concerning my probation, parole and the possibility of a full executive pardon. As I said it before while I was in your office, I want to repeat in writing most of the Spanish-Speaking people in the United States, would feel grateful if an executive pardon would be granted.
"In the meantime I want to offer my service or contribution, without reservation, to your service, all the Spanish-Speaking people and to harmony between our people and all others in the United States. Please do not hesitate to call me anytime for any service." (Armendariz, Ex. No. 24, p. 137.)

On the bottom of Ramirez' memorandum, Armendariz made the following handwritten notation: "HR talk to Lujan call 9-6-72." Armendariz testified that he took no action concerning the proposal but told Ramirez to call Congressman Manuel Lujan, Jr. concerning the problem (Armendariz, p. 140). Ramirez stated in a staff interview that he believed the Tijerina case should have been reviewed and that he sent the memorandum to Armendariz because he was a good "contact man" who could bring the problem to the attention of the right people. Ramirez claims his help was not conditioned upon campaign support. Armendariz and Ramirez stated that the Tijerina matter was not pursued further. Congressman Lujan was contacted by Committee staff. He said he could not recall discussing Tijerina with Armendariz or Ramirez.

(3) Alfred Hernandez Matter. Alfred Hernandez was head of the Spanish-speaking Democrats for Nixon effort. Evidence developed by the Select Committee suggests that while negotiations were under way to gain his support for the re-election effort, there were also discussions with him as to his interest in a federal position, particularly a federal judgeship. While all participants deny a *quid pro quo* arrangement, various memoranda and documents reflect the relationship between support and appointment.

A May 26, 1972 "Administrative-Confidential" White House memorandum from Marumoto to Colson and Malek (Ex. No. 262-19, 13 Hearings 5583-87) reads:

"Conde traveled to Houston with Armendariz to meet with an influential Mexican-American democrat who is thinking of supporting the President in November. Alex is to continue the discussions with him and work out the scenario if he comes aboard." (Ex. No. 262-19, 13 Hearings 5586.)

On June 8, 1972, Armendariz wrote a memorandum (recipient not indicated) regarding Hernandez. After describing Hernandez' Democratic credentials, the memorandum continued:

"Impressed with the President's record in assisting Spanish-speaking and disenchanted with a lack of recognition from Democrats, Mr. Hernandez is considering taking action in public support of the President. . . . Mr. Hernandez has hopes that this move will bring him better recognition than he has received from Democrats." (Ex. No. 262-44, 13 Hearings 5665)

The following day, June 9, Armendariz, Conde and Marumoto met with Hernandez regarding his potential support of the President. Then, on June 12, Marumoto wrote Hernandez a letter:

"It was good to have seen you again and particularly to hear of your interest in supporting the re-election of the President.
"I want to emphasize that if you implement your plans

371

as we discussed, the President will adequately recognize you." (Ex. No. 262-44, 13 Hearings 5664)

Finally, a memorandum dated August 18, 1972, from Marumoto to John Clarke reads:

"If any vacancies come up for the federal bench in Texas, 1701 and our operation would like to see Judge Hernandez appointed.
"He is a Democrat who is presently heading the Spanish-speaking Democrats for the President and is a three-time past National President of LULAC, the largest Chicano service organization in the country.
"It would be a real coup if we could appoint him." (Ex. No. 262-44, 13 Hearings 5663)

The propriety of the handling of the Hernandez matter was pursued by Senator Talmadge in his questioning of Marumoto:

TALMADGE   Were you not aware of the provision of title 18, section 600, of the United States Code that makes it a crime to promise Federal employment or other benefits under consideration for political support for a candidate or political party?
MARUMOTO   Yes, sir.
T   Isn't that the indication of these documents that I have just shown you?
M   One moment, sir. I would like to reemphasize that there was no promise or no offer whatsoever `to Judge Hernandez about a Federal judgeship.
T   The letters speak for themselves. But I understood that you made a specific pledge that he would be appropriately recognized.
M   That is right.
T   And shortly thereafter, you recommended him for a Federal judgeship. (13 Hearings 5318)

In fact, Hernandez was not offered a federal judgeship after the election. He was, however, offered a Commissionship on the Consumer Safety Products Commission, which he declined.

(4) Ed Pena Matter. The evidence before the Committee indicates that certain Administration and campaign officials sought to discharge Ed Pena, Director of Compliance with the Equal Employment Opportunity Commission, for favoring Democratic candidates. On May 19, 1972, Marumoto

372

wrote an "Administrative-Confidential" memorandum to Colson and Malek (Ex. No. 262-17, 13 Hearings 5579-82) which reads:

"Working with Kingsley, Ramirez and Rodriguez re: the dismissal of Ed Pena, Director of Compliance at EEOC."*

Two weeks later, on June 2, 1972, in a similar memorandum, Marumoto wrote:

Continuing to work on the following vacancies:
Developing a case re Ed Pena, Director of Compliance at EEOC (GS-17) who has been violating the Hatch Act." (Ex. No. 262-21, 13 Hearings 5588-5592.)

Then, on August 25, 1972, Pena became the subject of an entire "Confidential" memorandum from CRP staffer David E. Florence to Armendariz, which dealt with Pena's activities at a convention of the supposedly non-partisan LULAC Supreme Council.** Pena was accused therein of "attempting to undermine our efforts." The memorandum continued:

"Later, Pete Villa commented to me that Ed Pena thought LULAC was getting too Republican and that he, Ed, wanted LULAC to invite Shriver to the October Supreme Council meeting in Washington.
"It is my belief that one of the reasons Pete Villa, and Roberto Ornelas follow Ed Pena around speak up for him is so that they will be in the "thick" with the McGovern Administration if McGovern is elected President. It is my belief that it would be wise to terminate Ed Pena from his position as a GS-18 at EEOC." (Ex. No. 262-47, 13 Hearings 5669)

When questioned at public hearings concerning Pena, Marumoto testified as follows:

MONTOYA   Tell me about Ed Pena, why were some people anxious to get him fired?
MARUMOTO   He was just vocally expressing anti-administration sentiments.

* LULAC stands for League of United Latin American Citizens. Pena is the individual who recommended that EEOC investigate the University of Texas, an action described as potentially "disastrous" in a White House memorandum. See Section V 3, A *infra*.
** Marumoto described LULAC as "the largest Mexican-American Association, called the Elite of the United Mexican-American Citizens." (13 *Hearings* 5293).

MON   Did the White House have a policy of doing that to every employee in the government who was against the President?

MAR   No, sir.

MON   Why did you pick on Mr. Pena?

MAR   I guess he was the most visible.

* * *

MON   Was there anything different from what Mr. Pena was doing than from what various persons were doing who were working in similar positions who may have been Republicans?

MAR   I don't think so. (13 Hearings 5294, 5303-5304.)

Mr. Pena, in fact, retained his position.

(5) Request for a Demonstration. The evidence presented to the Committee indicates that, in one instance, Marumoto asked an official of a federal grantee—NEDA—to supply people to stage a demonstration in support of the mining of Haiphong Harbor in front of the offices of the Los Angeles *Times*. Marumoto testified as follows:

DASH   Who was Mr. Alfred Villa-Lobos?

MARUMOTO   He was at that time the executive vice president of that organization [NEDA].

D   Did you ever ask him to stage a phony demonstration in front of the Los Angeles Times office?

M   Yes, sir. I don't know if I agree with the term "phony."

D   What term would you use?

M   I was asked, on that particular occasion by Mr. Colson, when the Los Angeles Times came out with an anti-administration editorial, I believe—I can't recall the particular subject, but we had asked if Mr. Villa-Lobos would organize a group to demonstrate in front of the Los Angeles Times.

D   Did you receive cooperation in that request?

M   I think after a couple of days, he called back and said he just could not do it. (13 Hearings 5280)

In a staff interview, Villa-Lobos indicated he did not think Marumoto's request proper and therefore decided not to honor it.

(6) Holding Back Census Data. In one instance, the campaign team unsuccessfully attempted to delay the release

374

of information by the Census Bureau which was considered detrimental to the re-election effort. An "Administrative-Confidential" White House memorandum from Marumoto to Colson and Malek, dated July 7, 1972, relates:

"Conde discussed with Census Bureau the upcoming social and economic report on the SS. The report will show that the SS are doing better by comparison than the Blacks and the question is whether the report should show the comparison. It will have a SS-Anglo comparison which [of] course will show the Whites in a dominant position. The representative also talked to Des Barker on this. Conde discussed this with Alex Armendariz of 1701 and the inclination is not to show SS-Black comparisons. Report is due out July 20 and Conde will look over the figures with the Census representative and determine if other than Census media dissemination is warranted." (Ex. No. 262-32, 13 Hearings 5626)

A July 12, 1972 CRP document from Armendariz to Marumoto entitled "Selected Characteristics of Persons and Families of Mexican, Puerto Rican, and other Spanish Origin: March, 1972" reads:

"We have reviewed Mr. Joseph R. Wright, Jr.'s memo to Mr. Desmond Barker on the subject matter and offer our views on the subject, hoping some action can be taken to stop publication for the reasons mentioned below.
". . . *Our position is that any statistical data which show the Spanish-Speaking community lagging behind other elements of the population will be construed as the fault of the incumbent government.*" (Ex. No. 262-34, 13 Hearings 5627) (emphasis in original.)

Two days later, Marumoto, in a July 14, 1972, White House "Administrative-Confidential" memorandum, wrote Colson and Malek that:

"Armendariz and I reviewed Census material on the SS that is to be released soon. Recommended some information be held back." (Ex. No. 262-35, 13 Hearings 5632.)

Marumoto, in public testimony, confirmed that an attempt was made to restrain publication of census data that might have an adverse political impact in the Spanish-speaking community. (13 *Hearings* 5324) However, in a Committee interview, Desmond Barker of the Census Bureau recalled no contact from White House or campaign officials concerning this data. He stated that the information concerned was not held back but released.

2. ACTIVITIES RESPECTING BLACK CONSTITUENTS

While activities of a Responsiveness nature in pursuit of Black votes appear not as numerous as those regarding the Spanish-speaking, documents obtained by the Select Committee indicate that there were nonetheless certain efforts in this area. Several examples follow.

A. James Farmer Matter. On April 18, 1972, Jones wrote a "Confidential" memorandum to Malek entitled "Meeting with James Farmer" (Malek Ex. 27) that stated, in full text:

"In the Brown-Jones meeting with James Farmer, the following points of interest were discussed:
1. Farmer's willingness to work in support of the President. (It was agreed he might better serve at this time by maintaining a 'non-partisan' posture.) Jim expects to build on the attitude coming out of Gary.
2. His speaking engagements (he is to send a list of his engagements). We will seek to arrange media interviews in connection with his key appearances.
3. Farmer's interest in funding for his think tank proposal. He's seeking $200,000 seed money from HEW. (This should be moved on but should allow for a final Brown-Jones check-off in order to re-inforce Farmer's involvement. Additionally, there is some need that the think tank initially focus on key issues of interest to Black voters." *

On April 28, Frank Herringer submitted to Malek a "Confidential" talking paper for use in briefing John Mitchell on the basic tenets of the Responsiveness Program. This document—which, as Malek at his executive session testified, (p. 77), fairly represented the briefing given Mitchell—contained the following statement:

"Paul Jones wants favorable action on an HEW grant for James Farmer that would enable Farmer to have time to speak in support of the re-election."

Mr. Farmer did receive a $150,000 HEW grant as the communications from that Department found at Ex. 20 indicate.

* Robert Brown, at the time of this meeting, was Special Assistant to the President; Paul Jones was a campaign official.

Jones, in his executive session before the Committee, denied that he had any "check-off" powers relating to the Farmer grant or any other governmental grant. (The question, of course, remains as to the propriety of this CRP official participating in governmental grant processes.) Although Jones admitted in executive session that certain officials—e.g., Brown—were attempting to influence federal funding processes for campaign reasons, he claimed that he was personally not involved in such activities. (Jones 127-31) Brown, on the other hand, claimed in executive session, that, while he did involve himself in the grant-making process, he never promoted a grant for re-election purposes. (See, e.g., Brown, 36-7, 49)* Malek testified that, in regard to the Farmer transaction, he believed he took no action to ensure that Farmer's application was approved and instructed no one to do so. He denied that any improper *quid pro quo* was involved in the Farmer grant. (Malek 169-173)

After Malek testified, the Committee obtained a May 2, 1972, memorandum (Ex. 20) from Malek to Bob Finch, former Secretary of HEW and White House aide, which is reprinted here in its entirety:

"Following our conversation I have had several meetings with Jim Farmer and have had him meet with Bob Brown and Paul Jones (the head of the campaign's Black Vote Division). The results of these meetings and follow-up actions *which I have instigated* are as follows:

1. Farmer has been given a grant from OE to fund his project here in Washington.

2. He will now be able to spend a major part of his time on the above project while also making time available to the re-election efforts.

3. He has agreed to do speaking on our behalf and also to talk to key black leaders in an effort to gain their loyalties.

I feel that Jim is in a position to make a major contribution to our effort and am confident that he will. At the same time we are going to try to maintain his in-

* Brown testified that:
. . . I did not call in people and say, Well, we are just going to help all Republicans this time, or are we going to help all people that's going to vote for Nixon next time. None of that was ever done, and there is nobody who can ever say that Bob Brown called him up and said we are going to give you a contract over here if you vote for the President down the road here, or if you come over here, we are going to do this. There was no quid pro quo kind of deals made, particularly in view of the fact that there were many people, I would say, that most of them who got the money as the record will clearly show, were working . . . Democrats.

volvement in a manner that is not overtly partisan and does not harm his credibility.

Many thanks for getting this started and for putting me onto it." (emphasis added)

Upon apprisal of this memorandum, Mr. Malek maintained his contention that there was no improper *quid pro quo* respecting this grant, but stated that the memorandum indicated that he or his staff "checked" on this matter before the award was finalized. Mr. Farmer, by both affidavit and letter (Ex. 20), also has denied that there was any *quid pro quo* involved in this grant, stating that "it was not payment for any services rendered to the campaign". He has, in fact, averred that "I did no campaigning whatever, in any shape, manner or form. That fact is a matter of the public record."

B. Charles Wallace Matter. On July 14, 1972, Jones, in the memorandum that is Ex. 21, reported to Malek under the heading "Major Accomplishments" that:

"Thru White House contacts initiated new efforts to assist Charles Wallace, President, Wallace & Wallace Fuel Oils, in overcoming present constraints to expand his business. This has, for the time being, allowed us to assist a staunch Nixon supporter."

Neither Mr. Jones nor Mr. Wallace was able to inform the Committee exactly what "constraints" were overcome by the "new efforts" that were initiated. Mr. Wallace, in an affidavit dated April 13, 1974, which has been submitted to the Committee (Ex. 21) states that on October 26, 1972, he received a SBA 8(a) contract for an estimated $2,146,-220.* Wallace, in this affidavit, claims there was no *quid pro quo* arrangement that promoted this contract and the Select Committee has received no substantial evidence of such an arrangement. However, the Committee notes that on September 12, 1972, Wallace sent approximately 2000 letters to minority SBA 8(a) contractors seeking their support for the President's re-election, as the documents collected at Ex. 21 demonstrate.

C. Additional Involvement of Campaign Officials in Governmental Processes. Other documents obtained by the Select Committee reveal election-motivated involvements by campaign officials in decision making processes respecting the

* A letter from Mr. Wallace's counsel is also found at Ex. 21.

expenditure of federal funds to aid Blacks. For example:

(1) In a January 17, 1972, "Weekly Report" (Ex. 22) Jones wrote Robert C. Odle, CRP Administrative Director, that:

"Data was collected in connection with setting up briefing books on (1) black communities throughout the Nation, (2) list of key contacts by states and (3) minority recipients of grants, loans and contracts. (A need is to develop coordination with agencies on future grants and contracts *to insure maximum benefits.*)" (Emphasis added)

This communication was passed on verbotem to Mr. Mitchell, then the Attorney General, in a "Confidential" January 19 memorandum by Mr. Odle.*

(2) In a "Confidential" "Weekly Report" dated March 24, 1972, to Malek from Jones (Ex. 23), the latter wrote:

"A meeting in the office John Evans resulted in agreement on strategy to effectively deal with OMBE."

(3) An April 4, 1972, "Weekly Activity Report" (Ex. 24) from Jones to Odle stated:

"We met during the week with members of the Washington Team in review of OMBE grants *to work out strategy for greater impact in connection with the campaign.* We also were in contact with local trade association representatives who offer possible funding alternatives—and developed a proposal in this regard." (emphasis added)

(4) Jones, in a "Weekly Activity Report" to Malek dated September 7, 1972 (Ex. 26), stated:

"Attended White House OMBE meeting to clarify status of minority-oriented proposals *that have been submitted by active supporters.*" (emphasis added)

(5) In another "Weekly Activity Report" dated February 22, 1972, (Ex. 27), Jones wrote Odle:

"We attended the national meeting of Opportunity Industrialization Centers (OIC—minority employment program). OIC is presently receiving approximately 80% of

---

* Mr. Odle does not recall this matter, or any of the items discussed in this section. He stated he was the designated recipient of various weekly reports, the substance of which he would send to Mr. Mitchell after the secretarial staff had put them in the proper format. He said he often would not read the reports he received.

379

its budget [from Administration programs] yet scheduled speakers who were critical of the President (Roy Wilkins, NAACP; Ralph Abernathy, SCLC; Vernon Jordan, National Urban League). We are pursuing, and are in definite need of, assuring [that] future grants, loans, contracts and appointments serve the Black community in a more positive manner than in the past. Examples of such funding coming back to haunt us is [sic] seen in the Model Cities, OMBE and OEO programs."

An almost identical paragraph is contained in a February 25, 1972, "Memorandum For The Attorney General Through: Jeb S. Magruder" from Robert Odle. In an earlier "Confidential" memorandum dated February 18, 1972, to Magruder (Ex. 28), Jones had recommended:

"That the Administration bring under closer scrutiny its program of grants and loans and specifically that Labor Department manpower personnel follow-up with OIC."

(6) In a January 10, 1972, "Weekly Report" (Ex. 29), Jones wrote Odle:

"In Chicago Jones conferred with the Reverend Jesse Jackson (formerly of S.C.L.C.'s Operation Breadbasket) of the recently formed organization PUSH. Jackson is now seeking financial support for the new group (which has an economic thrust) and is also anxious to meet with the President. His support and/or "neutrality" (lack of active support of another candidate) could go far in favorably swinging black votes to RN. He is considered a definite possibility and appears anxious to move. Some early decision, policy-wise, should be made regarding follow-up posture (and Jones suggests that it should include input from Bob Brown). At Jackson's invitation Jones attended a luncheon of leading black businessmen of Chicago. A number are ready to assist us and had praise, during a press conference, for the Administration's efforts and assistance for minority owned banks. Jones suggests an additional area that should be considered for federal deposits is with minority-owned Savings and Loan Associations!—and at an early date."

Rev. Jackson, however, has informed the Select Committee that he never sought or received federal funding for PUSH. For a time he was a supporter of Senator McGovern.

(7) On May 11, 1972, Jones sent a "Weekly Activity Report" to Malek that declared: (Ex. 30)

"Coordination and developing with Bob Brown's office a strategy for a 30 million dollar negotiation for the Dept. of Labor."

Neither Jones nor Brown were able to provide significant details to the Committee as to the subject matter of this negotiation (Jones 103-03; Brown 55)

D. Solicitation of Contributions from Black Recipients of Federal Monies. There is evidence that campaign contributions were sought from Blacks whose firms held government contracts, grants and loans. The most prominent example of this activity concerned the solicitations for a $100-a-plate campaign dinner for Blacks in Washington on June 10, 1972. (See Malek 144-5; Brown Ex. Sess. 66) Contributing to this dinner, for example, were Jack Crawford and Charles Wallace who have been previously identified in this Report as government contractors.

Another individual solicited was Sam Harris, who is president of the Trade Association of Minority Management Consulting Firms and also president of Sam Harris and Associates, a Washington-headquartered firm with government contracts. Harris, in a Committee interview, indicated that, in regard to solicitation for this dinner and other approaches in 1972 for campaign contributions by Paul Jones and others, he was made to feel that his continued success in obtaining government contracts would, in significant degree, be dependent on his contributing to the President's re-election. Harris testified that he did make several contributions to the President's campaign. He said he was also asked, in regard to the June 10th dinner, to assist in arranging the attendance of other Black government contractors.

One incident related by Harris is particularly relevant. Harris states that the day before the election he was called by Norris Sydnor, an assistant to Brown at the White House, and told that his company was on an HEW list for a quarter million dollar HEW contract, a circumstance that surprised Harris since he had never submitted a proposal to HEW. Harris said Sydnor then asked for a $1,000 contribution to the campaign, which Harris subsequently made after Sydnor observed that the HEW award would more than cover the amount of the contribution. Several months later, having heard nothing from HEW, Harris asked Sydnor about the contract, but did not receive a satisfactory response. The contract never materialized.

Sydnor, in a staff interview, denied calling Harris the day before the election to inform him he was under consideration for HEW funding. He also denied soliciting Harris for $1,000 on that day, although he admitted requesting contributions from numerous people—perhaps including Harris—at various times.

3. THE RESPONSIVENESS PROGRAM PROGRESS REPORT

Mention has been previously made of the June 7, 1972 "Confidential Eyes Only" progress report on the Responsiveness Program from Malek to Haldeman. (Malek Ex. 16) While this report, in an attachment apparently written by Robert Davison,* details twelve separate "results" of the Responsiveness Program for the week ending June 2, 1972, the present discussion is limited to several of these specifics.

A. EEOC-University of Texas Matter. Two paragraphs of the report deal with an EEOC investigation concerning the University of Texas; the first was prepared by Rob Davison, the second is Malek's summary of Davison's account:

> "Senator Tower was informed by Vice Chairman Holcomb that Ed Pena, Director of Compliance, had recommended to Bill Brown that EEOC sue The University of Texas. Brown appeared to agree. If such a suit took place, the result would be a serious negative impact in a key state. Brown denies that the suit is under consideration. This should be followed carefully.

> * * *

> "We garnered from reliable sources in the Equal Employment Opportunity Commission that the Commission was preparing to sue the University of Texas for discrimination in the hiring of faculty. This could be disastrous in Texas. When queried, Bill Brown, Chairman of EEOC, agreed not to pursue it. I will continue to follow this situation closely."

Chairman Brown of the EEOC has submitted an affidavit to the Select Committee (Malek Ex. 18) denying the specifics of these paragraphs and presenting his account of the events that transpired concerning this matter. His statement

---

* Davison, in a staff interview, admitted that the projects described in this attachment were his. See also Malek, 85. The Committee has learned that at least one other progress report was forwarded to Mr. Haldeman by Daniel Kingsley, who assumed administrative responsibility for the Responsiveness Program when Mr. Malek move to CRP in July, 1972. In fact, Mr. Kingsley, in a Committee interview, indicated that several other progress reports were prepared. The Committee has not obtained these documents and it appears that all copies were destroyed. See Section VII *infra*.

is that the only contact with him in this regard was from someone seeking information. He states that he was not pressured by anyone to forego an EEOC proceeding.

Malek has testified that the statements in this memorandum constitute "puffing" on his part and that he did not personally keep abreast of this matter as claimed. (Malek 99, 101.) In any event, several observations should be made. A contact of some nature was made with the EEOC. (It should be recalled that affecting "legal or regulatory actions" for re-election purposes was one of the goals of the Responsiveness Program set forth in the March 17, 1972, Malek to Haldeman memorandum.) (Malek Ex. 4) Malek claimed to Haldeman that his forces had squelched this proceeding. Both Malek and Haldeman testified that Haldeman did not express disapproval of this action or instruct Malek to cease endeavoring to influence proceedings before regulatory agencies. (Malek 57; Haldeman 16-17) *

B. Dock and Wharf Builders Investigation. The progress report contains another apparent claim of interference with a regulatory proceeding, this time in the Labor Department. First Davison's statement of the matter in the back-up document, then Malek's:

> *"Local 454, Dock and Wharf Builders, Philadelphia, Pennsylvania, requested 5/10/72.* Herman Bloom, Spector's assistant at the Pa. CRP requested that the subpoenaed records of Local 454 be returned. The Business Agent of the Union is a Republican supporter and could be very helpful to the Administration in impacting the blue collar vote in a key county. The books were returned on 5/23/72 and the Union given a clean bill of health."

* * *

> "The Department of Labor ruled that Local 454 of the Dock and Wharf Builders Union in Philadelphia, whose steward is an active backer of this Administration, was not responsible for the illegal actions of its President. This action was requested by the Pennsylvania Committee for the Re-Election of the President, and they report that this action had a very strong impact on the local ethnic union members."

The request for action in this regard came to Malek from Al

---

* There is no evidence that Haldeman expressly stated his approval of Malek's claimed actions in this regard. Haldeman does not recall discussing this progress report with the President. (Haldeman, 18)

Kaupinen, a CRP staffer, in a memorandum attached. (Malek Ex. 17)

While Mr. Davison did make contacts with Labor on this matter, the Select Committee has not established that his contacts actually produced the result claimed, at least by implication, in the progress report. But the evidence does suggest that an attempt to influence the Labor proceeding was made. Further, there is testimony that Haldeman. when this "result" was reported to him, did not criticize Malek for his actions nor order him to refrain from operations of this nature. (Malek 94-98, 107; Haldeman 17-18)

C. Fannie Mae Inquiry. On March 29, 1972, Harry Flemming of CRP sent Malek the following "Confidential" memorandum:

"Our Pennsylvania Committee for the Re-Election of the President has brought to our attention that Michael Stack, a Democrat Ward Leader, last year earned $58,000 in mortgage foreclosure from Fannie May. Mr. Stack happens to be the ward leader in the same ward as William Austin Meehan, who is the Republican leader in Philadelphia. Meehan can't understand why the type of work that Stack is doing has to be given to a Democrat ward leader who is working against our interests. Perhaps a qualified Republican could be found who could handle Fannie May business in that particular area. Any help your office can give rectifying this situation would be helpful."

The progress report to Haldeman supplies certain details of the response to this request.

"William Meehan, Philadelphia, Pennsylvania; requested 3/29/72. William Meehan, Republican ward leader in Philadelphia, has requested that his Democratic counter, Michael Stack, be prohibited from receiving the substantial compensation he earns as a fee attorney for Fannie May. The impact of such action would not be of great benefit to the re-election. It is not possible for us to significantly change Mr. Stack's earnings as he is a close friend of Congressman Barrett, a member of the key HUD committee that appropriates funds for Fannie May."

Further information respecting contacts by Rob Davison on this matter is found in the affidavit of former HUD official Richard Goldstein. (Malek Ex. 21; Malek 110)

4. GSA MATTERS

A. Campaign Involvement in GSA Contract Awards. Evidence received by the Select Committee indicates that campaign officials were participating in the selection process for the awards of GSA architectural and engineering design contracts. The following passage is from an affidavit (Malek Ex. 21) obtained by the Select Committee from John E. Clarke, a former White House staffer who, as his affidavit confirms, had certain responsibilities relating to the Responsiveness Program.

> "The Responsiveness Program generated activity with architectural engineering contract awards by GSA. When contract awards were to be made, which are non-bid awards, the Architectural Engineering Contract Award Board would select 3 to 5 firms who were technically qualified to fulfill the contract and these firms were recommended to GSA. I would then be contacted by Larry Roush of the GSA and Roush would give me the names of firms who were being considered for an award. I would call Lee Nunn at the Finance Committee to Re-elect the President (FCRP) and ask Nunn if the Committee had any preference as to which of the firms should receive the award. It is my understanding that Nunn would then check with various sources on the Hill as well as other political sources who might be affected by the contracts to be awarded and ascertain whether or not there was any preference as to the award. In a day or two, Nunn would call me and state that there was no preference, if there was none, or indicate which firm was preferred if they had a preference. I would relay the message to Roush at GSA."

Mr. Clarke told the Committee that there were 8 to 10 instances in which this procedure was followed. He also expressed his view that the Responsiveness concept respecting GSA worked well. Mr. Roush, in an affidavit submitted to the Committee (Malek, Ex. 20), admitted that "Mr. Clarke's recommendations were accorded considerable weight."* He could not recall during a Committee interview a specific situation where Mr. Clarke's recommendation was rejected. Mr. Roush gave the Committee a list of nine contracts where Mr. Clarke had an input. Mr. Nunn, however, could not recall any specific instance where the names of potential GSA contractors were submitted to him for comment, even

---

* In a Committee interview he used the term "great weight."

though he conceded this very well could have happened. Mr. Clarke stated that a second progress report to Haldeman (which the Select Committee has not obtained) contained information as to his activities respecting GSA contracts.

B. Solicitation Of Political Contributions. The following finding of facts is from the Civil Service Commission's opinion in *In The Matter of Lewis E. Spangler, Etc.,* CSC No. F-1783-72, etc., March 29, 1972, (Ex. 28) in which six GSA employees were found to have taken an active part in political management in violation of §4.1 of Civil Service Rule IV and 5 U.S.C. § 7324 (a) (2):

> The record shows that during a meeting in his office on November 4, 1971, Lewis E. Spangler, Acting Commissioner of the Federal Supply Service, General Services Administration (GSA), advised George W. Dodson, Assistant Commissioner, Office of Automated Data Management Services, Federal Supply Service, GSA, that a "Salute to the President Dinner" was scheduled for November 9, 1971, that tickets were available, and that he (Mr. Dodson) and his subordinate employees could purchase, or contribute toward the purchase, of the tickets. Mr. Dodson relayed this information to his division chiefs at a meeting held in a conference room adjacent to his office on the same or the following day. Respondents Elliot Gold, Reuben T. Morgan, Joseph A. Weisgerber, and Stephen White were present at this meeting. Mr. Dodson informed them that they had a "management objective" to meet, namely, the purchase of one and one-half tickets for a total of $750; that employees who contributed toward the purchase of a ticket would have their names placed in a hat and the person whose name was drawn would attend the dinner. Thereafter, Mr. Gold solicited and received contributions by check from four employees totaling $225. Three checks were for $25 and a fourth for $150; Mr. Morgan solicited and received one $25 contribution by check; Mr. Weisgerber solicited and received two $25 contributions by check; and Mr. White solicited and received a check for $25. The checks received by Gold were turned over to Dodson at the latter's office; Weisgerber delivered his checks to Dodson at a local restaurant.
>
> The record does not show what disposition Dodson, Morgan and White made of the checks received by them. However, the "no contest" plea in each case under the Stipulation and Waiver of Hearing is taken as an im-

386

plied admission of the truth of the allegations contained in the Letters of Charges. *Wigmore on Evidence*, sec. 1066. It is found, therefore, that the "Salute Dinner" was a Republican Party political fund-raising affair, and that the proceeds of the sale of tickets to the "Salute Dinner," as shown above, were channeled by the Respondents to the Republican Party pursuant to a plan communicated by Lewis E. Spangler to George W. Dodson, Jr., on November 4, 1971.

The six individuals involved were given suspensions without pay ranging from 30 to 60 days.*

5. ACTIVITIES REGARDING THE STAFFING OF FEDERAL POSITIONS

As remarked, one objective of the Responsiveness Program was to ensure that personnel placements with the government were made to benefit the President's re-election campaign. In fact, the White House Personnel Office (WHPO) under Malek and Dan Kingsley had been engaged in a program to ensure that political considerations were taken into account in government staffing long before the 1972 election campaign began.** The evidence suggests that WHPO personnel intended that political considerations be taken into account not only in regard to placement on part-time boards and commissions and the employment of other non-career personnel, but also concerning the staffing of positions in the competitive service—that is, executive branch positions governed by Civil Service laws and regulations. In fact, as subsequently discussed, Mr. Malek's testimony in executive session indicates that the Departments and Agencies were asked by the WHPO to give special consideration to politically important prospects even in regard to career positions. (Malek 67-9)† The political use of government positions in regard to the Spanish-speaking community has been treated previously, but it is useful here to note other aspects of the government staffing process.

* See section V.7.A. *infra* regarding similar alleged conduct in the Veterans Administration.
** Mr. Kingsley has stated that the operations of the WHPO were never part of the Responsiveness Program, but remained an entirely independent process. But the relevant documents, such as the March 17, 1972, Malek to Haldeman memorandum (Malek Ex. 4) that sets out the basic Responsiveness plan, indicate that WHPO personnel actions were part of that program.
† Mr. Ehrlichman testified in Executive Session that there was a general "itch, on our part, to get friends in the Departments rather than the people we found there," an "itch," he said, that extended to competitive service positions. (Ehrlichman 88)

A. Part-time Boards and Commissions. A March 1, 1971,
memorandum from White House staffer John Freeman to
Dan Kingsley (copy to Malek) discusses "Staffing Strategy
for Part-Time Boards and Commissions." (Ex. 32) While this
memorandum complains about the absence of staffing programs "for strengthening and broadening support for the
'72 elections", it does note that:

> "Al Kaupinen did establish a procedure for securing the
> appointment of major financial contributors. This has
> been successful and should be continued."

The memorandum contains recommendations to meet 1972
campaign needs. One proposal was to ensure that a large
percentage of appointments were made from states crucial
to the President's re-election. The recommendations also contained the following entry:

> "III. Financial contributor—list compiled by WHPO
> with inputs from RNC, senior WH staff, Stans, etc.;
> would be placed primarily on Presidential Boards or
> given appropriate patronage rating and referred to De-
> partments."*

Also of interest is an August 31, 1972, memorandum from
Clayton Yeutter of CRP to Frank Herringer that states:

> ". . . [O]ne of the names I submitted to you several
> weeks ago for a possible appointment to a committee
> of some kind was a man named Wenk from South Da-
> kota. Obie O'Brien, our Nixon chairman, says that he
> believes we will get a very large contribution from him
> if an appointment comes through. Can you check on
> this for me? Or should I just call Kingsley?" (See Ex.
> 33)

On September 6, 1972, Herringer wrote Dan Kingsley that:

> "Clayton Yeutter and the Nixon Chairman from South
> Dakota believe that Mr. Wenk (resume attached) will
> be a big help to us if we can appoint him to an advisory
> board or commission.
> "I assume that a departmental in Agriculture would be
> the only alternative. Of course, time is of the essence
> —the quicker we can get a commitment, the better.
> Please let me know the prospects. I would rate this as

---

* John Clarke, who also worked in the WHPO, has confirmed that frequent
attempts were made to place financial contributors on regulatory boards and
commissions.

a MUST." (See Ex. 33) *

B Non-Career Personnel Generally. On February 17, 1971, Horton transmitted a memorandum to Malek and Kingsley to which was attached a document entitled "Talking Points On Changes In Management Of Non-Career Personnel." (Ex. 34) This memorandum, here quoted in full text, appears to indicate White House views as to how non-career appointments by the Departments should be made:

> "Because this paper will be left with the Departments, we deleted direct references to making patronage placements. However, the concept of setting Departmental patronage targets and the responsibilities for follow-through should be made clear verbally. The following points should be made clear to the Department and Agency Heads:
> 1. Informal targets will be established on how many full-time and part-time placements each Department can reasonably absorb.
> 2. Following these guidelines and reflecting the skills of the individuals, the WHPO would assign selected politically important candidates to appropriate Departments for placement.
> 3. It would be the Department's responsibility to match the individual to an appropriate job and report the results back to the WHPO."

Both Kingsley and Stanton Anderson, a former WHPO staffer, stated that this passage accurately stated that office's concept as to how non-career staffing should be handled.**

C. Competitive Service Positions. The evidence accumulated by the Select Committee suggests that the WHPO was referring applicants for competitive service positions to the Departments and Agencies with the urging that political considerations be taken into account in the employment determination. Several documents discovered by the Select Com-

---

* Mr. Wenk stated he was not offered a federal appointment and did not make a significant contribution to the President's reelection. O'Brien stated he never mentioned the possibility of a contribution to Yeutter. Yeutter, however, said he only passed on the information O'Brien gave him.
** The Civil Service laws and regulations relating to competitive service positions do not apply to appointments to Presidential boards and commissions and other non-career assignments. However, appointments to such non-competitive positions for political reasons at the least must still be judged in light of hat provision of the Hatch Act that makes it unlawful for an employer of an executive agency to "use his official authority or influence for the purpose of interfering with or affecting the result of an election." See 5 U.S.C. §732 (a) and Section VIII *infra*.

mittee are particularly informative in this regard. The first is a form used by certain senior Administration officials to instruct the WHPO concerning the political value to the President of a particular placement. Malek Ex. 10 is an August 30, 1971, memorandum using this form from Clark MacGregor (at that time head of White House Congressional relations) to Dan Kingsley concerning a particular applicant. This form contained the following entry to be completed by the sender:

IV. Value of Placement to the President Politically
☐ Highest Political Value (Must place)
☐ High Political Value (Place if possible)
☐ Moderate Political Value (Handle courteously)
☐ Little Political Value (Handle routinely)

Upon receipt of an important request for placement, the WHPO would make a staffing recommendation to a particular Department or Agency that included a grading respecting the political value of placing the individual in question. The WHPO operated in part through special referral units established in the Departments and Agencies. The Civil Service Commission, at this writing, is pursuing disciplinary action against a number of HUD and GSA officials who were connected or worked with the special referrals units in those institutions. The CSC claims that these persons, on requests from the White House and others, took political considerations into account in the staffing of competitive service positions.

An example of a WHPO request to the Departments and Agencies is Malek Ex. 12, a November 9, 1971, memorandum from Stanton Anderson of WHPO to Mack Warren of GSA re a Leslie Cohen, which reads:

"Attached is the resume of Leslie Cohen. Mr. Cohen comes highly recommended to this office and consequently is rated a 1 or Must Placement. We would appreciate your investigating the possibilities for him in your department in California. We would also appreciate it if you would keep my office closely informed of your progress on his behalf."

Records received by the Select Committee indicate that Mr. Cohen was treated as a "must" case and offered a position by GSA but declined to accept.

Mr. Anderson, in an affidavit submitted to the Select Committee dated June 4, 1974, (Ex. 35), has denied he asked the GSA to consider political factors in determining whether

Mr. Cohen would be offered a career position. His affidavit continues:

"More generally, all referrals that were sent from me to the departments and agencies under the standard White House rating and referral system were for non-career Schedule C job. This was always my intent and my expectation. In some instances, of course, these White House referrals were qualified for career employment and their applications were processed in accordance with normal career procedures if the candidate was interested in a career appointment and he completed the necessary Civil Service employment forms. At no time, however, did I ever ask a department or agency to violate the law or Civil Service regulations to place a person in a career position."

It should be noted, however, that the Cohen referral quoted above does not specify that it was for a non-career job. Moreover, a May 7, 1971, memorandum to Jack Lemay at GSA from Anderson (Ex. 36) calls into question certain assertions in his affidavit. This document reads:

"Enclosed is the resume for Mr. George M. Shirey, Jr. He is looking for a GS-13 or 14, PIO type position. He will be qualified with the Civil Service *so he can fill either a career or non-career slot. He is a Must.* Please consider his qualifications and get back to me with the possibilities as soon as possible. Thank you." (emphasis added)*

When read this document, Mr. Anderson contended that Mr. Shirey was a "Must" only for a non-career slot and reiterated that he had no intention to pressure any Department or Agency to violate Civil Service standards.

Mr. Kingsley has stated to the Committee that must or high priority referrals were not in reference only to non-career jobs. He said it was left to the agency involved to determine where a recommended individual would be placed.** Malek's testimony appears to comport with Kings-

* Exhibit 36 also contains a follow-up document by Lemay to other GSA officials stating that Mr. Shirey was a "must" and that the recipients should get back to him on this matter "as soon as possible." Another "must" referral by Anderson and a "high priority" referral by Rob Davison are included, with related papers, in Exhibit 36. The Davison referral appears clearly to relate to a career position. Exhibit 36 is a No. "3" or courtesy referral by Anderson to CSC of an individual for a specific job that, according to CSC is a career position.

** Kingsley, however, denied any intent to pressure the agencies to violate Civil Service laws and regulations.

ley's statement in this regard and provides other evidence respecting what was expected from the Departments and Agencies:

HAMILTON . . . Is it true . . . that you were instructing the agencies and departments when you referred names to them whether or not the placement was a "must" political placement, or a "high priority" political placement—

MALEK During my tenure in that particular position, we did. use the term "must place" occasionally. Rather than taking that literally, it meant that it was the highest priority and that we would want the agency to search very hard for an appropriate position. (pp. 67-8)

* * *

H But the basic question is, whether or not your staff was asking the agencies and departments to take into consideration political considerations in hiring, and I take it the answer to that is yes. Is that correct?

M Now I think we have to differentiate here. There are two different ways to approach this. One would be to say that for this particular career position we want you to hire this person because of his political —the political advantages, regardless of who else is qualified. That, we were not doing.

What we were doing in the case of a career position is we would be submitting the name of a person to a department and asking them to determine where this person would be qualified to serve. And, then once determining that, that they were qualified and competitive, to serve in that position, to try to get them into it.

So, what we were really doing is facilitating the personnel process in getting somebody in that door, where without the political push, they may not have been getting into the door. But we were not interfering with the competitive process of filling a particular position. (p. 69)

* * *

H Are you saying that, before the campaign, these Referral Units [at HUD and GSA] were not handling career personnel? Competitive service personnel?

M No, I am not saying that. What I am saying is that these Referral Units existed throughout much of the Administration and they had two purposes.

One was to do the screening and assist in the recruiting and evaluation and placement of people into non-

career positions. And, secondly, to take all of the patronage requests that were sent to them directly by the
Congress or through us to them and funnel them to the
appropriate place in the department for consideration.
So that if we would forward to them, or if a Congressman would forward to them, a particular recommendation, they would then either evaluate that person for a
non-career position, or if it was determined that there
were no non-career positions and that a career position
was desired, and it was important to place the person,
they would then circulate that person through the department so that he could be evaluated for various
career positions.

And, if he qualified, and was competitive, for one of
them, brought on board. I think that is a distinction.

H   Was it your understanding that the Referral Units
in the various agencies were to give special consideration
to names sent over by the White House that were designated "must"?

M   Yes. Yes, they were to give special consideration.
Absolutely. But the special consideration was not in
competition for a specific job, but to ensure that the
person was exposed to a range of jobs for which he or
she was qualified.* (pp. 71-2)

6. ACTIVITIES REGARDING THE ELDERLY

A. Use of Federal Resources. The evidence the Committee
has gathered indicates that federal resources were employed
to secure the support of Older Americans. Exhibit 38 is a
November 9, 1972, memorandum from Webster (Dan) Todd,
director of the CRP Older Americans Voter Bloc group, to
then Campaign Director Clark MacGregor. This document,
which is a final report on campaign activities respecting the
elderly, states, under the heading "Strong Points":

I doubt if there has ever before been such a massive
effort by a political organization to involve itself di-

* The Committee has received evidence from Stephen C. Royer, a former
ACTION Staff Recruitment Officer during 1971-72, indicating that the
ACTION personnel office, under the direction of Mr. Alan M. May and
at the urging of White House officials, was taking political contributions
into account in the staffing of competitive service positions. Mr. May has
stated to the Select Committee that it was not his intent or purpose to politicize the procedure for filling competitive service positions. Mr. May, however, is the author of a draft "Federal Political Personnel Manual" (Ex. 37)
dated 1972 and found in Mr. Malek's CRP files that discusses methods by
which non-supportive career civil servants could be removed from competitive service positions so that those positions could be filled by persons loyal
to the President to his political benefit.

rectly in the daily lives of so many. This effort, of course, can only be accomplished in an encumbent [sic] situation and the available resources of the Administration through Arthur Flemming, Elliot Richardson and the Domestic Affairs Council were maximized . . .

Elsewhere in the same memorandum, Todd refers to "an extensive and coordinated use of USG resources."

(1) Government Brochures. Todd, in a staff interview, stated that several Departments and Agencies prepared, for campaign use and at government expense, brochures reflecting their services for the elderly. Todd stated that the requests for these brochures originated with him, but were funneled through the Domestic Council.* Todd was unaware whether the Departments and Agencies involved had perceived that the requests actually came from CRP.

Various documents obtained by the Select Committee also indicate that government brochures were prepared for political purposes. Evans Exhibit 6 is an April 14, 1972, document entitled "Proposed Communications Support Program For the Older Americans Division Committee for the Reelection of the President." Under subsection "E", entitled "Brochures/Direct Mail", the following entry appears:

Government Agencies—each agency who has senior citizen programs will be asked to produce an informational brochure stating just exactly what the agency can do for older Americans. One will be released every two weeks beginning September 1. The agencies who will be asked to participate are:
—ACTION
—HEW
—HUD
—DOT
—OEO
—AGRICULTURE
—LABOR
—DOD

On the cover of this document Todd wrote: "Gangbusters! Lets make it happen".**

* As subsequently discussed, L.J. (Bud) Evans, who was in Charles Colson's White House staff and specialized in aging matters, disputes that Todd was the progenitor of these brochures. (See Evans 66 and Ex. 41)
** Exhibit 39 is a March 7, 1972, "Confidential" memorandum to John Mitchell from Todd attaching a "Campaign Plan For Older Americans," which indicates (p. 6) the intention "to maximize all of the resources at the disposal of the Administration" to publicize the President's efforts for older Americans. It continues:

It appears that at least HEW, HUD, DOA, DOL, ACTION, OEO and VA actually produced brochures. Copies of these brochures are contained in Exhibit 40.* The Comptroller General has stated that the costs of producing and mailing the DOA, HUD, DOL, ACTION, OEO and VA brochures totalled around $263,000. (See Exhibit 40) The Comptroller General also noted that these six publications were distributed in accordance with lists and preprinted mailing labels supplied by the White House. (See also Evans, 83). He also reported the assertions of various agency officials that this was the first time a concerted effort to produce a number of aging brochures had been made by an incumbent Administration.

Other campaign and White House documents strongly suggest a political purpose behind the brochures. On June 7, 1972, William Novelli of CRP wrote a "Confidential" memorandum entitled "Government White Papers and Brochures on Older Americans," (Evans Exhibit 10) to Todd and L. J. Evans. This memorandum is a review of the brochures project as of that date and also contains suggestions as to how to proceed. Under the heading *"Background"*, Novelli wrote:

We are all in agreement that brochures produced and distributed by government departments and agencies will be important in persuading older voters to re-elect the President. These brochures will be non-partisan enough to break through the election year aversion to political rhetoric, but will be strongly supportive of the President.

After outlining his views as to the contents of the brochures, Novelli, under the heading *"Distribution, Timing and Coordination"*, stated:

The agencies and departments should be requested to develop the brochures immediately, along with a plan for mass distribution.
We can indirectly check copy and also stagger the release of the brochures to insure a steady stream between now and late September.

"These resources include the use of printed materials, films, personalized direct mail, commercial and public service radio and TV time, editorial and other print exposure, etc."

* Exhibit 40 contains two memoranda from Des Barker of the White House staff to various Department and Agency Information Officers indicating that additional brochures were contemplated. This assumption is supported by a May 23, 1972, Evans memorandum found at Ex. 42. There was also a HEW brochure prepared in 1971. (Evans Ex. 20) The preparation of this brochure was a separate matter and most of the memoranda discussed below do not relate to this publication.

Exhibit 43 is an August 4, 1972 CRP memorandum for Clark MacGregor from Fred Malek entitled "Older American Progress." Under the caption "Administration Support," Malek stated:

The Older Americans project team has been particularly imaginative in the use of administration resources to support the re-election. Specifically, they have arranged for each Department and Agency with programs that help the elderly to develop and distribute a brochure that explains these programs. The first of the brochures (Department of Agriculture) is off the presses, and mentions the President prominently—not surprising since we control the content of each brochure. This brochure and subsequent ones will be direct mailed to approximately one million persons. . . .*

Mr. Evans, in his executive session before the Committee on May 28, 1974, vigorously denied that he perceived the primary purpose for these brochures as political. The main goal, he said, was to inform the elderly of the benefits and programs available to them and, he contended, the brochures were mainly informational, not political. He stated that the idea for most of these brochures evolved in 1971 before aging activities at CRP materialized. He said he made no attempt to stagger distribution of brochures for political benefit although he felt it would be advantageous if periodic distribution eventuated. He conceded that others in the White House and CRP may have supported the preparation of the brochures mainly for political reasons but emphasized that this was not his chief motivation. He stated that his memoranda re these publications often sound in political terms because he was trying to convince others to support this project. (Evans, 64-8, 72-4, 83-6, 100, 112-14).

These comments by Evans should be compared with the remarks in a May 23, 1972, "Confidential-Eyes Only" memorandum written by him to Todd and others on the subject "Government Brochures":

I have been informed of disgruntlement expressed at this morning's breakfast concerning the development of government "aging" brochures. *So that we will be united in our efforts to make this a successful program on behalf of the President,* I would like to take your time to review the history regarding the development of these

* Additional documents that indicate a political purpose behind these brochures and show that CRP personnel were participating in the planning for both their preparation and distribution are found at Evans Exhibits 7-17.

brochures.

In late February, Chuck Colson and I decided that the Departments and Agencies involved with "aging" were not letting older voters know, as well as they should or could, what was being done *by the President* on their behalf. One of the vehicles we decided to utilize to overcome this was the development of a series of pamphlets for mass distribution. (Ex. 42) (emphasis added)

The record contains a number of other documents authored by Evans indicating political motivations behind these brochures. While these are collected at Evans Exhibit 7-17, a few illustrations are useful here. Thus, in response to Todd's requests of July 14 and 24, 1972, as to a schedule for production and publication of certain brochures, Evans responded on July 24 with a detailed schedule indicating when each of the brochures then under consideration would be mailed. And on July 27 he sent Malek (then at CRP) a memorandum that read:

Attached is the first government aging brochure to come off the printing press. It still has a slight bureaucratic flavor to it, but I think it gets across the President's concern as well as emphasizes his help in solving the problems of older persons.

The original mailing will distribute 950,000 of these brochures. This will leave us 550,000 remaining brochures for distribution to Senators and Congressmen, *field organizations,* and other groups we may want to reach. We will be sending out seven additional brochures at a rate of approximately one every two weeks, and I will forward these to you as they come off the press. (emphasis added) * (Evans Ex. 15)

Evans explained his memoranda stating that distribution of the brochures would be staggered for maximum impact with the assertion that, since it appeared the brochures would inadvertently be finalized at different times, he told those interested they would be produced at intervals to reduce the pressure from persons concerned with political impact. (Evans 85-6)

Evans also reported to Colson on these brochures as reflected in a June 30, 1972, "Weekly Staff Report". (Malek, Ex. No. 29). Colson wrote "Excellent" by Evans' account of

---

* The term "field organizations" refers to various CRP operations. (Evans p. 86) Malek, on the top of this document, wrote in hand:
"Bud—This is really great work & should have major impact. I'll look forward to seeing the additional brochures. Fred."

the progress on these publications.

Colson, however, apparently became concerned about the political nature of the brochures. An unsigned memorandum to Malek dated August 3 states in part:

> . . . Danny called this a.m. and said that Evans told him at breakfast today that "Colson is having second thoughts (cold feet) about the seven additional brochures." Apparently, Volpe called Colson and said DOT didn't want to do a brochure, too .political w/a quote from the P on the cover, etc.—and this must have gotten Colson thinking.
>
> Danny is quite alarmed—and just wanted you to be aware of the above in case he makes a desperate plea to you to put in a strong call to Colson to get him to back off.

It appears that DOT did not produce a brochure but the other six pamphlets involved in this note—those from HUD, DOA, DOL, ACTION, OEO and VA—were prepared and distributed. (See further Evans, 91-3)

Evans earlier had entertained doubts concerning government production of brochures that were too political in nature. Exhibit 44 is a March 16, 1972, "Confidential" memorandum from Evans to Todd entitled "Older American Pamphlets" which sets out various options for the preparation of a brochure entitled "The President Speaks to Older Americans . . . Again", which was to consist entirely of quotations from and photographs of the President. (See Evans Ex. 20)* Evans recognized that preparation of a political pamphlet by GPO could result in a charge that "the Republicans got the GPO to do its campaign literature". He also noted that the purchase of a government pamphlet for use by the campaign organization "would have to be made through some dummy organization" to avoid the contention that the pamphlet was "political."

(2) Other Uses of Government Funds. The Evans to Col-

---

* This brochure was prepared by HEW but was never printed. An earlier pamphlet of the same nature entitled "The President Speaks to Older Americans" was printed and mailed in 1971. (Evans Ex. 20) Regarding these two documents the following exchange occurred with Mr. Evans:

HAMILTON Neither one of these has a great deal of informational value. In other words, they don't just tell you about programs.

EVANS No, but they say that the President is going to do something on behalf of older people for programs. They say that there is concern at the highest level of the federal government on their behalf. I would think that would be something that older people would want to know about. (Evans 113)

son "Weekly Staff Report" referenced above (Malek Ex. 29) contains other examples of proposed expenditures of federal funds for what appear to be primarily campaign purposes. At p. 2 Evans wrote:

> It appears that HEW has agreed to produce 60 copies of the Richardson, Flemming, Rocha TV program taping. This will then be distributed simultaneously *to the top TV stations in all of our key states. It is a very political show* which stresses time and time again the fantastic things the President has done for older people, which is why the need for simultaneous distribution. This should be shown in late July or early August. In any event, it will be shown before the President is nominated. (emphasis added)

There is a handwritten "good" by this entry written by Colson.* This document also comments that, with Malek's help, an individual, paid by HEW, would be "brought on board to act as [Arthur] Flemming's scheduling-advanceman from now until the election". An earlier memorandum from Evans to Malek (Evans Ex. 18) indicates that this individual was hired as a "Consultant at HEW" and suggests that he maintain close ties with the "Tour Office at the Re-election Committee".

B. The Federation of Experienced Americans. Particularly significant are the Administration's activities concerning the Federation of Experienced Americans. This organization, which was created on March 29, 1972, on White House initiative (Evans 43-6)** was the recipient in 1972 of two major federal awards:

1. A DOL contract for $1,540,000 for services from June 30, 1972, to January 31, 1974, to train and provide work for 350 poor, elderly persons.
2. An OEO grant of $399,839 for the period November 1, 1972, to February 28, 1974, for developing new methods to overcome the special problems of the Spanish-speaking elderly poor.

The GAO, concerning these two awards, has now concluded that:

"The grant and contract awards were processed outside

* According to both Todd and Evans, the Richardson/Flemming/Rocha tape was made but was of such poor quality it was never used. (Evans pp. 99-101)
** Evans had prior association with one of FEA's directors. (Evans p. 28)

normal procedures. Officials of Labor and OEO said that both the grant and the contract had substantial White House backing." *

As to the Labor Department contract, the GAO report (p. 13) contained the following statement:

The former Assistant Secretary [Malcolm R. Lovell, Jr.] advised us that the White House took an active role in directing the Labor Department as to how the expansion moneys were to be spent. [**] The White House staff member involved was identified as L. J. Evans, Jr. According to the former Assistant Secretary, the White House wanted $13 million in expansion moneys to go to organizations considered friendly to the administration. Labor's initial allocation plan did not satisfy this requirement and, according to the former Assistant Secretary, Mr. Evans and the former executive assistant [to the Assistant Secretary—Brad Reardon] worked out a compromise plan which called for awarding a $1 million contract to an organization to be selected by the White House. This occurred in February, 1972.

The GAO report continues (p. 13):

The former executive assistant told us the White House wanted to cut back and/or terminate funding for two of the operation mainstream contractors—National Council on Aging and the National Council of Senior Citizens.

Funding to these two contractors, considered "enemies" of the White House, was not terminated by DOL, even though the record shows that on February 28, 1972, they were given substantially less funding than the amounts originally

* Report to the Special Committee on Aging and the Subcommittee on Aging, Committee on Labor and Public Welfare, United States Senate, May 13, 1974, p. 1. (Evans Ex. No. 3) As Evans Ex. 1 (an August 31, 1972 memorandum from Evans to Rob Davison) indicates, an attempt was also made by the White House to achieve HEW-AOA funding for FEA. AOA, however, refused to fund this organization apparently because it considered the project—which was a public information program—too "political." (Evans 61-2) In fact, Evans' memorandum to Davison emphasized that the project "could be a highly effective tool between now and November 7." A September 11, 1972 "Confidential" memorandum from Todd to Malek indicates that Secretary Richardson's office was also concerned with the "legality" of the proposed contract (which was for $750,000). This memorandum states that the proposal "is highly unusual and the expenditure is not justified."
** In November, 1971, the President personally announced that the funds for "Operation Mainstream", a program to train and place elderly Americans, would be doubled from 13 to 26 million dollars.

recommended on December 18, 1971, by Robert J. Brown, Associate Manpower Administrator for the United States Training and Employment Service.* However, the White House-sponsored FEA—which was not incorporated until March 29, 1972—did receive a $1 million plus contract to begin on June 30, 1972.**

The GAO also found White House involvement concerning the OEO grant. Its report reads in pertinent part:

> . . . An OEO official advised us that a White House staff member, L. J. Evans, Jr., directed OEO to fund the proposal from FEA which was for a major project concerning elderly, Spanish-speaking people.
>
> OEO officials told us that Mr. Evans also instructed OEO to limit its forthcoming contract extension with the National Council on the Aging to 6 months after which OEO would be expected to award a grant or contract to FEA to provide a full range of professional training and technical assistance for OEO aging programs that had been provided by the National Council on the Aging for many years with funds from OEO and other agencies. (p. 15)

* * *

> The executive assistant told us the FEA proposal was first brought to his attention by the OEO Deputy Director and that he met FEA's president at the initial meeting at Mr. Evans' office. He said that, after OEO received the proposal, Mr. Evans telephoned him to express his support for FEA and then had frequent contact with him until the grant was awarded . . . (p. 17).

A memorandum to the record dated November 17, 1972, by Irven M. Eitreim, Chief, Older Persons Programs, Office of Operations, OEO, (Evans Ex. 4) sets out at length his view of the circumstances surrounding the FEA award:

> All of the circumstances surrounding the processing and awarding of the above grant have been so irregular that I am taking this means to record and document some of those circumstances to protect myself and perhaps some other people within the agency in the event of possible future embarrassing disclosures.

* Exhibit 45 (the Brown Memorandum) and Exhibit 46 (a DOL directive of February 28, 1972) show that Brown recommended $3.4 million for NCSC, which received $1.8 million, and $1.1 million for NCOA, which received $0.7 million.
** A memorandum dated June 15, 1972, prepared by Fred E. Romero, Acting Director, Office of Training and Employment Opportunities, that details the history of the approval of this contract is found at Exhibit 47.

I was informed by a staff member of the Office of Program Review in the early part of September that:

1) The agency had been ordered by a junior White House Staff member to fund a proposal from the Federation of Experienced Americans (an outfit of which I had never heard despite my intimate familiarity with all recognized national organizations in the aging field) to conduct a major project concerned with elderly Spanish-Speaking people.

2) That the same White House Staff member had instructed OEO to limit its forthcoming contract extension (effective September 24) with the National Council on the Aging to a six-month period after which we would be expected to award a grant or contract to the Federation of Experienced Americans to provide the full range of professional training and technical assistance for our aging programs that have been provided by NCOA over a period of years.

* * *

Late on the afternoon of October 30 I was given a copy of a letter from [David] Brody [President of FEA] dated October 20 which contained some modifications of the work plan and a loosely constructed budget amounting to a few dollars under $400,000. I was told the grant must be completely processed and signed by the end of the following day, October 31 . . . I was informed that the work program and budget were to be accepted as presented with no further opportunity for negotiating work or budget provisions.

At a small briefing session on the morning of October 31, conducted in an atmosphere of conspiracy and attended by Brody, we were told that the normal agency requirement for Review Board approval had been waived, that normal approval of the Mayor of Washington and certain governors would be handled informally and perhaps by telephone and that standard procedures for announcing the grant were to be by-passed at least for the time being.

* * *

In summary I have the following reservations about the grant.

1) I consider the grantee totally unqualified to do the job.

2) I think the grant can produce nothing that is not already well researched and tested. It is a weak, poorly

designed plan and quite inappropriate for the use of Sec. 252 funds.

3) The budget of $399,839 is grossly excessive. A planning grant of this nature should not exceed $75,000 to $90,000.

4) The urgency and secrecy with which the grant was pushed through were highly irregular. Never in my long experience in the Federal Government have I experienced anything approaching the impropriety of this grant transaction.

5) I sense that I have been "used" as a professional program specialist and titular head of OEO's Older Persons Programs and as a veteran civil servant to give this grant some semblance of legitimacy and suspect that my professional reputation may be damaged as a result.

6) I am appalled by the remaining possibility that we may have to award a grant or contract to FEA for the highly complex and sophisticated professional T & TA services needed by our aging program grantees. FEA does not have and cannot within a period of several years if ever acquire an acceptable degree of competence to perform these functions. I am convinced this course would be utterly destructive to our aging programs. An award to FEA for this purpose would offend the entire aging constituency in the country, knowledgeable members of both parties in the Congress and our own GAAs and SOS programs. No service at all would be preferable to a contract with FEA both from the programatic and political standpoints.

It appears that Dan Todd was also concerned about the White House sponsorship of FEA. In a handwritten memorandum to Malek (Ex. 48)—apparently prepared after the Watergate breakin, June 17, 1972, but before June 30, 1972, —Todd stated:

The Federation of Experienced Americans has become a matter of great concern to those of us working the elderly.

I have done as much leg work as is possible from my position and believe the matter now deserves fast attention from higher up:

1. I anticipate an extremely unfavorable reaction among aging organizations when this group begins to move—such that it could totally undermine the President's credibility with the OA's and cost considerable votes.

2. Involvement of White House personnel in questionable activities involving a million dollars of USG funds funneled through dubious outsiders could make the Watergate episode look tiny—this has every potential of a major scandal, if not brought under control.

3. ASF wants to talk directly with Secretary Hodgeson as DOL funds are involved—once he does this, I'm afraid the whole thing will be public.

All that I have are allegations—nothing that would stand up in court, but this will be aimed at the press where proof isn't needed—particularly following ITT and Watergate.

I urge your attention to this matter. I've done all I can from my shop. If there is any possibility, I would recommend that the grant be cancelled.

In hand on this document Malek wrote: "Discuss w/Colson." "What does Evans say to all this?" Todd, in a staff interview, stated that Malek told him Colson had advised that FEA was a legitimate organization. Todd, however, continued to be disturbed by the FEA matter as demonstrated by memoranda from him to Malek on this subject on September 11 and November 6, 1972. (Ex. 49)*

The June 30 "Weekly Staff Report" to Colson from Evans also reflects Todd's concern and reveals a White House purpose to injure anti-Administration organizations receiving federal funding:

I met with Malek, concerning the new aging organization, and *he was very impressed and very cooperative in getting his guys to move out in assuring us funding at our foe's expense.* However, after having chatted with Todd, he raised cries of alarm that such an organization would hurt us politically because we would cut funds to Democratic groups, thereby leading them to criticize us. As you are well aware, groups like NCSC are going to criticize us anyway. Unfortunately, while I told Todd about the organization in confidence, he immediately told Flemming, who was particularly upset and called

---

* The September 11 memorandum claims that a report by Evans on FEA:
[O]verlooks the potential liabilities (siphoning off competitive funds from legitimate established organizations with which we have made great progress over the last 18 months; possible tracing of the operation to the White House, which in light of the Watergate and ITT Affairs can't help our image much; questionable legal status of the grants themselves which even Bud admits to; difficult public posture if we are forced to defend the FEA and the questionable backgrounds and relationships of the people involved; outright cancelling of existing grants and contracts which can and will only be interpreted as politically motivated, etc.).

Malek. Malek seems to understand the value of the organization, and is still working with us, but I have had to do some shoring operations with Flemming. I don't think this requires any action on your part but you should be aware of it. (emphasis added)*

Colson wrote in hand by this entry: "Keep Malek on board."

Mr. Evans confirmed in his testimony that he was involved in some degree in the processes leading to the DOL and OEO awards. He denied, however, that he directed either DOL or OEO to fund FEA. While admitting that he expressed his view that funding would be desirable, Evans claimed he lacked the power to direct either institution to make an award. He also denied that he attempted to induce DOL and OEO to terminate or cut back existing funding to the National Council on Aging or the National Council of Senior Citizens, but did concede that he endeavored to limit any additional funding they might receive. (Evans 10-1, 13, 17 26-7, 35-6, 49, 57).**

GAO has conducted a programmatic review of FEA's DOL contract. It concluded that, in significant respects, FEA's operations were ineffective, deficient or in violation of its DOL contract. GAO also performed a financial review of FEA's activities regarding both the DOL contract and the OEO grant. It concluded that FEA's accounting system and related internal controls were inadequate. As a result of these deficiencies, GAO questioned expenditures of approximately $184,000 under the DOL contract and $30,000 under the OEO grant. Both DOL and OEO have concluded that

---

* A handwritten document found in Mr. Malek's CRP files, apparently written on June 17, 1872, entitled "Bud Evens—Aging Groups" (Exhibit 50), declares that one "Purpose" of FEA was to "Soak up money now going to Democratic Organizations—Nat'l Council on Aging; National Council of Sr. Citizens; and National Farmers Union."

** Exhibit 50 suggests that White House and campaign officials were interested in FEA's promotion because it could "serve political interests" even though it was "tax exempt" having convinced IRS that it was non partisan. In this regard certain facts are relevant. Before the November 1972 election, FEA, with a $5,000 "contribution" from 3M Company, prepared five radio spots advertising Administration programs that were favorable to the President. These spots were sent to selected radio stations in fourteen states considered crucial to the President's re-election. (See Evans 19-20 & Evans Ex. 5). (The Committee has no evidence that the 3M gift was intended to be a political contribution.) Copies of these spots were transmitted to Evans at the White House before they were sent to the selected stations (Evans 21-2, 59). Todd informed the Committee that, during the campaign, Evans requested that a brochure entitled "The President Cares" be delivered to FEA for distribution. Todd says he forbade this activity. Exhibit 48 may reflect his decision in this regard. Evans, however, denied he made this request, suggesting instead that it was Todd's idea that FEA distribute this material and that he (Evans) discouraged it. (Evans 31-2)

it would not be in the best interest of the government to refund FEA's present programs. (See Evans Exhibit 3)

7. OTHER RELATED ACTIVITIES

A. Conduct at the Veterans Administration. The Select Committee is in receipt of information indicating that in late 1971 and 1972 efforts were taken to politicize the Veterans Administration for purposes of the President's re-election. This information, which has been verified in all significant respects by the Select Committee, was first supplied to the Committee by Senator Alan Cranston, Chairman of the Subcommittee on Health and Hospitals of the Committee on Veterans Affairs. A complete report on the Subcommittee's investigation is found at Ex. 51.

It appears that in late 1971, Glenn C. Wallace, then Special Assistant to the Administrator, solicited $100 contributions for the President's election campaign from VA employees on federal facilities. The contributions were in connection with a $1,000 a plate dinner held to pay tribute to the President. A contribution of $100 gave the contributor the chance to draw for one of the two tickets to the dinner that, besides the ticket reserved for the Administrator, were available to VA personnel. The evidence collected by the Cranston Subcommittee also indicates that the Administrator, Donald Johnson, held a meeting in early 1972 of top VA officials where he indicated to those present that key officials in the agency would be expected to lend their full support to the reelection effort, including participation in campaign activities, and that the affairs of the agency until the election would be conducted with partisan considerations in mind.

Documents obtained by the Select Committee indicate that the VA was, to some degree, politicized during the 1972 campaign. Exhibit 52 is an undated document from CRP files concerning "Campaign Plans for Veterans' Leaders" apparently prepared by or for the Veterans Committee to Reelect the President. This document (at p. 20), under the heading "Administration Initatives and Activities", states:

"Veterans Administration. The VA is the point of contact for all civilian veterans who utilize any government veteran benefits and has received favorable responses from Vietnam-era veterans for their programs to assist returning veterans in recent years. Because of these factors the VA will be the primary agency used in the governmental effort to win the support of veterans. The VA Administrator and designated officials within his agency will be responsible for executing the VA communications activities presented in the Communications Plan. The VA will develop program activities in the medical and education areas and coordinate with labor and the Presidential advisory group on employment activities to focus attention on governmental initatives to aid the veteran. The VA will review major construction announcements, grants, opening of new facilities, and legislative actions and coordinate communication plans for these items with the Committee.* The VA will recommend program initiatives and action on special veterans issues and plan these activities with the Committee." See also at pp. 21-3.

Exhibit 53 is an undated "Final Report" for the CRP Veterans Division found in CRP files. At p. 4 it states:

"The campaign staff's effectiveness was significantly enhanced by its close liaison with the Veterans Administration and coordination of campaign activity with the agency. Frequent contact and planning with the Administrator of the VA to place spokesmen and start action programs made possible a positive veterans program throughout the campaign."

B. The Surrogate Program Advance School. The evidence shows that in early January, 1972, an "advance school" in connection with the Surrogate candidate program was held in the Executive Office Building under the direction of Bart Porter, head of the CRP Surrogate program. The 50-75 attendees were mainly "Schedule C" government employees from various departments and agencies. "Schedule C" employees are subject to the Hatch Act which forbids certain government employees from participating in political campaigns. (See the discussion in Section VIII below)

There is evidence that the purpose of the "advance school" was to train these employees for political missions. The advance manual for the Surrogate program (Ex. 54), which was distributed at the school, states at p. 4:

". . . [Y]ou should never lose sight of the political purpose of the trip and the fact that the actual events are in many cases only a vehicle for a more important purpose—namely exposure of the Administration's views to aid the President's reelection."

The Select Committee has received evidence regarding sev-

* "Committee" apparently refers to the Veterans Committee to Re-elect the President.

eral instances where "Hatched" government employees advanced for or accompanied Surrogates on political trips. It is significant that FCRP paid all bills for Surrogates and their aides on campaign trips thus underlining the political nature of the events in which "Hatched" government employees were involved. However, according to Jon Foust who, on April 15, 1972, joined CRP as chief of the advance team, advances handled by his office after that date were performed by CRP employees or persons in private life.

C. Activities Re Military Voters. Exhibit 55 is a July 12, 1972, "Administratively Confidential" memorandum from John Grinalds, then a Major in the United States Marine Corps and a White House fellow, to Malek concerning "Military Voters," which sets out a basic strategy for maximizing the President's support within that consituency. Attached to that memorandum is a "Recommended Action Plan For Career Military Voter Group"; the following entry appears in the "Plan":

ACTION STEP	PURPOSE	RESPONSIBLE ORGANIZATION	CONCEPT OF EXECUTION
4. Surrogate Speakers on Military Bases —DOD officials and U.S. Congressmen	To congratulate achievements of career military officers and NCO's on Vietnamization success and highlight President Nixon's leadership in process.	Committee * (McAdoo) in coordination with the Executive Branch (Colson) and Hill party leadership.	*Committee will select most populous bases;* then set up schedule with Defense for their officials and U.S. Congressmen from the respective states to visit the bases in Sept./Oct. tell the career force (who served in Vietnam) about how the President and the country appreciate their efforts and sacrifices in bringing about Vietnamization. *Strong highlight on President Nixon. Cost should be nil since it could be charged off as official business.* (emphasis added)

* The "Committee" referred to is CRP.

Malek indicated his approval of this proposal on the document but added the following comment in hand: "But discuss with Porter first". As noted, Bart Porter was in charge of CRP's Surrogate Program. Mr. Richard McAdoo, who is referred to in this document, has informed the Select Committee that no surrogate speakers were actually sent to military bases.

VI. Resistance in the Bureaucracy to the Responsiveness Concept

As the previous section demonstrates, the "results" of the Responsiveness program were many and varied. But the "successes" of the program were reduced because there was considerable resistance in the federal establishment to bending the system to fit re-election purposes. Without attempting to be exhaustive, the following examples give a flavor of the recalcitrance of some federal officials to requests made of them by White House and campaign officials.

1. THE FAILURE OF THE DEPARTMENTS AND AGENCIES TO SUBMIT RESPONSIVENESS PLANS

The basic document presenting the Responsiveness concept —the Malek to Haldeman memorandum of March 17, 1972 (Malek Ex. 4)—stated that the Departments would be required to submit plans to the White House outlining the ways in which each Department could respond to re-election needs. Accordingly, the Department and Agency heads, in their briefings with Malek and members of his staff, were instructed to prepare and present such plans. The Select Committee has been unable to establish that any formalized plans of this nature were actually submitted to the White House. In fact, it has received evidence that the White House did not receive a single written plan from a Department or Agency.

The experience at the Labor Department is instructive. The task of formulating Labor's plan was given by Secretary James Hodgson to Lawrence Silberman, then Under Secretary of Labor, now the Deputy Attorney General. After meeting with Malek, Mr. Silberman requested that various Assistant Secretaries and other high Labor officials submit to him their proposals as to how their operations could contribute to the President's re-election. Various plans were received, some of which are collected at Ex. 15, along with certain weekly reports submitted to Silberman's office respecting activity taken to support the campaign. But no comprehensive Labor plan

409

was drafted for submission to Malek. Silberman made an attempt but later assigned the task to his assistant, Richard Wise. Wise's unfinished handwritten draft is found at Ex. 56. Silberman testified at the confirmation hearing for his present position that he felt "uncomfortable" about submitting a formalized election plan to Malek and thus decided not to do so.

Nonetheless, the memoranda collected at Ex. 15 are instructive as to the potential for abuse that underlay the Responsiveness program. A June 19, 1972 "Memorandum For The Under Secretary" from Malcom R. Lovell, Jr., the Assistant Secretary for Manpower. details how many millions of dollars (up to $185 million) from Manpower Training Services and EEA money "can potentially be utilized for the purposes we discussed." The memorandum continues: "As we develop plans for the allocation of the discretionary funds, I will coordinate closely with you in order to get maximum beneficial utilization of these funds." However, both Mr. Silberman and Mr. Lovell have stated that the proposal for using Labor funds for campaign purposes discussed in this memorandum was never implemented.

A June 14, 1972 "Memorandum To The Under Secretary" from George C. Guenther, Assistant Secretary for the Occupational Safety & Health Administration, also contains several interesting statements:

(1) Guenther, under the heading "Action", stated that, during the campaign period:

> "While promulgation and modification activity must continue, no highly controversial standards (i.e., cotton dust, etc.) will be proposed by OSHA or by NIOSH.* A thorough review with NIOSH indicates that while some criteria documents, such as on noise, will be transmitted to us during this period, neither the contents of these documents nor our handling of them here will generate any substantial controversy.
>
> "While the activities of the Standards Advisory Committee on Agriculture will commence in July, the Committee · will concentrate on priorities and long-range planning, rather than on specific standards setting, during this period. Other standards advisory committees may be proposed during this period but again their activities will be low-keyed."

Mr. Silberman stated to the Select Committee that he did

---

* NIOSH is an acronym for National Institute for Occupational Safety and Health.

not instruct Mr. Guenther to discontinue the plan set forth in this paragraph and that publication of certain safety standards were withheld until after the election.

(2) Under the heading "Personnel", Guenther wrote:

"We are drafting an outline of OSHA's recruiting and hiring plan for the next six months. Subject to your approval, it is our intention to provide copies of this detailed plan to the Republican National Committee and the Committee to Re-elect the President. We can then consider applicants they propose."

The original document contains a "No" by this paragraph written by Mr. Wise to indicate his disapproval of this proposal.

(3) Finally Guenther stated:

"While I have discussed with Lee Nunn the great potential of OSHA as a sales point for fund raising and general support by employers, I do not believe the potential of this appeal is fully recognized. Your suggestions as to how to promote the advantages of four more years of properly managed OSHA for use in the campaign would be appreciated."

Apparently, no action was taken respecting this paragraph.

2. DOL MIGRANT LABOR GRANT

One "success" announced by Malek to Haldeman in the June 7, 1972, Progress Report Malek (Ex. 16) was actually resolved contrary to Malek's claim due to intransigence to White House pressure. This document contained the following statement:

"Senator Tower's office requested that the $2.2 million migrant worker program grant be given to the pro-Administration Lower Rio Grande Valley Development Council as opposed to the consortium of OEO CAP agencies. DOL has already announced that the OEO groups have the best proposal. If the Development Council were to receive the grant, there would be a significant plus for the Administration, as OEO's negative voice would be silenced, and the Council's positive feelings towards the Administration could be stressed. DOL has told Tower that the grant will be awarded to Tower's choice. Tower will confirm his decision this week."

Summarizing this "result", Malek wrote:

411

"The Department of Labor was asked to award a $2.2 million migrant labor program contract in Texas to a pro-Administration group. Labor had already publicly committed itself to a consortium of anti-Administration OEO/CAP agencies. Labor has reversed its stand."

But Labor Department records reveal that the OEO/CAP agencies were eventually funded (the project was approved on October 22, 1972) albeit at a lower rate of $1.7 million. While White House pressure caused a delay in funding, the grant did go to the group that Labor deemed superior.

3. APPROACH TO HUD

Richard Goldstein, in 1972, was a Special Assistant to Richard Van Dusen, the former Undersecretary of HUD. Mr. Goldstein has submitted an affidavit to the Committee Malek (Ex. 21) that included the following statement:

"Sometime in the summer of 1972, after Mr. Malek had left the White House staff to join the Committee to Re-elect the President, I received a telephone call from Mr. Davison in the course of which he asked that the Department set aside approximately $2-3 million that could be used in the State of California as part of the Responsiveness Program. Under Mr. Davison's proposal, an individual whom the White House would designate, but who would not be an employee of the Department of Housing and Urban Development with an appropriate delegation of authority from the Secretary, would make the decision as to how those monies were to be committed, i.e., which cities and towns in California would receive those funds. I told Mr. Davison that in my judgment such a program did not make sense; that it sounded illegal and certainly improper and I felt confident that HUD would not participate in such a program. I further told Mr. Davison that if he wanted a decision from a higher authority I would take the matter up with Under Secretary Van Dusen. Mr. Davison suggested that I do that. At the conclusion of my conversation with Mr. Davison, I spoke with Under Secretary Van Dusen about this matter. He agreed and told me that HUD would in no way participate in such a program."

Mr. Van Dusen has confirmed that he had the conversation with Goldstein reported in the latter's affidavit. Mr. Davison stated to the Committee's staff that he does not recall making the specific request set forth in the Goldstein affidavit.

412

4. DIFFICULTIES WITH OMBE

John L. Jenkins served as Director of the Office of Minority Business Enterprises (OMBE) at the Department of Commerce from August, 1971, until March, 1973. As indicated above, OMBE was a substantial source of federal funding for minority businessmen. Several memoranda reveal the dissatisfaction of White House and campaign officials respecting Jenkins' lack of responsiveness to campaign needs.

On March 3, 1972, Malek forwarded a memorandum to Bob Brown, Bill Marumoto, Paul Jones, and Alex Armendariz who were leaders in the campaign effort regarding Black and Spanish-speaking voters. (13 Hearings 5543) This memorandum stated:

> Each of you has expressed concern to me recently about the use of OMBE grants. This, obviously, represents an excellent opportunity to make a contribution and gain headway in the Black and Spanish-Speaking areas.
>
> I have discussed this situation with Ken Cole, and we are in agreement on the importance of this program to our efforts. However, if we are to be at all effective in the OMBE area, we must ensure that the White House speaks with a single voice. Ken and I are agreed that that single voice will be John Evans of the Domestic Council staff.
>
> I believe assigning John the complete responsibility in this area can be quite effective and helpful to our efforts. John has the same objectives that you do, and I am sure you will find him most receptive to your inputs and needs. In this regard, I think it would be helpful if at an early stage you each sat down with John to discuss the Blacks and Spanish-Speaking problems respectively to ensure he is fully apprised of your needs and that a meaningful liaison is established.

Later documents, however, indicate that the Jenkins-OMBE problem was not solved. On April 11, 1972, Jones sent a memorandum to Rob Odle (Ex. 57) which reported:

> We participated in meetings with White House Team members to resolve problems centering around OMBE activities in efforts to assure that maximum benefits flow from this program.

And, on July 21, 1972, Jones sent a memorandum to Malek containing the following entry: (Ex. 58)

PROBLEM
The inability, after repeated high level meetings, to get

favorable supportive responses from the Office of Minority Business Enterprises remains a continuing obstacle to best use of Administration resources to meet critical needs.

Jenkins testified before the Select Committee in executive session on February 8, 1974. He stated that, from time to time, he received telephone calls regarding grants from Marumoto or Rodriguez concerning pro-Administration Spanish-speaking firms and from Bob Brown or Paul Jones as to Blacks favorable to the Administration. (Jenkins, pp. 15-16) Jenkins testified he would inform the caller that the grants "were in the process" and then would proceed to follow proper procedures as laid down by legislation and regulations. He was aware, however, of the concern that he was not cooperative and of the "rumors that [he] was not directing the money into 'the right hands.' " (Jenkins, p. 15)

Jenkins testified at some length regarding the pressures brought to bear on him and his responses to them.

HERSHMAN   Is it not true, Mr. Jenkins, that pressures came from the White House and the Committee to Re-elect the President and the pressures took the form of influence centering around various grants and contracts awarded by your office?

JENKINS   I suppose they would term it pressure. They would exert effort towards getting a particular proposal. . . .

H   Did they not make it clear to you that they wanted to see grants and contracts going to firms, minority firms, who were supportive of the Administration?

J   Well, this was made in a statement, and maybe this is where my division with the White House came. We felt that even though this was made in a statement, that they still wanted us to follow the prescribed rules and regulations that had been established by the Congress to award a grant or contract to an individual firm. And that is very well where I probably fell in disfavor, if it was such, at the White House, because I did not deviate from that particular performance.

And we were told that we should be very attentive to those persons and organizations who were favorable to the President. And we took that under consideration within the guidelines of the requirements and criteria. (Jenkins, pp. 13-14)

When shown memoranda critical of his performance, Jenkins said:

I would say that it was all brought about because of a few small-minded people in the White House who felt that I had not cooperated with what they wanted done. (Jenkins, p. 57)

Jenkins said that he was not previously aware of the March 3 Malek memorandum quoted above relating to the appointment of John Evans as the OMBE contact, but continued:

. . . [S]ince I see the memo I can see some connection, because I was giving everybody a fit over there, and Marumoto would call me, Bob would call me, Norris Sydnor would call me . . . and I probably was not responding like they wanted me to, so . . . it was probably a memo . . . going to Malek, saying, We are not getting the juice out of OMBE that we should be getting out of it. And consequently this memo came out and they appointed John. (Jenkins, pp. 22-23)

Jenkins testified that he finally went to then-Department of Commerce Under-Secretary James Lynn to complain about the pressures on him. In a meeting attended by Marumoto, Rodriguez, Lynn and Jenkins, Lynn explained "that [Jenkins] had certain rules and regulations and requirements that had to be met and that [he] was moving on all projects that had some viability to them." (Jenkins, p. 24) See further Malek, 164-68. Lynn stated to the Committee that certain White House staffers were impatient with Jenkins but that he (Jenkins) was attempting to carry out his OMBE duties in a responsible manner.

VII. Purported Cancellation of the Responsiveness Program

Malek moved from the White House to the campaign as Deputy Director on July 1, 1972. Dan Kingsley, still at the White House, assumed responsibility for the Responsiveness Program at that time. A progress report from Kingsley to Haldeman (which the Select Committee has not obtained) apparently prompted the official—if not the actual—cancellation of the Responsiveness Program.

The events leading to this cancellation are set forth in an affidavit (Malek, Ex. 30) submitted to the Select Committee by Frank Herringer, a former Malek assistant, now the Administrator of the Urban Mass Transit Authority:

"Sometime later (probably during September 1972),

415

a carbon or Xerox copy of a 'progress report' on the Responsiveness project, from Kingsley to Haldeman, crossed my desk on its way to Malek. I do not recall any specifics of the report, but I believe it was similar to an earlier 'progress report' which was shown to me recently and which is in the [Select] Committee's possession. I scanned the report, or part of it, briefly and I recall that I was generally disturbed by the descriptions in the report of some of the individual actions that supposedly had occurred in the Responsiveness project. While I did not believe that anything inappropriate had actually occurred, I felt that the exaggerated tone of the report (as is equally true in the earlier report) could cause someone not familiar with the general staff practice of exaggerated writing to think that inappropriate activities were being carried on.

"I sent the copy of the Progress Report along to Malek, with a suggestion that he recommend to Haldeman that the project (or at least the reports) be discontinued, and possibly with a suggested draft memorandum for Malek to send to Haldeman, if he agreed.

"A few days later, Kingsley's secretary collected from my secretary materials in Malek's and my files relating to the early stages of the development of the 'Responsiveness' project. As far as I can recall, that was the last I ever heard of the project."

It appears that all Responsiveness documents collected by Kingsley were burned or otherwise destroyed because of their "politically sensitive nature". See Affidavit of John E. Clarke, Malek Ex. 19. The Select Committee obtained copies of the majority of the Responsiveness documents contained in this Report from CRP files of Malek and others that were preserved at the National Archives.

Malek essentially confirms the account set forth in the Herringer affidavit. Malek stated to the Committee that, after the Watergate affair broke, he felt the campaign should be free of all conduct that might be subject to "misinterpretation". (Malek p. 203)

It appears, however, from numerous documents the Select Committee has obtained, that activities of the Responsiveness type continued past September until the conclusion of the campaign. Without referencing all available documents, the Committee notes a November 2, 1972, "Confidential" memorandum from Alex Armendariz to Ken Cole (13 Hearings 5697) suggesting that La Raza Unida, a Spanish-speaking organization potentially hostile to the President, might remain neutral through the election if some of the government programs affecting its interests "could be sprung loose within the next few days". See further, e.g., 13 Hearings 5686, 5692.

VIII. Discussion

Throughout its investigation of the activities described in this Chapter, the Select Committee was met with the claim that this conduct is politics as usual, that other Administrations have similarly employed the resources at their command to ensure the incumbent's re-election. Because the Select Committee's investigation was limited by the Senate in S. Res. 60 to the 1972 campaign and election, the Committee cannot confirm or refute these charges.* But, to some degree, the contention that other Administrations have done the same thing misses the point. For, as the discussion that follows demonstrates, certain of the activities described not only appear to contravene the fundamental notion that our nation's citizens are entitled to equal treatment under the laws, but also raise questions as to the applicability of specific federal civil and criminal statutes.

It is useful to begin this discussion by referencing the admonition of the Supreme Court in the recent case of *United States Civil Service Commission et al v. National Association of Letter Carriers, AFL-CIO, et al.*, 413 U.S. 548, 564-5 (1973).

"It seems fundamental in the first place that employees in the Executive Branch of the Government, or those working for any of its agencies, should administer the law in accordance with the will of Congress, rather than in accordance with their own or the will of a political party. They are expected to enforce the law and execute the programs of the Government without bias or favoritism for or against any political party or group or the members thereof . . .

". . . [I]t is not only important that the Government and its employees in fact avoid practicing political justice, but it is also critical that they appear to the

* One could, however, speculate with some confidence that no other Administration was as victimized by its passion to commit its plans and strategems for using federal resources to paper as was the present one. Of interest in this regard is a May 24, 1972, "Confidential-Eyes Only" memorandum from L. J. Evans to Malek carrying the prescription "Burn Before Reading" by which Malek wrote "Always." (Evans Ex. 1) Perhaps unfortunately for those involved, many documents unearthed by the Committee were not "always" burned, before or after reading.

public to be avoiding it if confidence in the system of representative Government is not to be eroded to a disastrous extent."

In this case the Supreme Court affirmed the Constitutionality of a portion of the Hatch Act, 5 U.S.C. § 7324 (a) (2), which proscribes political activities by most federal employees.

The Hatch Act, in fact, contains another broad prescription that would seem to prohibit many of the activities described above. Section 7324 (a) (1) of Title 5 provides that an employee of an executive agency may not "use his official authority or influence for the purpose of interfering with or affecting the result of an election." Violation of this provision can result in dismissal from federal service. See 5 U.S.C § 7325. While this provision suffers from some vagueness and has never received an authoritative interpretation by the courts, its applicability must nontheless be considered in determining the propriety of the conduct presented in this Chapter.

Moreover, the question is raised whether certain conduct described in this Chapter may have amounted to a conspiracy to defraud the United States under 18 U.S.C. § 371. The most authoritative definition of this crime appears in the Supreme Court's decision in *Hammerschmidt v. United States*, 265 U.S. 182 (1923) (Taft ChJ.). There the Court said:

"To conspire to defraud the United States means primarily to cheat the Government out of property or money, but *it also means to interfere with or obstruct one of its lawful governmental functions by deceit, craft or trickery, or at least by means that are dishonest*. It is not necessary that the Government shall be subjected to property or pecuniary loss by the fraud, but *only that its legitimate official action and purpose shall be defeated by misrepresentation, chicane or the overreaching of those charged with carrying out the governmental intention*." (emphasis added)

See also, e.g., *Dennis v. United States*, 384 U.S. 885, 861 (1966), where the court observed that § 371 "reaches 'any conspiracy for the purpose of impairing, obstructing or defeating the lawful functions of any department of Government' "; *Hass v. Henkel*, 216 U.S. 462 (1910); *Tyner v. United States*, 23 U.S. App. D.C. (1904).

The evidence accumulated by the Select Committee presents the issue whether those Administration and CRP officials who agreed on plans to use federal resources for political ends were engaged in a conspiracy "to interfere with or obstruct . . . lawful government functions" and whether "legitimate official action and purpose [was] defeated by . . . the overreaching of those charged with carrying out the governmental intention." It is also relevant that the major documents promulgating Responsiveness plans were classified "Confidential," "Extremely Confidential" and/or "Eyes Only" and noted that secrecy in the implementation of the proposal was of paramount necessity in order to avoid adverse publicity. Thus, a question exists whether there was agreement to interfere with the lawful functions of government by "deceit, craft or trickery or . . . means that are dishonest."

In any event, there are specific federal criminal and civil statutes that appear applicable to the conduct herein described. And, of course, any agreement to violate a federal criminal law could also be prosecuted under 18 U.S.C. § 371 as a conspiracy to commit an offense against the United States.* Certain criminal and civil statutes that appear relevant to the activity portrayed in this Chapter are now discussed.**

1. The evidence suggests that one area of emphasis in the Responsiveness Program was the allotting or "rechannelling" of federal money—funds for grants, contracts, loans and subsidies—to target groups and areas in order to enhance the President's re-election chances, and to individual applicants who were supportive of, or would thereafter support, the President.

Section 595 of Title 18 makes it illegal for "a person employed in any administrative position by the United States, or by any department or agency thereof, . . . in connection with any activity which is financed in whole or in part by loans or grants by the United States, or any department or agency thereof, [to use] his official authority for the purpose of interfering with, or affecting, the nomination or the election of any candidate for the office of President [etc]". The offense is a misdemeanor and is penalized by a fine of not more than $1,000 and/or imprisonment of not more than one year. (There are, however, no reported cases under this section.)

2. The Committee has received evidence raising the possibility that certain individuals were offered government

* A conspiracy to commit certain *civil* offenses against the United States would also be prosecutable under this statute. *See, e.g.* United States v. Hutto, 256 U.S. 524 (1921); United States v. Wiesner, 216 F. 2d 739 (2nd Cir 1954).
** No attempt has been made exhaustively to catalogue all possible statutes that may conceivably apply, but the principal provisions that appear pertinent are discussed.

benefits in exchange for political support, or at least, political neutrality. Section 600 of Title 18 makes it a misdemeanor punishable by a fine up to $1000 and/or imprisonment up to one year to promise any government benefit "or any special consideration in obtaining such benefit, to any person as consideration, favor or reward for any political activity or for the support of or opposition to any candidate or any political party" in connection with a federal election.

3. There is evidence that plans were laid for government officials and others to solicit campaign contributions from minority recipients of federal grants, loans, and contracts. Moreover, the Committee has obtained evidence that these plans were in part consummated. It also appears from Civil Service Commission findings and otherwise that certain federal employees were solicited for campaign contributions by other federal employees on federal facilities. Several provisions of the federal criminal code are relevant regarding this conduct.

a. Section 611 of Title 18 provides that anyone "entering into a contract with the United States . . . for the rendition of personal services or furnishing any material, supplies or equipment . . . if payment for performance of such contract or payment for such material, supplies [or] equipment is made in whole or in part from funds appropriated by the Congress . . ." may not "directly or indirectly mak[e] any contribution of money or other thing of value, or promis[e] expressly or implicitly to make any such contribution, to any political party, committee, or candidate for public office or to any person for any political purpose or use". A contribution or promise to contribute is only illegal if made during the time period from the beginning of negotiation on a government contract to the completion of the contract or the termination of negotiations respecting the contract, whichever is later. It is also illegal *to solicit* "any such contribution from any such person for any such purpose during any such period". Penalty for violation is a fine of not more than $5,000 and/or imprisonment for not more than five years.

b. Section 602 makes it criminal for "an official or employee of the United States . . . or a person receiving any salary or *compensation for services* from money derived from the Treasury of the United States, directly or indirectly [to] solici[t], receiv[e], or [be] in any manner concerned in soliciting or receiving, any . . . contribution for any political purpose whatever, *from any other such . . . person*" (emphasis added). This statute carries a fine of up to $5,000 and/or imprisonment up to three years.

c. Section 603 makes it illegal for anyone "in any room or building occupied in the discharge of official duties by any person mentioned in section 602 . . . [to] solici[t] or receiv[e] any contribution of money or other thing of value for any political purpose". The penalties are the same as enumerated in section 602.

d. Section 607 makes it illegal for a federal employee to give a campaign contribution to another federal employee. The penalties are the same as in sections 602 and 603.*

4. The March 17 Malek to Haldeman memorandum (Malek Ex. 4) setting forth the basic precepts of the Responsiveness Program indicates that one of the goals of that program was the shaping of legal and regulatory proceedings to benefit the President's re-election campaign. And, in a Malek to Haldeman memorandum dated June 7, 1972 (Malek Ex. 16) Malek appears to claim that, for campaign purposes, his forces achieved successful results respecting EEOC and Labor Department proceedings.

Section 1505 of Title 18 provides that "[w]hoever corruptly . . . influences, obstructs, or impedes or endeavors to influence, obstruct or impede the due and proper administration of the law under which [a] proceeding is being had before [a] department or agency of the United States . . . [s]hall be fined not more than $5,000 or imprisoned not more than five years, or both". (emphasis added)

5. The evidence indicates that various federal employees were actively engaged in the President's re-election campaign. It appears that some of these employees were *not* exempt from the provisions of the Hatch Act, 5 U.S.C. § 3724 (a) (2), which provides that "[a]n employee in an Executive agency . . . may not . . . take an active part in political management or in political campaigns." Violation of this provision may result in dismissal from office. See 5 U.S.C. § 7325.

6. The Select Committee has received evidence suggesting that White House and campaign officials, acting through special personnel referral units established in various departments and agencies, were engaged in a program to place political supporters of the Administration in government positions regulated by the Civil Service merit system (i.e., com-

* See also the Hatch Act, 5 U.S.C. §7323, which provides:
An employee in an Executive agency (except one appointed by the President, by and with the advice and consent of the Senate) may not request or receive from, or give to, an employee, a Member of Congress, or an officer of a uniformed service a thing of value for political purposes. An employee who violates this section shall be removed from the service.

petitive service positions). It is unlawful for a department or agency to make determinations on staffing for competitive service positions on the basis of political considerations. For example, section 4.2 of Executive Order No. 10577, which was issued pursuant to U.S.C. § 3301 provides that:

"No discrimination shall be exercised, threatened or promised by any person in the executive branch of the Federal Government against or in favor of any employee in the competitive service, or any eligible or applicant for a position in the competitive service because of his . . . political affiliation . . . except as may be authorized or required by law."

Other similar statements of the law are found at § 7.1 of Executive Order No. 10577, § 9.5 of Executive Order No. 11598 (Nov. 17, 1966) and 5 C.F.R. § 300.103 (c), 330.101.

———————

The Committee rejects the proposition that much of the conduct described in this Chapter should be viewed as acceptable political practice. The Responsiveness concept involved the diverting of taxpayers' dollars from the primary goal of serving all the people to the political goal of re-electing the President. To condone such activity would display a limited understanding of the basic notion that the only acceptable governmental responsiveness is a responsiveness to the legitimate needs of the American people.

IX. Recommendations

1. PROSECUTION FOR VIOLATIONS OF THE EXISTING CRIMINAL STATUTES SET FORTH ABOVE, INSOFAR AS THEY RELATE TO FEDERAL ELECTIONS, AND THE CRIMINAL STATUTORY ENACTMENTS RECOMMENDED BELOW SHOULD BE ENTRUSTED TO THE PUBLIC ATTORNEY, WHOSE ESTABLISHMENT IS ELSEWHERE RECOMMENDED.

The reasons supporting the Committee's recommendation for a permanent Public Attorney are presented elsewhere in this Report.

2. THE FEDERAL ELECTIONS COMMISSION (ELSEWHERE RECOMMENDED) SHOULD BE GIVEN AUTHORITY TO INVESTIGATE AND RESTRAIN VIOLATIONS OF FEDERAL CIVIL AND CRIMINAL STAT-

UTES INSOFAR AS THOSE VIOLATIONS RELATE TO FEDERAL ELECTIONS. THE COMMISSION SHOULD ALSO BE EMPOWERED TO REFER EVIDENCE OF SUCH VIOLATIONS TO THE PUBLIC ATTORNEY.

The reasons supporting the Committee's recommendation for the creation of a Federal Elections Commission are presented elsewhere in this Report, as are the specifics concerning the recommended powers of this Commission.

3. THE COMMITTEE RECOMMENDS THAT CONGRESS ENACT LEGISLATION MAKING IT A FELONY TO OBSTRUCT, IMPAIR OR PERVERT A GOVERNMENT FUNCTION, OR ATTEMPT TO OBSTRUCT, IMPAIR OR PERVERT A GOVERNMENT FUNCTION, BY DEFRAUDING THE GOVERNMENT IN ANY MANNER.

As indicated above, there is a question whether some of the conduct described in this chapter may have interfered with the lawful functioning of government. Certain of the endeavors described were pursued in concert. There is, for example, evidence that governmental officials and CRP personnel acted jointly in various attempts to use federal resources for re-election purposes.

As noted, there is currently in the federal code a statute (18 U.S.C. §371) making it unlawful to conspire to defraud the United States. The Supreme Court has ruled that a conspiracy to interfere with the lawful functioning of government is prosecutable under this provision. The Committee's recommendation, which is an elaboration of the suggested provision in section 1301 of S. 1400 (the McClellan Bill) now pending before the Senate, would make illegal *individual* conduct that fraudulently interferes with a lawful government function. This recommendation, coupled with existing 18 U.S.C. § 371, should cover completely all future attempts by campaign officials, government personnel and others to use federal resources to influence a federal election in a fashion that interferes with lawful government functioning.

4. THE COMMITTEE RECOMMENDS THAT CONGRESS PRESERVE AS PART OF THE UNITED STATES CODE U.S.C., § 595, WHICH MAKES IT ILLEGAL FOR A GOVERNMENT OFFICIAL CONNECTED WITH THE AWARDING OF FEDERAL GRANTS AND LOANS TO USE HIS OFFICIAL AUTHORITY TO AFFECT A FEDERAL ELECTION, BUT RECOMMENDS THAT THIS OFFENSE BE UPGRADED TO A FELONY. THE COM-

MITTEE RECOMMENDS THAT 18 U.S.C. § 600, WHICH MAKES ILLEGAL THE PROMISE OF GOVERNMENT BENEFIT FOR POLITICAL SUPPORT, BE UPGRADED TO A FELONY. THE COMMITTEE ALSO RECOMMENDS THAT THE SCOPE OF SECTION 595 BE EXPANDED TO INCLUDE MISUSE OF OFFICIAL AUTHORITY IN CONNECTION WITH THE DISPENSING OF OTHER FEDERAL FUNDS SUCH AS GOVERNMENT CONTRACTS PAYMENTS AND FEDERAL SUBSIDIES.

The major proposed revisions of the criminal code currently before Congress—S. 1 (the McClellan Bill), S. 1400 (the Department of Justice Bill), H.R. 10047 (the Brown Commission recommendations)—would either seriously limit the scope of 18 U.S.C. § 595 or altogether remove its strictures from the law. This result, in view of the factual findings in this Chapter and the necessity of preserving the sanctity of the electoral process, is undesirable. To the contrary, this provision and 18 U.S.C. § 600 should be upgraded to felony level better to protect the integrity of federal elections.

Section 595 as now written does not appear to deal with misconduct by certain federal officials who have important responsibilities for dispensing federal funds—e.g., those dealing with government contracts and various federal subsidies. In view of the evidence uncovered, the scope of the statute should be expanded to cover conduct by these influential federal officials.

5. THE COMMITTEE RECOMMENDS THAT CONGRESS PRESERVE IN THE UNITED STATES CODE 18 U.S.C. §611—WHICH PROSCRIBES POLITICAL CONTRIBUTIONS BY OR SOLICITATIONS TO GOVERNMENT CONTRACTORS—AND 18 U.S.C. §602 —WHICH MAKES ILLEGAL POLITICAL SOLICITATIONS BY PERSONS RECEIVING FEDERAL COMPENSATION, FOR SERVICES RENDERED, TO OTHER SUCH PERSONS—BUT APPROPRIATELY AMEND THESE PROVISIONS TO MAKE ILLEGAL CONTRIBUTIONS BY OR KNOWING SOLICITATIONS TO (a) ANY PERSON RECEIVING, DURING THE CALENDAR YEAR A CONTRIBUTION OR SOLICITATION IS MADE, OTHER FEDERAL MONIES (e.g. GRANTS, LOANS, SUBSIDIES) IN EXCESS OF $5,000, AND (b) THE PRINCIPALS OR DOMINANT SHAREHOLDERS OF CORPORATIONS RECEIVING, DURING THE CAL-

ENDAR YEAR A CONTRIBUTION OR SOLICITATION IS MADE, SBA 8(a) OR OMBE AWARDS OR OTHER SUCH FEDERAL FUNDING DESIGNED TO BENEFIT DISADVANTAGED AND MINORITY GROUPS.

Section 611 only makes illegal contributions by or solicitations to contractors compensated by federal dollars. It does not cover contributions by or solicitations to other recipients of significant federal funding, e.g., certain grantees and loan recipients. Moreover, the statute by its terms does not seem to cover contributions by or solicitations to principals or dominant stockholders of corporations receiving federal monies. Similarly, Section 602 only covers solicitations to those receiving federal compensation *for services rendered;* it does not condemn solicitations to those receiving federal funding without returning services, or solicitations to the principals or dominant shareholders in corporations that receive federal monies. The evidence before the Committee indicates that, respecting minority groups, plans were laid to solicit recipients of grants or loans. Also, there appear to have been particular pressures to contribute on minority businessmen whose corporations were quite dependent on government business. The law currently prohibits contributions by corporations to federal elections and we recommended elsewhere that a $3,000 limit be placed on the amount any individual can contribute to a presidential campaign. The proposal to prohibit contributions by and knowing solicitations to the principals and dominant shareholders of corporate recipients of SBA 8 (a) or OMBE awards, or other federal funding designed to benefit disadvantaged and minority groups, adds another protection to persons who are most dependent on federal funds and thus all the more susceptible to campaign solicitations by federal candidates or their representatives.

The current major bills to revise the criminal code before Congress—S. 1, S. 1400, H.R. 10047— generally weaken the proscriptions in Sections 602 and 611 and lessen the penalties for their violation. In view of the abuses discovered, a weakening of the law in this area seems unwise.

6. THE COMMITTEE RECOMMENDS THAT CONGRESS AMEND THE HATCH ACT TO PLACE ALL JUSTICE DEPARTMENT OFFICIALS—INCLUDING THE ATTORNEY GENERAL—UNDER ITS PURVIEW.

The evidence the Select Committee has gathered indicated that various federal officials took an active part in the President's 1972 re-election campaign. Some of the officials apparently involved were covered by the Hatch Act, which prohibits certain federal employees from engaging in political campaigns and political management, but some were not. Some of the federal officials involved in political activities were employed at the Department of Justice—e.g. Mr. Mitchell.*

Section 7324 (d) of Title 5 exempts certain Justice Department officials from Hatch coverage. The Committee, however, believes that Justice Department officials should administer the nation's laws totally removed from all political considerations. The Committee thus recommends that all Justice Department employees and officials, including the Attorney General, be placed under the Hatch Act.

7. THE COMMITTEE RECOMMENDS THAT THE APPROPRIATE COMMITTEES OF BOTH HOUSES OF CONGRESS, IN ACCORDANCE WITH THEIR CONSTITUTIONAL RESPONSIBILITIES, MAINTAIN A VIGILANT OVERSIGHT OF THE OPERATIONS OF THE EXECUTIVE BRANCH IN ORDER TO PREVENT ABUSES OF GOVERNMENTAL PROCESSES TO PROMOTE SUCCESS IN A FEDERAL ELECTION.

This proposal needs no discussion for a major lesson of Watergate is that vigorous Congressional oversight of the executive branch is essential.

* In addition to this Chapter, see also Chapter 1 of this report regarding the Watergate break-in and its coverup.

CHAPTER IV

THE HUGHES-REBOZO INVESTIGATION AND RELATED MATTERS *

Introduction

Senate Resolution 60 mandated the Senate Select Committee to conduct investigations relating to "any transactions or circumstances relating to the source, the control, the transmission, the transfer, the deposit, the storage, the concealment, the expenditure or use in the United States or in any other country, of any monies or other things of value collected or received for actual or pretended use in the Presidential election of 1972 . . ." That resolution further mandated this committee to determine whether any money as described above had been placed in any secret fund or place of storage for use in financing any activity which was sought to be concealed from the public, and if so, what disbursement or expenditure was made of such secret fund, and the identities of any person or group of persons or committee or organization having any control over such secret fund or the disbursement or expenditure of the same."

This report reflects the results of the Committee's investigation into the receipt, storage, concealment and expenditure of cash contributions by Charles G. Rebozo and related matters. The contributions examined included the receipt by Rebozo of $100,000 in cash from Howard Hughes and $50,000 in cash from A. D. Davis.

The investigation was extensive and touched, at times, on incidents involving Presidential aides and a wide diversity of government agencies, including the Department of Justice, the Internal Revenue Service, the Treasury Department, the Atomic Energy Commission, the Civil Aeronautics Board, the Federal Reserve Board, the Federal Bureau of Investigation, and the Central Intelligence Agency. Indeed, the list of witnesses interviewed by the Committee reflects the number of significant government officials, past and present, who both aided and inhibited the investigation of this matter.[1]

The Committee received complete, unstinting cooperation

* Chapter 8 in the Committee Report.
1. See Appendix for list of witnesses interviewed.

427

from certain departments and agencies, including the Department of Justice and its Anti-Trust Division, the AEC, the CAB, and the Securities and Exchange Commission, whose efforts contrasted sharply with other witnesses and departments of the government. However, significant conflicts in testimony could not be conclusively resolved by the Committee because crucial documents and testimony were not produced in response to subpoenas issued by the Committee. The principal witnesses who refused to comply fully with subpoenas and fully provide documents and testimony included Charles G. Rebozo (for personal documents and in his capacity as President of the Key Biscayne Bank), F. Donald and Edward Nixon and a number of Hughes's employees.

In addition, the Committee, in its letter to the President's counsel on June 6, 1974, provided substantial evidence relating to Rebozo's use of cash funds to the direct benefit of the President. The purpose of the letter, sent by Senators Ervin and Baker, was to provide "the President an opportunity to comment on this material prior to the filing of this report." The Committee also hoped to obtain information and documents that would assist in its review of the evidence set forth in the letter.[2] Unfortunately, Counsel to the President, in his response of June 20, 1974, chose not to respond to any of the specific evidence that the Committee sought clarification and additional information on except to deny that the President instructed "Rebozo to raise and maintain funds to be expended on the President's personal behalf."[3]

In addition, Chairman Ervin, by letter and subpoena, sought to afford Mr. Rebozo an opportunity to respond to the information contained in the letter to the President's counsel.[4] Any assistance Mr. Rebozo's testimony may have afforded the Committee in its review of these matters was precluded, however, when the witness left the country and became unavailable for service of the subpoena.

Section I of the report provides a brief description of the Hughes Nevada Operations and Hughes' interest in political contributions.

Section 2 describes the background and initial discussions of the principals that culminated in the delivery of $100,000 in cash to Rebozo from Hughes. An abortive effort by Hughes' representatives to deliver $50,000 in cash to President-elect Nixon is described in Section 3.

2. See letter from Senators Ervin and Baker to James St. Clair dated June 6, 1974. Exhibit 1.
3. See letter from James St. Clair to Senators Ervin and Baker dated June 20, 1974. Exhibit 2.
4. See Senator Ervin's letter to Mr. Rebozo, dated June 21, 1974. Exhibit 3.

Section 4 describes Rebozo's assignments on behalf of the Nixon Administrations in 1969 including his efforts to raise funds and his responsibilities for President Nixon's properties in Key Biscayne, Florida.

Section 5 includes an analysis of the delivery of two packages from Hughes of $50,000 each to Rebozo. This section also reviews evidence relating to whether Rebozo retained or used any part of the $100,000 cash contribution including the efforts by the Committee to determine whether any of the currency returned to Hughes had, in fact, been circulated after the dates of delivery to Rebozo.

Section 6 describes the attempt by Howard Hughes to acquire the Dunes Hotel and Casino in Las Vegas and the discussions about the pending acquisition between Hughes representative Richard Danner and then-Attorney General John Mitchell.

Rebozo's fund-raising role for the 1972 Presidential election is examined in Section 7 including his receipt of $50,000 in cash from A.D. Davis in April, 1972.

While Rebozo testified he retained the Hughes' $100,000 contribution past the 1972 election hoping it could be used in 1974 or 1976, Section 8 describes his efforts to return $100,000 after the Internal Revenue Service contacted him in 1973. This section reviews the contacts Rebozo had with a variety of individuals including the President and his aides during early 1973 regarding his ultimate decision to return funds to Hughes.

Secton 9 reflects evidence received by the Committee relating to the initial IRS investigation of Rebozo and communications the President and his aides had regardng that investigation.

The issue of the possible use of the Hughes' $100,000 is reviewed in Section 10 which includes an analysis of funds expended by Rebozo on behalf of President Nixon. The analysis reviews the use by Rebozo of his attorney's trust accounts at two banks to pay for expenditures incurred for improvements to the President's Key Biscayne properties.

Conflicts in testimony relating to significant issues in the report are analyzed in summary form in Section 11.

Section 12 is a brief summary of the matters related in this report including a review of the President's response, through his counsel, to Chairman Ervin and Vice-Chairman Baker's letter of June 6, 1974 and the failure of Mr. Rebozo to appear before the Committee to respond to matters set forth in the report.

Finally, Section 13 presents the legislative recommendations of the Committee based on this investigation.

1. HUGHES AND THE HUGHES NEVADA OPERATIONS

Howard Hughes moved to Las Vegas, Nevada in November of 1966. Thereafter, Robert Maheu, a former FBI agent, contracted with Hughes through his own company to provide management services for hotels, casinos and other holdings that Hughes began to acquire. Maheu has stated that he was to report on these management matters directly to Hughes and not to executives of Hughes Tool Company.[5]

Maheu testified that as part of his management responsibilities, he was consulted with regard to which political leaders should be supported through political contributions from Mr. Hughes. By 1969, Hughes' cash contributions were furnished from monies from the Silver Slipper Casino, since that entity was owned by Hughes as a sole proprietorship.[6]

Maheu has testified that Mr. Hughes was cognizant of and approved all political contributions which were perceived by Hughes to insure access and influence over significant political leaders.[7]

Because of evidence before the Committee that Mr. Hughes had pertinent testimony with regard to political contributions being investigated, the Committee requested his appearance by letter which was never answered.[8] Although a subpoena for Hughes' appearance before the Committee was approved by the Committee Chairman, it could not be served because Hughes has remained out of the country during the entire period of the Committee's investigation.

2. BACKGROUND OF THE CONTRIBUTION COMMITMENT

The Hughes contribution of $100,000 to President Nixon's 1972 re-election campaign, which Richard Danner delivered to C. G. Rebozo, was first committed, as to the first $50,000, during the 1968 Presidential campaign. Some facts relating

5. Robert A. Maheu, Civil Deposition, July 4, 1973, p. 201024 and affidavit.
6. Thomas Bell Interview, December 18, 1973; Robert L. Morgan Executive Session, December 11, 1973, pp. 24-38, 190-204; Robert Maheu Interview, January 20, 1974.
7. Robert Maheu, S.C.C. Deposition; March 9, 1973, Vol. 3, p. 303. See also memo Hughes to Maheu, undated; a copy of the memorandum can be found in the Committee files but one says in pertinent part:
   "Bob, as soon as this predicament is settled, I want you to go see Nixon as my special confidential emissary. I feel there is a really valid possibility of a Republican victory this year. If that could be realized under our sponsorship and supervision every inch of the way, then we would be ready to follow with Governor Paul Laxalt as our next candidate."
8. For copy of letter see Exhibit 4. Letter from Terry Lenzner to Chester Davis.

to the early social and political ties of Danner, Rebozo and the President, leading up to this commitment and the failure to fulfill it in 1968, are pertinent to an understanding of the ultimate delivery of the Hughes contribution.

Dick Danner served as the FBI Special Agent in charge of the Miami area from 1940 until January, 1946, when he resigned from that post to manage George Smathers' first primary campaign for Congress.[9] Danner recalls meeting Charles G. Rebozo in 1940, when he first came to Miami with the FBI.[10] Rebozo does not recall meeting Danner until 1940, when he saw him at the El Commodore Hotel in Miami when Smathers made his decision to run for Congress.[11] Rebozo, a friend of Smathers from elementary school days, also played an active role in the successful 1946 Smathers campaign.

President Nixon was also first elected to Congress in 1946, and he and then-Congressman Smathers became good friends in the House of Representatives. Congressman Nixon occasionally vacationed in Florida with Smathers, and on one of these visits in 1947, Smathers introduced Congressman Nixon to Dick Danner.[12] After the 1950 election, when both Smathers and Nixon were elected to the U.S. Senate, Smathers invited Senator-elect Nixon down to Florida for a vacation. After staying with Dick Danner in Vero Beach for a few days, Danner and Senator-elect Nixon drove to Key Biscayne where Danner introduced Nixon to Charles "Bebe" Rebozo.[12a]

A. Danner's Version of Contribution Commitment. Danner testified that in the mid-Summer of 1968, he met with candidate Richard Nixon and Rebozo, and was asked to determine if Howard Hughes would contribute to the Nixon campaign.[13] Danner was certain that he had *not* initiated discus-

9. Danner was Special Agent in charge from 1940 until 1946 except fir a year and a half when he had a Dallas FBI office. See also *Miami Herald,* Thursday, September 5, 1946, p. 1.
10. See Danner testimony in *Maheu* v. *Hughes Tool Co.,* U.S. District Court Central District of California, May 3, 1974, p. 7771.
11. See Rebozo interview, October 8, 1973, p. 3. See also Smathers interview, January 10, 1974, p. 1.
12. Danner interview, August 30, 1973, p. 1. See also Danner testimony in *Maheu* v. *Hughes Tool Company,* p. 7770.
12a. See Rebozo interview with *Miami Herald,* November 1, 1973, p. 23-A; see also Smathers interview, January 10, 1974, p. 3. See also Danner Testimony in *Maheu* v. *Hughes Tool Company,* pp. 7770-71.
13. Danner Executive Session, December 19, 1973, p. 5; pp. 19-20; see also Danner diary, 1968.
Danner placed his meeting with Rebozo and Nixon as a few weeks prior to his meeting with Ed Morgan, which was in late August of 1968. (Danner Executive Session, December 18, 1973, p. 22). However, Danner also recalled that at the same meeting, candidate Nixon or Rebozo also asked

sions with Rebozo about a Hughes contribution, since in 1968 Danner had no association with Hughes whatsoever, and "didn't know any of the principals involved." [14] Danner was sure that either Mr. Nixon or Mr. Rebozo first asked him to check on a possible Hughes contribution at their meeting in 1968.[15] Danner's diary reflects that this meeting with candidate Nixon, Rebozo, and Danner could have occurred as early as April 10, 1968, or as late as July 10, 1968.[16]

Danner testified that Rebozo "suggested the possibility that I discuss the matter with Ed Morgan." [17] Danner was unsure how Rebozo knew that Morgan represented Hughes, but Danner's diary from 1968 indicates a long distance call from Danner to Rebozo on July 23, 1968, during which they discussed Mr. Edward P. Morgan.[18] Danner agreed to talk to Morgan about a possible contribution from Hughes, since he had been working with Morgan on negotiating the sale of the Tropicana in Las Vegas to the Winn-Dixie Company (owned by A. D. Davis and brothers).

Danner's diary reflects that he saw Ed Morgan on August 20 and August 21, 1968, and Danner testified that he asked Morgan about a possible Hughes contribution to the 1968 campaign.[19] Morgan said he would check on the matter with Robert Maheu and get back to Danner as soon as possible.[20] Following this meeting with Morgan, Danner's diary shows a call to Rebozo and Richard Nixon to discuss the subject of campaign funds and Howard Hughes, among other topics.[21]

Morgan called Robert Maheu in Las Vegas and explained to him that Bebe Rebozo through Richard Danner, wanted to know whether Howard Hughes would be willing to make a contribution to the Nixon campaign.[22] Maheu also recalls that Morgan mentioned that $50,000 was the requested amount for the contribution and that the contribution should be transmitted in cash. Maheu said he told Morgan that he

---

him to check with Clint Murchison, Jr., about the possibility of a contribution from him. Danner's diary shows that he met with Murchison on or about Tuesday, June 4, 1968 which would place his meeting with Nixon and Rebozo prior to June 4, 1968.

14. Danner Executive Session, December 18, 1973, p. 21.
15. *Ibid.*, p. 22.
16. See Danner diary from 1968 on April 10, May 17, July 10.
17. Danner Executive Session, December 18, 1973, p. 5.
18. See Danner diary, July 23, 1968. Exhibit 6.
19. Danner Executive Session, December 18, 1973, p. 22. Also see Danner Diary August 20-21, 1968. Exhibit 7.
20. Morgan interview, December 5, 1973, p. 2; Danner Executive Session, December 18, 1973, pp. 6-8.
21. See Danner diary from August 20 and August 21, 1968. Ex. 7. See also interview with Ed Morgan, December 5, 1973, p. 2. See also Danner Executive Session, December 18, 1973, pp. 6-8.
22. Morgan interview, December 5, 1973, p. 2.

would take the matter up with Howard Hughes.[23]

According to Maheu, Hughes felt that contributing through Rebozo was a good means of insuring access to Nixon were he elected President. Therefore, Hughes authorized $50,000 cash delivery to the '68 Nixon campaign according to Robert Maheu.[24] Maheu relayed the approval of Hughes to Edward P. Morgan, and suggested that Morgan, Rebozo, and Danner meet to arrange the mechanics of the delivery.[25]

Morgan recalled that shortly after he had transmitted this information to Danner, Danner told him that a meeting was arranged at Rebozo's suite at the Mayflower Hotel to discuss the mechanics for delivering the contribution.[26]

B. Rebozo's Version. First, Rebozo states that it was *Danner* who first brought up the subject of a possible Hughes contribution, and not Rebozo or candidate Nixon.[27] Secondly, Rebozo denied that there was any meeting among Danner, Rebozo and Nixon to discuss such matters with Rebozo either during or after the 1968 campaign.[28]

Rebozo did acknowledge, however, that there were some occasions in the 1968 campaign when Danner, President Nixon, and Rebozo met together.[29]

President Nixon has also issued denials that he met with Dick Danner and Bebe Rebozo to discuss a contribution from Howard Hughes. On January 16, 1974, Gerald Warren, Deputy White House Press Secretary, responded to press accounts of Danner's testimony by saying, "We have denied that the President discussed [with Mr. Danner] a possible contribution of any amount from Hughes." [30] Warren also told the Washington Post that President Nixon has never "discussed finances with Mr. Danner." [31] However, the handwritten notes in Danner's own diary from 1968 indicate that on September 27, 1968, candidate Nixon called Danner "re finances." [32]

23. Maheu interview, January 20, 1974; it was also Edward Morgan's explicit understanding that the contribution was to be in cash. (Edward Morgan interview, December 5, 1973).
24. Maheu interviews, September 15, 1973, and January 20, 1974.
25. Maheu interview, January 20, 1974; Edward Morgan interview, December 5, 1973.
26. Edward Morgan interview, December 5, 1973.
27. Rebozo Executive Session, March 20, 1973, p. 9.
28. *Ibid.*, pp. 11, 13.
29. Rebozo interview, January 17, 1974, p. 1.
30. *New York Times*, January 17, 1974, p. 30.
31. *Washington Post*, January 17, 1974, p. A1.
32. See 1968 Danner diary, September 27, 1968. In addition Danner also testified that at his earlier meeting with candidate Nixon and Rebozo to discuss the possibility of a Hughes contribution, one of them asked Danner to contact Clint Murchison, Jr., about a possible campaign contribution. Danner agreed to make the contact, and did in fact solicit a contribution

C. Meeting among Danner, Rebozo and Morgan. Danner, Rebozo and Morgan met for breakfast on September 11, 1968.[33] At this meeting Morgan recalls explaining that a contribution from Hughes of $50,000 in cash would be made to the Nixon campaign if there were some assurance that Nixon would personally acknowledge the receipt of the cash.[34] On September 9, 1968, Robert Maheu had received $150,000 in two checks from Nadine Henley of the Hughes organization, which was to be used in part for a campaign contribution to Mr. Nixon.[35]

Rebozo testified that "Morgan wanted to hand the money to the President, himself," but that Rebozo explained to Morgan that the President would never personally accept a contribution.[36] In addition, Rebozo testified that he felt uneasy about accepting a large cash contribution from Howard Hughes through Edward Morgan because of the 1956 loan from Hughes to F. Donald Nixon and because Ed Morgan represented Drew Pearson.[37]

Danner recalled no request by Morgan to pay the money directly to candidate Nixon, as Rebozo claimed, but testified that the contribution "was to be made through ordinary sources, not to the President, not to the candidate, but whoever was handling his campaign funds." [38] Danner also recalled that Rebozo indicated his willingness to handle the Hughes contribution at this meeting.[39]

Morgan recalled that he had merely asked for an assurance that Hughes received an acknowledgement of the contribution, but that *neither Rebozo* nor Danner would give him such assurances at this meeting.[40]

D. New York Meeting. Danner testified that sometime after the meeting in Washington, D.C., when Edward Morgan explained that the contribution would be forthcoming, Danner was told by Morgan that Bebe Rebozo would be contacted to make arrangements for the contribution.[41] Danner said

from Murchison as reflected by Danner's diary on or about June 4, 1968, but Murchison had already made other arrangements to contribute to the 1968 campaign. (Danner Exec. Session, Dec. 18, 1973, pp. 23-24.)

Murchison has advised the Committee that he discussed a contribution with President Nixon who told Murchison to give the contribution to him or Rose Mary Woods. (Murchison interview).

33. See Danner diary, September 11, 1968. Exhibit 9.
34. See Morgan interview, December 5, 1973, p. 2.
35. See Henley Exhibits #2 and #3, and Henley interview, January 22, 1974.
36. See Rebozo Executive Session, March 20, 1974, p. 15.
37. Rebozo Executive Session, March 20, 1974, p. 15.
38. Danner Executive Session, December 18, 1973, p. 15.
39. *Ibid.*, p. 12.
40. Morgan interview, December 5, 1973, p. 2.
41. Danner Executive Session, December 18, 1973, p. 27.

that shortly after receiving this information, Danner traveled
to New York City to discuss some campaign matters with
John Mitchell and Maurice Stans. Danner initially testified
that Edward Morgan accompanied him on this trip,[42] but
after discussing the matter with Morgan, Danner stated that
Morgan was not present in New York.[43]

Danner recalled that Rebozo introduced him to Stans and
Mitchell in the New York campaign offices.[44] Danner recalled having a brief discussion with Stans, and a longer discussion with John Mitchell about the Florida Democrats for
Nixon Committee, as well as possible campaign strategy.
Danner testified that during his meeting with Mitchell and
Rebozo in the late morning, Rebozo was called out of the
meeting to answer a telephone call directing him to meet
with some Hughes representatives who were allegedly handling the cash contribution to the Nixon campaign.[45]

Rebozo returned sometime later,[46] according to Danner,
an was "very angry and upset" because he learned that the
meeting was to be with F. Donald Nixon, older brother of
President Nixon, and John Meier, an employee of Robert
Maheu and Howard Hughes an acquaintance of F. Donald
Nixon.[47]

Danner recalls Rebozo telling him that Rebozo was not
about to see, talk to, or associate with F. Donald Nixon and
John Meier or have anything to do with them in the area of
political contributions.[48] Therefore, Danner testified that
Rebozo did not have the meeting with John Meier and Donald Nixon and that no contribution from Hughes was delivered at that time. Danner knew of no other attempts to
deliver the $50,000 cash contribution prior to the 1968
election.

Donald Nixon recalled that early in the 1968 campaign,
John Meier had some conversations with him about how
Howard Hughes had made arrangements to make a contribution to Mr. Nixon. Nixon recalled that Meier commented
to him that Meier and Robert Maheu wanted to make some

42. See Danner interview, August 30, 1973, p. 3.
43. See Danner Executive Session, December 18, 1973, p. 28; Morgan also
denies that he was in New York on that occasion (Morgan interview,
December 5, 1973, p. 2.)
44. Danner Executive Session, December 18, 1973, p. 29.
45. Danner Executive Session, December 18, 1973, p. 32. In his affidavit
for the IRS on July 5, 1973, Danner stated that Rebozo spoke to John
Meier on the telephone. However, Danner testified before the Select Committee that he did not know with whom Rebozo spoke on the phone.
46. Danner was unsure whether he was still meeting with John Mitchell
when Rebozo returned. (*Ibid.*, p. 36.)
47. *Ibid.*, p. 27.
48. Danner Executive Session, Dec. 18, 1973, p. 33.

arrangements for a contribution.[49]

Nixon also recalled that John Meier wanted to get together with Bebe Rebozo and Donald Nixon in 1968 during the campaign. However, Nixon recalled that Bebe Rebozo cancelled the meeting that was supposed to be held among Meier, Nixon, and Rebozo when he found out that John Meier was going to be involved.[50] Rebozo testified that he met once with F. Donald Nixon and John Meier during the 1968 campaign, but that there was no connection between the meeting and his refusal to accept the $50,000 contribution.[51] Rebozo testified subsequently that the presence of Meier and Nixon in New York "would have added to my (Rebozo's) rationale", in refusing to accept the money.[52]

Danner testified that his meeting in New York with Rebozo and Mitchell occurred after his meeting with Morgan and Rebozo in Washington, D.C. However, hotel records from New York hotels from the summer and fall of 1968, indicate that the only dates on which both John Meier and F. Donald Nixon were staying in New York, were from July 7 through July 10, 1968, at the New York Hilton.[53] In addition, John Meier testified before the SEC that he had dinner with Donald Nixon on July 8, 1968, at which time he met Bebe Rebozo. [54] Furthermore, Danner's own 1968 diary shows that Danner was in New York City on Monday, July 8, 1968, for meetings with "John Mitchell, Tom Evans, et al." [55] Finally, former Attorney General John Mitchell recalled meeting Dick Danner in New York prior to the Republican Convention in the summer of 1968.[56] Mitchell recalled that Howard Hughes contributed to the 1968 campaign, but he could not recall any discussion of the contribution at his summer meeting with Danner.[57]

Nadine Henley, Senior Vice President of the Summa Corporation, testified that in July 30, 1968, three weeks after the New York meeting, Robert Maheu told her that Howard Hughes had approved a $50,000 contribution to both the Nixon and the Humphrey Presidential campaigns.[58]

---

49. See interview with F. Donald Nixon, Nov. 17, 1973, p. 5.
50. *Ibid.*, p. 6.
51. Rebozo interview, Oct. 8, 1973.
52. Rebozo Executive Session, March 21, 1973, p. 424.
53. See New York Hilton Hotel Records, July, 1968, Exhibit 10.
54. Meier Interview with the SEC, Oct. 23, 1973, p. 8.
55. See Danner diary, July 8, 1968, Exhibit 11.
56. The Republican Convention was from Aug. 5-8, 1968.
57. Mitchell interview, Oct. 18, 1973, p. 6. Mr. Mitchell refused to testify further about this matter after the Oct. 18 interview on advice of counsel pending he outcomes of his criminal trials.
58. See Henley interview, Jan. 22, 1974, p. 3. See also Nadine Henley Exhibit 1.

3. ATTEMPTED CONTRIBUTION
AT PALM SPRINGS

Robert Maheu's telephone messages indicate that he was called on November 22, 1968, by a Stephen Craig of President-Elect Nixon's office concerning a possible campaign contribution since the campaign had a deficit of $800,000.[59]

Maheu recalled having a conversation with Howard Hughes after the election in which Maheu was instructed to make arrangements through then-Governor Paul Laxalt to make the promised $50,000 cash contribution to President-Elect Nixon.

Maheu testified that he approached Governor Laxalt who agreed to do what he could to help Maheu effect the delivery of the contribution. Former Governor Laxalt, however, recalled that Maheu contacted him sometime after the 1968 election to discuss fulfilling a campaign pledge made through Robert Finch to National Republican Campaign Committee.[60]

Laxalt recalled that he agreed to set up a meeting between Maheu and representatives of President-Elect Nixon during the Republican Governors' Conference in Palm Springs, California, on December 6, 1968.[61]

Laxalt says that he had no plans to contact anyone in particular on the Nixon staff to arrange for the delivery and that he certainly did not contemplate or plan any Maheu-Nixon meeting.[62]

Robert Finch recalled only that former Governor Laxalt called him to set up a meeting of the Western governors with President-elect Nixon.[63]

Finch said he had no knowledge of any meeting between Robert Maheu and President-Elect Nixon.[64]

Nadine Henley recalled that in early December 1968, Robert Maheu requested $50,000 in cash from her in order to make a campaign contribution to Richard Nixon to cover campaign deficiencies in the 1968 campaign.[65]

In addition, on December 5, 1968, Robert Maheu received $50,000 in $100 bills from the cage at Sands casino.[66] Therefore, Robert Maheu appears to have received approximately $100,000 in $100 bills on or about December 5 and 6, 1968, prior to his trip to Palm Springs.

59. See Maheu's Telephone logs, November 22, 1968, Ex. 12.
60. Paul Laxalt Interviews, October 11, 1973 and December 20, 1973.
61. *Ibid.*
62. See Paul Laxalt Interview, October 11, 1973.
63. Finch interview, November 1973, pp. 1-2.
64. *Ibid.*
65. Nadine Henley Interview, pp. 3-4, Jan. 22, 1974. See later section for fuller explanation of source of money.
66. See fuller explanation in following section.

Perhaps coincidentally, on Thursday, December 5, 1968, Richard Danner flew from Miami to Las Vegas to have discussions with Robert Maheu about possible employment by the Hughes Tool Company as manager of the Frontier Hotel.[67]

Danner testified that he met with Robert Maheu and others in the late afternoon of December 5, 1968, and that he also saw Maheu again on December 6, 1968. Danner testified that the substance of their discussions solely concerned his possible employment. Danner emphasized that there was no discussion whatsoever of any campaign contributions, nor was Danner given any cash by Maheu during the time he was in Las Vegas.[68]

On November 29, 1972, Danner told an agent of the Internal Revenue Service that Danner and Maheu began discussing the prospective contribution "shortly after the 1968 election, which preceded his employment with Hughes Tool Company."[69]

Danner's diary from 1968 shows that on Thursday, November 21, Danner received a long distance call from Bebe Rebozo about the "house project." Danner's diary shows five more telephone conversations with Rebozo in the week following November 21, and then a call from Danner to Rebozo in the week following November 21, and then a call from Danner to Rebozo on Friday, November 29, about the "project."[70] Danner testified that he could not recall what the "house project" was or the substance of his conversations during that time with Rebozo. This time period in late November, shortly before Danner travelled to Las Vegas to meet with Robert Maheu, also coincided with the initial discussions on Florida about the purchase by President-Elect Nixon of the Key Biscayne home of former Senator George Smathers. However, Danner testified that he played no role in the purchase by President Nixon of his Key Biscayne home and that he could not recall what the "house project" was.[71]

President-Elect Nixon flew to Palm Springs for an appearance at the Republican Governors' Association Conference on December 6, 1968. There he met for talks with small groups of Governors on the terrace of the Walter Annenberg home where he was staying.[72] After receiving the money from Nadine Henley, Maheu recalled flying to Palm Springs with

67. See Danner Diary, December 5-6, 1968, Ex. 13.
68. Richard Danner Executive Session, June 12, 1974, pp. 1, 142-145.
69. IRS memo, November 29, 1972.
70. See 1968 Danner Diary, week of November 21-28 and November 29, Ex. 14.
71. Danner Executive Session, June 11, 1974, p. 90.
72. See *New York Times*, December 7, 1968, p. 1, col. 4.

Paul Laxalt. Maheu also recalled driving to the Annenberg residence where Nixon was staying, and while Maheu waited in the car with the money, Laxalt went in the home to make arrangements for the delivery. Maheu recalled that Laxalt returned to the car and said that Nixon's schedule prohibited any meeting with Robert Maheu.[73]

Danner testified that he was not aware of the attempted delivery at Palm Springs by Maheu until after he had joined the Hughes Tool Company in early 1969.[74]

When Richard M. Nixon was inaugurated President of the United States on January 20, 1969, the $50,000 contribution committed initially by Edward P. Morgan in the summer of 1968, and still not been delivered to the Presidential campaign.

4. REBOZO'S 1969 RESPONSIBILITIES

A. Introduction. There is evidence before the Committee indicating that in 1969 Charles (Bebe) Rebozo exercised a number of responsibilities on behalf of the White House and President Nixon. These simultaneous assignments included the following:

1. Fund-raising for the use of the administration;
2. The disbursal of funds for various administration-connected projects;
3. To act as agent for President Nixon in the purchase, improvement, and maintenance of his homes in Key Biscayne, Florida;
4. Fund-raising for the President's re-election campaign.

B. Fund-raising. On February 17, 1969, H. R. Haldeman wrote a "confidential" memorandum to John Ehrlichman which stated in part:

Bebe Rebozo has been asked by the President to contact J. Paul Getty in London regarding major contributions. Bebe would like advice from you or someone as to how this can legally and technically be handled. The funds should go to some operating entity other than the National Committee so that we can retain full control of their use.

Bebe would appreciate your calling him with this advice as soon as possible since the President has asked him to move quickly. Signed H.[75]

73. Robert Maheu Interview, January 20, 1974.
74. Danner Executive Session, June 11, 1974, p. 143.
75. See Haldeman memo to Ehrlichman, dated February 17, 1969. Exhibit 15.

H. R. Haldeman stated through his attorney that he recalled that Bebozo attempted to obtain a contribution from J. Paul Getty.[76]

Edward L. Morgan said in an interview that shortly after his appointment to the White House staff in early 1969, he was called by John Ehrlichman.[77] Morgan said that Ehrlichman requested his advice on whether a contributor like J. Paul Getty could give $50,000 to the administration to be used for social events at the White House until July, 1969, when a new budget appropriation would be available for such purposes.[78] Morgan stated that he called Chuck Stuart, a friend of his in the White House who also worked for Ehrlichman, to discuss the matter, and that they agreed that using private contributions to fund White House social functions was inappropriate.[79] Morgan also said that he advised Ehrlichman that he and Stuart agreed that private contributions for such social functions were inappropriate.[80]

Rebozo testified that Herb Kalmbach asked him to make an appointment for Kalmbach with J. Paul Getty for the purpose of obtaining a contribution for the 1972 election.[81] Rebozo testified that he had not been asked by anyone else to speak to Getty himself nor had he been requested by anyone else to obtain money from Mr. Getty.[82]

Herbert Kalmbach testified that Rebozo had asked Kalmbach to solicit funds from Mr. Getty for the 1970 senatorial campaign program.[83] Kalmbach also testified that Rebozo "set it up for him to see Mr. Getty in Europe." [84]

General Alexander Haig testified that President Nixon had advised him that Mr. Rebozo had received campaign contributions frequently, and that he "normally" or "generally" passed them on to the campaign.[85] Haig further testified that he assumed that the time period discussed by the President included 1969 through 1971.[86]

In addition to this evidence concerning the contact with J. Paul Getty in early 1969, Rebozo was also having discussions at about the same time with Richard Danner about the possibility of a cash contribution from Howard Hughes.

76. Information furnished by John Wilson to Terry Lenzner, May 17, 1974.
77. Edward L. Morgan interview, p. 1.
78. *Ibid.*
79. *Ibid.* Stuart confirmed the conversation with Morgan, but recalled that he thought the contributions should be made by check and not cash. (Stuart interview, June 20, 1974).
80. *Ibid.*
81. Rebozo Executive Session, March 20, 1974, pp. 89-90.
82. Rebozo Executive Session, March 20, 1974, p. 90.
83. Kalmbach Executive Session, March 21, 1974, pp. 1-2.
84. *Ibid.*
85. Haig Executive Session, May 15, 1974, pp. 59-61.
86. *Ibid.*

These discussions are covered more fully in a subsequent section of this report.

C. Disbursal of Funds. There is evidence indicating that Rebozo maintained a fund in Florida to pay for administration-connected costs. In a letter of April 28, 1969, from Rebozo to Kalmbach, Rebozo wrote in part:

> Over the weekend, I spoke with John Ehrlichman and explained to him that it had been decided that the larger balance which I mentioned to you will be kept here in order to take care of frequent administration-connected costs which arise from time to time.[87]

There is evidence indicating that the fund which Rebozo maintained in Florida consisted of campaign funds. Rebozo testified that he retained about $6,000 from the 1968 campaign because the campaign owed him that amount for expenses that he had covered during the campaign.[88] On April 15, 1969, Rebozo set up the Wakefield Special Account with a deposit of $6,000 from the "Florida Nixon for President Committee." [89] Thomas H. Wakefield testified that he did not know that this account was opened until later when Rebozo advised him that he had established the account and that both individuals were signators.[90]

Also on April 15, 1969, Jack Caulfield wrote to Herbert Kalmbach a letter which said in part:

> Listed below is a list of expenses incurred by myself and another individual who shall remain nameless with respect to matters of interest to J. D. E.[91]

Caulfield's bill totaled $320 and he concluded:

> I would appreciate a check in the amount indicated above to be mailed to my residence, 13 Carlton Road, Orangeburg, N.Y.[92]

On April 17, 1969, Kalmbach wrote a letter to John Ehrlichman which said in part:

> Confirming our conversation of a few minutes ago, I'm in the process of setting up one "trustee for clients" account at the Security Pacific National Bank's Newport

87. See letter from Rebozo to Kalmbach dated April 28, 1969, Ex. 16.
88. Rebozo Executive Session, March 20, 1974, pp. 22-23.
89. See Exhibit 17.
90. Wakefield Executive Session, June 10, 1974, pp. 43-44.
91. See Exhibit 18. The reference to J.D.E. apparently refers to John Ehrlichman.
92. *Ibid.*

Beach office here in the Newport Center. The initial deposit will be in the amount of $216.18 which was received from BeBe this date. I will write checks to Jack Caulfield and whomever else you may authorize to receive payments at such time as I receive the additional funds.[93]

Rebozo also sent Kalmbach an additional check for $200 on April 28, 1969, and a check from the Wakefield Special Account to Kalmbach for $1,000 on July 17, 1969.[94] These funds were subsequently used by Herbert Kalmbach to pay the expenses and salary of Anthony T. Ulasewicz.[95]

There is conflicting testimony concerning whether or not Rebozo was aware of the purpose of the funds that he forwarded in 1969. Rebozo testified that he had advised Kalmbach after the 1968 election that he had leftover funds available and that subsequently Kalmbach requested some of the funds to be sent to him.[96] Rebozo testified that Kalmbach did not indicate nor did Rebozo ask what the purpose of the funds was.[97]

Kalmbach said that he was authorized by John Ehrlichman to contact Rebozo about obtaining leftover campaign funds to pay for Caulfield's expense statement submitted to Kalmbach.[98] Kalmbach testified that he then contacted Rebozo to obtain funds to pay for the expenses of Caulfield and Ulasewicz.[99] Kalmbach testified that he discussed the nature of the activities of Caulfield and Ulasewicz with Rebozo and that Rebozo specifically knew that the money was for Caulfield and Ulasewicz.[100]

Kalmbach's notes also indicate that he called Rebozo during the week of July 14, 1969, and that they discussed the payment to Ulasewicz as well as the payment of his expenses.[101]

However, Rebozo testified that he was not aware of the purpose of the funds that he forwarded to Kalmbach.[102]

Rebozo also used funds to pay for personal expenses for President Nixon from 1969 through 1973. These expense items are more fully explained later in this report.

93. See Exhibit 19. See also Kalmbach Executive Session, May 5, 1974, Ex. 000.
94. See Kalmbach Executive Session, May 15, 1974, Ex. 00.
95. Kalmbach Executive Session, May 5, 1974.
96. Rebozo Executive Session, March 20, 1974, p. 44.
97. Rebozo Executive Session, March 20, 1974, p. 26.
98. Kalmbach interview, June 13, 1974.
99. Kalmbach Executive Session, May 5, 1974, pp. 156-157 (Galleys).
100. Kalmbach Executive Session, May 5, 1974, p. 16.
101. See Exhibit 20; see also Kalmbach Executive Session, May 5, 1974, p. 16.
102. Rebozo Executive Session, March 20, 1974, pp. 23-26.

Finally, Larry Higby, formerly H. R. Haldeman's administrative assistant, testified that on or about April 30, 1973, at about the time of Haldeman's resignation:

... Mr. Haldeman told me that during one of the discussions he had with the President at the time of, or immediately after, his resignation, the President indicated that Mr. Rebozo did have some funds that could be made available to Mr. Haldeman; and as I understand it, also to Mr. Ehrlichman for the purpose of assisting in a legal defense.[103]

Higby also testified that Haldeman advised him that Rebozo had somewhere "in the neighborhood of $400,000 available to assist on legal fees." [104] Higby testified that he had confirmed the substance of his testimony two weeks earlier in a telephone conversation with Haldeman.[105]

D. *Acting As Agent for President Nixon at Key Biscayne.*
On the day following President Nixon's inauguration in 1969, Thomas H. Wakefield testified that he met with the President and Bebo Rebozo at a White House staff reception.[106] Wakefield testified that at this meeting with President Nixon and Rebozo, Wakefield was given instructions concerning matters which resulted in expenditures incurred on behalf of President Nixon.[107] Wakefield refused to discuss these instructions, claiming they were protected by the attorney-client privilege. Wakefield also testified that this meeting with President Nixon and Rebozo was the first occasion when Wakefield was informed by the President that henceforth Rebozo would act as the President's agent for matters that Wakefield refused to describe.[108]

Wakefield also testified that he attended a second meeting at the White House with John Ehrlichman and Bebe Rebozo either later the same day or the following day after Wakefield's meeting with President Nixon.[109] Wakefield again refused to disclose the substance of this conversation on the grounds of attorney-client privilege and because "Mr. Rebozo was designated as agent in the beginning of the

103. Higby Executive Session, May 22, 1974, p. 4.
104. *Ibid.*, p. 22.
105. *Ibid.*
106. Wakefield Executive Session, June 10, 1974, pp. 127-131. Wakefield refused to answer a number of questions about his conversations with President Nixon and Charles G. Rebozo because of the attorney-client privilege Wakefield asserted with respect to both individuals.
107. *Ibid.*
108. *Ibid.*
109. Wakefield Interview, June 24, 1974, p. 5.

443

conversation by Mr. Ehrlichman." [110] Wakefield stated that some action was taken as a result of his meeting with Ehrlichman and Rebozo, but Wakefield declined to describe what occurred because of his attorney-client relationship with the President.[111] As will be described more fully in a section below, certain $100 bills were deposited among trust accounts held by Thomas H. Wakefield, and were applied for expenditures on behalf of the President's Key Biscayne homes at the instructions of BeBe Rebozo.[112]

In addition, Richard Danner's diary entry of November 21, 1968, reflects: "L. D. from C. G. R. Miami RE: house project." [113] Danner testified that this notation reflected a telephone call with Rebozo, but that Danner had "no recollection whatsoever of what house project had to do with that conversation." [114] Danner did recall his friend former Senator George Smathers telling him that Smathers was going to sell his house to President Nixon following the 1968 election, but Danner had no recollection of discussing this sale with BeBe Rebozo.[115]

Therefore, at the time in early 1969 when Rebozo and Danner again began to discuss a contribution from Howard Hughes, there is evidence indicating: Rebozo was already raising funds at the direction of the President; Rebozo was disbursing money from campaign funds for various administration projects; and Rebozo was acting as agent for President Nixon with respect to the purchase and maintenance of his Key Biscayne homes.

5. DELIVERY AND RETENTION OF THE CONTRIBUTIONS

Introduction and Summary of Facts. The contributions that were finally delivered to Rebozo were the culmination of the attempted deliveries during 1968 described earlier. A contribution was discussed during the 1968 election and continued to be an item of discussion thereafter among various parties, including Hughes, Maheu, Danner, and Rebozo. The discussions were intense in early December 1968 and continued into the spring and summer of 1969, when Rebozo chided Danner about Hughes' generous support of Democrats and less sizeable support of President Nixon and Maheu author-

110. Wakefield Executive Session, June 10, 1974, p. 57. Wakefield interview, June 24, 1974, p. 5.
111. Wakefield Interview, June 24, 1974, p. 5.
112. See section on Possible Use of the Money.
113. See Exhibit 14.
114. Danner Executive Session, June 11, 1974, pp. 90-93.
115. *Ibid.*

ized a contribution to Rebozo.

The testimony on the deliveries of the money is voluminous and often contradictory, and Danner, Maheu, and Rebozo maintained few written records of the transaction. Rebozo testified that the money he received from Danner remained unused in a safe deposit box from its delivery to him (in two installments) until he returned it to agents of Hughes in June 1973. That testimony has been challenged by other testimony and evidence before the Select Committee.

The available testimony and evidence point to the following facts:

1. The money for one of the deliveries to Rebozo was put together in early December 1968. There is considerable testimony from various principals indicating that the first delivery consisted of money made available in December 1968 and that it was maintained whole until the ultimate delivery.

—In early Decemebr 1968, Robert Maheu and others acting on behalf of Howard Hughes were deeply involved in attempts to make a Hughes to Nixon contribution.

—Robert Maheu received $100,000 in cash in early December, $50,000 of which he tried to deliver to President-elect Nixon or one of his aides at Palm Springs, pursuant to negotiations commenced earlier in the year by Rebozo and Danner.

—Danner was in Las Vegas during this December 1968 period talking about joining the Hughes organization and, according to one of Danner's recollections, discussing political contributions with Maheu.

—Fifty consecutively numbered $100 bills among those Rebozo identified as the first delivery were, according to Federal Reserve Board records and other documentary evidence, delivered to the Las Vegas bank used by Hughes casinos during this early December 1968 period.

2. The first delivery took place in 1969.

—In their initial interviews and testimony, the principals involved in the deliveries agreed that 1969 was the year of the first delivery. Maheu has continued to subscribe to that statement; Danner changed his testimony after consultation with Rebozo; and Rebozo changed from 1969 (in his first interview with the IRS) to 1970 (in subsequent testimony) as the year of the first delivery.

3. The first delivery to Rebozo occurred September 11 or 12, 1969, in Key Biscayne, Florida.

—When Danner joined the Hughes organization in February, 1969, there was an ongoing concern that the money be soon delivered.

—According to Danner, in the spring of 1969, he and Maheu noted that the 1968 money was still intact and available for Rebozo, and Danner told Rebozo that it was available. Not long before September 11-12, Maheu authorized a delivery to Rebozo.

—Robert Maheu has stated the first delivery took place in 1969.

—Danner's first statement regarding this contribution substantially comports with Maheu's recollection of the first delivery.

—Danner's testimony, until changed in July, 1973, after consultation with Rebozo, was that the first delivery was in September 1969.

4. There is considerable evidence suggesting that the second delivery took place on July 3, 1970 or August 19-20, 1970, and there is some evidence of a delivery on October 28-30, 1970.

—*July 3, 1970*—According to Rebozo and Danner, this was the date of a delivery at San Clemente. Both men have always contended that one of the two deliveries was at San Clemente, and Danner testified this is the only time he was there. Only Rebozo testified firmly that this was the *first* delivery. Maheu stated that both deliveries were at Key Biscayne.

—*August 19-20, 1970*—If the first delivery were on July 3, the second delivery would have been either August 19-20 or October 28-30. Danner and Maheu discounted the October date as too close to the 1970 election for the money to have been used for Congressional campaigns.

Rebozo testified that the second delivery was in Key Biscayne, following the July 3, 1970 delivery within a "matter of weeks . . . (it) could have been three months . . . I don't know. I think I saw somewhere where Danner had indicated it was in August and that would be correct."

—*October 28-30, 1970*—The strongest evidence supporting this late 1970 date is the statement of Thomas Bell, a Hughes lawyer, that he gave $50,000 to Danner on October 26. Danner testified that he did not receive money from Bell, however, and Danner and Robert Maheu doubted a delivery so close to the 1970 Congressional election.

5. There is evidence suggesting that there may have been more than two deliveries from Danner to Rebozo.

—The only way much of the conflicting testimony can be reconciled is to conclude there were more than two deliveries of funds.

—There are four likely delivery dates: Sept. 1969; July 3, 1970; Aug. 19-20, 1970; and Oct. 28-30, 1970.

—Four packets of money have been identified as posisble sources of the deliveries: early Dec., 1968 (Sands Casino); Dec. 5, 1968 (Nadine Henley); July 11, 1969 (Nadine Henley); and Oct. 26, 1970 (Thomas Bell—Silver Slipper).

6. Documentary evidence from the Federal Reserve raises a question whether Rebozo maintained the two deliveries intact (see below). The following summary paragraphs should help the reader understand the detailed information that follows:

Section A sets forth the testimony and statements of the principals. There are numerous contradictions among the principals, and most of them have contradicted themselves on key points.

Section B is an analysis of the possible sources of the contributions to Rebozo. Determining when and where the money for the two deliveries was put together is directly related to an examination of Rebozo's testimony that the money he received from Hughes was the same money he returned to Hughes in June 1973. The Hughes people involved in assembling the money for delivery to Rebozo, notably Robert Maheu, have stated that the money for each delivery remained intact from the time it was assembled until the dates of delivery to Rebozo by Richard Danner, Hughes' agent. The Select Committee attempted to determine the accuracy of that assertion, and it found no contradiitory evidence or testimony. In contrast, Rebozo's testimony that he did not disturb or use the money has been challenged by testimony and evidence received by the Select Committee.

The available evidence suggests that $50,000 for one of the deliveries was obtained in early 1968. In the money returned and identified as the Hughes contribution [116] are numerous $100 bills—in the package identified as the first delivery and in the package identified as the second delivery —that were not available for commercial circulation until *after* early December 1968. Therefore, either the money was

116. The serial numbers which the Select Committee and the Federal Reserve System have been tracing are those of the 1001 Federal Reserve Notes Rebozo returned. While the contribution is generally referred to as a $100,000 contribution, Rebozo returned $100,000. How and when the extra Note got into the money is an unresolved question. The Committee has no evidence that a list of serial numbers was prepared when the money was put together or when it was delivered.

not kept intact from time of origin in December 1968 until
its delivery to Rebozo, or it was not kept intact by Rebozo
between its receipt and its return.

Section C analyzes the possible delivery dates and reaches
the conclusions summarized above.

Section D analyzes the testimony and evidence relating to
the storage of the Hughes contributions by Rebozo.

Section E compares the testimony and evidence relating
to possible combinations of sources and delivery dates with
the available Federal Reserve records. The comparison raises
a question whether the money Rebozo returned was the same
money he received.

For all possible combinations of delivery dates save one,
there are $100 bills in the money returned and identified as
the Hughes contribution that were not available for commercial circulation until *after* one or both delivery dates.
For example, if the first delivery was on July 3, 1970 in San
Clemente and the second on August 19-20, 1970 in Key
Biscayne (a probable combination, according to testimony
by Danner and Rebozo), there are *35* bills in the money
returned and identified as the second delivery that were not
available for commercial circulation until *after* August 20,
1970. Those 35 bills, therefore, could not have been delivered to Rebozo on August 19-20, but instead would have
been inserted into the package identified as the second delivery at some later date before Rebozo returned the money.
The latest date of commercial distribution is October 1, 1970,
when a 1969 Series $100 bill, series number GO 2 134 916 A,
was released to the Lakeview Trust and Savings Bank in
Chicago by the Chicago Federal Reserve Bank. The 35 bills
are as follows:

FEDERAL RESERVE NOTES (IDENTIFIED AS PART OF SECOND
DELIVERY TO REBOZO) NOT AVAILABLE FOR COMMERCIAL
DISTRIBUTION UNTIL AFTER AUGUST 19-20, 1970 *

* For some of the Notes listed below, records exist showing date of distribution to commercial banks. (Comm. Bank) For other bills, however,
records exist only through the date of release to a Federal Reserve Bank's
Cash Department. The dates of commercial release for these Notes would
be on or after the dates of release to Cash Departments.

SERIES	SERIAL	DATE RELEASED TO CASH DEPT., FEDERAL RESERVE BANK	DATE RELEASED TO COMM. BANK
1969	G02 134 916 A	9/8/70 (Chicago)	10/1/70 (Lakeview Trust, Chicago)
1969	L02 012 307 A	9/3/70 (Los Angeles)	9/23/70 (New Nat'l Bank, Las Vegas, 4th and Bridger)
1969	B00 745 268 A	9/21/70 (New York)	—

448

SERIES	SERIAL	DATE RELEASED TO CASH DEPT., FEDERAL RESERVE BANK	DATE RELEASED TO COMM. BANK
1969	L02 044 519 A	9/3/70 (Los Angeles)	9/16/70 (New Nat'l Bank, Las Vegas, 4th and Bridger)
1969	L03 169 610 A	9/11/70 (Los Angeles)	9/14/70 (New Nat'l Bank, Las Vegas, 4th and Bridger)
1969	L03 201 320 A	9/11/70 (Los Angeles)	9/14/70 (New Nat'l Bank, Las Vegas, 4th and Bridger)
1969	L03 169 914 A	9/11/70 (Los Angeles)	—
1969	L03 169 915 A	9/11/70 (Los Angeles)	—
1969	L03 170 246 A	9/11/70 (Los Angeles)	—
1969	L03 170 247 A	9/11/70 (Los Angeles)	—
1969	L03 171 517 A	9/11/70 (Los Angeles)	—
1969	L03 171 653 A	9/11/70 (Los Angeles)	—
1969	L03 201 337 A	9/11/70 (Los Angeles)	9/14/70 (New Nat'l Bank, Las Vegas, 4th and Bridger)
1969	L03 202 841 A	9/11/70 (Los Angeles)	—
1963A	H00 933 849 A	9/8/70 (St. Louis)	—
1963A	L03 967 973 A	9/3/70 (Los Angeles)	—
1963A	L03 967 972 A	9/3/70 (Los Angeles)	—
1969	L01 996 101 A	9/3/70 (Los Angeles)	—
1969	L01 997 818 A	9/3/70 (Los Angeles)	—
1969	L01 997 820 A	9/3/70 (Los Angeles)	—
1969	L01 998 739 A	9/3/70 (Los Angeles)	—
1969	L02 006 342 A	9/3/70 (Los Angeles)	—
1969	L02 011 839 A	9/3/70 (Los Angeles)	—
1969	L02 013 297 A	9/3/70 (Los Angeles)	—
1969	L02 036 812 A	9/3/70 (Los Angeles)	—
1969	L02 038 013 A	9/3/70 (Los Angeles)	—
1969	L02 039 302 A	9/3/70 (Los Angeles)	—
1969	L02 039 303 A	9/3/70 (Los Angeles)	—
1969	L02 047 193 A	9/3/70 (Los Angeles)	—
1969	L01 998 424 A	9/3/70 (Los Angeles)	—
1969	K00 853 653 A	8/5/70 (Dallas)	9/2/70 (NW Nat'l Bank, Dallas)
1963A	L03 778 452 A	6/9/70 (Los Angeles)	9/2/70 (Valley Nat'l Bank, Las Vegas)
1963A	L03 778 219 A	6/9/70 (Los Angeles)	9/2/70 (Valley Nat'l Bank, Las Vegas)
1969	L01 455 291 A	8/27/70 (Los Angeles)	—
1969	L01 447 735 A	8/27/70 (Los Angeles)	—

It is possible that the second delivery was not made until late October 1970 (as discussed in Section IV), in which case the Federal Reserve evidence does not contradict Rebozo's testimony. The October date, however, is less probable than several other dates, as explained in Section IV.

A. Testimony and Statements of the Principals. The testimony and statements by the key participants concerning the deliveries of the Hughes $100,000 do not conform in many key respects. Most of the people involved have changed their testimony and statements as the investigation progressed. The only consistent assertion of all principals have been that there were only two deliveries.

When initially questioned about the deliveries, the various parties—Robert Maheu, Peter Maheu, Danner, and Rebozo —placed the date of the first delivery within about one year of the November 1968 election.[117] As the investigation intensified, from about the time Rebozo returned the money in June 1973,[118] the parties began recalling later delivery dates. Other differences in testimony have occurred, including significant changes regarding locations of deliveries anl number of people present. For example, Robert Maheu has stated that he was present at a delivery in Key Biscayne. Danner initially so testified, but later, after talking with Rebozo, changed his testimony to agree with Rebozo's testimony that Maheu was not present.

Testimony about the Hughes-Rebozo contribution has been extensive and varied. In addition to the staff interviews and sworn testimony in sessions before the Select Committee, testimony concerning the contribution can be found in the *Maheu v. Hughes Tool Company* civil litigation[119]; the interviews and depositions relating to the Securities and Exchange Commission's investigation of the acquisition of Air West by Hughes [120]; and the interviews and affidavits furnished the Select Committee by the Internal Revenue Service, pursuant to a Senate resolution.[121]

The following summary is not exhaustive and must be read in conjunction with the later sections of the report analyzing the contribution.

1. Richard Danner. In February, 1969, Richard Danner commenced his employment with Hughes Tool Company as General Manager of the Frontier Hotel.[122] His responsibilities also called for him to serve as liaison for the Hughes entities

117. Citations for the statements made by the various parties are in the lengthier discussions below.
118. The return of the money is described in Section 8 below.
119. *Robert A. Maheu v. Hughes Tool Company,* Civil No. 72-305 HP, United States District Court for the Central District of California.
120. Securities and Exchange Commission, Case No. HO596; information from the Commission was furnished to the Select Committee pursuant to a letter of disclosure. William Turner, a lawyer with the SEC, was particularly helpful.
121. *See* Senate Resolution 288, 93rd Congress, 2nd Session.
122. Richard Danner Executive Session, December 18, 1973, p. 40.

and the Nixon administration.[123] According to Robert Maheu, Hughes was especially pleased that Danner joined the Hughes operation inasmuch as the 1968 campaign contribution still remained undelivered, and Danner, with his connections with Rebozo, coull readily remedy this problem.[124]

While Danner's recollection has been unclear about the dates of deliveries, who was present and who provided the money to him, he testified with certainty about the circumstances leading up to the decision to make the $100,000 in cash available to Rebozo.

Danner testified that, in the spring of 1969, he had frequent contacts with Rebozo during which Rebozo was "needling" [125] him about Hughes' apparent favoritism towards the Democrats by making a large contribution available to then-Vice President Humphrey in 1968, by having Larry O'Brien on retainer, and by employing Senator Humphrey's son.[126] Danner testified that he brought Rebozo's comments to Maheu's attention and that shortly thereafter Peter Maheu, Robert's son, showed Danner cancelled checks reflecting payments to various Nixon-Agnew committees during the 1968 campaign.[127] Danner testified that he related that information to Rebozo and "he (Rebozo) still felt that that was not comparable to what they had done for Humphrey." [128]

Danner then told Rebozo that the $50,000 undelivered at Palm Springs was still intact and available.[129] According to Danner's testimony, Rebozo declined the offer.[130] The contribution came up a short time later, in May or June 1969, when Danner testified that Rebozo raised the "question of whether Mr. Hughes would contribute to funds to begin taking polls on candidates for the 1970 congressional elections . . ." [131] According to Danner, he then discussed this matter with Maheu, who said that the undelivered $50,000 was available and that an additional $50,000 could be committed.[132]

Danner's only other consistent testimony has been that there were only two deliveries, one at San Clemente and one at Key Biscayne.

Danner testified that Robert Maheu told him the money

123. Robert A. Maheu interview, January 20, 1974.
124. *Ibid.*
125. Richard Danner Executive Session, December 18, 1973, p. 43.
126. *Ibid.*, pp. 80-86.
127. *Ibid.*, p. 16.
128. *Ibid.*, p. 43.
129. According to Danner, Maheu said "They can have that if they want it." *Ibid.* at 44.
130. *Ibid.*, p. 50.
131. *Ibid.*, p. 51.
132. *Ibid.*, pp. 52-53.

for the *first delivery* was in the safety deposit box at the Frontier Hotel.[133] It was either brought to Danner by Peter or Robert Maheu, or Danner picked it up himself from the safe deposit box.[134] He did not count the bills upon receipt but did note that they were bundled in packages of $5,000 each.[135]

In a transcribed question and answer session with the IRS on May 15, 1972 the first time he was questioned on the $100,000, Danner stated that the first delivery took place at Key Biscayne in the late summer of 1969, where Robert Maheu handed the package to Rebozo, and that the second delivery was at San Clemente at an unspecified later date.[136]

According to a contemporaneous memorandum, he told an IRS agent on Nov. 29, 1972 (in a telephone conversation) that the *first* delivery in Key Biscayne was in September 1969, and the *second* delivery in San Clemente on July 3, 1970.[137]

In a July 5, 1973 affidavit filed with the IRS as a correction to his May 15, 1972 questioning, Danner changed his prior statement. He said he was certain that the *first* contribution, not the *second,* took place on July 3, 1970 at San Clemente, with only Rebozo and Danner present, and that the second contribution was made in Key Biscayne on August 19-20, 1970,[138] again with only Rebozo and Danner present.

He stated to the Select Committee that he had been to the Western White House at San Clemente only once, which his travel records show to be on July 3, 1970.[139] Danner testified that he met with the President and Rose Woods after the delivery to Rebozo at San Clemente. His discussion with the President, Danner testified, focused on "the problems at the White House getting entertainment . . . suitable for young audiences and so on" [140] . . . and that there was no mention of the contribution.[141] In his discussion with Rose Mary Woods, Danner testified that there was no talk about the purpose of Danner's visit.[142] Woods had no recollection of

133. *Ibid.,* pp. 90-93.
134. Danner has testified that, with regard to both contributions, he is uncertain who delivered the money to him, noting that either $50,000 package could have come from either Robert or Peter Maheu. *See* Richard Danner Executive Session, June 11, 1974, pp. 188-89. He has also testified that Thomas Bell did not deliver either packagee to him. *Ibid.,* p. 186.
135. Richard Danner Executive Session, December 18, 1973, p. 99.
136. Interview of Richard Danner by IRS, May 15, 1972, p. 18.
137. Interview of Richard Danner by IRS, November 29, 1972.
138. Affidavit of Richard Danner, July 5, 1973.
139. Danner Executive Session, Dec. 18, 1973, p. 104; Danner travel records. Exhibit 21.
140. *Ibid.,* p. 106.
141. *Ibid.*
142. *Ibid.,* p. 107.

meeting Danner in July 1970 and said, in a staff interview, that "I would not know Danner if he walked in." [143]

Danner testified that he was unable to explain why the first delivery would not have been made until the summer of 1970, rather than in the fall of 1969, shortly after the spring 1969 Rebozo-Danner discussions of a possible contribution and Maheu's authorization of the delivery.[144]

2. Robert A. Maheu. In his statements and testimony about the two $50,000 contributions, Robert Maheu has provided conflicting information about sources of the money and delivery dates.

a. First $50,000. When Danner joined the Hughes organization there were on-going discussions between Hughes and Maheu about the uncompleted 1968 contribution. Maheu suggested Danner as the courier for the funds, and Hughes agreed.[145] Maheu has provided conflicting statements on the origin of the money. In September 1971, Maheu told the IRS that the first $50,000 came from the cashier's cage at the Sands Hotel in early December 1968.[146] In a 1973 IRS interview, Maheu said the money consisted of the same bills he received from Nadine Henley on December 5 and 6, 1968, and turned over to Peter Maheu upon his return from the Palm Springs Governors' Conference.[147] In a later interview with Select Committee staff, he said that he received the money for the first delivery from Henley on July 11, 1969.[148]

As to the first delivery, in a 1973 civil deposition Maheu testified that: "Mr. Danner made the first delivery which would have been sometime in, to the best of my recollection, sometime in 1969." [149] Maheu told Select Committee investigators that the delivery was made shortly after Danner joined the Hughes corporation, which was in February 1969.[150] Later in the same interview, Maheu stated that the first delivery must have been sometime after July 11, 1969, the date on which Henley sent him $50,000.[151]

Similarly, Maheu has expressed uncertainty about the mechanics of the first transaction, recalling only that it was

143. Rose Mary Woods interview, February 20, 1974.
144. Danner Executive Session, Dec. 18, 1973, p. 94.
145. Robert Maheu interview, January 20, 1974.
146. Interview of Robert A. Maheu by the IRS, September 21, 1971. See later section for a discussion of this possible source.
147. Robert Maheu IRS interview, September 19, 1973. See p. 000 below for a discussion of this source.
148. Roberet Maheu Select Committee staff interview, January 28, 1974. See p. 000 below for a discussion of this source.
149. Robert Maheu Civil Deposition, July 4, 1973 p. 1037.
150. Robert Maheu interview, January 20, 1974.
151. Robert Maheu interview, January 20, 1974.

his son, Peter, who transmitted the money to Danner some time after the early December 1968 Palm Springs Governors' Conference.[152]

Maheu testified in a civil deposition that Key Biscayne was the place of the first delivery, recalling that Danner used the DeHavilland to go to Key Biscayne and he (Maheu) had to explain the trip to Hughes when Hughes reviewed the log.[153]

According to Maheu, the purpose of the first delivery was to fulfill the pledge that had been made to the Nixon campaign in 1968. He stated that both he and Hughes were concerned that they not appear to be reneging on their commitments.[154]

b. Second $50,000. Maheu has given different dates and different reasons for this delivery. He is, however, certain that he *was* present when an envelope filled with cash was passed to Rebozo in Key Biscayne.

Maheu first told the Committee staff he was contacted by Bob Hope concerning a possible contribution of $50,000-$100,000 to the Eisenhower Hospital. Maheu discussed it with Hughes, and Hughes suggested that Maheu contribute $10,000 to the hospital and, at the same time, pledge to the Nixon Administration that Hughes would make additional contributions to the Congressional races. Hughes felt that through that arrangement he would get more mileage out of the Administration.[155]

In his July 4, 1973 deposition, where he first publicly discussed Hughes' political contributions, Maheu noted that the decision to make the contribution was based on conversations with Danner, who told Maheu of the political necessity of the contribution, rather than on Hughes' instructions relative to Maheu's conversation with Bob Hope.[156]

In a civil deposition, Maheu testified that the money was transmitted to Danner by Thomas Bell, a Hughes lawyer in Las Vegas in early 1970.[157] Later, in a Select Committee staff interview, he said Bell delivered it to Danner in the summer of 1970.[158] In his second staff interview, he said that he had testified under oath to a federal grand jury investigating Hughes' acquisition of Air West that the delivery to Rebozo was made by Danner and him on February 3-5, 1970 in Key

152. Robert Maheu Civil Deposition, July 4, 1973, p. 1096.
153. Robert Maheu Civil Deposition, July 4, 1973, p. 000. For a discussion of the contribution during the 1968 campaign, see sections 2 and 3, *supra.*
154. Robert Maheu interview, January 20, 1974.
155. Robert Maheu interview, January 20, 1974.
156. Robert A. Maheu Civil Deposition, July 4, 1973, vol. XII, pp. 1025-27. See the discussion of the Dunes, sec. 6 *infra* for a more detailed discussion of what Maheu understood the political necessity of the contribution to be.
157. Robert Maheu Civil Deposition, July 4, 1973, p. 1026.
158. Robert Maheu inteerview, September 15, 1973, p. 15.

Biscayne.[159] Finally, in that same interview, he stated that Thomas Bell's testimony that the money was taken from the Silver Slipper on October 26, 1972, plus the trip he and Danner took to Florida about that time, led him to believe that the money could have been delivered in late October 1970.[160]

The second delivery, according to Maheu, occurred at Rebozo's home in Key Biscayne. Maheu saw the envelope pass from Danner to Rebozo, who opened it but did not count the money. Rebozo then took the envelope went into another room, and returned in a short time without the envelope. The only conversation was something by Danner to the effect of "here's the second 50." No one else was present and the three immediately left in Rebozo's car to dine.[161]

3. Peter R. Maheu. Peter Maheu has stated that he transmitted one $50,000 packet to Richard Danner. Robert Maheu, Peter's father, has testified he instructed him to do so,[162] and Richard Danner has testified that he possibly received money from Peter Maheu.[163]

Peter Maheu recalled that he received the money at his father's house in 1969 from his father, who asked Peter to take it because his (Robert Maheu's) safe was not working at the time. Peter Maheu stated that the money was wrapped in packets of 50 bills with a standard bank wrapper around each packet and that the bills were not new.[164]

Peter Maheu only recalled his father saying "something to the effect that the money was for political contributions, and to place it in my safe and disburse it at his direction."[165] Peter Maheu stated that the source of the money was the Silver Slipper Casino in Las Vegas, which Hughes owned in his own name and used for political contributions.[166]

Peter Maheu took the money home, removed it from the envelope, and put it in his safe.[167] He kept the money for a short period of time, perhaps three weeks,[168] at which time his father instructed him to deliver it to Danner, explaining, as Peter remembered it, that "Danner was bringing the

159. Robert Maheu interview, January 20, 1974.
160. Robert Maheu interview, January 20, 1974.
161. Robert Maheu interview, January 20, 1974.
162. Robert A. Maheu Civil Deposition, July 4, 1973, p. 1096. As noted in the sections detailing Robert Maheu's testimony, there is conflict concerning when Peter Maheu received this money from his father.
163. Richard Danner Civil Deposition, September 4, 1973, p. 48. Danner's recollection is not clear on the event.
164. Peter Maheu interview, November 29, 1973, p. 5.
165. Peter Maheu, Civil Deposition, March 29, 1973, p. 72.
166. Ibid., p. 74.
167. Peter Maheu interview, December 4, 1973, p. 5.
168. Ibid.

money to Mr. Rebozo. Mr. Rebozo was going to give the money to Mr. Nixon."[169] Peter then took the money to Danner at the Frontier Hotel. According to Peter, his meeting with Danner was "extremely short," and he just "dropped off the money. . . ." He may have told Danner to "have a good trip."[170] Peter Maheu was confident that Danner went to Florida to deliver the money[171] and was sure that his father did *not* accompany Danner on that trip.[172]

Finally, Peter Maheu (in his Select Committee staff interview) stated that someone in his father's office gave him a typed sheet of paper to be signed by Richard Nixon acknowledging Nixon's receipt of $100,000 from Hughes.[173] Danner told Peter Maheu that Nixon will "never sign it,"[174] and Maheu has been unable to find the document.

4. Thomas G. Bell. According to Robert Maheu,[175] the second $50,000 contribution was transmitted to Richard Danner by Thomas Bell, a Hughes attorney in Las Vegas. In a Select Committee staff interview, Bell stated that he was involved in only one delivery of money to Richard Danner, $50,000 delivered at the direction of Robert Maheu in October of 1970[176]. He arrived at the date by examining the Silver Slipper disbursement forms and noting that he delivered the money in one lump sum just prior to the Congressional election of 1970. Since he never had as much as $50,000 in a lump sum other than on October 26, 1970, when he withdrew $115,000 from the Silver Slipper, he stated that this withdrawal was the source of the money for Danner.[177]

On the date of withdrawal, he received a call from Robert Maheu, who, with a great sense of urgency, said that Hughes wanted the money delivered to Danner.[178] Bell went to the Silver Slipper, got the money and immediately delivered it to Danner in Danner's office at the Frontier Hotel. Bell recalled no conversation with Danner. Bell stated that the same day, or early on the next day, he made a local call to Maheu to announce that the money had been delivered.[179]

169. Peter Maheu Civil Deposition, March 29, 1973, p. 77.
170. *Ibid.*
171. Peter Maheu Civil Deposition, March 29, 1973, p. 80.
172. Peter Maheu interview, December 4, 1973, p. 6.
173. Peter Maheu interview, December 4, 1973, pp. 7-8. The document was an undated and unsigned white sheet of paper 8½" X 5½"," according to Maheu.
174. *Ibid.*
175. Civil deposition of Robert A. Maheu, July 4, 1973, pp. 1025-1027.
176. Thomas Bell Interview, December 17, 1973, p. 7.
177. *Ibid.*
178. *Ibid.*
179. *Ibid.*, p. 8.

Bell said there were 10 packages of $100 bills, totalling $50,000, and that most of the bills were fairly new and crisp. He is not certain whether the money was wrapped at a Las Vegas bank or at the Silver Slipper, but he was certain that the wrappers were initialed and dated.[180]

5. Charles G. Rebozo. Charles Rebozo testified that he had no official fund-raising responsibilities with regard to the 1972 Presidential campaign when he began to discuss the Hughes contribution with Richard Danner in 1969 [181] but that nonetheless, he told the Committee that the $100,000 contribution from Hughes was received on behalf of the 1972 Nixon re-election campaign.[182]

Rebozo's first discussion of the two contributions with a governmental agency took place May 10, 1973, when, according to an IRS memorandum of the interview, he stated that:

> he received the money on two separate occasions— each in the amount of $50,000. That he could not recall whether he received the first package in Key Biscayne or California, but that he had received one package in each location. The California location was San Clemente. We attempted to zero in on the dates that he received the money. To his best recollection, it was late 1968 or early 1969 and that there were two or three months between each delivery.
>
> Mr. Rebozo said he had been approached by Danner in the fall of 1968 before the election about a political contribution to Nixon. Rebozo had refused it because he did not think it would be proper. After the election, he was approached again by Danner about the contribution. Rebozo could not remember whether he approached Danner or Danner approached him. As far as Rebozo is concerned, the money was for President Nixon's 1972 campaign. Mr. Rebozo was asked if it could have been for senatorial or congressional campaigns in 1970. Rebozo stated not as far as he was concerned. What was in Danner's or Maheu's minds, Rebozo did not know.[183]

Rebozo testified before the Select Committee that, after

180. *Ibid.*
181. Charles G. Rebozo Executive Session, March 20, 1974, p. 87.
182. *Ibid.*, p. 65. In addition to Rebozo's receipt of $100,000 which he claims was for the 1972 Nixon campaign, records indicate that Hughes contributed $150,000 to the 1972 Nixon campaign, $50,000 of which appeared on the pre-April 7, 1972 list of contributors kept by Rose Mary Woods. The remainder was contributed after April 7 and duly recorded.
183. Interview of Charles G. Rebozo by IRS, May 10, 1973.

457

the 1968 election, Danner occasionally visited Rebozo in Florida and brought up the subject of a Hughes contribution to President Nixon.[184] During these conversations, Rebozo testified, he asked Danner why Hughes had hired Larry O'Brien and placed Hubert Humphrey's son on the payroll if he (Hughes) were genuinely interested in supporting President Nixon.[185]

Rebozo testified that Danner approached him on four or five occasions in 1969 to offer the contribution,[186] which, Danner later told Rebozo, was the same money earmarked for the 1968 campaign.[187] Rebozo remembered one instance when Danner appeared at Key Biscayne with $50,000, but Rebozo refused to accept it.[188] Rebozo had no recollection of discussing with Danner using the contribution for polling purposes in the 1970 congressional elections.[189]

a. First $50,000 Contribution. Rebozo testified that, after a number of conversations with Danner in 1969, he finally relented and agreed to accept the contribution.
His rationale was that:

> Danner then had been working for Hughes a couple of years or so. I had come to know Maheu, whom I didn't know when he first offered the money. Morgan was seemingly out of the picture, and I began to get a little confidence in the fact that maybe this money could be utilized, and it wouldn't present any embarrassing problems. So it was somewhere after he had been with them for some time they agreed to take it.[190]

After agreeing to accept the money, and shortly before the delivery, Rebozo testified that he talked with Danner, who said he would come to Miami to make the delivery. Rebozo responded that he was "going to be in California next week, and that would save [Danner] a trip".[191] Rebozo also recalled Danner saying at about the time of the first delivery that there would be more than $50,000 contributed, but he did not recall whether Danner mentioned a specific amount.[192]

184. Charles G. Rebozo Executive Session, March 20, 1974, p. 38.
185. *Ibid.*, pp. 44-46.
186. Charles Rebozo Executive Session, March 20, 1974, p. 41. Danner testified that he offered the $50,000 only once prior to discussing the possibility of a contribution for the 1970 Congressional campaign. Danner Executive Session, June 11, 1974, p. 000.
187. Charles Rebozo Executive Session, March 20, 1974, p. 94.
188. *Ibid.*, p. 42.
189. *Ibid.*, p. 39.
190. *Ibid.*, p. 59.
191. *Ibid.*, p. 60.
192. *Ibid.*, p. 60.

Although he initially told the IRS that he was not sure where the first delivery was made,[193] Rebozo later testified that the first contribution took place July 3, 1970, at San Clemente,[194] a conclusion he reached after checking hotel and airline records [195] and talking with Danner.[196]

Rebozo testified that he and Danner met alone at San Clemente, and that during this meeting, Danner gave him a manila envelope containing $50,000.[197] Rebozo took the envelope and put it in his bag.[198] He has no recollection of what occurred next, but he and Danner may have visited briefly with the President [199] or Rose Mary Woods.[200]

b. Second $50,000 Delivery. Rebozo testified that the second delivery took place soon after the first, within "a matter of weeks . . . [it] could have been three months . . . I really don't know. I think I saw somewhere Danner had indicated it was in August and that would be correct." [201]

Rebozo could not recall the discussion leading up to this delivery and was "inclined to think that he [Danner] just brought it, down to Key Biscayne." [202] Rebozo testified that he was not certain whether the delivery in Key Biscayne took place at his home or at his bank.[203]

Rebozo testified that he is uncertain about any conversation he had with Danner, although Danner may have said "here was another 50." [204] Rebozo testified that he did not open the envelope.[205]

Rebozo testified that Maheu "was never there when Danner gave me the money on either occasion." [206]

B. An Analysis of Possible Sources of the Contributions.
1. Pre-election 1968. As discussed elsewhere in this report,[207] there was, during the summer and fall of 1968, an unsuccessful attempt to arrange a $50,000 cash contribution from Hughes to then-candidate Nixon. Rebozo, Danner, and Robert Maheu, key figures in the later deliveries, were also

193. Interview of Charles Rebozo by IRS, May 10, 1973
194. Charles Rebozo Executive Session, March 20, 1974, p. 61.
195. *Ibid.*, p. 61.
196. *Ibid.*, p. 66.
197. *Ibid.*, p. 67.
198. *Ibid.*, p. 68.
199. *Ibid.*, p. 68.
200. *Ibid.*, p. 70.
201. *Ibid.*, pp. 109-110.
202. *Ibid.*, p. 110.
203. *Ibid.*, p. 111.
204. *Ibid.*, p. 112.
205. *Ibid.*, p. 000.
206. *Ibid.*, p. 112. IRS notes reflect that Rebozo told them that, while Maheu was not present at either delivery, he may have been in Florida. *See* Interview of Charles G. Rebozo by the IRS, May 10, 1973.
207. See sections 2 and 3, *supra.*

heavily involved in the 1968 attempt. The Committee has no evidence that there was $50,000 in cash put together for a contribution before the election in 1968.

2. The Sands Hotel Cage—early December 1968. In early December 1968, two Hughes employees, Lawrence T. Ryhlick and John Ianni, withdrew $50,000 in $100 Notes from the casino cage at the Sands Hotel in Las Vegas.[208] Ryhlick was then the Controller at the Sands, and Ianni was the Executive Assistant to General Edward Nigro, a top Hughes aide (now deceased) at whose direction the cash was withdrawn. Ianni delivered the cash to Robert Maheu.[209] This transaction was unknown to Select Committee investigators until recently, and the evidence gathered on the withdrawal is consequently incomplete. However, the available evidence suggests that this is a likely source of one of the deliveries.

During interviews with staff members [210] Robert Maheu did not list this transaction when responding to general questions about political contributions. His explanations of the Sands withdrawal given to the Internal Revenue Service have not been consistent, ranging from no recall to detailed recollection (see above).

The details of this withdrawal are particularly important vis-a-vis documentary evidence on the money Rebozo returned, as explained below. The check for $50,000 which was cashed by Ryhlick is dated December 4, 1968.[211] The request for the disbursement, signed by General Nigro and Ryhlick, is dated November 30, 1968.[212] Ryhlick prepared another request for disbursement for his own recordkeeping purpose (not a carbon or photostatic of the request). Ryhlick remembered preparing his disbursement record a day or two after receiving the check,[213] and his disbursement record is dated December 5, 1968.[214] He said he got the check on December 4.[215] In statements to the IRS, Ianni and Ryhlick placed the date of the withdrawal as December 5, 1968.[216]

208. Ryhlick telephone interview, May 21, 1974. Ianni telephone interview, June 3, 1974.
209. Ryhlick teleephone interview, *supra* note. Ianni interview, note *supra*. Ryhlick says he was not preseent at the delivery to Maheu, but that immediately after making the delivery, Ianni reported his success to Ryhlick and Nigro.
210. Robert Maheu interview, September 15, 1973, January 20, 21, and 28, 1974.
211. Exhibit 22.
212. Exhibit 23.
213. Rhylick Telephone interview, June 20, 1974.
214. A copy of the form is in the files of the IRS.
215. *Ibid.*
216. *Ibid.*

However, Ryhlick has recently indicated that December 5 was only an approximate date of withdrawal. His best recollection was that the check was cashed up to four days after December 4, on the date of one of General Nigro's staff meetings.[217] The exact date of that meeting has not yet been determined. The check cleared the Bank of Las Vegas on Monday, December 9, so it was cashed sometime between December 4 and December 9. Ryhlick is sure that it was not cashed on a Saturday or Sunday (December 7 or 8).[218]

The significance of these dates is as follows. In the money Rebozo returned and identified as the first delivery, there are 50 consecutively numbered $100 bills that arrived at the Bank of Las Vegas (now the Valley Bank of Nevada) on December 5, 1968 as part of a large money shipment from the Los Angeles Federal Reserve branch bank.[219] The bills were shipped to the office of the Bank of Las Vegas that was used by the Sands and other Hughes casinos.[220] The money would have been available for bank customers at 9 a.m. on Friday, December 6. According to a Valley Bank official most of the $100 bills available for customers go out to the customers for weekend use by the end of the day each Friday.[221] The Valley Bank does not keep serial number records on bills it provides to commercial customers,[222] but it is quite possible that the string of 50 bills could have been picked up from the bank by the Sands on December 6. If the December 4 check were not cashed until December 6, these 50 bills could, therefore, have been in the $50,000 packet Maheu received from Ianni.

If the 50 bills were in the packet that was delivered to Robert Maheu, then their presence in the money Rebozo returned and identified as the first delivery would establish the Sands as the source for that delivery to Rebozo. If the Sands withdrawal was the source, the Federal Reserve evidence shows that not all the money returned and identified as the first delivery could have been the same money assembled at the Sands. There are 88 bills in the money returned and identified as the first delivery that were not available for commercial distribution until *after* the time of the Sands withdrawal.

217. *Ibid.*
218. *Ibid.*
219. Exhibit 24. The bills were delivered by the Federal Reserve to Brinks, Inc., for shipment at 3:50 p.m. on December 4, 1968. According to R. H. Wynne, Sr. Vice President of the Valley Bank, the shipment would have arrived at the Las Vegas bank on the afternoon of Thursday, Dec. 5. Wynne interview, June 20, 1974.
220. Wynne interview, note 4 h *Supra*.
221. *Ibid.*
222. *Ibid.*

This circumstantial possibility is particularly interesting in light of the attempted delivery in Palm Springs of cash to the Nixon campaign on December 6 and Danner's visit to Las Vegas on December 5-8.[223]

In addition, Maheu's earliest recollection, according to a September 21, 1971 IRS memorandum of a meeting between IRS agents and James Rogers, a tax lawyer for Robert Maheu, was that the Sands was the source for a delivery to Rebozo. The IRS memorandum stated:

> Mr. Rogers said Hughes ordered Maheu to take $50,000 from the cage at the Sands and turn it over to President Nixon. He said that Maheu probably sent an employee to the cage who returned and gave the money to Maheu. Mr. Rogers said that Maheu was supposed to turn the money which was in a sealed envelope over to an aide of President Nixon but he missed his connections and gave the money to Richard Danner instead, who later turned the money over to an aide of President Nixon's.[224]

This recollection of Maheu's is important in several respects. First, it is the earliest record available on the subject. Thus, it presumably reflected a fresher recollection than, for example, Maheu's lack of recall about the transaction in an IRS interview some two years later.[225] Second, Maheu's recollection that he sent someone to the cage for the money matches Ryhlick's observation that Nigro's order to withdraw the money, following standard operating procedure, would have been prompted by a Maheu to Nigro order.[226] Similarly, Maheu's recollection that he received the money comports with what Ryhlick and Ianni have said.[227] Third, the reference in the memorandum to Maheu missing connections in the planned delivery to a Nixon aide corresponds to the unsuccessful Palm Springs delivery that occurred about the time of the withdrawal from the Sands. Finally, Maheu's recollection that he gave the money to Richard Danner, who delivered it to "an aide of President Nixon", would firmly establish this transaction as the source of one of the deliveries to Rebozo.[228]

3. Nadine Henley—December 5, 1968. In addition to the $50,000 from the Sands, Robert Maheu received two de-

223. Danner travel records. Exhibit 25.
224. September 21, 1971 IRS memorandum of meeting with James Rogers.
225. March 13, 1973 IRS memorandum of meeting with James Rogers.
226. Ryhlick telephone interview, May 21, 1974.
227. Note 2, *supra*.
228. See pp. 460ff. for an analysis of the Sands as a possible source.

liveries of $25,000 each in $100 Notes on December 5 and 6, 1968 from Nadine Henley, a Hughes aide who withdrew it on December 5 from Hughes' personal account in a Hollywood branch of the Bank of America.[229] Henley said that Maheu requested the $50,000 for a political contribution to President-elect Nixon.[230] Mr. Nixon was in Palm Springs on December 6, 1968. A note written by Henley on December 5, 1968, says that the money she sent to Maheu on December 5 and 6 was for "State Committees—Nixon's deficit." [231]

Maheu has always acknowledged receiving the above cash,[232] but he has given a number of differing statements of what he did with it. In March 1973 he told the IRS that it was delivered to campaign aides of Hubert Humphrey for use in the 1968 Presidential campaign.[233] By early December 1968, of course, the 1968 election had already occurred. On January 20 and 21, 1974, Maheu told Select Committee investigators that this $50,000 was taken to Palm Springs for the unsuccessful delivery to President-elect Nixon and that it later became the first successful delivery to Rebozo.[234] He questioned that statement on January 21, however, and a few days later stated that, after returning from Palm Springs with this cash obtained from Henley, he used it to reimburse himself for a $50,000 campaign contribution he made directly to Hubert Humphrey earlier in 1968.[235]

In sum, the evidence reflects that Maheu did receive $100,000 on December 5 and 6, 1968 (from the Sands and from Henley), the disposition of which has never been conclusively determined. Once regarding the Sands money [236] and once regarding the Henley money,[237] he stated that the same money was later used for the first delivery of $50,000 to Rebozo. Danner corroborated this possibility by testifying that Maheu told him the first delivery contained the same

229. See Henley Exhibit 4 provided to Select Committee by Chester Davis on June 11, 1974, in the Richard Danner Executive Session.
230. Nadine Henley interview, January 22, 1974.
231. Henley Exhibit 4, note 9 *supra*.
232. IRS interviews from 1971-73; Select Committee interviews Jan. 20-21, 1974; Los Angeles testimony. Maheu signed receipts for the cash on Dec. 5 and 6, which were labelled as receipts for "non-deductible contributions." Henley Exhibit 4, note 9 *supra*.
233. March 15, 1973, memorandum of meeting between IRS agents and James Rogers, Maheu's tax lawyer.
234. Robert Maheu int., Jan. 20, 1974.
235. Robert Maheu interview, Jan. 28, 1974. That contention conflicts with Henley's note of Dec. 5, 1968, which indicates that part of the $150,000 in check Maheu received on Sept. 9, 1968 was to cover the Humphrey contribution. Henley Exhibit 4, note 9 *supra*. Humphrey had denied personally receiving a cash contribution from Maheu.
236. Through his lawyer, to the IRS on Sept. 21, 1971. See p. 000 *supra* and note 5.
237. Maheu interview, Jan. 20, 1974.

money that was undelivered in 1968,[238] and Rebozo testified that Danner told him the first delivery was the same money they had discussed in 1968.[239]

A telephone message taken by one of Maheu's secretaries on November 22, 1968 showed a call from one Stephen Craig, with the Nixon election campaign in New York City. The message reads: "re: contribution—have deficit of $800,000." [240] The Select Committee learned of this note shortly before June 28 and therefore had no time to explore its full significance. Taken at face value, however, it shows a post-election interest of the Nixon campaign in soliciting funds from Hughes. On December 17, 1968, Maheu received a form letter from President-elect Nixon, thanking ". . . all of those who contributed so generously to our cause." [241]

In early December Maheu received $100,000 cash in two days, traveled to Palm Springs and, Maheu has stated, tried unsuccessfully to deliver it to Richard Nixon or an aide of his. In addition, Richard Danner was in Las Vegas from December 5-8, 1968,[242] talking with Maheu and other Hughes aides about possibly joining the Hughes Nevada Operation.[243] Danner is not sure whether he was aware of Maheu's trip to Palm Springs at the time it occurred,[244] and he denied receiving any money from Maheu or other Hughes agents at that time.[245] Further, Danner testified that this visit to Las Vegas, his only visit to the Hughes operation in 1968, ". . . had nothing to do with campaign, campaign contributions, none whatsoever." [246] However, on November 29, 1972, Danner told IRS Special Agent Donald Skelton that ". . . he thought he and Maheu began discussing the prospective contribution shortly after the 1968 election, which preceded his employment with Hughes Tool Company." [247]

4. Nadine Henley—June 27-July 11, 1969. On July 11, 1969, Robert Maheu acknowledged in writing the receipt of $50,000 cash from Howard Hughes "for non-deductible

238. Danner Executive Session, December 18, 1973, pp. 90-91. Danner's recollection is not now clear. He stated that he cannot testify with certainty that one of he $50,000 deliveries consisted of *exactly* the same money as was available in 1968. Danner Executive Session, June 12, 1974, p. 9.
239. Rebozo Executive Session, March 20, 1974, p. 94.
240. Notes from IRS files produced pursuant to S. Res. 288.
241. Notes from IRS files produced pursuant to S. Res. 288.
242. Danner travel records. Exhibit 25.
243. Danner Executive Session, June 11, 1974, pp. 139-41.
244. *Ibid.*, at 142-43.
245. *Ibid.*, at 141-44.
246. *Ibid.*, at 144.
247. This memorandum is discussed more fully at p. 452.

contributions," [248] the phrase used to cover money for political contributions.[249] Nadine Henley acknowledged sending the cash to Maheu at his request. She did not, however, know why Maheu requested the money and apparently did not make a note on the purpose of the transaction as she had done on the December 5, 1968 withdrawal.[250]

Maheu told Select Committee investigators that this cash may have *been* the source of the *first* contribution to Rebozo.[251] When first asked about the source of the first delivery, Maheu said that the source was the December 5, 1968 money from Henley,[252] which he said he gave to his son, Peter, immediately after his return from Palm Springs on December 6 or 7.

In a later staff interview, Maheu stated that, based upon his son's recollection that he held the money he received from his father only a short time,[253] the June-July 1969 money was the source of the delivery.[254] Maheu was not able to place the July 1969 date in relation to any other events, as he had done for the December 1968 money he received from Henley. He assumed it was the date only because he rejected the December 1968 date. There is no independent evidence corroborating the date.

When questioned about the July 11 money by the IRS (in March 1973), Maheu, through his lawyer, professed *complete ignorance* of the transaction.[255] Nevertheless, less than one year later he said it was the source of a delivery to Rebozo. Further, when he told Select Committee investigators that the July 11 money was the source of the first delivery after discounting the December 5 money from Henley, the investigators were not yet aware of the Sands withdrawal, and Maheu did not mention it. As the discussion on the Sands withdrawal showed, it is a likely source for the first delivery.[256]

5. Silver Slipper Casino—October 26, 1970. On October 26, 1970, Thomas Bell, a Hughes lawyer in Las Vegas, withdrew $115,000 from the Silver Slipper casino in Las Vegas.[257]

248. Henley Exhibit 6, Danner Executive Session, June 11, 1974.
249. Robert Maheu interview, Jan. 20, 1974.
250. Nadine Henley interview, Jan. 22, 1974. The note is part of Henley Exhibit 4 in the June 11 Danner Executive Session. See p. 000 *supra*.
251 Robert Maheu, Interview, January 20, 1974.
252. Robert Maheu, Interview, January 20, 1974.
253. Peter Maheu interview, Nov. 29, 1973.
254. Robert Maheu interview, Jan. 28, 1974.
255. IRS memorandum of interview with James Rogers, Maheu's lawyer, March 15, 1973.
256. See pp. 460-2.
257. Exhibit 26 is the withdrawal slip. Bell related his version of the withdrawal in an interview on Dec. 17, 1973. A fuller explanation of Bell's story is set forth at pp. 456-7.

According to Bell, he immediately gave $50,000 of that sum to Richard Danner in Danner's office with no one else present. Bell's withdrawal and delivery to Danner were made at Robert Maheu's request, according both to Bell [258] and Maheu. [259] This was the only time, Bell said, that he was asked to deliver money to Danner. Bell assumed, but was not told by Maheu or Danner, that the money was for a political contribution. Bell had no idea what Danner did with the money.

In his latest testimony, Danner denied ever receiving any money from Bell, [260] although he earlier testified that it was possible that Bell delivered money to him. [261] Danner and Maheu were in Key Biscayne shortly after the $50,000 was allegedly given to Danner. [262]

This money could be the source only of the *second* delivery; all other potential delivery dates were before October 26, 1970.

6. A Note on Storage of the Money Before Delivery to Rebozo. As the earlier section on the roles of key participants shows, [263] there is some question about where the money for at least one of the deliveries, most likely the first, was held and for how long between the time it was put together and the time it was delivered to Rebozo. Before the Select Committee, Danner testified as follows:

> My recollection is one, perhaps the first one, had been locked in a box in the Frontier cage. And it was obtained from that source. Whether I got it or Mr. Maheu got it or one of the secretaries got it, I don't recall.
>
> The second contribution, again, I don't recall whether it was Robert Maheu or his son, Peter Maheu, who delivered it to me, either in their office or my office. But I am reasonably certain that this is the way the two deliveries were made to me. [264]

In his November 29, 1972 telephone conversation with IRS Special Agent Skelton, according to the IRS memorandum, Danner told Skelton that the first delivery was in Key Biscayne in September 1969 [265] and that the money that was delivered then had been kept intact in the Frontier cage "for

258. Bell Interview, Dec. 17, 1973.
259. Robert Maheu Interview, Jan. 20, 1974.
260. Richard Danner Executive Session, June 11, 1974, p. 186.
261. Danner Executive Session, December 19, 1973, p. 2.
262. See p. 475.
263. See p. 452.
264. Danner Executive Session, June 11, 1974, pp. 188-189.
265. *Ibid.*

a[t] least six months," [266] which would mean at least since March 1969. The spring of 1969 was about the same time, according to Danner, that Rebozo was chiding him about Hughes' failure to support President Nixon.[267] Danner was apparently involved in storing the money. He told Skelton that he, Danner, had personally supervised the transfer of the money while it was in the cage from a manila envelope to a locked box.[268] The only sources for money that were intact as early as March 1969 were (a) the Sands in early December 1968 or (b) Nadine Henley on December 5, 1968. Thus, Danner's story to Skelton tends to support the view that the money for the first delivery was the same money that had been obtained in December 1968.

C. An Analysis of Possible Delivery Dates. 1. The Bahamas —December 1968. On the disbursement form Lawrence Ryhlick prepared regarding the withdrawal from the Sands in early December 1968,[269] Ryhlick wrote (at some later date) the following notation:

> The money was taken by John Ianni and given to Bob Maheu. I was told he was to give this to President Nixon on Maheu's trip to the Bahamas.[270]

That observation was hearsay information, and the Select Committee has been unable to determine conclusively the accuracy of the remark. According to Ryhlick,[271] he made the handwritten entry regarding the Bahamas as one of his periodic attempts to make a record of the purposes for cash withdrawals given to Maheu, should he later be questioned by Hughes officials or anyone else regarding his role in obtaining funds for Maheu. Ryhlick was not sure who told him the money was intended for then President-elect Nixon, but he thought it might have been Nigro himself or Jack Hooper, Chief of Security for the Hughes operation. Nigro is dead, and Hooper has apparently been seriously ill since at least the fall of 1973 and has not been questioned.[272]

266. Ibid. Danner told the Select Committee that Maheu told him the undelivered money from 1968 was in a safe deposit box at the Frontier and that he, Danner, was "fairly certain" that it was the 1968 money. Danner Executive Session, Dec. 18, 1973, p. 91.
267. See p. 451.
268. Ibid.
269. See p. 460.
270. Notes taken from the copy of the record in the possession of the IRS. The record itself is in the possession of the Summa Corp. A written request from the Select Committee staff, dated May 31, 1974, for a copy of it has gone unanswered.
271. Ryhlick Interview, May 21, 1974.
272. His doctor has consistently attested to Hooper's illness in communication with the Select Committee staff.

There is no evidence that Maheu was in the Bahamas after the Sands withdrawal. Danner originally testified that he visited Rebozo and President-elect Nixon on Robert Abplanalp's Bahamian island, Grand Cay, sometime between the 1968 election and the inauguration in 1969.[273] President-elect Nixon visited that island on November 18-19, 1968, and on December 26, 1968.[274] Danner's diary does not show him in the Bahamas or nearby at either time Mr. Nixon was there in late 1968. He was in Spanish Cay and Freeport in the Bahamas from December 10-15, 1968,[275] a visit that, Danner testified, had nothing to do with political contributions or the delivery of money to President-Elect Nixon or Rebozo.[276] Danner's latest testimony, based upon an examination of his 1968 diary, is that (1) he saw President Nixon in the Bahamas only once in 1968 and (2) that visit was on April 10-12, 1968, at Walkers Cay, part of Abplanalp's property.[277] Further, Danner testified that he did not receive any money from Hughes' representatives in December 1968.[278]

Danner was in Las Vegas from December 5-8, 1968,[279] which was the same time period as (1) the receipt by Maheu of $100,000 in cash,[280] (2) the unsuccessful delivery of $50,000 to President-elect Nixon or an aide in Palm Springs,[281] and (3) the shipment to the Las Vegas bank used by the Hughes-owned casinos of 50 consecutively numbered $100 bills that were in the money Rebozo returned and identified as the first delivery.[282] While no firm conclusions can be drawn, this evidence and Ryhlick's note establish an interesting set of coincidences.

2. April 2-10, 1969—Key Biscayne. No one has testified to this date as a delivery date. This was Danner's first trip to Miami after he joined the Hughes organization [283] and, according to Danner, it concerned business dealings in the Bahamas.[284] Maheu told Select Committee investigators that the first delivery was made in Key Biscayne not long after

273. Danner Executive Session, December 19, 1973, p. 22. Danner testimony in Maheu v. Hughes Tool Co., No. 72-305-HP (C. D. Cal.), May 3, 1974, p. 7781-82.
274. New York *Times*, November 19, 1968, p. 30; New York *Times*, November 20, 1973, p. 15; New York *Times*, November 27, 1968, p. 18.
275. Danner Diary. Exhibit No. 00.
276. Danner Executive Session, June 11, 1974, p. 104-06.
277. *Ibid.* at 151.
278. *Ibid.* at 141-44.
279. Danner Travel Records. Exhibit 25.
280. See p. 437.
281. See pp. 438-9.
282. See p. 461.
283. Danner travel records. Exhibit 27.
284. Danner Executive Session, Dec. 19, 1973, p. 56. The trip concerned business dealings regarding CaySal island, as reflected on his travel records.

Danner joined the Hughes operation,[285] but he was unable to pinpoint the date. There is no indication from available travel or hotel records that Maheu was with Danner in Florida at this time. In summary, this is a possible delivery date without substantial support.

3. June 26, 1969—Key Biscayne. Like the April 2-10 date, there was no testimony supporting this specific date. Danner had no specific recollection of this trip,[286] although he testified that in the Spring of 1969 Rebozo was "more or less needling" him about Hughes' financial support of Hubert Humphrey and Hughes' failure to contribute to President Nixon.[287] Danner testified that "around May, possible early in June" [288] 1969, after Rebozo had once refused a $50,000 contribution, Danner and Rebozo began discussing the possibility that Hughes would contribute funds for the 1970 Congressional campaign.[289]

4. September 11-12, 1969—Key Biscayne. There is evidence that makes this the most probable delivery date for the first contribution. The factors suggesting this as a delivery date include the following:

1. The Rebozo-Danner discussions about Hughes' failure to contribute had set the stage for a delivery.

2. According to Danner, Maheu, who was aware of the Danner-Rebozo conversations about a contribution, authorized a delivery to Rebozo "sometime during the summer . . . maybe as late as August [1969].[290]

3. By this time, Maheu had obtained an additional $50,000 in cash from Nadine Henley.[291]

4. When first questioned about the first delivery (by the IRS on May 15, 1972), Danner made statements that fit with a number of facts about the September 11-12 trip. He stated as follows:

Maheu showed me the envelope. I saw that it contained packets of money, I did not count it. As I recall, it was in his office in the Frontier Hotel. We took the DeHaviland, flew to Miami, went to Key Biscayne, met Rebozo at his house, Maheu handed him the package and says here's fifty thousand dollars, first installment. Rebozo thanked him, he told . . . Maheu told him then that there

285. Robert Maheu interview, Jan. 20, 1973.
286. Danner Executive Session, Dec. 18, 1973, p. 75-76. Danner's travel records show him in Key Biscayne on June 26, 1969. Exhibit 28.
287. Danner Executive Session, Dec. 18, 1973, p. 42.
288. *Ibid.* at 51.
289. *Ibid.* at 51-52.
290. *Ibid.* at 88.
291. See pp. 462-3.

would be more forthcoming later on, and that wound up that transaction. We thereafter went to dinner, we didn't discuss the campaign contributions any further that I recall, the next morning I left and flew back to Las Vegas. My recollection is on that trip Maheu stayed, kept the plane down there in Miami, he had some other business to look into.[292]

While Danner's recollection has changed, it is worthy of particular scrutiny because (a) it is his first recollection, i.e., closest in time to the event itself, (b) it was given free of consultation with Rebozo; (c) it comports substantially with Maheu's recollection of the event.

a. Maheu has stated that he was present at a Key Biscayne delivery.[293] Records of the Key Biscayne Hotel show that Danner and Maheu were there on September 11-12, 1969.[294] Records of the Hughes company plane show that it made a trip to Miami on September 11, returning to Las Vagas on September 12.[295] Danner's records,[296] however, show a $152 expense for travel on September 11-12, indicating the possibility that he traveled by commercial airliner on part of his trip to Miami and back. If he traveled by commercial carrier from Miami to Las Vegas on September 12, that fact would coincide with his statement to the IRS that he returned to Las Vegas alone while Maheu kept the Hughes plane.

On July 5, 1973, Danner signed an affidavit to correct his May 15, 1972 testimony to the IRS. In that affidavit he stated that the first contribution was made in San Clemente on July 3, 1970. However, in subsequent testimony in court [297] and before the Select Committee,[298] Danner testified that he is certain only that *a* delivery, not necessarily the first, was made on July 3, 1970. His testimony, therefore, still leaves open the possibility, particularly when considered in light of the

292. Danner testimony before IRS agents in Houston, Texas on May 15, 1972, p. 18 (question and answer 201).
293. Robert Maheu Interview, January 20, 1974.
294. Exhibit 29.
295. Exhibit 30.
296. Exhibit 31. The $152 is divided into two unidentified charges, one for $125, one for $27. The cost of a one-way coach flight from Miami to Las Vegas in September 1969 was $136 plus five per cent tax. Telephone conversation with Jim Green at the Civil Aeronautics Board, June 28, 1974. The logs of the DeHaviland show two passengers (no names given) on the Las Vegas to Miami flight and five on the return. There are no credit card records available for Danner's air travel as far back as September 1969.
297. Testimony in *Maheu* v. *Hughes Tool Co.*, note *supra* at 7791:
    Q Now, directing your testimony to the first delivery which you say was at San Clemente to Mr. Rebozo, was anyone else there?
    A Well, I hate to describe it as the first delivery, but the delivery.
298. Danner Executive Session, June 11, 1974, p. 184.

470

facts outlined here, that the first delivery was September 11-12, 1969.

b. In his initial IRS testimony quoted above, Danner testified that the delivery was made at Rebozo's house by Danner and Maheu and that the three of them "thereafter went to dinner." [299] Maheu's version of the Key Biscayne delivery at which he said he was present conforms to Danner's in two respects: Maheu told Select Committee investigators that the delivery was made in Rebozo's house and that the three men then went together to dinner. [300] Both Danner and Rebozo testified before the Select Committee that the delivery was at Rebozo's bank office without Maheu present, [301] and Danner cannot remember whether he and Rebozo dined together after the delivery was made. [302]

5. Finally, Danner once placed the time of the first delivery as September 1969. On November 29, 1972, after he had first answered questions before the IRS, Danner called IRS Special Agent Donald Skelton in response to IRS requests that Danner review his records regarding possible dates and places of delivery. Danner told Skelton, according to the contemporaneous memorandum Skelton prepared, [303] that:

a) as near as he, Danner, could tell, the first delivery was made in September 1969;

b) the money for the delivery was locked in a secure box in the Frontier Hotel cage for at least *six months* before the delivery;

c) at Danner's instructions, the money was once transferred within the cage from one box to another;

d) he *and* Maheu made the first delivery in Key Biscayne; and

e) the *second* delivery was in San Clemente on July 3, 1970; [304]

f) Maheu and Danner began talking about making a contribution to Rebozo shortly after the 1968 election, *before* Danner joined Hughes.

These facts would tend to establish the dates of the deliveries. In addition, it is worth noting that the information Danner provided on November 29, 1972, comports with his earlier testimony to the IRS and with the evidence summarized

299. See p. 452.
300. Robert Maheu Interview, Jan. 21, 1974.
301. See *supra* for Danner and Rebozo testimony.
302. Danner Executive Session, June 11, 1974, p. 185.
303. Notes from IRS.
304. In his May 1972 testimony before the IRS, Danner had placed the second delivery in San Clemente "[s]ometime later," Question and Answer 102, than the Key Biscayne delivery. He was not then more specific on the date.

in this section,[305] although he testified to the Select Committee that he was ". . . reasonably certain that no delivery of money was made on that date." [306] Taken together, the evidence described above indicates that September 11-12, 1969 was the date of the first delivery.

5. February 3–5, 1970—Key Biscayne. On February 3–5, 1970, Danner was in Key Biscayne, registered at the Key Biscayne Hotel.[307] According to Danner's expense records, he had "[c]ontact with Rebozo re: TWA suit, Air West matters" [308] on this trip; according to his testimony, the *TWA* v. *Hughes* case [309] was the subject of discussions with Rebozo at that time, as well as Air West.[310]

Although the hotel records subpoenaed by the Select Committee do not show Maheu in Key Biscayne on February 3–5, Danner testified that Maheu was with him on the trip,[311] which included a visit to Nassau by Danner, Rebozo, and perhaps Maheu. Robert Wearley, a pilot of Hughes' private plane, the DeHaviland, testified that Maheu might have been on the flight with Danner from Las Vegas to Miami,[312] and that Maheu was definitely on the plane when it left Miami and returned to Las Vegas via Washington, D.C.[313] Maheu told Select Committee investigators that he was on the flight to Miami with Danner and that he and Danner met with Rebozo on February 3–5, 1970.[314]

In addition, Maheu told the investigators that he testified before a Las Vegas federal grand jury investigating Hughes' acquisition of Air West that the *second* delivery to Rebozo was made in a meeting among Maheu, Danner and Rebozo on February 3–5, 1970.[315] Maheu, however, could not explain the basis of that testimony.

305. Danner is not clear on when he and Rebozo first discussed Danner's IRS testimony of May 1972, but he thinks it was before the November 1972 election. Danner Executive Session, June 11, 1974, pp. 210-211, hence before the call to Skelton on November 29. When he and Rebozo discussed the deliveries, Rebozo insisted that Maheu was not present at either one (Danner Executive Session, June 11, 1974, pp. 182-83). If Rebozo and Danner did in fact talk about the deliveries before the election, Danner was nonetheless reiterating his May 1972 story when he called Skelton in late November.
306. Danner Executive Session, June 11, 1974, p. 182.
307. Exhibit 32.
308. Exhibit 33. Air West and TWA are discussed elsewhere in this report.
309. Danner Executive Session, Dec. 19, 1973, pp. 28-30.
310. *Ibid*, p. 30.
311. *Ibid*. at 30.
312. Wearley Executive Session, Dec. 14, 1973, p. 49.
313. *Ibid*.
314. Robert Maheu Interview, Jan. 21, 1974.
315. Robert Maheu Interview, Jan. 21, 1974.

Rebozo may have been in Las Vegas shortly before the flight to Miami and may have flown with Danner and Maheu from Las Vegas to Miami.[316] When confronted with that possibility, Maheu stated that it was unlikely that he and Danner would have gone with Rebozo to Florida to make a delivery if Rebozo were already in Las Vegas.[317]

Aside from Maheu's testimony before a grand jury, there is no evidence that this was a delivery date (assuming only two deliveries) as strong as the evidence on other dates, such as September 11–12, 1969.

6. March 20–22, 1970—Key Biscayne. Danner and Maheu were in Key Biscayne on the above dates, [318] immediately after Danner received approval from Attorney General John Mitchell for Hughes' proposal to buy the Dunes Hotel.[319] All parties have denied that a delivery was made on this date. Maheu stated that he made a trip to Key Biscayne to see Rebozo sometime during March 1970 and that the purpose was to discuss AEC testing, not to deliver money to Rebozo.[320] Rebozo, of course placed the *first* delivery on July 3, some four months later.

Danner supported Maheu's recollection that the discussions with Rebozo were about AEC testing and that no contribution was made on that date.[321] In sum, there is no firm evidence that this was the date of a delivery, although all participants would have a substantial interest in not admitting to a delivery date so close to the Dunes decision by John Mitchell.

7. July 3, 1970—San Clemente. This is the only date upon which Danner and Rebozo agree that one of the contributions was made. When questioned initially by the IRS, Rebozo said that one delivery was at San Clemente and one at Key Biscayne, but that he could not remember which came first.[322] In later testimony before the Select Committee, Rebozo stated that the *first* delivery was at San Clemente on July 3, 1970.[323]

316. Maheu did not remember ever flying to Florida with Rebozo, *Ibid.*, but Robert Wearley, the DeHaviland pilot, testified that "I believe he [Rebozo] departed Las Vegas with us" on the early February trip to Florida. Wearly Executive Session, Dec. 14, 1973, p. 47.
317. Robert Maheu interview, Jan. 21, 1974.
318. Danner Travel Records, Exhibit 34, Sonesta Beach Hotel records, Exhibit 35.
319. See *infra.* John Mitchell was also in Key Biscayne during this period, Mitchell logs, Exhibit 36, but there is no evidence that he met with Danner, Maheu, or Rebozo.
320. Robert Maheu interview, January 20, 1974.
321. Danner Executive Session, p. 000.
322. May 10, 1973 IRS interview.
323. Rebozo Executive Session, March 20, 1974, p. 61.

Danner also placed the first delivery on this date in his IRS affidavit of July 5, 1973,[324] which changed his May 1972 IRS testimony that San Clemente was the second delivery. In later testimony, however, he testified only that *a* delivery, not necessarily the first, was in San Clemente.[325] Robert Maheu told Select Committee investigators that his understanding was that both deliveries were made in Key Biscayne.[326]

Both Danner and Rebozo testified in detail about the July 3 delivery,[327] which included, according to Danner, a visit with President Nixon immediately after the delivery.

8. August 19–20, 1970—Key Biscayne. This is also a likely delivery date. Based at least partly upon his travel records,[328] which show him in Key Biscayne August 19–20, 1970, Danner testified before the Select Committee that a delivery could have been made at this time.[329] In addition, in his July 5, 1973 affidavit for the IRS, he stated that he was "certain" that the second delivery was on August 19–20, 1970.[330] Danner originally thought the Key Biscayne delivery was in August 1969, but his travel records show no trip to Key Biscayne in that period. Danner remembered a ". . . lapse of time, the extent of which I'm unable to define more accurately," [331] between the first delivery and the second delivery. If the first delivery were on July 3, the second delivery would have been either August 19–20 or October 28–30 (a date discussed below). Danner discounted the October date as too close to the 1970 election for the money to have been used for Congressional campaigns,[332] and Maheu questioned the October date for the same reason.[333]

Rebozo testified that the second delivery was in Key Biscayne, following the July 3, 1970 delivery within a "matter of weeks . . . [it] could have been three months . . . I don't know. I think I saw somewhere where Danner had indicated it was in August and that would be correct."[334] August 19–20 was within "a matter of weeks" of July 3, 1970, while Octo-

324. Danner also expressed his confusion regarding this in December 1973. Danner Executive Session, Dec. 19, 1973, p. 88.
325. See notes 31 and 32 *supra*. Danner's only trip to San Clemente, his travel records show, was on July 3, 1970. Exhibit 21.
326. Robert Maheu interviews, Jan. 20, 1974.
327. See pp. 452, 459.
328. Exhibit 37. Danner Executive Session, June 11, 1974, p. 181. Danner Executive Session, Dec. 19, 1973, pp. 2-3.
329. Danner Executive Session, Dec. 19, 1973, p. 2.
330. IRS notes.
331. Danner Executive Session, June 12, 1974, p. 3.
332. Danner Executive Session, Dec. 19, 1973, p. 4.
333. Robert Maheu interview, Jan. 21, 1974.
334. Rebozo Executive Session, March 20, 1974, p. 110.

ber 28-30 is almost four months after July 3. Rebozo's recollection of "a matter of weeks" between deliveries plus his inclination to accept the August date lend credence to August 19–20, 1970 as a delivery date.

Danner's present recollection is that he made the trip to Key Biscayne alone, that Maheu was neither present at the delivery nor in the Key Biscayne area when it was made.[335] There is no indication that Maheu was in Key Biscayne on August 19–20, in contrast to September 11–12, 1969; February 3–5, 1970; March 20–22, 1970; and (see below) October 28–30, 1970. If Danner is correct about Maheu not being on the trip to Key Biscayne at which a delivery to Rebozo was made, then August 19–20 would be the date for a delivery.

9. October 28–30, 1970—Key Biscayne. There is substantial conflict in the testimony with regard to these possible dates. Robert Maheu has stated that he instructed Thomas Bell sometime in 1970 [336] to withdraw $50,000 from the Slipper casino in Las Vegas and deliver it to Danner. Bell, as noted earlier, told Select Committee investigators that, at Robert Maheu's direction, he withdrew $115,000 from the Silver Slipper casino in Las Vegas on October 26, 1970, and delivered $50,000 of that sum to Danner on the same day.[337] Danner's expense records show him in Key Biscayne for "conference with Rebozo" [338] as part of a trip to Washington, D.C., and Miami on October 26–30, 1970, and hotel records show Danner and Maheu in Key Biscayne on October 28–29, 1970.[339] President Nixon was also in Key Biscayne on October 27–28.[340] There is no evidence that he met with Danner or Maheu or was aware of a contribution made in Key Biscayne. Danner could not recall whether the President was in Key Biscayne when the delivery was made.[341]

The strongest evidence supporting this late 1970 date is Thomas Bell's statement, based upon the withdrawal slip from the Silver Slipper, that he gave $50,000 to Danner on October 26. On the other hand, Danner's testimony that he did not receive money from Bell,[342] plus the statements of

335. Danner Executive Session. June 11, 1974, p. 183.
336. Maheu has given different times for the instruction. See p. 454.
337. See p. 456.
338. Exhibit 38.
339. Exhibit 39. Further, records of the DeHaviland show a Las Vegas-Washington-Miami-Las Vegas trip on Oct. 27-29, 1970. Exhibit 40.
340. Information provided by Congressional Research Service, Library of Congress.
341. Danner Executive Session, June 11, 1974, p. 187.
342. *Ibid.* at 186. He earlier testified that he could have received money from Bell, Danner Executive Session. December 19, 1973, p. 2.

475

Danner [343] and Robert Maheu [344] that a delivery was probably not made so close to the 1970 Congressional election, cast doubt upon this date.

D. *Storage of the Money by Rebozo.* Richard Danner testified that he delivered the cash to Bebe Rebozo in manila envelopes and that the cash was wrapped with bank wrappers from the Valley Bank of Nevada.[345] Rebozo testified that he received the first $50,000 in a "letter-sized thick manila envelope," [346] which he then took without opening it and marked "H.H." in the corner. In addition, Rebozo recalled that he wrote instructions on the envelope addressed to Thomas H. Wakefield, General Counsel, telling him that if anything should happen to Rebozo, Wakefield should turn the funds over to the Finance Chairman of the '72 campaign.[347] Rebozo then took the envelope and put it in safe deposit box No. 224 in the Key Biscayne Bank and Trust Company.

Records from the Key Biscayne Bank and Trust indicate that safe deposit box No. 224 was rented on July 9, 1968 by C. G. Rebozo with Thomas H. Wakefield as the "lessee-deputy." [348] Rebozo testified that he subsequently prepared a letter of instructions to Thomas Wakefield concerning what to do with the money in box No. 224, which Rebozo placed in the Director's Safe Deposit box at the Key Biscayne Bank.[349] Rebozo testified that he prepared the letter that was in the Director's box a few weeks or possibly a month after he had placed the first envelope in safe deposit box 224.[350]

Thomas H. Wakefield declined to testify as to whether Rebozo gave him any instructions regarding the safe deposit box because he claimed the information was privileged under the attorney-client relationship with Rebozo.[351] However, Wakefield stated in an interview on October 18, 1973, that sometime in 1968 or 1969 Rebozo gave him a key to the box and explained that in case of Rebozo's death, Wakefield should open the box and follow the instructions.[352]

Rebozo testified that the second contribution was also in a manila envelope that he placed in the safe deposit box 224, and that he placed rubber bands around the two envelopes.[353]

343. Danner Executive Session, December 19, 1974, p. 4.
344. Robert Maheu interview, January 21, 1974.
345. Danner Ex. Session, June 11, 1974, p. 186.
346. Rebozo Ex. Session, March 20, 1974, p. 47.
347. *Ibid.* p. 72.
348. See Rebozo Exhibit No. 3, March 20, 1974.
349. *Ibid.* pp. 73-74.
350. March 20, 1974, Rebozo testimony, p. 103.
351. Wakefield Ex. Session, June 10, 1974, p. 19.
352. Wakefield interview, Oct. 18, 1973, p. 2.
353. Rebozo Ex. Session, March 20, 1974, p. 75.

Rebozo testified that he told Rose Mary Woods about the first Hughes contribution either at the time of delivery at San Clemente or immediately thereafter.[354] Rebozo also testified that he probably informed Woods of the second contribution at the White House.[355] Rebozzo added that he may have spoken to Woods about the Hughes contributions "three or four times."[356]

In a letter dated Oct. 18, 1973 to Special Agent John Bartlett, of the IRS, Woods recalled,

"Mr. Rebozo told me that he had put this campaign contribution in a safe deposit box and further that he had given his attorney the instructions in the event of his death that he should open the box and follow the instructions therein. It was my understanding that those instructions were to deliver the contents to the Campaign Chairman or Finance Chairman of the next campaign."[357]

In addition, Woods gave testimony concerning Rebozo's conversation with her about the contribution as follows:

MR. LENZNER   And do you know how soon after he received the money he told you he received it?
MISS WOODS   No sir.
L   In other words—
W   I'm sorry, I do not.
L   I'm sorry, . . . finish your answer, go ahead.
W   I do not recall because I don't recall when he told me, I don't recall when he got the money, so I do not know how soon after.[358]

Woods also testified that when Rebozo advised her of the contribution, he did not specify the campaign for which the contribution was designated.[359]

Rebozo testified that at some point after he received the contributions, he thought he should take a look at the money itself. He testified that the money had "Las Vegas wrappers" on it, which he removed and replaced with rubber bands [360] because of "the stigma that is applied to anything from Las Vegas."[361]

Herbert Kalmbach testified that he met Bebe Rebozo on

354. *Ibid.*, p. 151.
355. *Ibid.*
356. *Ibid.*, p. 153.
357. See Exhibit 1, Woods Ex. Session, March 22, 1974.
358. Woods Ex. Session, March 22, 1974, p. 20.
359. *Ibid.* p. 21.
360. *Ibid.*, p. 107.
361. *Ibid.*, pp. 108-09.

January 8, 1974, and that Rebozo told him words to the effect that:

> "Undoubtedly, Herb, I have not told you that after you and I talked last spring regarding the Hughes money [April 30, 1973] I found that I had not, in fact, dispersed any of the Hughes cash to the several people I named. When I went into the safe deposit box, I found that the *wrappers around that cash had not been disturbed, and so it was clear that no part of this money had been used during the several years it was in my box."* [362] (emphasis added)

Since Rebozo's discussion with Kalmbach was on April 30, 1973, then either his statement that he removed the bank wrappers and placed rubber bands around the money is not true or his statement to Kalmbach was not true.

In this regard, it is significant to note the comments of Kenneth Whitaker, the FBI agent who was present on June 18, 1973—at Rebozo's request—when Rebozo opened the safe deposit box and had a list of serial numbers made.[363] According to Whitaker, there were ten-twelve packets of money in two envelopes. Some of the packets were held together by rubber bands, as Rebozo has testified, but Whitaker said, some of the packages were still in bank wrappers.[364] Thus, according to Whitaker, at least some of the money in Rebozo's possession was still wrapped in bank wrappers shortly before its return.

Rebozo testified that he again entered the safe deposit box to destroy the original envelopes in which the money was contained after "the signals changed." [365] Rebozo said that the signals changed when he decided not to contribute the cash to the campaign sometime after the Hughes-Maheu split in 1970 and before the campaign.[366] Although Rebozo has testified that the money was for the 1972 Nixon campaign, FBI agent Whitaker told the Select Committee that, on June 18, 1973, Rebozo told him that the contribution had been for 1970 Congressional campaigns.[367] Danner testified it was for 1970.[368] The Hughes-Maheu split was not until December 1970, one month *after* the 1970 Congressional election. Therefore, if the money were for that election, the Hughes-

362. Kalmbach Executive Session, March 21, 1974, p. 52, (Galleys).
363. Whitaker interview, November 20, 1973. Whitaker's role in the return of the money is discussed at p. 000 *infra.*
364. Whitaker interview, November 20, 1973.
365. *Ibid,* p. 74.
366. *Ibid,* p. 75.
367. Whitaker Interview, November 20, 1973.
368. See p. 000 above.

Maheu split offers no reason for Rebozo not contributing the cash to appropriate campaign committees in 1970.

Rebozo recalled that after the signals changed he took the safe deposit box into his office and placed the packets of money in large "brown envelopes" that replaced the envelopes with instructions on them. Rebozo thought this occasion—when he destroyed the envelopes with the instructions to Wakefield on them—was probably in 1972.[369] Rebozo testified that the sole purpose for changing envelopes was "to eliminate the instructions" [370] on the original envelopes. He could not recall if he placed any markings on the envelopes to keep the two contributions separate.[371]

The occasions when Rebozo entered his safe deposit box are difficult to determine from his records, since his visitation record card from safe deposit box 224 shows 5 visits between December 26, 1969 and June 5, 1970, but no visits between June 5, 1970 and June 18, 1973 when the money was removed from the safe deposit box to be counted.[372] Rebozo testified that there was no record of his entry into the safe deposit box because he got the key himself without signing the access card required for other customers.[373] At some time Rebozo destroyed the original envelopes containing the instructions to Wakefield. He destroyed the letter to Wakefield in the Directors' box at some later time.[374]

Rebozo testified that he once lost all of his keys to his safe deposit boxes.[375] In July 1973, Rebozo informed the IRS that he had lost his keys approximately a year before he talked to them.[376] Rebozo testified that his bank uses interchangeable locks on the boxes, so he switched locks for the boxes with lost keys.[377]

Rebozo testified that he then requested "from Mr. Wakefield his key" so that he could get into the safe deposit box.[378] After the lock was changed, Rebozo testified that he then gave Wakefield another key that was a replacement.[379]

Wakefield testified that after he first received a safe deposit key from Rebozo, he placed it in an envelope in his safe, where it remained until June 18, 1973.[380]

369. *Ibid.*, p. 83.
370. *Ibid.*, p. 124.
371. *Ibid.*, pp. 124-126.
372. Rebozo Exhibit #3, *Ibid.*
373. *Ibid.*, p. 84.
374. *Ibid*, p. 81.
375. *Ibid.*, p. 174.
376. See IRS interview, July 10, 1973.
377. Rebozo Executive Session, March 20, 1974, p. 174.
378. *Ibid*, p. 177.
379. *Ibid*, p. 178.
380. See Wakefield Executive Session, June 10, 1974, pp. 24-25.

According to Wakefield, (1) he received the key sometime in 1968 or 1969, (2) Rebozo never asked him for the key, (3) Rebozo never gave him another safe deposit key, and (4) Rebozo never told him he had changed the lock on box 224.[381]

Rebozo could recall nothing else that was done to the money or to Safe Deposit Box 224 until he returned the money in 1973.

E. The Federal Reserve Evidence Compared to the Sources and the Deliveries.* 1. The Mechanics of Tracing the $100,100. *a. Federal Reserve Recordkeeping.* Each $100 Federal Reserve Note (hereafter Note) has a series number (1928, 1950, etc.) and a serial number, which together make the Note unique. Serial numbers are often repeated in different series, however. The money Chester Davis produced before the Select Committee on December 4, 1973 contained Notes from several series, beginning in 1928. Federal Reserve records on the earlier series are almost non-existen,t but the Federal Reserve assured the Select Committee staff that Notes from those series would have been in circulation well before the relevant 1968–1970 time period. Consequently, subpoenas were issued only for Notes in two later series represented in the $100,100—the 1963A series and the 1969 series.** Federal Reserve Notes go through several steps before reaching commercial customers, as shown on Chart A, attached.

CHART A

DISTRIBUTION OF FEDERAL RESERVE NOTES

Step 1	Step 2	Step 3
a) Printed in Washington by Bureau of Engraving and Printing; b) Sent to Agent's Representatives at Federal Reserve Banks around the country.	Transferred by the Agent's Representatives to the Federal Reserve Banks (Cash Departments) upon demand by the Cash Departments.	Shipped from the Federal Reserve Banks (Cash Departments) to commercial banks upon demand by the commercial banks.

381. *Ibid.*, pp. 25-26 .

* The White House has apparently had at least a general knowledge of the Select Committee's work with the Federal Reserve System. By letter of June 6, 1974, a lawyer in Kenneth Gemmill's law firm informed the Select Committee that twice in 1974 General Alexander Haig told Gemmill that "there might be a problem" with the evidence produced by the Federal Reserve. Letter of Mathew J. Broderick to Terry F. Lenzner.

** Some of the Notes in the money Rebozo returned are "star" Notes, which are printed and numbered separately and used as replacements for regular Notes that are damaged during printing. It is impossible to trace "star" Notes.

For Notes on which the Select Committee subpoenaed information (except non-traceable "star" Notes), the Federal Reserve supplied the dates of step (1) and step (2) in the distribution process from detailed records maintained by the Federal Reserve Agents' Representatives.

The record-keeping for step (3) was inadequate, however, despite a Federal Reserve regulation * that requires the maintenance of complete records. At the time packages of new $100 Notes are shipped from a Federal Reserve Bank to a commercial bank, personnel in the Cash Department of the Federal Reserve Bank are required to record the beginning and ending serial numbers marked on each package of Notes. However, Cash Department records often fail to show serial numbers. Therefore, not every 1963A or 1969 Note can be traced to a particular commercial bank on a particular date. The poor record-keeping was most unfortunate in the San Francisco Federal Reserve Bank and its branch offices, especially Los Angeles. Approximately 60 percent of the Notes returned and identified as the first delivery and 50 percent of the Notes returned and identified as the second delivery passed through San Francisco or one of its branches, but, because of failure to record serial numbers, less than half of those Notes were traced to commercial banks.

In the materials that follow, those Notes that have as their latest distribution date the date of step (2) above are Notes for which no date of commercial shipment is available.

b. The Search for Records. Records showing steps (1) and (2) in chart A are kept in numerical order by series, thus making possible almost instant retrieval of information on a given Note. Records of commercial shipment, step (3) in chart A, are filed by date only, not by denomination, series, or serial number. In addition, Notes of a particular denomination and series are not so regularly distributed in numerical order as in steps (1) and (2). Consequently, Federal Reserve personnel who searched for commercial shipment information on a particular Note had to look at every commercial shipment form from the date of step (2) until the serial number was found or, if none were found, up to the present.

When a form recording the correct serial number was found, the search was not necessarily over, for in most Federal Reserve Banks the shipment forms show only serial numbers, not series numbers. If the lapse of time between step (2) and step (3) was great—*e.g.*, over one year—the strong possibility existed that the serial number on the commercial shipment form was for a Note from a different series.

---

* Regulation 2060.10, Federal Reserve Loose Leaf Service.

An example from one of the Notes Rebozo returned and identified as the first delivery follows:

Series	Serial No.	(Step (2)) Date Released to Federal Reserve Bank	(Step (3)) Commercial Shipment Date
1963A	L02 935 922A	3/24/69	4/19/71

The above information was submitted to the Select Committee by the Los Angeles branch of the San Francisco Federal Reserve Bank. If true, it would contradict Rebozo's testimony that he returned the same money he received. No one has ever claimed that a delivery was made as late as 1971, so this Note would have been inserted in one of the packets of money *after* Rebozo received it. The two-year lapse between (2) and step (3) seemed inordinately long to the Select Committee staff,* so the Federal Reserve was asked to check its records for the same serial number in the 1969 series. The officials in Los Angeles quickly discovered that a $100 Note in the 1969 series with a serial number identical to the 1963A Note was released to the Los Angeles branch (step (2)) on March 15, 1971, about one month before the commercial shipment date of April 19. No definite statement can be made about which of the Notes was recorded on the April 19 form, but the likelihood, according to Federal Reserve officials, is that the commercial shipment form is for the 1969 Note, which was released to the Federal Reserve Bank much closer to April 19 than was the 1963A Note in which the Select Committee was interested.

The San Francisco Federal Reserve Bank and its Los Angeles branch provided incorrect information to the Select Committee of the kind described above on some 17 Notes. In each case, if the date originally given as the commercial shipment date for the Note subpoenaed had been correct, then Rebozo's testimony that he returned the same money he received would have been clearly contradicted. The double-checking of the dates, as described above, was done by the Federal Reserve at the Select Committee's request. It should have been done by the Federal Reserve as a matter of course.

2. Some General Facts about the Money Rebozo Returned.

a. The 1,001 Federal Reserve Notes were distributed among the Country's 12 Federal Reserve Banks after they were printed by the Bureau of Engraving and Printing. About 60 percent of the Notes in the first delivery and 50 percent in the second delivery went to San Francisco or one of its branch banks, primarily the Los Angeles branch.

* By letter of February 1, 1974, A. S. Carella, Vice President of the San Francisco Federal Reserve Bank, formally confirmed that suspicion by estimating that the average time between steps (2) and (3) is two to three months.

b. There are very few records of commercial shipment available from Federal Reserve Banks other than San Francisco.

c. Because the San Francisco Bank and its branches have more records of commercial shipment available, and because so many of the Notes passed through those banks (especially Los Angeles), their records of commercial distribution have been analyzed in detail. The lopsided preponderance of Notes that went to Las Vegas commercial banks in both packets of money Rebozo returned suggests that a sizeable portion of the returned money was put together in Las Vegas. Most of the Las Vegas Notes went to the bank that was, during 1968–1970, used by the Hughes-owned hotels for supplying their casinos with cash.

d. The money identified and returned as the first delivery contains Notes ranging from the 1934 series through the 1963A series. No commercial shipment information is available on any Notes before the 1963A series. Most of the pre-1963A Notes were released to Federal Reserve Banks in the mid-1960's; a few as late as the end of 1967. The 1963A Notes on which records were found were available for commercial distribution from late 1967 through June 12, 1969. The latest date of commercial distribution is June 12, 1969 when three $100 Notes identified and returned as part of the first delivery were released to the Cash Department of the Los Angeles Federal Reserve Bank by the Agent's Representative. No record of commercial shipment was found for this Note.

e. The money returned as the second delivery contains Notes ranging from the 1928 series through the 1969 series. About three-quarters are from the 1963A and 1969 series. Notes from those series on which records were found went into commercial distribution from early 1967 through October 1, 1970. The latest date of commercial distribution is October 1, 1970, when a $100 Note identified as part of the first delivery. was released from the Federal Reserve Bank of Chicago to the Lakeview Trust and Savings Bank, Chicago. The next Note closest to October 1, is September 23, 1970, when a $100 Note was shipped from the Los Angeles Federal Reserve branch office to the Nevada National Bank, 4th and Bridger, Las Vegas. There are some 33 additional Notes that were not available for commercial distribution until late August or early September 1970. Therefore, there were 35 notes not available for commercial distribution until after August 19–20, 1970.

f. The money Chester Davis made available to the Select Committee on December 4, 1973, was the money returned to Hughes in June 1973. According to Danner,[382] each delivery to Rebozo consisted of ten packages of $5,000 each, the standard size of $100 bill packages. The money Chester Davis produced was divided into five packages per delivery, not ten. The five packages described as the second delivery contained 100 Notes each. The first delivery packages, however, were uneven, ranging from 50 Notes in one package to 150 in another. The extra Note in the 1001 Notes was in one of the first delivery packages. How it got there has never been explained.

3. The "Matching" Numbers. Comparing the serial numbers of the bills in the first delivery with those of the bills in the second delivery produced two examples of a phenomenon that subsequently contradicts Rebozo's story that he kept the two deliveries separated in the safe deposit box and did not disturb either of them until the withdrawal in 1973.

In the two examples charted below, the bills traveled through the Federal Reserve together and, as indicated on the chart, were shipped to the same commercial bank in the same package of money on the same day. That is, the dates and places described in steps (1), (2), and (3) in the distribution system described earlier [383] "matched" one another. However, the matching bills appear in *different* packages of the money Rebozo returned, one in the package identified as the first delivery and one in the second delivery. The two deliveries were apparently packaged on separate dates from eight months to almost two years apart, as the preceding discussions noted.[384] They were either put together from different sources in Las Vegas (the Sands and the Silver Slipper), or according to Maheu, in different cities (one delivery in Las Vegas, one in Los Angeles). According to a professional economist who analyzed their circumstances, the likelihood that the matching bills would end up coincidentally in separate deliveries that were kept segregated is "highly remote, verging on zero." [385]

The evidence on the matching numbers is summarized in Exhibit A on the following page. Back-up documents supporting these dates are in the Select Committee's possession.

There are several other pairs of what could be "matching"

382. See, *e.g.*, his May 3, 1974 testimony in the *Maheu v. Hughes Tool Company case*, pp. 7791-93.
383. See *supra*.
384. See *supra*.
385. See letter to the Select Committee from Dr. John Tucillo, Economics Department, Georgetown University, dated June 28, 1974. (Exhibit 41.) This conclusion, however, must be viewed in light of a number of caveats which are set forth in the above letter.

EXHIBIT A—"MATCHING" NUMBERS

Delivery—as identified by Rebozo	Series	Serial #	Date of Commercial Shipment	From	To
I. First	1963A	L02285857A	12/4/68	Los Angeles Federal Reserve	Nevada National Bank, 4th & Bridger, Las Vegas
Second	1963A	L02287969A			
II. First	1963A	L03248254A	5/21/69	Los Angeles Federal Reserve	Sunrise Branch, Bank of Las Vegas, Las Vegas
Second	1963A	L03248821A			

Notes on which the Federal Reserve evidence is incomplete, i.e. there are no records of commercial shipment for the Notes. Each of the incomplete sets went through steps (1) and (2) in the distribution system on the same dates. However, without the records for step (3) no conclusions can be drawn about whether the Notes "matched" completely, as in the two examples discussed above.

4. The Facts Compared with Possible Sources of the Deliveries. The Select Committee has received evidence and testimony pointing to four possible sources of funds for the deliveries. *If either of the first two sources—both in early December, 1968—was a source for a delivery, evidence produced by the Federal Reserve shows that the money returned by Rebozo was not kept intact from December 1968 until its return in 1973.* The third source (Nadine Henley, mid-1969) is doubtful (if the money remained intact at all times) because of where it originated—Los Angeles. Most of the money the Federal Reserve was able to trace went to Las Vegas commercial banks, not Los Angeles. The Federal Reserve evidence on the fourth source—the Silver Slipper on October 26, 1970—does not contradict the testimony that the money was kept intact from origin to return.

The discussion of Federal Reserve evidence on sources for the deliveries should be read as an introduction to the following section on delivery dates, for a full understanding of the significance of the Federal Reserve evidence is possible only when the all-important delivery dates are considered.

a. *Las Vegas—Sands Hotel, early December 1968.* If this was the source of the *first* delivery, all the money Rebozo returned as the first delivery could not have come from the Sands. There are 88 Notes in the money returned and identified as the first delivery that were not available for commercial distribution until *after* the Sands withdrawal and therefore would have been put into the $50,000 at a later date or later dates. The latest Notes were released to the Los Angeles Federal Reserve bank on June 12, 1969, some seven months after the Sands withdrawal.

If this withdrawal was the source of the *second* delivery, most of the Notes Rebozo identified as that delivery were not in circulation until well after the Sands withdrawal.

The Notes that went into circulation after the Sands withdrawal show that the money Rebozo returned could not be the exact money obtained in December 1968. There are three possible explanations: (a) the money did not stay intact from time of withdrawal by Hughes' agents to time of delivery to Rebozo; (b) it did not stay intact after Rebozo received it; or (c) some combination of (a) and (b).

b. *Los Angeles—Bank of America, December 5, 1968* (sent to Robert Maheu by Nadine Henley on December 5 and 6, 1968, in two $25,000 installments). As with the Sands withdrawal of the same date, there are 88 Notes in the money identified as the first delivery that were not in commercial circulation until after the money was obtained from the Bank of America, and even more post-December 5 Notes in the second delivery. In addition, most of the Notes Rebozo returned (for both deliveries) that could be traced went to commercial banks in Las Vegas. Few went to Los Angeles commercial banks, and almost none went to the Bank of America.

This withdrawal almost certainly could not have been the source of the first delivery (assuming the accuracy of Maheu's and Rebozo's statements about keeping the money intact) because of the 50 consecutively numbered Notes discussed earlier. Those 50 Notes identified by Rebozo as part of the first delivery arrived in Las Vegas on the same day the Henley money was withdrawn from the bank in Los Angeles and were not in circulation until the next day. Therefore, they could not have been part of the withdrawal in Los Angeles.

c. *Los Angeles—Cash from Bank of America*, probably obtained June 27, 1969 (sent to Robert Maheu by Nadine Henley, receipt acknowledged by Maheu on July 11, 1969.) If this withdrawal was the source of the first delivery, there is no contradictory Federal Reserve evidence. The latest distribution date for Notes returned and identified as the first delivery is June 12, 1969. If it was the source of the second delivery, however, a sizable proportion of the Notes returned and identified as that delivery could not have been in commercial circulation until after the June 27–July 11, 1969 period.

This possible source suffers from the same problem of location as does the earlier Henley money discussed in (2) above. If a delivery originated at a Bank of America branch in Los Angeles, one would expect to find a significant number of Notes in the delivery that were sent to that bank or at least to banks in Los Angeles. Such is not the case with the money Rebozo returned. In contrast, most of the Notes that were traced went to commercial banks in Las Vegas.

In addition, in the money returned and identified as the first delivery are 50 consecutively numbered $100 Notes that were shipped together from the Los Angeles Federal Reserve to a Las Vegas commercial bank on December 4, 1968. If this June–July 1969 money was the source of the first delivery, and if Rebozo returned the same money he received, then those 50 bills had to stay together from December 4, 1968 and find their way to Los Angeles for withdrawal by Henley some seven months later. Such a phenomenon seems unlikely.

Taken together, the evidence either makes this source unlikely—or indicates that the money returned and identified as the first delivery was not all the same money withdrawn by Henley in June 1969 and used for a delivery to Rebozo.

d. *Las Vegas—Silver Slipper Casino, October 26, 1970.* This withdrawal is a source only for the possible second delivery on October 28–30, 1970, since all other possible delivery dates were before October 1970. None of the available Federal Reserve evidence contradicts the testimony on this date. The latest commercial circulation date on money Rebozo returned as the second delivery is October 1, 1970, for a Note sent to a commercial bank in Chicago.

5. The Facts Compared with Possible Dates of Delivery. The following is an analysis of possible combinations of delivery dates based upon Federal Reserve evidence. Although the reader's patience may be tested, the most comprehensible format is to analyze each possible combination of delivery dates in light of what the information obtained from the Federal Reserve shows. Rebozo and Danner have testified that one delivery was in San Clemente on July 3, 1970. Consequently, to lend some coherence to the story, that date will be used throughout this analysis, sometimes as the first delivery, sometimes as the second.

The evidence from the Federal Reserve contradicts Rebozo's testimony that the money he returned was the money he received for all possible combinations of delivery dates save one. The only set of dates on which the Federal Reserve evidence does not contradict Rebozo's testimony is one of the variations under section 7 below, and the evidence tends to suggest that set of dates is less likely than several others.

Further, as discussed in the preceding section on sources, both the early December 1968 sources (Nadine Henley and the Sands) do not support the testimony that the money was held intact from time of origin until its return in 1973. There are some 88 Notes in the first delivery, and even more in the second, that were not in commercial circulation until after early December 1968.

(a) First delivery: Key Biscayne, April 2–10, 1969
Second delivery: San Clemente, July 3, 1970
Sources: a) Sands Casino, early Dec. 1968 (for either delivery), or
           b) Nadine Henley, Dec. 5–6, 1968 (for either delivery), and
           c) Nadine Henley, July 11, 1969 (for the second delivery)

488

None of the participants has suggested the April 1969 period as a possible time of delivery, and Danner testified that his trip to Florida, which included a business visit to Nassau, could not have been the occasion for a delivery.[386] If a delivery did occur at this time, Rebozo's testimony that he did not disturb the first delivery from time of receipt until June 1973 would be incorrect. There are some 50 Notes in the money returned and identified as the first delivery that could not have been in commercial circulation until after April 2, 1969. In addition, the evidence on this pair of dates would contradict Rebozo's testimony that the money he received as the second delivery was the money he returned in June 1973, for there are 72 Notes in the money returned and identified as the second delivery that could not have been in commercial circulation until after July 3, 1970.

    (b) First delivery: Key Biscayne, June 26, 1969
            Second delivery: San Clemente, July 3, 1970
            Sources: a) Sands, early Dec. 1968 (for either delivery), or
                        b) Nadine Henley, Dec. 5–6, 1968 (for either delivery), and
                        c) Nadine Henley, July 11, 1969 (for the second delivery)

The June 26 date has never been suggested by any of the parties as a possible delivery date, although Danner testified that he and Rebozo discussed campaign contributions about this time (Dec. 18, 1973, Executive Session, pp. 77–78). If this combination is correct, the source for the first delivery would have to be one of the early December 1968 withdrawals, since the July 11 money came after June 26. There are a number of Notes in the money identified as the first delivery that were not in circulation until later dates, thus contradicting Rebozo's testimony. Rebozo's testimony would also be incorrect as to the second delivery, for the same reason explained in possibility 1 above, *i.e.*, there are 72 bills in the money returned and identified as the second delivery that were not in circulation until after July 3, 1970.

    (c) First delivery: Key Biscayne, Sept. 11–12, 1969
            Second delivery: San Clemente, July 3, 1970
            Sources: a) Sands, early Dec. 1968 (for either delivery), or
                        b) Nadine Henley, Dec. 5–6, 1968 (for either delivery), or
                        c) Nadine Henley, July 11, 1969 (for either delivery)

386. Danner Executive Session, Dec. 19, 1973, p. 56.

489

This is a probable combination of dates, as discussed earlier.[387] Rebozo's testimony reconciles for the first delivery *only* if the money for that delivery was the money Maheu received on July 11, 1969. However, if the source were one of the early December 1968 withdrawals, the testimony would not stand up because a number of bills returned and identified as the first delivery were not in circulation until after early December 1968. In addition, as with possibilities 1 and 2, the Federal Reserve evidence on the money returned and identified as the second delivery contradicts Rebozo's testimony on the second delivery because there are 72 Notes in the money Rebozo returned and identified as the second delivery that were not in circulation until after July 3, 1970.

(d) First delivery: Key Biscayne, February 3–5, 1970
    Second delivery: San Clemente, July 3, 1970
    Sources: a) Sands, early Dec. 1968 (for either delivery), or
               b) Nadine Henley, Dec. 5–6, 1968 (for either delivery), or
               c) Nadine Henley, July 11, 1969 (for either delivery)

If this is the correct combination, Rebozo's testimony stands up for the first delivery *if* the money was put together on July 11, 1969, but not if it was put together in early December 1968, for the reasons listed in the preceding sections. Further, as with earlier possibilities 1, 2 and 3, the evidence on the money returned and identified as the second delivery contradicts Rebozo's testimony.

(e) First delivery: Key Biscayne, March 20–22, 1970
    Second delivery: San Clemente, July 3, 1970
    Sources: a) Sands, Dec. 5, 1968 (for either delivery), or
               b) Nadine Henley, Dec. 5–6, 1968 (for either delivery), or
               c) Nadine Henley, July 11, 1969 (for either delivery)

Again, Rebozo's testimony stands up for the first delivery only if it consisted of the money Maheu received in July 11, 1969. Similarly, as with the earlier discussions of July 3, the evidence on the money returned and identified as the second delivery contradicts Rebozo's testimony on the second delivery because of the 72 bills returned and identified as the second delivery that were not in circulation until after July 3.

387. See *supra* (for Sept. 11-12, 1969); *supra* (for July 3, 1970). 1970).

(f) First delivery: San Clemente, July 3, 1970
Second delivery: Key Biscayne, August 19–20, 1970
Sources: a) Sands, Dec. 5, 1968 (for either delivery), or
           b) Nadine Henley, Dec. 5–6, 1968 (for either delivery), or
           c) Nadine Henley, July 11, 1969 (for either delivery)

This is the first possible arrangement in which the *first* delivery is in San Clemente. Once again, Rebozo's testimony stands up for the first delivery only if the money delivered to Rebozo was the money Maheu received in July 1969. In addition, if the second delivery was on August 19–20, Rebozo's testimony could not be correct. There are *35* Notes in the money he returned as the second delivery that were not available for commercial distribution until *after* August 20, 1970.

(g) First delivery: San Clemente, July 3, 1970
Second delivery: Key Biscayne, October 28–30, 1970
Sources: a) Sands, Dec. 5, 1968 (for first delivery), or
           b) Nadine Henley, Dec. 5–6, 1968 (for first delivery), and
           c) Nadine Henley, July 11, 1969 (for first delivery), and
           d) Silver Slipper, October 26, 1970 (for second delivery)

This is the *only* one of the seven possible combinations under discussion that can conform to Rebozo's testimony that the money he returned was the exact money he received. Even this combination reconciles with his testimony *only if* Source (c), *the July 11, 1969, money from Henley, was the source of funds for the first delivery* AND IF Source (d) was the source of the funds for the *second* delivery. If the first delivery was put together from Sources (a) or (b), the general problem with these dates applies here, *i.e.*, there are 88 Notes in the money returned and identified as the first delivery that were not available for commercial distribution until after the early December 1968 transactions. If the first delivery was put together on or about July 11, 1969, and delivered on July 3, 1970, Rebozo's testimony is not contradicted by the Federal Reserve records.

If the second delivery was put together on October 26, 1970, Rebozo's testimony is not contradicted for that date. The latest date of commercial distribution available on the money returned and identified as the second delivery is October 1, 1970, for a Note sent to a commercial bank in Chicago.

6. DUNES REPORT

Introduction. Howard Hughes was a significant contributor to President Nixon's 1972 campaign. Although other principals in the Hughes-Rebozo contribution have disputed him,[388] Rebozo testified that the $100,000 in cash he received from an agent of Hughes was for President Nixon's 1972 campaign.[389] In addition to the secret contribution to Rebozo, Hughes contributed some $150,000 directly to the Nixon re-election campaign. The Rose Mary Woods list of pre-April 7, 1972 contributors shows a total of $50,000 from Hughes. The remaining $100,000 was contributed to various state Finance Committees to Re-elect the President after April 7 (generally after the election) and duly recorded.[390]

Besides being a contributor to Nixon campaigns in 1968 and 1972, Hughes was also a man whose numerous business activities were under frequent government review. As part of its investigation of Hughes' contributions to the 1972 campaign pursuant to S. Res. 60, the Select Committee investigated Hughes' relations with federal agencies from the date of the 1968 Presidential election through 1972.

The circumstances surrounding Hughes' efforts in 1970 to buy the Dunes Hotel in Las Vegas show questionable conduct at high levels of the Executive Branch and raise serious questions about the relation between campaign contributions by Hughes and federal action affecting Hughes. The problems inherent in difficult-to-trace cash contributions are emphasized in the Dunes case, where Richard Danner, the man who delivered the Hughes cash to Charles G. Rebozo, the President's close friend, also presented Hughes' case on the hotel purchase directly to the Attorney General in a series of secret meetings.

In early October 1973, the Select Committee staff began examining documents and interviewing the parties involved in the case. Over 50 interviews were conducted during the course of the investigation. The Antitrust Division of the Department of Justice cooperated freely and generously with the inquiry by providing copies of its files on the Dunes and the two other hotel cases involving Hughes and by making staff lawyers available for interviews.

---

388. See the discussion on the deliveries to Rebozo in Sec. 5(c) *supra.*
389. *Ibid.*
390. See GAO list of 1972 contributors. Hughes contributed $50,000 to the 1968 Nixon campaign.

I. *Prior Antitrust Division Review of Hughes' Hotel Activities—The Stardust and Landmark Cases.* Between early 1967 and early 1968 Hughes bought four resort hotels in Las Vegas,[391] as well as a substantial amount of land on the "Strip," and there was the widespread thought that Hughes wanted to buy up all of Las Vegas. As shown in memoranda written to and by Hughes, Hughes was keenly interested in the hotel negotiations undertaken on his behalf by Robert Maheu, chief of Hughes' Nevada operations. Copies of some of the 1968 Hughes-Maheu memoranda in which hotel purchases were discussed have come into the Select Committee's possession.[392]

By March 1968 Hughes was actively pursuing several possible hotel purchases, including the Stardust in Las Vegas, and was concerned about whether the State Gaming Commission would approve any purchases he made.[393]. Hughes' interest in the financial details of the proposed purchases was typified in Maheu's March 6, 1968 memorandum to Hughes on the Stardust[394] and in Hughes' memorandum to Maheu of March 17, 1968,[395] which set forth the men's evolving understanding of the proposed purchase terms. In a memorandum to Maheu dated March 14, 1968,[396] Hughes explained his strategy for obtaining Gaming Commission approval of his proposed purchases, which essentially was to promise the Commission that the Stardust would be Hughes' last major hotel-casino acquisition in Las Vegas. The Dunes was apparently of interest to Hughes at this early date,[397] but nothing happened until 1970.

In early April 1968 the Antitrust Division of the Department of Justice, aware of Hughes' interest in the Stardust and other Las Vegas hotels, began a formal investigation, or Preliminary Inquiry. The Preliminary Inquiry, which consisted of statistical research and analysis of the Las Vegas hotel

391. The Desert Inn, the Sands, the Castaways, and the Frontier. Hughes also bought the Silver Slipper casino, which has no hotel attached to it, in mid-1968.
392. Although the Select Committee has no copies of Hughes-Maheu memoranda written during the Dunes negotiations, there is reason to believe, based upon testimony received, that Hughes was as intimately involved in the Dunes negotiations as he was in the earlier purchases. Many of the memoranda were handwritten. Copies of the handwritten documents are appended to this report.
393. See Exhibit 1.
394. See Exhibit 2.
395. See Exhibit 3.
396. See Exhibit 4.
397. Exhibit 5. Hughes' handwritten notes following Maheu's information on the Dunes concern an unrelated matter, Hughes relations with Bill Gay, an aide of his.

industry and interviews of Hughes representatives,[398] was conducted primarily by James J. Coyle, then a staff lawyer in the Antitrust Division's San Francisco office and now chief of the Los Angeles office. As a result of his investigation, Coyle developed an expertise in the area of hotel acquisitions that was later used in evaluating other proposed purchases by Hughes, including the Dunes.

In a mid-April memorandum, Richard Gray, a Hughes lawyer from Houston, told Hughes of a Justice Department request that the planned May 1 purchase of the Stardust and the Silver Slipper casino (also in Las Vegas) be delayed until June 30 to give the Antitrust Division time to review the case.[399] By April 20, Hughes was apparently confident that the Justice Department review would present no problems,[400] but he was wrong. Although the Nevada Gaming Commission approved Hughes' plan to buy the Stardust,[401] The Justice Department inquiry led to a civil complaint, signed by the required Justice Department personnel, including Attorney General Ramsey Clark, and scheduled for filing in late June 1968.[402] Faced with the prospect of a lawsuit, Hughes' representatives postponed the merger shortly before the complaint was to be filed. Consequently, the suit was not filed. Hughes did not try again to purchase the Stardust, although Hughes' representatives tried in vain to obtain a reversal of the Department's position in the following months.

The gist of the complaint was that adding the Stardust to Hughes' other hotel holdings would violate Section 7 of the Clayton Act[403] by increasing his share of the relevant market —defined in the complaint as resort hotel rooms in Las Vegas

398. The *Antitrust Division Manual*, (pp. 54-56) an internal document for staff lawyers written several years ago, speaks of Preliminary Inquiries, involving no more than one week's work by one person, and Full Investigations, involving more time. The two categories have in fact been merged, according to present Antitrust Division officials. All investigations, up to the point of filing a complaint, are now termed Preliminary Inquiries.
399. Exhibit 6.
400. See Exhibit 7, an April 30, 1968, Hughes to Maheu memorandum in which Hughes says, without elaboration, "I am truly impressed with what you tell me about Justice."
401. On April 30, 1968, by a 3-2 vote. Under questioning by George M. Dickerson, chairman of the Gaming Commission, Richard Gray (Hughes' lawyer) reiterated a pledge made earlier by Robert Maheu that Hughes planned no more acquisitions of major hotels or casinos in southern Nevada if allowed to buy the Stardust. Transcript of Nev. Gaming Commission meeting, April 30, 1968, pp. 76-77. Attached as Exhibit 8. Maheu made the pledge to the Nevada Gaming Policy Board, the investigative arm of the Commission, on March 15, 1968. Transcript of Gaming Policy Board meeting, p. 5.
402. The complaint is contained in the official file on the Stardust case, given to the Select Committee by the Antitrust Division. The complaint and supporting memorandum attached as Exhibit 9.
403. 15 U.S.C. § 18.

—to almost 40 per cent, well beyond the percentages allowed by leading antitrust cases and by the Merger Guidelines promulgated by the Department on May 30, 1968,[404] and hence to an unlawfully anticompetitive level. The proposed complaint and accompanying legal memorandum are important reference points for the later handling of the Dunes case by the Justice Department.

In the Fall of 1968 Hughes became seriously interested in buying the Landmark Hotel in Las Vegas,[405] a then unfinished structure that was beset with substantial financial problems. Hughes' lawyer, Richard Gray, and lawyers for the owner submitted to the Antitrust Division a written request for advance approval, called a "business review letter," contending that the Landmark was a "failing company" that could be saved from bankruptcy only by Hughes' offer. The failing company doctrine is an explicit exception to the strictures of the Merger Guidelines.[406] The procedures for processing and granting requests for business review letters are set forth in Antitrust Division regulations.[407]

The Landmark File is extensive.[408] As in the Stardust case, the proposed purchase was found to violate the Merger Guidelines. The Antitrust Division expressed to the buyer and seller serious doubts about whether the "failing company" defense, necessary to override a violation of the guidelines, had been adequately established and demanded more proof.

A full-scale investigation was launched by the Antitrust Division, including numerous interviews of possible alternative purchasers by Antitrust Division lawyers, particularly James Coyle, who had worked on the Stardust case. On January 17, 1969, the Antitrust Division formally approved the purchase—in writing—having decided that an exception to antitrust rules was justified because no other alternative to

404. Relevant portions of the guidelines on horizontal mergers, of which the Stardust purchase would have been an example, are appended as Exhibit 10.
405. This interest emerged despite the pledge of no more southern Nevada purchases made to the Nevada Gaming Commission earlier in the year. See note 11, *supra*.
406. See Merger Guidelines, pp. 11-12, attached as Exhibit 11.
407. Volume 28, Code of Federal Regulations, section 50.6. The regulations require submission of all relevant data to the Antitrust Division including collateral oral agreements, and state that only written clearance can be given by the Department and relied upon by the parties to a proposed transaction. The regulations in effect at the time of the Landmark review are set forth in Exhibit 12. Revised regulations designed to increase public access to business review letters went into effect on February 15, 1974 as amendments to section 50.6.
408. The Antitrust Division gave the Select Committee the official Landmark File, containing the exchange of letters between the Antitrust Division and the parties to the Landmark transaction and the internal memoranda prepared by Antitrust Division lawyers.

bankruptcy existed besides Hughes.[409] Hughes now owns the Landmark.

II. The Dunes. A. How It Began. Hughes' proposed purchase of the Dunes Hotel in Las Vegas was handled by Hughes' representatives and by the Justice Department—very differently than were the Stardust and Landmark cases. In early 1970, Hughes instructed Robert Maheu to negotiate to buy the Dunes. According to Maheu, the instruction, like so many from Hughes, came without prior notice and with no explanation of Hughes' reasons.[410] (The Select Committee has discovered no Hughes-Maheu memoranda covering the Dunes negotiations.) Maheu says that Hughes, with whom he was frequently in touch regarding the Dunes, instructed him to send Richard Danner, then manager of the Hughes-owned Frontier Hotel in Las Vegas, directly to John Mitchell to obtain Justice Department approval of the purchase.[411]

Maheu stated that, after being thwarted by the Antitrust Division in the Stardust case, Hughes decided that he would never again "talk with any Assistant Attorneys General," but instead would deal only with "the boss," *i.e.* the Attorney General.[412] Maheu's explanation does not square with Hughes' approach to the Antitrust Division in the Landmark case, where, shortly after the Stardust confrontation, Maheu and Richard Gray formally approached the Assistant Attorney General, Antitrust Division, with a written business review request.

A more likely reason for sending Danner directly to Mitchell was that Danner knew Mitchell from the 1968 campaign.[413] According to Robert Maheu, Hughes, who had to pass upon the hirings of all top executives, was pleased with the hiring of Danner in early 1969 and was aware of Danner's political contacts.[414] Hughes-Maheu memoranda talked specifically about Danner being a liaison to the Nixon Administration, and Hughes instructed Maheu to supplement Danner's income some $10,000-$12,000 per year to compensate him for his liaison activities.[415]

B. The Mitchell-Danner Meetings. John Mitchell's decision to approve the Dunes purchase apparently rested on a series

409. See Exhibit 13 for the letter sent to the interested parties by the Antitrust Division.
410. Robert Maheu interview, Jan. 21, 1974.
411. *Ibid.*
412. Robert Maheu interview, Jan. 21, 1974.
413. The friendships among Danner, Mitchell, Rebozo, and President Nixon are covered elsewhere in this report. See chapter on campaign contributions.
414. Robert Maheu interview, Jan. 20, 1974.
415. Robert Maheu interviews, January 20, 28, 1974.

of secret meetings between Mitchell and Danner in early 1970. The following summary is based upon interviews with Mitchell and Danner, Mitchell's logs, and Danner's expense records. Significantly, there is *no* record of the Danner-Mitchell meetings, which no one else attended, in the Dunes File maintained by the Antitrust Division. Further, none of the Antitrust Division lawyers who knew or might have known about the case had any recollection of meeting with Danner on the Dunes, and none of them ever learned of the Danner-Mitchell meetings.

Danner, Rebozo, and Mitchell have denied that there was any connection between the discussions regarding the Dunes and the Hughes contribution to Rebozo. Mitchell said that his first knowledge of the Hughes contributions to Rebozo came from newspapers reports,[416] not from Danner, Rebozo, or anyone else involved in the transaction. Danner testified that he and Mitchell did not discuss political contributions or the 1972 Presidential campaign[417] and could not recall discussing the Dunes with Rebozo.[418] Rebozo testified that he never talked with Danner about the Dunes [419] or with Mitchell about any problems related to Hughes.[419a]

1) *Danner's Testimony*. Mitchell was aware that Danner was working in Las Vegas for Hughes. He called Danner in

416. John Mitchell interview, Oct. 18, 1973. The first news story on the $100,000 was a Jack Anderson column of Aug. 6, 1971, over a year after the Dunes.
417. Danner Executive Session, Dec. 19, 1973, p. 65.
418. *Ibid* at 64.
419. Rebozo Executive Session, March 21, 1974, p. 247. Although Danner and Rebozo testified that they did not discuss the Dunes during 1969-1970, they did talk about several other areas of governmental policy that were of interest to Hughes.
Danner testified that at various times he and Rebozo discussed Hughes' desire to stop atomic testing in Nevada and Hughes' purchase of Air West Airlines. See Danner Executive Sessions, Dec. 19 and 20, 1973. Rebozo testified that they discussed atomic testing but denied any discussions of Air West. See Rebozo Executive Session, March 21, 1974. According to Robert Maheu, in March 1970, Hughes instructed him to pledge to Rebozo a $1,000,000 contribution if the atomic tests in Nevada were halted. Maheu stated that he did not make the pledge and convinced Hughes to drop the idea. Robert Maheu interview, January 20, 1974.
Danner also testified that he talked with Rebozo about a possible negotiated settlement in the *TWA v. Hughes* litigation since Rebozo knew the principals of TWA. Danner Executive Session, December 19, 1973, pp. 25-28, 36. Rebozo Executive Session, March 21, 1974, pp. 256-57.
In addition, Danner testified that he gave Rebozo a memorandum outlining Hughes' views on an ABM system and that Rebozo later told him that the President and Dr. Kissinger had read it and wanted to brief Hughes. (Hughes declined the offer). Danner Executive Session, December 20, 1973, pp. 13-18. Rebozo recalled that the Hughes people wanted to brief President Nixon and Kissinger on some subject Rebozo could not recall and that Kissinger was willing to brief the Hughes people. Rebozo Executive Session, March 21, 1974, pp. 253-55.
419a. *Ibid.* at 249

497

late 1969 and asked to see him when Danner was next in Washington. On his next trip (date uncertain) Danner saw Mitchell and discussed a Justice Department Strike Force being set up to combat organized crime in Las Vegas. Mitchell was doubtful that Hughes' control over the casinos affected the influence exerted by organized crime in Las Vegas. At Danner's suggestion the Attorney General sent a Strike Force into the Frontier Hotel to review its operations. Danner testified that a Strike Force was sent and that it determined that the operation of the casino was not under "Mob" influence.[420]

The Select Committee found no evidence that any Justice Department lawyer was sent to the Frontier Hotel for such a purpose or that anybody in the Justice Department ever approved the Hughes operation at the Frontier. One Justice Department lawyer did visit the Frontier in early 1970 Nissen, who was an Assistant United States Attorney in Los Angeles in 1970, visited the Frontier on either January 21, 1970, or March 9, 1970, *solely* to examine records from the pre-Hughes days, then in the custody of Hughes' employees that were relevant to a case in Los Angeles. Nissen never discussed the merits of Hughes' operation with Hughes personnel or with anyone in the Department of Justice, including John Mitchell.[421]

Danner's first meeting with Attorney General Mitchell regarding the acquisition of the Dunes was in January 1970.[422] Danner has stated:

> "At about that time, the acquisition of the Dunes Hotel had come up. The Dunes was for sale. I was asked [by Robert Maheu] to talk to the Attorney General and ascertain what the guidelines might be, now or then at the time, relative to whether or not we would be in violation of antitrust, bearing in mind that at a former time when they [the Hughes Organization] were negotiating for the purpose of purchasing the Stardust Hotel, the Justice Department had threatened an antitrust suit if they took it."[423]

420. Danner Executive Session, December 19, 1973, pp. 42-43.
421. David Nissen telephone interviews, Jan. 31 and Feb. 12, 1974. For a discussion of anti-crime considerations in the Dunes decision, see section E below.
422. Danner's travel records place the meeting between January 7-10, 1970. Exhibit 14. However, Mitchell's logs show their first meeting to have been January 23, 1970, at 3:45 p.m. Exhibit 15. Danner's records (Exhibit 14) show a meeting with Mitchell sometime between January 22 and January 25, 1970 to discuss the Dunes. The January 7-10 meeting may have been the one at which Mitchell and Danner discussed the Strike Force. Danner could not place the time of the meeting as January 7-10 when asked directly. Danner Executivee Session, Dec. 19, 1973, pp. 46-48.
423. Danner Executive Session, Dec. 19, 1973, p. 43.

Danner testified that Mitchell asked him to get ". . . all the figures on hotel rooms in the State of Nevada, and those owned by Mr. Hughes.[424] Mitchell told Danner he was unfamiliar with the Department's earlier position on Hughes' proposed hotel purchases, so Danner briefed him.[425]

Danner met again with Mitchell regarding the Dunes on February 26, 1970.[426] Danner brought with him what he remembers as a one-page statistical memorandum showing ". . . the total number of hotel rooms, total number of motel rooms, total number of rooms in Hughes' hotels, and any percentage."[427] When questioned by the Select Committee staff, Danner thought the memorandum had been prepared by Al Benedict, then an aide of Maheu's.[428] However, the memorandum was prepared by Edward P. Morgan, a Washington lawyer who then represented Hughes and had represented the owners of the Stardust during the 1968 negotiations with Hughes.[429] The five-page memorandum (two of text, three of statistics), which was observed in the official Dunes File provided by the Antitrust Division, was undated and unidentified as to source of recipient. Further, there is no indication of how or when it was put into that file. The copy provided to the Select Committee by Morgan was attached to a cover letter from Morgan to Robert Maheu, written on February 27, 1970, one day after what the letter refers to as the Danner-Mitchell "conference."[430]

Interestingly, none of the Antitrust Division lawyers who worked on or theoretically had jurisdiction over the case, including then Assistant Attorney General Richard McLaren[431] remembers seeing this memorandum.

The lack of a stamped date of receipt on the copy in the Dunes File indicates that the memorandum was hand-delivered to the Department and placed directly into the file, not routed through the mail room. A memorandum setting forth similar

424. *Ibid.* at 43-44.
425. *Ibid.* at 55.
426. Danner travel records. Exhibit 16; Mitchell logs. Exhibit 17. The logs show that the meeting was at 4:15 p.m. and lasted up to 55 minutes.
427. Danner Executive Session, Dec. 19, 1973, p. 44.
428. *Ibid.* at 59.
429. Edward P. Morgan Interview, Dec. 7, 1973.
430. Exhibit 18.
431.Richard McLaren Interview, Dec. 6, 1973. Other key Antitrust Division personnel who cannot recall ever seeing the memorandum are Baddia Rashid, Director of Operations, through whom all investigations and proposed complaints are normally routed. Rashid interview, November 21, 1973; William Swope, an assistant of Rashid's. Swope interview, Nov. 23, 1973; Bruce Wilson, then Special Assistant to McLaren and now Deputy Assistant Attorney General. Wilson interview, November 23, 1973; Robert Hummel, then Deputy Director of Operations and now Director of Planning and Budget. Hummel interview, Nov. 28, 1973.

statistics and arguments was submitted to the Antitrust Division on Hughes' behalf by Edward Morgan during the Landmark case.[432] The date of receipt, origin of the memo, and official reaction to it are noted in handwritten comments on the memorandum made by an Antitrust Division lawyer, unlike the Dunes memorandum submitted by Morgan. The memorandum submitted to Mitchell by Danner in effect argues for two changes in the market definition used by the Antitrust Division in the Stardust and Landmark cases: first, instead of defining the market as resort hotel rooms in Las Vegas, the Antitrust Division should instead consider all guest rooms (i.e. *all* hotel and motel rooms) in Las Vegas or, secondly, all guest rooms in the entire state of Nevada. According to the unsubstantiated figures in the Danner memorandum, Hughes' purchase of the Dunes would not have violated the Merger Guidelines if one of the alternative market definitions were used.

There is nothing in the Justice Department Dunes file to indicate that any analysis was done on the memorandum delivered by Danner. Both James Coyle[433] and Baddia Rashid,[434] Director of Operations in the Antitrust Division, have noted that such a significant policy change should not have been made without an extensive analysis by lawyers in the Division.

Upon receipt of the memorandum on February 26, Mitchell told Danner, according to Danner's testimony, that he would "let the boys look this over and give you an answer later."[435] The only substantive discussion during the meeting apparently concerned the statistical information Danner had provided. Danner testified that the question whether the Dunes was being managed by criminal elements was not discussed.[436]

Mitchell promised to get in touch with Danner about the Dunes, which he did when he asked Danner, in a telephone conversation,[437] to see him the next time Danner was in Washington.[438] That conversation was probably on March 9, 1970.[438]

Danner came to Washington and met with Mitchell on March 19, 1970[439] Danner recalled the conversation as

432. Exhibit 19.
433. James J. Coyle interviews, Nov. 14, 1973, and Jan. 10, 1974.
434. Baddia J. Rashid interview, Jan. 17, 1974.
435. Danner Executive Session, Dec. 19, 1973, p. 61. See p. 44 of the same day's Executive Session for a similar statement.
436. Danner Executive Session, Dec. 19, 1973, p. 57.
437. *Ibid.* at 44.
438. Mitchell logs. Exhibit 20; Danner recalled that he called Mitchell. Executive Session, Dec. 19, 1973, p. 61. The March 9 entry is consistent with that recollection.
439. Mitchell logs. Exhibit 21; Danner travel records. Exhibit 22.

500

follows:

> I went to his office, I cannot recall whether there was
> anybody else present, whether he called anyone up to
> meet with me, but in a very perfunctory manner he said,
> from our review of these figures, we see no problems.
> Why don't you go ahead with the negotiations.[440]

During the same conversation, Danner testified that Mitchell told him the proposed purchase "met the guidelines" [441] (The Merger Guidelines). Danner testified that he could not recall Mitchell showing him, during the March 19 meeting, any documents reflecting an analysis of the proposed purchase by Justice Department lawyers.[442] In addition, Mitchell did not mention anything about removing organized crime from the Dunes or say that the decision had anything to do with that consideration.[443] Danner has no recollection that anyone else was involved in his conversations with Mitchell about the Dunes.[444]

Immediately after the meeting with Mitchell, Danner reported the favorable result to Robert Maheu and Edward P. Morgan.[445] Although neither man can remember how or where the message was delivered, both Danner and Maheu were registered at the Madison Hotel on March 19, 1970.[446] Maheu remembers Danner telling him that the case "was taken care of in Washington and there would be no interference beyond that."[447]

After Danner met with Mitchell and reported to Maheu, he flew to Florida for the weekend.[448] Maheu does not remember being in Florida then, but records from the Sonesta Beach Hotel in Key Biscayne show Danner and Maheu registered there from March 20-22, 1970.[449]. On March 20, 1970, at

440. Danner Executive Session, Dec. 19, 1973, p. 44.
441. Danner Executive Session, Dec. 19, 1973, p. 61.
442. *Ibid.*
443. *Ibid.* at 63.
444. Danner stated on earlier occasions that he met with the head of the Antitrust Division in addition to the Attorney General during these trips to Washington. *See, e.g.,* his deposition before the SEC on August 4, 1973, and his interview with Select Committee staff on August 30, 1973, p. 7. McLaren does not remember ever meeting with Danner. McLaren interview, Dec. 6, 1973.
445. Danner Executive Session, Dec. 19, 1973, pp. 61-62.
446. Madison Hotel records, Exhibit 23.
447. Robert Maheu interview, Jan. 21, 1974.
448. Robert Maheu interviews, Jan 20 and 21, 1974. Maheu does remember being in Florida for one weekend in March 1970, having been sent by Hughes to promise to Rebozo $1,000,000 in return for an Administration decision to stop Nevada AEC testing (Maheu never made the promise.) Maheu doesn't connect that weekend with any discussions of the Dunes.
449. Sonesta Beach Hotel records. Exhibit 24.

3:30 p.m., Mitchell left Union Station in Washington on a train trip to Florida.[450] Mitchell returned to Washington on the evening of March 23. At noon the next day he went "back to Key Biscayne," in the words of his log.[451] Thus, he was apparently in Key Biscayne when Danner and Maheu were.

President Nixon was not in Key Biscayne during this time period.[452]

Danner asserts that he did not discuss the Dunes with Rebozo during March 20-22, 1970, despite the just-completed meeting with Mitchell, or at any other time.[453] Danner does not remember whether he saw Mitchell in Key Biscayne over this March weekend.[454] Rebozo also denies any discussion of the Dunes with Danner.[455]

Maheu, on the other hand, has raised the distinct possibility of a quid pro quo arrangement.

On July 4, 1973, Maheu testified that, after Danner returned from one of his meetings with Mitchell in Washington, Maheu set in motion one of the two $50,000 contributions to Rebozo. According to Maheu:

> . . . I believe I informed Mr. Bell (Tom Bell, then a Hughes lawyer in Las Vegas) in the presence of Mr. Danner upon the return of Mr. Danner from Washington, D.C. that certain political obligations had to be met as the result of the trip which Mr. Danner had made. I believe I requested that Mr. Bell make those funds available to Mr. Danner.[456]

The recollections of Danner and Bell on this subject are set forth in the section on the deliveries of the $100,000.[457] While uncertain about Danner's talks with Mitchell, Maheu is certain that he commented about the $50,000 in conversations with Danner about the Dunes Hotel. When telling Danner that Hughes wanted to see Mitchell about the antitrust problems relative to the acquisition of the Dunes, Maheu noted:

> I remember telling Danner that we had authority from Hughes to make a commitment to help the Administration in some of the congressional races they'd be inter-

450. Mitchell logs. Exhibit 25.
451. Mitchell logs. Exhibit 26.
452. Information supplied by Cong. Research Service, Library of Congress.
453. Danner Executivee Session, Dec. 19, 1973, p. 64.
454. Danner Executive Session, June 11, 1974, p. 188.
455. Rebozo Executive Session, March 21, 1974, pp. 247-48.
456. Civil deposition in *Maheu v. Hughes Tool Co., Civil* No. 72-305-HP (C.D.Col.), Vol. XII, pp. 1025-26. Danner denied telling Maheu that political obligations had to be met as a result of his visits with Mitchell. Danner Executive Session, Dec. 20, 1973, p. 36.
457. See p. 000.

ested in. But I don't know to this day if he took the matter up with Mitchell or someone else.[458]

After one of Danner's trips to Washington to see Mitchell, he and Maheu, according to Maheu, talked about a planned delivery to Rebozo.[459]

2) Mitchell's Statement. Mitchell remembers only one meeting with Danner and with Antitrust Division officials sometime in the summer of 1970. Mitchell claims that the Antitrust Division preferred to have public corporations, rather than criminal figures, owning hotels. The question on the Dunes, however, was *not* one of criminal influences, but rather whether the market definition should be Las Vegas hotels or hotels throughout Nevada. Mitchell cannot remember whether he or anyone in the Department ever made a decision on the Dunes. In general, Mitchell says he remembers almost nothing about the Dunes.[460] There is nothing in the Dunes File written by Mitchell or indicating in any way his opinion on the case.

C. What Happened in the Antitrust Division. In early March 1970,[461] Mitchell called Richard McLaren, then head of the Antitrust Division. According to McLaren,[462] Mitchell emphasized that the Governor of Nevada was pushing for Justice approval of the Dunes purchased by indicating that the Dunes was hoodlum-owned and that Hughes would buy it and "clean it up." Mitchell told McLaren that he was inclined to go along with the purchase and asked McLaren to determine if Hughes could buy the Dunes without doing too much violence to the Merger Guidelines. McLaren interpreted this as a casual inquiry.

Soon after the call from Mitchell, McLaren met with James Coyle, who had developed a knowledge of the Las Vegas hotel situation in his work on the Stardust and Landmark cases. Coyle was in Washington working on the ITT case. McLaren's memory of his conversation with Coyle is vague.[463]

458. Maheu interview, Jan. 21, 1974.
459. *Ibid.*
460. Mitchell Interview, Oct. 18, 1973.
461. McLaren's and Mitchell's logs show a phone call beteween them on March 3, 1970. Exhibits 27 and 28, respectively.
462. McLaren Interview, December 6, 1973. McLaren, now a Federal District Judge in Chicago, based his recollection upon handwritten notes he took during the call from Mitchell. Exhibit 29. Those notes were provided to the Select Committee by the Antitrust Division as part of its Dunes File. On June 24, 1974, Judge McLaren submitted an affidavit to the Select Committee setting forth his recollection of the Dunes matter. Exhibit *28a* and attachments.
463. Indeed, McLaren's recollection of the entire Dunes case is hazy. He based his statements to the Select Committee staff and his affidavit primarily upon his notes and memoranda made at the time the case was before him.

In fact, until reminded of it during his interview, he could not remember meeting with Coyle; he thought he had called Coyle at Coyle's California office. Coyle's recollection is much clearer. According to Coyle,[464] McLaren told him that he (McLaren) might have to approve the Dunes purchase. This was the first time Coyle had heard of the possibility. McLaren told Coyle that the Governor of Nevada was putting pressure on for approval by arguing that Hughes would drive the Mafia from the Dunes, and he asked Coyle for his opinion of the purchase. Coyle remembered saying that approval could not be reconciled with the Department's 1968 position on the Stardust and that the job of controlling crime should be handled by the Nevada authorities, not by making exceptions to antitrust policies. Coyle offered to write a memorandum for McLaren based upon market shares and the Merger Guidelines and upon his recollection of the pertinent facts in the Stardust and Landmark cases. McLaren accepted the offer.

Coyle wrote a five-page memorandum[465] and gave it to McLaren's secretary on March 6, 1970, just before he returned to Califronia. He had no other involvement in the Dunes case and, hearing nothing about it, assumed that McLaren had been able to kill the idea of a Hughes purchase. The Coyle memorandum, after outlining the Stardust and Landmark cases, pointed out that the proposed purchase would increase Hughes' share of the Las Vegas resort hotel market to about 28 percent.[466] Coyle also noted that the proposed acquisition ". . . is bound to create controversy" and that, because of prior involvement with Hughes' hotel purchases, the Antitrust Division ". . . will be asked to take a position."[467] The memorandum concluded on an equivocal note, with Coyle suggesting a possible alternative to outright approval:

> If there are overriding considerations which make it necessary to modify our prior position on Hughes' acquisitions in Las Vegas we should tie the acquisition to the changing and unsettled market structure as suggested by Parvin Dohrman [another hotel case] and preserve our right to secure divestiture at a later date if it becomes necessary.[468]

464. Coyle Interviews, November 14, 1973, and January 10, 1974.
465. Exhibit 30.
466. pp. 4-5. While Coyle did not state directly that such an increase would violate the Merger Guidelines (see Exhibit 10) McLaren was presumably familiar with them and aware that 28 percent of the market would be a violation.
467. Exhibit 30, p. 5.
468. *Ibid.* Coyle, in his January 10, 1974, interview, said that he substituted the word "modify" for the word "reverse" in the final paragraph of his memorandum. He also stated in that interview that the only "overriding

On March 8, 1970, a Sunday, McLaren worked on the Dunes matter in his office for one-half hour,[469] presumably evaluating Coyle's memorandum.

Four days later, on March 12, 1970, McLaren and Mitchell met at 5:00 p.m.[470] and discussed the Dunes for approximately fifteen minutes.[471] McLaren told Mitchell that the purchase would violate the Merger Guidelines and would make the Department look bad because of its prior position on the Stardust.[472] McLaren also suggested that Nevada could act on its own against criminal figures running casinos by instituting license revocation proceedings. McLaren told Mitchell that the Antitrust Division could accept the Hughes purchase if ". . . there were no other legitimate and reasonable bids."[473] According to McLaren:

> My remarks did not express and were not intended by me to express my approval nor to substitute for the formal investigation and report procedure which precede Division action on acquisitions of this kind.[474]

The meeting concluded without Mitchell indicating what his reaction to McLaren's presentation was or what his position on the purchase would be. This was the last discussion on this subject McLaren remembers having with Mitchell.

Danner testified that on March 19, as noted earlier, Mitchell conveyed oral approval of the proposed purchase to Danner. McLaren says that he never met Danner or any Hughes people, that he knows of no Mitchell meetings with Hughes' representatives, and that he knows of no approval given to Hughes by Mitchell. On March 26, unaware that Mitchell had given oral approval to Danner one week earlier, McLaren wrote a two-page memorandum to Mitchell reviewing their early March phone conversation and their March 12 meeting.[475] With one possible exception,[476] no one

---

469. McLaren diary. Exhibit 31.
considerations" he had in mind were the anti-hoodlum concerns expressed to him by McLaren. Coyle did not report on his work for McLaren to his superior in San Francisco, Marquis Smith. Coyle interview, Jan. 10, 1974; Marquis Smith interview, October 16, 1973.
470. Mitchell's logs and McLaren's logs. Exhibits 32 and 33, respectively.
471. McLaren diary. Exhibit 34.
472. McLaren's recollection of this conversation is based almost entirely upon the memorandum he wrote to the Attorney General on March 26, 1970. Exhibit 35. The circumstances surrounding that memorandum and its discussion of other events are discussed below.
473. Exhibit 35, p. 2.
474. McLaren affidavit, pp. 4-5.
475. Exhibit 35.
476. Baddia Rashid says he may have seen the memorandum at some point, but he also says that he may be confusing some of the language in it with material he read on the Stardust case. January 17, 1974, interview.

in the Antitrust Division remembers seeing McLaren's March 26 memorandum or talking with McLaren about it. McLaren insists that, in his March 26 memorandum, as in his March 12 meeting with Mitchell, he in no way intended to approve the proposed Dunes purchase or to relinquish his control of any future investigation if what McLaren saw as a casual inquiry turned into serious negotiations for the sale.[477]

D. The FBI's Role. McLaren's March 26 memorandum was prompted by a March 23 memorandum written to him by FBI Director J. Edgar Hoover (with copies to no one else.)[478] According to the memorandum, on March 19, the day Mitchell gave the go-ahead to Danner, someone representing Hughes told a Dunes representative that the Antitrust Division would not object to the purchase.

Because McLaren had not given his approval, he wrote the memorandum to Mitchell so that Mitchell could clarify any misimpressions he might have had.[479] It was McLaren's impression that Mitchell had talked with the Governor of Nevada about the Dunes (an impression traced back to what Mitchell told him in their first conversation in early March), and that the Governor had in turn talked to representatives of Hughes, who in turn had approached the Dunes. The end result of this chain was the clearly erroneous impression, held by the Hughes and Dunes representatives, that the Antitrust Division had approved the purchase. McLaren attached the March 23 Hoover memorandum to his memorandum to Mitchell and concluded the memorandum as follows:

> I trust that the attached FBI report inaccurately records the understanding which the State Government received from the Department.[480]

Unfortunately, the FBI has been unable to provide further explanation of the Hoover memorandum and any interest it may have had in the Dunes. There are no FBI memoranda in either the Stardust File or the Landmark File. One Antitrust Division official has stated that this kind of apparently self-initiated FBI involvement in an antitrust case is unusual.[481] Another Antitrust Division official said that a memorandum directly to the Assistant Attorney General from the FBI Director was unusual.[482]

477. Richard J. McLaren interview, Dec. 6, 1973.
478. Exhibit 36.
479. Richard McClaren interview, Dec. 6, 1973.
480. Exhibit 35, p. 2.
481. Robert Hummel interview, Nov. 28, 1973.
482. Baddia Rashid interview, Jan. 17, 1974.

Hughes and his representatives were interested in enlisting FBI support for Hughes' hotel purchases at least as far back as the time of the Stardust. In a February 12, 1968, memorandum[483] to Maheu, Hughes urged Maheu to meet with Dean Elson, then head of the Las Vegas FBI office and later a Hughes employee, and George Dickerson, Chairman of the Nevada Gaming Commission, to convince Dickerson that Hughes should be allowed to buy the Stardust because he would drive out criminal elements. James Coyle, in one of his Stardust memoranda, dated April 26, 1968, reported that the FBI was pleased to see Hughes enter the Las Vegas hotel market.[484]

Harold Campbell, who headed the Las Vegas FBI office at the time of the Dunes, said that he may have written one memorandum to Washington on a report he received—sometime after the Dunes negotiations terminated—that the negotiations had taken place, but he did not remember hearing about any Antitrust Division interest in the case.[485]

E. The "anti-crime" factor in the Dunes decision. As the preceding discussion showed, John Mitchell told his Antitrust Division chief, Richard McLaren, that he (Mitchell) wanted to approve Hughes' plan to buy the Dunes because Hughes would drive out criminal elements present there. Mitchell told McLaren that the Governor of Nevada was pushing for approval of the purchase on this anti-crime ground, and McLaren relayed that information to Coyle.[486] When talking wtih Danner about the Dunes, however, Mitchell never mentioned the anti-crime argument or the Governor of Nevada,[487] and Danner never approached Mitchell from that angle. According to Danner, he simply gave Mitchell a statistical memorandum on hotel rooms in Nevada,[488] a memorandum that neither McLaren nor any other Antitrust Division lawyers who should have or might have seen and evaluated it remembers. According to Danner, the only Danner-Mitchell discussion regarding criminal elements in Las Vegas hotels was the discussion they had in late 1969 about the Frontier Hotel.[489] In an attempt to determine where Mitchell got the information he conveyed to McLaren in early March 1970 and whether it was correct and relevant to the approval he gave Danner, the Select Committee conducted numerous interviews.

483. Exhibit 37.
484. Exhibit 38, p. 5.
485. Harold Campbell interview, December 18, 1973.
486. See Sec. C, *supra*.
487. See Sec. B, *supra*.
488. See Sec. B, *supra*.
489. See Sec. B, *supra*.

Paul Laxalt was Governor of Nevada at the time of the Dunes and, according to McLaren, the source of pro-Hughes pressure on the Dunes. He was interviewed twice and later submitted an affidavit to the Select Committee. His statements flatly contradict every aspect of Mitchell's apparent assertion to McLaren that Laxalt was promoting Hughes. Laxalt *had* supported Hughes in his early hotel purchases in Las Vegas,[490] but the Dunes presented a different case. In his affidavit to the Select Committee, Laxalt denied discussing the Dunes with any officials in Washington, stated that he would have opposed Hughes' plan if he had heard about it because Hughes had reached his limit of gaming licenses in southern Nevada, and indicated that the Dunes was, in his opinion, a "well-operated hotel, free of any problems."[491] Laxalt's position was supported by Frank Johnson, who at the time of the Dunes was Chairman of the Nevada Gaming Policy Board, the investigative arm of the Gaming Commission. He, too, never heard about the Dunes plan and would have opposed it.[492]

Thinking that Mitchell might have been getting the anti-crime argument he used with McLaren from within the Justice Department, the Select Committee staff interviewed numerous Justice Department lawyers to determine what, if any, feeling there might have been in the Department that a Hughes purchase of the Dunes in 1970 would have been desirable. The following people were interviewed:

1. Will Wilson, Assistant Attorney General in charge of the Criminal Division at the time of the Dunes;[493]

2. Henry Petersen, present Assistant Attorney General, Criminal Division, Deputy Assistant Attorney General at the time of the Dunes;[494]

3. John C. Keeney, present Deputy Assistant Attorney General, Criminal Division, Chief of the Fraud Section at the time of the Dunes;[495]

4. William Lynch, Chief of the Organized Crime and

490. On July 25, 1968, one month after Hughes had pulled back from buying the Stardust in the face of the threatened Justice Department suit, Laxalt wrote Attorney General Ramsey Clark to urge reconsideration of the Department's position. Exhibit 40. The letter promoted Hughes as a beneficial presence on the Las Vegas hotel scene. Writing for the Attorney General, the Assistant Attorney General, Edwin Zimmerman, replied to Laxalt on August 13, politely rejecting his arguments and emphasizing the Department's ". . . responsibility for the consistent enforcement of the anti-trust laws." Exhibit 41.
491. Paul Laxalt affidavit, Feb. 28, 1974, Exhibit 42. That portion of the affidavit dealing with the attempted delivery of $50,000 to then President-elect Nixon or an aide of his is covered elsewhere in this report. See p. 00.
492. Frank Johnson interview, Dec. 19, 1973.
493. Will Wilson interview, Feb. 6, 1974.
494. Henry Petersen interview, Feb. 19, 1974.
495. John Keeney interview, Feb. 14, 1974.

Racketeering Section, Criminal Division, now and at the time of the Dunes;[496]

5. Fred Vinson, Jr., Assistant Attorney General, Criminal Division, 1965-69;[497]

6. Richard Crane, head of Los Angeles office of Justice Department Strike Force, 1970-present;[498]

7. David Nissen, Assistant United States Attorney, Los Angeles; at the time of the Dunes involved in a Las Vegas prosecution;[499] and

8. Mike deFeo, head of the Kansas City Strike Force, Department of Justice; a Special Assistant United States Attorney in Los Angeles at the time of the Dunes, with responsibilities for organized crime prosecutions in Las Vegas.[500]

None of these men was aware of any Hughes interest in buying the Dunes during 1970 or talked with Mitchell about the matter.

As a result, the source of John Mitchell's argument for approving the Hughes purchase that he conveyed to McLaren has not been determined.[501]

Hughes' representatives had made the anti-crime argument in 1968 at the time of the Stardust case. There was some discussion between Edwin Zimmerman, Assistant Attorney General, Antitrust Division, and Fred Vinson, Jr., Assistant Attorney General, Criminal Division, about Hughes' plan to buy the Stardust, with Vinson deferring to the Antitrust Division but seeing merit in Hughes' argument.[502]

496. William Lynch interview, Jan. 31, 1974.
497. Fred Vinson, Jr. interview, Dec. 17, 1974.
498. Richard Crane interview, Jan. 31, 1974.
499. David Nissen interview, Jan. 31, 1974.
500. Mike deFeo interview, Jan. 15, 1974.
501. If Mitchell had asked officials in the Criminal Division about the Dunes and about how Hughes ran his casinos, he would have learned that the casino manager at the Dunes, Sidney Wyman, and several other principals of the Dunes were then under investigation by the IRS and the Justice Department for possible criminal violations of the federal tax laws stemming from the casino operations. Wyman and the others were later indicted and acquitted at trial on October 31, 1972, in Criminal No. LV-2434 (D. Nev., filed December 14, 1971 in Reno.)
  Further, if Mitchell had initiated a thorough investigation of Hughes' practices regarding casinos, he would have learned that retaining key personnel was Hughes standard practice when he bought casinos and hotels. Robert Morgan Executive Session, Dec. 12, 1973, pp. 238-39. (Morgan is assistant comptroller of the Summa Corporation. From 1967-73 he was in charge of the Las Vegas accounting office of the Hughes Tool Company.) The tentative contract later drawn for the sale of the Dunes to Hughes contained a clause for the retention of Wyman. Hughes was so interested in keeping Wyman that he offered him a $3 million dollar loan in addition to the retention clause. Interview of Wyman and Morris Shenker, lawyer and principal in the Dunes. Dec. 20, 1973.
502. Exhibit 44.

The anti-hoodlum argument was rejected by the Antitrust Division.[503]

F. What Happened After The March 26 Memorandum. McLaren said that, after March 26, he heard nothing about the Dunes from Mitchell or anyone else and talked with no one about the case until late in November (discussed below). However, Walker B. Comegys, then McLaren's deputy, had a different recollection.[504] Comegys distinctly remembered McLaren stopping by his office just before McLaren left Washington on a trip. McLaren told Comegys, according to Comegys, that Mitchell had decided not to oppose Hughes' plan to buy the Dunes because all other potential purchasers had Mafia connections. This was the first and only time Comegys heard about any concern about the Dunes within the Justice Department. According to McLaren's logs, he left for Europe on May 21, 1970.[505] McLaren, emphasizing that he cannot remember Mitchell telling him he had approved the Dunes purchases, was willing to accept Comegys recollection and said he would be terribly surprised if Mitchell granted approval without consulting him, since, as far as he knew, Mitchell never double-crossed him.[506]

Although Mitchell's log for May 21 shows no call to or from Danner,[507] Danner's telephone records show a call to the Justice Department on May 21.[508] Danner recalled only that the negotiations fell through sometime after March 19,[509] but it is possible that he called Mitchell on May 21, as the Hughes-Dunes negotiations were apparently nearing completion, and thus prompted a Mitchell-McLaren conversation and McLaren's apparent conversation with Comegys. This chain of events is speculative, of course, but it may provide an explanation of the otherwise coincidental Danner call and McLaren comment, both on May 21.

At 5:05 p.m. on Friday, May 22, Comegys received a phone call[510] from Howard Adler, a Washington lawyer who was calling on behalf of lawyers for the Rapid-American Corporation, which, like Hughes, was then negotiating a possible purchase of the Dunes. As Comegys recalls the conver-

503. See Zimmerman's memorandum to Vinson, Exhibit 45, and a memorandum prepared by Coyle, Exhibit 30, p. 10.
504. Walker B. Comegys interviews, Nov. 5, 1973, and Dec. 19, 1973.
505. Exhibit 46.
506. McLaren interview, Dec. 6, 1973. In his affidavit, at p. 5, McLaren stated that he could recall no conversation with Comegys regarding the Dunes after March 26, 1970.
507. Exhibit 47.
508. Exhibit 48.
509. Danner Executive Session, Dec. 19, 1973, pp. 62, 76.
510. Comegys log. Exhibit 49.

sation,[511] Adler, whom Comegys knew, told him that the people he was calling for represented another potential buyer of the Dunes who had no Mafia connections. Comegys told Adler he had gotten the message; Comegys made no comment to Adler on the Antitrust Division's position. Comegys did not remember whether he reported this call to anyone in the Antitrust Division, to Mitchell, or to McLaren when he returned from Europe in early June. Mitchell's log shows a conversation with Comegys at 12:15 p.m. on May 22, before Adler called,[512] and both Mitchell's and Comegys' logs[513] show a telephone conversation between them on May 25, the next business day after May 22.

The Adler to Comegys call came about as follows. Les Jacobsen, a New York lawyer for Rapid American and partner in Fried, Frank, Harris, Shriver and Jacobsen, who was in Las Vegas negotiating with Dunes representatives,[514] learned that Hughes was also interested in buying the hotel. Jacobsen remembered that Hughes had had antitrust problems with his Las Vegas hotel interests in the past and wanted to make the Antitrust Division aware of another purchaser. Jacobsen called Milton Eisenberg in the firm's Washington office and told him to call the Antitrust Division. Eisenberg then called Adler, because he knew that Adler, who had been in the Antitrust Division, would know whom to call.[515] (Adler was not in the same firm as Jacobsen and Eisenberg.)

Adler told Comegys that he hoped the Antitrust Division would consider not only antitrust questions on the Dunes, but would also look to the question of criminal influences in Las Vegas hotels.[516] Neither Jacobsen nor Eisenberg remembered saying anything about the anti-Mafia argument.

The Select Committee staff discovered no direct link between the May 22 Adler to Comegys call and the May 22 letter described below.

On May 22, 1970, as the Hughes-Dunes negotiations appeared to be nearing agreement,[517] James Hayes, a New York City lawyer (partner in Donovan, Leisure, Newton & Irvine) representing Hughes on the *TWA v. Hughes* case, wrote a letter to the presiding federal judge, the Honorable Charles Metzner of the Southern District of New York, informing the judge that Hughes was about to buy the Dunes for $35 million in cash and that the Attorney General had approved the pur-

511. Comegys interviews, note 122 *supra.*
512. Exhibit 50.
513. Exhibits 51 and 52, respectively.
514. Les Jacobsen interview, Dec. 14, 1973.
515. Milton Eisenberg interview, Dec. 17, 1973.
516. Howard Adler interview, Oct. 23, 1973.
517. As described in Section G below.

chase.[518] Hayes was instructed by Robert Maheu to write the letter.[519] Hughes had recently suffered a big monetary defeat in the district court and was before Judge Metzner on the question of how large the supersedeas bond should be for appeal. The judge was concerned that Hughes was tying up too many of his assets in non-liquid items, which could present problems of liquidity if the judgment against Hughes were upheld on appeal. Maheu remembered telling Hayes, at Hughes' request, to write the letter,[520] but did not remember telling Hayes that Mitchell had approved the deal.[521] Edward P. Morgan, who was in Las Vegas with Maheu on May 22 negotiating the deal for Hughes, remembered[522] talking with Hughes' lawyer Chester Davis when Maheu brought him into a Maheu-Davis telephone call. Morgan told Davis that the deal was on the verge of final agreement. Davis told Morgan that he needed the information for Judge Metzner; Morgan assumed that Danner relayed the information to Hayes.[523] Richard McLaren was unaware of the letter until apprised of it by Select Committee staff members. Based upon the integrity and reputation of Hayes' firm, Donovan, Leisure, Newton & Irvine, McLaren was sure that Hayes would not have written the letter without receiving assurances that Mitchell had approved the deal.[524]

G. The Negotiations And Their Collapse. Shortly after Danner received approval from Mitchell and gave the news to Maheu, Maheu (as always, at Hughes' request) called Edward P. Morgan and told him to begin negotiations with representatives of the Dunes. Morgan described the call this way:

> I got a call from Mr. Maheu, saying that Mr. Hughes was most interested in acquiring the Dunes Hotel, and I remember my reaction was, in effect, how in the hell does he expect to do this, when he was turned down on the Stardust deal by the Antitrust Division, and in the intervening period, acquired the Landmark under an exception, and then I learned, as I had learned in other areas, that mine was not to know the reason why, that

518. Exhibit 53; referred to by Judge Metzner in his opinion setting the amount of bond. *Trans World Airlines, Inc. v. Hughes*, 314 F. Supp. 94, 98 (S.D.N.Y. 1970).
519. James Hayes telephone interview, Dec. 6, 1973.
520. Robert Maheu deposition, an. 29, 1973, Vol. VII in *Maheu v. Hughes Tool Co.*, Civ. No. 72-305-HP (C.D. Cal., filed Feb. 10, 1973), pp. 570-71; Maheu interviews, Jan. 20 and 21, 1974.
521. Maheu interviews, note 135 *supra.*
522. Edward P. Morgan interview, Dec. 7, 1973.
523. *Ibid.*
524. McLaren interview, Dec. 6, 1973.

Mr. Hughes wanted it done.[525]

Maheu assured Morgan that Hughes was satisfied that there would be no Justice Department objections.[526]

Morgan, assisted by Tom Bell, Hughes' personal lawyer in Las Vegas, negotiated with Morris Shenker, the St. Louis lawyer who represented the Dunes, and Sidney Wyman, casino manager at the Dunes. Shenker provided the Select Committee with documentation on the negotiations. The deal fell through in late May 1970.

The course of the negotiations themselves is unimportant, but several points are noteworthy. All participants agreed that financial considerations alone led to the break-off of negotiations in late May 1970, shortly after the May 22 letter was set to Judge Metzner.[527] Shenker produced updated profit-and-loss figures on the Dunes,[528] which showed a substantial loss for the preceding months (due to a loss of business during remodeling and an employees' strike).[529] Antitrust considerations played no part in the termination. In fact, Shenker and Wyman did not remember questions about the Justice Department's antitrust policy ever arising during the negotiations.[530] Morgan remembered Shenker once asking him if there would be any antitrust problems; Morgan told him that he, Morgan, had been assured there were none.[531]

On November 24, 1970, some seven months after the negotiations between Hughes and the Dunes broke off, J. Edgar Hoover wrote a still unexplained memorandum [532] to the Attorney General, with copies to the Deputy Attorney General Richard Kleindienst and McLaren. Hoover reported that Hughes had renewed his interest in the Dunes and that Edward P. Morgan was implying to someone that the Antitrust Division would not object to the purchase. The late date of this memorandum makes no sense in terms of the statements and documentation the Select Committee has been given; because the FBI provided no further evaluation, the basis of this memorandum is not available.

McLaren remembered receiving a copy of the memorandum, which to him did not constitute firm enough information

525. Morgan deposition in *Maheu v. Hughes Tool Co.*, Vol. 00, April 3, 1973, pp. 84-85.
526. Morgan interview, Dec. 5, 1973.
527. Morgan interviews, Dec. 5 & 7, 1973; Shenker and Wyman interview, Dec. 20, 1973; Tom Bell interview, Dec. 17, 1973.
528. Exhibit 54.
529. Shenker-Wyman interview, footnote 86 above.
530. Shenker-Wyman interview, footnote 86 above.
531. Morgan interview, Dec. 5, 1973.
532. Exhibit 55.

to warrant initiating a Preliminary Inquiry.[533] McLaren did write a note[534] to Baddia Rashid, Director of Operations, when he received the Hoover memorandum. He asked Rashid who had worked on Las Vegas hotels earlier, saying that he wanted to talk with him. It is not clear whether Rashid ever received the memorandum (note that his name is crossed out and replaced by the word "File" in McLaren's handwriting). At any rate, Rashid remembered[535] telling McLaren that Coyle was the Las Vegas hotel expert. Having learned that, McLaren apparently did nothing. Neither he[536] nor Coyle[537] remembered discussing this second Hoover memorandum. Coyle remembered seeing the memorandum, the *original* of which, *i.e.*, presumably Mitchell's copy, was for some unexplained reason sent to California and routed to Coyle.

The memorandum may have been, in the juxtaposition of the following two paragraphs, Hoover's oblique way of asking Mitchell why there had been a change in the Department's position since the Stardust case:

> It was reported that Morgan has strongly implied that there will be no objection from the Antitrust Division of the Department of Justice concerning Hughes' efforts to purchase another Las Vegas casino.
>
> As you will recall the Antitrust Division objected to Hughes' attempt to purchase the Stardust Hotel-Casino in Las Vegas in 1968.[538]

Morgan,[539] Robert Maheu,[540] and E. Parry Thomas,[541] the Las Vegas banker mentioned in the Hoover memorandum, denied that—as reported in the memorandum—they visited the SEC as a group to seek approval for a cash purchase of the Dunes by Hughes.

Conclusion. In contrast to the immediately preceding case involving Hughes' hotel plans (the Landmark), the initial approach to the Justice Department on the Dunes was made directly to the Attorney General, not to the Antitrust Division.

533. McLaren interview, Dec. 6, 1973; McLaren affidavit, p. 6 (Exhibit 28a).
534. Exhibit 56.
535. Rashid interview, Jan. 17, 1974.
536. McLaren interview, Dec. 6, 1973. McLaren affidavit, p. 6 (Exhibit 28a).
537. Coyle interviews, Nov. 14, 1973; Jan. 10, 1974.
538. Exhibit 55.
539. Morgan interview, Dec. 7, 1973.
540. Robert Maheu interview, Jan. 21, 1974.
541. E. Parry Thomas interview, Dec. 18, 1973. Thomas is chairman of the Board of Continental Connectors, the company that owns the Dunes. He was aware of the Hughes-Dunes negotiations, but not of any communications between Hughes' agents and the Justice Department.

It was made by the courier of $100,000 to Rebozo, a friend of Rebozo's, Mitchell's, and the President's. Although Danner and Mitchell contend that their discussions concerned anti-trust questions regarding the hotel market in Las Vegas, Mitchell apparently did not invite his antitrust chief, Richard McLaren, to any of the meetings with Danner, advise him of the meetings, or submit Danner's statistical memorandum to the Antitrust Division for analysis. In fact, the Danner-Mitchell meetings were kept so secret that McLaren wrote his one memorandum to Mitchell on the Dunes one week *after* Mitchell gave Danner approval of the purchase.

As the evidence demonstrates, the apparent decision by Mitchell to approve the Dunes purchase is clothed with the appearance of impropriety:

1) Secret meetings were held in lieu of the existing procedures for providing appropriate antitrust analysis;
2) An ad hoc decision was made by the Attorney General which reversed the position of the professionals in the Antitrust Division, a position based upon considerable study and statistical analysis; and
3) Except for the fact that the purchase negotiations ultimately fell through for financial reasons wholly unrelated to antitrust considerations, this is a classic case of governmental decision-making for friends.

7. REBOZO'S 1972
CAMPAIGN FUND-RAISING ROLE

On December 20, 1973, Charles G. Rebozo testified in a civil deposition as follows:

"I am not a fund-raiser. I never have been."[542]

However, evidence before the Select Committee indicates that:

1.) Rebozo solicited funds at the request of President Nixon.[543]

2.) Rebozo opened and maintained an account at the Key Biscayne Bank and Trust Company for the retention of 1972 campaign funds.[544]

3.) Rebozo used his personal safe deposit box at the Key Biscayne Bank and Trust Company to store cash campaign contributions for the 1972 campaign.[545]

4.) Rebozo was aware of other "in kind" contributions and

542. Deposition of C. G. Rebozo in *Common Cause* et. al. v. *Finance Committee to Re-elect the President* et. al. December 20, 1973; p. 21.
543. See Exhibit 15.
544. See Exhibit 42.
545. Rebozo Executive Session, March 20, 1974, pp. 40-45.

cash contributions.[546]

5.) Rebozo personally handled at least $190,000 in campaign contributions for the 1972 Presidential campaign.[547]

Rebozo's discussions with Richard Danner about a cash contribution from Howard Hughes began shortly after the 1968 election.[548] In addition, a memorandum from early 1969 states that Haldeman informed Ehrlichman that President Nixon asked Rebozo to contact J. P. Getty for purposes of soliciting "major contributions" to be controlled by the White House.[549] Edward L. Morgan has said that he was approached by John Ehrlichman in the spring of 1972 with the question of the legality of such a contribution from J. P. Getty.[550]

Rebozo testified that he contacted Mr. Getty and arranged an appointment for Herbert Kalmbach to solicit contributions at Mr. Kalmbach's request.[551] On March 21, 1974, Herbert Kalmbach testified that Rebozo had asked him to solicit funds from Mr. Getty for the 1970 Senatorial Campaign Program.[552] Public documents from the Committee to Re-elect the President reflect a contribution to the 1972 campaign of $125,000 by Mr. Getty.[553]

Rebozo testified that he also arranged an appointment for Kalmbach with Mr. Raymond Guest to solicit contributions.[554] Public records reveal a $200,000 contribution by Guest to the 1972 campaign to re-elect the President.[555]

On April 5, 1972, Rebozo opened an account at the Key Biscayne Bank and Trust Company for the purpose of retaining 1972 campaign contributions.[556] Entitled the "Committee for the Re-election of the President" account, Rebozo stated that he opened the account "to beat the April 6 deadline with respect to a $10,000 contribution which had been made."[557]

On April 6, 1972, Rebozo deposited $10,000 in the account, which was later wired the same day to the Finance Committee to Re-elect the President's account at the First National Bank of Washington, D.C.[558] The source of this contribution was

546. See exhibit 43.
547. This figure includes $100,000 from Howard Hughes, $50,000 from A. D. Davis, and nearly $40,000 which went through the FCRP account at the Key Biscayne Bank and Trust Company.
548. See Section on delivery of the money.
549. See exhibit 15.
550. See Morgan interview, June 3, 1974; see also interview of Charles Stuart, June 20, 1974.
551. Rebozo Executive Session, March 20, 1974, p. 31 (galleys).
552. Kalmbach Executive Session, March 21, 1974, pp. 44-45 (galleys).
553. Paul Barrick interview, May 16, 1974, pp. 12-13.
554. Rebozo Executive Session, March 20, 1974, p. 31 (galleys).
555. See Paul Barrick interview, May 16, 1974, pp. 14-15.
556. Deposition of Rebozo, *op. cit.*, p. 8.
557. Eee Exhibit 44 (Rebozo letter to Maurice Stans, Aug. 2, 1972).
558. See Exhibit 42.

Atlantic Investors of Miami, Ltd., a partnership of J. Kislak and Alek Courtelis.[559]

Rebozo's campaign account in the Key Biscayne Bank and Trust also served as a repository after April 7, 1972, for $29,740 in other campaign contributions. These contributions were finally transferred to the Finance Committee's main account in Washington, D.C., on April 2, 1973. Rebozo was the recipient of each of these contributions that were forwarded to Washington, and he acknowledged the receipt of each contribution with a personal note.[560] Rebozo, however, did not forward to the campaign committee any portion of the $100,000 cash contribution from Howard Hughes.

On December 20, 1973, Rebozo testified that he did not receive any other pre-April 7 campaign contributions besides the Hughes and Kislak contributions and "others that are reported."[561] However, only when asked specifically about a contribution from A. D. Davis six months later before the Select Committee, did Rebozo acknowledge receipt of a $50,000 cash contribution from the Davis brothers on "April 4 or 5," 1972.[562] This contribution from A. D. Davis and J. E. Davis was not reported in any records of the Finance Committee to Re-elect the President,[563] nor was it deposited in the account Rebozo established for 1972 contributions.

Mr. A. D. Davis subsequently testified that he delivered $50,000 in one hundred dollar bills to Rebozo on April 5, 1972 which was intended only for President Nixon's 1972 re-election campaign.[564] Davis also testified he and Rebozo discussed the importance of the April 7 date and that Rebozo indicated to him that he would speak to the President about this contribution.[565]

Rebozo testified that he received the contribution from Davis, called the Finance Committee office in Washington, D.C., and that the Finance Committee dispatched Fred La Rue to Miami to pick up the contribution.[566] In fact, La Rue testified that he did not discuss nor receive any campaign contributions from Rebozo until October, 1972,[567] a full six months after the Davis contribution was received.

La Rue testified that he was contacted by Mr. John Kerr of the Nunn-for-Senate campaign in Kentucky in September,

559. See Exhibit 45.
560. See Exhibit 46.
561. Rebozo deposition, *op. cit.*, pp. 54-56.
562. Rebozo Executive Session, November 21, 1974, pp. 413-17.
563. See Barrick interview, May 16, 1974, p. 16.
564. Davis Executive Session, April 11, 1974, pp. 5, 9-10, 64.
565. *Ibid.*, p. 12.
566. Rebozo Executive Session, March 21, 1974, p. 415.
567. La Rue Executive Session, May 28, 1974, pp. 7-8.

1972, concerning the possibility of sending additional funds from the Committee to Re-elect the President to the Nunn campaign.[568] Mr. Kerr, however, denies any such request was made by him. (See Exhibit   ) La Rue testified he subsequently discussed the subject with former Attorney General John Mitchell, who had initially committed support to the Nunn campaign.[569] La Rue testified that Mitchell suggested that he contact Rebozo for possible funds.[570] When La Rue called him, Rebozo told La Rue that the funds were immediately available, and La Rue arranged to pick them up on his way back to Washington from his home in Jackson, Mississippi.[571] La Rue's travel vouchers from CRP indicate that his trip from Jackson to Miami to pick up the cash did not occur until October 12, 1972.[572] Finally a letter dated October 13, 1972, from Maurice Stans to Mr. A. D. Davis states, "Through Bebe Rebozo, I learned of the encouragement you have indicated for this year's election." The letter makes no reference to any contribution from Mr. Davis.[573] La Rue testified that he picked up an envelope containing cash on that date from Rebozo and that he probably told Rebozo that the money would go to a "senatorial campaign" without specifying which one.[574]

La Rue said in an interview on April 9, 1974, that he received about $25,000-$30,000 from Rebozo in October. However, in subsequent sworn testimony, La Rue could not rule out the possibility that he received much more than $50,000 from Rebozo.[575] However, the date on which La Rue picked the money up from Rebozo was more than six months after Rebozo received the cash contribution from A. D. Davis and Rebozo did not tell La Rue that the money he gave him was a contribution from A. D. Davis to the President's campaign. Further, there are no records of the contribution in Rebozo's campaign account.

La Rue testified that he returned to Washington, D.C., with the cash, and comingled it with the cash already in his file cabinet which was being used to pay the Watergate defendants.[576] La Rue testified that subsequently a courier for the

568. La Rue Executive Session, p. 8.
569. Ibid., pp. 9-10.
570. Ibid., p. 10.
571. Ibid., pp. 33-34, p. 11.
572. Exhibit 47.
573. See Exhibit 48. All other FCRP donors of similar amounts obtained by the Committee indicates acknowlegement for contributions was made by specific reference to the contributions.
574. Ibid., p. 40, pp. 33-34; Staff interview of Fred La Rue, April 9, 1974, p. 3.
575. La Rue Executive Session, May 28, 1974, p. 13.
576. La Rue Executive Session, May 28, 1974, p. 36.

Nunn campaign picked up a sum of cash of about the same amount that he had picked up from Rebozo during this campaign period in 1972.[577] The Nunn campaign, however, denies receiving any such cash.[578]

Several issues remain unresolved concerning the Davis contribution and related events. Furthermore, Mr. Rebozo refused to appear on June 26, 1974, pursuant to a subpoena and letter dated June 21, 1974,[579] from Chairman Ervin to clarify the record concerning these and other issues. Major outstanding issues, therefore, remain:

1) Why Mr. Rebozo failed to deposit the Davis contribution in the bank account opened expressly for the purpose of receiving pre-April 7 contributions?

2) When, if ever, did Rebozo notify the Finance Committee concerning his receipt of the Davis contribution?

3) Where did Rebozo store the cash in the period of time between the receipt of the money from Davis and his payment of funds to La Rue?

4) Were the funds that were turned over to La Rue in the same amount and the original bills given to Rebozo by A. D. Davis?

5) Were any funds furnished by Rebozo to La Rue paid to Watergate defendants, and did Rebozo have any knowledge of that?

8. RETURN OF THE HUGHES CONTRIBUTION

George P. Shultz, Secretary of the Treasury, received a sensitive and confidential memo from Johnnie M. Walters, Commissioner of the International Revenue Service, on February 23, 1973.[580] The purpose of this memo, was to alert Secretary Shultz that the IRS investigative team had concluded that there was a need to interview Charles "Bebe" Rebozo.[581] Shultz sent this information to John Ehrlichman.[582] In this memo, Walters explained that the IRS had received testimony from Richard Danner about a political contribution Danner made on behalf of Howard Hughes to Rebozo.[583] While the IRS had received this testimony from Danner on May 15, 1972, a formal request to interview Rebozo was not made

577. La Rue interview, April 9, 1974, p. 3.
578. See Affidavits of Governor Louie Nunn and John Kerr.
579. Counsel to Rebozo has acknowledged to Committee Counsel that he received the Chairman's letter.
580. Shultz Interview, January 24, 1974, p. 4. Also see Walters Interview, June 14, 1974, p. 64.
581. Walters Interview, June 14, 1974, p. 63.
582. Shultz Interview, January 24, 1974, p. 4. Also see Barth Executive Session, June 6, 1974, pp. 10-11, 26.
583. Walters Interview June 14, 1974, p. 64.

until February 23, 1973, ten months later. Although field agents of the IRS had requested permission to interview Rebozo as early as the summer of 1972, these requests were not authorized until April of 1973. According to Walters, this delay resulted from a policy decision that he and other top-ranking officials within the IRS made during the summer of 1972.[584] The IRS had concluded that in an effort to conduct business as free of politics as possible, all matters that were politically sensitive, would be postponed until after the 1972 elections.[585] When requests were made to interview Rebozo during the summer of 1972, these requests were postponed by Walters personally in accordance with the above policy.[586]

Requests from the IRS field agents to interview Rebozo came to Walters on a continuing basis.[587]. On February 22, 1973, after the elections, Johnnie Walters discussed these requests with William Simon, who at that time was Deputy Secretary of the Treasury. Simon suggested that Walters compose a memo for Secretary Shultz, informing him of the need the IRS had to interview Rebozo. According to Walters, Simon told him that Secretary Shultz would be meeting with President Nixon later that day in Camp David and the IRS' request to interview Rebozo could be brought to the President's attention during this meeting.[588] At the time, the IRS wanted to talk with Rebozo only to verify information with regard to whether he had received $100,000 from Danner.[589] Walters stated that the purpose of this memo was not to ask for permission but merely to alert the Administration that Rebozo was to be interviewed by the IRS. Walters emphasized, however, that the request to interview Rebozo would be postponed until Walters himself received the go-ahead from Secretary Shultz.[590]

As of March 8, 1973, Walters still had not heard from Shultz concerning his request to interview Rebozo. Walters, therefore, spoke again with Simon to emphasize the need to interview Rebozo. Walters finally received approval from Shultz on April 7, 1973.[590]

As of March 8, 1973, Walters still had not heard from Shultz concerning his request to interview Rebezo. Walters, therefore, spoke again with Simon to emphasize the need to interview Rebezo. Walters finally recived approval from

584. Walters Interview, June 14, 1974, p. 52.
585. Walters Interview, June 14, 1974, pp. 48-50.
586. Walters Interview, June 14, 1974, p. 52.
587. Walters Interview, June 14, 1974, p. 61.
588. Walters Interview, June 14, 1974, p. 63.
589. Walters Interview, June 14, 1974, p. 66.
590. Walters Interview, June 14, 1974, p. 76.

Shultz on April 7, 1973.[591]

Although Walters did not officially inform the White House of the IRS interest in Rebozo until February of 1973, the White House actually had received this information as early as the spring of 1972. Sometime between March and June of 1972, a sensitive case report which mentioned the names of Don Nixon, Charles "Bebe" Rebozo, Larry O'Brien and others involved in the Hughes investigation, was brought to John Ehrlichman's attention by Roger Barth, who was an Assistant to the Commissioner of the IRS. Barth, in fact, provided a copy of the sensitive case report to Ehrlichman.[592] Barth testified that Ehrlichman requested to be kept informed as the case progressed and expressed specific interest in Larry O'Brien's involvement.[593] Ehrlichman recalls that he was continually receiving sensitive case reports concerning the Hughs investigation but that he did not tell Rebozo of the IRS' interest in Rebozo until Barth requested him to do so.[594]

After Walters received a go-ahead from Shultz concerning the IRS request to interview Rebozo, Walters asked Barth to notify Rebozo of this.[595] Before notifying Rebozo, however, Barth first spoke with Ehrlichman to get his approval of this matter.[596]. Ehrlichman has testified that when the sensitive case report came over,

> . . . it came over with a note from Barth saying that I need to talk to you about this and so I immediately called him and he said at that time 'I need to have a green light on interviews of Rebozo . . .' I said, 'you know, OK, I think it is from my standpoint indicated. I will give you the green light if you are satisfied with that' . . .[597]

According to Barth, he met with Ehrlichman and Ehrlichman showed him a copy of Walter's February 23, 1973 memo. Ehrlichman asked Barth if Rebozo was in trouble and Barth explained that as far as he knew this was just a third party interview and that the IRS was not planning to do an audit or a criminal investigation of Rebozo. With these assurances, Barth had testified that Ehrlichman approved the interview. Ehrlichman has testified that because of the close

591. Walters Interview, June 14, 1974, pp. 65-67.
592. Barth Executive Session, June 6, 1974, p. 4. *Also see* Ehrlichman Executive Session, February 8, 1974, p. 103.
593. Barth Executive Session, June 6, 1974, p. 4.
594. Ehrlichman Executive Session, February 8 1974, p. 114.
595. Walters Interview, June 14, 1974, p. 71.
596. Ehrlichman Executive Session, Feb. 8, 1974, p. 113. *Also see* Barth Executive Session, June 6, 1974, p. 26.
597. Ehrlichman Executive Session February 8, 1974, p. 113.

relationship between Rebozo and the President, Barth was reluctant to call Rebozo directly. Ehrlichman, therefore, agreed to call Rebozo.[598]

Shortly after Rebozo was informed by Ehrlichman that the IRS wanted to interview him, Rebozo began to make a concerted effort to return the $100,000. Rebozo testified that in March and April he attempted to contact Richard Danner to arrange for the return of the contribution.[599] Danner, however, does not recall any contacts between Rebozo and himself concerning the return of this money until may 1973.[600] While Rebozo discussed his decision to return Hughes' contribution with various people including the President, Rebezo has testified that the ultimate decision to return the money was his alone.[601]

Rebozo testified that after Hughes left Nevada in November 1970, and fired Maheu, Rebozo became very apprehensive about the Hughes contribution.

. . . So as time went on (Rebozo) just thought it better not to use that money for the '72 campaign and try to see if things cleared up and to hold it for the '74 or '76, some point where I could turn it over to the properly appointed authority. But matters went from bad to worse with the Hughes organization . . .[602]

Rebozo was also very concerned that this Hughes contribution would be disclosed and then any association between '72 campaign and Howard Hughes would be a source of embarrassment to the President as it had in his 1970 campaign. Rebozo testified that:

. . . I didn't want to risk even the remotest embarrassment of Hughes' connection with Nixon. I was convinced that (the Hughes loan to Don Nixon) cost the President the '60 election and didn't help him in '62 in Calif. . . .[603]

Although Rebozo claimed that dramatic organizational changes within the Hughes organization caused him concern, he made no effort to discuss this in the context of the contribution with Danner or any other Hughes employee, nor did he seek advice from any Administration or campaign

598. Barth Executive Session, June 6, 1974, p. 26. Ehrlichman Executive Session, February 8, 1974, pp. 113-114. Also see Rebozo Executive Session, March 21, 1974, p. 354.
599. Rebozo Executive Session, March 21, 1974, pp. 282, 294. Also see Rebozo Interview, October 17, 1973, p. 18.
600. Danner Executive Session, December 19, 1973, p. 16.
601. Rebozo Executive Session, March 20, 1974, p. 120.
602. Rebozo Executive Session, March 20, 1974, p. 76.
603. Rebozo Executive Session, March 20, 1974, p. 115.

officials. Finally when Ehrlichman told Rebozo that he was going to be interviewed by the IRS, that Rebozo began to make a concerted effort to return the money. Although Rebozo said the contribution was for President Nixon he had been hopeful that this campaign contribution could be used in 1974 or 1976. Now, with the IRS requesting to interview him, Rebozo decided that the money could not be used for any campaign purposes and that the best course of action would be to return it.[604]

Rebozo has testified that he discussed the Hughes contribution with the President on two occasions prior to its return. The first conversation took place in Key Biscayne some time after the 1972 Presidential election. During this conversation Rebozo has stated that he "explained the whole picture" to the President.[605] Rebozo testified that he could not recall what the President's reaction was to this information but stated that the President did not offer any advice about whether or not the money should be returned.[606]

Rebozo's second conversation with the President was in March or April, 1973. This discussion occurred after Ehrlichman had told Rebozo that the IRS would be interviewing him. Rebozo has testified that during his second conversation with the President Rebozo told him that he had decided to return the Hughes contribution and that President Nixon agreed with his decision.[607]

Rebozo has testified that the next conversation which he had was with Herb Kalmbach on April 30, 1973.[608] The Senate Select Committee has interviewed Rebozo three times and also questioned him in a two day Executive Session. While Rebozo in each of his sessions with the Committee spoke freely about his conversation with Kalmbach on April 30, 1973, he never once asserted that his conversation related in any manner to information which he later claimed was protected by the attorney client privilege.

Rebozo has testified that while he was in the west wing of the White House on the morning of April 30, 1973, he ran into Kalmbach in the halls. According to Rebozo, their meeting was not arranged and Rebozo was not seeking Kalmbach's advice. Rebozo testified that:

604. Rebozo Executive Session, March 21, 1974, pp. 355-357.
605. Rebozo Interview, October 17, 1973, p. 23. *Also see* Rebozo Executive Session, March 21 1974, p. 353. *Also see* Rebozo Executive Session, March 20, 1974, p. 134.
606. Rebozo Executive Session, March 21, 1974, pp. 353-354.
607. Rebozo Executive Session, March 20, 1974, pp. 133-134.
608. Rebozo Interview, October 17 1973, p. 20. *Also see* Rebozo Executive Session, March 21, 1974, p. 403. *Also see* Kalmbach Executive Session, March 21, 1974, p. 49. (Galleys)

. . . I think it was just a general discussion. You see, Kalmbach and I have numerous discussions, naturally on the San Clemente interest. He and I worked on the Yerba Linda House and Whittier property. We talked about things like that . . . I believe I told him about [the Hughes contribution] . . . he had been involved in fund raising and it wasn't going to be any secret. I guess I just felt the key people should know about it . . .[609]

During an interview with the Senate Select Committee, on October 17, 1973, Rebozo stated that he did not ask Kalmbach for any advice or counsel concerning the return of the money because by

. . . April 30, 1973, the decision was already made. If I did ask, it was just for his opinion. As I recall, the part about the Hughes money was just an irrelevant part of the conversation . . .[610]

Rebozo, during an Executive Session on March 20-21, 1974, testified that on April 30, 1973, he did ask Kalmbach for his judgment and Kalmbach told him he thought Rebozo should give it back. Rebozo does not recall discussing this topic again with Kalmbach.[611]

Kalmbach was also questioned on three occasions by the Committee concerning his meeting with Rebozo on April 30, 1973. In each of these sessions with the Committee, Kalmbach responded to specific questions about this meeting and indicated that it related to discussions concerning the re-financing of San Clemente, and the issue of whether the $100,000 was used in the purchase of San Clemente. During these first three interviews with the Committee, Kalmbach never asserted an attorney-client privilege concerning his meeting with Rebozo on April 30, 1973. On a fourth and fifth occasion, in an interview on March 8, 1974, and an executive session on March 21, 1974, Kalmbach, for the first time refused to testify with regard to this specific conversation because of attorney-client privilege.

Senator Ervin, however, on March 21, 1974, ruled that based on the above-described testimony of Rebozo, he and Kalmbach had not entered into a valid attorney-client relationship. Because of the significance of Kalmbach's testimony, pursuant to Senator Ervin's instructions, it is set out at length as follows:

609. Rebozo Interview, October 17, 1973, p. 20. *Also see* Rebozo Executive Session, March 21, 1974, pp. 391-403.
610. Rebozo Interview, October 17, 1973, pp. 19-21.
611. Rebozo Executive Session, March 21, 1974, pp. 403-404.

". . . sometime during the week of April 23, 1973, Bebe Rebozo called me at my office in Newport Beach, I think he was calling from Key Biscayne and told me he had a matter he wanted to discuss with me and asked when I would be next in the East. I told him I too had some items I wanted to go over with him and that I was scheduled to be deposed in Washington at 10:00 AM Monday, April 30 and perhaps we could meet sometime during my one or two day stay in the Capitol . . . (Rebozo) said he would be in Washington over the weekend and suggested that we get together Sunday evening, April 29. . .

At about 7:30 on Monday morning, April 30, I took a cab from the Madison to the Pennsylvania Avenue front entrance of the White House . . . the person on the desk called Bebe and announced my arrival and within five or ten minutes, he came out and met me. He decided we should use the Fish Room, which is just off the lobby. We went together and sat in the corner nearest the door. After we had spent 10 or 15 minutes covering (various) points, Bebe went into the matter he wanted to discuss. (Bebe) said the president had asked him to speak to me about this problem, and not Maurice Stans. He said he had personally received $100,000 in campaign contributions from Dick Danner representing Howard Hughes. He said that he had received two cash contributions of $50,000 each in 1969 and 1970. He said that the IRS had scheduled a meeting with him on this very subject which would be held two or three weeks hence. He said that he had dispersed part of the funds to Rose Woods, to Don Nixon, to Ed Nixon and to unnamed others during the intervening years, and that he was now asking for my counsel on how to handle the problem.

In response to my questions, he reiterated that the money had been given to him as a contribution by Hughes and that the expenditures he had made to the several individuals including Rose and to the President's two brothers had come from the Hughes cash.

I then said that my advice was that he should get the best tax lawyer he could, and give him not only the entire story but also the balance of the Hughes cash for return to Hughes and a list of everyone to whom he had given money from these funds to which list should be attached, whatever backup could be obtained to show the use to which the funds had been put by the recipients. I said that he and his attorney should then lay out the facts of the matter exactly out to the IRS.

Bebe in reply to my advice expressed grave reservations about so doing for the stated reason that, 'this touches the President and the President's family, and I just can't do anything to add to his problems at this time, Herb.'

I then said I would like to check the validity of my advice with Stanley Ebner, who I identified as then General Counsel at OMB in the White House, indicating further that Stan had been counsel to Maurice Stans' Finance Committee during the 1972 campaign, and that he had begun his duties with Stans after the new finance law tool effect on April 7, 1972.

Bebe was very queasy about my talking to anyone about this matter and I assured him I would not mention his name to Stan and I would talk to "Stan" only on a hypothetical basis . . . finally, Bebe agreed and we said goodbye to each other after agreeing to meet the next morning at 8:30 in the lobby of the West Wing of the White House. Immediately after Bebe and I parted, I used the phone in the lobby and called Stan at his office in the Executive Office Building. I found him in and in response to my request for a few minutes of his time, he suggested that I come right over.

I went over to Stans' office and after a very brief exchange of amenities, I asked him to let me check my judgment against his as to special situation that had arisen. And then recounted the facts as earlier expressed to me by Bebe . . . Stan agreed completely as to what I had advised Bebe, and expressed himself, that he could not see any other course. . .

I again met with Bebe the next morning. I arrived by cab from the Madison and was in the lobby around 8:30. When Bebe came out to see me, I remember that he—we wandered around the lobby floor looking for a private meeting place. Finally with Rose Woods along, we went into a small room on the ground floor of the West Wing. Rose left us, and we sat down behind a closed door.

I began recounting my visit with Stan, including his confirmation of my suggested course of conduct for Bebe to follow, and before I had completely finished, Bebe cut short further discussion of the matter with a somewhat baffling comment, that he saw no problem but he thanked me for my thoughts . . .

Our entire conversation that Tuesday morning did not last longer than 15 or 20 minutes and I recall that I left the White House around 9:00 AM . . .[612]

Ebner has stated that he did meet briefly with Kalmbach on April 30, 1973. Ebner recalls that Kalmbach discussed a hypothetical situation at that time. Ebner cannot recall specific hypothetical facts furnished him since Kalmbach apparently discussed hypothetical situations with him on a number of occasions.[613]

In a sworn affidavit, James O'Connor, Kalmbach's attorney, stated that following the meeting with Rebozo, Kalmbach immediately told O'Connor all of the details of this meeting including the fact that Rebozo had disbursed some of the $100,000 Hughes campaign contribution to Rose Mary Woods and the Nixon brothers.

In October 1973, after Kalmbach was interviewed by the Committee, O'Connor dictated a brief memo to his secretary, Margaret Blakely, which he then asked her to read over the telephone to Rebozo. The purpose of this memo was to inform Rebozo that Kalmbach had acknowledged to the Senate Select Committee, that he had met with Rebozo on April 30, 1973, and that he testified that the prime purpose of the meeting was to review certain matters involving the President's personal affairs and indicated that Kalmbach had not given any additional information concerning this meeting to the Committee.[614]

On January 25, 1974, O'Connor once again asked his secretary to call Rebozo and tell him that if Kalmbach was pressed as to any details of a conversation between himself and Rebozo on April 30, 1973, and/or May 1, 1973, that he would state that the discussions were pursuant to the attorney-client relationship.[615]

Margaret Blakely has also provided a sworn affidavit to the Committee that on two occasions she was requested by O'Connor to contact Rebozo. According to Blakely, both O'Connor and Kalmbach felt it best if she contacted Rebozo rather than either of them and that if Rebozo had any questions, she would attempt to get the answers for him. During her first conversation with Rebozo, in October, 1973:

> . . . she was simply advising him that Mr. Kalmbach was asked on October 12th by Mr. Lenzner to furnish the number and location of all bank accounts in the name of the President and on which he was signatory; that Mr. Kalmbach was concerned about any possible violation of

612. Kalmbach Executive Session, March 21, 1974, pp. 49-52. (Galleys)
613. Ebner Interview, April 15, 1974, p. 1.
614. O'Connor Affidavit, May 14, 1974, Exhibit 49.
615. O'Connor Affidavit, May 14, 1974, Exhibit 49.

the Attorney-Client Privilege; that Mr. Kalmbach was questioned by the Special Prosecutor's office and by Mr. Lenzner on October 11 and 12 as to a meeting on April 30 with Rebozo and Mr. Kalmbach acknowledged the meeting took place at or about that time; Mr. Kalmbach further advised both investigative bodies that the prime purpose of the meeting was to review certain matters involving the President's personal affairs, including the sale of the Whittier property and the refinancing of the San Clemente property, among other things: That Mr. Kalmbach was disturbed about reports that campaign funds were used in the acquisition of the San Clemente property . . .[616]

Blakely's second conversation with Rebozo was on January 24, 1974. At this time she told him:

. . . if Mr. Kalmbach is pressed as to any details of the conversation between himself and Mr. Rebozo on April 30 and/or May 1, he, of course, would have to tell the truth; that in the unlikely event he is pressed on this matter, he will, of course, state that these discussions were pursuant to the attorney-client relationship and therefore subject to the attorney-client privilege . . .[617]

Blakely indicated that during both of her conversations with Rebozo, he made no comment and had no questions.

Although Rebozo had denied any other conversations with Kalmbach concerning this matter, Kalmbach has testified that:

. . . A third meeting was held with Bebe on Tuesday morning, January 8, 1974. He and I had talked by telephone once or twice after he arrived in San Clemente to be with the President during his stay in California. Never at any time during these telephone conversations did Bebe mention directly or indirectly our discussions in the White House on April 30, May 1. . . .
And finally he called and asked me to meet with him on Tuesday January 8. I agreed to meet him at 8:30 in the morning at Mess at the Western White House. On that date when I arrived at the gate, the guard told me that Rebozo had left word that I should proceed directly to the Guest House in the living compound. This I did and arrived at the Guest House, which is directly across a court from the Presidents' quarters, at 8:30.

616. Blakely Affidavit, May 15, 1974, see Exhibit 50.
617. Blakely Affidavit, May 15, 1974, see Exhibit 50.

When I entered the Guest House, Bebe told me the reason he had switched our meeting place was because he had learned that a great number of the press were over at the offices, and we would be afforded greater privacy within the compound. Our meeting lasted about one hour and fifteen minutes and ranged across a number of subjects. . . .

At one point somewhat near the end of the meeting, Rebozo said words to me to the effect that:

'undoubtably Herb, I have not told you that after you and I talked last spring regarding the Hughes money, I found that I not in fact disbursed any of the Hughes cash to the several people I named. When I went into the safe deposit box, I found that the wrappers around the cash had not been disturbed, and so what was clear that no part of this money had been used during the several years it was in my box!

I didn't make any comment at all to Bebe when he made this statement other than to acknowledge what he had said. We then went on to other items on the agenda and I left him around 9:45 and drove up Los Angeles. . . .[618]

In late April or early May, 1973, Rebozo called William E. Griffin and asked Griffin to fly to Florida to discuss a problem that Rebozo had. Rebozo did not indicate what the problem was except that he had something he wanted to discuss with Griffin that was very important. Griffin met with Rebozo in Florida on May 3, 1973, where Rebezo told him for the first time of the Hughes $100,000 campaign contribution. According to Griffin, Rebozo told him that he had received two $50,000 cash campaign contributions from Richard Danner. These contributions were made in 1969 and 1970. Rebozo also explained to Griffin that he had maintained the $100,000 in a safe deposit box and that he still had the identical bills which Danner had earlier given to him. Rebozo's concern at this time was how he should handle the matter with the IRS.[619]

Griffin testified he did not offer any advice to Rebozo during the May 3, 1973 meeting because he wanted an opportunity to research certain problem areas which he felt Rebozo may have concerning his retention of the $100,000. Griffin stated he told Rebozo he was concerned with problems of unreported income, gift tax, campaign statutes, and the election statutes. Griffin testified he could recall that Rebozo stressed that the bills in his safe deposit box were the exact

618. Kalmbach Executive Session, March 21, 1974, p. 52. (Galleys)
619. Griffin Executive Session, March 28, 1974, pp. 86-87. (Galleys)

same bills he received from a Hughes representative in 1969 and 1970.[620]

Griffin testified he returned to New York to do some research for Rebozo. In early May, 1973, Griffin met again with Rebozo at Key Biscayne. Griffin testified he told Rebozo that he should immediately obtain an independent individual who could act on Rebozo's behalf to count the money, identify the bills, verify that the money was in a safe deposit box, and that this individual should arrange for the return of the money. Rebozo, according to Griffin, accepted his advice and asked Griffin if he could act on Rebozo's behalf. Griffin declined because of his close association with Robert Abplanalp who was also a very close friend of the President's. Griffin felt that any representation that he made on Rebozo's behalf would be tainted with partisanship.[621]

According to Rebozo, he did discuss the return of the Hughes contribution with William Griffin. Rebozo, however, did not recall ever asking Griffin to act in Rebozo's behalf to facilitate the return of the money, nor could Rebozo recall any specific advice Griffin offered to him concerning the need for an independent third party to arrange for the return of the money. Rebozo does recall that Griffin did some research for him and then later advised Rebozo to turn the money back.[622]

On May 10, 1973, Rebozo was interviewed by IRS agents Donald Skelton and Albert Keeney. The agents explained to Rebozo that they were investigating the Hughes Tool Company, Robert A. Maheu, John Meier, and other people associated with the Hughes Association, and that their purpose of interviewing Rebozo was to verify some information that they had received concerning a campaign contribution which had allegedly been given to Rebozo by Richard Danner. Rebozo told the agents that he had, in fact, accepted a contribution from Richard Danner and that he still had the money in a safe deposit box. According to the IRS, Rebozo stated that the only persons who knew of the Hughes contribution were Rebozo, and the agents. Rebozo also told the IRS that he had considered contacting Danner in an effort to return the money but did not do so because he feared additional publicity.[623] Rebozo has testified that he cannot recall when he first told Danner that he wanted to return the money but stated he believed he told him in March or April 1973.[624]

620. Griffin Executive Session, March 28, 1974, pp. 87-89. (Galleys)
621. Griffin Executive Session, March 28, 1974, pp. 95-96.
622. Rebozo Executive Session, March 21, 1974, pp. 358-360.
623. IRS Interview of Rebozo, May 10, 1974, pp. 1-4.
624. Rebozo Executive Session, March 20, 1974, p. 133. *Also see* Rebozo Interview, October 17, 1973, p. 18.

Rebozo, however, later testified that it was not until after his May 10, 1973 interview with the IRS that he actually tried to contact Danner to ask him to take the money back.[625] Danner has stated that he met with Rebozo in Las Vegas, April 1973, but that this meeting was purely social.

According to Danner, there were no discussions about the return of the Hughes contribution at this time.[626] Danner has testified that he specifically recalls the first conversation he ever had with Rebozo concerning this matter took place over the weekend of May 18-20, 1973.[627] Rebozo also recalls meeting with Danner at this time and discussing the return of the Hughes contribution.[628]

During an executive session with the Committee, Rebozo testified as follows concerning his May 18-20, 1973, meeting with Danner:

1. Over the weekend of May 18-20, 1973, Rebozo stayed at the Madison Hotel where he met with Danner and discussed the return of the Hughes contribution.

2. According to Rebozo, both he and Danner were in Washington to attend some social function but Rebozo cannot remember what it was. Rebozo did not request Danner to come to Washington.

3. In addition to discussing the return of the Hughes contribution, Rebozo and Danner also discussed the political feelings on the West Coast concerning Watergate.

4. Rebozo left Washington on May 19, 1973 to join the President at Camp David. On May 20, 1973 Rebozo invited Danner to come to Camp David and discuss with the President what the political feelings were on the West Coast. Rebozo arranged for a White House limousine to pick Danner up and drive him to Camp David.

5. Danner met with Rebozo for approximately one-half hour before the President joined them. Prior to the President's arrival, Danner and Rebozo discussed the return of the Hughes contribution. Throughout the weekend, Danner refused to accept the return of the Hughes contribution but promised Rebozo he would talk to his superiors and arrange for it to be returned.

6. The President joined Danner and Rebozo, in Rebozo's cabin at Camp David and remained with them for approximately five to ten minutes. During their conversation, there was no mention of the return of the Hughes

625. Rebozo Executive Session, March 21, 1974, p. 357.
626. Danner Executive Session, December 19, 1973, pp. 15-16. *Also see* Danner Executive Session, June 11, 1974, pp. 176-179.
627. Danner Executive Session, December 18, 1973, p. 124.
628. Rebozo Executive Session, March 21, 1974, pp. 362-368.

contribution. The only subject which Danner discussed with President Nixon was the political mood on the West Coast concerning Watergate.

7. After the President left, Danner and Rebozo visited for a short while and then Danner returned to Washington.

8. On May 18, 1973, Danner, Rebozo, and Mr. and Mrs. Abplanalp, flew to the Adirondack Fisheries in Abplanalp's private jet and had lunch. After lunch, Danner and Rebozo returned to Washington. While they were with the Abplanalps, there was no discussion whatsoever concerning the Hughes contribution.[629]

Danner testified as follows concerning his May 18-20, 1973 meeting with Rebozo.

1. Danner met with Rebozo in Washington during the weekend of May 18-20, 1973 at Rebozo's specific request that he do so.

2. Danner met with Rebozo at the Madison Hotel and during this meeting, Rebozo told him for the first time that he wanted to return the $100,000 Hughes contribution. This information came as a complete surprise to Danner.

3. Danner refused to take the money back because he felt it wasn't his money to accept. Danner promised Rebozo that he would make the necessary inquiries to determine who the money should be properly returned to. During this weekend, there were extensive conversations between Danner and Rebozo concerning the return of the Hughes contribution.

4. Danner has testified that he also spoke with Rebozo about the political feelings on the West Coast concerning Watergate. Rebozo asked Danner if he would stay over and come to Camp David on the following morning. Danner agreed.

5. On May 20, 1973, Danner met with Rebozo at Camp David and prior to the President's arrival, discussed the return of the Hughes contribution. Danner once again refused to accept the return of the money.

6. After the President joined Danner and Rebozo, in Rebozo's cabin, there were no discussions of the Hughes contribution or any other campaign contributions. During their meeting, Danner expressed to the President what the political feelings were on the West Coast. After the conversation, the President took Rebozo and Danner on

629. Rebozo Executive Session, March 21, 1974, pp. 362-368. *Also see* Rebozo Executive Session, March 21, 1974, pp. 378-379.

a brief tour of Camp David.

7. Danner's meeting with the President and Rebozo lasted for one to one and a half hours.

8. After the President left, Danner and Rebozo had lunch together and then Danner returned to Washington.

9. Danner testified that he has never discussed the Hughes contribution with President Nixon.

10. On May 18, 1973, Danner, Rebozo, and Mr. and Mrs. Abplanalp flew to the Adirondacks in Abplanalp's private jet to have lunch. While the four were together, there were no discussions concerning the Hughes campaign contribution.[630]

Deputy Press Secretary Gerald L. Warren in a statement made to the Press on January 26, 1974, stated that:

. . . Mr. Danner was in Washington to talk with Mr. Rebozo and did pay a brief visit to the President at Camp David. The meeting lasted only five or ten minutes and Danner reported on the mood of the people in the West . . .[631]

General Haig testified that while he was not aware at the time that Danner and Rebozo met with President Nixon at Camp David on May 20, 1973, he learned of it when it became a public relations issue in the White House. Haig discussed this matter with Ron Ziegler, who informed him that the purpose of the meeting at Camp David was to enable Danner to express his support for the President at a time when the President had been under heavy attack. Ziegler stated to Haig that he had discussed this meeting with the President. Haig felt confident that Ziegler ". . . was on top of the matter and had the details."[632] Ziegler has stated that he consulted with both the President and Rebozo to confirm that the May 20, 1973, Camp David meeting was only five or ten minutes long.[633]

Warren stated that Ziegler confirmed that Rebozo and Danner had met with President Nixon at Camp David for five or ten minutes. Warren did not check either the Cardex or the Presidential logs to determine the length of the meeting.[634]

Danner, in subsequent testimony to the Senate Select Com-

630. Danner Executive Session, December 18, 1973, pp. 124-132. *Also see* Danner Executive Session, June 11, 1974, p. 177, pp. 200-207. *Also see* Madison Hotel records, May 17-20, 1973, Exhibit 51. Neither Danner or Rebozo mentioned this meeting in staff interviews until the Committee obtained hotel records which showed that they were both at he Madison Hotel during this time.

631. Washington *Post,* January 26, 1974, p. A-12.

632. Haig Executive Session, May 15, 1974, pp. 30-31.

633. Ziegler Interview, June 24, 1974.

634. Warren Interview, February 26, 1974, p. 8.

mittee, has reconfirmed his testimony that the meeting he attended with President Nixon and Rebozo lasted at least one hour.[635]

Abplanalp has stated that he had no knowledge of the $100,000 Hughes contribution which Rebozo received from Danner. Abplanalp recalls that he has only seen Danner three times in his life. The third time was in May 1973. Abplanalp has never had any conversations with Danner concerning the Hughes contribution.[636]

Shortly after the May 20, 1973 Camp David meeting, Rebozo told Haig of his involvement in the Hughes contribution. This is the only conversation Rebozo recalls having with Haig concerning the Hughes contribution.[637]

Haig has testified that Rebozo did tell him of the Hughes contribution, and his involvement with it. Haig did not counsel Rebozo to return the money.[638]

On May 23, 1973, William Simon received a telephone call from General Haig. Haig, at this time, requested an update of information concerning the Hughes contribution which Rebozo received. Simon recalled that this information had been given to the White House long ago since Rebozo's name had appeared on sensitive case reports. After the time of Haig's telephone call, Simon called Don Alexander, Commissioner of the IRS and asked for an update on the IRS investigation into the Hughes $100,000 contribution to Rebozo. Alexander immediately sent a memo to Simon which detailed the facts of the case. After receiving this memo, Simon called General Haig to inform him that Rebozo was going to be investigated by the IRS concerning his involvement with the Hughes contribution. Simon stated that he thought this was a matter Simon should discuss with the White House Counsels, Buzhardt and Garment.[639]

After Simon's conversation with Haig on May 23, 1973, Simon testified he discussed with Len Garment the status of the IRS investigation of Rebozo. During his conversation with Garment, Simon used the memo that Alexander had previously supplied to him. According to Simon's log, he was in contact with General Haig, Len Garment, and Don Alexander on May 23, 1973.[640]

635. Danner Executive Session, June 11, 1974, pp. 200-207. *Also see* Danner Executive Session, December 18, 1973, pp. 124-132.
636. Abplanalp Interview, Nov. 1, 1973, p. 41. *Also see* Exhibit 51.
637. Rebozo Executive Session, March 21, 1974, pp. 395-397.
638. Haig Executive Session, May 15, 1974, pp. 37-44.
639. Simon Interview, May 10, 1974, p. 15. *Also see* Haig Executive Session, May 15, 1974, pp. 14-15. *Also see* Exhibit 52, Simon's logs.
640. Simon Interview, May 10, 1974, p. 28. *Also see* Garment Executive Session, May 17, 1974, pp. 15-18.

Sometime after May 23, 1973, Haig met with White House Counsel Garment, Chapman Rose, and Fred Buzhardt to be briefed on the IRS investigation of Rebozo. This meeting took place in Haig's office. It was decided that Haig should inform the President of this investigation since it was a matter which could be potentially embarrassing to the President. It was also decided that there should be no discussions between White House counsel and Rebozo concerning the IRS investigation. Garment suggested to Haig that Rebozo should get a qualified tax attorney, and that if Rebozo needed a recommendation Garment would provide one.[641]

Haig testified he thereafter met with President Nixon to brief him on the IRS investigation of Rebozo. Haig told the President that the White House counsel felt that Rebozo should have a competent tax attorney and that if necessary they could suggest someone for him. The President told Haig to "tell them to do so." It was Haig's general impression that the information he furnished President Nixon concerning the IRS investigation of Rebozo did not come as news to President Nixon. Haig stated that "[President Nixon] just shrugged it off, and as a matter of fact, handled it with a number of on going problems that [Haig] was discussing at the time."[642]

Two or three days later, Haig told the President that Garment had recommended Kenneth Gemmill as a possible attorney for Rebozo. The President then told Haig to give this name to Rebozo on the following weekend when both Haig and President Nixon would be in Key Biscayne.[643]

On the following weekend, which would be either the last weekend in May or the first weekend in June 1973, Haig gave the name and address of Kenneth Gemmill to Rebozo. Haig testified that "[a]t that time Mr. Rebozo took it and said he did not know what he would do with it, but he obviously was well aware at that time of the IRS interest in the Hughes $100,000, there is no question about it."[644] Rebozo has testified that someone in the White House suggested Kenneth Gemmill to him as a good tax attorney. "I had heard of [Ken Gemmill] before and I had been told when all of this business started that I would probably need Washington Counsel. So I got hold of him."[645]

On June 8, 1973, Gemmill received a telephone call from Rebozo. Gemmill testified that Rebozo told him that Garment

641. Garment Executive Session, May 17, 1974, pp. 16-20; *also see* Haig Executive Session, May 15, 1974, pp. 14-16.
642. Haig Executive Session, May 15, 1974, p. 19.
643. Haig Executive Session, May 15, 1974, p. 16.
644. Haig Executive Session, May 15, 1974, pp. 16-17.
645. Rebozo Executive Session, March 21, 1974, p. 286.

says that I should come see you about a problem." Rebozo did not give any details to Gemmill concerning his problem at this time. He merely set up an appointment to see Gemmill on June 11, 1973.[646]

Both Gemmill and Rebozo have testified that they met on June 11, 1973 in Gemmill's Philadelphia office. During this meeting, Rebozo explained to Gemmill that he had been interviewed by two IRS agents concerning the $100,000 campaign contribution. Rebozo then described to Gemmill the events surrounding his acceptance of the $100,000. Gemmill has testified that at no time did Rebozo ever indicate to him that Rebozo had consulted with other lawyers.[647]

Gemmill recalled that on June 12, 1973, he also called Len Garment to tell him that Rebozo had been in to see him. Gemmill recalled that Garment said, " 'I am glad he is in good hands. You handle him as a privileged client and do not tell me anything about it.' [Gemmill] said I am to handle him as a privileged client, and [Garment] said 'yes, do not tell me anything about it,' and that was the end of that."[648] General Haig recalls that during a subsequent conversation he had with Garment, Garment had told him Gemmill had been acquired by Rebozo to represent him in the IRS matter.[649]

Gemmill stated that on June 18, 1973, he called Rebozo and told him that he and Wakefield should go to the safe deposit box which they held jointly that contained the $100,000 Hughes contribution. Both Wakefield and Rebozo were to count the $100,000 and make a list of the serial numbers from each of the bills to be used as a receipt and also a way to identify the bills that were returned. Rebozo asked Gemmill if he thought it would be advisable to have someone from the government there, such as the head of the FBI in Miami, to witness this operation. After some consideration, Gemmill told Rebozo that this may be a good idea since an FBI agent may be able to determine whether the money has been in the same location for a given period of time.[650]

Kenneth Whitaker, SAC-Miami, FBI has testified that Rebozo called him on June 18, 1973 and, offering no explanation, asked him to come to the bank immediately. At around 10:00 a.m., Whitaker met with Robozo and Wakefield at the Key Biscayne Bank. Rebozo then explained to Whitaker that in 1969 or 1970 he had received $100,000 in campaign contributions from Danner, a representative of Howard Hughes.

646. Gemmill Executive Session, May 29, 1974, p. 4.
647. Gemmill Executive Session, May 29, 1974, pp. 6-8.
648. Gemmill Executive Session, May 29, 1974, p. 7.
649. Haig Executive Session, May 15, 1974, p. 23.
650. Gemmill Executive Session, May 29, 1974, pp. 8-9. *Also see* Rebozo Executive Session, March 20, 1974, pp. 78-82.

Rebozo told Whitaker that this contribution was placed in a bank vault and had never been used or disbursed. Whitaker has testified that Rebozo wanted him to see if he could determine the age of the money. After discussing the money, Rebozo, Wakefield, and Whitaker joined Margaret Barker, Rebozo's sister, and entered the bank vault. Each of them signed the access card and then Rebozo removed the safe deposit box. Whitaker has stated that the safe deposit box had two large brown envelopes, the contents of which Rebozo emptied on the tables. These envelopes contained ten to twelve packets of money approximately ¾ of an inch thick. These packets were all one hundred dollar bills and appeared to be new. Whitaker has stated that after he saw the money he told Rebozo that there was no way he could determine the age of the bills. Whitaker stated that he did initial six or seven of the $100 bills in the upper lefthand corner for identification purposes only.[651]

After they had completed counting the money and making a list of serial numbers, they discovered that there was an extra $100 bill. Rebozo called Kenneth Gemmill to tell him that the list had been completed. Gemmill suggested that Rebozo try to contact Danner and that both of them should be in Philadelphia the following morning.[652]

On June 19, 1973, Rebozo met with Gemmill in Philadelphia. Danner, however, did not show up. Gemmill stated that in a telephone call Danner said that Chester Davis would call. When Davis did call Gemmill explained to Davis that Rebozo wanted to return the Hughes contribution. Gemmill and Davis agreed to meet in Washington, D.C. on June 21, 1973.[653]

After Gemmill's conversation with Davis, Rebozo told Gemmill that he had the money with him in a briefcase. Since Gemmill was not willing to accept responsibility for the money, Rebozo decided to bring it with him to New York and have Griffin hold it until its return could be arranged. Rebozo then gave Gemmill Griffin's name and telephone number and asked him to contact Griffin after a date was arranged for the return of the money. Gemmill agreed.[654]

651. Whitaker Interview, November 20, 1973, pp. 2-3. Kelley who is the director of the FBI, in a letter which he wrote to the Commissioner of the IRS, stated Whitaker had reported to him that: Danner had given Rebozo this money in 1969 for congressional elections. *Also see* Rebozo Executive Session, March 20, 1974, pp. 78-82.
652. Gemmill Executive Session, May 29, 1974, p. 9. *Also see* Rebozo Executive Session, March 20, 1974, pp. 78-82.
653. Gemmill Executive Session, May 29, 1974, pp. 9-11. *Also see* Danner logs June 1973, Exhibit 53. *Also see* Rebozo Executive Session, March 21, 1974, p. 284.
654. Rebozo Executive Session, March 21, 1974, pp. 284-286. *Also see* Gemmill Executive Session, May 29, 1974, pp. 10-12.

Rebozo has testified that later that afternoon he met with Griffin at the Hudson Valley National Bank in Yonkers, New York. Rebozo explained to Griffin that he had just left a meeting in Philadelphia with Gemmill where he was, in hopes of returning the money. Rebozo's efforts, however, were frustrated, and he wanted Griffin to hold it until its return could be arranged. Griffin agreed to hold the money in his safe deposit box at the Hudson Valley National Bank. Griffin testified that while Abplanalp was in the area during this conversation, he didn't hear it. Rebozo assured Griffin that within the next few days he would receive a call from Ken Gemmill who would tell him when the money should be returned and where.[655]

On June 21, 1973, Gemmill has testified that he met privately with Chester Davis in Davis' room at the Madison Hotel. After reviewing Danner's statement to the IRS, Gemmill and Davis discussed the discrepancies between Danner's and Rebozo's recollection of the delivery of the money. Gemmill has stated that as far as he was concerned, none of these discrepancies affected the return of the money.

Davis agreed to arrange for the return of the money and promised to be in contact with Gemmill within a few days.[656]

Gemmill has stated that on Monday, June 25, 1973, Davis called and told him that the money could be returned to the Marine Midland Bank, 140 Broadway, New York City, New York, on Wednesday, June 27, 1973. Since Davis was planning on being out of town on June 27, 1973, he told Gemmill that Walter Glaeser, the office manager at Davis' law firm, would accept this money on behalf of Howard Hughes, and, as previously agreed upon, the money would remain in a safe deposit box until IRS agents had an opportunity to examine it.[657] Gemmill called William Griffin and asked him to meet in New York on June 27, 1973, at the Marine Midland Bank. Since Griffin and Gemmill had not met, Gemmill agreed to produce a copy of the list of the bills which Rebozo, Wakefield and Barker had prepared earlier as a form of identification.[658]

Griffin met with Gemmill and Glaeser at the Marine Midland Bank on June 27, 1973. After Gemmill provided him with the receipt which Rebozo had earlier prepared, Griffin turned the money over to them. After a brief discussion,

655. Griffin Executive Session, March 28, 1974, pp. 7-9. (Galleys) *Also see* Rebozo Executive Session, March 21, 1974, pp. 283-285.
656. Gemmill Executive Session, May 29, 1974, pp. 11-12. *Also see* Davis Executive Session, December 4, 1973, pp. 1-10.
657. Gemmill Executive Session, May 29, 1974, pp. 11-12.
658. Griffin Executive Session, March 28, 1974. pp. 10-11. *Also see* Gemmill Executive Session, May 29, 1974, p. 11.

Griffin left.[659]

After Griffin's meeting at the Marine Midland Bank, he called Rebozo to tell him the money had been returned.[660] Rebozo has testified that shortly thereafter, Rebozo told the President that the Hughes contribution had been returned and the President once again assured Rebozo that that was the right thing to do.[661]

9. THE IRS INVESTIGATION OF REBOZO

The evidence set forth below indicates that the Internal Revenue Service investigation of Rebozo:

—was postponed several times

—was handled through oral rather than the normal written reports

—included advance notice to the President and Rebozo

—did not inquire into the relevant periods given in testimony and evidence available

—allowed Rebozo's attorney, rather than the IRS, to obtain information from third party witnesses

—did not include additional interviews with Rebozo even after IRS had learned Rebozo had altered his previous statements

—included notice to Rebozo that the IRS did not intend to pursue any criminal investigation of the matter

—included notice by the IRS to Rebozo and his attorney that the Special Prosecutor's Office had sought and obtained disclosure of evidence regarding Rebozo

—involved use of extra personnel at the request of the taxpayer

The Internal Revenue Service first learned of a relationship between Charles G. Rebozo and the Hughes Tool Company in December of 1971 during the investigation of John H. Meier. Meier, an employee of Robert Maheu working for Howard Hughes, had allegedly received millions of dollars from the fraudulent sales of mining claims to Hughes. Because of Meier's relationships with a variety of political figures, including F. Donald Nixon and Edward Nixon, IRS sensitive case reports were prepared on a monthly basis relating information to alert IRS officials and the Secretary of the Treasury of an IRS investigation that might touch upon

659. Griffin Executive Session, March 28, 1974, p. 11. (Galleys) *Also see* Gemmill Executive Session, May 29, 1974, pp. 12-13. Gemmill has provided the Committee with copies of the envelopes which held the money.
660. Griffin Executive Session, March 28, 1974, p. 12. (Galleys)
661. Rebozo Executive Session, March 21, 1974, p. 287.

prominent and, therefore, newsworthy individuals.[662] Former Secretary of the Treasury Shultz determined whether information from the sensitive case reports should be brought to the President's attention.

The December 1971 Sensitive Case Report indicated that Mr. Rebozo had instructed Meier to be unavailable for an IRS interview because it was feared Meier might disclose his association with Donald Nixon in connection with the sale of mining claims and rebates from the claims. Former Commissioner of IRS, Johnnie M. Walters, stated to the Committee that he advised Secretary of the Treasury, John Connally, on March 3, 1972, of the allegations relating to Rebozo's advice to Meier to "make himself unavailable."[663]

In addition to the Meier investigation, the IRS was also conducting an intensive investigation of the Hughes organization, which investigation was described by former Commissioner Walters; "This Hughes project, investigation, was a mammoth undertaking because the Hughes organization is so diverse and so widespread that we required a substantial number of agents, special agents, and others to carry on the investigation. I forget, but I have a recollection that at one point we had approximately 50 people on this thing; and I could see it going on forever."[664]

As part of the above investigation, special agents of the IRS interviewed Danner on May 15, 1972, in the offices of the Hughes Tool Company in Houston, Texas. On that occasion, the IRS received testimony under oath from Danner that he had, in fact, delivered two packages containing a total of $100,000 in cash to Charles G. Rebozo. Examination by this Committee of sensitive case reports provided by the IRS reflects no mention of the information received concerning the receipt by Rebozo of the $100,000 until an entry on April 26, 1973, which referred to a telephonic contact made by the IRS with Rebozo. The sensitive case reports do reflect, however, on a continuing basis, information relating to amounts paid to former Chairman of the Democratic National Committee, Larry O'Brien, from the Hughes Tool Company, pursuant to a contract. Former Commissioner Walters recalls Mr. Rebozo's name surfacing in the late spring or early summer of 1972 and a request by the IRS to interview both Rebozo and F. Donald Nixon with regard to matters previously mentioned. However, Walters stated that he decided,

662. Interview of George Shultz, January 24, 1974. Shultz indicates in the interview that he felt the sensitive case reports were a good check system so that the IRS would be aware that the handling of prominent indiivduals would be scrutinized by the public.
663. Johnnie M. Walters Interview, June 14, 1974, p. 20.
664. Johnnie M. Walters Interview, June 14, 1974, p. 26.

as is reported more completely in this report elsewhere, that the policy of the IRS should not be to interview sensitive political figures during the campaign year of 1972.[665] It is also pertinent to note, however, the IRS policy did not prohibit the continued investigaton of Larry O'Brien after communications were received from John Ehrlichman.[666]

Rebozo was finally contacted by IRS agents from the Las Vegas office on April 26, 1973, and interviewed on May 10, 1973. After the results of that interview were furnished to the Washington, D.C. National Headquarters, a decision was reached to conduct an investigation and audit of Rebozo, but that the investigation would be conducted by the Jacksonville, Florida office. The district director of the Intelligence Division, Troy Register, assigned agent John Bartlett to be in charge of Intelligence Division (criminal fraud) side of the investigation. Bartlett and agent Burt Webb, from the Audit Division, met with Rebozo's attorney, Kenneth Gemmill, on July 10, 1973, and advised Gemmill that they were assigned to make an examination of returns of Rebozo for the years 1968 through 1973.[667] Mr. Gemmill objected to any examination of 1968 or 1969 or 1973 records, claiming that the Statute of Limitations had already run on 1968 and 1969 and that 1973 records were not relevant. Agent Bartlett responded by indicating that Rebozo had previously told the IRS that he thought the money had been delivered in 1968 and 1969 and that there was other information relating to money in 1968.[668] Despite this initial position, the Internal Revenue Service ultimately agreed not to require production of records relating to 1968, 1969, or 1973. In addition, on that same date, Bartlett's notes indicate that he advised Gemmill that the IRS would not contact third-party witnesses, but would allow Gemmill and Rebozo to obtain information needed by the IRS from third parties. Had the IRS, in the spring of 1973, required the production by Rebozo of the 1969 records, the agents would have observed then that Rebozo had provided payments for the personal expenses of President Nixon.

Bartlett and Webb again met with Rebozo on July 24, 1973, apparently to discuss leaks of information Rebozo charged came from the IRS. According to Bartlett's notes, the IRS agents asked Rebozo, for reasons not explained, whether he had been contacted by "Cox's commission" and he answered

665. Johnnie M. Walters Interview, June 14, 1974, p. 49.
666. This matter is explained more fully below.
667. See Notes Taken from Interview in Meeting as Provided by IRS and as Prepared by Agent Bartlett.
668. See Bartlett notes, *Ibid.*

in the negative.

Agents Bartlett and Webb again met with Rebozo on August 17, 1973, at which time Rebozo advised them that the President was flying in that night to see Rebozo and wanted to go out to California with him, but Rebozo did not think he would go because he wanted to stay and finish up the IRS business.[669] Mr. Rebozo indicated to the IRS agents that day that he would like to pay to have additional agents put on the investigation in order that it be finished more quickly. After making that request the second time, Rebozo mentioned to the IRS agents that the President had phoned him 15 minutes after his speech on the previous Wednesday. Mr. Bartlett had advised this Committee that pursuant to Rebozo's request, Bartlett discussed this issue with his superiors and additional agents were added to the investigation.

On October 10, 1973, IRS agents met with Attorney Gemmill at the University Club in New York City and advised Gemmill that the investigation had developed nothing new. Mr. Gemmill then requested that the IRS furnish him with a copy of the interview previously conducted by the IRS on May 10, 1973, with his client. Bartlett provided a copy of that interview to the taxpayer's lawyer who made notes of his client's prior statements. During the October 10 meeting in New York, agent Bartlett inquired of Mr. Gemmill as to whether Mr. Rebozo had ever informed President Nixon of the receipt of the $100,000. In response to that request, Mr. Gemmill phoned agent Bartlett at 10:00 a.m. on October 12, 1973, and related to him that he had talked to Rebozo who now indicated that he in fact had told Rose Mary Woods that he had placed the $100,000 in the safe deposit box. Agent Bartlett's response was to ask Rebozo's lawyer if Woods would be available for an interview. Gemmill said he didn't know but that he would find out if they so desired. Bartlett indicated that he did not need the information at that time.[670]

Gemmill again telephonically contacted agent Bartlett on October 16, 1973, and talked between 9:30 and 9:32 a.m. At that time, Gemmill advised Bartlett that after their conversation the prior week in New York, Gemmill called and asked Rebozo whether he had discussed the money with the President. Gemmill said Rebozo told him that he had told the President in Key Biscayne between the election and when the money was returned, which Rebozo believed was in the

669. This information again is based on notes taken by the Committee of Bartlett's Memorandum of the Interview of Rebozo of August 17.
670. Information obtained from handwritten notes of agent John Bartlett provided by IRS.

spring of 1973. Bartlett asked Gemmill when it was that Rebozo had advised Miss Rose Mary Woods, and Gemmill said "shortly after receipt of the money." Bartlett then asked about access to Miss Woods and was told that they probably could get a statement from her as to what she knew about it.[671]

Bartlett had another telephonic communication with Gemmill on the following day, October 17, and Gemmill advised Bartlett that he would get on the phone the next day with regard to the letter from Rose Mary Woods. Bartlett advised Gemmill, "I told him that we had nothing new basis at present—that I thought nothing serious would develop but we had to wait to see what might come up in Watergate or Cox before making a final decision."[672] Barlett has indicated to the Committee that he intended to mean by the quoted language that the IRS could not state they had cleared Rebozo while another investigative body had an ongoing investigation. Gemmill testified that he had no recollection of any discussion of the Special Prosecutor at all with agent Bartlett.[673]

Agents Bartlett and Webb met with Rebozo at his bank on October 18, 1973 and indicated that they had advised Gemmill about the results of the investigation "and I don't anticipate at this time any action by intelligence, final decision still pending." Bartlett has explained that that information was communicated to Rebozo so that he would understand there would be no continuing criminal investigation by IRS of the matter. Bartlett's handwritten notes further indicate that on that date he advised Rebozo that disclosure of information and evidence obtained by the IRS had been granted to Special Prosecutor Cox's office. Agent Bartlett has indicated to the Senate Committee that he disclosed this information to warn the taxpayer under investigaton that anything he might say might be evidence against him in the grand jury. Agent Bartlett conceded, however, that when he read the taxpayer his *Miranda* warning rights on his earlier interview on July 10, 1973, the taxpayer was then advised the information he provided could be used against him in a criminal proceeding.[674]

Agent Bartlett's notes also reflect that he had a prior telephonic communication with Gemmill on October 18, between

671. Information taken from handwritten notes of agent John Bartlett.
672. Information taken from handwritten notes of Agent John Bartlett provided by the IRS. Observations by investigators of the Committee indicate that the above quoted statement appeared to have other words which were erased and covered over by the quoted language.
673. Kenneth Gemmill Executive Session, May 29, 1974, p. 000.
674. Information relating to meeting of October 18, 1973, comes to some extent from handwritten notes of agent Bartlett, as provided by IRS.

9:30 a.m. and 9:38 a.m., and the notes include the words, "Call after meeting with Cox, Fred Buzhardt, White House 486-1414" (sic) and "l. I told Gemmill about disclosure to Cox." According to Bartlett, these notes indicate that Gemmill was informed by Bartlett even before Mr. Rebozo that Special Prosecutor Cox's office had received a disclosure of IRS information with regard to the receipt by Rebozo of $100,000. The notation, with Buzhardt's name on it, according to Bartlett, refers to the fact that Gemmill was to contact Buzhardt to obtain a letter from Rose Mary Woods, reflecting her information with regard to the receipt of $100,000 by Rebozo.

While Attorney Kenneth Gemmill could not recall discussions with Bartlett with regards to Special Prosecutor Cox, he admitted to having a conversation with White House Counsel Fred Buzhardt but refused to discuss the substance of it on the grounds that it was protected by the attorney-client privilege. White House Counsel Fred Buzhardt testified that he recalled having:

"... received a request from Mr. Kenneth Gemmill to see if I could get some answers to some questions for an Internal Revenue agent. I believe that pertains to this, from Miss Rose Mary Woods. I think you submitted to me a list of questions which I provided to Miss Woods. Miss Woods gave me the answers. I drafted a letter for her to a Revenue agent or somebody with the IRS and I believe it was Jacksonville, Florida, but I do not recall for sure. That is the only thing I recall doing with respect to this at all." [675]

Fred Buzhardt further testified that he did not remember the questions that the IRS wanted answered, that he recalled "... the subject was about whether Miss Woods had a conversation with Mr. Rebozo," but he could not recall the subject matter of the alleged conversation.[676] Buzhardt did not recall whether he saw Woods in person or contacted her by telephone but he did recall:

"I discussed the questions with her and I asked her what the answers were and would she answer them for the IRS. And she said, Yes. She gave the information and I prepared the letter for her as I recall, or a draft, and sent it over to her. And as I recall, she sent it back to me and I mailed it. I think as I recall I sent her the draft and I sent an envelope addressed to the IRS."[677]

675. Fred J. Buzhardt Executive Session, p. 4 (May 7, 1974).
676. Fred J. Buzhardt Executive Session, p. 9 (May 7, 1974).
677. Fred J. Buzhardt Executive Session, pp. 11-12 (May 7, 1974).

Buzhardt did not recall whether Woods answered the questions orally or in writing and, also, did not recall that after the letter was prepared, typed and signed, that he had taken it back from Woods, had made some changes on it, had it re-typed and re-signed by her.[678] Buzhardt did not recall whether between the time the letter was typed and the time it was sent, he contacted any other individual with regard to the contents of the letter but admitted, "it is possible."[679] Buzhardt could not recall how long it was between the time Gemmill requested the letter and Buzhardt's first contact with Woods with regard to the letter. He did not recall whether any changes had been made "in the substance, content or body of the letter" prior to the time it was sent and when asked, "Did you furnish a copy of that letter to any other individual?", Buzhardt replied, "I do not know."[680] Buzhardt, when asked if he had made any changes on the letters that was to be signed by Woods, answered:

"Well, I don't have a recollection of it, Mr. Lenzner. I am sure I wouldn't have made changes unless there was some outside input because I didn't know anything about the matter. I had no idea what the answers to the questions were, so I would have had to have some input from outside, if I made changes. They had to come from Miss Woods. They couldn't have come from me because I had no earthly idea about the matter one way or the other."[681]

Buzhardt could not recall whether he ever asked Woods, the President's personal secretary, if she had ever discussed the matter of the $100,000 from Mr. Rebozo with President Nixon or anyone else at the White House.[682] Woods testified concerning the letter that:

"Mr. Buzhardt came in and said that the IRS is apparently in there checking all or they're going over Mr. Rebozo's files. He wanted—Mr. Buzhardt wanted to give

678. Fred J. Buzhardt Executive Session, p. 13 (May 7, 1974).
679. Fred J. Buzhardt Executive Session, pp. 13-14 (May 7, 1974).
680. Fred J. Buzhardt Executive Session, p. 19 (May 7, 1974). See also Exhibit 54 for a copy of the letter from Miss Woods to Agent Bartlett.
   Buzhardt was also asked by Senator Weicker:
   "So in October of 1973, Mr. Rebozo's $100,000 contribution was not of particular significance to the counsel of the President; is that correct?"
   and Mr. Buzhardt responded:
   "Certainly not to me, no."
   See p. 21 of Executive Session.
681. Fred J. Buzhardt Executive Session, p. 24 (May 7, 1974).
682. Fred J. Buzhardt Executive Session, p. 26 (May 7, 1974).

them a letter on the Hughes loan, I mean the Hughes contribution and he asked if I would be willing to sign a letter they could give to the IRS and I said, 'Yes, I would,' and I gave him the best of my knowledge on it. He wrote the letter and then, as I say, it was typed twice because he just changed a couple of words in the letter. There was no major change. I don't even remember whether he changed 'to' or a 'by' or what it was, because he prepared the letter and Mrs. Acker typed it."[683]

Woods testified that she did not know whether Gemmill had asked for the letter. Miss woods was sure, however, that Fred Buzhardt left her office with the letter and then returned, after a period of time, with some changes.[684] Woods did not recall what changes were made in the body of the letter.

In addition to the fact that Miss Woods' letter was signed and sent to the IRS on October 18, 1973, General Alexander Haig, the Chief of Staff of the White House and H. R. Haldeman's successor, telephonically communicated to Attorney General Elliot Richardson on that same date, a "re-expression of the President's concern about the extent to which Mr. Cox was getting into things that he thought were outside the charter." Former Attorney General Richardson testified before the United States Senate Judiciary Committee that Haig advised hm of the President's concern and "he didn't see what Mr. Cox's charter had to do with the activities of Mr. Rebozo, especially when there had already been an investigation of the whole matter by the Internal Revenue Service."[685] Richardson further testified that General Haig expressed not only that "the investigation was outside of Mr. Cox's charter," but also that "the Internal Revenue Service was giving Mr. Rebozo a clean bill, that it was the most thorough investigation in years, and that they are intimidated. This is no longer an acceptable basis for a government to run. That was October 18. But there was no request that anything be done about Rebozo and I had no conversation about Rebozo with Mr. Cox and all." When asked specifically about the October 18, 1973 telephone call with then-Attorney General Richardson, General Haig answered as follows:

"Yes, I do and again in the context of an indication. At the time we were very concerned about another matter with respect to Mr. Cox and Mr. Cox's failure to give us

683. Rose Mary Woods Executive Session, pp. 22-23 (March 22, 1974).
684. Rose Mary Woods Executive Session, pp. 24-25 (March 22, 1974).
685. Hearings before the Judiciary Committee, United States Senate, Elliott Richardson witness, November 8, 1973, see pp. 386-387.

a response and the whole subject of Mr. Cox's frame of reference, activities and investigations came up.

"As I recall Mr. Richardson mentioned to me something about a Cox activity at that time that I knew nothing about involving Abplanalp and his discussions with Mr. Cox about that. Well I did not raise that, Elliot raised it. I raised this strictly in the context of the problems we were having with Mr. Cox on another issue, and what I would want to make very, very clear is that the Rebozo matter had nothing to do with the considerations and deliberations made with respect to Mr. Cox in that week of October."[686]

General Haig was also asked if he called Attorney General Richardson at the instruction of the President on October 18, and he responded as follows:

"No, it was not in that specific sense. And again you have to put yourself, if you can, to portray the kind of dialogue that was going on during that week. . . . I was frequently in the habit that week and at other times of having a discussion with the President and picking up the phone and calling Elliot Richardson. On that occasion, I may have expressed this as being of presidential concern and I'm sure if I did that I would have had reason to know that either because I knew the President's thinking or because he specifically told me so."[687]

General Haig further denied that the President ever expressed any concern about Special Prosecutor Cox's investigation of Rebozo and, in fact, could not recollect any statement that the President made in discussing the $100,000 furnished to Rebozo, except the President's concern about the way the investigations were being handled. In indicating that the President had not expressed concern with regard to the Special Prosecutor's investigation of Rebozo, General Haig did state, however:

"The concerns I had about it were very limited. In the fall, there was some concern about a number of areas that the Special Prosecutor may or may not have been involved in, in the context of his charter. Mr. Buzhardt, I know, has discussed it with me and I know he discussed it with the Attorney General at that time, Elliot Richardson."[688]

686. General Alexander Haig Executive Session, p. 51 (May 15, 1974).
687. Alexander Haig Executive Session, pp. 53-54 (May 15, 1974).
688. Alexander Haig Executive Session, p. 49 (May 15, 1974).

General Haig was also asked the following:

MR. LENZNER Do you recall representing to Mr. Richardson that the President was concerned that Mr. Cox was getting into an investigation of Mr. Rebozo?
GENERAL HAIG I may have. I know our counsel were concerned about it.
L Which counsel was that?
H Mr. Buzhardt and I discussed it. We discussed that and we discussed another area of activity that Mr. Cox was into and I know there was some on-going discussions with Mr. Buzhardt and Mr. Richardson.[689]

Mr. Buzhardt, however, testified directly in conflict with the above testimony.

L Now on or about the same date as this letter (the October 18 letter of Miss Woods), do you recall having any discussions with any other inividual with regard to the initiation by Special Prosecutor Cox of an investigation into the receipt by Mr. Charles G. Rebozo of $100,000 from the Hughes Tool Company?
B No.
L Have you, at any time, become aware of the fact, aside from the news media, that Mr. Cox had initiated an investigation into this matter?
B I may have been. I don't recall it.
L Do you have any recollection of ever discussing that issue, the issue of the Cox investigation of the Rebozo receipt of $100,000, with General Haig?
B No, I don't recall it.[690]

Mr. Buzhardt further testified that he did not recall whether he was aware that General Haig had made the October 18 call at the time it was placed.

Gemmill also testified that Bartlett made an agreement with him that when he received the results of the Federal Reserve Bank's search of the dates of the currency returned by Rebozo to Hughes, he would furnish that information to Gemmill.[691] In addition, agent Bartlett's handwritten notes of November 25, 1973 reflecting a telephonic contact with Gemmill indicate "have we heard from the Federal Reserve concerning the money—answered in the negative."[692] Gemmill also asked Bartlett if IRS had any evidence of funds

689. Alexander Haig Executive Session, p. 50 (May 15, 1974).
690. Fred J. Buzhardt Executive Session, p. 28 (May 7, 1974).
691. Kenneth Gemmill Executive Session, p. 73, May 29, 1974.
692. This information was obtained from handwritten notes provided by the IRS.

going to a trust account of the President, and Bartlett told Gemmill that they had not.

Following Gemmill's testimony on May 29, 1974, his counsel furnished additional information Gemmill received from General Haig to wit:

"Mr. Gemmill now recalls two additional conversations with General Haig concerning the $100,000 contribution. One occurred a few days before Mr. Gemmill left for China and the other occurred possibly two months earlier. To the best of Mr. Gemmill's recollection, General Haig in both conversations indicated that the Federal Reserve Bank report was on the way and 'there may be a problem.' On both occasions, Mr. Gemmill recalls that he replied the revenue agents had agreed to give Mr. Gemmill a copy of the Federal Reserve Bank report and that he would wait and see what the report said.[693]

In addition to agreeing to provide the taxpayer not only with a copy of his interview but with a copy of the results of the Federal Reserve Bank report, the IRS apparently obtained access to only a limited number of cashier's checks purchased by Mr. Rebozo despite the fact that a considerable number of cashier's checks were purchased by the taxpayer under the names of Charles Gregory and Anita Reynolds. The IRS further agreed not to photocopy any of the cashier's checks to which they had access and did not obtain information from the checks themselves regarding who received the proceeds of such checks for the purpose for which the checks were issued.

General Haig testified that he discussed the IRS investigation of the Hughes contribution with President Nixon several times: "I would say there were several brief discussions when it came to my attention—to my knowledge. Then there was a prolonged period when it never came up at all. Then I may have discussed it once or twice when the investigation was nearing a conclusion." [694] Haig also testified that he was present at discussions in Key Biscayne between the President and Mr. Rebozo regarding the investigation of Mr. Rebozo. On one occasion Haig said the President advised him that Rebozo had been before the Select Committee for testimony.[695] General Haig further testified that on one occasion the President advised him of information the President received from Mr. Rebozo: "I think he probably said that Mr.

693. Letter of June 6, 1974 to Terry Lenzner from Matthew J. Broderick of the law firm of Dechert, Price and Rhoads.
694. Alexander Haig Executive Session, May 15, 1974, p. 87.
695. Haig Executive Session. pp. 85-89.

Rebozo did not use the money because he was afraid it would be troublesome and he put it in the safe deposit box and left it there. I know more recently the President expressed to me his absolute conviction that none of that money was given to Miss Woods or his family, his brothers."[696]

Finally, Secretary Shultz stated to the Committee that the only person he discussed the Rebozo tax audit with was General Haig and this occurred in late 1973.[697]

IRS Audit of Larry O'Brien. It was during the course of the IRS investigation of the Hughes Tool Company that special agents of the IRS, in a sensitive case report, stated that their investigation had disclosed that the Hughes Tool Company made substantial payments to Lawrence F. O'Brien and Associates during 1970. This same sensitive case report also referred to possible improprieties by Rebozo, Don Nixon, John Meier and others. Because some of the names mentioned were politically prominent, this information was summarized in a sensitive case report brought to the Secretary of Treasury's attention.[698] Roger Barth, who was assistant to the Commissioner of the IRS, testified that in May, 1972, he received a sensitive case report which arose out of the Hughes Tool Company investigation.

> ... Now, when I received this report, I of course went through the normal procedure of taking it to Secretary Shultz, and either he or I transmitted a copy of the sensitive case report of the Hughes project to John Ehrlichman at the White House, because of the fact that there were allegations or representations in the report of possible wrongdoing by Mr. Rebozo and Mr. Nixon, the President's brother or brothers ...
>
> Sometime thereafter, not very long thereafter, I was either called on the phone or went over—I can't remember which—to Mr. Ehrlichman's office, and I think I went over there, as a matter of fact ... and he asked that he be kept advised of the development of this Hughes project as it related to Mr. Robozo and the Nixon brother or brothers. And in the conversation about that, he raised the question of whether, you know, what would be the tax treatment or the implication of the payments to Larry O'Brien. If this were a political contribution by the Hughes Tool Company, it could conceivably be a violation of the Corrupt Practices Act,

---

696. Haig Executive Session, pp. 75-76.
697. Interview with former Treasury Secretary, George Shultz, January 24, 1974.
698. Sensitive Case Report—IRS—Chronology, April 26, 1974, pp. 1-5.

and if it were deducted by the corporation, it could be a violation of the tax laws. On the other hand, if it were compensation for consulting services for Mr. O'Brien or his firm, then he raised the question of would this be reported by Mr. O'Brien.

I thought this was the reasonable question that he asked and I told him I would check it out, but I did not want to make any contact with our field personnel through normal channels because I did not want to give the impression I was on behalf of the Commissioner trying to instigate any audit of Mr. O'Brien. So what I did was go to the Assistant Commissioner of Inspection, Frank Geibel and asked for Lawrence O'Brien's tax returns ... I asked that they get them in a way that the agents working on the case in the field wouldn't know that I requested them. And they did this, and what I did, I just looked at the tax returns of Mr. O'Brien and his consulting firm and made sure that there was enough gross income reported for those years, to cover the amount reported.[699]

Ehrlichman has testified that he received sensitive case reports beginning in 1969 when he was Counsel to the President and continuing throughout his tenure at the White House. Ehrlichman stated that the President and the Secretary of the Treasury had worked out the arrangement whereby sensitive case reports would be transmitted to the White House through Ehrlichman.[700] Johnnie Walters, who was Commissioner of the IRS from August 1971 through May 1973 has testified that it would be quite proper for the Secretary of the Treasury to alert the White House to sensitive case reports. Walters, however, has also testified that he had no knowledge that Barth was providing copies of sensitive case reports to Ehrlichman. Walters stated that "it would have been out of the routine, and I would worry about it."[701]

Ehrlichman testified that he received the sensitive case report from Barth, and that after receiving it, called Shultz to find out what the status of the O'Brien audit was. Shultz, at this time, had only been Secretary of the Treasury for a few weeks and was not even aware that O'Brien was being audited. Shultz told Ehrlichman he would get this information and report back to him.[702]

After his conversation with Ehrlichman, Shultz called

699. Barth Executive Session, June 5, 1974, pp. 4-5.
700. Ehrlichman interview, January 10, 1974, pp. 1-2.
701. Walters interview, June 14, 1974, pp. 18-22.
702. Shultz interview, January 24, 1974, p. 2.

Walters to get the status of the O'Brien audit. Walters has testified that:

> ... Secretary Shultz stated to me that the White House had information that indicated that Mr. O'Brien may have received large amounts of income which possibly might not have been reported properly. The Secretary asked me if I could check, and I said I would check. I then asked the Assistant Commissioner of Compliance, Mr. Hanlon if he would determine whether Mr. O'Brien had filed returns, and the status of those returns. A few days later, Mr. Hanlon reported orally to me that IRS had checked, that Mr. O'Brien had filed returns; that those returns reflected large amounts of income; that the returns had been examined; that a small, relatively small deficiency was indicated in one which Mr. O'Brien had paid; and that the audit and examinations were closed.
>
> Now I reported this to the Secretary at some point and told him just that, which meant that there was nothing else; that IRS has performed its function and responsibility ... Sometime later, the Secretary indicated that that had not completely satisfied Mr. Ehrlichman and, wasn't there anything else that could and should be done; and, of course, by this time, IRS had already concluded that it should interview Mr. O'Brien in connection with these repayments from Hughes.
> ... I told the Secretary ... that we could interview Mr. O'Brien and just be sure that the amounts reflected in the return covered the particular amounts from the Hughes organization ... [703]

Walters has stated that at a later date Shultz confirmed to him that it was Ehrlichman who told Shultz about the money O'Brien received from Hughes.[704]

Walters testified that in late 1971 or early 1972, the top management team of IRS discussed the approaching 1972 Presidential elections. The IRS deliberately concluded that anything that was politically sensitive should be postponed until after the election. Walters said they did not want to be involved in politics on either side and so wherever possible, politically sensitive interviews were to be postponed until after the election. Because of this policy, the IRS did not interview Rebozo or Don Nixon until six months after the election. The IRS, however, did succumb to pressures from

703. Walters interview, January 14, 1974, pp. 43-44.
704. Walters interview, June 14, 1974, p. 46.

the Administration and interviewed O'Brien before the 1972 election. Walters further testified that:

> ...With that policy in mind, it's obvious that any interview of Larry O'Brien would have been postponed until after the election. So, I think IRS would not have conducted that interview until after the election had it not been for the generation of pressure from the White House, Ehrlichman;...[705]

In the meantime, both Barth and Shultz had kept Ehrlichman apprised of the status of O'Brien's audit. Shultz stated that there had been an unspoken feeling that the IRS tended to be rather easy on Democrats while they were particularly hard on Republicans. Ehrlichman had especially expressed these kinds of feelings to Shultz. It was Shultz's objective, therefore, to be sure that a proper audit was conducted on O'Brien. From time to time, Shultz called the IRS to see how the proceedings were going and he would then call Ehrlichman to report on the status of the O'Brien audit.[706] Barth has testified that he advised Ehrlichman that after Barth checked O'Brien's tax returns, there appeared to be enough gross incomes to cover the amounts that Hughes reported he had paid O'Brien. According to Barth, this was the first and only time that he had ever obtained an individual's tax returns to verify information he obtained through a sensitive case report. Barth testified that Ehrlichman knew he was going to obtain O'Brien's tax returns and in fact encouraged him to do so.[707]

Ehrlichman testified that there were good political reasons to go after O'Brien since O'Brien was the head of the Democratic party. After Ehrlichman saw O'Brien's name in the sensitive case report, he said he brought this information to President Nixon's attenion. The President was quite interested in the audit of O'Brien and was especially interested in the fact that O'Brien was on retainer to the Hughes organization, according to Ehrlichman. Ehrlichman, however, did not recall if the President made any specific requests for Ehrlichman to follow up on this matter.[708]

Haldeman has testified that the information coming from the Hughes tax audit concerning Larry O'Brien may have revived the White House interest in O'Brien. Haldeman further stated that from the Administration's perspective, Larry O'Brien was the only effective Democratic politician in

705. Walters interview, June 14, 1974, p. 49.
706. Shultz interview, January 24, 1974, p. 3.
707. Barth Executive Session, June 5, 1974, pp. 13-16.
708. Ehrlichman Interview, January 10, 1974, p. 3.

the country and therefore, there was some interest in attacking O'Brien to lessen his effectiveness from a political standpoint.[709] Ehrlichman has testified that Haldeman filled in many of the informational gaps that were left from the sensitive case report concerning O'Brien. For example, Ehrlichman learned from Haldeman that the amount of the retainer O'Brien was receiving from Hughes was quite significant, and recalls that both were impressed by the possibility of embarrassing O'Brien because of a possible overlap of his retainer with Hughes and his tenure as Chairman of the Democratic National Committee.[710]

On August 17, 1972, Larry O'Brien was interviewed by the IRS. A written report of this interview was sent to Walters who in turn transmitted the report to Secretary Shultz. By this time, Walters felt that the IRS' interest in O'Brien should be concluded because the taxpayer had filed his returns, reported his income, and paid his taxes. Walters said he had insisted to Shultz that the IRS had conducted an audit and the case was closed. Walters added that "it appeared that [Shultz] was being pressed..."[711]

On August 29, 1972, Shultz told Walters that he wanted to meet with both Walters and Barth to discuss the O'Brien audit. Walters testified that both he and Shultz thought they were being "back doored" in some fashion and that in this situation it would be advisable for Barth to be apprised of the specifics concerning the O'Brien matter. During this meeting with Schultz and Barth, Walters explained to Barth that information had come to the IRS from the White House concerning large amounts of money O'Brien made that were possibly not reported. Walters further explained to Barth that the IRS had checked O'Brien's return and that it appeared that everything was proper and the examination was closed.[712] Barth testified that he said that he had read the report on the matter and he felt it was a thorough job. Shultz then called Ehrlichman to give him a final report on the O'Brien audit. Both Walters and Barth were on telephone extensions during this joint telephone call. Shultz and Walters reported to Ehrlichman that the audit report on O'Brien was completed and that everything was in order. Ehrlichman asked Barth if he had read the report and that if everything appropriate had been done on this audit. Barth testified he told Ehrlichman that it looked like an appropriate audit and there was nothing worth pursuing any further. Barth recalls that Ehrlichman

709. Haldeman Interview, November 9, 1973, p. 4.
710. Ehrlichman Interview, January 10, 1974, p. 2.
711. Walters interview, June 14, 1974, p. 45.
712. Walters interview, June 14, 1974, pp. 6-9.

seemed to take his word for it and that the only reaction Ehrlichman seemed to have was that he was annoyed that it had taken so long for this report to be prepared.[713]

Walters testified that toward the end of the conversation, Ehrlichman expressed very strong feelings to Walters concerning the manner in which the O'Brien audit was conducted. Walters testified that as this conversation became more offensive to him personally, he hung up his extension.[714] Shultz recalls that during this conversation, Ehrlichman told Walters that Walters would not go after prominent Democrats even if the facts were there. According to Shultz, this was the only challenge to the thoroughness of the O'Brien audit that he could recall.[715]

Ehrlichman stated that the purpose of this joint telephone call was to report to him that the audit on O'Brien had been completed and that it had disclosed no improprieties or delinquencies. Ehrlichman testified that:

> "...my concern was throughout, that the IRS down in the woodwork was delaying the audit until after the election and that seemed to be the case, that there was a stall on..."[716]

Ehrlichman also testified that "I wanted them to turn up something and send [O'Brien] to jail before the election and unfortunately it didn't materialize." During this joint telephone conversation Ehrlichman said he had his first opportunity to articulate to Walters what his opinion was concerning the job Walters did on the O'Brien audit.

> "...it was my first crack at [Walters]. George wouldn't let me at him. George wanted to stand between me and his commissioner and this was the first time I had a chance to tell the Commissioner what a crappy job he had done...."[717]

Ehrlichman did accept the Commissioner's view that the O'Brien audit was closed. He says he did not suggest that they reopen the audit on O'Brien at any time because as far as he was concerned, the matter was closed.[718] Barth, however, has testified that shortly after the Aug. 29; 1972 joint telephone conversation with Ehrlichman, Ehrlichman called him a few hours later. Barth recalls that Ehrlichman just wanted to

713. Barth Executive Session; June 5, 1974, pp. 6-9.
714. Walters Interview; June 14, 1974, p.57.
715. Shultz Interview; January 24, 1974, p. 3.
716. Ehrlichman Executive Session; Feb. 8, 1974, p. 42 (gallies).
717. Ehrlichman Executive Session; June 5, 1974, p. 10.
718. Ehrlichman Executive Session; Feb. 8, 1974, p. 42 (gallies).

check to make sure that Barth honestly felt that the IRS audit of O'Brien was conducted properly. Barth told Ehrlichman that he was satisfied with the audit and according to Barth, Ehrlichman thanked him for his judgment on the matter and that was the end of the conversation.[719]

On September 15, 1972, however, John Dean and H. R. Haldeman met with President Nixon and, according to evidence received by the Committee, discussed the IRS investigation of Larry O'Brien. The details of this discussion, however, were not provided to the Committee by the White House. In addition, this particular conversation was deleted from the White House tapes provided to the Special Prosecutor and the House Judiciary Committee as well as the transcripts released to the public.[720]

10. THE ISSUE OF USE OF THE MONEY

Background. As discussed in Section 4 above, in February, 1969, Charles G. Rebozo was asked by the President to contact J. Paul Getty "regarding major contributions."[721] Evidence obtained by the Senate Select Committee indicates that the President, Rebozo, Haldeman and Ehrlichman sought to establish a fund to be controlled by the White House staff rather than by the Republican National Committee.[722] Evidence obtained by the Committee indicates that Rebozo controlled funds during 1969 which he used for "administration-connected costs."[723]

The Committee has ascertained that pursuant to communications with John Ehrlichman, Rebozo, between April and July, 1969, transmitted $1,416.18 from his fund to Kalmbach for payments to Caulfield and Ulasewicz. These funds originally derived from 1968 campaign contributions in the Florida Nixon for President Committee account.[724] Rebozo has also testified that he received $150,100 in cash contributions from Howard Hughes and A. D. Davis.[725] In the case of the Hughes funds, the Committee has received evidence and testimony indicating that those funds were never transferred to the appropriate campaign officials or committees.[726]

719. Barth Executive Session, June 5, 1974, p. 10.
720. See Thompson Affidavit and "Memorandum of Substance of Dean's Calls and Meetings with the President." 4 *Hearings* 1794-1800.
721. See exhibit 15 for memo from Haldeman to Ehrlichman of February 17, 1969 and also interview of Edward L. Morgan.
722. Ibid.
723. See exhibit 16.
724. See Kalmbach Executive Session, May 5, 1974, p. 00.
725. See Rebozo Executive Session, March 21, 1974, p. 415.
726. See Rebozo Executive Session, March 20, 1974, p. 76.

According to CRP's records, the funds contributed by A. D. Davis were never received by the Committee to Re-elect the President on whose behalf Mr. Rebozo accepted them.[727]

Herbert Kalmbach has testified that on April 30, 1973, Rebozo told him that Rebozo had spent some of the $100,000 received from Hughes on F. Donald Nixon, Edward Nixon, Rose Mary Woods, and other individuals.[728]

In an effort to confirm or deny Kalmbach's testimony, the Committee sought, through a series of subpoenas, to obtain financial records from Rebozo and from his Key Biscayne Bank and Trust Co. Rebozo refused to produce all documents requested, thus frustrating the Committee's investigation work and preventing it from obtaining necessary and relevant documents.[729]

The Committee, therefore, found it necessary to subpoena the documents and records of third parties. In order to determine if Rebozo has made expenditures with "hidden" funds, the Committee subpoenaed a few typical Key Biscayne contractors and vendors who were likely to have served either Rebozo or the President during the period in question.[730] Time did not permit an exhaustive inquiry.

This limited survey of contractors and vendors proved fruitful since it revealed that Rebozo was using four trust accounts in his attorney's name through which his funds moved.

Three of these accounts are at Rebozo's bank and Rebozo again refused to produce lawfully subpoenaed records relating to said trust accounts.[731] Nevertheless, based on records provided by those few vendors and contractors contacted and the limited documents and records available to the Committee, a detailed analysis was prepared.

Summary of Facts. The Committee has received testimony and evidence that:

1. Rebozo ordered and paid for expenses totalling over $50,000 for President Nixon during the periods following both the 1968 and 1972 Presidential elections.

2. These payments were made by Rebozo despite the fact

727. See A. D. Davis Executive Session, p. 000. See La Rue Executive Session, May 28, 1974, pp. 7-8. See also interviews with Paul Barrick, Fred LaRue and memo of conversation with Robert Barker, attorney for Maurice Stans.
728. See Kalmbach Executive Session, March 21, 1974, p. 49-52 (Galleys).
729. See Exhibit 00.
730. The Committee staff pursued this route after learning Rebozo was reimbursed for expenditures on one occasion by the President.
731. Rebozo, individually and as President of the Key Biscayne Bank, was subpoenaed to produce certain records reflecting payments he made on behalf of the President and others. Rebozo never complied with this subpoena. See Exhibit 00.

that all other expenses of President Nixon were paid for by check issued against his bank accounts or by debit memos drawn against his bank accounts. Rebozo has the authority to draw against the President's account at the Key Biscayne Bank by issuing debit memos for cashiers' checks and bank transfers. Although he has regularly used this procedure, he did not do so for these transactions.

3. Substantial payments furnished by Rebozo on behalf of President Nixon were made in cash and, when Rebozo paid the same companies for work done for his own benefit, he paid by check.

4. Expenses paid for by Rebozo included $45,621.15 for improvements and furnishings at the President's 500 and 516 Bay Lane properties in Key Biscayne, Florida. The records reflecting expenditures for these improvements were withheld from the firm of Coopers and Lybrand and do not appear in their August, 1973 examination of the President's assets and liabilities, which covered the period from January 1, 1969 to May 31, 1973.

5. Currency totalling at least $23,500 was deposited by Rebozo in trust accounts not in his name to pay for the President's expenses, thus concealing the true source of these payments. All currency so deposited was in $100 bills.

6. In addition to Rebozo's role as the President's personal agent regarding the Key Biscayne property,[732] President Nixon was aware of and concurred in at least some of these improvements to his properties.

7. Substantial funds used to pay for expenses and gifts of the President were transmitted to trust accounts in the name of Rebozo's attorney, a process which concealed the source of the funds.

8. $4,562 which originated as campaign contributions was passed by Rebozo through three bank accounts and a cashier's check, none in his name, to purchase jewelry given by the President as a gift to his wife.

9. Throughout the period during which these expenditures were made on the President's behalf, Rebozo had access to substantial amounts of cash retained from campaign contributions received.

10. The Coopers and Lybrand examination of the President's assets and liabilities as of May 31, reflects no liabilities payable to Rebozo.

11. Rebozo did not file a United States Gift Tax Return[733]

732. See Section 4 above.
733. See Internal Revenue Service Form 709; these returns must be filed on or before the 15th day of the second month following the close of the calendar quarter during which the gift or gifts were made [IRC §6075 (b)].

for calendar years 1969, 1970, 1971 or 1972 as required by the Internal Revenue Code Section 6019(a).

12. The President reimbursed Rebozo in the amount of $13,642.52 for a portion of the cost for construction of a pool on the President's property. This reimbursement occurred after Rebozo returned funds to representatives of Hughes and despite the fact that the Coopers and Lybrand report reflected no liability payable to Rebozo.

13. During November 1972, Rebozo expended at least $20,000 in currency on the President's behalf.

14. According to Rebozo's testimony and financial records, the only apparent sources available to Rebozo for a substantial portion of the $20,000 in currency used in November 1972 were campaign contributions.

The Coopers and Lybrand Report. On August 20, 1973, the accounting firm of Coopers and Lybrand issued a report on the President's assets and liabilities. They reported in a letter to the President on improvements and furnishings to his properties at 500 and 516 Bay Lane that: "Through May 31, 1973, you paid from your personal funds for improvements to these properties in the amounts of $37,942 with respect to 500 Bay Lane, and $38,479 with respect to 516 Bay Lane as follows: [734]

Property	Improvements	Furnishings	Total
500 Bay Lane	$24,734	$13,208	$37,942
516 Bay Lane	29,687[735]	8,792	38,479
Total	$54,421	$22,000	$76,421

The details of these expenditures are as follows:

IMPROVEMENT COSTS PAID BY PRESIDENT NIXON
ON HIS KEY BISCAYNE PROPERTIES [736]

CONTRACTOR AND SERVICE	DATE PAID	500 BAY LANE	516 BAY LANE	TOTAL
Babcock Company Builders, Inc.	4-14-69			
Remove existing bedroom and construct Executive office	5-16-69		$14,765.00	$14,765.00
Alterations and Repairs	5-2-69 to 5-13-69	$3,224.19		3,224.19

734. See Coopers and Lybrand letter to President Nixon, August 20, 1973, p. 000.

735. Included in the improvements for 516 Bay Lane were loan charges of $368.50 on the property, therefore the total actual costs per the President's records are $76,053.

736. These figures are from the Presidenet's accounting records for the period January 1, 1969 through May 31, 1973 as maintained by Arthur Blech.

CONTRACTOR AND SERVICE	DATE PAID	500 BAY LANE	516 BAY LANE	TOTAL
Alterations and Repairs	4-24-69 and 5-2-69		799.49	799.49
Alterations—Executive Office	8-11-69		11,307.12	11,307.12
Alterations and Repairs	11-12-69	6,299.44		6,299.44
Caldwell Scott Construction Co. Remodeling	7-28-69 and 8-26-69	15,210.38		15,210.38
Little, Lair & Pilkington	4-14-69 and 6-17-69		2,132.60	2,132.60
Metals Tech. Inc. Panels	10-1-69		314.80	314.80
Rablen-Shelton Furnishings	7-31-69	10,000.00		10,000.00
	10-31-70	3,208.23	8,791.77	12,000.00 737
Loan charges per records		37,942.24	38,110.78	76,053.02
			368.50	368.50
		$37,942.24	$38,479.28	$76,421.52

—The above Expenditures totaling $76,421.52 were made from the President's personal funds, usually by debit memo against his bank accounts at the Key Biscayne Bank and Trust Company, for cashiers checks or bank checks issued to the suppliers.[738]

Expenditures by Rebozo Concealed from Accountants. The Committee's investigation, however, reflects actual expenditures for the same period on the President's properties as follows:

Property	Improvements	Furnishings	Total
500 Bay Lane	$54,364	$14,939	$ 69,303
516 Bay Lane	42,441	9,930	52,371
Total	$96,805	$24,869	$121,674

As noted in the above schedules, costs for improvements and furnishings reported by Coopers & Lybrand amounted to $76,053 (plus $368.50 in loan charges) whereas actual expenditures for improvements and furnishings amounted to at least $121,674. Expenditures for improvements and furnishing amounting to $45,621 were not included in the President's records when the records were presented to the accounting firm. These expenditures made for improvements on and

737. Payments made by check drawn against President Nixon's account; the remaining payments to suppliers was done by cashiers check or Key Biscayne bank check.
738. Information obtained from interviews with Kalmbach, DeMarco, Marilyn Parent, Ann Harvey and Arthur Blech.

furnishings of the President's properties at 500 Bay Lane and 516 Bay Lane from 1969 to 1972 include the following:[739]

Conversion of garage into living quarters....	$11,978.84
Swimming pool and accessories	18,435.18
Extension of roof	6,508.11
Fireplace	3,586.00
Architectural model of 500 Bay Lane	395.65
Putting green	243.57
Billiard table...	1,138.80
Architect fees and tile repairs	3,335.00
Total	$45,621.15

These improvements were directed and paid for by Charles G. Rebozo, with funds derived from the following sources:

1. By personal checks of Charles G. Rebozo (Acct. #1-34)	$13,361.21
2. By checks from Trust Accounts	23,213.01
3. By currency	5,065.28
4. By form unknown—believed to be currency	3,981.65
Total	$45,621.15

Funds deposited in the above mentioned Trust Accounts included currency amounting to $23,500. Thomas Wakefield stated the currency deposited in the Trust account consisted of $100 bills.[740] Accordingly, the total currency which may have been used to finance these expenditures amounted to $32,259.94.

The Improvements on the President's Key Biscayne Properties. In December, 1968, President Nixon, Mrs. Nixon, Mr. and Mrs. David Eisenhower, and Mr. Rebozo met with Mr. Jaime Borrelli, of the architectural firm of Bouterse, Borrelli and Albaisa, (BBA), to discuss possible alterations to the 500 Bay Lane property.[741] Plans were thereafter prepared and revisions made from time to time. On most occasions, Rebozo would take the plans to Washington, D.C. for review by the President and his family.[742]

Documents in the files of the Committee reflect that Rebozo was consulted and made decisions on every aspect of modifi-

739. These expenditures were obtained by contacting vendors which provided services to the Key Biscayne properties.
740. Interview of Thomas H. Wakefield, June 24, 1974, p. 1.
741. Interview of Jaime Borrelli; June 1, 1974, p. 1.
742. Ibid.

cation and alterations to 500 Bay Lane.[743]

Architect Fees and Tile Repairs—$3,335. The architectural firm of Bouterse, Borrelli and Albaisa, was formed in the latter part of 1968. Donald A. Bouterse is a nephew of Rebozo. Rebozo always paid this firm for improvements on the President's properties with currency. According to the architects records furnished to the staff the following currency payments were made by Rebozo.[744]

Date	Amount
February 10, 1969	$ 400
March 7, 1969	400
March 19, 1969	300
April 2, 1969	581
Total	$1,681

Rebozo also paid $1,654 in cash for the work done by Designers Flooring Company. The payments were made as follows:[745]

Date	Amount
April 11, 1969	$ 754
May 26, 1969	300
July 22, 1969	600
Total	$1,654

The President's records through May 31, 1973 and Rebozo's records do not reflect any reimbursement to Rebozo by President Nixon. It is also of interest that when Rebozo made a $500 payment to Donald Bouterse on Jan. 6, 1969, and $273 on March 6, 1969, to Designers Flooring Company in connection with work on his own property at 490 Bay Lane, payment was made by personal check.[746]

743. Exhibit 55 contains a number of documents reflecting the firm BBA's work done at the order of Mr. Rebozo for President Nixon's residence. For example, the bill sent to Rebozo for payment of Feb. 3, 1969 notes "additions and alterations, 500 Bay Lane, Key Biscayne COM. No. 68-120" and estimates the cost of construction at $8,000. A standard form agreement between owner and contractor dated February 18, 1969 indicates an agreement between Mr. Rebozo as agent for the owner of 500 Bay Lane and the Caldwell Scott Engineering Construction Company which was contracted to do certain work on the President's home.
744. See Exhibits 00, 00, and 00. Specifically, Mr. Rebozo ordered certain work to be done in 1969 by Borrelli's firm which was for "additions and alterations, 500 Bay Lane, Key Biscayne" which work he assumed the obligation for payment. In a letter to Mr. Borrelli on July 7, 1969, Rebozo makes reference to a dispute with regard to payment for a subcontractor, Caldwell-Scott, and notes "as you know, the original statement was forwarded more than two months after I had requested it of Mr. Scott. This, of course, made payment therefore impossible for me."
745. See Exhibits 00, 00, and 00.
746. See Exhibit 000.

Architectural Model of 500 Bay Lane—$395.65. Bouterse, Borrellia & Albaisa, architects, received two payments from Rebozo amounting to $395.65 for a model of 500 Bay Lane in connection with remodeling work on President Nixon's properties. The payments were made by Rebozo as follows:[747]

Date	Amount
January 18, 1969	$295.65
March 14, 1969	100.00
Total	$395.65

Although the BBA representative contacted was unable to state whether payment was made in currency, no charge was found on Rebozo's bank statement indicating that a check from Rebozo had been issued in payment.

Conversion of Garage into Living Quarters—516 Bay Lane—$11,978.84. Robert Little, former senior partner in the architectural firm of Little, Lair & Pilkington, stated that he met with President Richard Nixon and Charles G. Rebozo in 1969 at the Key Biscayne Compound to discuss remodeling of the President's property at 516 Bay Lane. This discussion initially entailed plans to be drawn by Little's firm in the construction of a bedroom and general remodeling. Later, Little was directed by Rebozo to revise these plans since Mrs. Nixon wanted the garage on the 516 Bay Lane property converted into living room, bedroom and bath.[748]

The fees paid to Little, Lair & Pilkington were made by check from the President's bank account and thus are included in the records furnished to the Coopers & Lybrand accounting firm.

The conversion itself was described in documents furnished the Committee as "516 Bay Lane, convert two-car garage into efficiency with living room, bedroom and bath—starting date, May 25, 1969." The work was done by Babcock Company Builders, Inc. and payment of $11,978.84 was made on August 6, 1969 by Rebozo's personal check number 4169 drawn on his account #1-0034 in the Key Biscayne Bank. Although Rebozo purported to make all 1969 canceled checks available to the Committee staff, *this check for $11,978.84 was not included.*[749]

The financial records of Rebozo and the President show no reimbursement of this expenditure to Rebozo by President Nixon through May 31, 1973.

747. See Exhibit 000 for copies of receipts.
748. Interview of Robert Little, June 1, 1974, p. 1.
749. See exhibits 00 and 00 for description of work in on invoice.

Putting Green at 516 Bay Lane—$243.57. The Bartlett Construction Company installed an "Arnold Palmer Putting Green" at President Nixon's 516 Bay Lane property. The bill submitted amounting to $243.57 was paid by Rebozo's personal check (account #1-34) on June 17, 1969.[750] Again, records reviewed by the staff do not reflect reimbursement by the President to Mr. Rebozo for this expenditure.

The President's Payments for Work on his Key Biscayne Properties—$76,053.02. While the preceding payments represent amounts paid by Rebozo in 1969 for work on the President's properties, he continued to oversee and ordered other work to be done at the President's homes. Payments were made for these other expenses from the personal account of the President in the Key Biscayne Bank. In most of these instances, an advice of charge, authorized by Rebozo, was made against the President's account for a cashier's check or Key Biscayne Bank check issued to the supplier or contractor.[751] In two instances, a personal check was drawn on the President's account. (These payments, all of which were charged to the President's account #2-527 in the Key Biscayne Bank are shown above on page 560.) Rebozo was, therefore, in a position to charge the President's bank account for any expenditures affecting the President's properties.[752]

The Wakefield Trust Accounts. Within the ten months following the 1968 election, Rebozo paid expenses of the President totalling $17,091.86 with cash or with checks charged to Rebozo's account. Within the three months following the 1972 campaign, Rebozo paid for $28,529.29 of expenses incurred on the President's behalf from funds concealed in trust accounts under the control of Rebozo's attorney, Thomas H. Wakefield.

In mid-November of 1972, Jack Brown, an employee of the Key Biscayne Bank and Trust Company who is regularly used as an agent by Rebozo, ordered from J. H. Clagett, Inc. a general contractor, the extension of the existing roof at 500 Bay Lane to cover the patio.[753] At that time, Brown, acting on the instructions of Rebozo, represented himself to be an agent of the President.[754] On November 17, 1972, an application for a building permit was filed with the Metropolitan Dade County Building and Zoning board in the name

750. See exhibits 00 and 00 for copy of billing and check.
751. See interviews of Arthur Blech, the President's accountant.
752. *Ibid.*
753. See Brown Executive Session, 00, p. 00 and Clagett interview, June 14, 1974, p. 12.
754. *Ibid.*, p. 13.

of Charles G. Rebozo for 500 Bay Lane.[755] Rebozo's name was subsequently crossed out and the name of Richard M. Nixon written above it.[756] On November 24, 1972, $10,000 in $100 bills were deposited to the Thomas H. Wakefield Trust Account (#05-791-19) at the First National Bank of Miami on behalf of Rebozo.[757] This trust account had remained inactive from October 31, 1968 to November 24, 1972 with a balance of $76.24.[758] On November 30, 1972, J. H. Clagett, Inc. submitted an invoice for $6,508.11 to Jack Brown at the Key Biscayne Bank and Trust Company as a "bill for Rebozo Compound."[759] On December 7, 1972, Thomas H. Wakefield, representing C. G. Rebozo, drew a check to J. H. Clagett, Inc. for $6,508.11 against the account in which $10,000 was deposited two weeks previously in the Thomas H. Wakefield Trust Account.[760] There is no record of any reimbursement for this expense to Rebozo by the President.

Thomas H. Wakefield is a signator on the following accounts:

BANK	NAME OF ACCOUNT	ACCOUNT NUMBER	DATE OPENED
First National Bank of Miami	1. Wakefield, Hewitt and Webster Trust Account	11-611-1	5/18/70
	2. Wakefield and Underwood Trust Account	6-681-1	
	3. Thomas H. Wakefield Trust Account	05-791-9	6/24/47
Key Biscayne Bank and Trust Company	4. Wakefield, Hewitt and Webster Trust Account	1-673	Not available
	5. Thomas H. Wakefield Special Account	2-691	4/15/69
	6. Wakefield, Hewitt and Webster Special Account	1-067	Not available

Testimony and documents received by the Committee indicate that Rebozo, as a client of Wakefield, has had transactions related to at least five of these trust accounts.[761] Thomas Wakefield refused to produce any records relating to transactions on behalf of Rebozo or of the President in his trust

755. See Exhibit 00.
756. *Ibid.*
757. See Wakefield interview, 00, p. 00 and Exhibit 00.
758. *Ibid.*
759. See Exhibit 00.
760. See Wakefield interview, 00, p. 00 and Exhibit 00.
761. See Thomas H. Wakefield Executive Session, documents attached as exhibits from the Wakefield, Hewitt, and Webster Trust Account.

accounts on the grounds of attorney-client privilege.[762] He
also invoked this privilege in response to questions regarding
these transactions during an Executive Session of the Committee, although he did provide some information at interviews.[763] Rebozo refused the Committee's request that he
waive the attorney-client privilege and allow Wakefield to
explain these transactions. In order to obtain information
regarding these transactions, it has been necessary to serve
subpoenas directly on the banks involved. Although some
records were provided for one account on a previous occasion,
Rebozo, as president of the Key Biscayne Bank and Trust Co.,
failed to produce records for the remaining trust accounts
when they were subpoenaed in October, 1973 and again in
June 1974.[764]

Construction of Swimming Pool and Accessories—
$18,435.18. Rebozo signed a contract with the Catalina Pool
Company of Miami, Florida on November 14, 1972 for a
20′ x 40′ pool to be constructed at President Nixon's residence
at 500 Bay Lane, Key Biscayne.[765] A permit for the construction of this swimming pool was obtained by a representative
of Catalina Pools, Inc., from the Metropolitan Dade County
Board on November 15, 1972.[766] The permit reflects the pool
to hold 31,000 gallons and the cost is estimated to be $9,000.
Construction on the pool began on November 17 and was
completed on November 28, 1972. The documents received
by the Committee indicate that the bills for this work were to
be sent to Wakefield, Hewitt and Webster, attorneys, Miami,
Florida.[767]

The expendiures relating to this pool amounted in the
aggregate to $18,435.18, as follows:[768]

Paid To	For	Amount
Catalina, Inc.	Construction	$10,100.00
Belcher Oil Co.	Pool Heater	1,727.26
Climatrol Inc.	Screening around swimming pool	3,600.00
Paul's Carpets	Pool Carpet	1,277.64
Brown Jordan	Pool Furniture delivered to 478 Bay Lane	1,730.28
	Total	$18,435.18

762. *Ibid.*
763. *Ibid.*
764. See Exhibit 00, Committee Subpoena dated 00.
765. See Exhibit 00 for copy of contract.
766. See Exhibit 00 for Metropolitan Dade County Building Permit Application.
767. See Exhibit 00 for copy of notes of Catalina Pool Co.
768. See discusson below.

The pool bills were paid from the following sources:[769]

Wakefield, Hewitt & Webster — Trust Account
    First National Bank of Miami #11-611-1 .... $14,977.64
    Key Biscayne Bank #1-673 .... 1,727.26
Cash from Rebozo 1,730.28

    Total $18.435.18

The payments to Catalina Pools, Inc., were made from the Wakefield, Hewitt and Webster—Trust Account in the First National Bank of Miami, as follows:

Date	Amount
11-20-72	$ 1,000.00
11-22-72	5,935.00
11-23-72	2,000.00
12-18-72	1,165.00
Total	$10,100.00

Each check has a notation reflecting that the transaction is on behalf of C. G. Rebozo.[770] Wakefield also indicated that Rebozo was his client in the case of each check. Ann Harvey, Herbert Kalmbach's secretary, stated that in the summer or fall of 1972, she received an inquiry from Mr. Rebozo asking for specification of the pool that had been constructed at the President's San Clemente estate.[771]

Pool Heater. Documents, obtained pursuant to a subpoena duces tecum on the Belcher Oil Company, indicate that Mr. Rebozo ordered a heater for the President's pool at 500 Bay Lane on or about November 15, 1972. The heater was paid for on February 20, 1973 by a check in the amount of $1,727.26 drawn on funds in the Wakefield, Hewitt and Webster Trust Account #1-673, located at the Key Biscayne Bank. The check has a notation on it "invoice dated 1/31/73 — Rebozo, C. G."[772]

The committee has not been furnished with the details of this Trust Account #1-673 since Mr. Rebozo, who was served with a subpoena in his capacity as President of the Key Biscayne Bank, has refused to comply with a subpoena duces

769. See Exhibits 00 through 00.
770. See Exhibit 00 for copy of checks issued to Catalina Pool. E.g., 11/20/72 check has notation "deposit on swimming pool contract for 500 Bay Lane, Key Biscayne, Florida; REBOZO, C.G." and the file # in Mr. Wakefield's office for Rebozo.
771. See interview of Ann Harvey, p. 00.
772. See Exhibits 00 and 00 of the Belcher Oil Company and the check in payment of the pool heater.

tecum. The Committee, however, received evidence that substantial amounts on behalf of Rebozo have been deposited in this account including at least $3,500 in $100 bills.[773] Wakefield indicated the Key Biscayne Trust involved significantly greater sums related to Rebozo than his trust account at the First National Bank. Wakefield estimated deposits through his Key Biscayne Bank trust account on behalf of Rebozo of approximately $200,000.[774]

Screen Enclosure at Pool. The evidence in possession of the Committee reflects that on or about November 16, 1972, Mr. Charles G. Rebozo ordered from Climatrol Corporation a "screen enclosure installed at 500 Bay Lane, Key Biscayne, Florida."[775] Rebozo requested plans for the screens to be provided for the President's review at Camp David, Maryland.[776] Payments to Climatrol Corporation were made as follows:

Date	Bank	Account Number	Amount
12/22/72	First National Bank of Miami	11-611-1	$1,500[777]
12/22/72	First National Bank of Miami	05-791-9	$1,100
12/28/72	First National Bank of Miami	05-791-9	$1,000[778]

It will be noted that the first check was drawn on the Wakefield, Hewitt & Webster—Trust Account while the remaining checks were drawn on the Thomas H. Wakefield Trust Account. Thus, Climatrol was paid $3,600 in three checks signed by Thomas H. Wakefield on two different trust accounts that he used to pay for work ordered by Rebozo.

With respect to the payment of $1,500 on December 22, 1972, it is noted that Rebozo's funds in Trust Account 11-611-1 were overdrawn on December 18, 1972 in the amount of $100. On December 22, 1972, currency amounting to $1,600 was deposited, which cured the overdraft and provided the funds for the $1,500 check to Climatrol. The deposit of cash funds in the law firm trust accounts and subsequent issue of checks from said trust accounts concealed the fact that cash payments furnished by Rebozo were provided to pay for work on behalf of President Nixon. As indicated before, this method of payment was totally unnecessary since checks could have been written on the President's Key Biscayne

773. See Wakefield interview, 6/24/74, p. 2.
774. *Ibid.*, p. 3.
775. See invoice of Climatrol Corporation as Exhibits 00 and 00.
776. Interview of Lee Latham, Climatrol salesman; May 17, 1974; p. 1.
777. See Exhibit 00 for copy of check #172 referred to above which has on the face of it the words "Rebozo, C. G."
778. See Exhibit 00 for copy of related checks.

accounts or debit memos drawn against these same accounts by the Presidents' lawyers who had been assigned that role.

Pool Carpet. The payment of $1,277.64 was made to Paul's Carpet, Inc., by check dated December 8, 1972 signed by Thomas H. Wakefield and drawn on his Trust account in the First National Bank of Miami.[779] This check was for work ordered by Rebozo on November 21, 1972 which was to provide for the installation of 182 yards of green grass, 100% polypropelene, for Cementing at the pool at the President's home at 500 Bay Lane. Mr. Rebozo was billed at the Key Biscayne Bank for this expense.

Pool Furniture. Documents received by the Committee indicate that Mr. Rebozo on January 26, 1973 ordered furniture for the "pool area" to be delivered to "Mr. Robert H. Abplanalp, 478 Bay Lane, Key Biscayne, Florida." [780] Interviews and testimony before the Committee, however, indicate that while Mr. Abplanalp is the owner of the property at 478 Bay Lane, he immediately leased it after purchase to the U.S. government and this property does not have a pool.[781] In addition, Mr. Fabergas, an interior designer for the BBA Architectural firm and Mr. Steve Morrison, Assistant Sales Manager for the Brown-Jordan Company, who supplied the furniture at a cost of $1,730.28, stated to the Committee that Mrs. Nixon insisted that the fabric of the furniture match exactly with the fabric of the Presidential pool furniture, which had been purchased for the San Clemente property.[782]

The Committee has ascertained that Rebozo paid the BBA Architectural firm for expenditures made to Brown-Jordan Company deposits directly to their account at the Key Biscayne Bank.[783] The first deposit was made in the BBA account on February 1, 1973 in the amount of $1,519.50. The second payment was disclosed to the BBA firm in a letter dated February 20, 1973 from Mr. Rebozo's bookkeeper, who enclosed a deposit ticket from Mr. Rebozo to the firm's account for $210.78. The deposit tickets and letter reflect the initials "CGR" and $210.78 was deposited in cash.[784] The BBA firm did not have in their files the deposit ticket for the $1,519.50, and, in an effort to determine if that deposit was also made in cash, a subpoena duces tecum was served on Mr. Rebozo but he has refused to comply with the subpoena.

779. See Exhibit 00 for copy of related check.
780. Exhibit 00 is an order form for the furniture from BBA Architectural firm.
781. See interviews of Mr. Purdue.
782. See interviews of Fabergas and Morrison of 000.
783. See Exhibit 00.
784. See Exhibit 00.

Summary of Wakefield Trust Account Payments. A composite summary of the transactions relating to the construction of the pool and extension of the roof at 500 Bay Lane as noted in the two Trust Account records received from the First National Bank of Miami disclose the following:

Item	Amount
Total currency deposited	$23,500.00
Payments to	
Catalina Pools Inc.	$10,100.00
J. B. Clagett, Inc.	6,508.11
Paul's Carpets Inc.	1,277.64
Climatrol	3,600.00
Belcher Oil Co.	356.25
	$21,842.00
Funds transferred to	
Wakefield, Hewitt & Webster	
Trust Account #1-673 in	
Key Biscayne Bank	$ 2,255.52
Total disbursements	24,097.52
Excess disbursed from	
Firm-Trust Account 11-611	(597.52)
Funds in Firm-Trust Accounts	
#05-791-9 from Oct. 31, 1968	
to October 31, 1972	76.24
Balance of excess disbursements	$ (521.28)

It is noted that the trust account #05-791-19 in the name of Thomas H. Wakefield, contains only transactions relating to Rebozo's activities. However, the trust account #11-611-1 in the firm's name is utilized by the law firm for more clients than just Rebozo.

The Currency amounting to $23,500 was deposited on Rebozo's behalf to trust accounts as follows:

Date	Amount	Account Number
Nov. 16, 1972	$10,000	11-611-1
Nov. 24, 1972	10,000	05-791-8
Dec. 22, 1972	1,600	11-611-1
Jan. 25, 1973	200	11-611-1
Apr. 4, 1973	1,700	05-791-9
Total	$23,500	

Other currency deposited in the Trust accounts as revealed
from the records furnished by The First National Bank of
Miami and per interview of Thomas H. Wakefield are as
follows:

Account	Date	Amount
In First National Bank of Miami		
Wakefield, Hewitt & Webster-	7/21/72	$3,500.00
Trust Account, 11-611-1	7/2/73	2,150.00
		5,650.00
In Key Biscayne Bank		
Wakefield, Hewitt & Webster-	not	
Trust Account, 1-673	known	3,500.00
	Total	$9,150.00

Accordingly at least $32,650 in currency has been de-
posited in three trust accounts on behalf of Rebozo.

According to Thomas H. Wakefield, the currency deposited
as indicated above consisted of $100 bills.[785] Wakefield in-
voked attorney-client privilege as to the source of the funds
and indicated that his client was Rebozo.[786]. However, Wakefield has stated that he never deposited currency on behalf
of any client other than Rebozo.[787] The currency received by
Rebozo from Richard Danner, representative of Howard
Hughes, and at least half of that from A. D. Davis consisted
of $100 bills.

Furthermore, Rebozo reported in his September 1972 financial statement a total of $12,234.72 cash on hand and in
unrestricted bank accounts of which $2,453.78 is the balance
in Rebozo's six bank accounts.[788] According therefore to
Rebozo's own figures currency on hand would be approximately $9,780.94.[789]

Rebozo's only known source of currency during this period
was his bank salary for the months of September, October
and two weeks in November 1972. The cash he received from
this source amounted to $3,844.80 and *assuming he spent no
part of it*, the full amount is being included in this computa-
tion as being available to Rebozo. Rebozo did not during this

785. Interview of Thomas H. Wakefield, June 1, 1974; p. 2, June 24, 1974,
p. 2.
786. Mr. Wakefield did state that $21,600 in $100 bills deposited in the
First National Bank trusts were on behalf of Mr. Rebozo; *Ibid.*
787. Wakefield interview June 24, 1974, p. 2.
788. See Affidavit of Carmine Bellino.
789. *Ibid.*

period or at any time since January 1, 1969 draw a check to cash for his own use nor is there any indication that he received currency from business transaction. Therefore, Rebozo had a maximum of $13,665.74 in currency on hand at the November 15, 1972 salary date which was just prior to the deposit of $20,000 in currency in the Wakefield Trust Accounts. According to Rebozo's testimony and financial records made available to the Committee, Rebozo did not have sufficient funds available on November 16 and November 24, 1972 at which time he made two ten thousand dollar ($10,000) cash deposits. These funds, amounting to $20,000 were subsequently used for the President's behalf.

A summary of information available to the Committee pertaining to the above analysis follows:

Cash on hand and in unrestricted bank accounts per financial statement of C. G. Rebozo, at Sept. 1, 1972		$12,234.72
Balance in Rebozo bank accounts at Sept. 1, 1972:		
Acct. 1-34		
In Key Biscayne Bank	1,241.61	
Acct. 1-262		
In Key Biscayne Bank	70.97	
Acct. 4-4179		
In Key Biscayne Bank	472.56	
Acct. 1-0886		
In Key Biscayne Bank	7.08	
Acct. 4 In Greater Miami		
Fed. S. & Loan	461.56	
Acct. 5-28170 In Mfrs. Hanover	200.00	
Total cash in banks		2,453.78
Currency on hand, Aug. 31, 1972		9,780.94
Currency from Salary Payments		
September 15, 1972	776.96	
September 30, 1972	776.96	
October 15, 1972	776.96	
October 31, 1972	776.96	
November 15, 1972	776.96	
Total currency, assuming none spent		3,884.80
Cash available at Nov. 15, 1972....		13,665.74

572

Deposit in Wakefield, Hewitt & Webster Trust Account, First Nat'l Bank of Miami, Account #11-611-1, Nov. 16, 1972, in currency	$10,000.00
Deposit in Thomas H. Wakefield Trust Account, First Nat'l Bank of Miami, in currency, Account #05-791-9, Nov. 24, 1972	10,000.00
Total Currency Payments	$20,000.00
Currency used in excess of currency from known sources	($6,334.26)

An additional analysis using earlier records also shows a shortage of currency.

Rebozo reported in his September 1971 financial statement a total of $47,520.49 cash on hand and in unrestricted bank accounts. His bank balances were in excess of this amount and therefore, no currency was reported by Rebozo as being on hand as of September 1, 1971.[790] Rebozo's only known source of currency from September 1, 1971 through November 30, 1972 was his bank salary. During this period, Rebozo received $23,246.52 in currency for his bank account never issued any checks or debits from which currency was derived for his use. Assuming that Rebozo spent no part of his salary other than what he deposited, he had only $12,446.52 in currency from known sources (other than campaign funds) available to him during a period when he deposited $23,500 in the Wakefield Trust accounts on the President's behalf. Therefore, Rebozo must have had available to him at least $11,053.48 from some previously undisclosed source at a time when he had access to currency derived from campaign contributions.[791]

The information is summarized below:

Cash on hand and in bank at September 1, 1971 per financial statement	$47,520.49
Currency (All of above is accounted for in banks)	none

790. See Exhibits 00.
791. See Bellino affidavit, p. 00. Also note that according to an Intangible Personal Property report filed by Rebozo with the State of Florida, as of January 1, 1972, he declared cash on hand of $1000.00.

Currency received as a salary from Key Biscayne Bank from September 1, 1971 to November 30, 1972	$23,246.52
Currency deposited during above period	10,800.00
Currency available from known sources	12,446.52
Currency payments for President Nixon's Properties in Key Biscayne	23,500.00
Currency used in excess of available currency from known sources	($11,053.48)

These two analyses indicate that Rebozo had some previously undisclosed source of currency from which he drew funds on the President's behalf. According to his testimony and records, the only such source of currency available to him were campaign contributions.

Rebozo's Financial Situation. According to documents available to the Committee, a substantial percentage of Rebozo's reported gross income went for the payment of interest on loans. A study of Mr. Rebozo's financial statements covering the period from September 1, 1968 to September 1, 1973, reflects a constant borrowing of funds from various banks and individuals in Dade County and also outside of Florida. His principal assets include stock in the Key Biscayne Bank and Fisher's Island, Inc.

Rebozo's total interest payments on loans during the five year period amounted to almost one-half million dollars while his reported gross income during this period averaged to only $24,000 a year above his itemized deductions.[792] Therefore, a considerable portion of his reported gross earnings, averaging approximately 72%, went to the payments of interest on Rebozo's loans.

No Record of Pool Costs in President's Books. Although at least $18,435.19 was expended in connection with the swimming pool on the President's property at 500 Bay Lane, no record whatsoever appeared in 1972 or the 1973 accounting books of the President maintained by Arthur Blech, the President's certified public accountant.[793] However, when Blech

792. Documentation for the above analysis may be found in the Committee's files. The Committee did not feel it appropriate to reveal extensive personal financial data.
793. See Arthur Blech interview of 00, p. 00.

was reviewing the accounts in early 1974, in connection with the preparation of the President's 1973 income tax return, he found a check, signed by Rose Mary Woods—the first she had ever signed on the President's account.[794]

The check was dated August 18, 1973 and was of further interest because it was payable to Mr. Rebozo, in the amount of $13,642.52. Blech noted also that the check was typewritten and that two different typewriters had been used since the typing on the check. As he had no idea what this check could have been for, he posted the item to Account 999—Suspense. Thereafter, he inquired of Harvey and Frank De Marco and learned the payment was for the construction of a swimming pool which had occurred in December, 1972, and the check to Rebozo for $13,642.52 dated August 18, 1973 was a reimbursement for payments he had made.[795]

It is of interest to note that at the time of issue of this check in August 1973, Rebozo had returned $100,000 to Hughes, was under active investigation by the Internal Revenue Service and the staff of the Committee was indicating interest in the Hughes contribution.

The Fireplace. Other documents received by the Committee indicate that Rebozo ordered the construction of a fireplace for the President's home at 516 Bay Lane[796] and instructed the contractor, J. H. Clagett, Inc., that the billing should be sent to Thomas H. Wakefield.[797] The records received from Clagett indicate that the bill of $3,586 was paid on March 26, 1973, but Clagett has been unable to provide the form of the payment, i.e., whether it was cash deposited in his Key Biscayne Bank account or whether it may have been a Wakefield Trust Account check. This item was not paid from the President's bank accounts; nor was it paid from Rebozo's bank accounts furnished to the Committee.[798]

The Committee attempted to determine how payment was made by service of a subpoena on Mr. Charles G. Rebozo as President of the Key Biscayne Bank but he has failed to comply with the subpoena.

The Pool Table. The Committee has also received documents and information that Mr. Rebozo paid $1,138.30 by personal check on March 19, 1970 to William Brandt's Billiard Supply Company for a "pool table" order by Mr. Rebozo at 490 Bay Lane.[799] This pool table has a gold

794. *Ibid.*
795. Arthur Blech interview.
796. Exhibit 00 reflects copy of estimate furnished for construction.
797. J. H. Clagett interview;
798. See Bellino affidavit, p. 000.
799. Exhibit 00 is copy of billing from Brandt's. See Bellino affadavit.

covering.[800] However, Mr. James Perdue, who assisted in the work being done on the President's properties home at 490 Bay Lane, stated there is a pool table in President Nixon's home at 516 Bay Lane and his description of this cover was identical to the one ordered by Rebozo as described above.[801]

Fuel Oil Payments. In addition to the payments to Belcher Oil Company for the pool heater, three payments were made to them from the two trust accounts in the First National Bank of Miami as follows:

Date	Amount
1/25/73	138.50
4/24/73	75.88
5/16/73	141.87

These checks are in payment of fuel oil delivered to the President's home at 500 Bay Lane and believed to have been used in the pool heater mentioned above.[802]

More recent invoices included as exhibits, for example the invoice of June 29, 1973, indicate billings to Key Biscayne Bank for work performed at the President's home on 500 Bay Lane. Indeed, exhibit 00 includes a copy of a cashier's check signed by Vernon L. Tucker, an officer of the Key Biscayne Bank, in the amount of $38.16 payable to the Belcher Oil Co. The space provided for the remitter was not filled in, and thereby does not disclose who furnished the funds for the purchase of the cashier's check.

The Florida Nixon for President Committee Account. Rebozo maintained an account in the Key Biscayne Bank in the name of The Florida Nixon for President Committee account #1-0455. Although efforts have been made to obtain a copy of this account and Rebozo promised to furnish a copy of the account to the Committee, he has failed to do so. Rebozo was a signator to this account and at least $426.87 was used from this campaign fund for the personal benefit of President Nixon. February 19, 1969 Rebozo issued his own check in this amount of $426.87 to reimburse the campaign account.[803] The check stub for check number 3867 reads "Reim. of various bills advanced for RMN, Pers."

On April 14, 1969, Rebozo issued check #1150, against funds in the Florida Nixon for President Committee account, payable to Herbert W. Kalmbach in the amount of $216.18.

800. Interview with Mrs. Brandt; June 4, 1974; p. 1, See Exhibit 00.
801. See Perdue interview.
802. See Exhibits 00, 00, and 00 for copies of checks and bills.
803. See Bellino affidavit.

Part of these funds were subsequently used to pay expenses of Jack Caulfield, who conducted special investigatory work for John Ehrlichman.

The following day, Rebozo issued a check for $6,000 payable to Thomas H. Wakefield—Special Account, drawn on the Florida Nixon for President Committee, and thereupon opened a new account, the Thomas H. Wakefield—Special Account #2-1691 in the Key Biscayne Bank.[804] The signators were Thomas H. Wakefield and Charles G. Rebozo,[805]—with either *one* authorized to sign. No address was shown for the mailing of statements—the only notation being "Hold Statements."[806]

Rebozo has testified that the $6,000 represented funds that were owed to him for "one thing or another." He further testified that he was "worried about how it might look" if he wrote a check to himself. He testified that he created this special account in his attorney's name and wrote a check to it in order to receive the funds "without drawing them to attention."[807]

Rebozo continued to sign all checks or authorized charges until the final closing of this account. The funds in this account were disbursed by Rebozo in the same manner as he handled the funds in the Florida Nixon for President Committee account except that now the nature of the funds i.e. campaign funds, was concealed through the use of said special account.

Disbursements from this account were as follows:

Date	Paid to	Amount	Remarks
May 6, 1969	Herbert W. Kalmbach	$ 200.00	Subsequently paid to Jack Caulfield
May 23, 1969	Bank charge for checks	4.66	
May 29, 1969	Pitney-Bowes Inc.	124.80	Invoice # 65-182408
July 25, 1969	Herbert W. Kalmbach	1,000.00	Subsequently paid to Tony Ulasewicz
Sept. 10, 1969	Thunderbird Studio	108.16	Balance due, pictures at reception of President Nixon
June 28, 1972	Wakefield, Hewitt & Webster Trust Acct. # 1-673	4,562.38	Use discussed below
		$6,000.00	

804. Wakefield was not aware of this account until Rebozo told him *after* it was opened. Wakefield was not aware of the source of the funds originally deposited in this account. See Wakefield Executive Session, p. 44.
805. See Exhibit 00 for signator card.
806. See Exhibit 00 for statements.
807. See Rebozo Executive Session, March 20, 1973, p. 27. Rebozo agreed to produce the Florida Nixon for President Commitee records supporting his statement but as mentioned above later refused to produce them for the Committeee.

Rebozo has refused a Committee request that he provide documents showing the purpose of the original transfer of $6,000.00 of campaign funds to the Thomas H. Wakefield Special Account.

It will be noted that this special account, derived from 1968 campaign funds, maintained a balance of $4,562.38 for almost three years. On June 28, 1972, Rebozo closed it out by transferring the funds through an advice of charge[808] to the Wakefield, Hewitt & Webster Trust Account #1-673 in the Key Biscayne Bank. The same day, a check was issued for $5,000 against account 1-673, and the proceeds of this check were deposited in the Wakefield, Hewitt & Webster Trust Account #11-611-1 in the First National Bank of Miami.[809] Also on the same day, a check was issued from this account purchasing a Cashier's Check from the First National Bank of Miami, payable to Harry Winston in the amount of $5,000.[810] These funds were used to purchase platinum diamond earrings, a birthday gift to Mrs. Nixon from President Nixon, as indicated hereinafter.

Purchase of Earrings for Mrs. Nixon from Harry Winston. The records of Harry Winston, a jeweler in New York City, reflect that on March 17, 1972, a set of platinum diamond earrings containing

> *"Tops*
> 16 Pear shape diamonds
>
> *Bottoms*
> 2 Pear shape diamonds
> 2 Tapered baguette diamonds"

were delivered to Lieutenant Commander Alex Larzelere who was then attached to the White House staff. The consignment slip of March 17, 1972, indicates in handwriting "Rose Mary" in the upper left hand corner. Lieutenant Commander Larzelere delivered the earrings to his superior at the White House and was told that they were for President Nixon's gift to his wife on her birthday.[811] On the copies of the bills addressed

808. Exhibit 00 is a copy of the advice of chargee of June 28, 1972, which transferred the $54,562.38 from the Wakefield Special Account in the Key Biscayne Bank to the Wakefield, Hewitt & Webster Trust Account, in the First National Bank.
809. Exhibit 00 is a copy of the deposit ticket reflecting that transaction.
810. Exhibit 00 is a copy of the check which purchased the cashier check to Harry Winston.
811. Exhibit 00 reflects records of Harry Winston and the purchase of $5,000 earrings. Winstons' records further reflect that the earrings were ordered on the President's account and that a bill was sent to President Richard M. Nixon at the White House which was delivered by hand by a salesman who

to President Richard Nixon is indicated in handwriting of the salesman, "please send to Rose Mary Woods."

The full cost of these earrings is shown as $5,650, with payment being made as follows according to Harry Winston's records:

President Richard M. Nixon	$5,000
First National Bank of Miami	
President Richard M. Nixon	560
Riggs National Bank	
Rosemary Woods	90
First National Bank of Washington	
	$5,650

The $5,000 check, as previously stated, was a cashiers check drawn on the First National Bank of Miami and derived from the Wakefield, Hewitt & Webster, Trust Account #11-611-1 in the First National Bank. The funds in this account were transferred from the Wakefield firm Trust Account #1-673 in the Key Biscayne Bank and $4,562.38 was received by the firm Trust Account from the Thomas Wakefield-Special Account #2-1691 in the Key Biscayne Bank. The funds in the special account were derived from the Florida Nixon for President Committee. Therefore, $4,562.33 of funds originally derived from campaign contributions were used to purchase platinum diamond earrings.

This complex four stage process of payment for this gift, concealed the fact that the funds originated from contributions to the 1968 campaign and were ultimately used by Rebozo on behalf of President Nixon.

President Nixon Beneficiary of Loan Note Signed by C. G. Rebozo. The examination of the President's assets and liabilities dated August 20, 1973, by the accounting firm of Coopers and Lybrand noted that the President had purchased property at 500 Bay Lane, Key Biscayne, Florida "consisting of land, building and furnishings" on December 19, 1968 from Senator George A. Smathers for $125,000. Their report also noted the President had purchased land at 516 Bay Lane for $127,928 and the down payments for these properties came from the proceeds of a loan obtained in the amount of $65,000 on December 19, 1968 from the First National Bank of Miami.

---

is now deceased. See also interview of Lt. Cdr. Alex Larzelere; June 19, 1974; p. 1. Mrs. Nixon, in fact, had her 60th birthday on March 17, 1972. See *Who's Who*, Inc., 1972, p. 374.

When President Nixon acquired the Key Biscayne properties, he assumed the existing mortgages and a note for $65,000 which was executed by C. G. Rebozo with the First National Bank of Miami. This note was dated December 19, 1968, payable 32 days later at 7% interest.[812] The proceeds of this note were used to pay the owners of the property as follows:

Paid to	Amount
Senator & Mrs. George A. Smathers	$43,497.00
Manuel Arca, Jr. & Evora Bonet de Arca	20,243.00
Closing expenditures	643.00
	64,383.00
Cash remitted to President Nixon	617.00
Total	$65.000.00

Wakefield stated that Rebozo paid him legal fees incurred for the purchase of 500 and 516 Bay Lane and he considered Rebozo to be his client for said purchase.[813]

This transaction handled by Rebozo not only provided the President with the Key Biscayne properties without the investment of any funds on his part (in fact the President received $617) but the obligation on the $65,000 note was accepted by C. G. Rebozo. In this connection, the liability ledger includes this $65,000 loan in the name of Richard M. and Patricia R. Nixon,[814] while the demand tickler sheet was in the name of C. G. Rebozo.[815]

Although this loan was due January 20, 1969, it was on that date made a demand loan and was not paid until September 4, 1969. On that date Mr. Richard Stearns, Senior Vice-President of the Key Biscayne Bank forwarded a Cashier's Check charged to the President's account in the Key Biscayne Bank with letter reading as follows:

"Enclosed you will find our Cashier's Check No. 10864 in the amount of $65,763.75 of which $65,000 is payment on the principal note of Mr. C. G. Rebozo and $763.75 for interest."[816]

In the report of the Joint Committee on Internal Revenue Taxation on their examination of President Nixon's tax returns, evidence was adduced that on March 12, 1973 the sum of $65,000 was transferred to the President's account to Mr. Rebozo as a three year loan payable to Mrs. Patricia Cox at

812. Exhibit 00 is a copy of the note referred to.
813. Wakefield interview; June 25, 1974; p. 00.
814. See Exhibit 00 for liability ledger sheet.
815. See Exhibit 00 for demand tickler file.
816. See Exhibit 00 for copy of letter dated September 4, 1969.

8% interest. This amount was part of the proceeds of the sale of property on December 28, 1972, which property had been acquired by the President from Cape Florida Development, Inc.

While the Committee has been unable to determine, based on documents received to date, if the transfer of $65,000 to Mr. Rebozo on March 12, 1973 was related in any way to the note Mr. Rebozo signed on behalf of President Nixon for $65,000, the Committee's letter to Mr. St. Clair of June 6, 1974, asked for any information or documents from the President which might clarify any relationship between the two transactions. The letter inquired, "The Committee would appreciate learning under what circumstances Mr. Rebozo incurred the above described obligation(referring to the signing of the note) and what if any, consideration he received for incurring said obligation." At noted below, the Committee received a response to its letter from counsel St. Clair which failed to respond to any of the specific issues raised by the Committee's inquiry.[817]

Summary of Total Payments on Behalf of President Nixon. A summary of the payments made by Rebozo on behalf of the President as disclosed from documents and interviews discussed herein reflects a pattern of Rebozo expenditures of at least $50,000. The Committee has obviously not been able to identify conclusively all the payments made by Rebozo as the pertinent records desired from Rebozo and his Biscayne Bank & Trust Company, have never been produced and Rebozo has refused to comply with subpoenas duces tecum served on him. Any further investigations by other investigatory bodies should focus initially on obtaining the trust account records from the Key Biscayne Bank that this Committee has been unable to obtain.

$20,000 Cash Funds in Rebozo's Possession—September, 1969. Since 1964, Rebozo has followed the practice of preparing and mailing to banks from whom he has received loans, a financial statement as of September 1 of each year, showing his assets, liabilities, net worth and other financial data.

Of interest in connection with his September 1, 1969, financial statement is the fact that he included therein cash on hand of $20,000. As the evidence tended to show, this is the month during which Richard Danner delivered a $50,000 campaign contribution from Howard Hughes to Bebe Rebozo.

817. Exhibit 1 is a copy of the letter to Mr. St. Clair of June 6, 1974.

Specifically, the financial statement executed on Oct. 9, 1969 and mailed to the Manufacturers-Hanover Trust Company[818] showing his assets, liabilities, and net worth as of Sept. 1, 1969 includes as "cash, on hand and unrestricted in banks, $23,741.36."

Rebozo's checking account #1-34 in the Key Biscayne Bank shows a balance as of September 1, 1969 of $3,741.36. The difference between the amount in the bank ($3,741.36) and the amount shown on his financial statement, ($23,741.-36) is $20,000, which sum would have to be currency. It is of interest to note that the following year, September 1, 1970, Rebozo's financial statement shows "Cash on hand and unrestricted in banks, $44,691.20." [819] This amount agrees to the penny with the balance in Rebozo's bank account #1-34 at the Key Biscayne Bank.

When questioned at Executive session on March 21, 1974[820] Rebozo denied the $20,000 represented cash. Stated funds in a savings account in a bank in Key West were included in his cash. However, the documentation he forwarded to us does not support his statement since the amount in the savings account of the First Federal Savings & Loan of Key West, Florida is in the name of Monroe Land and Title Co. and the balance is less than $2,000.[821]

When questioned on March 21, 1974, Rebozo also denied that the $20,000 was cash that Richard Danner had brought to him as part of the Hughes contribution.

In addition, Rebozo was asked at his Executive Session if he ever had a sum of $50,000 in cash since January 1, 1969 to which Rebozo answered, "No, I never had that much cash, not deposited."[822] Mr. Rebozo was also questioned as to whether he had ever loaned any money to the President since January 1, 1969, and answered, "I haven't but the bank has. Wait a minute, not since January of 1969, though." [823] Rebozo was also asked, "And have you ever given any gifts of cash or stock or any other negotiable commodity of value in excess of $1,000 to the President?" Mr. Rebozo answered, "No." Rebozo was also asked, "Have you ever cashed any checks in excess of $10,000 in the President's behalf for cash?" and again Rebozo answered "No."[824]

In addition to the expenditures already commented upon, Rebozo's personal bank records furnished to the Committee,

818. Exhibit 00 is a copy of the financial statement referred to.
819. Exhibit 00.
820. See pp. 8-10 Rebozo Executive Session, March 21, 1974.
821. See Exhibit 00 for details in pass book.
822. Rebozo Exec. Session, p. 8, March 21, 1974.
823. Rebozo Ex. Session p. 56, March 21, 1974.
824. Rebozo Ex. Session, p. 56, March 21, 1974.

reveal he issued personal checks for a variety of expenses incurred on President Nixon's Key Biscayne properties between January 24, 1969 and May 12, 1970, which checks total $832.32[825] Of this sum, Rebozo's records reflect he received one reimbursement from the President, in the amount of $127.77 on February 14, 1969. The records maintained by the President's accountant reviewed by the Committee also reflects that the President had made only one reimbursement of $127.77 through May 31, 1973.

The President's Response. In a letter of June 6, 1974, Chairman Ervin and Vice-Chairman Baker furnished most of the above described information to Mr. James St. Clair, Counsel to the President. The letter noted as its purpose that:

> The Committee has received certain evidence that may relate to information and documents in posession of the President or his representatives. We wish to afford the President an opportunity to comment on this material prior to the filing of this report. We would appreciate any assistance you can provide in clarifying the issues set forth below and in aiding us in reviewing of this evidence. Information provided will be especially helpful in those areas where the Committee has not had access to all available documents, and where systematic analysis has been impossible since only random documentation has been provided us.[826]

On June 24, 1974, the Committee received a response to its letter from Mr. St. Clair in behalf of the President. After characterizing the Committee's letter and indicating he had reviewed it with the President on June 20, 1974, Mr. St. Clair makes two general responses:

> "The President has made public an audit of his affairs dated August 20, 1973, certified by Cooper and Lybrand, which he is confident, reflected fully his receipts and expenditures for the period covered.
> I believe that the only useful comment that can be made in response to your letter is to convey the President's assurance that he never instructed C. G. Rebozo to raise and maintain funds to be disbursed for the President's personal behalf, nor so far as he knows was this ever done."[827]

825. See schedule of the payments referred to above in the Committee's files.
826. Exhibit 1 is a copy of the Committee's letter to the President's Counsel, Mr. St. Clair on June 6, 1974.
827. See Exhibit 2 for copy of St. Clair's letter to Senator Ervin and Senator Baker.

As a result, the President through his counsel has failed to respond to any of the specific inquiries delineated in the Committee's letter and, therefore, has not provided information that might assist the Commitee in is review of these matters.

Rebozo's Response. When Mr. Rebozo was questioned at an Executive Session[828] the Committee did not have in its possession information which disclosed Rebozo's substantial expenditures on behalf of President Nixon. He was asked if on occasion he had paid "miscellaneous bills for 500 Bay Lane." Rebozo replied in the affirmative and when he was asked if he had been reimbursed for these expenditures, he answered, "Yes, I say, usually I'm not going to knitpick with the President. If there's something I think he should have, I might just go ahead and do it without even him knowing about it. He just doesn't concern himself at all with financial problems ever; never has."

The Committee has subpoenaed from Rebozo and from the Key Biscayne Bank and Trust Company records of expenditures during the relevant periods paid for on behalf of President Richard Nixon, Rose Mary Woods, F. Donald Nixon, Donald A. Nixon, and Edward Nixon. Rebozo had, both individually and in his capacity as president of the Key Biscayne Bank and Trust Company, refused to produce these records.[829] After the facts discussed above were developed by the Committee, a subpoena was issued for Rebozo's appearance and served on his attorney, thus providing Rebozo with an opportunity to respond. His attorney informed the Committee that Rebozo had left the country and that he was no longer authorized to accept service on Rebozo's behalf.

Other Recipients of Campaign Funds. As noted above, the Committee received evidence that Rebozo advised Kalmbach that he had furnished part of the funds received from Hughes to the President's brothers.

Both F. Donald and Edward Nixon have denied under oath to the Senate Committee, having received any funds or gifts from Mr. Charles G. Rebozo.

The Committee, however, has been unable to make a conclusive determination as to whether Messrs. Edward or F. Donald Nixon received any of the proceeds of the Hughes contribution due to the failure and refusal of both to comply with the subpoena *duces tecum* which sought certain docu-

---

828. Rebozo Executive Session, March 21, 1974, p. 14.
829. See Exhibit ——, subpoenas of the Select Committee dated ——
——, 1974.

ments and records deemed by the Committee pertinent to its inquiry,[830] and to testify after being advised questions would relate to whether either received the proceeds of campaign contributions.

The chart on the following page traces currency and bank funds controlled by C. G. Rebozo and expended for the benefit of President Nixon and others. The figures reflected in the chart do not reflect necessarily all such possible transactions due to Mr. Rebozo's failure to comply fully with subpoenas served on him for records relating to those transactions.

The chart does reflect, however, the flow of cash currency in and out of three trust accounts and a special account, all in the name of Rebozo's attorney, Thomas H. Wakefield. The chart also reflects amounts expended for alterations, additions, and improvements on the President's Key Biscayne properties and for other items purchased in his behalf.

The chart, for example, shows that $6,000 of campaign contributions were deposited in the Florida Nixon for President Committee, which funds were later transferred to the Thomas H. Wakefield Special Account at the Key Biscayne Bank. The chart then shows the flow of $4,562.38 from the Wakefield Special Account to the Wakefield, Hewitt & Webster Trust Account, and on the same date $5,000 was withdrawn from said trust account and deposited in the Wakefield, Hewitt & Webster Trust Account at the First National Bank of Miami. On the same date as that transfer, a cashier's check was purchased at the First National Bank of Miami, which was furnished to Harry Winston, a jeweler in New York, for the purchase of platinum and diamond earrings, furnished by President Nixon to his wife on her birthday in March of 1972.

830. See Exhibits 00 and 00 for copies of subpoena duces tecum served on F. Donald and Edward Nixon for financial records and other documents sought to determine if they had received the proceeds of any cash contributions.

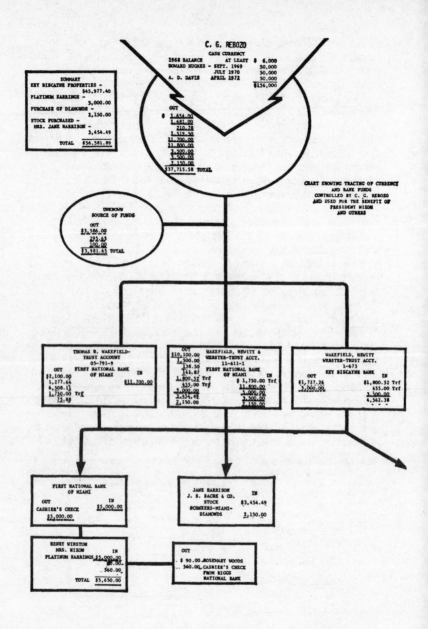

C. G. REBOZO
CASH CURRENCY

1968 BALANCE	AT LEAST	$ 6,000
HOWARD HUGHES – SEPT. 1969		50,000
	JULY 1970	50,000
A. D. DAVIS	APRIL 1972	50,000
		$156,000

SUMMARY
KEY BISCAYNE PROPERTIES – $45,977.40
PLATINUM EARRINGS – 5,000.00
PURCHASE OF DIAMONDS – 2,150.00
STOCK PURCHASED –
MRS. JANE HARRISON – 3,454.49
TOTAL $56,581.89

OUT
$ 1,654.00
1,681.00
210.78
1,519.50
11,700.00
11,800.00
3,500.00
3,500.00
2,150.00
$37,715.58 TOTAL

CHART SHOWING TRACING OF CURRENCY
AND BANK FUNDS
CONTROLLED BY C. G. REBOZO
AND USED FOR THE BENEFIT OF
PRESIDENT NIXON
AND OTHERS

UNKNOWN
SOURCE OF FUNDS
OUT
$3,586.00
295.65
100.00
$3,981.65 TOTAL

THOMAS H. WAKEFIELD–
TRUST ACCOUNT
05-791-9
FIRST NATIONAL BANK
OF MIAMI
OUT   IN
$2,100.00
1,277.64
6,508.13 $11,700.00
1,750.00 Trf
75.89

WAKEFIELD, HEWITT &
WEBSTER–TRUST ACCT.
11-611-1
FIRST NATIONAL BANK
OF MIAMI
OUT
$10,100.00
1,500.00
138.50
141.87
1,800.52 Trf $ 1,750.00 Trf
455.00 Trf   11,800.00
5,000.00   5,000.00
3,454.49   3,500.00
2,150.00   2,150.00

WAKEFIELD, HEWITT
WEBSTER–TRUST ACCT.
1-673
KEY BISCAYNE BANK
OUT   IN
$1,727.26 $1,800.52 Trf
2,000.00   455.00 Trf
             3,500.00
             4,562.38

FIRST NATIONAL BANK
OF MIAMI
OUT   IN
CASHIER'S CHECK $5,000.00
$5,000.00

JANE HARRISON   IN
J. S. BACHE & CO.
STOCK $3,454.49
SCHREZERS–MIAMI–
DIAMONDS   2,150.00

HENRY WINSTON
MRS. NIXON   IN
PLATINUM EARRINGS $5,000.00
                  90.00
                  560.00
TOTAL $5,650.00

OUT
$ 90.00 ROSEMARY WOODS
560.00 CASHIER'S CHECK
FROM RIGGS
NATIONAL BANK

586

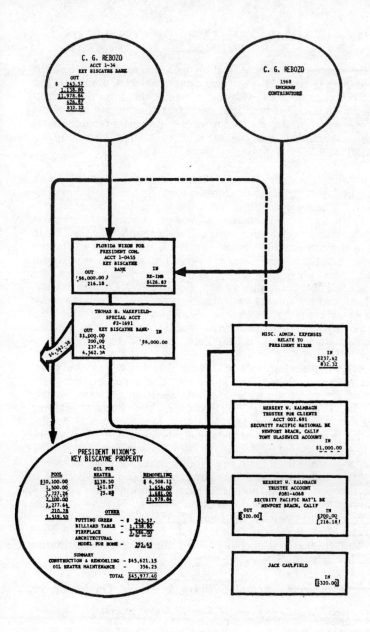

C. G. REBOZO
ACCT 1-34
KEY BISCAYNE BANK
OUT
$ 243.57
    1,138.80
    11,978.84
    426.87
    832.32

C. G. REBOZO
1968
UNKNOWN
CONTRIBUTORS

FLORIDA NIXON FOR
PRESIDENT COM.
ACCT 1-0455
KEY BISCAYNE
BANK
OUT   IN
$6,000.00)   RE-IMB
    216.18 . $426.87

THOMAS H. WAKEFIELD-
SPECIAL ACCT
#2-1691
OUT   KEY BISCAYNE BANK   IN
$3,000.00
    200.00 $6,000.00
    237.62
    4,562.38

$4,562.38

MISC. ADMIN. EXPENSES
RELATE TO
PRESIDENT NIXON
IN
$237.62
    832.32

HERBERT W. KALMBACH
TRUSTEE FOR CLIENTS
ACCT 002.691
SECURITY PACIFIC NATIONAL BK
NEWPORT BEACH, CALIF
TONY ULASEWICZ ACCOUNT   IN
$1,000.00

PRESIDENT NIXON'S
KEY BISCAYNE PROPERTY

POOL	OIL FOR HEATER	REMODELING
$10,100.00	$138.50	$ 6,508.11
1,500.00	141.87	1,654.00
2,727.76	75.88	1,681.00
2,100.00		11,978.84
1,277.64		
210.78		
1,519.50		

OTHER
PUTTING GREEN   - $ 243.57
BILLIARD TABLE   -   1,138.80
FIREPLACE   -   3,585.00
ARCHITECTURAL
MODEL FOR HOME   -   295.65

SUMMARY
CONSTRUCTION & REMODELING - $45,621.15
OIL HEATER MAINTENANCE   -   356.25

TOTAL $45,977.40

HERBERT W. KALMBACH
TRUSTEE ACCOUNT
#081-4068
SECURITY PACIFIC NAT'L BK
NEWPORT BEACH, CALIF
OUT   IN
($320.00] $200.00
                       216.18)

JACK CAULFIELD
IN
[$320.00]

587

11. A SUMMARY ANALYSIS OF CONFLICTING EVIDENCE

In the course of its investigation into the receipt by Rebozo of $100,000 from Hughes, the Senate Select Committee has received considerable evidence, a significant portion of which reflects conflicts in principal witnesses's testimony. To allow for an appropriate review of rather complex factual materials, a summary analysis of said conflicting testimony on important issues is presented here.

Initiator of the contribution. When asked on March 20, 1973, who brought up Hughes' contribution first, Mr. Rebozo replied, "Danner brought it up with me. I had no reason to bring it up with Danner. He was a practicing lawyer in Washington and was not even connected with Hughes." [831] In his testimony on December 18, 1973, Mr. Richard Danner was asked if it was Danner "who initiated the discussions about the possibility of getting a contribution from the Hughes Tool Company or Mr. Hughes." [832] Danner replied, "No, I had no contact with the Hughes Tool Company, none whatsoever in that respect. I didn't know any of the principals involved. And when the question arose as to whether I could do anything in that light, I agreed to talk to Morgan." [833]

Rebozo also testified on March 20, 1974, that he never met with candidate Nixon and Richard Danner to discuss the possibility of obtaining a contribution from Howard Hughes in the 1968 campaign.[834] However, Mr. Richard Danner testified on December 18, 1973 that Mr. Nixon was present at the first discussion of a possible Hughes contribution and that either candidate Nixon or Mr. Rebozo first asked Danner to ascertain if Hughes would make a contribution.[835]

After Rebozo denied that candidate Nixon was present in the first discussion about the Hughes contribution in 1968, Danner was asked again about candidate Nixon's presence in an executive session on June 12, 1974. Danner again confirmed that President Nixon and Rebozo had both been present in the first meeting when the Hughes contribution was brought up.[836]

Facts Concerning Actual Delivery of Funds. On March 20,

831. Rebozo Testimony, Executive Session, March 20, 1974, p. 9.
832. Danner Executive Session, December 18, 1973, p. 21.
833. *Ibid.* pp. 21-22.
834. Rebozo Executive Session, March 29, 1974, p. 10.
835. Danner Executive Session, Deceember 18, 1973, pp. 20, 22.
836. Danner Executive Session, June 12, 1974, p. 000.

1974, Mr. Rebozo testified that he received the first $50,000 cash contribution from Richard Danner on July 3, 1970 at the staff mess at San Clemente, and that he received the second $50,000 cash contribution from Richard Danner in August, 1970, at his office in the Key Biscayne Bank in Key Biscayne, Florida.[837]

However, when Rebozo first met with IRS agents on May 10, 1973, he testified that he received the first delivery in late 1968 or early 1969 and that he received the second delivery two or three months later. At that time, Rebozo could not recall whether he received the first package in Key Biscayne or San Clemente, but that he had received one package in each location.[838]

Rebozo also told the IRS agents on May 10, 1973, that Robert Maheu may have been present in Florida when Rebozo received the contribution in Florida, but was not present at the time of the delivery.[839]

On July 10, 1973, when Rebozo met again with IRS agents, he recalled that the first contribution had been in 1969 at the San Clemente Inn since, to the best of his knowledge, Danner had never been inside the San Clemente compound.[840] It was not until his October 8, 1973, interview with the Senate Select Committee that Rebozo finally fixed on July 3, 1970 as being the date of the first contribution and the San Clemente Western White House as being the place for that delivery.[841]

However, on June 18, 1973, Rebozo told Kenneth Whittaker, special agent in charge of the Miami FBI office, that he had received $50,000 in cash from Richard Danner in 1969.[842]

In addition, Richard Danner testified before the Senate Select Committee on December 18, 1973, that he could not recall whether the first delivery of cash was in the late summer of 1969 in Key Biscayne, Florida, or on July 3, 1970, at San Clemente.[843] Similarly, Robert Maheu also places the first delivery of $50,000 in 1969. Maheu testified in a deposition on July 4, 1973, that, "Mr. Danner made the first delivery which would have been some time in 1969." [844] Simlarly, Robert Maheu was certain that he was present at the delivery of the cash in Key Biscayne. He recalls seeing

837. See Rebozo Testimony, March 20, 1974.
838. IRS Interview, May 10, 1973, p. 2.
839. *Ibid*, p. 2.
840. IRS Interview, July 10, 1973, p. 6.
841. See October 8, 1973, Interview with Rebozo.
842. See letter from FBI Director Clarence Kelly to Commissioner Donald Alexander, 000.
843. Danner Executive Session, December 18, 1973, p. 88.
844. Robert Maheu, Civil Deposition, July 4, 1973, Vol. 12, p. 1037.

the envelope containing the cash passed from Danner to Rebozo, and recalls that Danner, Rebozo, and Maheu left Rebozo's home in Rebozo's car to dine at Sol Mandel's Restaurant after Danner had given Rebozo the cash.[845]

Richard Danner completely supported Maheu's version of the first delivery in Danner's first interview with the I.R.S. on May 15, 1972.[846] Danner subsequently changed his I.R.S. testimony on July 5, 1973, after he had discussions about the matter with Rebozo in the summer of 1972.[847]

In one of his interviews with the Select Committee staff, Rebozo also stated that it was his recollection that he received the Key Biscayne contribution at his home rather than at his bank office.[848] On December 20, 1973, Rebozo testified that he received the second $50,000 contribution at his home in August 1970.[849]

Initiator of First Delivery. On March 20, 1974, Mr. Rebozo testified before the Select Committee that Danner had offered the $50,000 contribution to Rebozo on numerous occasions after the 1968 election.[850] However, on May 10, 1973, Mr. Rebozo told IRS agents that after the 1968 election, Rebozo could not remember whether he approached Danner or Danner approached him about making the contribution.[851]

Mr. Danner testified on Tuesday, December 18, 1973, that after the 1968 election in early 1969, Rebozo "needled" Danner about the fact that the Hughes people had not made a subtantial contribution to the 1968 campaign. Danner testified that in 1969 Rebozo asked Danner whether Hughes would contribute funds to begin taking polls on candidates for the 1970 congressional elections.[852] Danner also testified that this occurred after Rebozo had refused Danner's offer in early 1969 to deliver the $50,000 contribution that had been promised for the 1968 campaign.[853]

Purpose of the money. On March 20, 1974, Mr. Rebozo testified that the two contributions he received from Richard Danner were to be used for the 1972 Presidential campaigns, since he "did not accept contributions from anybody for anything else." [854] However, on June 18, 1973, Rebozo ap-

845. Robert Maheu interview, January 20, 1973.
846. See May 15, 1972 IRS interview with Danner, p. 18.
847. Danner Executive Session, June 11, 1974, p. 210.
848. See January 17, 1974, Rebozo Interview.
849. See Deposition of Charles G. Rebozo, December 20, 1973, in *Common Cause* vs. *FCRP*, p. 28.
850. See Rebozo Testimony, March 20, 1974.
851. See IRS Interview, May 10, 1973, p. 2.
852. Danner Testimony, December 18, 1973, p. 51.
853. *Ibid.*
854. See Rebozo Testimony, March 20, 1974, p. 55.

parently told Kenneth Whittaker that the money Rebozo was taking out of the safe deposit box in the Key Biscayne Bank was from Howard Hughes and was to be applied to the Republican Congressional elections in 1970.[855] In addition, Rebozo apparently told Whittaker that a short time after receiving the first contribution, he received another $50,000 from Richard Danner to be used for the same purpose.[856]

Richard Danner has insisted throughout his staff interviews and his sworn testimony before the Select Committee, that the funds he contributed on behalf of Howard Hughes were requested by Rebozo to be used for the 1970 Congressional campaigns or for polls for those elections, and that this was the purpose of the contributions.[857] Robert Maheu has testified that the purpose of the first $50,000 contribution was to fulfill the pledge made in the 1968 campaign, and that the second contribution was made to insure that the Hughes people had an entree with the Nixon administration.[858]

Finally, Richard Danner testified that in March or April, 1972, he received a telephone call from Bebe Rebozo, asking him if Howard Hughes was going to make a contribution to the 1972 campaign.[858a]

Individuals Who Had Knowledge of the Receipt of the Hughes Contribution. On March 20, 1974, Bebe Rebozo testified under oath to the Select Committee that he had informed Rose Mary Woods of the Hughes contribution shortly after he received it.[859]

On May 10, 1973, Rebozo told Internal Revenue Service special agents who were interviewing him that he and the two agents were the only individuals who "knew about the money." [860] Furthermore, on July 10, 1973, Rebozo told Internal Revenue special agent John Bartlett and Revenue agent Bert Webb that he did not notify anyone of the receipt of the money.[861]

It was not until his October 8, 1973, interview with the Senate Select Committee that Rebozo testified that he told Rose Mary Woods that he had a contribution from Howard Hughes totalling $100,000 in his safe deposit box which he

855. See Letter from FBI Director Clarence Kelley to Commissioner Alexander of the IRS.
856. *Ibid.*
857. Danner Interview, August 30, 1973; Danner Executive Session, December 18, 1973; Danner Executive Session, June 12, 1974.
858. Robert Maheu Interview, September 15, 1973; and January 20, 1974.
858a. Danner Executive Session, December 18, 1973, p. 110.
859. Rebozo Executive Session, March 20, 1974, p. 98.
860. See Rebozo Interview with IRS, May 10, 1973, p. 4.
861. See July 10, 1973, Interview by IRS.

shared with Thomas Wakefield.[862] In that interview, Rebozo stated that he told Miss Woods about the contribution at about the time he became apprehensive about retaining it.[863] In addition, Rebozo stated in that interview that he thought that he told Herb Kalmbach at some point when discussing 1972 campaign contributions that he received a 1968 contribution from Howard Hughes.[864] Finally, in that same interview, Rebozo recalled that he also informed President Nixon about the campaign contribution from Howard Hughes in one of his visits at Key Biscayne after the 1972 election.[865]

Then in Rebozo's interview with the Senate Select Committee on October 17, 1973, Rebozo stated that he did not discuss the contribution with any other individuals besides Rose Mary Woods between the time he received it and the time when he decided to return the contribution.[866] Rebozo added that he talked wth several other individuals about the contribution after he had decided to return the money. Rebozo also testified that he talked to Herbert Kalmbach about the Hughes contribution on April 30, 1973.[867]

Then on March 20, 1974, Rebozo swore under oath before the Senate Select Committee that President Nixon had counseled Rebozo to give the money back in early 1973.[868]

Rebozo also testified on March 20, 1974, that he discussed what he should do with the money with William Griffin, a New York lawyer, and the attorney for Robert Abplanalp.[869] Furthermore, Rebozo testified on March 20, 1974, that he had several discussions of the Hughes contribution with Rose Mary Woods, and estimated that he discussed it with her on three or four separate occasions.[870] Rebozo also stated in an interview on October 17, 1973, that he told Miss Woods that the Hughes contribution was for the 1972 campaign and that he discussed the problems of the Hughes organization with her.[871]

Miss Woods testified on March 22, 1974, "I don't think we had several discussions, there was nothing to discuss so far as I know." [872] In addition, she testified that Rebozo never offered any details with regard to the contribution [873] and

862. Rebozo Interview, October 8, 1973, p. 6.
863. Ibid.
864. Ibid.
865. Ibid.
866. Transcript of October 17, 1973, p. 17.
867. See Transcript of Rebozo Interview, October 17, 1973, p. 31, third section.
868. Rebozo Executive Session, March 20, 1974, p. 133.
869. Rebozo Executive Session, March 20, 1974, p. 132.
870. Rebozo Executive Session, March 20, 1974, p. 153.
871. Rebozo interview, October 17, 1973, pp. 48-49.
872. Woods Executive Session, March 22, 1974, p. 29.
873. Ibid., p. 33.

that she did not know for which campaign the contribution was intended.[874]

Rebozo also testified that he discussed the $100,000 with Thomas H. Wakefield after he decided to return the money.[875] In addition, Rebozo testified he told the President about having the Hughes money sometime prior to March or April, 1973 when the President visited Key Biscayne, Florida.[876]

On October 17, 1973, Rebozo told the Select Committee staff that after he had decided to return the money, Rebozo mentioned the Hughes contribution to John Ehrlichman and H. R. Haldeman.[877] Ehrlichman, however, said in a January interview that he did not know anything at all about the $100,000 contribution until he read about it in the newspaper in the fall of 1973.[878]

Ehrlichman recalled that he did discuss the general subject of Hughes contributions with Rebozo. Although he could not recall the date, he recalled that Rebozo told him that the Hughes people had misled him into thinking that they would make a very large contribution, but had ended up making a contribution very much under $10,000.[879]

Ehrlichman said that Rebozo had indicated to him that Rebozo had received only a "de minimis" contribution from the Hughes people.[880] Then on March 21, 1974, Rebozo testified that neither Haldeman nor Ehrlichman knew anything about the $100,000 in 1972 or 1973. Rebozo testified that, "they knew nothing about it, to my knowledge." [881]

On March 20, 1974, Rebozo testified that after receiving the cash, he marked H. H. in the corner of the envelope containing the cash, wrote a letter to Thomas H. Wakefield that was placed in the directors' safe deposit box with instructions on what to do with the money should anything happen to Rebozo, marked similar instructions on the manila envelope containing the money, and placed the envelope in his safe deposit box No. 224 at the Key Biscayne Bank.[882] However, Rebozo also testified that he destroyed the original envelope in which the Hughes money was contained "some time after the Hughes problem started and the campaign got underway." [883] Rebozo also testified that he destroyed the letter to Wakefield in the Director's box at a later time.[884]

874. Ibid., p. 21.
875. See Rebozo Executive Session, March 20, 1974, p. 293.
876. Rebozo Executive Session, March 21, 1974, p. 353.
877. Interview of Charles G. Rebozo, October 17, 1973, p. 2.
878. See Ehrlichman interview, January 10, 1970, p. 20.
879. Ehrlichman interview, January 10, 1974, pp. 24-25.
880. Ibid.
881. Rebozo Executive Session, March 21, 1974, p. 297.
882. See pp. 71-74, Rebozo Executive Session, March 20, 1974.
883. Rebozo Executive Session, March 20, 1974, p. 80.
884. See Rebozo Executive Session, March 20, 1974, p. 83.

Rebozo further testified that some time after he placed the Hughes contribution in his safe deposit box, he took the bank wrappers off the money and placed rubber bands around the packets.[885]

However, on March 21, 1974, Herbert Kalmbach testified that he met Rebozo on January 8, 1974, and that Rebozo then told him:

> Undoubtedly, Herb, I have not told you that after you and I talked last spring regarding the Hughes money, I found that I had not in fact disbursed any of the Hughes' cash to the several people I named. When I went into the safe deposit box, I found that the wrappers around that cash had not been disturbed, and so it was clear that no part of this money had been used.[886]

In addition, Ken Whittaker stated in an interview on November 20, 1973, that when he observed the counting of the money on June 18, 1973, "some of the packets were held together by rubber bands, while others were in bank wrappers." [887] Whittaker did not recall any identification on the wrappers.

Rebozo also testified that Thomas H. Wakefield had a duplicate key to safe deposit box No. 224, where the money was kept during the entire time that the money was stored in a safe deposit box.[888] Rebozo testified that some time during the period after he received the Hughes contribution, he lost all of his keys to his safe deposit boxes and that the locks were changed after he lost his keys.[889] Rebozo testified that he gained access to Box No. 224 on this occasion by requesting the second key from Mr. Wakefield, so that Rebozo could get into the box. (*Ibid*, p. 177) Rebozo also testified that he gave Wakefield the replacement key for the new lock after the new lock was installed.[890]

However, Thomas H. Wakefield, under oath before the Senate Select Committee on June 10, 1974, testified that Rebozo never came to him to request his copy of the key of the safe deposit box No. 224, and that he was never given any replacement key to get into the box after the locks were allegedly changed.[891] Wakefield stated in an interview that sometime in 1968 or 1969 Rebozo gave him a key to the safe deposit box and told him that in case of Rebozo's death,

885. Rebozo Executive Session, March 20, 1974, p. 114.
886. Kalmbach Executive Session, March 21, 1974, p. 52 (galley).
887. Whittaker Interview, November 20, 1973, p. 3.
888. See Rebozo Executive Session, March 20, 1974, p. 167.
889. *Ibid*, p. 175.
890. *Ibid*, p. 178.
891. See Wakefield Executive Session, June 10, 1974, p. 26.

Wakefield should open the box and follow instructions.[892]

Rebozo also testified that it was not the custom of the bank to ask Rebozo to sign the access card each time he went into his safe deposit boxes. Therefore, the safe deposit box records produced by Rebozo did not represent each time that he went into the box.[893]

Other Contributions. On March 21, 1974, Rebozo testified that A. D. Davis made a $50,000 cash contribution to Rebozo on April 4 or 5, 1972. Rebozo further testified that he called the Finance Committee to Re-Elect the President after receiving the contribution and the committee sent Fred LaRue down to pick the money up.[894]

However, Fred LaRue testified that he did not discuss any contribution with Bebe Rebozo until October, 1972, and that on that occasion, LaRue called Rebozo to request contributions for the Nunn campaign in Kentucky at the request of John Mitchell.[895] In addition, LaRue's plane ticket showing the trip during which he picked up the money from Rebozo is dated October 12, 1972.[896]

However, on December 20, 1973, Rebozo testified in a civil deposition that he received campaign funds for President Nixon's re-election campaign from January 1, 1971 through April 6, 1972, "which have already been listed." [897] It is interesting to note, however, that the A. D. Davis contribution was never noted on any list of contributors to the 1972 campaign, nor was any help from Davis acknowledged by Maurice Stans, the chairman of the FCRP, until October 13, 1972. Rebozo also testified that he set up a separate bank account for all contributions he received for the 1972 campaign.[898] However, Rebozo testified before the Select Committee that he did not place the Hughes $100,000 contribution nor the A. D. Davis $50,000 in the special account that he had set up.

On July 10, 1973, Rebozo told IRS Special Agent Jack Bartlett that "In 1972, Rebozo put all contributions received by him in the bank account (special bank account he set up for contributions)." [900] In addition, Rebozo also testified on December 20, 1973, that aside from the Kislak contribution and the Hughes contribution, he received other con-

892. Wakefield interview, October 18, 1973, p. 2.
893. Rebozo Executive Session, March 28, 1974, p. 180.
894. March 21, 1974, p. 415.
895. See LaRue Executive Session, May 28, 1974, pp. 7-8.
896. See plane ticket exhibit.
897. Civil Deposition of Charles G. Rebozo, December 20, 1973, *Common Cause et al. v. the FCRP*, p. 4.
898. *Ibid*, pp. 8-9.
900. See IRS Interview, July 10, 1973.

tributions, but those were "others that are reported, but they are a matter of record." [901] Rebozo added, "I believe, however, they are subsequent to the April 7th date." [902]

Then, Rebozo was asked:

Q There should be no pre-April 7, 1972 contributions that are not in the material you submitted. Is that correct?

A That's correct, to the best of my recollection. If you are getting at something specific you want to ask me about, go ahead.[903]

On March 20, 1974, Rebozo was asked if Herbert Kalmbach asked him to see any specific individual with regard to contributions for the 1972 campaign. Rebozo replied, "Yes. I think that later on, I don't know whether it was 1969 or 1970—it might have been 1970—he asked me to make an appointment with him with a couple of people that I knew. One was Paul Getty and another was Raymond Guest.[904] Rebozo also testified that the purpose of contacting these individuals was for the purpose of obtaining contributions for the 1972 election. The following exchange occurred:

MR. LENZNER Had you been asked by anybody else to speak to Mr. Getty yourself?

MR. REBOZO No.

L You had not been requested by anybody else to seek to obtain money from Mr. Getty?

R No.[905]

However, in a memorandum dated on February 17, 1969, from H. R. Haldeman to John Ehrlichman, Mr. Haldeman stated that Bebe Rebozo has been asked by the President to contact J. P. regarding major contributions.[906]

Herbert Kalmbach testified on March 21, 1974, that Rebozo had asked Kalmbach to solicit from Mr. Getty funds for the 1970 Senatorial campaign program.[907] Kalmbach also testified that Rebozo "set it up for him to see Mr. Getty in Europe." [908]

On November 9, 1973, H. R. Haldeman told staff in an interview that he recalled that Rebozo was responsible for raising funds from former Senator George Smathers and his

901. *Ibid*, pp. 54-55.
902. *Ibid*.
903. *Ibid*. p. 56.
904. Rebozo Executive Session, March 20, 1974, p. 89.
905. Rebozo Executive Session, March 20, 1974, p. 90.
906. See Exhibit 15, and information furnished by John Wilson to Terry Lenzner.
907. Rebozo Executive Session, March 21, 1974, pp. 44-45 (galleys).
908. Ibid, p. 44.

friends "and may have been J. P. Getty contact." [909]

In addition, Rebozo testified that he sent left over 1968 campaign funds from the Florida Nixon for President Committee to Herb Kalmbach pursuant to Kalmbach's request. Rebozo testified that he did not know what Kalmbach was going to do with the money:

> . . . I wasn't concerned with the purpose. He was just a little late in asking me and I thought everything was paid . . .[910]

Kalmbach testified that Rebozo had a special account in Key Biscayne that had left-over 1968 campaign funds in it. Kalmbach said he asked Rebozo to send these funds to him in order to pay Caulfield and Ulasewicz. Before requesting this money from Rebozo, however, Kalmbach said he first cleared this procedure with John Ehrlichman. Kalmbach recalls that Ehrlichman approved that the funds Rebozo held from 1968, should be used to pay Caulfield and Ulasewicz. Kalmbach testified that he discussed the need for these funds with Rebozo and that Rebozo specifically knew they were for Caulfield and Ulasewicz.[911]

Return of the Money. Rebozo testified on March 20, 1974, that he first decided to return the Hughes contribution in March of 1973.[912] Rebozo also testified that he began trying to contact Danner in order to convince Danner to take the money back "around March or April," 1973.[913] However, later on at the same executive session, Rebozo testified that he in fact made no efforts to contact Danner to have him take the money back until after he met with the Internal Revenue Service.[914]

Rebozo's first interview with the Internal Revenue Service was not until May 10, 1973, thereby placing his efforts to have Danner take the money back after that date. Rebozo also testified that after he talked to the IRS, William Griffin was the first lawyer to whom he spoke about the money.[915] Rebozo also said that the time at which he first spoke to the lawyers that he mentioned in his testimony was after he met with the Internal Revenue Service.[916]

In his first interview with the Internal Revenue Service on

909. Haldeman Interview November 9, 1973, p. 2.
910. Rebozo Executive Session, March 20, 1974, pp. 23-26.
911. Kalmbach Executive Session, May 5, 1974. p. 16.
912. Rebozo Executive Session, March 20, 1974, p. 122.
913. *Ibid*, March 21, 1974, p. 294.
914. Rebozo Executive Session, March 21, 1974, p. 357.
915. Rebozo Testimony, March 21, 1974, p. 354.
916. *Ibid.*

May 10, 1973, Rebozo asked the agents interviewing him "what he should do with the money—whether he should give it to us [the agents]." [917] In that same interview, Rebozo also told the agents that, "he had considered calling Danner several times and offering to return the money, but that he had never done so because he was afraid that he would create some additional publicity." [918]

On October 17, 1973, Rebozo told the Select Committee staff that he had decided to return the Hughes contribution prior to his discussion on April 30, 1973, with Herbert Kalmbach. In addition, on October 17, 1973, Rebozo stated, "I know I had a little trouble trying to get it back, and exactly when that was I don't know, but it probably was in 1973, it's very likely that it was. And once that decision was made, I'm sure I mentioned it to a number of people, but up until then, even Wakefield himself who was on the box didn't know, well not up until the time we took the money out he didn't know what he was on that box for." [919] Rebozo also testified on that occasion that it was March or April 1973 when he first told Danner that he wanted to return the money.

In addition, Rebozo testified about his meeting with Herbert Kalmbach as follows:

LENZNER   Yes, how about Mr. Kalmbach, did you ever discuss this with him?
REBOZO   I probably told him about it. He was involved in . . . saw him several times at the White House . . . and in California.
L   And do you remember how it was, were you seeking his advice or counsel?
R   I don't think so. I think it was just a general discussion. You see, Kalmbach and I have business discussions, naturally on the San Clemente interest. He and I worked on the Yorba Linda House.[920]

Rebozo later on testified further about his meeting with Kalmbach:

L   Do you recall if the two $50,000 contributions came up?
R   Yeah, I believe I told him about it . . . that may be.
L   Do you recall specifically what you told him about it? And why you told him at that time?
R   No, other than, I mean, he had been involved in

917. See Internal Revenue Service Interview, May 10, 1973, p. 2.
918. *Ibid*, p. 4.
919. Transcript of October 17, 1973, Interview, p. 18.
920. *Ibid*, p. 19.

fund raising and it wasn't going to be any secret. I guess I just told the key people that should know about it.

L   Did you ask whether you should send the money back, did that question arise?

R   Well, that was April 30, 1973, and I think the decision was already made then. If I did ask, it was just for his opinion.

L   Since, you had already decided, did you communicate—tell him that you had already decided to send the money back?

R   I don't know. No. Because as I recall the part about the Hughes money—it was just an irrelevant part of the conversation.

L   The purpose of the meeting was not to discuss that.

R   No.

L   Did he ask you specifically about the Hughes money? [Kalmbach?]

R   He didn't ask me. I told him and I think that's the first time that I told him. I'm not sure, it may have been earlier. I don't know. Just like there may have been some others I told at that time. It's a bit of a dilemma. I hated to see it go back if it could be used. But I had clung to vain hope longer than perhaps I should have.

L   Did you have other discussions with Kalmbach?

R   I don't think so.

L   Do you remember any reaction that Kalmbach had at that time when you told him about the funds?

R   No. I can't say that I do.

L   Was he concerned that there may have been a problem your having received these funds—any concern about that?

R   I don't know. I think he had enough. I think he had enough concern of his own to be concerned about the fact that I had . . . I don't recall.

L   Did he discuss any of his problems he was facing?

R   No, I was reading about this.

L   Did he seem surprised to learn of these funds or did he appear to know about them?

R   If he was I don't recall his showing it. I think in the campaign as I told you last time, that I was asked, if Hughes had made a contribution in 1968. I said he had.

R   But nobody questioned that a check turned in. In 1972 I handled this as best I could.

L   Who asked you about the Hughes thing . . .

R   I think that Herb did, can't be sure, but I think

he had.[921]

Richard Danner testified on Tuesday, December 18, 1973, that the first occasion on which he was informed that the money had not been used and that Rebozo wanted to return the money, was on May 18, 1973, at the Madison Hotel in Washington, DC, in a discussion that Danner had with Rebozo.[922] Mr. Danner also responded to further questioning about the return of the money as follows:

> LENZNER Did Mr. Rebozo indicate whether he had discussed the return of the money with anybody else?
>
> DANNER No, he didn't mention that. And I asked him if he had consulted with an attorney or tax man or anyone of that sort, and he said no, he hadn't and I suggested that he had better do that.[923]

On March 28, 1974. William Griffin testified under oath before the Senate Select Committee that he met with Bebe Rebozo in either late April or May 3, 1973, and that Mr. Rebozo explained to him that he had $100,000 in a safe deposit box at the Key Biscayne Bank and that the money was the same money he had been given in 1969 and 1970.[924] Griffin could not recall whether Rebozo said that he was going to meet with the Internal Revenue agents or he had just met with them.[925] Griffin placed the date of his first meeting with Rebozo in late April, 1973, but his first airplane ticket showing a trip down to Key Biscayne from New York was dated May 3, 1973. [926] However, both of those dates are prior to May 10, 1973, when Rebozo first met Internal Revenue agents and told them that they were the only ones that knew that the money was still in the safe deposit box in the Key Biscayne Bank.

On March 21, 1974, Herbert Kalmbach testified that on the evening of April 29, 1973, he received a call from Bebe Rebozo who requested a meeting with him the following morning.[927] Kalmbach said he met with Rebozo on the following morning, April 30, 1973, at about 8:00 in the morning and after they discussed such matters as refinancing of San Clemente and the President's taxes, Rebozo asked Kalmbach if he could go on "attorney-client basis" "in discussing a personal problem." Kalmbach testified that Rebozo said

921. Transcript of October 18, 1973, Rebozo Interview, pp. 20-21.
922. Danner Executive Session, December 18, 1973, p. 124.
923. Ibid, p. 126.
924. Griffin Executive Session, March 28, 1974, p. 87 (galleys).
925. Ibid, p. 88.
926. Ibid, p. 86.
927. Kalmbach, Executive Session, March 21, 1974, p. 50, (galleys).

"The President had asked him to speak to me about this problem and not Maurice Stans." [928] Kalmbach stated that Rebozo said the IRS had scheduled a meeting with him on the subject of a $100,000 contribution from Howard Hughes which Rebozo received in 1969 and 1970.[929] Kalmbach then testified that Rebozo said that "he had disbursed part of the funds to Rose Woods, to Don Nixon, to Ed Nixon and to unnamed others during the intervening years . . ." [930] Kalmback further testified, "In response to my questions, he reiterated that the money had been given to him as a contribution by Hughes, and that the expenditures he had made to several individuals including Rose and the President's two brothers had come from the Hughes cash." [931]

Kalmbach then testified that he advised Rebozo to get the best tax lawyer he could and to lay out the facts exactly to the Internal Revenue Service. Kalmbach said that Rebozo replied to his advice, expressing grave reservations about following it for the stated reason that, "This touches the President and the President's family and I can't do anything to add to his problems at this time, Herb."

Kalmbach testified that he checked with another attorney, Stanley Ebner, in the White House, who agreed completely with his advice when presented in a hypothetical context.[932]

Kalmbach stated that he met Rebozo again the following morning, May 1, 1973, at around 8:30 a.m. Kalmbach testified that he began to recount his visit with Stan Ebner, but before he had finished, Rebozo "cut short further discussion with a somewhat baffling comment that he saw no problem but he thanked me for my thoughts." [933]

Kalmbach also testified that he had a third meeting with Bebe Rebozo on Tuesday, January 8, 1974, at about 8:30 in the morning at the San Clemente Western White House.[934] Kalmbach recalled taht at one point toward the end of his meeting on January 8, Rebozo told him words to the effect that: Undoubtedly, Herb, I have not told you that after you. and I talked last spring regarding the Hughes money, I found that I had not in fact disbursed any of the Hughes cash to several people like me. When I went to the safe deposit box, I found that the wrappers around that cash had not been disturbed, so it was clear that no part of this money has been used during the several years that it was in

928. *Ibid*, p. 50.
929. *Ibid*, p. 51.
930. *Ibid*.
931. *Ibid*.
932. *Ibid*, p. 51.
933. *Ibid*, p. 52.
934. *Ibid.*, p. 52.

my box." [935]

In an affidavit sworn on May 14, 1974, Mr. Jim O'Connor, Kalmbach's attorney, stated that following Kalmbach's meeting with Rebozo on or about April 30, "Mr. Kalmbach discussed with affiant [Jim O'Connor] the fact that after discussing the San Clemente matter and the handling of the tax affairs of the President, that thereafter and after stating that the attorney-client relationship did indeed exist, Mr. Rebozo advised Mr. Kalmbach that he had given some of the $100,000 in question which had been given to him by Danner, to Rose Mary Woods and to the Nixon brothers, and Mr. Rebozo asked Mr. Kalmbach what he should do." [936]

In addition, Margaret C. Blakely, Jim O'Connor's secretary, filed an affidavit on May 15, 1974, which stated that on or about the middle of October, 1973, she was asked by Mr. O'Connor to call Mr. Rebozo to inform him that Mr. Kalmbach had been questioned by the Special Prosecutor's office and by Terry Lenzner on October 11 and 12 concerning a meeting on April 30, 1973 with Mr. Rebozo, "and Mr. Kalmbach acknowledged the meeting took place at or about that time; Mr. Kalmbach further advised both investigating parties that the prime purpose of the meeting was to review certain matters involving the President's personal affairs, including the sale of the Whittier property and the refinancing of the San Clemente property, among other things; that Mr. Kalmbach was disturbed about reports that campaign funds were used in the acquisition of the San Clemente property, etc." [937]

Blakely also swore that on or about January 25, 1974, she was again asked to contact Rebozo, and when Mr. Rebozo returned her call, she read to him a memorandum as follows: "If Mr. Kalmbach is pressed as to any details of a conversation between himself and Mr. Rebozo on April 30 and/or May 1, he of course would have to tell the truth; that in the unlikely event he is pressed on this matter he will of course state that these discussions were pursuant to the attorney-client relationship and therefore subject to the attorney-client privilege." [938]

On March 20, 1974, the following exchange occurred during Mr. Rebozo's testimony:

MR. LENZNER   Did you ever make the statement to anybody that you had used the money or had somebody else use it on behalf of other individuals?

935. Ibid, p. 52.
936. See O'Connor Affidavit, Exhibit 49.
937. See Blakely Affidavit, Exhibit 50.
938. *Ibid*, p. 2.

MR. REBOZO No sir. I don't think anybody else did, either.[939]

Rebozo also testified on March 21, 1974, that he ran into Herb Kalmbach at the White House on April 30, 1973, and asked for his judgment on whether or not Rebozo should return the money.[940] Then the following exchange occurred on March 21, 1974:

L   Did you explain to him again that you had received the funds and that you had kept them and why you kept them?
R   I think I passed over that.
L   And I take it you did tell him you kept ti because you were asking for his judgment on whether you should return them or not?
R   That's right.
L   Did you ask him to do anything other than giving you his judgment at that time?
R   No.
L   Did you ever discuss with him again the $100,000 contribution from Hughes?
R   I don't think so. I've seen very little of him. That may be the last I saw him.

There was further discussion on March 21, about Rebozo's meetings with Kalmbach. The exchange follows:

L   We talked, I think, to Mr. Kalmbach some time in October or November of 1973. Did he ever advise you of those discussions?
R   No, I don't think so. I don't know. I don't think I've seen Kalmbach—yes, I did see him once in California since that meeting we just referred to [April 30, 1973]. That simply had to do with the grounds, the Presidential grounds out there, the certain repairs that need to be made and so on.
L   There was no discussion on that occasion about the Hughes contribution of $100,000?
R   No.
L   I'm sorry sir?
R   No.
L   You told him, then, on April 30, that, basically that you had retained the same funds that had been given to you previously. Did you tell him when you had received these funds—Mr. Kalmbach, on April 30, Mr. Rebozo?

939. Rebozo, March 20, 1974, p. 192.
940. Rebozo Executive Session, March 21, 1974, p. 403.

603

R No. Actually at that time I wasn't even sure when I'd receive it. That was established later.

L And you did tell him they were the same funds and you wanted to know what to do about it?

R Yes.[941]

Later, on March 21, Rebozo was asked if he ever discussed with Haig, Garment, Ehrlichman, Griffin, and Kalmbach the issue of whether the funds had been used or not. Mr. Rebozo replied, "That was not an issue. They had not been used. I still have the funds." Lenzner added, "So the answer is no, you had never discussed that with any of those individuals?" Mr. Rebozo. "No."

Rebozo also testified on March 21, 1974 that he had no financial or business transactions with Edward Nixon, the President's brother.[942] Rebozo denied that he had given Edward Nixon any gifts in excess of $1,000.[943] Rebozo also denied that he ever had any financial or business transactions with Rose Mary Woods except for the Fisher's Island transaction.[944] Rebozo also denied that he had ever given money in excess of $1,000 to Rose Mary Woods.[945] Rebozo denied ever furnishing any money to F. Donald Nixon.[946]

Rebozo also testified that he had not given any gifts of cash or stock or any other negotiable commodity of value in excess of $1,000 to the President.[947]

Camp David Meeting. On March 21, 1973, Rebozo testified that he recalled meeting Richard Danner in Washington in May 1973, but he did not recall asking Danner to come to Washington for the meeting.[948] Rebozo also testified that after talking to Danner on May 18th or 19th, Rebozo decided to have President Nixon talk personally to Danner about the "mood of the people" he was seeing in Las Vegas, and so he called an aide to have him bring Danner up to Camp David in a courier car.[949] Rebozo also testified that he asked the President to come over to Rebozo's cottage to have Danner relate to the President the mood of the people of the west.[950] Rebozo testified that he did not recall

941. Rebozo Executive Session, March 1, 1974, pp. 406-07.
942. *Ibid,* p. 453.
943. *Ibid.*
944. *Ibid.,* p. 454.
945. *Ibid.,* p. 455.
946. *Ibid,* p. 421.
947. *Ibid,* p. 452.
948. *Ibid,* p. 362.
949. *Ibid,* p. 364.
950. *Ibid,* p. 365.

that the President was present at the meeting for more than 10 minutes.[951] Rebozo could also not recall the kind of day it was on Danner's visit, nor did he recall taking a walk with Danner and President Nixon on the Camp David grounds.[952]

Richard Danner testified on December 18, 1973, that Rebozo had been "wanting to see me" prior to Danner's coming into Washington on May 18, 1973. Danner also testified that Rebozo told him that President Nixon wanted to talk to Danner, and that he was picked up by a car and driven to Camp David on May 29, 1973.[953] Danner testified that he met with Rebozo and the President beginning around 12:00 noon, and that "we talked in the room for perhaps an hour. And then we took a walk. I remember it, because it was misting rain, and I didn't have a raincoat, but we took quite a walk around the compound, and he was showing me various places and what was being done. And this probably lasted until 2:00, something like that." [954]

Danner reconfirmed his testimony of December 18, 1973, in another executive session on June 11, 1974, in which he detailed the walk that he and President Nixon and Rebozo took around the compound.[955] Danner also testified that his meeting with President Nixon was certainly more than a 5-minute meeting.[956] Finally, weather reports indicate that on May 20, 1973, a light rain fell on Camp David, Maryland.[957]

IRS Investigation. Mr. Rebozo testified in the morning of March 21 that he first learned about the IRS investigation into the Hughes matter when "the agent called from Las Vegas and wanted to come and see me, and we set up an appointment." [958] Rebozo denied that he ever talked with Ehrlichman about the $100,000 contribution or that Ehrlichman ever called to alert him that the IRS would soon call and request an interview about the Hughes matter.[959]

However, in the afternoon session on March 21, Rebozo testified:

> . . . I think that perhaps I ought to correct a misunderstanding I may have made to Senator Weicker earlier,

951. *Ibid,* p. 373.
952. *Ibid,* p. 374.
953. *Ibid,* p. 128.
954. *Ibid,* pp. 130-31.
955. Danner Executive Session, June 11, 1974, pp. 200-01.
956. *Ibid.,* p. 201.
957. NCAA Weather Report for Catoctin Mountain Park.
958. Executive Session of C. G. Rebozo; March 21, 1974; p. 299.
959. *Ibid;* p. 303.

because I was asked about Ehrlichman and I do recall that Ehrlichman did mention the IRS to me. I didn't recall any specific conversation, but now I do remember that he [Ehrlichman] had said something about the IRS was going to check this out . . ." [960]

Ehrlichman testified on February 8, 1974, that he called Mr. Rebozo at the request of Roger Barth of the IRS to notify Rebozo that the IRS wanted to interview him.[961] Ehrlichman testified he told Rebozo to interview him about "whether or not Rebozo had received funds from the Hughes organization . . ." [962]

Finally, Roger Barth testified that he called Rebozo to notify him of the IRS request for an interview.[963] Barth testified that he acted at Ehrlichman's request.[964]

12.   SUMMARY

The transmittal of $100,000 in $100 bills from Howard Hughes to the President's close friend, Charles G. Rebozo, several years prior to the 1972 election, reflects a number of classic issues inherent in the furnishing of large cash contributions to political campaigns:

1. Why were cash funds furnished to a closed friend of the President rather than to any campaign official or organization?

2. Why were the funds contributed several years prior to the 1972 campaign for which they were allegedly intended, especially since Howard Hughes ultimately contributed another $150,000 in 1972 to the Finance Committee to Re-Elect the President?

3. Did Howard Hughes profit in any way by his contribution to Rebozo on behalf of the President?

Mr. Rebozo's testimony about the matter steadfastly rejects any notion of impropriety in his receipt and handling of the two $50,000 cash contributions. He has testified:

—that he finally agreed to accept the Hughes contribution in 1970 after rejecting it many times in 1968 and 1969 because of the possible embarrassment it might cause President Nixon;

960. *Ibid;* 354; It should be noted that Mr. Rebozo and Mr. Ehrlichman presently retain the same counsel, Mr. William Snow Frates of Miami, Florida.

961. Executive Session of John D. Ehrlichman; February 8, 1974; p. 39. (Galley.)

962. *Ibid;* p. 39. (Galley.)

963. Executive Session of Roger Barth; June 6, 1974; p. 26.

964. *Ibid,* p. 26. See Section on Delivery and Sources of Money, above.

—that the contribution was intended solely for the President's 1972 re-election campaign;

—that he placed the two $50,000 cash contributions in his safe deposit box without counting them and with instructions to his attorney to turn the money over to the President's campaign in case anything happened to Rebozo;

—that he subsequently destroyed these instructions sometime after the December, 1970, split between Hughes and Maheu, thereby leaving $100,000 in one hundred dollar bills in his safe deposit box with no evidence of the money's origin or purpose;

—that he subsequently removed the wrappers with the words "Las Vegas" from the money and wrapped the money in rubber bands while again not counting the money;

—that he did not use any of this money for any purpose, and that he returned the same identical $100 bills to Mr. Hughes in the spring of 1973;

—that he told only Rose Mary Woods of the receipt of the funds until after the 1972 election, when he informed President Nixon, and that he informed others of the contribution after he decided to return the money; and

—that he had *no* discussions about the money with President Nixon and Mr. Danner on May 20, 1973, at Camp David, despite the fact that the meeting occurred *after* Rebozo had decided to return the money and *before* Danner agreed to accept it.

Indeed, Rebozo has maintained in all his testimony that his initial apprehension over accepting the cash contribution from Howard Hughes was exacerbated by the very public conflict that had erupted in late November, 1970, between Robert Maheu and Howard Hughes. Had Rebozo understood the funds to be intended for the Congressional races, he could easily have turned them over to the appropriate Congressional campaigns prior to the conflict that later caused him such apprehension. And while the publicized confrontation between the Hughes factions may have deterred Rebozo from applying the funds to any campaign for three to four years, Rebozo testified that he never once attempted to contact any representative of Hughes, any representative of the Republican National Committee, or any representative of the President's reelection campaign to seek advice with regard to the funds until well after the 1972 Presidential election.

In fact, in early 1972, Rebozo began receiving and accepting a variety of contributions, properly established a bank account for such funds, and acknowledged the receipt of such funds to both the donors and the Finance Committee to Re-Elect the President. At no time, however, did he acknowledge in writing to Hughes or his representatives the receipt of the $100,000 nor did he ever notify, as he did with other contributions in 1972, any campaign officials the receipt of $100,000 until after the election. While Mr. Rebozo has always maintained that the funds were intended for the President's campaign, he has also testified that he maintained the $100,000 well after the 1972 election because he believed it could be used for the 1974 Congressional campaign or 1976 Presidential election.

Mr. Rebozo also insists that he never discussed the contribution with the President until well after the 1972 election and that Danner is mistaken in stating that he, Rebozo and the President met in 1968 and discussed the possibility of obtaining a contribution from Howard Hughes. Rebozo has testified that while he met with Mr. Danner on May 18 and May 20, 1973, in Washington to discuss the return of the contribution, at no time was the contribution discussed in the presence of President Nixon on May 20 at Camp David. Rebozo concedes that one of the issues discussed with Danner both at a hotel in Washington and at Camp David before the President arrived was his desire to return the funds to Danner, but Rebozo insists that the only topic discussed *after* the President arrived was Danner's perception of the mood on the West Coast with regard to Watergate. The President, of course, knew by the time he met with Danner at Camp David that Rebozo had in fact been the recipient of a substantial contribution from the Hughes organization. The President, therefore, would have been fully aware that he was in the presence of the principals who had been involved in a contribution in which the IRS had suddenly expressed an interest. In any event, the President through his press spokesman has denied any conversation ensued during that meeting with regard to the Hughes' $100,000.

In addition, of course, the Committee received evidence indicating that the President, prior to his meeting on May 20, 1973 with Danner and Rebozo, requested Rebozo to discuss with Herbert Kalmbach the issue of the receipt, use, and possible return of the Hughes $100,000 on or about April 30, 1973. The Committee also received testimony from Larry Higby that on or about April 30, 1973, H. R. Haldeman told Higby that the President informed Haldeman that Rebozo had available approximately $400,000 to defray legal fees for both Haldeman and John Ehrlichman.

Much of the above information was contained in a letter Chairman Ervin and Vice-Chairman Baker sent to the

President's counsel, Mr. St. Clair on June 6, 1974. This letter contained additional specific information including evidence that the President requested that Rebozo contact J. Paul Getty regarding major contributions, evidence that Rebozo maintained a fund in Key Biscayne to take care of "administration-connected costs," and a list of specific expenditures on behalf of the President exceeding $45,000 that were ordered and paid for by Rebozo. These listed expenses on the President's Key Biscayne properties included substantial alterations of the President's home and the construction and equipping of a pool for the President. In his letter on behalf of the President dated June 20, 1974, St. Clair conveyed "the President's assurance that he never instructed C. G. Rebozo to raise and maintain funds to be expended on the President's personal behalf, nor, so far as he knows, was this ever done." In addition, the President through St. Clair, declined to comment with regard to any of the expenditures amounting to over $45,000 that Rebozo furnished on behalf of the President.

On the basis of the evidence reflected in the letter of Mr. St. Clair, Chairman Ervin sought to provide Rebozo with an opportunity to furnish information and documents to assist the Committee in reviewing the evidence obtained by the staff. On one occasion in fact, Rebozo and his counsel agreed to provide the Committee with certain documents the Committee had sought through subpoena and to provide additional information through testimony. Instead of complying with the subpoena and furnishing the documents pursuant to the agreement entered into, however, Rebozo and counsel moved to quash the subpoena both in Court and before the Committee. The Committee, by unanimous vote rejected Rebozo's application and the Federal District Court for the District of Columbia recently denied an effort to enjoin the Committee's subpoena and investigation of Rebozo. Indeed when an additional subpoena and letter was issued by Chairman Ervin in an effort to obtain Rebozo's responses to questions based on the above described information, Rebozo was in Europe and therefore unavailable for the process of the subpoena. As a result, certain crucial testimony and documentation which was deemed necessary by the Committee to clarify the factual matters related in this report have been denied the Committee and the discrepancies and conflicts in testimony have not been finally resolved.

As a result, the Committee has before it evidence which suggests a number of possible alternative resolutions of the factual material presented herein:

1. That Rebozo paid for the President's expenses out of his own funds. Since Rebozo declined to furnish the Committee with all personal documents and with pertinent document from his bank, the Committee has been unable to make a judgment with regard to this matter except to the extent of determining, based on the records thta were provided by Rebozo, that the great portion of expenditures made for the President were not made out of Rebozo's bank account, and those made in currency were not made from Rebozo's personal funds derived from known sources.

2. That the President in effect paid for these expenses himself by later reimbursing Rebozo. While Rebozo's refusal to produce records and the President's failure to respond to specific issues in the letter of June 6 has hampered the Committee's ability to make a judgment on this issue, the Committee finds only one reimbursement, the $13,642 check discussed in the body of the report. Moreover, the Committee notes that the Coopers and Lybrand report to the President made no mention of any outstanding liabilities due Rebozo.

3. That Rebozo paid for the expenditures on behalf of the President from another source of funds. The testimony and evidence before the Committee indicates that the only other sources of funds available to Rebozo were campaign contributions. Again, the failure of key witnesses to comply with subpoenas frustrated the Committee's efforts in conclusively resolving this issue.

The Select Committee diligently attempted to determine which one of these three alternative conclusions is accurate.

It could have undoubtedly made such a determination if Rebozo had made all of the records controlled by him or his bank relating to these matters available to the Committee or if the President had availed himself of the opportunity to clarify or explain these matters which was extended to him in the June 6, 1974 letter from Senator Ervin, the Committee Chairman, and Senator Baker, Vice-Chairman, to his lawyer, Mr. St. Clair.

Rebozo persisted in his refusal to make records controlled by him or his bank relating to these matters available to the Committee and placed himself beyond the reach of the Committee by traveling to Europe when he had reason to know that the remaining life of the Committee precluded it from enforcing further subpoenas on him or others.

And unfortunately, the President did not avail himself of the opportunity to clarify or explain the matters arising out of his dealings and relationship with Rebozo.

In view of the above, the Committee finds it appropriate

that the matters set forth herein be pursued further by relevant investigative bodies.

13. LEGISLATIVE RECOMMENDATIONS

I. COMMUNICATIONS BETWEEN THE WHITE HOUSE AND THE INTERNAL REVENUE SERVICE SHOULD BE MORE STRICTLY REGULATED. SPECIFICALLY:

1) ANY REQUESTS, DIRECT OR INDIRECT, FOR INFORMATION OR ACTION MADE TO THE IRS BY ANYONE IN THE EXECUTIVE OFFICE OF THE PRESIDENT, UP TO AND INCLUDING THE PRESIDENT, SHOULD BE RECORDED BY THE PERSON MAKING THE REQUEST AND BY THE IRS. REQUESTS AND RESPONSES BY THE IRS (I.E. WHETHER INFORMATION WAS PROVIDED), SHOULD BE DISCLOSED AT LEAST ONCE A YEAR TO APPROPRIATE CONGRESSIONAL OVERSIGHT COMMITTEES;

2) ON "SENSITIVE CASE REPORTS," WHICH COVER SPECIAL CASES, THE IRS SHOULD BE PERMITTED TO DISCLOSE TO PERSONS IN THE EXECUTIVE OFFICE OF THE PRESIDENT, UP TO AND INCLUDING THE PRESIDENT, *ONLY* THE NAME OF THE PERSON OR GROUP IN THE REPORT AND THE GENERAL NATURE OF THE INVESTIGATION.

3) ALL PERSONS IN THE EXECUTIVE OFFICE OF THE PRESIDENT, UP TO AND INCLUDING THE PRESIDENT, SHOULD BE PROHIBITED FROM RECEIVING INDIRECTLY OR DIRECTLY ANY INCOME TAX RETURN.

4) ALL REQUESTS FOR INFORMATION OR ACTION AND ALL IRS RESPONSES SHOULD BE DISCLOSED PERIODICALLY TO THE APPROPRIATE CONGRESSIONAL OVERSIGHT COMMITTEES.

Discussion. There were numerous efforts by the White House to use the IRS for political purposes between 1969 and 1972. Particularly striking examples, such as attempts to use the IRS to harass persons perceived as "enemies," have already been exposed and discussed at great length by the Select Committee and other groups. In addition, there was misuse of the IRS by the White House regarding the IRS investigations of Rebozo, the President's brothers, and people connected with the Hughes operation. Because of the close relationship of several of the parties to the President, questions of improper White House influence in this case are particularly acute.

Recommendation 1 was prompted by example of White House requests made regarding, among others, Larry O'Brien. In the Spring of 1972 the IRS Commissioner, Johnnie Walters, decided to postpone until after the November election any further investigation of several people who had close relations to prospective Presidential nominees. These people included Larry O'Brien, the President's brothers, and Charles G. Rebozo. The decision was made as an effort to avoid any charges that the investigations were politically motivated. Roger Barth, then Assistant Commissioner of the IRS and a source of information for the White House, had told John Ehrlichman that O'Brien, the Nixon brothers, and Rebozo were or would be under investigation. At some point in the Spring of 1972, Barth gave Ehrlichman a copy of a "sensitive case report" listing these names as subjects of interest to the IRS.

Although it is not clear whether Ehrlichman was told about Walters' decision to postpone the investigations, it is clear that Ehrlichman pressured Barth, Walters, and George Shultz, Secretary of the Treasury, into pursuing intensely the O'Brien investigation in the hope that information damaging to O'Brien might be uncovered before the election. Understandably, Ehrlichman did not push the IRS on the investigations of Rebozo or the Nixon brothers. O'Brien was pursued and interviewed, but Rebozo and the Nixon brothers were not.

Rather than trying to ban such requests from the White House or delineate those requests that are proper, the most straightforward approach is to require disclosure of all requests. Those that are clearly improper, such as the Ehrlichman request on O'Brien, are less likely to be made if the requesting party knows they will be disclosed to Congress. There have been, of course, proper White House requests to the IRS in this and preceding Administrations. There is no reason to think that the effective functioning of the White House or the IRS will be impaired by the disclosure of such requests.

Recommendation 2 was prompted by the Select Committee's discovery that "sensitive case reports" on people involved in some way with Hughes were given regularly to John Ehrlichman by Roger Barth, apparently without the knowledge of Barth's superiors, including Commissioner Walters. Because some of those reports touched upon Rebozo, hence possibly on the President himself, the potential value of those reports to the White House is obvious. There is no sound policy reason for providing the White House with the details of ongoing investigations, and such disclosure could seriously mar the IRS's reputation for impartiality.

There are, however, legitimate reasons for providing the White House with enough information on sensitive cases to identify the person or group involved and the general nature of the IRS inquiry. For example, if the President were considering someone for appointment to a high federal position, he should be able to know whether that person's tax status is under any particular scrutiny. Similarly, the President should be able to learn whether any of his aides or intimates are under investigation. Limiting disclosure by the IRS to identification of the party under investigation and a general statement about the investigation should provide enough information for the White House to decide what to do about the situation, *e.g.*, continue to support, or perhaps withdraw, a nomination. Requests for this basic information on "sensitive case reports" and the IRS's responses to the requests would, of course, be disclosed to the appropriate Congressional committees under Recommendation 1.

Recommendation 3 was prompted by those instances where individuals in the executive office of the President would seek and receive copies of income tax returns. Generally these were the returns of individuals perceived as "enemies" of the White House. That the returns were oftentimes sought and used for improper political purposes is clear. A statute prohibiting the receipt of income tax returns by those in the executive office of the President would do much to curb these improper practices.

In addition, by making receipt—rather than distribution—criminal, the statute would eliminate those instances where returns could be obtained indirectly from a governmental agency, e.g. a U.S. Attorney General's Office, which has free disclosure with the IRS.

II. CONGRESS SHOULD ENACT LEGISLATION REQUIRING FULL FINANCIAL DISCLOSURE BY THE PRESIDENT AND VICE PRESIDENT OF THE UNITED STATES TO THE GOVERNMENT ACCOUNTING OFFICE EACH YEAR OF ALL INCOME, GIFTS, AND THINGS OF VALUE THAT THEY OR THEIR SPOUSES HAVE RECEIVED DURING THE YEAR OR EXPENDITURES MADE FOR THEIR PERSONAL BENEFIT OR

THE BENEFIT OF THEIR SPOUSES BY OTHER INDIVIDUALS.

Discussion. Presently, legislation requires that Congressmen and Senators file statements of financial disclosure each year. Certainly, the head of the Executive Branch of the government should be held to no less a standard than the members of the Legislature, and perhaps even held to a higher standard of disclosure because of the significance of his position.

Full financial disclosure by the President and Vice President to the public each year would also help protect the Office of the President, ensuring that no individual occupying the Office would be the object of any speculation, innuendo, or suggestion of impropriety regarding income, gifts, and expenditures. In addition, such a standard of full public disclosure would help to raise the ethical standards by which the public views its elected officials and would restore a measure of confidence in the workings of government.

Examples of items which should be disclosed include the following:

(a) Copies of tax returns, declarations, statements, or other documents which were made individually or jointly for the preceding year in compliance with the provisions of the Internal Revenue Code;

(b) The identity of each interest in real or personal property having a value of $10,000 or more which the President or Vice President or spouses owned at any time during the preceding year;

(c) The identity of each trust or other fiduciary relation in which the President or Vice President or spouses held a beneficial interest having a value of $10,000 or more, and the identity, if known, of each interest of the trust or other fiduciary relation in real or personal property in which he or she held a beneficial interest having a value of $10,000 or more at any time during the preceding year;

(d) The identity of each liability of $5,000 or more owned by the President or Vice President or by them jointly with their spouses, at any time during the preceding year; and

(e) The source and value of all gifts received by the President, Vice President, or spouses in the aggregate amount or value of $50 or more from any single source received during the preceding year.

The information required to be filed with the GAO would be made public automatically unless there were some overriding reasons to protect the confidentiality of the information. In such a case, the information would still be available to any standing, select or special committee of either House of Congress upon the receipt by GAO of a resolution requesting the transmission of such information.

STATE AND LOCAL BAR ASSOCIATIONS SHOULD CONDUCT A STUDY OF THE ATTORNEY-CLIENT PRIVILEGE IN LIGHT OF THE ABUSES OF THE PRIVILEGE UNCOVERED DURING THE SELECT COMMITTEE'S INVESTIGATIONS.

Discussion. A strong attorney-client privilege is essential to the effective functioning of our legal system. It must be broad enough to encourage full disclosure by client, including disclosure of past criminal conduct. At the same time, the privilege should not be used to protect from disclosure communications involving violations of law and near violations that have nothing to do with the offering of legal advice by a lawyer. Providing information to a person who happens to be a lawyer, or involving him or her in one's affairs should not automatically cloak the transaction with the protections of the privilege.

In at least four instances during the Select Committee's investigations, the lawyer-client privilege has been pleaded as part of an attempt to cover up illegal or questionable activities that had nothing to do with the rendering of legal advice:

(1) Mardian and Liddy in the Watergate cover-up;
(2) Dean and Segretti in the Watergate-dirty tricks cover-up;
(3) Kalmbach and Rebozo in the Hughes-Rebozo cover-up;
(4) Wakefield-Rebozo, also in the Hughes-Rebozo area.

A review of these cases by the various bar associations should help to clarify the proper limits of the privilege and provide more detailed guidance for lawyers, clients, and legislative and investigative bodies.

Exhibits

I. Letter from Senator Ervin and Senator Baker to James
St. Clair, Counsel for the President. Dated June 6, 1974

UNITED STATES SENATE
Select Committee on
Presidential Campaign Activities
Washington, D.C. 20510

June 6, 1974

Mr. James St. Clair
The White House
Washington, D.C.

Dear Mr. St. Clair:

The Senate Select Committee on Presidential Campaign
Activities has been conducting investigations pursuant to
Senate Resolution 60 for the purpose of recommending
legislation regarding, among a number of issues, the receipt,
concealment, and use of cash campaign contributions for
the Presidential election of 1972. The Committee is
presently attempting to conclude its investigative efforts and
file its report by June 30, 1974.

The Committee has received certain evidence that may
relate to information and documents in possession of the
President or his representatives. We wish to afford the
President an opportunity to comment on this material
prior to the filing of this report. We would appreciate any
assistance you can provide in clarifying the issues set
forth below and in aiding us in reviewing of this evidence.
Information provided will be especially helpful in those
areas where the Committee has not had access to all available documents, and where systematic analysis has been
impossible since only random documentation has been
provided us.

The information described below relates to apparent
instructions from President Nixon to Mr. Charles G. Rebozo
to raise and maintain funds which, the evidence implies,
were expended on President Nixon's behalf.

A. *Rebozo Fundraising for Use of the Administration
and the President*

1. The Committee has received evidence and testimony
that in early 1969 the President personally requested Mr. Charles G. Rebozo to contact large

contributors, including Mr. J. Paul Getty, for the purpose of maintaining a fund to be controlled by the White House staff rather than by the Republican National Committee. (See Exhibit A)

2. The Committee has also received evidence that both Mr. John Ehrlichman and Mr. H. R. Haldeman were aware of the President's instructions to Mr. Rebozo. (See Exhibit A)

3. The Committee has received testimony that Mr. John Ehrlichman attempted to determine the propriety and legality of receiving such funds.

4. The Committee has also documented that by April 28, 1969, Mr. Rebozo was responsible for maintaining a fund in Key Biscayne, Florida, to "take care of frequent administration-connected costs." (See Exhibit B) Both Mr. Ehrlichman and Mr. Herbert Kalmbach were apparently advised of these facts.

5. The Committee has received sworn testimony that, on or about April 30, 1973, Mr. H. R. Haldeman advised Mr. Lawrence Higby that the President had informed Mr. Haldeman that Mr. Rebozo had approximately $400,000.00 available to defray the legal expenses of Mr. Haldeman and Mr. Ehrlichman.

B. *The Receipt of Hughes' $100,000 Cash Contribution*

1. The Committee has received sworn testimony from Mr. Richard Danner that he met with the President and Mr. Rebozo in the summer of 1968 to discuss a possible Hughes contribution and that either President Nixon or Mr. Rebozo asked him to determine if Mr. Hughes would contribute to the 1968 campaign.

2. Mr. Danner further testified that in the spring of 1969, Mr. Rebozo contacted him on a number of occasions seeking funds from Howard Hughes.

3. Mr. Danner has also testified that he met with President Nixon in San Clemente on July 3, 1970, on the same visit when he delivered the $50,000.00

in cash to Mr. Rebozo, but that he did not discuss the contribution with the President.

4. The Committee has received sworn testimony from both Mr. Charles G. Rebozo and Miss Rose Mary Woods that Rebozo informed the President's personal secretary, Miss Rose Mary Woods, of the receipt of the $100,000.00 in cash shortly after he received it, and that Mr. Rebozo testified that he had discussed the contribution with her on possibly four occasions.

5. Mr. Rebozo has further testified, however, that he did not discuss the receipt of the $100,000.00 with President Nixon until after the 1972 campaign.

C. *Approval by Attorney General Mitchell of the Acquisition of the Dunes Hotel by the Hughes Tool Company*

1. Mr. Richard Danner testified before this Committee that he met with Attorney General John Mitchell on March 19, 1970, and received verbal approval for the Hughes Tool Company to acquire the Dunes Hotel and Casino.

2. The Committee has received further evidence that this assurance from the Attorney General that the Anti-Trust Division of the Justice Department would not prosecute this Hughes purchase was directly contrary to the policy established by the Anti-Trust Division in reviewing prior applications for hotels purchased by Mr. Hughes in Las Vegas.

D. *Receipt of the $50,000.00 Cash Contribution from Mr. A. D. Davis*

1. The Committee has received sworn testimony that Mr. Rebozo received an additional $50,000.00 in cash from Mr. A. D. Davis for President Nixon's 1972 campaign on or about April 5, 1972. Mr. Rebozo testified that he then called the Finance Committee after receiving the contribution and that they sent Fred LaRue down to Florida to pick up the money.

2. The Committee has reviewed all available records, including those of the Finance Committee to Re-Elect the President, and there is no evidence that

the contribution from Davis to Rebozo was ever transmitted to the Finance Committee.

3. The Committee has received further evidence that Mr. Maurice Stans, formerly the Director of the Finance Committee, has no recollection of ever having been advised of any contributions from Mr. A. D. Davis.

4. Mr. Fred LaRue testified before the Committee that he called Mr. Rebozo at the request of Mr. John Mitchell in October, 1972, to solicit a contribution for a Senatorial campaign, and that he received an estimated $25,000.00 in cash from Mr. Rebozo on or about October 12, 1972, which was to be used in the Nunn-for-Senate campaign in Kentucky. Mr. LaRue denied receiving any cash contributions from Mr. Rebozo prior to October, 1972.

E. *Expenditures Paid for Improvements and Furnishings at 500 and 516 Bay Lane and Not Reported in Coopers and Lybrand Report*

1. On August 20, 1973, Coopers and Lybrand reported to President Nixon that, through May 31, 1973, the President spent "personal funds for improvements" for his properties in Key Biscayne as follows:

Property	Improvements	Furnishings	Total
500 Bay Lane	$24,734	$13,208	$ 37,942
516 Bay Lane	29,687	8,795	38,479
Total [1]	$54,421	$22,000	$ 76,421

2. Documents received to date by this Committee based on a limited number of available records reflect, through May 31, 1973, actual expenditures on the President's properties as follows:

Property	Improvements	Furnishings	Total
500 Bay Lane	$50,777	$14,938	$ 65,715
516 Bay Lane	46,027	9,931	55,958
Total	$96,804	$24,869	$121,673

1. Available records reflect an interest payment of $368.50 included in the total expenditures for "improvements and furnishings." Therefore, the total expenditure according to the President's records made available to Coopers and Lybrand for improvements and furnishings was $76,053.

3. Expenditures for improvements and furnishings at the President's 500 and 516 Bay Lane properties, which were not included in the President's records when examined by Coopers and Lybrand, total $45,620. (See Footnote 1)

4. Total expenditures reflected in available documents total $121,673. In a statement issued by the White House on May 12, 1969, the 500 and 516 Bay Lane properties were reflected as having a purchase price of $252,800. (See Exhibit C for items received to date.)

F. *Expenditures on 500 and 516 Bay Lane Paid for by Charles G. Rebozo*

1. The Committee has received evidence that in December, 1968, President Nixon met with Mr. Borrelli, Mr. Rebozo, Mrs. Nixon, and Mr. and Mrs. David Eisenhower to discuss possible alterations to his home at 500 Bay Lane. Thereafter, in 1969, Mr. Rebozo ordered work to be done by the architectural firm of Bouterse, Borrelli, Albaisa, for "additions and alterations, 500 Bay Lane, Key Biscayne." Mr. Rebozo paid for this work in cash on the following dates in the following amounts:

February 10, 1969	$ 400.00
March 7, 1969	400.00
March 19, 1969	300.00
April 2, 1969	581.00
TOTAL	$1,681.00

In addition, payments of $295.65 and $100.00 were made on January 18, 1969, and March 14, 1969, respectively, by Mr. Rebozo to B.B. & A. architects for "job expenses" incurred on work for the President's house. Although records reflect that Mr. Rebozo apparently did not make these payments by personal check, we have not been able to determine conclusively that Mr. Rebozo made these payments in cash. The records received by this Committee to date do not reflect any reimbursement to Mr. Rebozo for the above-listed payments. Evidence furnished the Committee further indicates that when Mr. Rebozo

620

paid the same firm for work done on his home at 490 Bay Lane, he did so by personal check.

2. The Committee has received evidence that Mr. Rebozo paid $754.00 in cash on or about April 11, 1969, to Designers Flooring Company for work done at the President's 500 Bay Lane home. The evidence obtained further reflects that Mr. Rebozo paid $300.00 and $600.00 in cash to the same company in May and July, 1969, for work done at the President's house at 516 Bay Lane. Again, records received to date reflect no reimbursement to Mr. Rebozo for the $1,654.00 cash payments that he made. Also, Mr. Rebozo ordered tile work from the above-named company for his residence at 490 Bay Lane, for which he paid by personal check in the amount of $273.00 on March 6, 1969.

3. Evidence obtained by this Committee reflects Mr. Rebozo paid the Babcock Company $11,978.84 for work at President Nixon's house at 516 Bay Lane. Documents received by us indicate the work was to "convert two car garage into efficiency with living room, bedroom and bath . . ." Mr. Rebozo's check to Babcock has on it the notation "516 Bay Lane (Garage)." [2] Again,

2. This check was missing from records provided by Mr. Rebozo to the Committee.

records received to date reflect no reimbursement by the President to Mr. Rebozo for his payments.

4. The Committee has received documents reflecting that Mr. Rebozo was billed by the Bartlett Construction, Inc. at the Key Biscayne Bank Building for the installation of an "Arnold Palmer putting green" at President Nixon's 516 Bay Lane property. Bartlett Construction was paid $243.57 by Mr. Rebozo's personal check on or about June 17, 1969. Again, records reviewed by the Committee do not reflect reimbursement to Mr. Rebozo for this expenditure.

5. The Committee has received documents reflecting Mr. Rebozo's order, shortly after the November 1972 Presidential election, for the construction of a swimming pool at President Nixon's 500 Bay Lane property. The aforesaid documents reflect

payment to Catalina Pools, Inc. in the amount of $10,100.00, in checks dated between November 20 and December 18, 1972, written on the "Wakefield, Hewitt and Webster Trust Account" at the First National Bank of Miami. Notations appearing on the November 20, 1972, check of $1,000.00 include "Deposit on swimming pool contract for: 500 Bay Lane . . . Rebozo, C. G." Further evidence obtained indicates that approximately eight months after the above expenditures were made, and after the President was advised of the IRS investigation into the receipt and return by Mr. Rebozo of the Hughes' $100,000.00, reimbursement was made to Mr. Rebozo for the swimming pool out of the President's personal funds. Evidence received reflects that on August 18, 1973, a check to Mr. Rebozo in the amount of $13,642.52 was signed by Rose Mary Woods on President Nixon's bank account 2-0527-4.

6. The Committee has obtained evidence that on or about November 15, 1972, Mr. Rebozo ordered a heater from Belcher Oil Co. for the pool at the President's 500 Bay Lane property. The heater was paid for on February 20, 1973, by a check in the amount of $1,727.26 drawn on funds in the "Wakefield, Hewitt and Webster Trust Account" at the Key Biscayne Bank. Further evidence before this Committee indicates that this Trust Account included a deposit of $4,562.50 from an account entitled Florida Nixon for President. This last account consisted of campaign contributions received and retained from the 1968 Presidential election. As a result, it appears that Belcher Oil Co. may have been paid with funds originally obtained as campaign contributions.

7. The evidence obtained to date reflects that on or about November 16, 1972, Mr. Rebozo ordered from Climatrol Corporation a "screen enclosure" to be installed around the pool at the President's 500 Bay Lane property. Between, on or about November 27, 1972, and December 28, 1972, Climatrol received three checks totaling $3,600.00 drawn against the "Wakefield, Hewitt and Webster Trust Account" in the First National Bank of Miami. The documents available to the Committee to date do not reflect conclusively whether the

aforementioned check to Mr. Rebozo of $13,642.52 drawn against the President's funds on August 18, 1973, was intended to repay Mr. Rebozo for the $3,600.00 expended on the screens.

8. Evidence received by the Committee reflects that on November 21, 1972, Mr. Rebozo ordered from Paul's Carpet Co., Inc., the installation of 182 yards of carpeting for the pool area at the President's 500 Bay Lane property. Mr. Rebozo was billed at the Key Biscayne Bank for this expenditure and payment of $1,277.64 was made from a Wakefield, Hewitt and Webster Trust Account. Again, records available to date are not conclusive as to whether the President reimbursed Mr. Rebozo for this expense.

9. Documents received by this Committee further reflect that on or about November 17, 1973, Mr. Rebozo ordered from J. H. Clagett work to be done at the President's 500 Bay Lane property. The work is identified in the documents as "extending existing roof to cover patio." Information furnished the Committee indicates that this expenditure amounted to $6,508.11 which was not furnished from President Nixon's personal funds. According to records received to date, the $6,508.11 was paid by "Thomas H. Wakefield" in December of 1972.

10. Evidence received by the Committee indicates that Mr. Rebozo ordered on January 26, 1973, furniture for the "pool area" to be sent to "Mr. Robert H. Abplanalp, 478 Bay Lane, Key Biscayne, Florida." Information obtained by the Committee, however, indicates that the furniture was actually ordered for the President, was intended to match the fabric of similar furniture at his San Clemente home, and that 478 Bay Lane, while owned by Mr. Abplanalp, was leased to the U.S. Government. Further information indicates that the 478 Bay Lane property does not include a pool. Documents received by the Committee indicate the firm of Bouterse, Borrelli and Albaisa was paid by Mr. Rebozo making deposits to their account at the Key Biscayne Bank. The first deposit for $1,519.50 was made on February 1, 1973. The second payment was disclosed to the

623

firm in a letter of February 20, 1973, from Mr. Rebozo's bookkeeper enclosing a deposit by Mr. Rebozo to the firm's account of $210.78. Again, based on evidence available, we are unable to determine if President Nixon reimbursed Mr. Rebozo for these payments.

11. Evidence received by the Committee reflects that a fireplace was added to the President's home at 516 Bay Lane at a cost of $3,586.00, which was paid on March 26, 1973. The review of records available to date does not reflect that President Nixon's personal funds were used for payment to either J. H. Clagett, Inc., the contractor, or Artistic Stone, the subcontractor.

12. The Committee has received documents and testimony that Mr. Rebozo paid $1,138.80 by personal check on or about March 20, 1970, to Well Brandt's Billiard Supply Inc. While records indicate the order for a "pool table" was from Mr. Rebozo at 490 Bay Lane, the evidence before the Committee indicates that Mr. Rebozo does not have a pool table at his 490 Bay Lane residence. Further evidence indicates that a pool table was obtained for President Nixon's home at 516 Bay Lane.

13. Evidence received by the Committee to date reflects that neither of President Nixon's attorneys, Messrs. Kalmbach and DeMarco, were aware of the above-listed expenses and the President's accountant, Mr. Arthur Blech, learned only of the expenditure for the construction of a swimming pool when, a year later, a check appeared payable to Mr. Rebozo.

G. *Purchase of 500 and 516 Bay Lane, Key Biscayne, Florida*

1. On August 20, 1973, Coopers and Lybrand reported to President and Mrs. Nixon that the proceeds of a $65,000 loan from the First National Bank of Mimai were applied the purchase of properties at 500 and 516 Bay Lane, Key Biscayne, Florida. The Coopers Lybrand Report reflects that personal funds of President Nixon went to repay the $65,000 loan and the $3,504.00 interest on September 4, 1969.

2. The Committee has received evidence that the note of January 20, 1969, for the $65,000 loan was signed by "C. G. Rebozo." The First National Bank of Miami's ledger sheet for said loan bears the notation next to Mr. Rebozo's name "For Richard M. and Patricia Nixon."

3. The Committee has also received a copy of a letter from the Senior Vice-President of the Key Biscayne Bank dated September 4, 1969, to the First National Bank of Miami which reads, in pertinent part, as follows:

   "Enclosed you will find our Cashier's Check no. 10864 in the amount of $65,763.75 of which $65,000 is payment on the principal note of Mr. C. G. Rebozo and $763.75 for interest."

4. The Committee would appreciate learning under what circumstances Mr. Rebozo incurred the above-described obligation relating to President Nixon's property and what, if any, consideration he received for incurring said obligation.

5. The Committee has also received evidence that on March 12, 1973, the sum of $65,000 was transferred from the President's account to Mr. Rebozo as a three-year loan payable to Mrs. Patricia Cox at 8% interest. This amount was apparently part of the proceeds of a sale of property by President Nixon on December 28, 1972. Based on the evidence available to it, the Committee is unable to determine if the transfer of $65,000 to Mr. Rebozo on March 12, 1973, is related in any way to the note for $65,000 described in the preceding paragraphs.

H. *Other Expenses Paid from Campaign Contributions*

1. The Committee has obtained documents which reflect that Mr. Rebozo, on February 19, 1969, reimbursed the Florida Nixon for President campaign account for "various bills advanced RMN, Pers." Mr. Rebozo's check in the amount of $426.87 appears to have been a reimbursement for contributions used to pay certain of President Nixon's personal expenses.

2. Documents and testimony received by the Committee indicate Mr. Rebozo, pursuant to instructions of Mr. Ehrlichman, transmitted approximately $1,416.18 to Mr. Kalmbach for payment to Messrs. Jack Caulfield and Tony Ulasewicz. The above amount was furnished from 1968 campaign contributions remaining in the Florida for Nixon account and was withdrawn in April 1969.

I. *Other Expenses Paid by Mr. Rebozo*

1. Evidence obtained by the Committee to date reflects that Mr. Rebozo issued personal checks for a variety of expenses incurred by President Nixon between January 24, 1969 and May 12, 1970, which totaled $831.60. Further, other documents reviewed to date reflect only a single possible reimbursement to Mr. Rebozo of $127.77 on February 14, 1969.

J. *Return by Mr. Rebozo of the $100,000.00 Hughes Contribution*

1. Mr. Rebozo has testified that President Nixon advised him to return the $100,000 contribution in the spring of 1973 after Mr. Rebozo had been contacted by the Internal Revenue Service.

2. Mr. Herbert Kalmbach has testified that on April 30, 1973, Mr. Rebozo told him that the President had advised Mr. Rebozo to speak to Mr. Kalmbach, rather than to Mr. Maurice Stans, concerning the $100,000 in cash that Mr. Rebozo had received from Mr. Hughes.

3. Mr. Kalmbach further testified that Mr. Rebozo told him at their meeting on April 30, 1973, that he had disbursed part of these funds to "Rosemary Woods, to Don Nixon, to Ed Nixon, and to unnamed others during the intervening years," and that he was to meet with the IRS to discuss the contribution shortly thereafter.

4. The committee received further testimony from Mr. Kalmbach that he indicated to Mr. Rebozo that he should get the best tax lawyer he could find and "lay out the facts of the matter exactly to the I.R.S." According to Mr. Kalmbach, Mr.

626

Rebozo expressed "grave reservations" about following that course of action since Mr. Rebozo said "this touches the President and the President's family, and I just can't do anything to add to his problems at this time."

5. The Committee has also received sworn testimony mentioned earlier, that on or about April 30, 1973, Mr. Lawrence Higby was advised by Mr. H. R. Halderman that President Nixon had informed Mr. Haldeman that Mr. Rebozo had approximately $400,000.00 that was available to defray legal expenses incurred by Messrs. Haldeman and Ehrlichman in the future.

6. While the Committee has been unable to determine conclusively whether any of the individuals allegedly specified by Rebozo to Kalmbach in their conversation of April 30, 1973, actually received any part of the Hughes' $100,000.00 it has received evidence that portions of cash contributions have been provided in the past to Messrs. Edward and Donald Nixon. For example, Mr. Kalmbach testified under oath that on or about April 29, 1969, Mr. Ehrlichman approved the payment of $3,000 in cash to Mr. Ed Nixon from a $25,000 cash contribution from Mr. D. K. Ludwig. In addition, Mr. F. Donald Nixon "had been paid expenses of $6,500 in late 1968" from campaign contributions left over from 1968 and stored at the Riggs National Bank Safe Deposit Box No. E429 according to documents received by the Select Committee. (See Exhibit D)

7. The Committee has received evidence that Mr. Rebozo was first interviewed by the Internal Revenue Service about the receipt of the $100,000.00 contribution, on or about May 10, 1973, and the Committee has received testimony that the contact by the Internal Revenue Service had some effect on Rebozo's decision to return the $100,000.00.

8. The Committee has received evidence that on or about May 19, 1973, Mr. Rebozo met with Mr. Richard Danner in Washington, D.C., to discuss the $100,000.00 contribution and to request that Danner take the contribution back. Furthermore, the Committee has received sworn testimony that

627

on the following day, May 20, 1973, Mr. Danner and Mr. Rebozo met with President Nixon at Camp David, Maryland, for a period of time that is in dispute. Mr. Rebozo has testified that at this particular time, he was having great difficulty in persuading Mr. Danner to take back the contribution.

K. *Knowledge of the Internal Revenue Service and Special Prosecutor Investigation*

1. The committee has received sworn testimony from Mr. John Ehrlichman that he informed Mr. Rebozo that the IRS was going to contact him prior to their first contact.

2. In addition, the Committee has received testimony that there were, apparently, discussions between President Nixon, Mr. Rebozo and General Haig relating to the nature of the IRS investigation into the receipt of the $100,000.00.

3. The Committee has also received testimony that on May 23, 1973, one day after The President's statement on Watergate to the Nation, General Alexander Haig and The President's counsel, Mr. Leonard Garment, apparently spoke with Mr. William Simon, then Deputy Secretary of the Treasury, regarding the status of the IRS investigation of Mr. Rebozo. This matter was apparently further discussed between General Haig, Mr. Garment, Mr. Fred Buzhardt and Mr. Chapman Rose, and General Haig apparently reported on this discussion to President Nixon with the recommendation that Mr. Rebozo obtain "a qualified tax attorney."

4. Testimony before the Committee indicates that the President requested General Haig to obtain the name of a qualified tax attorney and to furnish it to Mr. Rebozo. Mr. Rebozo thereafter retained Mr. Kenneth Gemmill, an attorney who also represented President Nixon on tax matters during this same period.

5. The Committee has received information that on one occasion General Haig apparently advised Mr. Gemmill that a Federal Reserve Board report relating to Mr. Rebozo might create problems, which Mr. Gemmill apparently assumed related to the

Board's examination of the serial numbers of the $100 bills actually returned by Mr. Rebozo to Mr. Hughes on June 27, 1973.

6. General Haig has testified before this Committee that he received reports "periodically" from Mr. Gemmill on the status of the IRS investigation of Mr. Rebozo. In addition, General Haig testified that President Nixon had advised him that "Mr. Rebozo frequently received money, campaign money, which he normally would process through to the proper campaign recipients," and the President stated that Mr. Rebozo had done this for "a number of years."

7. Former Attorney General Elliot Richardson testified before the Senate Judiciary Committee on November 8, 1973, that General Haig called him on October 18, 1973, two days before Special Prosecutor Cox was dismissed, to advise him of President Nixon's concern that Special Prosecutor Archibald Cox had begun an investigation into the receipt by Mr. Rebozo of the Hughes' $100,-000.00 cash contribution. On or about the same date, the President's counsel, Mr. Fred Buzhardt, prepared a letter to the IRS for the signature of Miss Rose Mary Woods, President Nixon's executive secretary. The letter related to Miss Wood's knowledge of Mr. Rebozo's receipt of the $100,-000.00, which information she allegedly received at the time Mr. Rebozo received said payments.

As noted above, the Committee will appreciate receiving relevant information and documents that the President is able to furnish that will assist in clarifying the above-described matters.

Sincerely,

s/Sam J. Ervin, Jr.   s/Howard H. Baker, Jr.

Sam J. Ervin, Jr., U.S.S.   Howard H. Baker, Jr. U.S.S.

MEMORANDUM

THE WHITE HOUSE
WASHINGTON

CONFIDENTIAL

February 17, 1969

MEMORANDUM FOR: MR. EHRLICHMAN

BeBe Rebozo has been asked by the President to contact J. Paul Getty in London regarding major contributions.

BeBe would like advice from you or someone as to how this can legally and technically be handled. The funds should go to some operating entity other than the National Committee so that we retain full control of their use.

BeBe would appreciate your calling him with this advice as soon as possible since the President has asked him to move quickly.

s/H.

C. G. REBOZO
Key Biscayne, Florida

April 28, 1969

Mr. Herbert W. Kalmbach
Kalmbach, DeMarco, Knapp & Chillingworth
Suite 900 Newport Financial Plaza
550 Newport Center Drive
Newport Beach, California 92660

Dear Herb:

Enclosed find an additional check in the amount of $200.00. This will at least take care of the $320.00 statement which you now have.

Over the weekend, I spoke with John Ehrlichman and explained to him that it had been decided that the larger balance which I mentioned to you will be kept here in order to take care of frequent administration-connected costs which arise from time to time. Let me know, if you need more help.

Thank you very much.

Sincerely,

s/C. G. Rebozo

C. G. Rebozo

CGR:lh
Enclosure

RECEIVED
APR. 30, 1969
KALMBACH, DeMARCO,
KNAPP & CHILLINGWORTH
LAW OFFICES

Exhibit C

Itemized Expenditures on the Presidential Homes (500 and 516 Bay Lane) in Key Biscayne According to Documents in the Possession of the Select Committee

Vendor and Type of Work	Date of Payment	Amount	Site of Work	Agent	Means of Payment
B.B.A. Architects 1 (job expenses)	1-18-69	295.65	500 Bay La.	Rebozo	Payment by Mr. Rebozo. Form of Payment Unknown
B.B.A. Architects (fee)	2-10-69	400.00	500 Bay La.	Rebozo	Cash from Mr. Rebozo
B.B.A. Architects (fee)	3-7-69	400.00	500 Bay La.	Rebozo	Cash from Mr. Rebozo
B.B.A. Architects (job expenses)	3-14-69	100.00	500 Bay La.	Rebozo	Payment by Mr. Rebozo. Form of Payment Unknown
B.B.A. Architects (fee)	3-19-69	300.00	500 Bay La.	Rebozo	Cash from Mr. Rebozo
B.B.A. Architects (fee)	4-2-69	581.00	500 Bay La.	Rebozo	Cash from Mr. Rebozo
Designer's Flooring (Repair and Replace Tile)	4-11-69	754.00	500 Bay La.	Rebozo	Cash from Mr. Rebozo
L.L. & P Architects (fee) 2	4-14-69	1,297.30	516 Bay La.	Rebozo	Payment by the President 3
Babcock Construction Company	4-14-69	6,500.00	516 Bay La.	Rebozo	Payment by the President
Babcock Construction Company	5-5-69	1,210.36	500 Bay La.	Rebozo	Payment by the President
Babcock Construction Company	5-13-69	463.08	500 Bay La.	Rebozo	Payment by the President
Babcock Construction Company	5-13-69	1,550.75	500 Bay La.	Rebozo	Payment by the President
Babcock Construction Company	5-14-69	320.33	516 Bay La.	Rebozo	Payment by the President
Babcock Construction Company	5-14-69	479.16	516 Bay La.	Rebozo	Payment by the President
Babcock Construction Company	5-16-69	8,265.00	516 Bay La.	Rebozo	Payment by the President
Designers Flooring	5-27-69	330.00	516 Bay La.	Rebozo	Cash from Mr. Rebozo
Bartlett Const. (Putting green)	6-17-69	243.57	516 Bay La.	Rebozo	Mr. Rebozo's Personal Check

1. "B.B.A. Architects" is an abbreviation for Bouterse, Borrelli, and Albaisa Architects—Planners; Miami, Florida.
2. "L.L. & P Architects" is an abbreviation for Little, Lair, and Pilkington, Architects, formerly of Miami, Florida.
3. This notation reflects the Committee staff's understanding that these payments were made by the President.

Vendor and Type of Work	Date of Payment	Amount	Site of Work	Agent	Means of Payment
L,L, & P Architects (fee)	6-19-69	835.00	516 Bay La.	Rebozo	Payment by the President
Rablin-Shelton (furnishings)	6-19-69	10,000.00	500 Bay La.	Rebozo	Payment by the President
Designer's Flooring	7-19-69	600.00	516 Bay La.	Rebozo	Cash from Mr. Rebozo
Caldwell-Scott Construction	7-31-69	14,622.13	500 Bay La.	Rebozo	Payment by the President
Babcock Construction Company	8-11-69	11,978.84	516 Bay La.	Rebozo	Mr. Rebozo's Personal Check
Babcock Construction Company	8-11-69	11,307.12	516 Bay La.	Rebozo	Payment by the President
Caldwell-Scott Construction	8-21-69	588.25	500 Bay La.	Rebozo	Payment by the President
Rablin-Shelton	10-2-69	12,000.00	500&516 Bay La.	Rebozo	Payment by the President
Babcock Construction Company	10-10-69	6,299.44	500 Bay La.	Rebozo	Payment by the President
Metal Tech., Inc.	?	314.80	516 Bay La.	?	Payment by the President
Brandt Billiards	3-20-72	1,138.80	516 Bay La.	Rebozo	Rebozo personal check
Catalina Pool Co.	11-20-72	1,000.00	500 Bay La.	Rebozo	Payment from W,H, & W 4 Trust Account
Catalina Pool Co.	11-22-72	5,935.00	500 Bay La.	Rebozo	Payment from W,H, & W Trust Account
Catalina Pool Co.	11-28-72	2,000.00	500 Bay La.	Rebozo	Payment from W,H, & W Trust Account
Catalina Pool Co.	12-18-72	1,165.00	500 Bay La.	Rebozo	Payment from W,H, & W Trust Account
Climatrol, Inc. (Screening for Pool)	12-28-72	2,600.00 (1500 and 1100)	500 Bay La.	Brown 5	Payment from W,H, & W Trust Account
Climatrol, Inc.	12-29-72	1,000.00	500 Bay La.	Brown	Payment from W,H, & W Trust Account
Paul's Carpet, Inc. (Pool Carpet)	12-72	1,277.64	500 Bay La.	Brown	Payment from W,H, & W Trust Account

4. "W,H, & W Trust Account" is an abbreviation for Wakefield, Hewitt, and Webster Trust Account. This Miami law firm used trust accounts held at both the First National Bank of Miami and the Key Biscayne Bank and Trust Company to make these payments.
5. Mr. Jack W. Brown is the auditor of the Key Biscayne Bank and Trust Company. Mr. Brown testified he was acting as an agent for Mr. Rebozo in these instances.

Exhibit C (continued)

Itemized Expenditures on the Presidential Homes (500 and 516 Bay Lane) in Key Biscayne According to Documents in the Possession of the Select Committee

Belcher Oil Co. (Pool Heater)	2-20-73	1,727.26	Brown	Payment from W,H, & W Trust Account
B.B.A. Architects (Pool Furniture)	2-1-73	1,519.50	Rebozo	Payment by Mr. Rebozo. Form of Payment Unknown
B.B.A. Architects (Pool Furniture)	2-20-73	210.78	Rebozo	Cash from Mr. Rebozo
Clagett Const. (Pool related const.)	12-8-72	6,508.11	Rebozo	Payment by "Thomas H. Wakefield"
Clagett Const. (Fireplace)	5-73	3,586.00	Rebozo	Unknown

Exhibit D *

Riggs National Bank Safe Deposit Box No. E 429
Main Office, 1503 Pennsylvania Avenue
Washington, D.C.
Attn: Mrs. Amanda Sweeney, Safe Deposit Department
Telephone: (202) ST. 3-5600, Extension 311

Chronology of receipts and disbursements:

·1/24/69 HWK and WDR opened box with an initial
deposit of $733,952.20

5/28/70 TWE and FMR withdrew $300,000 ($200,000
brought out to California by FMR for initial
deposit to the Crocker-Citizens box in Los Angeles;
the other $100,000 was used to (a) reimburse the
Security Pacific box in NB for $45,000 of the
$100,000 earlier disbursed in California and
$55,000 was disbursed to KDKC as reimburse-
ment to the firm for a loan of that amount
obtained by the firm which was needed to enable the
earlier $100,000 disbursal). Balance: $433,952.20

7/17/70 HWK and FMR withdrew $333,952.20 ($16,500
was paid over to JAG * that date by HWK;
$258,452.20 was taken to California by FMR for
deposit in the Crocker-Citizens box—when such
was deposited on 7/21/70 by HWK and FMR
and a complete count made, it was found that
the total was actually $253,452.20, i.e. $5,000
short which was probably due to an inaccurate
pencil notation on a sealed envelope in the box
from which envelope FDN had been paid expenses
in late 1968 of $6,500; and $59,000 went to the
Security Pacific box in NB). Balance: $100,000

* (covered $9,000 for Massachusetts poll (MC). MC special
of $1,000, $1,500 to California for recount, $3,500 to JAG
for expenses, and $1,500 for Magruder Youth Committee)

Two box keys issued, one to each of the following:

Thomas W. Evans
France M. Raine, Jr.

Joint access authorized to any two of the following:
Herbert W. Kalmbach
Thomas W. Evans,
France M. Raine, Jr.

II. Letter from James St. Clair to Senator Ervin and Senator
Baker, dated June 20, 1974.

THE WHITE HOUSE
WASHINGTON

June 20, 1974

Dear Senators Ervin and Baker:

I am sorry for the delay in responding to your letter of
June 6, 1974, requesting comment form the President on
certain matters set forth therein. As you will understand,
there has been very little opportunity to review it with
the President in view of his recent trip to the Middle East.
However, during the President's absence I did review your
letter with his counsel and today reviewed it with the
President.

The staff summaries contained in your letter of evidence
described as being before your Committee are so uninforma-
tive and obscure that intelligent comment is not possible.
Nor would any useful purpose be served by entering upon
a point-by-point discussion of the nature and purported
support for the many wholly unjustified innuendoes and
inferences stated or suggested by the materials in your
letter and the misleading manner in which they are arranged.
In this connection, I note that extensive materials from the
Committee investigation paralleling portions of your letter
appear in a lengthy and detailed article in today's *New York
Times*. As to matters referred to of which the President
might be expected to have first-hand knowledge, such as
any major expenditures on his properties at Key Biscayne,
the summary reflects only unidentified "evidence" or "documents" received by the Committee, the source and authenticity of which are undisclosed. The President has made
public an audit of his affairs dated August 20, 1973, certified
by Coopers and Lybrand, which, he is confident, reflected
fully his receipts and expenditures for the period covered.

I believe that the only useful comment that can be made in
response to your letter is to convey the President's assurance

that he never instructed C. G. Rebozo to raise and maintain funds to be expended on the President's personal behalf, nor, so far as he knows, was this ever done.

Sincerely,

s/ James D. St. Clair

James D. St. Clair
Special Counsel to the President

Honorable Sam J. Ervin, Jr., U.S.S.
Honorable Howard H. Baker, Jr., U.S.S.
United States Senate
Select Committee on Presidential
Campaign Activities
Washington, D.C. 20510

Appendix

LIST OF INDIVIDUALS INTERVIEWED

Individuals Interviewed by SSC Staff During Course of Hughes-Rebozo Investigation

NAME	DATE	NAME	DATE
ABPLANALP, Robert	11-1-73	CERNY, Howard	1-5-74
ACKER, Marjorie	3-25-74	CHOTINER, Murray	8-9-73
	5-6-74		8-17-73
ANDREWS, Vince, Jr.	12-7-73		12-7-73
BACON, Donald	1-31-74	CLAGETT, J. H.	6-14-74
BAKER, Buehl	6-3-74	CLARK, John	1-10-74
BAKER, Donald	11-26-73	CLARK, Thos. R.	10-15-73
BARKER, Bernard	11-13-73	CLIFFORD, George	10-15-73
	1-4-74	COMEGYS, Walter	11-5-73
BARRICK, Paul	5-16-74	COMER, Katherine	11-73
BARTH, Roger	7-31-73	COYLE, James	11-14-73
	6-6-74		1-10-74
BARTLETT, Jack	5-16-74		1-31-74
BARTLEY, Evelyn	1-17-74	CRANE, Richard	2-14-74
BAUTZER, Greg	1-22-74	CROMAR, Jack	12-3-73
BEANS, Robert		CROMAR, Jack (cont.)	12-12-73
BELL, Thomas	12-17-74		5-7-74
BENEDICT, Alvin	12-10-73	"D", Mrs.	8-22-73
BENNETT, Gen. John	5-18-74	DAHL, Norman	10-23-73
BENNETT, Robert	7-27-73	DANNER, Richard	8-30-73
	9-6-73		12-18–20-73
	9-13-73		12-18 & 19-73
	12-28-74		6-11–12-74
	1-2-74	DAVIS, A. D.	3-19-74
BIRD, Robert	10-21-73		4-11-74
BISHOP, Alvin	12-20-73	DAVIS, Chester	10-10-73
BLECH, Arthur	10-26-73		12-3–4-73
	11-14-73		6-12-74
	4-18-74	DAVIS, Irving, "Jack"	2-5-74
	6-3-74	DAWSON, Ann	2-7-74
BOGGS, "Pat"	7-19-73		2-11-74
BRANDT, William		DEAN, John	7-31-73
BRIGGS, William			9-73
BRINN, Lawrence	5-22-74		10-24-74
BROWN, Howard	10-25-73	DEBOER, Franklin	8-8-73
BROWN, Jack	5-13-74	DEFEO, Mike	2-14-74
BROWN, Secor	1-15-74	DEMARCO, Frank	11-13–14-73
BROWNHILL, Ruth	1-15-74		1-31-74
BRUMMETT, Jean	12-21-73		2-74
BUTTERFIELD, Alexander	9-18-73		4-17-74
BUZHARDT, Fred	4-10-74		7-23-73
	4-23-74	DEMOTT, Howard	
	5-7-74	DENT, Robert	
CAMPBELL, Harold	12-18-73	DESAUTELS, Claude	10-29-73
CANTOR, Arthur	12-4-73	EBNER, Stanley	3-74
CARNEY, Tom	3-18-74	EHRLICHMAN, John	1-10-74
CAULFIELD, John	5-15-74		2-8-74
	9-11–12-73	ELLIS, Richard	12-18-73
	9-18-73	ELSON, Dean	9-11-73
	3-15-74	EVANS, Harry	10-28-73
	3-23-74	FIELDING, Fred	7-12-73
			2-8-74

NAME	DATE	NAME	DATE
FINCH, Robert	11-15-73		10-12-73
FIRESTONE, Leonard	4-17-74		11-13-73
FLANIGAN, Peter	11-20-73		3-8-74
FOLEY, Joseph	10-11-73		3-21–22-74
GARMENT, Leonard	4-4-74		5-5-74
	5-17-74		6-13-74
GAY, Bill	10-9-73	KEENEY, John C.	2-14-74
GEMMILL, Kenneth	12-3-73	KIRBY, Esther	8-27-73
	5-29-74	KLEIN, Herb	8-27-73
GILLER, Gen. Edward	10-16-73		11-16-73
GLAESER, Walter	12-3–4-73	KLEINDIENST, Richard	10-19-73
GOLDEN, James	10-16 & 19-73	KONOWALSKI, Diane	9-7-73
	1-2-74	LAROCCO, Anthony	9-21-73
	6-27-74	LARUE, Fred	7-6-73
GONZALES, Virgilio	11-10-73		7-7-73
	12-10-73		10-15-73
GRACE, David	10-30-73		4-9-74
GREENSPUN, Hank	8-25 & 28-73		5-28-74
	4-18-74	LATHAM, Lee	5-17-74
GRIFFIN, William	12-7-73	LAXALT, Paul	10-11-73
	1-8-74		12-19-73
	3-28-74		1-2-74
	4-19-74	LEE, Jean	
GRIBBEN, Dave	12-3–4-73	LINDENBAUM, Sol	12-26-73
HAIG, Gen. Alexander	5-2-74	LYNCH, W.	
	5-15-74	MAGRUDER, Jeb Stuart	8-16-73
HALDEMAN, H. R.	7-25-73	MAHEU, Peter	11-29-73
	7-30-73	MAHEU, Robert	8-30-73
	11-9-73		9-15-73
	1-31-74		1-20–21-74
HALL, Joan	1-21-74		1-28-74
HALLOMORE, Barry	11-15-73	MAILLOUX, Pierre	12-15-73
	4-25-74	MALEK, Fred	4-18-74
HAMILTON, Wayne		MARTIN, Susan	2-4-74
HARRISON, Jane Lucke	1-16-74	MARTINEZ, Eugenio	12-10-73
HARTMAN, June	1-21-74	MESSICK, Hank	1-15-74
HARVEY, Ann	5-4-74	MIDDENDORF, J. W.	5-14-74
HAYES, Jim		MILLER, Clifford	1-22-74
HEALY, Ray		MITCHELL, John	10-18-73
HELMS, Richard	3-8-74	MONCOURT, Nicole	4-1-74
HENDERSCHEID, Robert		MOORE, Richard	2-27-74
HENLEY, Nadine	1-22-74	MORGAN, Edward P.	9-7-73
HEWITT, Robert	6-10-74		12-5
HIGBY, Lawrence	5-22-74		3-6-74
	6-24-74		5-2-74
HILLINGS, Patrick	11-7-73	MORGAN, Robert	12-11–12-73
HINKLE, Sgt. Earl	11-15-73	MURPHY, Charles	1-10-74
HOLLINGSWORTH, Robert	10-17-73	MURRAY, Thomas	10-73
HOLM, Molly	7-24-73	McCORD, James	9-17-73
HULLIN, Tod	1-11-74		10-23-73
HUMMEL, Robert	11-30-73	McKIERNAN, Stanley	4-15–16-74
HRUSKA, Janet	7-12-73		5-15-74
HUNT, E. Howarl	7-25–26-73	NIXON, Edward	11-10-73
	9-10–14-73		11-16 & 17-73
	12-17–18-73		4-15-74
HILL, George		NIXON, F. Donald	11-8-73
JACKSON, Morton	8-23-73		11-16 & 17-73
JOHNSON, Frank	12-19-73		4-16-74
JONES, Linda Lee	9-6-73	NEWMAN, Ross	10-19-73
JULIANA, James	11-5-73	NOFZIGER, Lyn	
KALMBACH, Herbert	9-24-73	NORTON, Jim	

639

NAME	DATE	NAME	DATE
O'BRIEN, Lawrence	10-9-73	STUART, Charles	5-74
	12-7-73	STURGIS, Frank	3-7-74
OLEJNIK, Virginia	2-15-74	SUCKLING, John R.	10-25-73
PELOQUIN, Robert	12-28-73	SULLIVAN, William	9-73
	3-15-74		2-74
PEREZ, Jenaro	12-3-73	SWOPE, Wm.	11-23-73
PERKINS, Mahlon	12-7-73	TAMMERO, Robert	
PETERSEN, Henry	2-19-74	TAYLOR, Robert	10-27-73
PFEIFER, Miss		THOMAS, E. Parry	12-20-73
RAMEY, James T.	10-16-73	THOMAS, Jane	1-5-74
RASHID, Babbia	11-21-73	"T"	8-25-73
REAL, Jack	12-1-73	TODD, Webster	12-3-73
REBOZO, Charles G.	10-18-73	ULASEWICZ, Anthony	7-9-73
	10-17-73	VAL, Claudia	1-8-74
	3-20-21-74	WAKEFIELD, Thomas	10-18-73
	5-9-74		1-16-74
REYNOLDS, Anita Rebozo	2-5-74		6-10-74
RICHARDSON, Elliott	4-30-74	WALTERS, Johnnie	6-14-74
ROSELLI, John	2-20-74	WARREN, Gerald	2-26-74
RYAN, James	6-6-74	WEARLEY, Robert	12-2-73
SABATINO, Lewis	5-22-74	WEBB, Thos., Jr.	
SAMPLE, Alexander, Jr.	12-18-73	WESTMAN, Burton	12-20-73
SCHEMMER, Ben	10-10-73	WHITTAKER, Kenneth	11-20-73
SCHULTZ, George	11-21-73	WHITTINGHILL, Charles	12-6-73
	1-25-74	WILSON, Bruce	11-23-73
SCOTT, Regina	2-5-74	WITWER, Allan	1-14-74
SHENKER, Morris	12-20-73	WINTE, Ralph	8-28-73
SIMON, William	5-7-74		8-30-73
SINNOT, William	10-15-73	WOODS, Rosemary	2-20-74
	12-19-73		3-22-74
SLOAN, Hugh	4-26-74	WYMAN, Sidney	12-20-73
SMATHERS, George	1-10-74	YOUNG, Carl	
SPRAGUE, Robert		YOWELL, Susan	2-27-74
STEARNS, Richard	10-3-73	ZIEGLER, Ron	6-24-74
	12-10-73	ZIMMERMAN, Ed	2-7-74
STRACHAN, Gordon	8-8-73		

Individuals Interviewed by Telephone

NAME	DATE	NAME	DATE
ADLER, Howard	10-23-73	COMEGYS, Walter	10-23-73
	12-6-73	DANIEL, Mr.	
AGNEW, Spiro	6-24-74	DEKREEK, Janet	12-3-73
ALBASIA, Aldolpha	5-14-74	DELAUER, Magel	10-22-73
	6-1-74	DEMARCO, Frank	6-3-74
	6-3-74	DESKIN, Ruth	4-5-74
ALBRIGHT, Barbara	6-3-74	DESROSHER, M. A.	
AYER, William	11-26-73	DONNEM, Roland	10-23-74
BARKER, Dez	1-4-74	DOUGLAS, Stephen	
BARKER, Robert		EBNER, Stanley	4-15-74
BARRY, William		EISENBERG, Milton	12-13-73
BLECH, Arthur	5-8-74	FEINBERG, Joseph	6-6-74
	6-22-74		6-10-74
BLITCH, Albert		FIGENSHAW, James	1-15-74
BONELLI, Jaime	6-1-74	FRESH, Larry	
BRANDT, Mrs.	6-4-74	GAYLE, Thos	
BUZZELLA, R. W.		GUSTAFSON, Tom	6-4-74
CANTOR, Arthur	10-17-73	HALL, Joan	5-74
CASTRO, June	6-3-74	HALLOMORE, Barry	11-7-73
CHAMBERS, R. W.	1-11-74	HALLOMORE, Lloyd	11-6-73
CLEVELAND, Geraldine	5-18-74	HAMAND, Joy	10-25-73

NAME	DATE	NAME	DATE
HAYES, Jim	12-6-73	ROCHE, Lois	
HEAL, Terry		ROTH, George	11-20-73
HERNANDEZ, Renaldo		SALKOF, Godwin	
HOOPER, Ray		SCHADE, Paul	10-29-73
IANNI, John	1-10-74	SCHAEFFER, Don	
	6-21-74	SCHEINBAUM, Stan	11-4-73
JACKSON, Robert		SCOTT, Robert	
JAFFE, Col.	11-2-73	SCOTT, William	6-12-74
JONES, Lyle	1-15-74		6-19 & 20-74
JONES, Richard		SHELTON, Robert	5-29-74
JURY, Mr.		SHERMER, Robert	
KESTENBAUM, Lionel	10-17-73	SIEGEL, Ronald	
KOTOSKE, Tom	2-19-74	SILBERMAN, Irwin	
KRAUSHAAR, I. N.	4-10-74	SMITH, Marquis	10-16-73
LAMBERT, Harry		SNEAD, Robert	
LITTLE, Robert	6-1-74	SPIRA, Slyvan	
MASUR, Wayne		STEWART, Chas. W.	
MORGAN, Edward L.		STUART, Charles	6-20-74
MORRISON, Sue	1-18-74	SUCKLING, John R.	10-11-73
MURCHISON, Clint, Jr.	6-2-74	SULLIVAN, Margaret	2-16-74
MURRAY, Gene		TAYLOR, Paul, Jr.	
MURRAY, Rita	10-18-74	THRELKIND, Major	
McCAUGHLIN, Robert	6-4-74	TILLOTSON, Mr.	
McDONALD, Robert	12-4-73	ULASEWICZ, Anthony	4-20-74
McKIERNAN, Stanley	12-10-73	VINSON, Fred, Jr.	12-17-73
McKILLOP, Roy, Sr.		VAGLIOTTI, Gabriel	
McLAREN, Richard	10-17-73	WAGGONER, Mr.	
NISSEN, David	1-31-74	WAKEFIELD, Thomas	6-26-74
	2-12-74	WEISS, Leonard	10-31-73
NUNN, Gov. Louis		WHITTINGHILL, Charles	12-11-73
PLYLER, Robert		WILSON, Mrs.	
REAGAN, Robert		WILSON, Will	2-6-74
RHYLICK, Lawrence	5-22-74	YORK, William, Jr.	
	6-20-74	ZIMMERMAN, Ed.	10-17-73
RIX, H. John			

SENATOR LOWELL P. WEICKER, JR.

A STILLNESS

In the early 1970s, several independent events took place in the United States of America. On the surface they appeared to lack a common bond.

In June of 1969, a Louis Harris poll found that 25% of all Americans felt they had a moral right to disregard a victim's cry for help. Over the next several years, this mood took the form of countless incidents of "looking the other way" when men and women were assaulted and murdered in full view of entire neighborhoods.

On May 4, 1970 at Kent State University in Ohio, a group of students who refused an order to disperse were fired upon by the National Guard, killing William Schroeder, Sandy Scheuer, Jeffrey Miller, and Allison Krause, and wounding nine others. Ten days later, at Jackson State University in Mississippi, police who had been called in to protect firemen from violence, opened up a 28-second fusillade into and around a dormitory killing Phillip Gibbs and James Earl Green, and wounding twelve others.

During 1971, a decision was reached by the Administration to conduct the President's re-election campaign with a special committee totally separate and insulated from the political party which would renominate that President.

In early 1972, a young radio reporter in Miami stood outside a supermarket trying to get people to sign a copy of the Bill of Rights. Seventy-five percent refused, many saying it was "Communist propaganda."

In February of 1972, it was revealed that International Telephone and Telegraph had allegedly offered a campaign contribution of $400,000 in return for the Justice Department dropping an anti-trust suit against ITT. The suit was dropped on Presidential order, but when the Attorney General was questioned about the President's role by a Senate Committee in March, he lied.

On June 17, 1972, burglars employed by the Committee to Re-elect the President were arrested inside the headquarters of the Democratic National Committee with bugging equipment and large sums of cash.

In December of 1972, having failed to get Congressional approval for a reorganization of the Cabinet, the Administration moved autonomously to establish three or four "super Secretaries" and to place various Executive Office employees in key sub-Cabinet posts. The obvious goal was to create a White House-directed network of decision-making and reporting quite different from the formal Cabinet structure which remained subject to Congressional scrutiny.

In February of 1973, the White House held a Peace-with-Honor reception to celebrate the end of the Vietnam War. Only those Congressmen who had supported the President's Vietnam policies were invited, implying that those who had questioned our involvement in Vietnam were either against peace or were dishonorable men and women.

Some of these incidents were matters of life and death and were well publicized. Others were matters of principle and were little noticed at the time.

In each instance a significant outrage had taken place.
What was common to all?
In each instance no one complained.
A Constitutional stillness was over the land.

THE UPROAR

That American decency, idealism, honesty and reverence for the Constitution that some thought bought off has been stirring and reasserting itself for many months now.

Yes, a few still shout treason when questions are asked.
A few still espouse the end as justifying the means.
A few still goggle at an American title rather than the title of American.
But it was only yesterday, June 17, 1972 to be specific, that today's few were part of a large American majority.
Why the turnaround?
The truth!
Because Frank Wills discovered taped doors at the Watergate, America's doors didn't close in all our faces.

CONSTITUTIONAL DEMOCRACY IN THE ERA OF WATERGATE

For this Senator, Watergate is not a whodunit.
It is a documented, proven attack on laws, institutions, and principles.
The response to that attack was and is a nation of laws

at work, determining whether men shall prevail over the principles of a Constitutional democracy. It has been and will be the testing of a great experiment in government begun some two hundred years ago.

Laws, institutions, and principles were squarely before this Committee, to be debated, probed and documented, in order to assert remedies and reassert time-honored concepts. Guilt or innocence was not an issue. This was a fact-finding body; it was a legislative body; and those duties go to the heart of what Watergate was all about.

In keeping with the Committee's duties, this is a report of facts and evidence, leading to legislative recommendations. To document the abuse of laws, institutions, and principles, the facts and evidence are presented, first, as they bear on the basis of our laws, the Constitution; second, as they relate to the institutions of our Government; and third, as they affect the principles of our political system.

I. The Constitution

One of the most disturbing facts about the testimony presented to this Committee is that so much of it went relentlessly to the heart of our Constitution.

To appreciate what happened to the Constitution, it is useful to divide the seven Articles and 26 Amendments into substantive versus procedural provisions. The substantive sections lay out rights, powers, and duties. The procedural areas address somewhat more technical and administrative matters. The important point is that the essence and strength of the Constitution springs from its substantive areas, primarily the first three Articles, the first ten Amendments and the Fourteenth Amendment.

Evidence presented to this Committee can and will demonstrate every major substantive part of the Constitution was violated, abused, and undermined during the Watergate period.

It is a record built entirely on the words of the participants themselves. Tragically, it focuses on the most prodigious Article of the Constitution, Article II, which sets out the powers and duties of the Executive; it includes the most significant individual rights guaranteed by the first ten Amendments, our Bill of Rights; and it encompasses the Fifth and Fourteenth Amendments' guarantees of due process of law, the foundation of our system of justice.

A. THE EXECUTIVE

Of all the issues confronting the Constitutional Convention at Philadelphia, the nature of the Presidency ranked as one of the most important. The resolution of that issue was one of the most significant actions taken.[1]

Most state constitutions prior to that time had weak executives and strong legislatures.[2] The decision to create a President, as opposed to plural administrators,[3] was a reluctant recognition of the advantages of a strong executive.

Nevertheless, the Convention took steps to contain presidential power. Only after deciding the method of selecting a President, his term, mode of removal, and powers and duties did the Convention agree to the concept of a strong President.[4]

This bit of history, indicating that the delineation of the President's office and powers preceded the creation of his position in the Constitutional scheme, is quite important. It demonstrates that executive power is to be exercised within the framework of the Constitution, and particularly, within the guidelines of Article II, which lays out the powers and duties of that office.

This is much of what Watergate is all about, and it bears a close look at Article II.

The issue at stake is the exercise of potentially awesome Presidential power. As to that issue, Article II contains two points of significance.[5] First, its opening words state: "The

1. Congressional Research Service, Library of Congress, *The Constitution of The United States of America* (1973), p. 429. Background on the Convention from C. Thach, *The Creation of the Presidency, 1775–1789* (Baltimore: 1923).

2. As a result of experience with the royal governors, not only did most states have weak executives, but the Articles of Confederation (which was the agreement by which the national government was functioning at the time of the Constitutional Convention) vested all powers in a one-body Congress. C. Thach, chs. 1–3. The Virginia Plan, which was the basis of discussion, offered a weak executive, with only power to "execute the national laws" and to "enjoy the Executive rights vested in Congress." Id., ch. 4; Congressional Research Service, p. 430.

3. It was not until the closing days of the Convention that there was any assurance the executive would not be tied to the legislature, devoid of power, or headed by plural administrators. Although the discussion about the executive opened on June 1, 1787, as late as September 7, 1787, eight days before the final Constitution was ordered printed, the Convention voted down a proposal for an executive council that would participate in the exercise of all the executive's duties. M. Farland, *The Records of the Federal Convention of 1787* (New Haven: 1937), 21 & 542.

4. The eventual basis of Article II was the New York Constitution. On June 1, 1787, James Wilson moved that the executive should be one person. A vote on the Wilson motion was put off until the other attributes of the office had been decided. The decision resulted largely from experience with the Articles of Confederation "that harm was to be feared as much from an unfettered legislature as from an uncurbed executive and that many advantages of a reasonably strong executive could not be conferred on the legislative body." Congressional Research Service, p. 430.

5. According to Alexander Hamilton, "The second Article of the Constitution of the United States, section first, establishes this general proposition, that 'the Executive Power shall be vested in a President of the United States of America.' That same article in a succeeding section, proceeds to delineate

executive Power shall be vested in a President of the United States of America." [6] This grant of executive authority, with no words of limitation, has, from the time of Jefferson, been the basis for expanding the presidential office and activities.[7]

However, the initial broad authority is offset by a second significant factor, the enumeration of executive powers later in Article II.[8] These declare in part that the President is to be Commander-in-Chief, make treaties, appoint ambassadors and other officers, grant pardons, and take care that the laws are faithfully executed.

It is worth noting that experience has eventually placed limits on the general powers. The President has been allowed, as a practical matter, to exercise those additional powers that fall naturally within his range of activities.[9]

The important point, however, is that no President has been, or can be, allowed to conduct the executive branch in conflict with the Constitution taken as a whole, and certainly not in conflict with express sections of the Constitution, such as the Bill of Rights, or Article I (the legislature), or Article III (the judiciary). This then is the proper context for examining facts.

Article II of the Constitution, by which the Presidency was created, was violated from beginning to end by Watergate.

There is massive evidence of misuse of the awesome general powers that reside in the executive department.

There is equal evidence documenting abuses of the enumerated duties.

1. General Powers and Duties. The facts show an executive branch that approved a master intelligence plan containing proposals that were specifically identified as illegal,[10] that proposed setting up a private intelligence firm with a "black bag" or breaking and entering capability as secret investiga-

---

particular cases of executive power." 32 *Writings of George Washington*, J. Fitzpatrick ed. (Washington: 1939) 430; 7 *Works of Alexander Hamilton*, J.C. Hamilton ed. (New York: 1851) 76.

6. U.S. Constitution, Article II, Section 1.

7. The practice of expanding presidential powers has continued steadily, but was irrevocably set when the "Strict constructionists" came to power in 1801 and did not curb executive power, but rather enlarged it. The modern theory of Presidential power was conceived by Hamilton, but it is interesting to note his qualification "that the executive power of the nation is vested in the President; subject only to the *exceptions* and *qualifications*, which are expressed in the instrument." 7 *Works of Alexander Hamilton*, 80–81; see Congressional Research Service, 433 & 437.

8. U.S. Constitution, Article II, Sections 2–4.

9. See note 7 supra.

10. See Vol. 3, Ex. 35, p. 1319. This is a plan submitted by Tom Charles Huston to the President and approved in July, 1970. Presidential Statement, May 22, 1973. Part D., entitled "Surreptitious Entry," reads: "Use of this technique is clearly illegal: it amounts to burglary." Id., at 1321.

tive support for the White House,[11] that set up its own secret police,[12] that used its clandestine police force to violate the rights of American citizens,[13] that hired a private eye to spy on its enemies, including their personal lives, domestic problems, drinking habits, social activities and sexual habits,[14] that circulated an enemies list,[15] that developed plans to "use the available federal machinery to screw our political enemies,"[16] that knew of an illegal break-in connected with the Ellsberg case and concealed that fact rather than report it to appropriate authorities,[17] that used a presidential increase in milk support prices to get $5,000 from the milk producers to pay for the Ellsberg break-in,[18] that recruited persons for that break-in on the false pretense of national security,[19] that offered the presiding judge in the Ellsberg trial the FBI Directorship at a clandestine meeting in the midst of the trial,[20] that ordered a warrantless wiretap on a news columnist's telephone,[21] that wiretapped 17 newsmen and government officials in an operation that was outside proper investigative channels,[22] that suggested firebombing the Brookings Institute,[23] that set up an Intelligence Evaluation Committee outside the legitimate intelligence community to disseminate information that should have been restricted to individual agencies,[24] that used the Secret Service to wiretap

11. Operation Sandwedge, drawn up by John Caulfield in late 1971, to infiltrate campaign organizations, with a "Black bag" capability, "surveillance of Democratic primaries," and "derogatory information investigative capability, world-wide." See Ex. and pp. 00–000, Campaign Practices, supra.
12. See, THE INTELLIGENCE COMMUNITY, infra. (discussion of the establishment and functions of the secret so-called Plumbers unit in the White House).
13. On June 21, 1974, Mr. Charles Colson was sentenced to one to three years in jail for, among other things, activities of the Plumbers "to influence, obstruct, and impede the conduct and outcome of the criminal prosecution of Daniel Ellsberg."
14. See, the list of investigations by Anthony Ulasewicz. THE INTELLIGENCE COMMUNITY, infra; see also, Ulasewicz testimony, Vol. 6, pp. 2219–2277.
15. See, Vol. 4, Exhibits 44, 48–65.
16. Vol. 4, Ex. 48, p. 1689.
17. When the prosecutors finally learned of the break-in 18 months after it occurred, they were told by the President, "you stay out of that," even though it was a crime for which at least one defendant has been convicted. Vol. 9, p. 3631.
18. Ellsberg Break-in Grand Jury Proceedings, 652–656.
19. Testimony of Bernard Barker, Vol. 1, p. 358.
20. Testimony of John Ehrlichman, Vol. 6, pp. 2617-2619.
21. At Ehrlichman's instructions, Caulfield had John Regan tap columnist Joseph Kraft's home telephone. John Caulfield Executive Session, March 16, 1974.
22. See, testimony of Robert Mardian, Vol. 4, pp. 2392-2393; John Ehrlichman, Vol. 4, p. 2529; and John Dean, Vol. 3, p. 920.
23. John Caulfield Executive Session, March 23, 1974; testimony of John Dean, Vol. 3, p. 920.
24. Notwithstanding the fact that the statutes prohibit the CIA from participating in any domestic intelligence function they were called upon to

648

the President's brother,[25] that kept $350,000 in left-over 1968 campaign funds in a safe in the Chief of Staff's office,[26] that used most of those funds as "hush money" for the Watergate burglars,[27] that approved a large contribution from the milk producers association after being told it was meant to gain access to and favors from the White House,[28] that received and passed on information about an IRS audit of one of the President's friends,[29] that arranged for a tax attorney for the friend,[30] that contacted the IRS as well as the Justice Department in a number of other tax cases involving friends of the President,[31] that planned and possibly carried out a break-in at the office of a Las Vegas publisher,[32] that suggested a break-in at the apartment of the man who attempted to assassinate Governor Wallace,[33] that contemplated a break-in at the Potomac Associates offices,[34] that tried to rewrite history by making up bogus State Department cables to falsely connect the Kennedy Administration with the assassination of President Diem,[35] that attempted to get reporter William Lambert to use the phony cables in a story,[36] that tried to plant false stories connecting the President's opponent with communist money and the crimes

evaluate domestic intelligence-gathering by other agencies, when the Intelligence Evaluation Committee was set up. Testimony of John Dean, Vol. 4, p. 1457.
25. In a Press Conference on November 17, 1973, the President stated: "The Secret Service did maintain a surveillance. They did so for security reasons, and I will not go beyond that. They were very good reasons, and my brother was aware of it."
26. Testimony of H. R. Haldeman, Vol. 7, p. 2879; Gordon Strachan, Vol. 6, pp. 2442, 2461.
27. Testimony of Fred LaRue, Vol. 6, p. 2343.
28. Mr. Kalmbach testified that he reported the original milk producers' contribution, and their request in return for 90% parity, a Presidential address at their Convention, and a Presidential audience, to Messrs. Ehrlichman, Flanigan, Gleason, and Dent. Herbert Kalmbach, Executive Session.
29. Gen. Alexander Haig, White House Chief of Staff, was called by William Simon of the Treasury Department and told that Mr. Rebozo was to be audited. Gen. Haig met with White House attorneys on the matter, resulting in a decision to tell the President and volunteer to use the White House attorneys to find a tax lawyer for Mr. Rebozo. Gen. Alexander Haig, Executive Session.
30. Id.
31. This help was extended to Dr. Kenneth Riland. Testimony of John Dean, Vol. 4, pp. 1550, 1559. It also went to the Rev. Billy Graham and actor John Wayne. Id., at 1529–1530.
32. Testimony of Howard Hunt, Vol. 9, p. 3687. See also, Transcripts of Presidential Conversations.
33. Testimony of Howard Hunt, Executive Session, July 25, 1973, pp. 129-133.
34. A White House memo, dated July 6, 1971, from John Caulfield to John Dean, stated: "Building appears to have good security with guard present in lobby during day and evening hours. However, a penetration is deemed possible if required."
35. Testimony of Howard Hunt, Vol. 9, p. 3732.
36. Id., at 3672.

alleged in the Ellsberg case,[37] that installed an elaborate system of taping conversations between the President and his staff or visitors,[38] that told federal investigators to stay out of the Ellsberg matter,[39] that undertook a clandestine operation to hide a key witness in the ITT case in a Denver hospital where she was interrogated by Howard Hunt in disguise,[40] that authorized and funded from within the White House a dirty tricks operation including scurrilous literature, late night telephone campaigns and advertising designed to offend local interests, seemingly sponsored by Democratic candidates, and physical disruptions directed against Presidential opponents,[41] that planted spies, hecklers, and pickets in the Muskie and Humphrey campaigns,[42] that participated in discussions of a campaign against Democrats to include prostitutes, mugging, kidnapping, bugging, and burglary,[43] that pressed for adoption of Liddy's Watergate plan,[44] that was told of the authorization and budget for Liddy's plan,[45] that believed it had received transcripts of illegal wiretaps and never reported that crime,[46] that was warned of the planned break-in at the Watergate and did nothing to stop it,[47] that knew the

37. Vol. 10, Ex. 194, p. 4259 (A memo from Pat Buchanan recommending, "The Ellsberg Connection, tying McGovern to him and his crime—as soon as the indictment come down.") A Dean to Haldeman memo stated, "We need to get our people to put out the story on the foreign or Communist money that was used in support of demonstrations against the President in 1972. We should tie all 1972 demonstrations to McGovern. . . ." See, Vol. 8, p. 3171.
38. Testimony of Alexander Butterfield, Vol. 5, p. 2074.
39. Testimony of Henry Petersen, Vol. 9, p. 3631.
40. Testimony of Robert Mardian, Vol. 6, p. 2359; Testimony of Howard Hunt, Vol. 9, pp. 3752-53.
41. See, THE ELECTORAL PROCESS, infra (description of the Segretti operation).
42. See, Executive Session, Herbert Porter, April 2, 1973 (the activities of Sedan Chair I and Sedan Chair II).
43. Testimony of John Mitchell, Vol. 5, p. 1610.
44. Testimony of Jeb Magruder, Vol. 2, p. 835. (phone call by Mr. Colson to Mr. Magruder, to "get on the stick and get the Liddy project approved so we can get the information from O'Brien.")
45. For example, on March 30, 1972, a few days after the Liddy plan was allegedly approved, a memo from Strachan to Haldeman reported, "Magruder reports that 1701 (CRP) now has a sophisticated political intelligence gathering system with a budget of 300." Testimony of Gordon Strachan, Vol. 6, p. 2441. An April 4, 1972, talking paper for a meeting between Mitchell and Haldeman included the intelligence plan and its $300,000 budget. *Id.*, at 2454.
46. Mr. Strachan testified, "I did not tell Mr. Dean that I had, in fact, destroyed wiretap logs, because I was not then sure what they were, I only had suspicions." Testimony of Gordon Strachan, Vol. 6, p. 2442. Mr. Strachan had also had access to all the Watergate wiretap transcripts. Testimony of Jeb Magruder, Vol. 2, p. 827.
47. Mr. Strachan, according to Mr. Magruder, was as well briefed, on the evening of June 16, 1972, on the intelligence operation (including the plan for a second break-in on June 17) as anybody at the Committee to Re-Elect. Testimony of Jeb Magruder, Vol. 2, p. 827.

full scope of Liddy's activities shortly after the Watergate arrests and kept those facts from proper authorities,[48] that shredded Watergate evidence in the Chief of Staff's files,[49] that tried to use one of its executive branch agencies as a "cover" for the Watergate operation,[50] that was the scene of meetings at which high officials plotted to use the power and influence of the presidency to cover up crimes and obstruct justice,[51] that saw advisors invoke the power of the presidency to use an FBI Director in ways that would eventually cause him to resign,[52] that used the President's fundraising powers to collect illegal corporate contributions,[53] to raise funds to finance a crime,[54] and to collect bribes for a criminal case,[55] that discussed using the President's clemency prerogatives as early as July 1972, to keep the lid on Watergate and other crimes, while misleading the American people by calling Watergate a "third rate burglary," [56] that made offers of clemency for improper purposes,[57] that announced, in a Presidential statement, a Dean investigation clearing the White House, when there had in fact been a coverup not an investigation and the President had never, ever talked to Dean about Watergate,[58] that discussed, in the Oval Office, unethical out-of-court contacts with the

48. The White House counsel, among others, was fully briefed by Liddy himself three days after the break-in, and given the full story of Liddy's Plumbers' activities as well. Testimony of John Dean, Vol. 3, p. 933.

49. Testimony of Gordon Strachan, Vol. 6, p. 2458.

50. Both Mr. Helms and Gen. Walters of the CIA testified that at a meeting on June 23, 1972, with Mr. Haldeman and Mr. Ehrlichman, they were instructed to use the CIA to interfere with the FBI investigation of Watergate. Testimony of Richard Helms, Vol. 8, p. 3238; testimony of General Vernon Walters, Vol. 9, p. 3405.

51. As soon as Mr. Dean returned to Washington after the break-in, he began meeting with White House officials, such as his meetings on June 19, 1972, with Messrs. Ehrlichman, Colson, and others to discuss how to handle Liddy and the contents of Hunt's safe. Testimony of John Dean, Vol. 3, p. 934.

52. Patrick Gray testified that he took the Hunt files and destroyed them because the order came from "the counsel to the President of the United States issued in the presence of one of the two top assistants to the President of the United States." Testimony of Patrick Gray, Vol. 9, p. 3467.

53. See, testimony of eight corporate executives convicted of illegal corporate contributions, Nov. 13–15, 1973. Vol. 13.

54. Not only was the Ellsberg break-in financed by milk producers' money (see, note 18, supra), but the Watergate break-in was financed by money from the Committee to Re-Elect. Testimony of Hugh Sloan, Vol. 2, p. 539; testimony of Maurice Stans, Vol. 2, p. 795.

55. Mr. Kalmbach was asked to raise funds for the Watergate burglars. Testimony of John Dean, Vol. 3, p. 950; confirmed by Transcripts of Presidential Conversations, April 14, 1973, p. 494.

56. Presidential Statement of August 15, 1973, p. 3; testimony of John Ehrlichman, Vol. 7, pp. 2848-2849.

57. On at least three occasions Watergate defendant James McCord received offers of executive clemency if he would remain silent and plead guilty. Testimony of James McCord, Vol. 1, pp. 131, 132, 135, 139–141.

58. Testimony of John Dean, Vol. 3, p. 955.

presiding judge in one of the Watergate civil suits,[59] that purposely lied to the FBI and a federal grand jury,[60] that encouraged campaign officials to commit perjury and plead the Fifth Amendment to obstruct justice,[61] that used the President's personal attorney and White House staff to pay criminal "hush" money,[62] and to pay for a private eye operating out of the White House,[63] that used its influence to get raw FBI files for improper purposes,[64] that prevailed upon the FBI not to interview certain witnesses,[65] that used patriotic concern for the presidency to pressure defendants to plead guilty in a criminal case,[66] that used its influence to get special treatment for high officials before a federal grand jury,[67] that plotted to cover up the Segretti story and denounced in the harshest terms those who uncovered the story,[68] that noted "it would assuredly be psychologically

59. Testimony of John Dean, Vol. 3, p. 958. "He (Judge Ritchie) has made several entrees off the bench—one to Kleindienst and one to Roemer McPhee to keep Roemer abreast of what his thinking is. He told Roemer that he thought Maury (Maurice Stans) ought to file a libel action." Transcripts of Presidential Conversations, September 15, 1972, p. 60.
60. Herbert L. Porter pleaded guilty, on January 28, 1974, to one count of making false statements to FBI agents. Gordon Strachan testified that he was expressly asked to do something he knew was improper related to his grand jury testimony of April, 1973. Testimony of Gordon Strachan, Vol. 6, p. 2443. See also testimony of Jeb Stuart Magruder, Vol. 2, pp. 801, 802, 804, 831–832.
61. Dean attempted to get Sloan's lawyers to have Sloan take the Fifth Amendment. Testimony of Hugh Sloan, Vol. 2, pp. 585, 586. Herbert Porter testified that he was asked to perjure himself by Magruder concerning the amount given Liddy—asked to say he gave $100,000 to pay surrogates. Porter, subsequently, perjured himself to the grand jury and in the trial. Testimony of Herbert L. Porter, Vol. 2, pp. 635–637.
62. Testimony of John Dean, Vol. 3, p. 950. Kalmbach recollected that Dean stressed secrecy with respect to raising funds for the defendants, that he made a very strong point that there was absolute secrecy required, confidentiality, indicating that if this became known, it might jeopardize the campaign and cause misinterpretation. Testimony of Herbert Kalmbach, Vol. 5, p. 2098.
63. Mr. Caulfield worked on his intelligence projects with Mr. Ehrlichman and Mr. Kalmbach. He hired Mr. Ulasewicz on July 9, 1969, who was paid on a monthly basis through the Kalmbach law firm. Testimony of John Caulfield, Vol. 1, p. 251.
64. Testimony of John Dean, Vol. 3, pp. 944–945. Testimony of L. Patrick Gray, Vol. 9, p. 3479.
65. At the request of Mr. Dean, Mr. Gray held up FBI interviews with such valuable witnesses as Mr. Dahlberg, Mr. Ogarrio and Kathleen Chenow. On June 28, Dean requested Gray to hold up an interview with Kathleen Chenow on grounds of national security. Testimony of L. Patrick Gray, Vol. 9, p. 3455.
66. Testimony of Bernard L. Barker, Vol. 1, p. 358.
67. Petersen testified that he received a telephone call from Ehrlichman asking that Mr. Stans be excused from going to the grand jury and telling Petersen to stop harassing Stans. Testimony of Henry Petersen, Vol. 9, p. 3618.
68. Testimony of Clark MacGregor, Vol. 12, p. 5019.

satisfying to cut the innards from Ellsberg and his clique,"[69] that obstructed Congressional investigations of Watergate and related matters,[70] that filed Watergate counter suits for the distorted purpose of using subpoena powers to delve into the financial and sexual activities of political opponents,[71] that made numerous misleading or false statements about Watergate to the American people,[72] that failed to promptly inform proper authorities about knowledge of crimes involving White House officials,[73] that forced the resignation of a special prosecutor, Attorney General, and Assistant Attorney General when their Watergate prosecution took an independent position,[74] that suggested using the Attorney General's powers to keep a Republican opponent off the primary ballot in Florida,[75] that used the executive's authority over the media's regulatory agencies to intimidate the media,[76] that ordered a personal tax audit, surveillance by an FBI agent and Secret Service agents, and an anti-trust action, all in response to a newspaper article about one of the President's friends,[77] that tried to punish foundations with views different

69. Memorandum of July 8, 1971, from Patrick L. Buchanan to John Ehrlichman.
70. Mr. Mitchell testified that there were many discussions of preventing the House Banking and Currency Committee hearings from getting off the ground, including possible use of assistance from the Justice Department. Testimony of John Hitchell, Vol. 5, p. 1897. The Lacosta meetings, which discussed the use of executive privilege to prevent testimony of people from the White House, could well be concluded to evidence an intention to prevent the facts from becoming known, according to Mr. Dean. Testimony of John Dean, Vol. 4, p. 1460.
71. Testimony of John Dean, Vol. 3, p. 957.
72. For example, a meeting on October 15, 1972, at the White House, with Ehrlichman, Ziegler, Buchanan, Moore, Chapin, and Dean was held to prepare a press response to Segretti stories. It was decided to attack and deny the stories even though an intense investigation within the White House had already established the basic truth of the stories. The same denial was issued again in succeeding months. Testimony of John Dean, Vol. 3, pp. 1202, 1206, and 1209; notes of the meetings, Vol. 3, p. 1200.
73. Aside from the coverup in general, the President claims to have learned of crimes on March 21, 1973, but did not tell the prosecutors about this evidence until they came to him on April 15, 1973. Testimony of Richard Kleindienst, Vol. 9, pp. 3579–3580; testimony of Henry Petersen, Vol. 9, p. 3628.
74. On October 20, 1973, Attorney General Richardson and Assistant Attorney General Ruckelshaus resigned in response to the President's demand that they fire Special Prosecutor Cox, who wanted to appeal a court decision involving Watergate evidence to the Supreme Court. See also, Executive Session of General Alexander Haig.
75. Memo to the Attorney General from Mr. Magruder, August 11, 1971: "Pat Buchanan suggested that maybe we could have the Florida State Chairman do whatever he can under this law to keep McCloskey (Rep. McCloskey, R—Calif.) off the ballot." Vol. 10, Ex. 177, p. 4194.
76. Memo from Charles Colson to H. R. Haldeman, September 25, 1970, recommending that he "pursue with Dean Burch the possibility of an interpretive ruling by the FCC . . . this point could be very favorably clarified and it would, of course, have an inhibiting impact on the neworks. . . ."
77. When the newspaper Newsday decided to run an in-depth article on

than White House policy by pressuring the IRS to review their tax exempt status,[78] that set up a program to insure that government contracts, grants, and loans would, as a matter of government policy, be political rewards,[79] that treated the Presidential pardon as a political tool,[80] that used its power over the tax collection agency to gather intelligence on and harass political opponents,[81] that issued instructions to hire a shaggy person to sit in front of the White House with a McGovern button, and counter demonstrators at the funeral of J. Edgar Hoover,[82] that infiltrated a Quaker vigil in front of the White House,[83] that used the agency that is supposed to guard the President to spy on the President's political opponent,[84] that ordered 24 hour surveillance of a political opponent,[85] that used the Departments to dredge up potentially embarrassing information on presidential contenders, and then leaked it to the press,[86] that used White House influence to obtain CIA equipment for the Ellsberg break-in,[87] that used its entrustment with our national security to convince four Cubans to burglarize a political party,[88] that ordered an FBI investigation of an unfriendly newsman to

Mr. Rebozo, the reporter writing the story was audited at White House request, an FBI agent investigated the newspaper's offices, an anti-trust suit was recommended, and the Secret Service investigated the reporters' activities while they were writing the story. Testimony of Senator Lowell P. Weicker, hearings on Warrantless Wiretapping and Electronic Surveillance, April 8, 1974 (Exhibit 7).

78. Memo to the President from Patrick Buchanan, March 3, 1970. Vol. 10, p. 4114.

79. Memo from Fred Malek to H. R. Haldeman, March 17, 1972, entitled "Increasing the Responsiveness of the Executive Branch."

80. For example, a request that a prominent Jewish figure in Florida be pardoned for political benefit. In a memo to John Dean, Charles Colson recommends, "If there is anything we can do properly, we should . . . this has to be handled with extreme care." Testimony of Senator Lowell P. Weicker, hearings on Warrantless Wiretapping and Electronic Surveillance, April 8, 1974. The pardon was granted and a $30,000 contribution followed. Interview with Calvin Kovens, October 25, 1973.

81. See, Vol. 4, Ex. 44, pp. 1682, 1694, 1695.

82. Testimony of Robert Reisner, Vol. 2, pp. 500, 512.

83. Interview with Jeb Magruder, August 8, 1973.

84. White House memo from Steve Karalekas to Charles Colson, August 16, 1972, referring to the activities of Agent Bolton. See also, testimony of John Dean. Vol. 3, pp. 923, 1071.

85. "It was my understanding, based on my discussion with John Dean, that there was to be a 24-hour tail on Senator Kennedy." Testimony of Gordon Strachan, Vol. 6, p. 2492.

86. See, memo from Fred Malek to H. R. Haldeman, entitled "Increasing the Responsiveness of the Executive Branch," dated March 17, 1972.

87. On July 7, 1971, John Ehrlichman called General Cushman, Deputy Director of the CIA, to arrange CIA assistance to Howard Hunt for disguise purposes. Hunt told Cushman that he (Hunt) had been charged with a "sensitive mission" by the White House to "interview a person whose ideology he was not certain of." Testimony of General Robert Cushman, Jr., Vol. 8, pp. 3290–92.

88. Testimony of Bernard Barker, Vol. 1, p. 358.

harass him,[89] that proposed leaking confidential FBI files to embarrass the producer of a satirical movie,[90] that used its control of important Watergate evidence and the privilege known as executive privilege to aid those supporting the President and to deprive or delay those in opposition,[91] that made plans to eliminate professionals in government service who placed their professional responsibilities above questionable White House political demands,[92] that participated actively and formally in a campaign organization while drawing White House staff salaries,[93] that ran secret letter-writing campaigns against Republican Senators, and that generally emasculated the Republican Party.[94]

That . . . all of that . . . violated the concept of executive power in Article II of the Constitution. Extensive as the record is, it is only selected examples.

It is certainly not what our founding fathers had in mind when they envisioned the presidency.

2. Enumerated Powers and Duties. The so-called enumerated powers and duties of the President's office are set forth beginning with Section 2 of Article II. That Section grants the President direct power over Cabinet officers,[95] and much testimony before this Committee demonstrated how those officers were used on behalf of the President's office.

An Attorney General, for a significant period of time, ran the President's re-election campaign while still in office at the Justice Department.[96] His reason for this role was that, "it is very, very difficult to turn down a request by the President of the United States." [97] even though the Attorney General himself later testified that he felt such

89. Mr. Haldeman ordered an investigation of newsman Daniel Schorr. See Vol. 4, p. 1490.
90. Memo from John Caulfield to John Dean, dated June 25, 1971, subject: Emile de Antonio, producer of "Millhouse"; New Yorker Films, Inc.; and Daniel Talbot, film distributor. "I recommend that it is time to move on the above firm and individuals, as follows: A) Release of de Antonio's FBI derogatory background to friendly media. B) discreet IRS audits of New Yorker Films, Inc., de Antonio and Talbot."
91. Mr. Haldeman testified that he had access to various tapes of Presidential conversations. (See Vol. 8, pp. 3050–51); compare with testimony of John Dean, Vol. 4, p. 1503.
92. See Vol. 4, Exhibit 44, p. 1682.
93. Testimony of Robert Odle: "those people who were at the White House had influence over the (Committee for the Re-Election of the President), they gave it direction, they assisted it." See Vol. 1, p. 23.
94. See, THE PARTY PROCESS, supra.
95. U.S. Constitution, Article II, sec. 2.
96. Mr. Mitchell testified that he "had frequent meetings with individuals (from CRP) dealing with matters of policy," before he resigned as Attorney General. Testimony of John Mitchell, Vol. 5, p. 1653.
97. Testimony of John Mitchell, Vol. 5, p. 1859.

a role in politics while still in office was wrong.[98] Memos from CRP, such as one entitled "Grantsmanship," suggesting an effective method of "insuring that political considerations" be used in Federal programs,[99] were sent to the Attorney General from May 1, 1971, onward.[100] At one point, it was even suggested that the Attorney General wield the power of his office to keep a Republican contender off the primary ballot in Florida.[101] That campaign role also included an extraordinary meeting in the Attorney General's very office, to review plans for bugging, mugging, burglary, prostitution, and kidnapping.[102]

Another Attorney General was placed in the awkward position of being asked immediately after the Watergate break-in to help get Mr. McCord out of jail before he was identified. He was soon thereafter warned of White House concern with a too aggressive FBI investigation.[103] He was then asked to provide raw FBI Watergate files, perhaps improperly, to the White House. That same Attorney General was later used as a secret contact with this Committee's investigation of Watergate, and was then removed from office in an apparent connection with the Watergate affair.[104] He eventually became the first Attorney General in history convicted of a crime, for his testimony about the ITT matter.[105]

A third Attorney General was forced to resign his office when he backed the Special Prosecutor's procedure for obtaining Watergate evidence from the White House.[106]

An Assistant Attorney General was also asked to provide raw FBI Watergate files, again improperly, to the White House,[107] and was later told by the President not to investigate the Ellsberg break-in.[108] Another Assistant Attorney General was forced to resign when he backed the Special Prosecutor's decisions in the Watergate case.[109] Still another Assistant Attorney General gave confidential Justice Department and FBI intelligence information to the President's re-election

98. Id.
99. Vol. 1, Ex. 1, p. 449.
100. See, testimony of Robert C. Odle, Vo. 1, pp. 40-41.
101. See, note 75 supra.
102. Testimony of John Mitchell, Vol. 5, p. 1610.
103. Testimony of John Dean, Vol. 3. p. 936.
104. See, testimony of Richard G. Kliendienst, Vol. 9, p. 3597.
105. Richard G. Kliendienst pleaded guilty, on May 16, 1974, to one count of refusing to testify about ITT; sentenced June 7, 1974 to one month unsupervised probation.
106. On October 20, 1973, Attorney General Richardson resigned in a dispute with the President over the firing of Special Prosecutor, Archibald Cox.
107. Testimony fo John Dean, Vol. 3, pp. 944-945.
108. Testimony of Henry Petersen, Vol. 9, p. 3631.
109. On October 20, 1973, Assistant Attorney General William Ruckelshaus resigned in response to the President's request to fire Special Prosecutor Archibald Cox.

campaign, at the direction of the White House.[110]

Three Attorney Generals and three Assistant Attorney Generals. And all this was done on behalf of the presidency, which has a Constitutional responsibility to "take Care that the Laws be faithfully executed." [111]

A Secretary of Commerce with all the authority as to corporate affairs that goes with that position, was placed in charge of raising funds for the President's re-election, including, as it turns out, a number of illegal corporate contributions.[112] A Secretary of Treasury met with a milk producers association and supported their request for higher price supports. After the President granted higher support prices, the milk producers arranged for him to be offered at least $10,000 in cash for his personal use. He later aided them in tax and antitrust matters at a time when a large contribution to the President from the milk producers was being arranged.[113]

The Commissioner of the Internal Revenue Service was criticized because "practically every effort to proceed in sensitive areas is met with resistance, delay and the threat of derogatory exposure." [114] The Director of the CIA, according to his own testimony and that of his assistant, was called to the White House and asked to use the CIA to cover up Watergate.[115] The Acting Director of the FBI was brought to the White House and given material from the safe of one of the Watergate burglars, to keep it hidden, an act which resulted in his eventual resignation.[116] That same Acting Director turned over raw FBI files on Watergate to the White House,[117] perhaps illegally,[118] when assured it was at the President's request,[119] which request the President has confirmed in public statements.[120] He was rewarded by being

110. With the approval of the Attorney General John Mitchell, Mr. McCord testified that he received information, on a daily basis, from the Internal Security Division of the Justice Department, which information included FBI data and data on individuals of both a political and non-political nature. Testimony of James McCord, Vol. 1, pp. 178-183.
111. U.S. Const., Art. II, sec. 3.
112. Testimony of Maurice H. Stans, Vol. 2, p. 734.
113. See, MILK FUND INVESTIGATION, supra. [See Vol. Two of this edition.]
114. Transcripts of Presidential Conversations, Sept. 15, 1972.
115. Testimony of Richard Helms, Vol. 8, p. 3238. Testimony of Lt. Gen. Vernon Walters, Vol. 9, p. 3405.
116. Testimony of L. Patrick Gray, Vol. 9, p. 3467. Testimony of John Ehrlichman, Vol. 7, p. 2674.
117. Testimony of John Dean, Vol. 3, p. 945.
118. John Dean pleaded guilty to an "information" charge that included a conspiracy to obtain FBI Watergate files. (U.S. v Dean, D.D.C., No. 886-73).
119. See testimony of L. Patrick Gray, Vol. 9, pp. 3479-81.
120. Presidential statements of March 2, 1973, April 5, 1973, and October 19, 1973.

left to "twist slowly, slowly in the wind" [121] while his nomination to permanent Director was pending before the Senate, even though the President had reportedly already abandoned him.[122]

This is how the officers in the departments and agencies were used by the White House, and it is clear that those activities did not pertain to "any subject relating to the Duties of their respective offices," [123] as the Constitution requires in its grant of Presidential authority in this area.

Immediately following the Section in Article II granting authority over departments and agencies, is a section giving the President the "power to grant Reprieves and Pardons for Offenses against the United States." [124]

There is undisputed testimony that defendants in the Watergate criminal case were offered clemency in exchange for their silence.[125] Aside from the issue as to who authorized the offers, they were particularly firm in the case of one defendant who was apparently ignoring the "game plan." [126]

There is the well-documented case of a request from a former Senator, and close friend of the President, for a pardon on behalf of a prominent Jewish figure in Florida, because of the political advantage that would follow.[127] That pardon was granted. The beneficiary then gave the President's campaign $30,000.[128]

Article II also gives the executive the power to appoint ambassadors. Whereas this has often been a source of political reward, there is substantial evidence of an unusually well-organized and enforced program of "ambassadorships-for-sale," in return for specific support in the 1972 Presidential campaign.[129]

Along with appointive power for ambassadors, the executive has appointive power over lesser "Officers of the United States." [130] This power was used, for example, as a reward

121. Testimony of John Ehrlichman, Vol. 7, p. 2679.
122. See, Vol. 7, Ex. 102, p. 2950.
123. U. S. Const., Art. II, sec. 2.
124. U. S. Const., Art. II, sec. 2.
125. McCord testified that Mr. Caulfield assured him of executive clemency, support for the family and rehabilitation after prison on numerous occasions. Testimony of James McCord, Vol. 1, p. 131.
126. On January 13, 1973, Mr. McCord met Mr. Caulfield and another message was conveyed as to clemency, along with statements that the President's ability to govern was at stake, another Teapot Dome scandal was possible, the government may fall, and everybody else was on the track but McCord, who was not following the "game plan," and who should get "closer to your attorney" and keep silent. Testimony of James McCord, Vol. 1, pp. 139-140.
127. See, testimony of Senator Lowell Weicker, Jr. Hearings on Warrantless Wiretapping and Electronic Surveillance, pp. 151-155.
128. Interview with Calvin Kovens, October 25, 1973.
129. See, Use of the Incumbency-Responsiveness Program, supra.
130. U. S. Const., Art. II, sec. 2.

for at least one participant in Watergate, who received a prominent position in the Department of Commerce.[131] Another CRP official in charge of certain spy activities pointedly reminded the White House of the work he had done when he applied for employment after the election.[132] Plans were also drawn up to use this appointive power in the President's second term to get rid of officials, across the board, who rightfully placed their professional responsibilities in the way of White House political demands.[133]

These enumerated powers and duties of the executive are followed with the duty to "take Care that the Laws be faithfully executed." [134] Evidence was presented to this Committee of a break-in by a White House unit, which break-in contributed to a mistrial in a major national security case, the Ellsberg case. Illegal use of wiretaps and agent provocateurs by the administration was the direct cause of mistrials or dismissals in most major conspiracy cases brought by the federal government during this same period.[135]

This was an executive branch that conspired to present perjury, lie to the FBI, and pay for the silence of key witnesses in the Watergate case. This was the executive that knew of a break-in related to the Ellsberg case and failed to take any action or report that fact.[136] This was the executive that told an Assistant Attorney General not to investigate the Ellsberg matter.[137] This was the administration that learned of the Watergate planning sessions, budget approval, that received illegal wiretap transcripts, and covered up or failed to promptly report White House involvement in Watergate as those facts became known.

This is the White House that pressured the IRS, the Antitrust Division of Justice, the CIA, the FBI, the Secret Service, and the FCC to enforce laws not "faithfully," but "selectively." [138]

131. Jeb S. Magruder was appointed to the office of Deputy Director of Communications in the Department of Commerce after numerous discussions, with H. R. Haldeman and John Mitchell among others, as to the sensitivity of the administration and its need to take care of Magruder. Testimony of Jeb Magruder, Vol. 2, p. 806.
132. Testimony of Herbert Porter, Vol. 2, p. 653; see also, testimony of Jeb Magruder, Vol. 2, p. 806.
133. Vol. 4, Ex. 44, p. 1682.
134. U. S. Const., Art. II, sec. 3.
135. On May 13, 1974, in an unanimous ruling, the Supreme Court affirmed a decision prohibiting the use, against more than 600 defendants in Federal criminal cases of evidence obtained under wiretapping applications that were improperly signed by executive assistant rather than the Attorney General. (No. 72–1057, United States v. Giorando).
136. Testimony of Henry Petersen, Vol. 9, pp. 3630-3631; see also, testimony of Richard Kleindienst, p. 3574.
137. Testimony of Henry Petersen, Vol. 9, p. 3631.
138. See, note 77 supra; testimony of Howard Hunt, Vol. 9, pp. 3752-53; testimony of Patrick Gray, Vol. 9, p. 3467; and note 84 supra.

This is the same White House in which the President said in a conversation with John Dean on September 15, 1972, "We have not used the power in this first four years as you know. We have never used it. We have not used the Bureau (FBI) and we have not used the Justice Department but things are going to change now." The following months may or may not have been a change from what had been going on in 1970, 1971, and 1972, but they certainly were a sad chapter for our system of laws.

B. SEPARATION OF POWERS

The separation of powers between three constitutionally equal and mutually independent branches of government is one of our foremost Constitutional doctrines.[139] It is often expressed as the concept of "checks and balances." Its success depends to a large degree on self-adherence and restraint by those in a position to upset the balance.

The record of Watergate reflects a conscious attempt to undermine the responsibilities of the other two branches, as set forth in Article I, which established the legislature, and Article III, which established the judiciary.

The first Congressional body to take an interest in the Watergate matter was the House Banking and Currency Committee. Every attempt was made to use executive power and influence, not to legitimately respond to that Committee's investigation, but rather to obstruct, block, and actively mislead it.[140] The executive branch had sole possession of critical evidence necessary to that investigation. Its overt attempts to undermine the Committee's work were therefore of great significance.

A different type of obstacle to the exercise of Congressional powers occurred when nominees for high executive branch positions were sent before Senate Committees for confirmation. In a number of instances, those nominees consciously misled Committee inquiries and prepared testimony in such a way that relevant facts would be concealed.[141] To the extent that the nomination process was subverted, those who participated or were responsible deprived the Congress of a fundamental Constitutional duty, the duty to advise and consent.

Discussions by senior White House officials of what were termed Watergate tactics, and meetings at LaCosta, California,

139. It is an historic concept of government derived from Aristotle and Montesquieu, based on the contention that "men entrusted with power tend to abuse it." For a good discussion of this concept, see Locke, *The Second Treatise on Civil Government*, section 141; Duff and Whiteside, 4 *Selected Essays on Constitutional Law*, 291–316 (1938).
140. Testimony of John Dean, Vol. 3, pp. 961, 1575.
141. Testimony of John Dean, Vol. 3, pp. 1007–1008.

focused on ways of obstructing an investigation of Watergate by the Senate. This included tactics such as the use of executive privilege to prevent the testimony of people from the White House,[142] efforts to influence members of the Senate Committee conducting the investigation, and the compiling of campaign financing data from those members' past campaigns in an effort to embarrass them.

The attack group, a media-oriented White House group, arranged to meet with people from North Carolina thought to have embarrassing information about the Chairman.[143] Members of the administration were used as clandestine contacts with Republicans on the Committee to either give "guidance" or gather intelligence on what facts the Committee possessed.[144] John Dean was suggested as a liaison with the Committee after he had admitted wrongdoing in the coverup,[145] and efforts toward having a "White House" minority counsel were put forward.[146]

Separation of powers also encompasses Article III, the judiciary. Here again, the executive subverted the Constitutional balance. As an example, on September 15, 1972, in a conversation in the Oval Office, the President was told by Mr. Dean that ex parte (out-of-court) contacts had been made with the judge in one of the Watergate-related civil suits.[147] These contacts were for the purpose of obtaining an advantage in the case by keeping apprised of inside

142. "The White House will take a public posture of full cooperation, but privately will attempt to restrain the investigation and make it as difficult as possible to get information and witnesses." Testimony of John Dean, Vol. 3, p. 984.

143. Dean testified that there was a discussion that one of the ways of pressuring the Ervin committee was to review contributions made by the White House to members of the committee in the 1970 election, and that with this in mind records of those contributions were placed by Mr. Colson in Mr. Dean's safe so they could be looked into. Testimony of John Dean, Vol. 4, pp. 1501–1502. Dean recalled a conversation with Mr. Baroody, of the attack group (media-oriented White House group), in which Baroody told Dean that either that night or the next night he was meeting with some people from North Carolina who thought they might have some interesting information on Senator Ervin. Testimony of John Dean, Vol. 4, p. 1534.

144. Attorney General Kleindienst was directed to meet with Senator Baker and provide guidance. Transcripts of Presidential Conversations, March 22, 1973.

"P John, you would have no problems to talk with Pat Gray and ask him what the hell Weicker is up to. Do you mind?

E Not at all." Transcripts of Presidential Conversations, March 27, 1973. (discussion between the President and Mr. Ehrlichman).

145. "Mitchell: I think it would be appropriate for your Counsel to be present.

Dean: That's right.

President: Alright. Now that that is done let's get down to the questions—" Transcripts of Presidential Conversations, March 22, 1973.

146. Testimony of John Dean, Vol. 3, p. 984.

147. See, note 59, supra.

661

information, and they could well be unethical.[148] There was no evidence that the White House took any steps to stop that activity.

Still another abuse of the separation between the executive and judicial branches, was a contact made with the presiding judge in the Ellsberg case. That judge was asked if he would be interested in becoming Director of the FBI. Significantly, the offer was made in rather clandestine circumstances, at the very time the Ellsberg case was being tried, and at a time when it was becoming ever more possible that the break-in at Ellsberg's psychiatrist might become known to the judge and jeopardize the case against Ellsberg.[149] A contact under such circumstances, by one of the top White House officials and briefly by the President himself,[150] once again threatened the concept of mutual independence intended by the separation of powers.

C. THE BILL OF RIGHTS

Unlike other amendments to the Constitution, the Bill of Rights was drawn up as something of a cohesive declaration of rights. It comprises the first ten amendments, and represents a guarantee of individual freedoms that are fundamental to democracy.

The First, Fourth, Fifth, and Sixth Amendments are the bulwark of the substantive guarantees in our Bill of Rights. They were, without exception, attacked and violated by Watergate and related events.

That attack focused on the First Amendment, which by its very words, as well as the prominent role it has taken in our history, mark it as a profoundly important statement of individual rights. Specifically, it protects freedom of expression in four forms—freedom of speech, press, assembly, and petition.

Those who spoke out against the administration, whether it was the Chairman of the Democratic Party or Senators expressing their opposition, whether it was a prominent or unknown citizen, or whether a member of the administration itself, often found themselves the target of official retaliation for having exercised their freedom of speech.

"People who were most vocal and could command some audience were considered enemies or opponents." [151]

One witness testified that the White House was continually seeking intelligence information about demonstration

148. Canon 7 of the Code of Professional Responsibility, Ethical Considerations, pp. 7–35.
149. Testimony of John Ehrlichman, Vol. 6, pp. 2617–2619.
150. Id.
151. Testimony of John Dean, Vol. 4, p. 1459.

leaders and their supporters that would either discredit them personally or indicate that the demonstration was in fact sponsored by some foreign enemy. There were also White House requests for information regarding ties between major political figures (specifically Members of the U. S. Senate) who opposed the President's war policies and the demonstration leaders.[152]

Interference with the freedom of speech of such opponents took a wide variety of forms. It included a program run by Donald Segretti, in which his operatives were asked to "obtain hecklers," to be used to disrupt the speeches of Democratic presidential candidates.[153]

According to Mr. Haldeman, the "enemies list" was drawn up to deprive those "who were expressing vocal opposition" to the White House of any "platform for getting extraordinary publicity for their expression of opposition." [154] Thus, they were labeled as "enemies," their names circulated through the government, and as a group, identified for semi-official executive branch action.

Aside from the enemies or opposing candidates, selected individuals who expressed opposition were subjected to questionable tactics. As an example, Alfred Baldwin conducted surveillance of various outspoken Senators and Congressmen, including Representatives Abzug, Chisholm, Koch, and McCloskey, and Senators Javits, Kennedy, and Proxmire.[155]

Senator Kennedy was not only subjected to the Baldwin surveillance. He was also a target of Anthony Ulasewicz and John Caulfield, who investigated his political contributors, his accident at Chappaquidick, and a trip to Hawaii on official business.[156] Howard Hunt was asked by Mr. Colson to get information from a Kennedy friend in Rhode Island, and was provided with a CIA disguise for the operation.[157] Mr. Haldeman, according to multiple testimony, asked that Senator Kennedy be subjected to 24-hour surveillance. Literally dozens of citizens who spoke out in opposition were targets of Ulasewicz investigations, which were paid for by the President's personal attorney, supervised by Mr. Ehrlichman, and conducted outside law enforcement channels, because legitimate law enforcement was not involved.

152. Testimony of John Dean. Vol. 3, p. 915.
153. Testimony of Robert M. Benz, Vol. 11, p. 4404.
154. Testimony of H. R. Haldeman, Vol. 8, p. 3155.
155. Testimony of Alfred Baldwin. Vol. 1, pp. 396–397.
156. Testimony of John Dean. Vol. 3. pp. 922–23: see also, testimony of Howard Hunt, Vol. 9, pp. 377-78. This resulted in a written report by Caulfield of Senator Kennedy's trip to Honolulu in August. 1971. See, Vol. 3, Ex. 34–4. p. 1117.
157. Executive Session of John Caulfield, March 16, 1974, p. 85.

The Watergate break-in itself, according to Jeb Magruder, was an attempt to find embarrassing information about Lawrence O'Brien, because "Mr. O'Brien had been a very effective spokesman against our position on the ITT case." [158] Magruder testified that because of O'Brien's effectiveness in speaking out, "we had hope that information (from the illegal break-in and wiretap) might discredit him." [159] This is an interesting use of the power and influence of the presidency, in light of the First Amendment. It has what is often called, in Supreme Court, First Amendment cases, "a chilling effect." To the extent government actions intimidate free speech, they violate the Constitution.

Those who chose to exercise constitutionally recognized "symbolic" speech, such as displaying a placard, were likewise interfered with. There was testimony that "during the late winter of 1971, when the President happened to look out the windows of the residence of the White House and saw a lone man with a large 10-foot sign stretched out in front of Lafayette Park," [160] Mr. Higby told Mr. Dean of the President's displeasure with the sign. Mr. Haldeman said the sign had to come down, and when Dean came out of Higby's office he "ran into Mr. Dwight Chapin who said that he was going to get some 'thugs' to remove that man from Lafayette Park. He said it would take him a few hours to get them, but they could do the job." [161]

This was the White House, and its apparent version of First Amendment rights of free speech. It also is indicative of the White House attitude to the First Amendment's "right of the people to peaceably assemble, and to petition the Government for a redress of grievances," [162] an attitude that likewise runs through much of its attack on the press.

The press, however, came in for especially intensive intimidation. A memo from Mr. Magruder to Mr. Haldeman, entitled "The Shot-gun versus the Rifle," [163] set out a plan for influencing news coverage of the White House. It gives some idea of the executive branch concept of our free press.

Among its specific suggestions was a recommendation to "utilize the anti-trust division (of the Justice Department) to investigate various media relating to anti-trust violations. Even the possible threat of anti-trust action I think would be effective in changing their views." [164] Such a recommendation is clearly wrong, an abuse of government, and an abuse of

158. Testimony of Jeb Magruder, Vol. 2, p. 790.
159. Id.
160. Testimony of John Dean, Vol. 3, p. 917.
161. Id.
162. U. S. Const., Amend. I.
163. Memo from Jeb Magruder to H. R. Haldeman, October 17, 1969.
164. Id., at 2.

the First Amendment. In at least one case, involving an in-depth story on Charles G. Rebozo, an anti-trust action was recommended against the Los Angeles Times, which owned the paper doing the story.[165]

Another recommendation in "The Shot-gun versus the Rifle" was "utilizing the Internal Revenue Service as a method to look into the various organizations that we are most concerned about. Just the threat of an IRS investigation will probably turn their approach." [166] It would again be illegal. And again in the Rebozo story, the newsman in charge of the story was in fact audited, at the specific request of the White House.[167]

Newscaster Chet Huntley wrote a piece in *Life* magazine, containing what were considered unfavorable remarks. The suggestions for retaliation against Huntley, in a White House memo by Mr. Higby, contained a telling statement of broad philosophy: "What we are trying to do here is tear down the institution." [168]

The broader tactics used against the press included meetings between Mr. Charles Colson and media representatives. In a summary of his meetings with the three network chief executives, he observed that they were terribly nervous about the Federal Communications Commission. He stated that, "although they tried to disguise this, it was obvious. The harder I pressed them (CBS and NBC) the more accommodating, cordial and almost apologetic they became." [169] He concluded by observing that "I think we can dampen their ardor for putting on 'loyal opposition' type programs." [170] One of the basic guarantees of a free press is that government power *not* be used as prior restraint on the content of news.

Individual newsmen that were apparently critical of the administration were likewise intimidated. One such newsman, Daniel Schorr of CBS, was investigated by the FBI. When the investigation became known, the false story that he was being considered for a high administration position was put out, and Mr. Malek took the blame for the investigation even though it had been ordered by Mr. Haldeman.[171]

Newspapers and reporters that uncovered the Watergate

165. Memo from David Wilson to John Dean. December 1, 1971.
166. Memo from Jeb Magruder to H. R. Haldeman, October 17, 1969.
167. Testimony of Senator Lowell Weicker, hearings on Warrantless Wiretapping and Electronic Surveillance, April 8, 1974. (Ex. 7).
168. "The point behind this whole thing is that we don't care about Huntley—he is going to leave anyway. What we are trying to do here is tear down the institution. Huntley will go out in a blaze of glory and we should attempt to pop his bubble." Memo from L. Higby to Jeb Magruder, July 16, 1970.
169. Memo from Charles Colson to H. R. Haldeman, Sept. 25, 1970.
170. *Id.*
171. Testimony of John Dean, Vol. 4, p. 1490.

story were publicly attacked and ridiculed. In one case, four months after the break-in, the "official White House position" was that stories about Donald Segretti were "stories based on hearsay, character assassination, innuendo or guilt by association." [172] That statement was later called "inoperative," after the White House had been unable to cover up the truth in the story.

Newspapers were exploited, by using them to put out stories known to be misleading, improper, and in some cases totally false. For example, Mr. Hunt testified that he used confidential FBI files to prepare a derogatory article on Mr. Leonard Boudin, an attorney in the Ellsberg case, which information Mr. Colson passed on to the working press.[173]

A memo from Mr. Haldeman stated that "we need to get our people to put out the story on the foreign or Communist money that was used in support of demonstrations against the President in 1972. We should tie all 1972 demonstrations to McGovern and thus to the Democrats as part of the peace movement." [174] Even though there was no evidence to support such stories, the memo went on to recommend, "we could let (columnists) Evans and Novak put it out and then be asked about it to make the point that we knew and the President said it was not to be used under any circumstance." [175]

Falsely tying Senator McGovern to Communist money was not the only false connection that was suggested. Mr. Patrick Buchanan recommended a number of campaign news strategies including, "The Ellsberg connection, tying McGovern to him (Ellsberg) and his crime," because "if the country goes to the polls in November scared to death of McGovern, thinking him vaguely anti-America and radical and pro the left-wingers and militants then they will vote against him— which means for us." [176] This is a clear abuse of executive power as to the press.

One of the most cold-blooded memos to come out of the White House during this period was written by Patrick J. Buchanan. It analyzed the pros and cons of a press attack on Dr. Ellsberg.

The memo begins, "having considered the matter until the early hours, my view is that there are some dividends to be derived from Project Ellsberg." Giving his personal view, Buchanan stated, "To me it would assuredly be psychologically

---

172. Testimony of Clark MacGregor. Vol. 12, p. 5019.
173. Testimony of Howard Hunt, Vol. 9, p. 3673; see also, Executive Session of Howard Hunt. pp. 121-122.
174. Memo from John Dean to H. R. Haldeman, Vol. 8, p. 3171.
175. Id., at 3172.
176. Vol. 10, Ex. 194, p. 4259.

satisfying to cut the innards from Ellsberg," an attitude which has brought his fellow White House staffer, Mr. Colson, a jail term.

Nevertheless, Buchanan concluded that the Ellsberg issue would not "be turned around in the public mind by a few well-placed leaks." Lest there be any doubt about his position, he then stated, "This is not to argue that the effort is not worthwhile—but that simply we ought not now to start investing major personnel resources in the kind of covert operation not likely to yield any major political dividends to the President." [177]

No legal or moral problems for Buchanan; just an objection to the management end of it.

Mr. Buchanan also testified, as to documents surreptitiously taken from the Muskie campaign and photographed by "Fat Jack." Buchanan testified that he "did get the material on two occasions, and (he) did recommend that it be sent to columnists Evans and Novak. Evans and Novak did print, on two occasions, I believe, material from Muskie's campaign." [178] Here again was a high official, using the credibility of the White House, to peddle wrongfully obtained confidential information.

Material obtained secretly from the Commerce Department relative to Senator Muskie's apparently legitimate attempts to help the Maine sugar beet industry as their Senator was leaked to the press, for political purposes, when that industry began to fail.[179]

Information from the Department of Defense as to Senator McGovern's personal and confidential war records was recommended for leak to press.[180]

Testimony was received that Mr. Colson ordered the fabrication of State Department cables relative to the Kennedy Administration's handling of President Diem's assassination, and recommended that this false information be leaked to Mr. William Lambert of *Life* magazine.[181] All this was a blatant attempt to improperly use government power and responsibilities to distort the constitutional role of the press.

Finally, the official press spokesman for the White House consistently told the press and the American people versions of Watergate that were not true, when he and those who pre-

177. White House memo from Patrick Buchanan to John Ehrlichman, July 8, 1971.
178. Testimony of Patrick Buchanan, Vol. 10, p. 3921.
179. Memo to Charles Colson from Thomas Thawley, Deputy Assistant Secretary of Commerce, April 16, 1971.
180. Memo from Richard Howard to Fred Fielding, May 12, 1972 (this memo had an unusual instruction at the top: "PLEASE BURN BEFORE READING").
181. Testimony of Howard Hunt, Vol. 9, p. 3672.

pared him were in a position to know, or in fact knew, that his statements were untrue. The President himself misled the press in news conferences and official statements, as to the investigation, its results, and the substance of evidence involving himself and the Watergate matter.

The Fourth Amendment fared no better.

It guarantees the "right of the people to be secure in their persons, houses, papers, and effects, against unreasonable searches and seizures. . . ." [182] It was expressly violated by burglaries and warrantless wiretaps.

As an example, this constitutional safeguard was at the center of illegalities contained in the so-called 1970 Intelligence Plan. In a colloquy during the course of this Committee's hearings, the Chairman and Mr. Dean discussed the elements of that Intelligence Plan. It was described as recommending 1) techniques for removing limitations on electronic surveillance and penetration, 2) the use of mail coverage, 3) a technique designated as surreptitious entry, 4) development of campus sources of information, and 5) the use of military undercover agents. The Chairman rightly noted, and the witness concurred, that resort to burglary, electronic surveillance and penetration without a court order is a clear violation of the Fourth Amendment.[183]

Nevertheless, on July 5, 1970, a memo written by Mr. Haldeman indicated that the President of the United States gave his approval to the plan.[184] There is additional evidence that events took place which closely parallel the recommendations in the 1970 plan. In contrast with the evidence that the plan was approved, there is no documentary evidence that the plan was at any time officially withdrawn, although one witness claimed it was.[185]

The instances of burglaries and wiretapping have been well-documented. They include the break-in at Ellsberg's psychiatrist's office, the possible break-in at publisher Hank Greenspun's office, the four attempts and two successful break-ins at the Democratic National Committee headquarters, the plans to break-in at McGovern's campaign headquarters, proposed penetrations of the Potomac Associates and The Brookings Institute, questionable wiretaps of newsmen and government officials, wiretaps of Spencer Oliver, Lawrence O'Brien, and columnist Joseph Kraft. This disregard for the Fourth Amendment proceeded in spite of apparently severe

182. U. S. Const., Amend IV.
183. Vol. 4, p. 1455.
184. Memo to Mr. Huston from H. R. Haldeman, July 14, 1970, Vol.3, Ex. 36, p. 1324; Presidential Statement, May 22, 1973.
185. Mr. Haldeman testified that the President approved the Huston plan, and that it was rescinded five days later with notification of the agency heads. Testimony of H. R. Haldeman, Vol. 8, p. 3030.

warnings and objections by one of the most experienced figures in law enforcement in this nation's history, J. Edgar Hoover.[186]

The Fifth Amendment was likewise violated. However, it is more appropriately discussed along with the Fourteenth Amendment in the next section examining Due Process of Law.

The Sixth Amendment guarantees the right to a speedy trial, the right to the evidence of witnesses, and the right to subpoena evidence from witnesses,[187] an important principle in our system of justice.

While it may be temporarily obscured by the plight of high officials in Watergate, history will record that seven men were brought to trial in 1973 for the Watergate break-in. Six of those men spent considerable time in jail. To date no persons have paid a higher price for Watergate, through the justice system. When history judges our system of laws, the fairness of the trial those men went through will be at the fore.

Viewed in that light, the so-called coverup takes on a somewhat different significance. It was nothing less than a massive interference with the constitutional right of seven American citizens to a fair trial. They were categorically denied the testimony of witnesses who possessed evidence that was critical to their defense. Perjury was planned and orchestrated from within the White House itself. Evidence was destroyed. Key witnesses were excused from giving testimony before the grand jury, avoiding their constitutional duty. A speedy trial was opposed, not because it would result in greater justice, but because it served the political ends of the White House. Even the defendants themselves were paid to not give testimony, thereby denying any hope to at least one of them who might have preferred a fair trial. Offers of clemency, family support, and rehabilitation were used for the same purpose.[188]

In an opposite sense, the Sixth Amendment's guarantees of a witness's testimony were again subverted when counter-lawsuits were undertaken against Democratic officials partly to use the power of taking witnesses' depositions, to get at embarassing information.[189] Here the tactic was to put political opponents under oath and use that circumstance and

186. Testimony of H. R. Haldeman, Vol. 7, p. 2874. Mitchell also expressed his disapproval of the 1970 Domestic Intelligence Plan to Mr. Hoover and Mr. DeLoach of the FBI and he "talked to both Mr. Haldeman and the President about the subject matter." Testimony of John Mitchell, Vol. 4, p. 1604.

187. U. S. Const., Amend. VI.

188. Testimony of James McCord, Vol. 1, p. 131.

189. Dean testified that the counter suits against the Democrats in the fall of 1972 demonstrate "the willingness to commence counteractions to avoid further prying into the situation at the White House." Testimony of John Dean, Vol. 4, p. 1473.

power to elicit confidential information. Those who denied witnesses to their own, could not apparently resist enforcing and invoking the Sixth Amendment's guarantees when it came to their opponents.

D. DUE PROCESS OF LAW

The concept of due process put simply means the right to fair and just treatment under the law.

It is rooted in Chapter 39 of the Magna Carta, in which King John declared that "no free man shall be taken or imprisoned . . . except by the lawful judgment of his peers or by the law of the land." [190]

Recent Supreme Court cases have described due process, which is guaranteed by the Fifth and Fourteenth Amendments, as embodying "a system of rights based on moral principles so deeply imbedded in the traditions and feelings of our people as to be deemed fundamental to a civilized society as conceived by our whole history." [191]

Due process has been even more succinctly described by the Supreme Court as "that which comports with the deepest notions of what is fair and right and just." [192] It is the backbone of justice in America, and it was dramatically missing in the evidence of not only the Watergate criminal proceedings, but in the Ellsberg case and countless other cases with political overtones in the period directly leading to Watergate.

The particular phraseology associated with due process has been generally used in close association with precise safeguards of accused persons. Nevertheless, it is equally a restraint on action by the government that unfairly discriminates against our citizens or the exercise of their rights. Those two guarantees have often been called procedural and substantive due process. Both were violated by the events leading to and including Watergate.

The obvious example of procedural abuses were the trials. In the Ellsberg case, information for use against the defendant was sought by means of a warrantless break-in, an act that eventually contributed to that case being dismissed. In addition, the presiding judge in that case was offered an attractive job, as FBI Director, in the midst of the trial. [193] The offer came from Mr. Ehrlichman, who was responsible for supervision of the so-called Plumbers, at a time when Ehrlichman knew about the break-in by the Plumbers, and presumably knew of its potential consequences. Dr. Ellsberg's right to a

190. Text and commentary on this chapter may be found in W. McKechinie, *Magna Carta—A Commentary on the Greater Charter of King John* (Glasgow: 1914).
191. Solesbee v. Balkcom. 339 U.S. 9, 16 (1950).
192. Id.
193. Testimony of John Ehrlichman, Vol. 6, pp. 2617–2619.

fair trial was also jeopardized by tactics that attempted to destroy his public image, discredit his associates, and attack publishers who printed the Pentagon Papers. One of the President's closest advisors has been sentenced to one to three years in jail for that tactic.

The direct interference with a fair trial for the Watergate defendants has already been documented. In addition, those defendants were subjected to prejudicial public statements that they were "third rate burglars," "blackmailers," and even "double agents." The important point is that the accusations came from the White House, and that the White House was in a position to remove those labels by following its legal duty of providing all relevant evidence.

Perhaps of even greater significance is the vast number of cases involving those accused of conspiracies against the United States. The improper use of wiretaps, agent provocateurs, and informers resulted in the dismissal of most of those cases.[194] While this was not directly a focus of the Watergate investigation, it became relevant in examining the climate and attitudes that led to the Watergate plan.

Criminal cases were not the only instances of due process violations. The "fair and right and just" application of our laws suffered when anti-trust actions were generated on the basis of political considerations, when income tax audits were ordered because a newsman wrote an article the White House did not like, when an enemies list was compiled so that the laws could be applied more strictly or to the disadvantage of opponents, when White House staff members had access to FBI files pertaining to their own investigation, when they were given special treatment before a grand jury, when the intelligence gathered by the various agencies of our government was collected, evaluated, and distributed in apparent violation of the agency statutes, when the military was used to spy on American citizens working for the Democratic Party.[195] All of this violated the Fifth Amendment and, in some cases, the Fourteenth Amendment. In the process, Watergate and its predecessor activities violated one of the broadest principles of our system of laws, a concept so fundamental that it is the basis of fully one quarter of all litigation that comes before the Supreme Court of the land.

This is apparently what happens when the witness who was the Attorney General during most of that period can be

194. In the White Panthers case, it was illegal wiretaps. In the Camden 28 case, it was the use of an agent provocateur; and in the 11 gambling, narcotics, and bribery cases in Miami it was illegal wiretaps.
195. See, GENERAL POWERS AND DUTIES, notes 10–94 supra. and accompanying text; see also, testimony of Senator Lowell Weicker, Jr., hearings on Warrantless Wiretapping and Electronic Surveillance, April 8, 1974.

asked whether he "exalted the political fortunes of the President before the President's responsibility to perform his constitutional duties to see that the laws are faithfully executed," and he responds, "I think that is a reasonable interpretation."[196]

II. The Government

One of the significant patterns of evidence that emerged from this Committee's investigation relates to the operation of government.

In the climate of Watergate there is a tendency to dismiss anything short of crimes. But there is great value to the facts that follow, not because they contain sensational crimes, but because they confirm a misuse of the intended functions of important institutions. It reflects a departure from legitimate government that if allowed to persist would be of far greater significance, over time, than any short-term criminal event.

A. THE INTELLIGENCE COMMUNITY

The attitudes and policies that led to Watergate had a profound impact on the intelligence community, from the FBI and the CIA to the lesser intelligence sections of other agencies.

Soon after the new administration took office in 1968, there seems to have been a basic dissatisfaction within the White House as to our existing intelligence capabilities. They were variously considered too timid, too bound by tradition, and generally incapable of acting effectively with respect to what the White House perceived as necessary intelligence.

One of the responses by the White House was to set up a plan, an intelligence plan, so that the objectives, methods, and results of the intelligence community would coincide with the White House. This plan was drafted by Tom Charles Huston in early 1970,[197] and came to be known as the 1970 Domestic Intelligence Plan, or the Huston Plan.

Much of the plan, which has been described previously,[198] was illegal, either in its objectives or in the methods it proposed. Nevertheless, there are numerous indications, in evidence received by this Committee, that the types of activities

196. Testimony of John Mitchell, Vol. 5, p. 1895.
197. According to Mr. Haldeman, "the President set up an interagency committee consisting of the Directors of the FBI, the CIA, the Defense Intelligence Agency and the National Security Agency," and "Mr. Huston, the White House staff man for this project, was notified by a memorandum from me of the approval of the President." Testimony of H. R. Haldeman, Vol. 7, 2875.
198. See, notes 183–186.

recommended in the plan were carried out in the following years. The net effect was to subvert or distort the legitimate intelligence functions of the government.

The plan recommended an expanded use of electronic surveillance. However, the expanded wiretapping that took place in succeeding years was done outside legitimate channels, such as the 17 so-called Kissinger taps,[199] the tap on Joseph Kraft,[200] the Watergate wiretaps, and even the wiretap on the President's brother.[201]

The second element of the plan called for surreptitious entries. Burglaries in fact took place at the office of Dr. Ellsberg's psychiatrist,[202] at the Democratic National Committee, at the office of publisher Hank Greenspun, according to multiple evidence; [203] and were suggested or planned for the offices of the Potomac Associates,[204] The Brookings Institute,[205] and Senator McGovern's campaign headquarters.[206]

Mail sent to an affiliate of the Democratic party was opened and photographed by the United States Army. in a well-documented and apparently massive operation,[207] and military agents spied on the Concerned Americans in Berlin, a group of McGovern supporters who were officially recognized by the Democratic party.[208]

The specific actions proposed by Huston are only one aspect of the plan. Equally important are the policy recommendations. The heart of this new policy was better coordination and use of existing intelligence from all areas of the government.[209] The means of carrying it out was to be a new intelligence "Committee" sitting above all the agencies. Again, the plan was carried out.

199. Testimony of Robert Mardian, Vol. 4, pp. 2392–2393; John Ehrlichman, Vol. 4, p. 2529; and John Dean. Vol. 3, p. 920.
200. Testimony of John Dean. Vol. 3, p. 919. In June, 1969, Ehrlichman directed Caulfield in lieu of the FBI to place a national security tap on Kraft's home phone. Caulfield contacted Jack Regan, former FBI agent, who ultimately installed the tap. Executive Session of John Caulfield, March 23, 1974.
201. Presidential Press Conference, November 17, 1973.
202. Testimony of Howard Hunt, Vol. 9, p. 3663.
203. Testimony of Howard Hunt, Vol. 9, p. 3687. See Transcripts of Presidential Conversations, Sept. 15, 1972.
204. White House memo, July 6, 1971, from John Caulfield to John Dean, stating in part, "a penetration is deemed possible if required."
205. Testimony of John Dean, Vol. 3, p. 920; Executive Session of John Caulfield, March 23, 1974.
206. Testimony of Howard Hunt, Vol. 9, p. 3686.
207. See, testimony of Senator Lowell P. Weicker, hearings on Warrantless Wiretapping and Electronic Surveillance, relating to intelligence activities of the United States military directed against "The Concerned Americans in Berlin," an affiliate of the American Democratic party. (Exhibit 8)
208. Id.
209. This was the final section of the 1970 Domestic Intelligence Plan, entitled "Measures to Improve Domestic Intelligence Operations." Vol. 3, Ex. 35, p. 1323. See testimony of John Dean, Vol. 4, p. 1457.

On September 17, 1970, an Intelligence Evaluation Committee was set up in the White House.[210] It was to receive information from the CIA, the FBI, the National Security Agency, and other intelligence sections. Notwithstanding the fact that the statutes prohibit the CIA from participating in any domestic intelligence function, it was called upon to evaluate domestic intelligence-gathering by the other agencies when the Intelligence Evaluation Committee was set up. This intelligence was to be digested by the CIA experts and then disseminated for use wherever useful, regardless of the statutory limits placed on the agency that collected the information.[211]

What was important about setting up that Committee was not the work it actually did, but rather the legitimization of a concept. That concept was that intelligence functions of the various agencies were there for whatever purpose the Executive decided it wanted, not for the purposes Congress decided by statute.

As an illustration, Mr. McCord testified that he eventually received information for use by CRP frim the Internal Security Division of the Justice Department, on a daily basis.[212] It included information from the FBI, pertained to individuals, and was of a political as well as non-political nature.[213] This arrangement was made pursuant to a request sent to Mr. Mitchell from Mr. McCord, which led to a call from Assistant Attorney General Mardian in which he relayed the Attorney General's approval and told McCord to work through the Internal Security Division.[214]

The Internal Security Division of the Justice Department also provided political legal assistance to the White House. For example, it provided information regarding demonstrators, and information that would embarrass individuals in connection with their relationship with demonstrators and demonstration leaders.[215]

Another illustration of misuse of intelligence was the request made to the IRS, on July 1, 1969, by Mr. Huston, to set up a means of "reviewing the operations of Ideological

210. The memo to the Attorney General describing the setting up of the IEC was quoted in full in the text of the hearings. Vol. 3, p. 1063.
211. Testimony of John Dean, Vol. 3, pp. 916–919, 1057–1074, and Vol. 4, p. 1457.
212. McCord received information, including FBI data, from the Internal Security Division of the Justice Department, upon his request to Attorney General Mitchell. Mitchell told Mardian to direct McCord to I.S.D., where McCord's contact was John Martin, Chief of the Evaluation Section. Testimony of James McCord, Vol. 1, p. 178.
213. Id., at 181.
214. Id., at 178
215. Testimony of John Dean, Vol. 3, pp. 916–919.

Organizations." [216] Soon the IRS had set up an "Activists Organizations Committee,"[217] collecting intelligence to "find out generally about the funds of these organizations." An internal memo pointed out that "its activities should be disclosed generally only to those persons who need to know, because of its semi-secretive nature." "We do not want the news media to be alerted to what we are attempting to do or how we are operating because the disclosure of such information might embarrass the Administration." "The type of organization in which we are interested may be ideological . . . or other." "In effect, what we will attempt to do is to gather intelligence data on the organizations in which we are interested and to use a Strike Force concept." [218] This was not tax collection; it was the IRS being converted into an intelligence agency; and it was stopped in the midst of this Committee's hearings in mid-1973.

The next step was when the IRS began gathering intelligence from other parts of the government, with no attempt made to restrict this to tax-related information. Arrangements were made with the military, the Internal Security Division of the Justice Department, and the Secret Service to turn over information on individuals or groups.[219] So long as the IRS has the power to be a potential harassment for the average citizen if audits are not conducted on an objective basis, this procedure of developing files on dissenting citizens must be questioned. The more important point is that IRS duties and responsibilities are spelled out by the Congress, and such an intelligence operation is not one of them.

The IRS and the Justice Department were not the only agencies pressured into assisting White House intelligence demands. A Secret Service agent spied on Senator McGovern,[220] when supposedly protecting him during the campaign. When the White House was informed of this, no objection was made.

216. Memo from Tom Huston to Roger Barth, Asst. Commissioner of IRS, August 14, 1970.
217. See testimony of Senator Lowell P. Weicker, hearings on Warrantless Wiretapping and Electronic Surveillance, April 8, 1974 (Exhibit 1, memo by D. O. Virdin of the IRS; report of meeting to set up an "Activists Organizations Committee").
218. Id.
219. For example, on December 4, 1969, D. W. Bacon, Asst. Commissioner, IRS, contacted Colonel Heston C. Cole, Counterintelligence Division, Directorate Office of Special Investigations; and on January 26, 1970 the IRS contacted Director Rowley of the Secret Service, in both cases to coordinate intelligence-gathering operations through the Activists Organizations Committee. See, testimony of Senator Lowell P. Weicker, hearings on Warrantless Wiretapping and Electronic Surveillance, April 8, 1974.
220. White House memo from Steve Karalekas to Charles Colson, August 16, 1972, referring to the activities of Agent Bolton. See also, testimony of John Dean, Vol. 3, pp. 923, 1071.

An FBI agent was used by a White House staff member to spy on a Long Island newspaper doing an article on one of the President's friends.[221] The Commerce Department was called on to provide commercial information in a project that it was hoped would embarrass Senator Muskie.[222] The Department of Defense was used to find out information as to Senator McGovern's war records, at a time when there were public charges that he may have acted with cowardice.

There was testimony to the effect that there was nothing short of a basic policy to use any governmental agencies to seek politically embarrassing information on individuals who were thought to be enemies of the White House. The so-called "enemies list" was maintained in the White House for this purpose, and a memo was prepared to implement a means of attacking these enemies.[223]

Apparently it was not enough to maneuver the intelligence community and related agency functions. Plans were made to take what is clearly a function of government outside the government, to set up an independent intelligence operation.

The first plan was put forth by Mr. Caulfield, in proposals to Messrs. Dean, Mitchell and Ehrlichman. He suggested a private security entity that would be available for White House special projects, thereby insulating the White House from its deeds. It was called Operation Sandwedge.[224]

Mr. Caulfield rejected the Sandwedge plan, and it was apparently replaced with an operation that came to be known as the "Plumbers." In the meantime, Caulfield began conducting intelligence functions from a position on the White House counsel's staff, functions that properly belonged in the agencies, if anywhere.

Caulfield was instructed, for example, to develop political intelligence on Senator Kennedy, including instructions from the Assistant Attorney General to obtain certain information

221. John Caulfield testified that he requested a New York City FBI agent to go out to the *Newsday* offices. This was done, and included a report of the newspaper's confidential publication schedule. Executive Session of John Caulfield, March 23, 1974.

222. Memo to Charles Colson from Thomas Thawley, Deputy Asst. Secretary of Commerce, April 16, 1971.

223. White House memo from John Dean, August 16, 1971, entitled "Dealing with our Political Enemies." Vol. 4, Ex. 48, p. 1689.

224. Drafted in late summer 1971, Operation Sandwedge called for an offensive intelligence-gathering operation for infiltration of campaign organizations and headquarters with undercover personnel, surveillance of Democratic conventions and meetings, derogatory information-seeking investigations, and "black bag" activities. Though dropped from active consideration by late 1971, Operation Sandwedge can be seen as a precursor of the Gemstone Plan which achieved the capabilities championed by Caulfield. See, Caulfield Executive Session, March 23, 1974; See also, Campaign Practices Section of Select Committee Report, exhibit of memorandum of Caulfield to Dean entitled "Operation Sandwedge." See also, Vol. 2, p. 786; Vol. 3, pp. 924-6; Vol. 6, p. 2537.

about the travels of Mary Jo Kopechne.[225] When he took the job, he told Mr. Ehrlichman that he would hire an ex-New York City policeman to do investigative work.[226]

Mr. Ulasewicz was then used to collect information on various enemies, political, ideological, and personal. A sample of his activities reveals not only why intelligence should not be outside the checks of a professional organization, but also the rather broad scope of what the White House was in fact doing. His investigations included such things as Richard Nixon's old apartment in New York, a Kennedy official trip to Hawaii, name checks on White House visitors, the President's brother, political contributors to a dozen Senators who opposed the administration, Jefferson Hospital in Philadelphia, Louis Harris Polls, the Businessmen's Education Fund, the Hoouse of Mercy home for unwed mothers, the U.S. Conference of Mayors, a comedian named Dixon, Mrs. Rose Kennedy's secretary, and Birmingham, Alabama City Council, Mayor, and Executive Staff.[227] And that is just a sample of the much larger number of his investigations. Many of them are clearly the responsibility of established agencies, if they are anybody's responsibility at all.

Eventually, a semi-official unit, the Plumbers, was established within the White House, with a combination of police and intelligence duties. It conducted what Mr. Mitchell referred to in his testimony as the "White House horrors." [228] According to Mitchell, these operations were so wrong that if the President had heard about them he would have "lowered the Boom", even though there is other evidence that the President did know about them and didn't lower any boom.[229]

The legitimate intelligence agencies were used to support

225. In the summer of 1969, when Dean was working at the Justice Department, "then Deputy Attorney General Kleindienst called (Dean) into his office and told (him) that the White House wanted some very important information . . . regarding the foreign travels of Mary Jo Kopechne." Dean was directed to obtain the information from Mr. De Loach, Deputy Director of the FBI, and give it to John Caulfield from the White House. Vol. 3, p. 922.
226. Ehrlichman appointed Caulfield to the White House staff on April 8, 1969, as a liaison with various law enforcement agencies, with the understanding that the services of Mr. Ulasewicz, a retiring New York detective, would be obtained. Commencing July, 1969, Ulasewicz reported on his investigatory activities to the White House through Caulfield, on the orders of Mr. Ehrlichman and Mr. Dean. Vol. 1, p. 251.
227. See, Committee interviews with Mr. Ulasewicz, Mr. Dean, Mr. Caulfield, Anne Dawson, Tony LaRocco.
228. Mr. Mitchell described the Plumbers' activities which he learned of from Mardian and Mr. LaRue, as the "White House horror stories." Vol. 4, pp. 1624–25.
229. On March 22, 1973, the day after Mr. Dean told the President of the Watergate-related White House horrors and other facts, the President, according to Mitchell, discussed the possibility of using Dean as a liaison with the Ervin Committee, rather than lowering any boom. Vol. 5, p. 1894.

this operation, specifically by providing materials for their operations. General Cushman of the CIA testified that after a personal request from Mr. Ehrlichman, CIA technical services people provided Mr. Hunt with a drivers license, social security card, wig, and speech altering device, which were delivered to a "safe house" off CIA premises per Hunt's instructions.[230]

Around August, 1971, Hunt began to make additional demands on the CIA: first, for a stenographer to be brought in from Paris, which Cushman and Director Helms considered merely a face-saving move and rejected. Later demands were made for a tape recorder in a typewriter case, a camera in a tobacco pouch, for film development, and for an additional alias and false papers for another man ("probably Liddy"), which requests came to Cushman's attention after they had been granted by the technical services people.[231]

After Hunt's additional demands and a subsequent request for a New York address and phone services, Cushman and Helms decided Hunt's requests had exceeded his original authority. On August 31, 1971, Hunt made a final request, for a credit card, which was denied.[232]

Mr. Young of the Plumbers unit asked the CIA to do a psychological profile of Dr. Ellsberg. It was clearly a domestic project, the only one of its type ever requested, according to Gen. Cushman of the CIA, who also testified that such profiles are reserved for foreign leaders. Nevertheless, it was done, but Mr. Young considered it unsatisfactory, so another profile was prepared and sent.[233] Other projects spanned a broad range, such as spiriting Dita Beard from the East Coast to a Denver hospital, and a subsequent trip to Denver by Hunt in disguise to question her about the ITT affair.[234] To bring the full influence of the White House to bear on this extraordinary activity, Mr. Ehrlichman testified that he personally introduced Messrs. Krogh and Young, who headed up the Plumbers to the heads of various agencies, such as the Secretary of Defense, the Attorney General, and the Director of the CIA.[235]

230. Vol. 8, pp. 3292–93.
231. Id.
232. Id.
233. Id., at p. 3311.
234. Shortly after the ITT memo was published in February, 1972, Mr. Liddy transported Dita Beard from Washington to a hospital in Denver. In his interview there, Mr. Hunt elicited from Dita Beard a public statement that the memo was a fraud. Testimony of Robert Mardian, Vol. 6, p. 2359; Howard Hunt, Vol. 9, pp. 3752–53.
235. Mr. Ehrlichman testifies further that Mr. Krogh and Mr. Young "described the function of the special unit" (the Plumbers) to the heads of the various agencies. Vol. 7, p. 2691.

Members of the Plumbers eventually went on to similar work for the Committee to Re-Elect. Although they were clearly outside the government, they again used the legitimate agencies. Ex-CIA employees were recruited on the basis of their loyalty to the CIA. National security responsibilities were misused. Mr. Barker was even told that the interests of national security he was serving were above the FBI and the CIA.[236] To reinforce this position, classified and critical information about the mining of Haiphong harbor was relayed to Barker the day before the President's announcement.[237] This was not only a misuse of secret Defense Department intelligence, but it also furthered a misuse of national security entrustment in the executive branch.

In a different type of situation, Mr. Haldeman was appointed "the Lord High Executioner of leaks". This technique of attacking and solving the leaks problem illustrates the contempt for normal government functions. It resulted in Mr. Caulfield, by his own testimony, being directed by Ehrlichman to wiretap a newsman's telephone (Joseph Kraft) in pursuit of a leak,[238] outside the safeguards of government wiretap procedures and regulations. There are capabilities within the legitimate operations of our government for handling such a problem. The attitude that these problems had to be treated independently was the same attitude that led to the 17 Kissinger taps being installed outside normal FBI channels and Mardian's instructions from the President regarding the disposition of those wiretap logs "that related to newsmen and White House staff suspected of leaking",[239] and that led to unusual and perhaps illegal White House involvement in the Ellsberg case itself.

There is a reason for demanding that government officials use only the tested and accountable facilities of government. It has been illustrated by the kind of projects undertaken independently by the White House.

The final contempt for the intelligence community can be seen in efforts to exploit them in the coverup. Mr. Ehrlichman said that he and Mr. Haldeman had spoken to General Walters and Mr. Helms of the CIA shortly after the Water-

236. Testimony of Bernard Barker, Vol. 1, p. 360.
237. Mr. Hunt testified that he was "in very general terms aware of" the President's speech announcing the bombing of Haiphong harbor prior to the speech. Hunt requested that Mr. Barker "attempt to have as many telegrams as possible sent to the White House . . . manifesting approval of the President's move." Testimony of Howard Hunt, Vol. 9, pp. 3745–46.
238. See, note 21, supra.
239. The President instructed Mr. Mardian in the fall of 1971 to transfer the logs from Mr. Sullivan, Assistant Director of the FBI, to Mr. Ehrlichman, who kept them in his safe for over a year. Testimony of John Dean, Vol. 3, pp. 920–21.

gate break-in.[240] Ehrlichman further said that Walters was a friend of the White House and was there to give the White House influence over the CIA.[241] Dean testified that Ehrlichman asked him to explore the possible use of the CIA with regard to assisting the Watergate burglars.[242]

On June 23, 1972, Mr. Haldeman and Mr. Ehrlichman met with Director Helms and General Cushman of the CIA. According to Director Helms, Haldeman said something to the effect that it had been decided that General Walters was to go talk to FBI Director Gray and inform him that "these investigations of the FBI might run into CIA operations in Mexico" and that it might be best if they were tapered off— or something like that.[243] According to General Walters, Haldeman directed Helms to inhibit the FBI investigation on grounds that it would uncover CIA assets in Mexico. Haldeman also indicated he had information the CIA did not have, and that five suspects were sufficient.[244] When Director Helms and Director Gray of the FBI scheduled a meeting between themselves on JJune 28, 1972, Mr. Ehrlichman intervened and canceled the meeting, thus preventing any independent contacts.

At a later time, Mr. Dean discussed with General Walters the possibility of using covert CIA funds to pay the Watergate defendants.[245] In February 1973, the CIA was asked by the White House to take custody of Justice Department files on Watergate, but the request was denied.[246]

Mr. McCord testified that at the time of the Watergate trial, pressure was brought on himself and other defendants to claim for purposes of a defense that Watergate was a CIA operation.[247]

The FBI was likewise abused in numerous ways. Some of these, such as turning over Hunt's files to Mr. Gray, have

240. Ehrlichman and Haldeman were instructed to insure that covert CIA activities were not exposed by the Watergate investigation being conducted by the FBI. Vol. 6, p. 2557.
241. On June 26, 1972, Mr. Dean on Mr. Mitchell's suggestion, sought through Mr. Ehrlichman to contact the CIA as to the Watergate break-in. Vol. 3, p. 946.
242. Mr. Dean indicated to Gen. Walters that witnesses were wobbling and could cause problems, and asked if the CIA could raise bail for some of these defendants. Testimony of John Dean, Vol. 3, p. 1037; Vol. 4, p. 1461.
243. Testimony of Richard Helms, Vol. 8, p. 3238.
244. Memorandum of General Walters, Vol. 7, Ex. 101, pp. 2948–49.
245. Testimony of John Dean. Vol. 3, p. 1037.
246. On February 9, 1973, Mr. Dean called the new Director of the CIA, Mr. Schlesinger, and suggested that the Justice Department be required to return to the CIA a package of all the materials turned over to Justice regarding Hunt and the break-in at Dr. Fielding's office. Mr. Schlesinger and General Walters decided this was "out of the question." Testimony of General Walters, Vol. 9, pp. 3417–19.
247. Testimony of James McCord, Vol. 1, pp. 193–98.

been well documented. But there were other examples. The FBI set up the so-called Kissinger wiretaps outside channels, effectively insulating them from routine discovery and accountability, and at the President's instructions, Mr. William Sullivan (who had supervised the wiretaps) turned over all evidence of them to the White House when it was reportedly related to the President that Hoover might use them to preserve his job.[248] The FBI ran an investigation of CBS newsman Daniel Schorr, in what was a White House tactic to embarrass him, according to one witness.[249]

Mr. Ehrlichman testified that he was instructed after the Watergate break-in to see to it that the FBI investigation did not uncover the Ellsberg break-in or get into the Pentagon Papers episode.[250]

In the end, the wake of Watergate left a distorted intelligence community whose historic professionalism had been badly damaged.

B. LAW ENFORCEMENT AGENCIES

The primary responsibility for law enforcement falls to the Department of Justice. To the extent that White House or political considerations interfered with that responsibility, it interfered with a critical part of our government.

There was considerable evidence of White House contacts, including pressure and interference, with respect to the Watergate investigation. It began almost immediately after the break-in, with a request to the Attorney General that he try to obtain the release of Mr. McCord.[251] In the following days, he was warned about a too aggressive investigation, he was warned in mid-1972 that Magruder might have to plead the Fifth Amendment, he was asked to provide raw FBI

248. In July, 1972, Mr. Sullivan, Associate Director of the FBI, informed Mr. Mardian of the existence of "some very sensitive national security surveillance logs that were not . . . in-channel," that Mr. Hoover might use to preserve his job. Mr. Mardian then flew by courier plane to see the President in San Clemente, who directed him to obtain the reports from Mr. Sullivan and deliver them to Mr. Ehrlichman. Testimony of Robert Mardian, Vol. 6, pp. 2392–93.

249. Mr. Haldeman requested Mr. Higby to direct the FBI to investigate Daniel Schorr. But "to the dismay of the White House, Mr. Hoover proceeded with a full field wide-open investigation" which became apparent and "put the White House in a rather scrambling position to explain what had happened." Ultimately the White House attempted to explain that Mr. Schorr was being considered for a Presidential appointment in the environmental field. Testimony of John Dean, Vol. 3, p. 1071.

250. Testimony of John Ehrlichman, Vol. 6, p. 2544.

251. On the suggestion of Messrs. Mitchell, LaRue, and Magruder, then Attorney General Kleindienst was contacted at the Burning Tree Country Club, while playing golf, by Mr. Liddy and Mr. Powell Moore, to "see if there was any possibility that Mr. McCord could be released from jail. The Attorney General rebuffed this request." Testimony of Jeb Magruder, Vol. 2, p. 798.

files on the case, and he was asked to be the White House secret contact with this Committee.[252] As noted earlier, an agency of the Justice Department, the FBI, was consciously lied to, was asked for raw files, its Director was given potentially embarrassing evidence from the safe of one of the Watergate burglars, with instructions he interpreted as a request to destroy that evidence.

The White House counsel testified that he in fact received information from the Justice Department and the FBI on the Watergate case. Mr. Dean stated that he was asked by Mr. Mitchell, after Mitchell had left CRP, to get FBI 302 reports of interviews with witnesses, and that Mr. Haldeman and Mr. Ehrlichman also thought it would be a good idea to get those reports. Mr. Mardian, attorneys O'Brien and Parkinson, and Mr. Richard Moore all viewed those files after Dean obtained them. Dean pleaded guilty to an "information" charge in October 1973, which charge included a conspiracy based on White House access to those files.[253]

There were similar pressures as to the whole Ellsberg matter. When Assistant Attorney General Petersen advised the President of the Ellsberg break-in, he was told, "I know about that," and "You stay out of that." [254]

The Anti-trust Division of the Justice Department received requests, which have been reviewed earlier as to the media, to go after targets of White House dislike.

After the association of milk producers pledged $2 million to the President's campaign, a grand jury investigation of their association was halted by the Attorney General.[255] Nevertheless, anti-trust violations were allowed to be pursued as a civil, as opposed to criminal, suit.[256] The anti-trust suit was

---

252. Between July 7 or 8, Ehrlichman called Kleindienst to tell him that Petersen had refused Ehrlichman's order to "not harass" Secretary Stans with respect to interrogations. Kleindienst told Ehrlichman to never again give orders to Justice Department personnel, and if this was the President's desire, then Kleindienst would resign as Attorney General. Testimony of Richard Kleindienst, Vol. 9, pp. 3564–3565.

Ehrlichman testified that, based on what Dean had told him about "the unfolding of this thing, that Mr. Magruder may have some involvement and that culminated in a meeting with the Attorney General at the end of July, on July 21 . . ." Testimony of John Ehrlichman, Vol. 6, p. 2554.

253. U.S. v. Dean, D.D.C. No. 886–73.

254. Mr. Petersen was so concerned about the President's directive that he consulted Attorney General Kleindienst and both of them considered going to the President and threatening to resign unless the Justice Department was allowed to investigate the Ellsberg matter. Testimony of Henry Petersen, Vol. 9, pp. 3631–2.

255. See Affidavit of Bruce Wilson to the Senate Select Committee on Presidential Campaign Activities.

256. See Letter from Richard W. McLaren to David M. Dorsen, Assistant Chief Counsel, Senate Select Committee on Presidential Campaign Activities, dated May 10, 1974.

in fact brought in February, 1972, in spite of much White House concern by Messrs. Colson and Haldeman.[257] The milk producers discussed their anti-trust suit with Treasury Secretary Connally in March, 1972, resulting in a call to the Attorney General.[258] Other contacts with the Attorney General were made on behalf of the milk producers, and an attempt was made to give additional contributions in return for dropping the anti-trust suit.[259]

A similar pattern of efforts to obtain favorable treatment from the Attorney General in an anti-trust matter followed the transfer of $100,000 by the Hughes Tool Co. to a friend of the President. The Hughes Corporation was involved in anti-trust problems related to pending purchases of a hotel in Las Vegas and an airline corporation.[260] At the time the money was being transferred, a representative of the Corporation met with the Attorney General. The anti-trust problems were subsequently resolved.[261]

The grand jury system, an essential element of the prosecution process, was subverted by members of the administration and CRP, even to the point of special favors for such officials when they were to be called before the grand jury. According to one witness, Mr. Ehrlichman attempted to prevent former Commerce Secretary Stans from appearing before the Watergate grand jury by directing Assistant Attorney General Petersen not to call Stans. Stans' testimony was eventually taken in private, as was the testimony of Messrs. Colson, Kehrli, and Young.[262]

It should be recalled that the Attorney General doubled as a campaign manager from July 1971, until he resigned in April 1972. When asked if it wasn't improper "for the chief law enforcement officer of the United States to be engaging in, directly or indirectly, managing political activities," the Attorney General responded, "I do, Senator." [263] He held

257. See the Milk Fund Investigation, Part VI, Milk Producer Contribution Activity in 1972 prior to April 7—and the Justice Department anti-trust suit against A.M.P.I., (supra.) particularly Strachan Exhibits 7–10.
258. Id., Part VI (D) (2).
259. Id., Part VI (E) (1, 2).
260. See, Hughes-Rebozo Report, Dunes Hotel case, of the Senate Select Committee on Presidential Campaigns (supra).
261. Id.
262. Mr. Dash: You said you did agree on a concession. Could you tell us where was Mr. Stans interrogated?
    Mr. Petersen: He was interrogated in my conference room by the prosecutors on the case with a reporter present and no one else.
    Mr. Dash: And not before the grand jury?
    Mr. Petersen: No, sir.
    Mr. Dash: Who else, by the way, was given a similar concession during the investigation?
    Mr. Petersen: Colson, Kehrli, and Young.
263. Testimony of John Mitchell, Vol. 5, p. 1856.

this dual role while a number of large campaign contributors, such as the association of milk producers, the Hughes Tool Co., and International Telephone and Telegraph had important cases under investigation by the Justice Department. The Attorney General who succeeded him pleaded guilty to a charge pertaining to the ITT matter.[264]

The prestige of the Attorney General's office was misused. Mr. McCord testified that a very important reason for his participation in the Watergate operation was "the fact that the Attorney General himself, Mr. John Mitchell, at his office had considered and approved the plan, according to Mr. Liddy." [265] Mr. Baldwin was told that if at any time he had trouble establishing his authority for being in a certain place or for having a weapon, he was to mention John Mitchell.[266] In an outrageous insult to our law enforcement institutions, it was in the Attorney General's office on January 27, 1972, and on February 4, 1972, that Liddy's plan was presented, including expensive charts outlining mugging, bugging, burglary, kidnapping, and prostitution.

The Justice Department was not alone.

Some of the most blatant attempts to pressure an agency charged with enforcing laws were aimed at the IRS. The conversation between the President and Messrs. Dean and Haldeman on September 15, 1972, states this clearly, criticizing the IRS for not being sufficiently "responsive" to personal and political demands.[267] It is buttressed with evidence that the IRS was contacted in relation to cases involving friends of the White House. [268]

264. Former Attorney General Richard Kleindienst pleaded guilty on May 16, 1974, to one count of refusing to testify, a misdemeanor, in the ITT case, receiving a suspended sentence of one month in jail and a $100 fine.
265. Testimony of James McCord. Vol. 1, p. 128.
266. Mr. Baldwin further testified: "I felt that I was in no posistion to question John Mitchell;" and Baldwin therefore did not question the legality of his own Watergate-related activities. Testimony of Alfred Baldwin, Vol. 1, p. 409.
267. Mr. Dean testified that on September 15, 1972, he discussed with the President "using the Internal Revenue Service to audit the returns of people," and that this was in keeping with earlier discussions with Haldeman wherein Dean was requested that "certain individuals have audits commenced on them." Dean replied to the President that the IRS had not been happy with the prior requests and, according to Dean, the President told him to keep a good list, so that "we would take care of these people after the election." Haldeman addd "that he had already commenced a project to determine which people in which agencies were responsive and were not responsive to the White House." Testimony of John Dean, Vol. 4, pp. 1480–81.
268. Mr. Dean testified to several requests made to him to intervene on behalf of "friend" tax reports. One case involved the Justice Department, and two other cases resulted from complaints by John Wayne and Billy Graham, who felt they were being harrassed by the IRS. Dean's assistant, Mr. Caulfield, contacted the IRS, which allowed him to see Graham's Sensitive Case Report out of Atlanta and which forced the local agent to justify his audit

The confidential tax return information of Mr. Harold J. Gibbons, Vice President of the Teamsters, was turned over to Mr. Colson. It is significant that the memo discussing Gibbons' taxes points out that he supported Senator McGovern;[269] in fact, he was the only major Teamster official to support McGovern, and the only one whose taxes were apparently sent to the White House.

The tax data for a prominent Jewish leader in Rhode Island was given to Mr. Dean's office, along with confidential tax return information on a number of prominent entertainers. Tax audits of Democratic party Chairman Lawrence O'Brien were sought in an attempt to come up with damaging information. In contrast, IRS contacts were used to help in audits of the President's friends, including actor John Wayne, the Reverend Billy Graham, and Mr. Charles G. Rebozo.[270]

A close friend of the President's, according to Mr. Dean, "thought he was being harassed by the agents of the Internal Revenue Service." Dean raised this with Mr. Walters (Commissioner of the IRS) who said that could not be the case. Dean kept checking the status of the case, because he "got questions on it with considerable regularity." Dean stated that "it was Rosemary Woods who kept asking me the status of the case because this individual was seeing the President a good deal." The case was referred to the Criminal Division of the Justice Department. Dean was told he had to do something about it, so he eventually saw Mr. Ralph Erickson at the Justice Department, who said "there is one more thing we can do; there are some weaknesses in the investigation and we may send it back to the Internal Revenue Service for one last look to see if this follows, it really is a solid case," which to Dean's recollection was done.[271]

Nevertheless, the President was not satisfied and suggested

of Wayne. Testimony of John Dean, Vol. 4, pp. 1530, 1559; Executive Session of John Caulfield, March 23, 1974, pp. 47–48; interview with Mike Acre, September 27, 1973, p. 7.
269. Mr. Colson's memo not only mentioned "that there are income tax discrepancies involving the returns of Harold J. Gibbons," but was also interested that "if there is an informer's fee, let me know." Vol. 4, Ex. 45, p. 1686. It is worth pointing out that none of the official duties of Mr. Colson at the White House would legally justify him having access to citizens' tax returns, except upon specific request of the President.
270. Sensitive cases, such as the President's friends, large contributors, or prominent political figures, were sent to the White House. Testimony of John Dean, Vol. 4, p. 1529. Roger Barth, Assistant to the IRS Commissioner, would also call John Ehrlichman directly, and the Secretary of the Treasury would contact the President directly, in the process of bringing Sensitive Case Reports to White House attention. Interview with Roger Barth, July 31, 1973, pp. 7–8.
271. Vol. 4, pp. 1530, 1539, 1559. This case involved Dr. Kenneth Riland. Dr. Riland was subsequently acquitted of income tax evasion by a federal jury.

that changes be made at the IRS after the 1972 election. In addition, Mr. Dean prepared a briefing paper for Mr. Haldeman with respect to a meeting with the head of the IRS, to make the IRS more responsive to the White House.[272] Mr. Strachan testified that Mr. Haldeman discussed a more politically responsive commissioner of the IRS so that it could be used against political opponents such as Clark Clifford.[273]

The IRS was not only contacted with respect to individual cases, it was also the focal point of certain questionable policies. One of these policies was to "punish" groups, tax exempt groups in particular, who were thought to hold ideological views different from the White House. There was no evidence that these organizations advocated or did anything illegal or unconstitutional, or that they in any way violated the tax laws. Nevertheless, they were singled out for challenge as to the tax exempt benefits they enjoyed under the law. Groups enjoying the same benefits who were sympathetic to the administration did not receive the same attack.

Use of the Secret Service to spy on Senator McGovern has already been reviewed.

The misuse of the CIA and the FBI have likewise been examined earlier.

It is quite a record for a "law and order" administration.

C. REGULATORY AGENCIES

The regulatory agencies, as much as any other area of government, fit the references in a White House memo which addressed the general problem of how to use the "incumbency" and power of the White House against opponents, or "how we can use the available federal machinery to screw our political enemies." [274]

We have already reviewed numerous misuses of the IRS against political opponents. We have likewise reviewed evidence of plans to make the IRS more responsive to White House problems and demands.

A prime example of the distortion of regulatory power is contained in the record of the administration's plans to attack the media. The agency at the center of this plan was the FCC.

The Federal Communications Commission licenses radio and television stations, and is thereby in a unique position to hurt the networks or any other organization such as a newspaper that owns a local station. The memos on this subject

272. One document submitted by Mr. Dean (Exhibit 44) is a briefing paper for H. R. Haldeman for a meeting with the head of the IRS, to make the IRS more responsive to the White House. Vol. 4, p. 1349.
273. Testimony of Gordon Strachan, Vol. 6, pp. 2486–2487.
274. White House memo from John Dean, August 16, 1971, entitled "Dealing with our Political Enemies." Vol. 4, Ex. 48, p. 1689.

which have been reviewed previously, were frightening at best. They demonstrate clear contempt for statutory restraints on the power given to the FCC by Congress.

A good sample of the attitude toward agencies is a memo from Mr. Jeb Magruder to Mr. Ken Reitz which notes that ACTION, the agency that coordinates government volunteer programs, "is an agency that we should be able to use politically." The memo recommends a meeting with ACTION's director to discuss how "we used their recruiters (who talked to 450,000 young people last year), advertising program, public relations effort, and public contact people, to sell the President and the accomplishments of the Administration. We should be involved and aware of everything from the scheduled appearances of ACTION's recruiters to the format and content of its advertising." [275]

D. THE DEPARTMENTS

The variety and scope of evidence bearing on the functions of the Departments stretches all the way from fabricating a false historical record of the State Department in the Vietnam war to using the Department of Interior to punish a newscaster.

The State Department incident shows the extremes that were followed to achieved the political ends of the White House. In apparent anticipation that Senator Kennedy would be the opposing nominee for the presidency, an attempt was made to falsify President Kennedy's role in the assassination of President Diem early in the Vietnam war.

The strategy used to implicate President Kennedy in Diem's death was to make up phony telegrams between the White House and South Vietnam during that critical period. One particular telegram indicated that Kennedy did not offer safe refuge to Diem, thereby insuring his assassination. To be able to do this, the State Department was contacted by Mr. Young of the White House Plumbers, resulting in Hunt's authorization to go over and review the appropriate cables between the United States and Saigon. Arrangements were made to "leak" the story to appropriate news persons.[276] When Hunt's safe was opened on June 20, 1972, the bulk of the papers, according to testimony, were classified cables from the State Department relating to the early years of the Vietnam war.[277]

The Department of Commerce was more directly used.

275. Memo from Jeb Magruder to Ken Reitz, Director of Young Voters for the President, November 28, 1971.
276. Testimony of Howard Hunt, Executive Sessions, July 25, 1973 and Sept. 10, 1973; also Vol. 9, pp. 3672, 3733, 3772, 3780.
277. Testimony of John Dean, Vol. 3, p. 937.

The Secretary of Commerce attended meetings on campaign matters and campaign contributions while still in office.[278] In order to put out a story demonstrating that help provided to the Maine sugar beet industry by Senator Muskie was going to cost taxpayers $13 million in defaults by that industry, the Department of Commerce was requested to provide the research material for that story. The correspondence flowed between the White House and Commerce, until the White House feared that their respective roles might be discovered.[279]

Because of a rather hostile comment former newscaster Chet Huntley once made regarding the President, there was an effort to make it as difficult as possible for him to get his Big Sky project in Montana moving. Apparently, Huntley needed assistance from the Interior Department, which was periodically contacted by the White House in this regard. For whatever reason, Huntley eventually agreed to back the President in the 1972 campaign and the attack was called off.[280]

The Department of Agriculture announced, on March 12, 1971, that price supports for milk would not be increased.[281] Board members of the Commodity Credit Corporation, which has responsibility for clearing such a decision, was unanimous in its recommendation not to increase supports.[282]

On March 25, 1971, the President reversed the decision of the Agriculture Department. There is much evidence of White

278. While still Secretary of Commerce, Mr. Stans met in several instances on campaign-related matters in January and February, 1972. Testimony of Maurice Stans, Vol. 2, pp. 733–4.

279. See, note 179 supra.

280. In a memo to Lawrence Higby, on July 16, 1970, Jeb Magruder expressed a need to get some "creative thinking" going on an attack on Huntley for his statements in *Life*. "Huntley will go out in a blaze of glory and we should attempt to pop his bubble." Vol. 10, Ex. 166, p. 4127.
In a memo to H. R. Haldeman on October 19, 1971, Lyn Nofziger notified Haldeman that "Huntley claims to be a Republican" and would support the Republican Senatorial candidate in Montana. John Whitaker, the White House liaison for the Department of Interior then ordered the Department of Agriculture to quit "dragging its feet on Big Sky," Vol. 4, p. 1703.

281. On March 12, Department of Agriculture announced Secretary Hardin's decision to maintain price support level at $4.66. Since in 1970 the Secretary granted the largest increase at the beginning of a marketing year, which led to increase in production, Secretary Hardin, after a careful review, felt the retention of price support levels was in the long term best interests of dairy producers. News Release, United States Department of Agriculture, March 12, 1971.

282. The Division of the Agricultural Stabilization and Conservation Service drafted its recommended decision in the form of a docket. The docket, based on recommendations of economists and superiors, recommended the $4.66 figure and supported it with a four page justification. The docket was then passed up line before going to the CCC Board of Directors for approval and undergoes "pre-Board clearance" by others in USDA. On March 3, 1971, the Board of Commodity Credit Corporation approved the docket. The recommended decision then went to the Secretary of Agriculture for final action.

House awareness and attention at that time to a $2 million campaign pledge by the milk producers.

Whether or not the President's decision was the result of a dairy industry bribe, it is important to note that the legitimate functions of the Agriculture Department were circumvented and interfered with. In the reversal process, none of the Assistant Secretaries at Agriculture or their staffs were consulted. These were the professionals who had the expertise, who knew the reasons for the initial decision, who would have to enforce and live with the new decision by the President. Their opinion or expertise as to the President's reversal was never given; it was never solicited, even indirectly.[283]

Instead, at 10:30 a.m. on March 23, 1971, the President met with the milk producers, saying, "I know, too, that you are a group that are politically very conscious. . . . And you are willing to do something about it." [284] After a flurry of meetings between other administration officials and milk producers representatives, the President changed the Department of Agriculture's position on March 25, 1971. Thus, regardless of other issues involved, the acceptable processes of government were evaded for apparently personal and political interests.

A memo was presented which revealed a Cabinet session in which Mr. Fred Malek told the assembled Cabinet members of a plan to make the Departments more "responsive" to the political needs of the administration. It was this program that led to some of the more unique abuses of the Departments and agencies.

It was this program that led to evidence of quid-pro-quos for the contracts from the Department of Health, Education, and Welfare, the Department of Housing and Urban Development, the Department of Labor, the Department of Interior, the Office of Economic Opportunity, the Office of Minority Business Enterprise, the Federal Home Loan Mortgage Association, the General Services Administration, ACTION, and the Veteran's Administration.[285]

283. Assistant Secretary Palmby stated that he was unaware of any reconsideration of the March 12 decision. Palmby summarized his role by stating: "I was part of the March 12 announcement. I was not part of the later announcement." Interview with Palmby, p. 22.
Furthermore, Assistant Secretary Richard Lyng indicated that his first knowledge of the reversal in decision came one hour before the formal announcement.
284. From, motion for Immediate Production of Records for Which Privilege Has Been Waived, at 2, Nader v. Butz, C.A. 148–72 (D.C.D.C., filed January 11, 1974).
285. An "Administrative Confidential" memo from Mr. Marumoto, Mr. Malek's Assistant in the responsiveness program, to Rob Davison, also of Mr. Malek's staff, July 19, 1972 (concerning a Washington, D. C., consulting firm under consideration for contracts from DOL and HUD); an "Ad-

For example, a June 3, 1971, White House memo noted that the head of the Federal Home Loan Bank Board "has given a great deal of thought to, and designed, a sound economical plan to use federal resources (projects, contracts, etc.) for advantage in 1972." [286]

A June 23, 1971, White House memo recommended that "In addition to designating 'must' grants from pending applications there may be occasions in which political circumstances require a grant be generated for a locality." [287] This, of course, is in direct contravention of equal treatment under the laws that control federal awards, which are supported by taxpayer funds and are to be distributed only on the basis of merit and need, by law.

By March 1972, this program, according to a memo to Mr. Haldeman citing success at the Commerce Department as an example, had "resulted in favorable grant decisions which otherwise would not have been made involving roughly $1 million." [288] It was then recommended that someone was

---

ministrative-Confidential" Weekly Report from Mr. Marumoto to Mr. Colson and Mr. Malek, Vol. 13, Ex. 262-28, p. 5615. (DOT grant applicants who were "unfriendly toward the Administration" were being identified); an "Administrative-Confidential" Weekly Report, from Mr. Marumoto to Mr. Colson and Mr. Malek, May 5, 1972, Vol. 13, Ex. 262-15, p. 5572 (concerning a $70,000 DOT grant to Joseph Reyes, National Hispanic Finance Committee, authorized by the Finance Committee for the Re-Election of the President; J. A. Reyes Associates also received a $200,000 sole source non-competitive contract from OEO in July, 1972); an "Administrative-Confidential" Weekly Report from Mr. Marumoto to Mr. Colson and Mr. Malek, May 19, 1972, Vol. 13, Ex. 262-17, p. 5581 (a $200,000 grant from the Office of Minority Business Enterprise); a "Confidential" memo from Harry Flemming of CRP to Mr. Malek, March 29, 1972 (concerning a Philadelphia Republican ward leader's complaint that his Democratic counterpart was being favored with Fannie Mae mortgage disclosure fees); an affidavit of John Clarke to the Senate Select Committee on Presidential Campaign Activities (indicating the process whereby architectural engineering contract awards by G.S.A. were given political clearance by Mr. Clarke of the White House staff); a memo by Dan Todd, director of the CRP Older Americans Voter Block group, entitled "Proposed Communications Support Program For the Older Americans Division Committee for the Re-Election of the President," April 14, 1972 (indicating federal agencies, such as ACTION, should prepare brochures on their senior citizen programs for frequent release during the two months prior to the election); "Final Report" of CRP Veterans Division, from CPP files ("The Campaign staff's effectiveness was significantly enhanced by its close liaison with The Veterans Administration and coordination of campaign activity with the agency.")

286. A "Confidential—Eyes Only" memo from Mr. Magruder to William Timmons of the White House staff, June 3, 1971, (indicating that Preston Martin, head of the FHLBB, was a "California-Nixon Republican" and "was a little put out that nobody has sought his political advice").

287. A "Confidential" memo by William Horton of Fred Malek's staff entitled "Communicating Presidential Involvement in Federal Government Programs" (which appears to be a "first draft" of the Responsiveness program).

288. Apparently the efforts of Mr. Gifford of the White House staff had influenced favorable decisions on a dozen contracts worth $1 million "which otherwise would not have been made"—"politically these actions have been

needed to take "the lead in the program to politicize the Departments and Agencies . . . and closely monitor the grantsmanship project to ensure maximum and unrelenting efforts." [289]

A December 23, 1971, memo to Mr. Haldeman noted that "this program, even if done discreetly, will represent a substantial risk. Trying to pressure 'non-political' civil servants to partisanly support the President's re-election would become quickly publicized and undoubtedly backfire. Consequently, the strategy should be to work through the top and medium-level political appointees who exercise control over most of the Departmental decisions and actions." [290]

By June 1972, Mr. Malek reported he had "reviewed the program with each Cabinet Officer (except Rogers) and with the heads of the key Agencies," and "had them name a top official who would be the political contact for this program," as well as "educate the loyal appointees . . . thus forming a political network in each Department." [291] Aside from abuse of the laws which authorize federal grants, there are numerous indications that this program violated the Hatch Act.[292] That Act specifically protests against politicizing the government, and makes such efforts criminally illegal. In addition, much of this conduct may have involved a conspiracy to defraud the United States, under the criminal laws of Title 18, United States Code, Section 371,[293] as well as criminal violations of at least three sections of the campaign laws.[294]

So much for our independent Departments and Agencies.

---

most favorable." An "Extremely Sensitive-Confidential" memo from Mr. Malek to Mr. Haldeman entitled "Increasing the Responsiveness of the Executive Branch," March 17, 1972.
289. A "Confidential" memo from Mr. Malek to Mr. Haldeman entitled "My Role in Support of Re-Election," January 28, 1972.
290. Mr. Malek sought "to minimize any direct links to the President," and therefore proposed "we stop calling it politicizing the Executive Branch and instead call it something like strengthening the government's responsiveness." A "Confidential" memo from Mr. Malek to Mr. Haldeman entitled "Redirecting the White House staff to support the President's Re-Election," December 23, 1971.
291. A "Confidential Eyes Only" memo from Mr. Malek to Mr. Haldeman entitled "Responsiveness Program—Progress Report," June 7, 1972.
292. For example, an unsigned "Confidential" memo on CRP stationery addressed to Attorney General Mitchell, concerning "heavy exploitation of the Cabinet Committee on Opportunity for Spanish-Speaking Peoples," Vol. 13, Ex. 362-3, p. 5534; a memo from Mr. Marumoto to Mr. Colson and Mr. Malek, April 28, 1972, concerning reorganization of the Cabinet Committee's media section to support the campaign, Vol. 13, Ex. 262-14, p. 5569; Manual for the Surrogate Program Advance School, directed by Brad Porter for "Schedule C" government employees subject to Hatch Act, supra.
293. *Hammer Schmidt, et al v. United States*, 265 U.S. 182 (1923); also, *Dennis v. United States*, 384 U.S. 855, 861 (1966).
294. Title 18, sections 595, 600, 602, 603, 607, 611, 1505; see also, Use of the Incumbency-Responsiveness Program, supra.

The executive department diverted a substantial portion of its payroll, privileges, and power into non-governmental activities. Mr. Frederick Malek, for example, held an official position at the Committee to Re-Elect the President as of June 1972, while on the White House payroll until September 1, 1972.[295] Mr. Gordon Strachan likewise was employed as a liaison to CRP, while being paid as an assistant to the White House Chief of Staff. Political advertising was supervised from the office that was supposed to be White House Chief of Staff.[296] Mr. McCord testified that he took part in Watergate partly because "the top legal officer in the White House" had participated in the decision to undertake the operation.[297]

The prerogatives granted the executive were misused, as has been detailed earlier. The effect is well summed up by Mr. McCord's testimony that he was told the President of the United States was aware of meetings offering him payoffs and clemency, that the results of the meetings would be conveyed to the President, and that at a future meeting there would likely be a personal message from the President himself. This supplemented threats that "the President's ability to govern is at stake," and "the government may fall" if Mr. McCord did not follow the "game plan."[298] Mr. Caulfield confirmed that when he met with Mr. Dean that Dean wanted to transmit the message to McCord that the offer of executive clemency was made with the proper authority, and that he made such representation to McCord.[299]

Not only were the department functions abused, but the executive power of appointing department officials was likewise used. It was Herbert Porter who testified that he reminded the White House of the things he had done in the campaign when they dragged a bit in finding him a new job after the election.[300] It was Jeb Magruder who was rewarded with a high ranking job at the Commerce Department for his misdeeds in the re-election campaign.[301]

295. Mr. Fred Malek according to Mr. Odle, became head of the citizens division of CRP between March and June 1972, exercising supervisory control, and had an office at CRP, even though he did not leave the White House until September 1, 1972. Testimony of Robert Odle, Vol. 1, pp. 31-32.
296. Mr. Odle's testimony was that Mr. Strachan (Mr. Haldeman's Assistant) participated rather actively in matters over at the Committee to Re-Elect. Vol. 1, p. 31.
297. Testimony of James McCord, Vol. 1, p. 129.
298. On January 13, 1973, Mr. McCord met Mr. Caulfield and another message was conveyed as to clemency, along with statements that the President's ability to govern was at stake, another Teapot Dome scandal was possible, the government may fall, and everybody else was on the track but McCord, who was not following the "game plan," and who should get "closer to your attorney" and keep silent. Testimony of James McCord, Vol. 1, pp. 139-140.
299. Testimony of John Caulfield, Vol. 1, p. 266.
300. See note 132, supra.
301. See note 131, supra.

These examples are minor compared to the general plans that were discussed to restaff the departments after the election to make them more subservient to the White House.[302]

As a final, rather tragic note, this is the White House that used its power over department appointments to nominate Mr. Gray to the FBI Directorship, decided not to support him any longer, and rather than tell him of that fact, decided to let him "hang there, and twist slowly, slowly in the wind." [303]

III. The Political System

Watergate challenged the very underpinnings of American politics and the American political condition. It happened in the natural clash and confusion of a free and open system of self-government; the same condition that despite its risks and vulnerability has given us many more moments of magnificence.

Nevertheless, whenever the nation approaches a Presidential election year we have especially good reason to recall our founding fathers' warnings against the "danger of factions." History teaches us that no matter how much a President may insist otherwise, an incumbent begins to measure policy decisions by their effect on his re-election and wields power in pursuit of his most advantageous position.

The system is designed to absorb this, but without question there is a line that cannot be crossed if the process is not to be abused.

The best way to observe how this happened to our political system in 1972 is to examine it in three component parts: the political party, the electoral process, and the democratic system.

A. THE POLITICAL PARTY

Political parties in America have their own life and status. They were expressly excluded from our Constitution, yet they have persisted since the nation's first generation.

The party has come to serve as a link between constituencies and men chosen to govern. They serve a valuable function, drawing competitive forces together to seek the

302. A December 23, 1971, "Confidential" memorandum from Malek to Haldeman entitled "Redirecting the White House staff to Support the President's Re-Election."
303. In a telephone conversation with John Ehrlichman, Mr. Dean made reference to the fact that the President said he was "not sure that Gray's smart enough to run the Bureau." Vol. 7, Ex. 102, pp. 2950-51. And yet the President apparently had no qualms about nominating a man not "smart enough to run the Bureau" to be Permanent Director of the FBI.

reconciliation so essential to intense issues. When the parties do not function well, individual citizens feel a loss of control over politics and government. They find themselves powerless to influence events. Voting seems futile; politics seems pointless. The political process crosses the line . . . and things go badly for America.

By any measure, the process that led to Watergate emasculated important party functions. It began with the decision to take the party's leader, and his re-election, out of the Republican party and into an independent entity, unresponsive to the checks and balances of party politics. From that point on, the Committee to Re-Elect the President was a political disaster.

There was a rationalization of CRP's existence, in some testimony, to the effect that it was needed for the primaries.[304] A number of Republican candidates entered the primaries, and it was considered unfair to use the Republican National Committee on behalf of the President. This theory ignored the President's massive popularity in the party at the time.

The fact is that CRP remained in operation throughout the campaign, long after it would have been proper for the Republican party to take over.

Significantly, all available evidence indicates that the traditional party organizations at the national level, the Republican and Democratic National Committees, did not undertake illegal or improper activities in the 1972 campaign. After 16 months of investigation, the staff of this Committee reported conclusively that there was no evidence of wrongdoing, directly or indirectly, by the Republican National Committee or its Chairman, Senator Robert Dole (R-Kan.) during the 1972 campaigns.

Evidence as to CRP's operation is in direct contrast.

By setting up an exclusive organization, concerned only with the President, the party was excluded from being properly aided by its titular head. The President was well-financed, and he won in a landslide. The Republican candidates for Congress and state offices did not have similar success in financing and campaigning against their Democratic opponents.

A good example of the tactics that hurt the party was the list of 100 Democratic Senators and Congressmen, "primarily

304. Mr. Odle justified the need for the CRP because the President was but a candidate for nomination prior to the Convention. Though, according to Odle, there was little doubt the President woul dtriumph, there was a distinct possibility of a challenge from Congressman Ashbrook and Congressman McCloskey. Odle felt it was not proper for the National Committee to work for President Nixon, with two challengers anticipated. Vol. 1, p. 23.

from the South, who had supported the President on the crucial votes on the Vietnam war," who would "not receive very strong opposition" from the White House.[305] Clearly this would not have been possible if the party had been involved in the President's campaign.

Not only did the White House undermine the Republican Party by supporting Democratic candidates. It likewise undermined the party from within, by attacking Republican candidates. A memo from Mr. Haldeman in October, 1969, outlined a letter-writing campaign to silence Republican Senators Percy, Goodell, and Mathias.[306] It consisted of "sending letters and telegrams, and making telephone calls to the Senators, blasting them . . ."[307]

A few days later it was reported to Haldeman that local groups in Illinois had begun sending critical telegrams and letters to Sen. Percy.[308] A handwritten note by Mr. Haldeman disclosed "this was an order . . . I was told it was being carried out and so informed the President."[309] Incredible as it may seem the Party was writing letters to itself, leaders of the Republican Party were being attacked by the head of their own party . . . in disguise.

An incident of serious significance was the suggestion by Mr. Patrick Buchanan that the Florida Republican State Chairman and the United States Attorney General attempt to use a provision in Florida law to keep a Republican challenger off the primary ballot, not because of legal considerations but for political advantage.[310] Earlier, that same challenger had been subjected to a bogus contribution to his New Hampshire campaign, in the name of the Young Socialist Alliance, staged by Mr. Colson, and leaked to the press to discredit his candidacy.[311] Again, a fellow Republican.

Negative politics were even taught to the young.

Mr. Ken Rietz organized the Young Voters for the President as part of CRP and designed projects for them such as the "McGovern-Shriver Confrontation" project.[312] This project used the Young Voters to confront Democratic candidates. to generate adverse press, and "upset the candidate."[313] The

305. Testimony of Gordon Strachan, Vol. 6, pp. 2483-2484.
306. Memo from Jeb Magruder to H. R. Haldeman, October 14, 1969.
307. Memo from H. R. Haldeman to Jeb Magruder, October 11, 1969.
308. Memo from Jeb Magruder to H. R. Haldeman. October 14, 1969.
309. Memo from Jeb Magruder to H. R. Haldeman, October 14, 1969. (handwritten note on the face thereof)
310. Note 75 supra.
311. Herbert Porter called Roger Stone and suggested that Stone travel to New Hampshire and contribute money to McCloskey's campaign under the name of an extremist group. Staff Interview with Roger Stone, pp. 2-3.
312. Memo from Edward Failor to Jeb Magruder, Sept. 23, 1972.
313. In a Sept. 22, 1972 progress report, Ken Rietz, Director of Young Voters for the Pressident, cited daily orchestrated demonstrations using YVP

result was that by September, 1972, they had "learned the McGovern organization and/or the Secret Service has reacted to our activities . . . the street walk was canceled and McGovern spoke in an area that was barricaded off." [314]

The Committee to Re-Elect the President violated the principles of good politics, beginning with its structure and staffing.

The separation between partisan politics and government was violated by the participation of White House staff, as well as department and agency officials, in the campaign operation of CRP. Testimony as to the structure was to the effect that "people who were at the White House had influence over the Committee, they gave it direction, they assisted it," and that the campaign director "came from the Justice Department." [315]

The role of the Assistant to the White House Chief of Staff "was to try to find out all of the things that were going on at the Committee and make Mr. Haldeman aware of them." [316] Mr. Fred Malek, according to the individual in charge of personnel at CRP, became head of the Citizens Division of CRP between March and June 1972, exercising supervisory control, and had an office at CRP, even though he did not leave the White House staff or payroll until September 1, 1972.[317]

Mr. Mitchell at the Justice Department and Mr. Haldeman at the White House "jointly made decisions in advertising."[318] In citing instances of so-called blame-taking, one witness cited an example where Mr. Colson took the blame for ads of questionable political ethics, whereas Mr. Haldeman was actually responsible.[319]

Campaign recommendations from CRP were sent to the Attorney General for his decision as early as July 3, 1971. That particular campaign memo was written by a staff member in Mr. Malek's White House office, with the assistance of an individual in the Office of Management and Budget

---

personnel to confront candidates McGovern and Shriver, in an attempt to generate adverse press coverage. Memo from Ken Rietz to Jeb Magruder, Sept. 22, 1972.
314. Memo from Edward Failor to Jeb Magruder, Sept. 23, 1972.
315. Testimony of Robert Odle, Vol. 1, p. 23.
316. Id., at 31.
317. Id., at 23, 31–32.
318. With respect to advertising, Mr. Odle stated that "Mr. Haldeman had an interest in advertising without any question," and Mr. Mitchell, or Mr. MacGregor "and Mr. Haldeman jointly made decisions in advertising." Vol. 1, p. 35.
319. Dean testified that Colson took the blame for ads of questionable political ethics which had been placed by a Mr. Shipley, whereas Mr. Haldeman was actually responsible. Vol. 4, p. 1490.

and an individual in Mr. Harry Dent's White House office.[320] Mr. Mitchell himself testified that he "had frequent meetings with individuals (from CRP) dealing with matters of policy" and staffing of CRP while he was still Attorney General.[321]

The hiring of personnel for the Committee was "cleared by Mr. Magruder (CRP), Mr. Mitchell (Justice Department), and Mr. Strachan, who would be looking out for Mr. Haldeman's (White House) interest in the clearance process." [322]

The Assistant to Mr. Haldeman was even well briefed on the Liddy plan long before the break-in, and in fact was called on June 17, 1972, to alert him to the pending break-in.[323]

The temptation and opportunity to abuse executive power thus existed, and the fact that such abuses took place has been demonstrated earlier in this report. For example, the use of government agencies to seek politically embarrassing information on individuals who were thought to be enemies of the White House, which was testified to repeatedly, was certainly facilitated by the presence of White House and agency staff within a non-party campaign committee. These tactics extended beyond the departments and agencies. Mr. McCord testified to phone calls and personal contacts to the effect that there would be executive clemency, financial support for the families, and rehabilitation after prison.[324] This was possible only through the facilities of the Presidency; little if any of it could have been offered by a political party.

A second aspect of staffing that caused problems and that

320. Memo on: Grantsmanship, dated July 3, 1971, from Magruder (CRP). It states: "Enclosed is a copy of a proposal to insure that the President and his Congressional supporters get proper credit for Federal Government programs. This proposal was written by Bill Horton in Fred Malek's office with the assistance of Bill Gifford, OMB, and Peter Millspaugh in Harry Dent's office. If implemented this should be an effective method of insuring that political considerations are taken into account." Odle testified that these types of memos were sent to the Atorney General from May 1, 1971, onward. Vol. 1, Ex. 1, p. 449.
321. Mitchell testified that he "had frequent meetings with individuals (from CRP) dealing with matters of policy" and staffing of CRP while he was still Attorney General, even though in a colloquy with Senator Kennedy during the Kleindienst confirmation hearings (which was entered into the record) Mitchell has testified that at that time he did not have any re-election campaign responsibilities. Exhibits 74 and 75 consist of a number of documents wherein Mitchell was "exercising his responsibility as director of the campaign" in June 1971, and January 1972, while still Attorney General. Vol 4, pp. 1653–1655.
322. Testimony of Robert Odle, Vol. 1, p. 72.
323. In his regular "political matters" memo to H. R. Haldeman, Strachan wrote: "Magruder reports that 1701 now has a sophisticated political intelligence gathering system with a budget of 300. A sample of the type of information they are developing is attached at tab 'H.' Testimony of Gordon Strachan, Vol. 6, p. 2441.
324. Testimony of James McCord, Vol. 1, p. 131.

could have been avoided by using the Republican Party, was the use of personnel that had little or no experience in elective politics. The danger with such a staff can be illustrated in the intelligence-gathering area. Candidates and campaign organizations have collected intelligence for generations. In the past, however, there has been something akin to an unwritten code as to the methods and content of information sought.

It is interesting to contrast Mr. Ehrlichman's description of discreet investigations, as intended to develop questionable facets of the personal lives of those being investigated, checking into domestic problems, drinking habits, personal social activities, and sexual habits.[325]

Somehow Mr. Ehrlichman tried to make a connection between the type of undercover prying into private lives of Ulasewicz and his "own knowledge" of Members of Congress who "totter onto the floor in a condition . . . of at least partial inebriation." [326]

Not only did Ulasewicz not investigate the behavior of officials while performing their public responsibilities, but Mr. Ehrlichman offered no evidence to substantiate his "own knowledge."

When Mr. Ehrlichman then testified that it was proper to have ad hoc investigators going into sexual habits, drinking habits, domestic problems, and personal social activities and then provide that information to the electorate, this Senator responded, "You definitely have two different concepts of politics in this country meeting head on." [327]

Significantly, the American people passed judgment on this issue shortly thereafter. A Harris poll exactly two months later reported: "By 83 to 8 percent, the public is massively critical about the hiring of private detectives by the White House to spy on the sex life, drinking habits, and family problems of political opponents." [328]

Whether caused by a lack of experience or by a lack of proper leadership, the staff of CRP had a tragic history. One employee recalled that "when you find that a person you trust and respect is in jail for doing something and that man worked for you, it is quite a serious thing." [329] It was summed up by Mr. Robert Odle, who testified that during his association with the Committee he came in contact with more than

325. Ehrlichman considered private investigators going into sexual habits, drinking habits, domestic problems and personal social activities are a proper subject for investigation in political campaigns. Vol. 7, pp. 2774–2775.
326. Testimony of John Ehrlichman, Vol. 7, p. 2777.
327. Id., at 2779.
328. *Wash. Post*, Sept. 27, 1973.
329. Testimony of Robert Odle, in reference to the arrest of Mr. McCord, Vol. 1, p. 29.

400 of its national staff, and "it now appears tragically that some of those people have acted unethically." Indeed at the time he testified on May 17, 1973, the opening day of hearings, two former members of the staff had been convicted of crimes.[330] To date, in mid-1974, seven former members have been indicted for or convicted of criminal conduct.[331] This is not what politics should be or has been about.

The second area in which CRP took over normal party functions was campaign financing.

Money was not propertly raised.

Instead, it was allegedly raised by Mr. Rebozo, a friend of the President, who had no official campaign responsibility. Money was raised by the President's personal attorney. During the 1970 campaigns, he was directed on three separate occasions by the White House staff to disburse funds from a trust fund in his control at the Chase Manhattan Bank in New York. He successively took $100,000, $200,000 and $100,000 from a safe deposit box, on which one of the signatories was a family relation of the White House Chief of Staff.[332]

The beginnings of the administration's relationship with the milk producers association, according to their testimony was a $100,000 contribution to the President's attorney to gain "access" to the White House, and to lay the groundwork for favorable treatment in certain specified ways for the milk producers and the dairy industry.[333] Messrs. Haldeman, Ehrlichman, and Colson, all of whom were senior White House advisors, held meetings to discuss fund-raising, including the $2 million pledge from the milk producers.

Money was raised by a Secretary of Commerce and a Secretary of the Treasury. All of which would have been unnecessary if financing had been left to the professionals in the Republican Party.

The handling of money was equally bad. Large amounts of cash were transferred and used. Secret funds were set up.

330. James McCord and Gordon Liddy. This refers only to employees of CRP.
331. James McCord, Gordon Liddy, Jeb Magruder, John Mitchell, Herbert Porter, Robert Mardian and Fred LaRue. This again refers only to employees of CRP.
332. Mr. Kalmbach delivered these funds, left over from the 1968 campaign, to a man he did not know, but could identify by means of clandestine signals at the Sherry-Netherlands Hotel in New York. Testimony of Herbert Kalmbach, Vol. 5, pp. 2142–44.
333. Mr. Kalmbach understood the $100,000 contribution from AMPI in 1969 to be tied to "access" to the President and Administration approval of new price supports for dairy farmers. Affidavit of Herbert Kalmbach, to the Senate Select Committee on Presidential Campaign Activities, supra.

Financial records were destroyed, on a number of occasions.[334] People with no campaign responsibility were receiving and distributing money. Illegal corporate contributions were given to CRP and accepted.[335]

Even though CRP represented itself as a Presidential reelection organization, it gave $25,000 to a congressional campaign in Maryland.[336] It gave $50,00 to a Vice Presidential donor in Maryland to make it appear that a Vice Presidential fund-raising event was more successful than it was, in what turned out to be an illegal transaction.[337] Mr. McCord's salary from the Committee was continued from July 1972, through January 1973.[338] One witness understood that in Governor Wallace's gubernatorial campaign in Alabama, Mr. Kalmbach provided Wallace's opponent with between $200,000 and $400,000.[339]

The intelligence activities of CRP were the greatest distortion of the political system undertaken by that Committee. The Republican Party had an information-gathering function of a research nature, but it was considered inadequate by the White House which had become used to the sophisticated techniques of law enforcement, national security and government intelligence. Unfortunately, by combining systems, they weren't able to draw the distinction between law enforcement and politics.

As a result, CRP found itself collecting and using secret intelligence from the FBI, and the Internal Security Division of Justice.[340] They developed a Security Unit that burglarized, photographed and wiretapped, that staked out Senators' and Congressmen's offices, and cased the Democratic headquarters.[341] They planned illegal acts against the Democratic Party chairman, at his residence and subsequently at his office. Similar plans were made for Senator McGovern's headquarters in Washington and at the Democratic Convention.[342] Electronic surveillance of Senator Muskie's campaign

334. Testimony of Herbert Kalmbach, Vol. 5, p. 2111; see also, testimony of Hugh Sloan, Vol. 2, p. 572.
335. See, testimony of eight corporate executives convicted of illegal corporate contributions Nov. 13–15, 1973. Vol. 13.
336. Testimony of Hugh Sloan, Vol. 2, p. 541.
337. Testimony of Maurice Stans, Vol. 2, p. 756.
338. Mr. McCord testified that he received $25,000 for legal fees and a continuation of his $3,000 monthly salary (through January 1975) from the Committee to Re-Elect the President via Mrs. Hunt, Vol. 1, p. 130.
339. Testimony of John Dean, Vol. 4, p. 1536.
340. Testimony of James McCord, Vol. 1, pp. 178–181.
341. This refers to the White House Plumbers (Vol. 3, pp. 919–924), the surveillance of Alfred Baldwin (Vol. 1, pp. 396, 397) and the aborted attempt of the Liddy-McCord team to break-in to McGovern headquarters, as well as the successful Watergate break-ins (Vol. 1, pp. 125–247).
342. These were the initial targets specified by Mr. Liddy to Mr. McCord. Testimony of James McCord, Vol. 1, p. 128.

office was discussed as a future target, according to McCord, but instead an office in an adjacent building was leased under the false name of John B. Hayes.[343]

Transcripts of illegally wiretapped phone calls were available to the Committee to Re-Elect.[344] The person transcribing the wiretaps was paid by payroll check from the Committee.[345]

A secretary on the CRP payroll typed up illegal wiretap transcripts, assisted Mr. Liddy in preparing a pass to enter McGovern headquarters, and eventually took part in the shredding of illegal intelligence documents.[346]

CRP built a capability to intercept and photograph memos in the Muskie campaign, and infiltrated not only Muskie's campaign but McGovern's suite at the Democratic Convention and Senator Humphrey's campaign (with an infiltrator known as Sedan Chair).[347] CRP became a group that had a .38 snub-nosed, Smith and Wesson revolver in its files that it handed out to one of its spies,[348] that was purchasing spy equipment from bugging equipment to microfilm machines for viewing its stolen documents, that was falsifying credentials, and shredding incriminating documents. Expensive charts were purchased, to display plans for bugging, mugging. burglaries and the like to the Attorney General. After that briefing, Liddy reported that Mr. Dean had asked him to destroy them, but because the charts were so expensive, Liddy decided not to. It found itself with an arrangement for two attorneys, Mr. Caddy and Mr. Rafferty, to appear at the second precinct following the Watergate arrests, when the participants did not return home from their night's work.

At one point the Committee was even instructed by the White House to hire a shaggy person to sit in front of the White House wearing a McGovern button.[349] This could only be matched by the hiring of counter-demonstrators for the funeral of J. Edgar Hoover,[350] hardly a political event.

343. Testimony of James McCord, Vol. 1, p. 153.
344. Testimony of Jeb Magruder, Vol. 2, p. 827.
345. Alfred C. Baldwin operated as an employee of the Committee to Re-Elect the President, was paid by payroll check from the Committee and was given an identification pin by the Committee. Testimony of Alfred Baldwin, Vol. 1, p. 393.
346. Testimony of Sally Harmony, Vol. 1, p. 463.
347. Interview with Herbert Porter, Aug. 20, 1973. Interview Roger Greaves, Aug. 21, 1973.
348. Mr. Baldwin was given a .38 snub-nosed revolver, Smith and Wesson, from the first or second drawer of a file cabinet at the Committee to Re-Elect the President. Testimony of Alfred Baldwin, Vol. 1, p. 392.
349. Robert Reisner testified that Charles Colson instructed Magruder to hire shaggy person to sit in front of White House with McGovern button. Vol. 2, p. 512.
350. Robert Reisner believed it was Charles Colson who initiated the hiring of counter-demonstrators at the Hoover funeral. Id.
Hunt testified to enlisting the aid of Mr. Barker and associates during Mr.

The Committee to Re-Elect the President not only under-mined the national Republican Party. The proper functioning of the Democratic Party was likewise subverted. The intelligence functions previously described were designed, among other things, to influence the choice of the Democratic nominee for President. As part of that tactic, the illegal or unethical capabilities that were set up were consistently focused on the strongest contender. The early attack was against Senator Kennedy. It shifted to Senator Muskie. As Muskie's strength diminished, instructions came from the White House to shift the attack to Senator McGovern. This included not just intelligence, but the so-called dirty tricks operation as well.

The attempts to undermine the Democratic Party went beyond the candidates. A memo entitled "Counter Actions" and dated September 11, 1972, noted that depositions could be taken in a civil suit against Larry O'Brien, covering "everything from Larry O'Brien's sources of income while Chairman of the DNC to certain sexual activities of employees of the DNC. They should cause considerable problems for those being deposed." [351]

Mr. Dean recalled Mr. Haldeman telling him that he hoped O'Brien would be Senator McGovern's campaign manager, "because we have some really good information on him. (Dean) believed he was referring to tax information at that time." [352]

B. THE ELECTORAL PROCESS

A whole range of activities during the 1972 campaign, in-cluding so-called dirty tricks, were aimed at the voter. To the extent that improper or illegal methods were used to influence votes, they interfered with the electoral process.

The task of influencing the final vote for President had its beginnings early in the campaign process. It was a complex operation, not simply questionable tactics to get people to vote for Mr. Nixon. Rather, its thrust was negative, to get people to vote against strong contenders.

To take away votes from Senator Muskie in New Hampshire, Mr. Colson (stating that he had the President's approval) drafted a letter urging a write-in campaign for Senator Kennedy. Between 150,000 and 180,000 of the letters were sent out, a press conference was staged in support of the bogus campaign, along with appropriate

---

Hoover's funeral. Hunt was informed by Liddy that in conjunction with demonstrations, an effort would be made to desecrate the catafalque of Hoover in the Capitol. Vol. 9, p. 3712.
351. Vol. 4, p. 1471.
352. Id.

advertising. All at a cost of some $10,000, paid for by contributors to a Republican President, not a Democratic write-in candidate.[353]

The President's campaign funds were also given to Democratic contenders Eugene McCarthy and Shirley Chisholm.[354]

Along this line, there was a project to finance the candidate for the Democratic nomination for Governor who was opposing former Governor George Wallace. This was to be financed by surplus funds from the 1968 campaign, which Mr. Haldeman testified that he "requested or approved . . . for funding support to a candidate for Governor in Alabama." [355]

Mr. Haldeman also approved "the funding of Donald Segretti."[356]

The story of Segretti and his henchmen illustrates more dramatically than anything else the efforts of the White House in the 1972 election to subject the voting privilege of American citizens to gutter politics.

Whether Segretti had any significant or measureable effect is not the question. It was an example, straight from the White House, of the worst in American politics.

It included informers planted in opponents' campaigns, stink bombs unleashed against voters attending a campaign picnic, against volunteers in a telephone bank operation and inside a campaign headquarters, a letter on a replica of Muskie stationery accusing Senators Jackson and Humphrey of sexual improprieties in the most vile language, flyers inviting voters to a non-existent open house at Muskie headquarters, a flyer advertising a free all-you-can-eat lunch with drinks at Humphrey headquarters, a small plane circling the Democratic Convention advertising "Pot, Peace, Promiscuity, Vote McGovern," adverse press that forced cancellation of a Muskie fund-raising dinner, printed cards with "If you like Hitler, you'll love Wallace—Vote for Muskie," stinkbombs thrown into a campaign headquarters, a forged letter on McCarthy stationery urging McCarthy delegates to switch to Humphrey, a letter on Yorty stationery blaming the McCarthy letters on Yorty, hired hecklers, pickets, and informers to disrupt, infiltrate, and spy on Senators Humphrey, Muskie, and Jackson, a false press release with the information that Muskie was using Government-owned typewriters and Federal employees not on leave of absence, a series of false anti-Muskie advertisements in the University of

353. Interviews with Jeb Magruder, August 18, 1973, p. 3, and October 1, 1973, p. 11.
354. Interview with Gordon Strachan, August 13, 1973, p. 8; interview with John Mitchell, June 27, 1973.
355. Testimony of John Dean, Vol. 4, p. 1536.
356. Testimony of H. R. Haldeman, Vol. 7, p. 2876.

Miami campus newspaper, the local Cuban newspaper, and on the local Cuban radio station insulting the Cuban people, a false press release on Muskie stationery with a vague stand on aid to Israel which did not go over well in Miami Beach, a flyer claiming Muskie favored busing while sending his children to private schools, rats and birds released at a Muskie press conference, a naked woman to run in front of Muskie headquarters yelling "I love Muskie," a flyer falsely advertising the appearance of Lorne Greene and Mrs. Martin Luther King at a Humphrey rally, hundreds of dollars worth of flowers, chicken, and pizzas delivered to Muskie headquarters, a set of invitations to Black Panthers, the Gay Liberation Front, the Hare Krishna movement and African diplomats for a Muskie fund-raising dinner, a chauffeur for the Muskie campaign, code-named "Ruby 1," who would turn over documents being delivered so they could be surreptitiously photographed, and eventually shown to Mr. Mitchell, a rented office near Muskie's headquarters to facilitate copying of documents, a group of infiltrators in Muskie headquarters in Milwaukee, Humphrey headquarters in Philadelphia, McGovern headquarters in Los Angeles, Washington, and Miami, a ploy to get campaign workers to drink beer and skip work, and an operation to switch phone-bank call sheets so the same people would be called repeatedly or the wrong message would go to selected groups.[357] This is not to mention similar operations by persons known as "Sedan Chair 1" and "Sedan Chair 2";[358] and "Ruby II."[359]

It was nothing short of a massive operation to deprive the American voter of information about Democratic candidates for President. It was significant not so much as an attack on politicians, but as an attack on voters and their opportunity to cast a fully-informed vote.

Dirty tricks were not the only means used to influence the electoral process improperly.

Misleading the voter by official conduct and statements was equally in evidence. This kept critical information hidden from voters, when there was a legal obligation to disclose it, thereby preventing a proper judgment of the incumbent administration.

The Watergate break-in was called a "third rate burglary"

357. This list was compiled from the testimony of Donald Segretti, Vol 10, pp. 3980–4054; Martin Kelly, Vol. 11, pp. 4376–4402; Robert Benz, Vol. 11, pp. 4403–4434; and John Buckley, Vol. 11, pp. 4435–4477.
358. See, interview with Herbert Porter, August 20, 1973; interview with Roger Greaves (Sedan Chair 1), August 21, 1973; testimony of Michael McMinoway, Vol. 11, pp. 4478–4535.
359. Testimony of Marc Lacritz, Vol. 11, p. 4636 (describing the activities of Thomas Gregory, a student hired by Howard Hunt).

at a time when the White House knew better, based on its briefings and discussions, including a discussion of executive clemency with the President in July 1972.[360]

Mr. Mardian testified that he even complained to Mr. Clark MacGregor, who had succeeded Mr. Mitchell as campaign manager, that statements being made regarding non-involvement of campaign personnel were untrue, and that he unsuccessfully attempted to brief MacGregor about the tremendous exposure of certain people in the campaign.[361]

On August 29, 1972, the President assured the nation that an investigation by John Dean had cleared the White House of any involvement. This statement was made in spite of the fact that the President had received no report from Dean, and never, ever talked with Dean about Watergate.[362]

In mid-September 1972, the President discussed possibly unethical out-of-court contacts that had apparently taken place with the judge in one of the Watergate lawsuits, as part of a strategy to keep the process of justice from operating.[363] Delay or obstruction of this process again insured that voters would not have the legal record before them in November.

In mid-October 1972, high level staff meetings at the White House were convened to decide how to handle news reports about Segretti. Even though those participating knew or had access to the full Segretti story, the decision was made to issue tough denials, and what Mr. Richard Moore described as "weasel words." [364] The story was basically correct, yet it was denounced as "hearsay, inuendo, and character assassination." No effort was made to tell the truth. The voters were kept in the dark.

Perhaps this tactic was best summed in testimony by Mr. John Mitchell. He was interviewed by the FBI on July 5, 1972, and stated that all he knew was what he read in the newspapers, despite testimony that he had been extensively briefed about Watergate by Mardian and LaRue. His explanation: "at that particular time, we weren't volunteering any information." [365] His reason: "the re-election of the President, this particular President, was uppermost in my mind without question." [366] One man was thereby elevated above the fundamental principles of this nation.

360. Presidential Statement, August 15, 1973, p. 3; testimony of John Ehrlichman, Vol. 7, pp 2848-2849.
361. Testimony of Robert Mardian, Vol. 6, p. 2430.
362. Testimony of John Dean, Vol. 3, p. 955.
363. Id., at 958; Transcripts of Presidential Conversations, September 15, 1972, p. 60.
364. Testimony of Richard Moore, Vol. 5, p. 2038.
365. Testimony of John Mitchell, Vol. 5, p. 1926.
366. Id., at 1827.

TRANSITION (FROM FACT TO OPINION)

At the conclusion of the fact-gathering phase of the Committee's mandate, I met with legislative assistant, A. Searle Field, and assistant minority counsel, H. William Shure, to discuss what shape our report on Watergate should take. We settled upon the following "woulds" and "wouldn'ts":

1. We would emphasize the known in order to impress upon the reader the importance of its implications rather than explode new facts of scandal. We were convinced White House strategy was (is) geared to numbing America past concern by innundating America with one White House horror after another.
2. We would report within a framework of principles and institutions rather than people.
3. We would opine and editorialize but separately from the factual presentation.
4. We would recommend remedial legislation.

1. We wouldn't try and resolve conflicting testimony.
2. We wouldn't make judgments on individual guilt or innocence.
3. We wouldn't cite "shaky" material as proof.

If what you've read up to now in these pages is not new, neither is it susceptible to argument.

The indisputable ugliness of Watergate is of such scope as to categorize it as a sheer insanity; either for those who participated in it or have since defended it.

I don't know, except as the courts have already passed judgment, who is guilty or who is innocent.

But I do know that to accept the *White House* version of your Constitution, your government and your politics is to counterfeit America.

UNDERSTANDING WATERGATE

Alright, what to do with the raw data of Watergate? Unless positive understandings and actions emanate from this negative sequence, then it seems to me nobody really was caught breaking into Watergate.

The gut question this summer is what do Americans now know and what are they going to do about it? By way of dramatizing the need for a proper answer to that question, let me cite the following example. I recently received a critical letter which read:

"Really, Senator, all is fair in 'love and war.'"

American elections—war?
Members of another party—enemies?
Politics—fear?
Is that the lesson America is taking home from the Watergate? Because if such is the case, then a whole new era in American politics will have dawned and Gordon Liddy will be recognized not as peculiar but as a visionary. Also at such time we of the Select Committee would have failed. Though a year has gone by between the time of the Senate Watergate hearings and this Senator's Watergate conclusions, it is a matter of Constitutional life and death that the American people make a connection between those two events.

What about the Constitution? Is it up to our times? Certainly it never before has obtained such visibility. But how about acceptance?

I. The Constitution

Later in this section I intend to editorialize on the abuses to our governmental and political institutions. However the pivotal struggle of Watergate is one between men who play for the moment and look upon the Constitution as a 4th of July interruption to their own charter and men who play for tomorrow and understand it to be the force that has given America success beyond America's natural abilities for success.

Never first in population, land mass or natural resources, why have we attained a national greatness and personal affluence beyond that achieved by any country or people?

Because we perjured? Because dissent was disloyalty? Because justice was political? Because our concern was developing fear? Because we burgled? Because we thought the worst of each other?

Or, because

"All men are created equal, that they are endowed by their Creator with certain unalienable rights, that among these are life, liberty, and the pursuit of happiness. . . ."

Or, because

"Congress shall make no law . . .abridging the freedom of speech or of the press; or the right of the people peaceably to assemble, and to petition the Government for a redress of grievances."

Or, because

"The right of the people to be secure in their persons,

707

houses, papers, and effects against unreasonable searches and seizures shall not be violated. . . ."

Or, because

"No person shall be deprived of life, liberty or property without due process of law. . . ."

Or, because

"In all criminal prosecutions the accused shall enjoy the right . . . to be confronted with the witnesses against him; to have compulsory process for obtaining witnesses in his favor. . . ."

Or, because

"The President . . . shall take the following Oath: 'I do solemnly swear that I will faithfully execute the office of President of the United States and will, to the best of my ability, preserve, protect and defend the Constitution of the United States.' "

I catch none of the "everybody's doing it" or "transcripts" spirit in any of those words.

The Constitutional history of Watergate to this date has been that of a President and his Ministers who de facto have tried to "yes—but" most sections of the Constitution.

I feel Article V to be preferable to Administration amending methods.

Several years ago many Americans were willing to silently tolerate illegal government activity against militants, terrorists or subversives as an expeditious way to circumvent the precise processes of our justice system. Though quick, it also proved to be only a short step to using such illegal tactics against any dissenting Americans. The result was we almost lost America. Not to subversives, terrorists or extremists of the streets but to subversives, terrorists and extremists of the White House.

That is why there can be no acquiescence, now, to a few "yes—buts" to the Constitution. To do so would be just as big a cop-out as those who espouse violence in the name of peace.

American Constitutional democracy is not the tidiest, most orderly, most efficient, most expeditious, quietest political system on earth. It is in fact raucous, off in a thousand directions of concern, involved with millions of individuals rather than a mass, revolutionary and querulous. But what some deem as flaws are precisely its genius. For those who have made it, it's a pain. For those who haven't, it rebuts predestination.

Our greatness will always be in direct proportion to our freedoms. Yes, that includes the freedom to be wrong.

Free spirits, not measured freedom, has been the promise of the Constitution. We can have peace in Vietnam, on campus and in the neighborhood without forfeiting that promise and no man or group of men deserve leadership if they would put the nation to such a choice.

II. Government

The offices of government in this nation are complex and awesomely powerful. Even if engaged in legal pursuits. It's not an exaggeration to state that a United States Senator needs every bit of his clout to move effectively within the bureaucratic maze. Insofar as the 99.9% of Americans who are not Presidents, Congressmen or Senators, if anything goes wrong with either end of the governed-government equation, the mismatch of the century ensues. And that's so even though the slip-up is innocently legal. Fully 50% of a Senator's time and staff are devoted to resolving the innocently legal slip-ups between his constituents and their government. And I'm sure those who speak up are no more than 5% of those being wronged.

What then if agencies and officers of the United States government become involved, not in innocently legal mistakes, but purposefully illegal vengeance? In light of the facts already presented, the greatest danger of this section is for me not to overeditorialize the case so as to engender disbelief. Of those who read this report, 99% of them know Senators, Congressmen, successful lawyers and other powerful persons. But America is not supposed to be about the powerful—rather the frail. And they're the ones who will eventually suffer the most if the White House record on using the government agencies politically to bring about conformity is allowed to go unchallenged.

The "enemies list", revealed in the dialogue I had with John Dean, has received much hoopla. But aside from the fact that today it has become a badge of honor, have you ever thought what it feels like to be an American and have the highest office in the land look upon you as an enemy? To be spied on, to be investigated, to be harrassed, to be reviled by your own country? It may be a badge of honor when revealed but it's frighteningly disheartening while it's going on and no one believes that these things are happening in America.

Oh, yes, I've heard the excuses for the illegal use of the federal law enforcement/intelligence community. National security, domestic security, terrorists, law and order, subversives, militants. But let me put the White House record in the proper factual context.

No administration within my lifetime has a worse record of convictions in relation to indictments than the Nixon Administration. Why? Because it tried to achieve law and order by lawlessness. It was the courts that said no, not the Justice Department.

In the matter of the Special Compliance Division of the IRS and their keeping tabs on "militants, subversives, terrorists, ideological and other organizations," it is fact that in all the IRS files that came into White House possession, there is not one militant, subversive, terrorist individual or organization. That is the lesson of a White House gone ape. Our lesson is that you can't protect the rights of anyone unless you protect the rights of everyone.

The differences between myself and this Administration on Watergate are not philosophical, political, historical, personal or regional. They are Constitutional, pure and simple. A better summation of our differences could not be found than the surreptitious entry language of the "1970 Spy/Huston/Sullivan Plan" and again in the words of the President on September 15, 1972:

"Use of this technique is clearly illegal: it amounts to burglary. It is also highly risky and could result in great embarrassment if exposed. However, it is also the most fruitful tool and can produce the type of intelligence which cannot be obtained in any other fashion."

You can't have that and democracy.

"I want the most comprehensive notes on all those who tried to do us in. They didn't have to do it. They are asking for it and they are going to get it. We have not used the power in this first four years as you know. We have not used the Bureau (FBI) and we have not used Justice. But things are going to change now. And they are either going to do it right or go."

You can't have that and democracy.
Remember what Pat Gray said?

"I said early in the game that I thought that Watergate would tarnish everyone with whom it came in contact and I am no exception. *I had a responsibility not to permit myself to be used, not to permit myself to be deceived* and I failed in that responsibility and I have never failed in anything that I have undertaken until this point in time. And it hurts."

710

The Congress and the American people, with more facts in hand than Pat Gray ever had, have an even greater responsibility not to be used or deceived in this matter of abuses to our governmental agencies and political processes.

Because most elected officials or citizens haven't had the FBI, IRS, CIA, MI, SS, Justice Department, Defense Department, Commerce Department, "Fat Jack" or Tony Ulasewicz on their tail does not mean the abuses of Watergate passed them by. It only means that if they don't speak out now, they've got no complaint later. A little less spectating Watergate and a little more speaking out is very much in order.

Admittedly to speak out is tough. Just as the Bill of Rights and democracy is tough.

But speaking out is a patriotism far better suited to 1974 than 1972's wearing of flag lapel pins by White House and CRP employees while they advocated burglary, wiretapping, committed perjury, politicized justice, impugned the patriotism of those who disagreed with them and threw due process in the shredder.

Americans of all generations have suffered and died at their best because they were uncompromising in the idealism they wished for their country. Who of this generation, then, wants to declare a lesser truth for America?

It is the answer we give to that question which matters. It will decide America.

III. Politics

In November, 1962 I was elected to my first public office— State Representative to the General Assembly in Hartford, Connecticut.

Now, some 12 years and 8 elections later, I am rounding out my first term in the United States Senate—a boyhood dream come true.

Yes, it's time consuming and rough on the family life. To that extent it's tough. But each dawn for 12 years has me looking forward to the day. Politics is a clean business with dedicated people. The terms "9–5" and "5-day week" are seldom heard. The winning politician is in the business of love and not hate. The average politician takes the cost of serving out of his pocket and not the public's taxes.

These things need saying to challenge the "end justifies the means" image, the "everybody's doing it" image that the White House knowingly and a few ignoramuses unwittingly would give politics.

We're replete with failings personally as I, my staff and my family know all too well. But with the public trust given us by our constituencies—we'd no more see that in the mud than the American flag.

Can I prove the above? Sure. Look at your America as I've asked the people of Connecticut to look at their State.

The truth of American politics is in the schools of this country, not a wiretap; in the hospitals, not a burglary; in the housing projects, not a scurrilous letter; in the parks, not in hush money; in facilities for the retarded, not in spying; in people who volunteer in a thousand ways, not in dirty tricksters; in politicians who reach for the weak first, the strong second, not in hatchet men. In short, dirt does not conceive so much tangible excellence as we have in our country.

The truth of America is not in the deeds of men and women at their worst but rather at their best. Government with its politicians and the people are not apart in a democracy. They are one.

And so it is we will not get any better ethics or more idealism in the Oval Office or on the Senate floor than we do in the voting booths.

Watergate was conceived in an ignorant apathy of the electorate and was executed in semi-conscious apathy. Its greatest danger is that it will be forgotten in an apathy of total knowledge. That kind of voting booth acquittal means that American politics has officially joined the Administration on the dark side of the manhole.

Thank you, no!

PEOPLE AND POWER

Watergate is not the story of one powerful man. It is a story of people. Though my efforts have been directed toward the principles and institutions of this nation, I am well aware that their existence or disappearance reflects human behavior.

It is no source of pride to me as an American that the coinage of responsibility has been in inverse measure to rank and power. I was taught early on, first by my Dad and then by the United States Army, that rank has its privileges because rank has its responsibilities.

Yet in the case of this President, I've heard the word "privilege" used over and over again as a dodge of responsibility.

The word "stonewall" has been used to describe the President's defense. Believe me, it has been and continues to be a "human wall."

712

REPUBLICANS

Obviously this has been rough duty in a Republican sense. However, from the outset I've operated on the basis that the best investigation was the best politics. I couldn't change the facts. I couldn't silence those who knew the facts. All I could do was to make sure that a Republican spoke the facts if not before, then simultaneously with a Democrat.

On page 103 of the "Transcripts", President Richard Nixon is talking to John Dean:

> "I don't know what we can do. The people who are most disturbed about this (unintelligible) are the (adjective deleted) Republicans. A lot of these Congressmen, financial contributors, et cetera, are highly moral. The Democrats are just sort of saying, '(expletive deleted) fun and games.' "

Richard Nixon understood the strong base of integrity that is a Republican heritage. Because he rejected it then is no reason for any Republican to do so now.

Because the Republican National Committee and its Chairman, Senator Robert Dole of Kansas, were in the traditional Republican mold of decency and honesty is exactly the why of a Committee to Re-Elect the President. At an executive session of the Select Committee held on Wednesday, June 19, 1974, I inquired of the staff and the Committee whether after one year of investigation there was evidence of wrongdoing by either the RNC or Senator Dole. The answer was a clear-cut "no" in both instances. Republicans who now state that "everybody does it" dishonor the men and women of their own official party organization and Bob Dole who didn't do it and wouldn't have done it.

One last comment.

The record establishes that:

1. The White House took a dive on the Congressional races of 1972 insofar as many Republican candidates were concerned.[367]

2. Democratic candidates were actively assisted in some instances.[368]

3. The White House expended considerable resources and energies zapping Republican Senators and Congressmen.[369]

---

367. Gordon Strachan testified that there was a list of approximately 100 Democratic Congressmen, primarily from the South, who were not to receive active opposition from the White House. Vol. 6, p. 2483.

368. Carmichael/Eastland campaign in Mississippi for the United States Senate, 1972.

369. As part of a White House campaign against Senators Percy, Mathias,

4. The Justice Department was consulted as to how to keep a Republican off the Florida primary ballot.[370]

Along with a will to pursue the truth, I would hope the will to win for the Republican Party is slightly stronger and fairer in its next titular head.

TOMORROW

No, this won't be the Watergate to end all Watergates.
Other men will tape the doors of America in other times.
Whether they succeed will be a matter of spirit.
For then as now, the state of our spirit will determine the state of this Union.

RECOMMENDATIONS

The necessary legislative and/or Constitutional steps should be initiated to:

1. MAKE ALL FORMS OF DOMESTIC ELECTRONIC SURVEILLANCE, INCLUDING WIRETAPPING, ILLEGAL.

2. HAVE THE OFFICE OF ATTORNEY GENERAL OF THE UNITED STATES BE AN ELECTED OFFICE.

3. MAKE ALL NOMINATIONS FOR FEDERAL ELECTIVE OFFICE BY DIRECT PRIMARY, WITH UNAFFILIATED VOTERS FREE TO PARTICIPATE IN THE PARTY PRIMARY OF THEIR CHOICE.

4. ESTABLISH A JOINT CONGRESSIONAL COMMITTEE, WITH COMPLETE INVESTIGATIVE POWERS AND ROTATING MEMBERSHIP, TO MONITOR DOMESTIC INTELLIGENCE-GATHERING AND LAW ENFORCEMENT ACTIVITIES THROUGHOUT THE EXECUTIVE BRANCH, AND BE ABLE, UNDER APPROPRIATE SAFEGUARDS, TO OBTAIN AND PROVIDE ACCESS TO RELEVANT MATERIALS REQUESTED

---

and Goodell, a confidential memo by Mr. Haldeman on October 11, 1969, ordered a program of: "sending letters and telegrams, and making telephone calls to the Senators, blasting them . . ."
370. Memo to Attorney General Mitchell from Jeb Magruder, August 11, 1971: "Pat Buchanan suggested that maybe we could have the Florida State Chairman do whatever he can under this law to keep McCloskey (Rep. McCloskey, R-Calif.) off the ballot."

BY ANY MEMBER OF CONGRESS. SIMILAR OVER-SIGHT FUNCTIONS NOW HELD BY CONGRESSIONAL COMMITTEES SHOULD BE TRANSFERRED TO THE JOINT COMMITTEE.

5. GRANT THE SUPREME COURT ORIGINAL JUR-ISDICTION OVER DISPUTES AS TO ANY PRIVILEGE ASSERTED BY THE PRESIDENT WITH RESPECT TO THE CONGRESS OR FEDERAL LAW ENFORCEMENT AGENCIES, THEREBY MAKING THE SUPREME COURT THE FIRST AND FINAL ARBITER OF THE ISSUE.

6. SUBJECT SENIOR WHITE HOUSE STAFF PER-SONNEL TO CONFIRMATION BY THE SENATE.

7. PROHIBIT WHITE HOUSE STAFF FROM MAK-ING RECOMMENDATIONS, INQUIRIES, OR EX-CHANGING CLASSIFIED INFORMATION WITH ANY DEPARTMENT OR AGENCY AS TO ANY CASE, AC-TION, OR FUNDING EXCEPT UPON WRITTEN AU-THORITY OF THE PRESIDENT, WHICH AUTHORITY SHALL BE IMMEDIATELY TRANSMITTED TO THE APPROPRIATE CONGRESSIONAL COMMITTEE, ALONG WITH A DESCRIPTION OF EACH INSTANCE IN WHICH THE AUTHORITY IS USED.

8. DRAFT A CODE OF CANDIDATE RESPONSI-BILITY, WITH APPROPRIATE DISCIPLINARY RULES AND GRIEVANCE PROCEDURES, TO BE ENFORCED THROUGH A FEDERAL ELECTIONS COMMISSION.

9. PROVIDE FOR "ACCREDITED CAMPAIGN REP-RESENTATIVES", EXCHANGED BY OPPONENTS FOR NOMINATION OR ELECTION TO FEDERAL OFFICE, TO BE ACCORDED THE PRIVILEGES OF TRAVEL, INTERVIEWS, AND NEWS RELEASES GRANTED TO ACCREDITED PRESS REPRESENTATIVES IN GEN-ERAL.

10. REQUIRE FEDERAL CANDIDATES AND OF-FICEHOLDERS TO FULLY DISCLOSE ALL SOURCES OF INCOME AND ASSETS OR LIABILITIES OVER $1,500, TO BE SUBMITTED BY FEBRUARY 15TH OF EACH YEAR, FOR THE CALENDAR YEAR PRECED-ING, FOR PUBLICATION IN THE CONGRESSIONAL RECORD. THIS TO SUPERCEDE ANY PRESENT STA-TUTES RELATIVE TO CONGRESSIONAL FINANCIAL DISCLOSURE.

11. REQUIRE CAMPAIGNS FOR THE PRESI-DENCY, AFTER A NOMINEE IS SELECTED, TO BE RUN BY THE PARTY OF THE CANDIDATE.

12. REQUIRE THAT CAMPAIGNS FOR NOMINA-TION OR ELECTION TO FEDERAL OFFICE BE CONDUCTED BETWEEN THE FIRST TUESDAY OF SEPTEMBER AND THE FIRST TUESDAY OF NO-VEMBER.

13. DESIGNATE ELECTION DAY AS A FEDERAL HOLIDAY, IN ORDER THAT THE VOTING FRAN-CHISE NOT BE RESTRICTED BY COMPETING CONCERNS ABOUT JOBS.

14. REQUIRE THAT CANDIDATES FOR FEDERAL ELECTIVE OFFICE REPORT ALL COLLECTIONS AND EXPENDITURES TWO WEEKS BEFORE ELECTION DAY, WITH NO COLLECTIONS THEREAFTER.

15. PROHIBIT CANDIDATES FOR FEDERAL ELEC-TIVE OFFICE FROM ACCEPTING CASH CONTRIBU-TIONS OVER $50 OR SPENDING MORE THAN $10,000 IN PERSONAL FUNDS.

16. RESTRICT CANDIDATES FOR FEDERAL ELEC-TIVE OFFICE TO ONLY ONE CAMPAIGN COM-MITTEE.

17. OPEN ALL CONGRESSIONAL HEARINGS AND SESSIONS TO THE PUBLIC, EXCEPT WITH RESPECT TO NATIONAL SECURITY, PROPRIETARY INFORMA-TION, OR PERSONALLY DEFAMATORY MATTERS. THE PRESENT RULE, LEAVING SUCH OPEN SES-SIONS UP TO EACH COMMITTEE'S DISCRETION, SHOULD BE MADE MANDATORY AND UNIFORM.

APPENDIX—SELECTED EXHIBITS

Exhibit 35

TOP SECRET
HANDLE VIA COMINT CHANNELS ONLY

OPERATIONAL RESTRAINTS ON INTELLIGENCE COLLECTION

B. Electronic Surveillances and Penetrations. (pp. 26-28)

Recommendation:

> Present procedures should be changed to permit intensification of coverage of individuals and groups in the United States who pose a major threat to the internal security.

Rationale:

> At the present time, less than 65 electronic penetrations are operative. This includes coverage of the CPUSA and organized crime targets, with only a few authorized against subjects of pressing internal security interest.

TOP SECRET

5/15/73

Exhibit 35 (*continued*)

TOP SECRET
HANDLE VIA COMINT CHANNELS ONLY

Mr. Hoover's statement that the FBI would not oppose
other agencies seeking approval for and operating
electronic surveillances is gratutious since no other
agencies have the capability.

Everyone knowledgable in the field, with the exception
of Mr. Hoover, concurs that existing coverage is grossly
inadequate.

C. Mail Coverage (pp..29-31)

Recommendation:

Restrictions on legal coverage should be removed.

Rationale:

There is no valid argument against use of legal mail
covers except Mr. Hoover's concern that the civil
liberties people may become upset. This risk is surely
an acceptable one and hardly serious enough to justify
denying ourselves a valuable and legal intelligence tool.

Covert coverage is illegal and there are serious risks
involved. However, the advantages to be derived from
its use outweigh the risks. This technique is particularl
valuable in identifying espionage agents and other contact
of foreign intelligence services.

D. Surreptitious Entry (pp. 32-33)

Recommendation:

ALSO, present restrictions should be modified to permit
selective use of this technique against other urgent and
high priority internal security targets.

TOP SECRET

5/15/73

718

Exhibit 35 (continued)

Rationale:

Use of this technique is clearly illegal: it amounts
to burglary. It is also highly risky and could result
in great embarrassment if exposed. However, it
is also the most fruitful tool and can produce the
type of intelligence which cannot be obtained in any
other fashion.

The FBI, in ~~the~~ Mr. Hoover's younger days, used to
conduct such operations with great success and with
no exposure. The information secured was invaluable.

Surreptitious entry of facilities occupied by subversive
elements can turn up information about identities,
methods of operation, and other invaluable investigative
information which is not otherwise obtainable. This
technique would be particularly helpful if used against
the Weathermen and Black Panthers.

E. Development of Campus Sources (pp. 34-36)

Recommendation:

Present restrictions should be relaxed to permit expanded
coverage of violence-prone campus and student-related
groups.

ALSO, CIA coverage of American students (and others)
traveling or living abroad should be increased.

5/15/73

Exhibit 35 (*continued*)

Rationale:

The FBI does not currently recruit any campus sources among individuals below 21 years of age. This dramatically . reduces the pool from which sources may be drawn. Mr. Hoover is afraid of a young student surfacing in the press as an FBI source, although the reaction in the past to such events has been minimal. After all, everyone assumes the FBI has such sources.

The campus is the battle-ground of the revolutionary protest movement. It is impossible to gather effective intelligence about the movement unless we have campus sources. The risk of exposure is minimal, and where exposure occurs the adverse publicity is moderate and short-lived. It is a price we must be willing to pay for effective coverage of the campus scene. The intelligence .community, with the exception of Mr. Hoover, feels strongly that it is imperative the we increase the number of campus sources this fall in order to forestall widespread. violence.

CIA claims there are no existing restraints on its coverage of over-seas activities of US nationals. However, this coverage has been grossly inadequate since 1965 and an explicit directive to increase coverage is required.

F. Use of Military Undercover Agents (pp. 37-39)

Recommendation:

Present restrictions should be retained.

Rationale:

The intelligence community is agreed that the risks of lifting these restraints are greater than the value of any possible intelligence which could be acquired by doing so.

5/15/73

·Exhibit 35 (*continued*)

TOP SECRET
HANDLE VIA COMINT CHANNELS ONLY

BUDGET AND MANPOWER RESTRICTIONS
(pp. 40-41)

Recommendation:

Each agency should submit a detailed estimate as to
projected manpower needs and other costs in the event
the various investigative restraints herein are lifted.

Rationale:

In the event that the above recommendations are concurred
in, it will be necessary to modify existing budgets to provide
the money and manpower necessary for their implementation.
The intelligence community has been badly hit in the budget
squeeze (I suspect the foreign intelligence operations are in
the same shape) and it may be well be necessary to make
some modifications. The projected figures should be
reasonable, but will be subject to individual review if this
recommendation is accepted.

MEASURES TO IMPROVE DOMESTIC INTELLIGENCE OPERATIONS
(pp. 42-43)

Recommendation:

A permanent committee consisting of the FBI, CIA, NSA,
DIA, and the military counterintelligence agencies should
be appointed to provide evaluations of dome.tic intelligence,
prepare periodic domestic intelligence estimates, and carry
out the other objectives specified in the report.

Rationale:

The need for increased coordination, joint estimates, and
responsiveness to the White House is obvious to the
intelligence community. There are a number of operational
problems which need to be worked out since Mr. Hoover is
fearful of any mechanism which might jeopardize his autonomy.
CIA would prefer an ad hoc committee to see how the system
works, but other members believe that this would merely delay
the establishment of effective coordination and joint operations.
The value of lifting intelligence collection restraints is
proportional to the availability of joint operations and evaluation,
and the establishment of this inter-agency group is considered
imperative.

5/15/73

TOP SECRET

Exhibit 36

July 14, 1970

<u>TOP SECRET</u>

MEMORANDUM FOR: MR. HUSTON

SUBJECT: <u>Domestic Intelligence Review</u>

The recommendations you have proposed as a result of the review have been approved by the President.

He does not, however, want to follow the procedure you outlined on page 4 of your memorandum regarding implementation. He would prefer that the thing simply be put into motion on the basis of this approval.

The formal official memorandum should, of course, be prepared and that should be the device by which to carry it out.

I realize this is contrary to your feeling as to the best way to get this done. If you feel very strongly that this procedure won't work you had better let me know and we'll take another stab at it. Otherwise let's go ahead.

H. R. HALDEMAN

<u>TOP SECRET</u>

Exhibit 37

WASHINGTON

August 5, 1970

TOP SECRET
HANDLE VIA COMINT CHANNELS ONLY

EYES ONLY

MEMORANDUM FOR H. R. HALDEMAN.

FROM: TOM CHARLES HUSTON

SUBJECT: DOMESTIC INTELLIGENCE

    In anticipation of your meeting with Mr. Hoover and the Attorney General, I would like to pass on these thoughts:

    1. More than the FBI is involved in this operation. NSA, DIA, CIA, and the military services all have a great stake and a great interest. All of these agencies supported the options selected by the President. For your private information, so did all the members of Mr. Hoover's staff who worked on the report (he'd fire them if he knew this.)

Exhibit 37 (*continued*)

-2-

3. We are not getting the type of hard intelligence we need at the White House. We will not get it until greater effort is made through community-wide coordination to dig out the information by using all the resources potentially available. It is, of course, a matter of balancing the obvious risks against the desired results. I thought we balanced these risks rather objectively in the report, and Hoover is escalating the risks in order to cloak his determination to continue to do business as usual.

4. At some point, Hoover has to be told who is President. He has become totally unreasonable and his conduct is detrimental to our domestic intelligence operations. In the past two weeks, he has terminated all FBI liaison with NSA, DIA, the military services, Secret Service -- everyone except the White House. He terminated liaison with CIA in May. This is bound to have a crippling effect upon the entire community and is contrary to his public assurance to the President at the meeting that there was close and effective coordination and cooperation within the intelligence community. It is important to remember that the entire intelligence community knows that the President made a positive decision to go ahead and Hoover has now succeeded in forcing a review. If he gets his way it is going to look like he is more powerful than the President. He had his say in the footnotes and RN decided against him. That should close the matter and I can't understand why the AG is a party to reopening it. All of us are going to look damn silly in the eyes of Helms, Gayler, Bennett, and the military chiefs if Hoover can unilaterally reverse a Presidential decision based on a report that many people worked their asses off to prepare and which, on its merits, was a first-rate, objective job.

5. The biggest risk we could take, in my opinion, is to continue to regard the violence on the campus and in the cities as a temporary phenomenon which will simply go away as soon as the Scranton Commission files its report. The one statement that Rennie Davis made at HEW which I thought made sense was that the Attorney

Exhibit 37 *(continued)*

-3-

General was kidding himself when he said the campuses would be
quiet this fall. Davis predicted that at least 30 would be closed
down in September. I don't like to make predictions, but I am
not at all convinced, on the basis of the intelligence I have seen,
that we are anyway near over the hump on this problem, and I
am convinced that the potential for even greater violence is
present, and we have a positive obligation to take every step
within our power to prevent it.

      6. Hoover can be expected to raise the following points
in your meeting:

      (a) "Our present efforts are adequate." The answer
is bullshit! This is particularly true with regard to FBI campus
coverage.

      (b) "The risks are too great; these folks are going to
get the President into trouble and RN had better listen to me."
The answer is that we have considered the risks, we believe they
are acceptable and justified under the circumstances. We are
willing to weigh each exceptionally sensitive operation on its
merits, but the Director of the FBI is paid to take risks where
the security of the country is at stake. Nothing we propose to
do has not been done in the past -- and in the past it was always
done successfully.

      (c) "I don't have the personnel to do the job the
President wants done." The answer is (1) he has the people and/or
(2) he can get them.

      (d) "I don't object to NSA conducting surreptitious entry
if they want to." The answer is that NSA doesn't have the people,
can't get them, has no authority to get them, and shouldn't have
to get them. It is an FBI job.

TOP SECRET

Exhibit 37 *(continued)*

-4-

    (e) "If we do these things the 'jackels of the press' and the ACLU will find out; we can't avoid leaks." Answer: We can avoid leaks by using trained, trusted agents and restricting knowledge of sensitive operations on a strict need to know basis. We do this on other sensitive operations every day.

    (f) "If I have to do these things, the Attorney General will have to approve them in writing." This is up to the AG, but I would tell Hoover that he has been instructed to do them by the President and he is to do them on that authority. He needn't look for a scape goat. He has his authority from the President and he doesn't need a written memo from the AG. To maintain security, we should avoid written communications in this area.

    (g) "We don't need an Inter-Agency Committee on Intelligence Operations because (1) we're doing fine right now -- good coordination, etc. -- and (2) there are other existing groups which can handle this assignment." The answer is that we are doing lousy right now and there aren't other groups which can do the job we have in mind because: (1) they don't meet; (2) they don't have the people on them we want or have some people we don't want; (3) they don't have the authority to do what we want done; (4) ultimately this new operation will replace them; and (5) they aren't linked to the White House staff.

    There are doubtless another dozen or so specious arguments that Hoover will raise, but they will be of similar quality. I hope that you will be able to convince the AG of the importance and necessity of getting Hoover to go along. We have worked for nearly a year to reach this point; others have worked far longer and had abandoned hope. I believe we are talking about the future of this country, for surely domestic violence and disorder threaten the very fabric of our society. Intelligence is not the cure, but it can provide the diagnosis that makes a cure possible. More importantly, it can provide us with the means to prevent the.

726

Exhibit 37 *(continued)*

-5.

deterioration of the situation. Perhaps lowered voices and peace
in Vietnam will defuse the tense situation we face, but I wouldn't
want to rely on it exclusively.

There is this final point. For eighteen months we have
watched people in this government ignore the President's orders,
take actions to embarrass him, promote themselves at his
expense, and generally make his job more difficult. It makes
me fighting mad, and what Hoover is doing here is putting
himself above the President. If he thought the Attorney General's
advice should be solicited, he should have done so before the
report was sent to the President. After all, Hoover was chairman
of the committee and he could have asked the AG for his comments.
But no, he didn't do so for it never occurred to him that the
President would not agree with his footnoted objections. He
thought all he had to do was put in a footnote and the matter was
settled. He had absolutely no interest in the views of NSA,
CIA, DIA, and the military services, and obviously he has
little interest in our views, or apparently even in the decisions
of the President. I don't see how we can tolerate this, but
being a fatalist, if not a realist, I am prepared to accept the
fact that we may have to do so.

Tom

TOM CHARLES HUSTON

Exhibit 48

August 16, 1971

MEMORANDUM

SUBJECT: Dealing with our Political Enemies

This memorandum addresses the matter of how we can maximize the fact of our incumbency in dealing with persons known to be active in their opposition to our Administration. Stated a bit more bluntly -- how we can use the available federal machinery to screw our political enemies.

After reviewing this matter with a number of persons possessed of expertise in the field, I have concluded that we do not need an elaborate mechanism or game plan, rather we need a good project coordinator and full support for the project. In brief, the system would work as follows:

-- Key members of the staff (e.g., Colson, Dent Flanigan, Buchanan) should be requested to inform us as to who they feel we should be giving a hard time.

-- The project coordinator should then determine what sorts of dealings these individuals have with the federal government and how we can best screw them (e.g., grant availability, federal contracts, litigation, prosecution, etc.).

-- The project coordinator then should have access to and the full support of the top officials of the agency or department in proceeding to deal with the individual.

Exhibit 48 (*continued*)

I have learned that there have been many efforts in the past to take such actions, but they have ultimately failed -- in most cases -- because of lack of support at the top. Of all those I have discussed this matter with, Lyn Nofziger appears the most knowledgeable and most interested. If Lyn had support he would enjoy undertaking this activity as the project coordinator. You are aware of some of Lyn's successes in the field, but he feels that he can only employ limited efforts because there is a lack of support.

As a next step, I would recommend that we develop a small list of names -- not more than ten -- as our targets for concentration. Request that Lyn "do a job" on them and if he finds he is getting cut off by a department or agency, that he inform us and we evaluate what is necessary to proceed. I feel it is important that we keep our targets limited for several reasons: (1) a low visibility of the project is imperative; (2) it will be easier to accomplish something real if we don't over expand our efforts; and (3) we can learn more about how to operate such an activity if we start small and build.

Approve _____

Disapprove _____

Comment _____

729

Exhibit 48 (*continued*)

MEMORANDUM

THE WHITE HOUSE
WASHINGTON

July 16, 1971

CONFIDENTIAL

MEMORANDUM FOR:

> Marge Acker
> Pat Buchanan .
> John Dean
> Dan Kingsley
> Gordon Strachen
> Van Shumway
> Jerry Warren
> Lucy Winchester
> Larry Higby

SUBJECT: OPPONENTS LIST

Please remove Raymond Gues from your copy of the Opponents List.
He appears on the page entitled, " Democrat Contributors of $25, 000
or More in 1968 Campaigns".

·Joanne L. Gordon

Exhibit 90

THE WHITE HOUSE
WASHINGTON
August 11, 1971

MEMORANDUM FOR: JOHN D. EHRLICHMAN

FROM: BUD KROGH AND DAVID YOUNG

SUBJECT: PENTAGON PAPERS PROJECT - STATUS
REPORT AS OF AUGUST 11, 1971

(1) Where things stand in the Grand Jury investigations.

The Los Angeles Grand Jury last week subpoenaed six people. Messrs.
Burt Wallrich, Arno Guilfoile, Spencer Marx and Jackie Barnet all
appeared and took the Fifth Amendment. Albert Appleby and Jane Youman
are presently outside of California on vacation and will be subpoenaed
when they can be served. Ellsberg's old telephone records were also
subpoenaed but were not available since the records were not kept back
that far. His Bankamericard records have also been subpoenaed but have
not yet been received.

The Boston Grand Jury will meet next week. Justice has not made a final
decision but is considering subpoenaing the following individuals:

> Mrs. Louis Marx (mother of Mrs. Ellsberg)
> Samuel Popkin (Harvard)
> Richard Falk (Princeton)
> Ralph Stavins (IPS)
> Richard Barnet (IPS)
> Marcus Raskin
> K. Dunn Gifford (A friend of Sheehan and Ellsberg who stayed
>   at Treadway Motor House March 20th, when Sheehan was
>   there.)
> Richard Steadman

It seems unlikely that Barnet, Raskin and Gifford will be called because
they have been overheard.

(2) We have received the CIA preliminary psychological study (copy
attached at Tab A) which I must say I am disappointed in and consider
very superficial. We will meet tomorrow with the head psychiatrist,
Mr. Bernard Malloy, to impress upon him the detail and depth that we
expect. We will also make available to him here some of the other information

Exhibit 90 (*continued*)

we have received from the FBI on Ellsberg. In this connection
we would recommend that a covert operation be undertaken to
examine all the medical files still held by Ellsberg's psychoanalyst
covering the two-year period in which he was undergoing analysis.

Approve _____E_____   Disapprove _____
if done under your assurance that it is not traceable.

(3) We have received a letter from Director Hoover confirming that
the Ellsberg case and related matters will be handled on a "Bureau
Special" basis.

(4) We have tasked CIA with doing a leak assessment on all leaks
since January, 1969, along the lines of the attached memorandum
at Tab B.

(6) We are continuing to press the FBI to determine whether the
report of a foot locker containing film magazines stored for Ellsberg
with Bekins Van and Storage Company in California is indeed accurate,
and what the content of the films is. The foot locker was apparently
picked up by a friend of Ellsberg, a reporter for Dispatch News Service,
David Obst, who indicated that the contents of the foot locker were
needed for a book to be published in New York.

(7) Attached at Tab C is a memorandum from Richard Smyser on
impact of (a) Ellsberg case, (b) an expose of the 1963 coup, and
(c) the drug situation in South Vietnam, on (a) South Vietnamese
election, (b) the U. S. election, and (c) on peace negotiations.

MINORITY REPORT ON CIA INVOLVEMENT *

SUBMITTED AT THE REQUEST OF
SENATOR HOWARD H. BAKER, JR.

Introduction

This report is submitted at Senator Baker's request to summarize the highlights of an investigation of CIA activity, if any, in connection with the Watergate incident and aftermath. It is based on material in the possession of the Committee, both classified and unclassified. It does not attempt to deal with all the matters deemed pertinent and important to a full and complete inquiry, but is designed to generally describe the areas of interest and concern pursued during the staff investigation and executive session interviews since the conclusion of the Committee's public hearings.

In view of the fact that the Committee has chosen to have no further public hearings; that the Committee staff is in the process of being reduced in size; that further cooperation by the Agency seems more likely on the request of the standing jurisdictional committees rather than on the request of the Watergate Committee, and that the total burden of additional work to complete the investigation thoroughly is probably beyond the competence of the remaining staff in terms of numbers and time, Senator Baker requested that this memorandum be prepared for submission to the full Committee for further disposition as the Committee may determine. It is pointed out that, while the report itself is not classified, it makes reference to, and in some instances quotes from, material which is classified. Therefore, each copy of this report has been treated for security purposes as if it were classified. They are numbered and accounted for as in the case of classified material.

The report is broken down into seven categories, tabbed as follows:

(1) Background. A recitation of the first references to CIA connections on the part of the Watergate burglars, reference to the possibility of CIA involvement by the President in his speech of May 22, 1973, and certain other published information and correspondence.

(2) Mullen. The fact that the Mullen Company and its president, Bob Bennett, had an established relationship with the CIA is described in some detail in this section of the report. Most of the information contained in this section was discovered after Volume IV was requested by Senator Baker. The CIA arranged to release this volume and subse-

---

* This is not part of the Committee's official report.

quent documents to the Watergate Committee in the custody of George Murphy serving as security officer for the Committee through an arrangement with the Joint Committee on Atomic Energy.

(3) Pennington. This section derives from a CIA supplied memorandum dated February 22, 1974, from the then Director of Security, detailing the information that Lee R. Pennington, a CIA operative, had entered James McCord's house and/or office shortly after the Watergate break-in for the purpose of destroying evidence of a CIA connection with McCord.

(4) Tapes. This section derives from information supplied to Senator Baker by Director Colby that there was a central taping capability at the CIA; that the tapes had been destroyed, and the possibility that some of the tapes may have been Watergate-related. Director Colby stated that he did not know whether Watergate-related tapes had been destroyed.

(5) TSD. The initials stand for Technical Services Division of the Central Intelligence Agency, and the section deals with rather extensive contacts between Hunt and the Agency and the support supplied by the Agency to Hunt and Liddy, which was used in a wide variety of undertakings. A number of factual discrepancies appear in this section which cannot be effectively reconciled on the basis of the information we now possess—such as Hunt's receipt of certain Agency technical assistance and contemporaneous participation in the preparation of the Ellsberg psychiatric profile.

(6) Martinez. This tab refers to Eugenio Martinez, one of the Watergate burglars. The section delineates the Martinez-Agency relationship, Hunt's early activities in Miami, the actions taken or not taken by the Agency's office in Miami, and certain unresolved questions.

(7) Recommendations. The seventh tab is self-explanatory and constitutes the recommendations of the staff for further inquiry.

Background

In a speech on May 22, 1973, President Nixon stated in part the following in connection with the Watergate matter:

> Within a few days, however, I was advised that there was a possibility of CIA involvement in some way.
>
> It did seem to me possible that, because of the involvement of former CIA personnel, and because of some of their apparent associations, the investigation could lead to the uncovering of covert CIA operations totally unrelated to the Watergate break-in.

In addition, by this time, the name of Mr. Hunt had surfaced in connection with Watergate, and I was alerted to the fact that he had previously been a member of the special investigations unit in the White House. Therefore, I was also concerned that the Watergate investigation might well lead to an inquiry into the activities of the special investigations unit itself.

* * *

I also had to be deeply concerned with insuring that neither the covert operations of the CIA nor the operations of the special investigations unit should be compromised. Therefore, I instructed Mr. Haldeman and Mr. Ehrlichman to insure that the investigation of the break-in not expose either an unrelated covert operation of the CIA or the activities of the White House investigations unit—and to see that this was personally coordinated between General Walters, the Deputy Director of the CIA, and Mr. Gray at the FBI.

One of the matters to which the President was evidently referring was explored by Senator Baker in his questioning of John Ehrlichman when Ehrlichman appeared before the Select Committee on July 26, 1973. Ehrlichman was questioned with regard to missing paragraph five of a memo from Egil Krogh and David Young to John Ehrlichman dated August 11, 1971.[1]

This was the same matter which had been brought to the attention of the Minority staff in July of 1973 which resulted in a briefing of Senator Ervin, Senator Baker, Sam Dash, and Fred Thompson by White House Counsels Fred Buzhardt and Leonard Garment. The subject of that briefing is what is now referred to as the "Admiral Moorer-Yeoman Radford Incident."

With regard to involvement of the CIA in the Watergate affair, it should be noted that since June 17, 1972, there have been numerous newspaper articles pointing out the fact that many of those involved in the Watergate break-in were former CIA employees; that CIA equipment was used by Hunt, and other possible CIA links to Watergate.

In the September 14, 1973, issue of the *National Review*, Miles Copeland wrote an article entitled "The Unmentionable Uses of a CIA," [2] suggesting that McCord led the Watergate burglars into a trap.

In the November, 1973, issue of *Harper's* Magazine, an

1. *See* Public Testimony of John Ehrlichman dated July 26, 1973, at 2702-2704.
2. *National Review*, September 14, 1973, "The Unmentionable Uses of a CIA," at 996.

article entitled "The Cold War Comes Home," [3] by Andrew St. George, indicated strongly that former CIA Director Helms had prior knowledge of the Watergate break-in. As a result of the St. George allegation, Senator Baker asked Senator Symington and the Senate Armed Services Committee to conduct the inquiry into those allegations. The Senate Armed Services Committee held hearings on this matter and heard testimony from CIA officials that the Agency was not knowledgeable of the Watergate break-in before it occurred; had not led the burglars into a trap; and, that the magazine allegations had no basis in fact.

It would appear that no information relative to this Committee's mandate was developed from the testimony adduced during the hearings before the Senate Armed Services Committee on the St. George matter.

However, in the aftermath of the St. George inquiry, Senator Baker propounded a number of questions to the CIA on November 8, 1973, one of which follows:

7. QUESTION: On or after June 17, 1972, did any of the individuals associated with these break-ins in any way communicate with any individual associated with CIA to discuss the Watergatet break-ins or the Ellsberg psychiatrist office break-in, other than Mr. McCord who wrote letters to CIA which are part of the Watergate hearing record?

ANSWER: On 10 July 1972 an officer of a commercial concern communicated to an employee of CIA information which had come to his attention concerning the "Watergate Five." The relationship of this informant and his company to the Agency was and is classified. Since this information was hearsay, contained a repetition of then current published speculation, and indicated that the informant had appeared before the Grand Jury on the matter, no action was taken. The employee's hand-written memorandum for the record on this matter is contained in sensitive material which Agency officers have made available for review, but not retention, by the staffs of the four CIA Subcommittees as well as the staffs of the Senate Select Committee on Presidential Campaign Activities and the Federal Prosecutor. Aside from this, the Agency had no communication of the type referred to in this question.

An examination of the aforementioned "sensitive material" [4] revealed more than was theretofore known about the scope

3. *Harper's* Magazine, November, 1973, "The Cold War Comes Home," at 82.
4. This material was produced as a part of Volume IV of the documents furnished to us by the CIA.

of the CIA's dealings with Robert Bennett and Mullen and Company and led to a further intensification of the staff's investigative efforts in other CIA-related areas.

Robert Bennett and Mullen and Company

The Mullen and Company has maintained a relationship with the Central Intelligence Agency since its incorporation in 1959.[1] It provided cover for an agent in Europe and an agent in the Far East at the time of the Watergate break-in.[2]

Hunt left the CIA in 1970 and joined Mullen and Company with what founder Robert Mullen understood to be Director Helms' blessing.[3] Hunt's covert security clearance was extended by the CIA [4]; he was witting of the Mullen cover [5]; and, on occasion he undertook negotiations with the Agency with respect to that cover—even after becoming employed at the White House (according to Agency records).[6]

Robert Bennett, who is Senator Bennett's son, joined Mullen and Company and became its President in 1971. He was introduced to the Mullen CIA case officer in April of that year.[7] Bennett brought the Hughes Tool account with him to Mullen.[8] CIA records indicate that Agency consideration was given to utilizing Mullen's Hughes relationship for a matter relating to a cover arrangement in [South America], and to garner information on Robert Maheu.[9]

Bennett's accessibility to the CIA has raised questions concerning possible Agency involvement in, or knowledge of, Bennett's activities in regard to Hunt/Liddy, to wit: Bennett suggested and coordinated the DeMott interview

1. Executive Session Testimony of Robert R. Mullen, February 5, 1974, at 3.
2. Executive Session Testimony of Robert F. Bennett, February 1, 1974, at 25-26; Executive Session Testimony of [Mullen and Company Case Officer], February 4, 1974, at 5.
3. CIA Memorandum, undated, Subject: Wrap-Up of Agency's Association with Robert R. Mullen and Company, found at Tab 3 of CIA Supplemental Material, Volume III, at 3; Executive Session Testimony of Robert R. Mullen, *supra* note 1, at 8; Executive Session Testimony of Robert F. Bennett, *supra* note 2, at 67.
4. *See* Memorandum for Deputy Director for Plans, October 14, 1970; Subject: E. Howard Hunt—Utilization by Central Cover Staff, found at Tab 16, CIA Supplemental Materials, Volume II.
5. *Id.;* Executive Session Testimony of Robert R. Mullen, *supra* note 1, at 9.
6. Executive Session Testimony of [Former Deputy Director of Plans, hereinafter DDP], February 5, 1974, at 6-10; CIA Memorandum, undated, Subject: Wrap-Up of Agency's Association with Robert R. Mullen and Company, *supra* note 3, at 2.
7. Executive Session Testimony of [Mullen and Company Case Officer], *supra* note 2, at 12.
8. Executive Session Testimony of Robert F. Bennett, *supra* note 2, at 132.
9. *See* [Mullen and Company Case Officer] Memorandum for Record, April 30, 1971, Subject: Association of Robert R. Mullen and Company with the Hughes Tool Company. This document is found at Tab 16, Supplemental CIA Material, Volume II.

regarding Chappaquidick; [10] Bennett coordinated the release of Dita Beard's statement from Denver, after contacting Beard's attorneys at the suggestion of a Hughes executive; [11] Bennett suggested that Greenspun's safe contained information of interest to both Hughes and the CRP; [12] Bennett asked for and received from Hunt a price estimate for bugging Clifford Irving for Hughes; [13] Bennett coordinated the employment of political spy Tom Gregory by Hunt and *discussed with Gregory the latter's refusal to proceed with bugging plans on or about June 16, 1972.* [14] Bennett received a scrambled from Hughes personnel for use on Mullen telephones; [15] Bennett and Liddy set up dummy committees as a conduit for Hughes campaign contributions; [16] and *Bennett served as the point of contact between Hunt and Liddy during the two weeks following the Watergate break-in.*[17] Furthermore, Robert Oliver, Mullen's Washington lobbyist for Hughes Tool, is the father of R. Spencer Oliver, Jr., whose telephone was tapped at the Democratic National Committee. Bennet met with the Olivers after the break-in to discuss the bugging.[18]

The true nature of Bennett's relationship to the CIA was not known to us until late November of 1973 when, at Senator Baker's request, the CIA produced another volume of CIA documents (Volume IV). The following information was adduced from this volume.

On July 10, 1972, Bennett reported detailed knowledge of the Watergate incident to his CIA case officer. The case officer's report of this meeting was handwritten [19] and carried

10. Executive Session Testimony of E. Howard Hunt, December 18, 1973, at 69-70; Executive Session Testimony of Robert F. Bennett, *supra* note 2, at 62-65.
11. Executive Session Testimony of Robert F. Bennett, *supra* note 2, at 93-94.
12. Executive Session Testimony of E. Howard Hunt, *supra* note 10, at 6-8; *But see* Executive Session Testimony of Robert F. Bennett, *supra* note 2, at 79-84. Bennett indicates that Hunt suggested Bennett coordination with Hughes.
13. Executive Session Testimony of E. Howard Hunt, *supra* note 10, at 72-73; Executive Session Testimony of Robert F. Bennett, *supra* note 2, at 121-124.
14. Staff Interview of Thomas J. Gregory, September 1, 1973, at 5; Executive Session Testimony of E. Howard Hunt, *supra* note 10, at 17; Executive Session Testimony of Robert F. Bennett, *supra* note 2, at 69-75.
15. Staff Interview of Linda Jones, September 6, 1973, at 3; Executive Session Testimony of Robert F. Bennett, *supra* note 2, at 140.
16. Staff Interview of Linda Jones, *supra* note 15, at 9; *See* Summarized Highlights of Linda Jones Interview, dated September 10, 1973.
17. Staff Interview of Linda Jones, *supra* note 15, at 8; Executive Session Testimony of Robert F. Bennett, *supra* note 2, at 153-157.
18. Executive Session Testimony of Robert F. Bennett, *supra* note 2, at 100-101.
19. [Mullen and Company Case Officer] Memorandum for Record, July 10, 1972, Subject: Meeting with Robert Foster Bennett and his comments con-

to Director Helms on or before July 14, 1972, in this form because of the sensitivity of the information.[20] It revealed that Bennett had established a "back door entry" to E. B. Williams, the attorney for the DNC, in order to "kill off" revelations of the Agency's relationship with the Mullen and Company in the course of the DNC lawsuit. He agreed to check with the CIA prior to contacting Williams.[21] Our staff has confirmed that Bennett did funnel information to Williams via attorney Hobart Taylor and *that this information was more extensive than the information Bennett had previously provided the Grand Jury.*[22] *The CIA has acknowledged paying one-half of Bennett's attorney fee for his Grand Jury appearance.*[23]

Although Bennett was supplying information to the CIA about many aspects of the Watergate incident and was at that time serving as liaison between Hunt and Liddy, there is no indication that these facts were disclosed to the FBI.

The aforementioned July 10 report contains mysterious reference to a "WH flap." [24] The report states that if the Mullen cover is terminated, the Watergate could not be used as an excuse.[25] It suggests that the Agency might have to level with Mullen about the "WH flap." [26] Nonetheless, a July 24, 1972 contact report shows that the CIA convinced Robert Mullen of the need to withdraw its Far East cover through an "agreed upon scenario" which included a falsified Watergate publicity crisis.[27] The Agency advises that the "WH flap" has reference to a [deletion at Agency request] that threatened to compromise Western Hemisphere operations,[28] but has not explained sufficient reason to withhold such information from Mullen nor explained the significance

---

cerning E. Howard Hunt, Douglas Caddy, and the "Watergate Five" Incident (sic), found in CIA Supplemental Material, Volume IV.

20. Executive Session Testimony of [Mullen and Company Case Officer], *supra* note 2, at 20-21, 28-29.

21. [Mullen and Company Case Officer] Memorandum for Record, *supra* note 19, at 11-12.

22. Robert F. Bennett, Memorandum for Record, dated January 18, 1973, at 17; Executive Session Testimony of Robert F. Bennett, *supra* note 2, at 129. *See also* Hobart Taylor Interview Report, dated February 11, 1974.

23. CIA Memorandum, undated, Subject: Wrap-Up of Agency's Association with Robert R. Mullen and Company, *supra* note 3, at 5.

24. [Mullen and Company Case Officer] Memorandum for Record, *supra* note 19, at 13-14.

25. *Id.* at 12-13.

26. *Id.* at 13.

27. [Mullen and Company Case Officer] Memorandum for Record, July 24, 1972, Subject: Withdrawal [Far East] Cover, found in CIA Supplemental Material, Volume V, at 1-2.

28. Executive Session Testimony of [DDP], *supra* note 6, at 39; Executive Session Testimony of [Mullen and Company Case Officer], *supra* note 2, at 43.

of same to Watergate developments. This Agency explanation is clouded by conflicting evidence. The Assistant Deputy Director of Plans has testified that he is very familiar with the matter and that it had no unique effect on Mullen's cover.[29] The Mullen case officer testified that the flap concerned cover.[30] Bennett, who thought the reference concerned a "White House flap," did advise of information received from the European cover that a [compromise] adversely affected a former Mullen cover [deleted at Agency request].[31]

A memorandum drafted by the Chief of the Central Cover Staff, CIA, on March 1, 1973, notes that *Bennett felt he could handle the Ervin Committee if the Agency could handle Hunt.*[32] Bennett even stated that he had a friend who had intervened with Ervin on the matter.[33] The same memorandum suggests that Bennett took relish in implicating Colson in Hunt's activities in the press while protecting the Agency at the same time.[34] It is further noted that Bennett was feeding stories to Bob Woodward who was "suitably grateful"; that he was making no attribution to Bennett; and that he was protecting Bennett and Mullen and Company.[35]

Pennington Matter

The results of our investigation clearly show that the CIA had in its possession, as early as June of 1972, information that one of their paid operatives, Lee R. Pennington, Jr., had entered the James McCord residence shortly after the Watergate break-in and destroyed documents which might show a link between McCord and the CIA. This information was not made available to this Committee or anyone else outside the CIA until February 22, 1974, when a memorandum by the then Director of Security was furnished to this Committee.[1]

The evidence further shows that in August of 1972, when the FBI made inquiry about a "Pennington," *the Agency*

29. Executive Session Testimony of [Former Assistant Deputy Director of Plans], February 28, 1974, transcript not presently available.
30. Executive Session Testimony of [Mullen and Company Case Officer], *supra* note 2, at 43.
31. Executive Session Testimony of Robert F. Bennett, *supra* note 2, at 17-24.
32. Memorandum for Deputy Director for Plans, March 1, 1973, Subject: Current *Time Magazine* Investigation of Robert R. Mullen & Company Connection with the Watergate Incident, found in CIA Supplemental Material, Volume IV, at 4.
33. *Id.*
34. *Id.*
35. *Id.*
1. *See* "Memorandum for Director of Intelligence," February 22, 1974; Exhibit 1 to the Executive Session Testimony of Lee R. Pennington, February 23, 1974.

response was to furnish information about a former employee, [with a similar name], who was obviously not the man the FBI was interested in, and to withhold the name of Lee R. Pennington, Jr.[2]

The Pennington information was known within the CIA at least at a level as high as the Director of Security, according to the [former Chief of the Security Research Staff, hereinafter referred to as Chief, Security Research Staff], by whom Pennington was retained at $250 per month until December of 1973.[3] In January of this year, [Director of Security] ordered that the Pennington materials be removed from the CIA Watergate files when those files were about to be reviewed by the CIA's Inspector General's office in connection with the CIA furnishing this and other Congressional committees certain information on the taping capacity at the CIA.[4] Our information is that, since the revelation of the Pennington matter in February of this year, [Director of Security's] early retirement has been "accepted."[5]

It seems that the Pennington matter was extremely sensitive not only bcause of the above-mentioned facts, but because Pennington may have been a "domestic agent," possibly in violation of the CIA's charter.[6] The Agency has advised that the Security Research Staff was abolished in August of 1973.[7]

All of the above information was produced by the CIA only as a result of the position taken by a staff employee of the Personnel Security Division, [Personnel Security Officer #1]. Because of the Senator's and the staff's request for documentation and information relating to the destruction

2. Executive Session Testimony of [Personnel Security Officer #1], February 25, 1974 at 11-14, 15, 17-18; Executive Session Testimony of [Assistant Deputy Director of Personnel Security], March 2, 1974 (transcription not presently available).
3. Executive Session Testimony of [Chief, Security Research Staff], February 24, 1974, at 25-26; Executive Session Testimony of Lee R. Pennington, *supra* note 1, at 29. (*Note:* The Chief, Security Research Staff, was the recipient of certain of the McCord letters.)
4. Executive Session Testimony of [Personnel Security Officer #1], *supra* note 2 at 46-49, 50-51, 52-54, 57-59, 69-72.
5. The CIA, through its legislative liaison, has informed this Committee that [Director of Security] "retired" on or about February 26, 1974, shortly after his Executive Session Testimony before this Committee on February 25, 1974.
6. *See* Executive Session Testimony of [Chief, Security Research Staff], *supra* note 3, at 25-26, 30; Executive Session Testimony of Lee R. Pennington, *supra* note 1, at 4-7, 10, 29. In this regard, Volume VIII CIA Supplemental Materials references an apparent CIA file on a United States citizen, Jack Anderson (#349691). This reference is contained in CIA memoranda in November and December of 1972 which discuss Pennington's providing his CIA case officer with a memorandum allegedly written by McCord about Jack Anderson and others. It should be noted that the CIA file on Mr. Pennington was not provided to this Committee and also apparently has portions "missing" from it, *see* Action Required section of this memorandum, *infra*, at Miscellaneous. No. 9.
7. Executive Session Testimony of [Director of Security], February 25, 1974, at 17-18.

of CIA tapes and other matters, Deputy Legislative Counsel prepared a statement for Director Colby's signature on February 19, 1974. In it was the blanket assertion that the CIA had produced all Watergate-related information for this Committee as well as its Congressional oversight committees.[8] Because he was aware of many of the above facts, [Personnel Security Officer #1] made it clear that he could not and would not subscribe to such a statement.[9] *[Personnel Security Officer #1] was so concerned that the documentary evidence of the Pennington information would be destroyed by others in the CIA that he and a co-employee copied the relevant memoranda and placed them in their respective personal safes.*[10] This matter was subsequently brought to the Inspector General's attention and the [Director of Security's] memorandum of February 22 was drafted and made available to this Committee, the oversight committees, and the Special Prosecutor's office.[11]

Our investigation in this area also produced the fact that, contrary to previous CIA assertions, the CIA conducted a vigorous in-house investigation of the Watergate matter, starting almost immediately after the break-in.[12] *As one member of the Security Research Staff stated they were in a state of "panic."* [13] In November and December of 1972, [Executive Officer to Director of Security] was specially assigned to then Executive Director/Comptroller Colby to conduct a very secretive investigation of several Watergate-related matters. *[Executive Officer to Director of Security] was instructed to keep no copies of his findings and to make no records. He did his own typing and utilized no*

8. Supplemental CIA Materials, Volume VIII; see also Executive Session Testimony of [Personnel Security Officer #1], *supra* note 2, at 61-63.
9. Executive Session Testimony of [Personnel Security Officer #1], *supra* note 2, at 45-52. In his Executive Session Testimony [Personnel Security Officer #1], states that, at a meeting on January 22, 1974, to discuss whether the "Pennington matter" should be withheld from or disclosed to the appropriate authorities and Congressional committees, he informed his supervisory CIA personnel that (tr. 52):
"Up to this time we have never removed, tampered with, obliterated, destroyed, or done anything to any Watergate documents, and we can't be caught in that kind of bind now. We will not do it." [Personnel Security Officer #1] added that he "didn't cross the Potomac on (his) way to work in the morning, and that the Agency could do without its own L. Patrick Gray" (tr. 53). Subsequently, [Personnel Security Officer #1] prevailed and the information was made available to this and other appropriate Congressional Committees.
10. Executive Session Testimony of [Personnel Security Officer #1], *supra* note 2, at 49, 45-52.
11. See "Memorandum for Director of Central Intelligence," *supra*, note 1.
12. Executive Session Testimony of [Personnel Security Officer #1], *supra* note 2, at 1-4; Executive Session Testimony of [Security Research Staff Officer], February 25, 1974, at 5, 31-32, 42, 49.
13. Executive Session Testimony of [Security Research Staff Officer], *supra* note 12, at 5.

secretaries.[14]

Less clear than the aforementioned efforts to suppress the Pennington information, is an understanding of Pennington's actual role or non-role in the destruction of documents at the McCord home shortly after the Watergate break-in. Pennington has testified that he did not go to the McCord home for the purpose of searching for or destroying CIA-related documents, but does acknowledge witnessing the destruction of documents by Mrs. McCord and others.[15] It is clear from the testimony of others [16] that the CIA received information, evidently from Pennington, indicating more active participation by operative Pennington.

Tapes

In a meeting in Senator Baker's office with Director Colby and George Murphy, following a discussion of the Cushman tape, Murphy asked Colby if there were other tapes, and he replied in the affirmative. In response to a question from Senator Baker, Colby further acknowledged the prior existence of a central taping capability at the CIA. Senator Baker then requested that relevant tapes be reviewed and delivered to the Committee, to which Colby agreed. Shortly thereafter, Colby confirmed to Senator Baker recent press accounts that the tapes had been destroyed. In that same connection it should be pointed out that the staff had previously interviewed Victor Marchetti, who stated upon questioning that he suspected that there was a central taping system at the CIA. When the staff broached this subject with the Agency's [Deputy Legislative Counsel], he stated that if there had been such a system, it was no longer in existence.

Shortly before Director Helms left office, and approximately one week after Senator Mansfield's letter requesting that evidentiary materials be retained,[1] *Helms ordered that the tapes be destroyed.*[2] Although the CIA is apparently unable

14. Executive Session Testimony of [Executive Officer to Director of Security], March 3, 1974 (transcription not presently available).
15. Executive Session Testimony of Lee R. Pennington, *supra* note 1.
16. Executive Session Testimony of [Security Research Staff Officer], *supra* note 12; Executive Session Testimony of [Personnel Security Officer #1], *supra* note 2; Executive Session Testimony of [Chief, Security Research Staff], *supra* note 3.
1. Letter from Senator Mansfield to DCI Helms, dated January 16, 1973.
2. Executive Session Testimony of [Director Helms' Secretary], February 6, 1974, at 14. See also CIA memorandum for Director of Security, dated January 31, 1974, at 3. She states that she told the technicians to destroy only Helms' tapes and not all of the tapes (Executive Session Testimony at 34-35). However, there seems to have been no doubt in the minds of the technicians that they were to destroy all of the tapes on hand. Executive Session Testimony of [Office of Security Technician #1], February 6, 1974,

to state with any degree of precision the date on which the tapes were actually destroyed, testimony indicates that it was during the week of January 22, 1973.[3] While the CIA claims that the destruction was not unusual and was one of several periodic destructions, two facts seem clear. First, the only other destruction for which the CIA has any record was on January 21, 1972, when tapes for 1964 and 1965 were destroyed (there are no records of periodic destructions);[4] and secondly, never before had there been a destruction of all existing tapes.[5] It should be noted that there exists a separate taping system for the Office of Security.[6] That system is still operative, and the O/S tapes presumably are still in existence. The Agency has advised that it has reviewed all Office of Security tapes, watch office tapes, and duty office tapes to determine the relevancy of same but has not provided these tapes to the Select Committee, despite the Committee's request. The Agency has provided the Committee with two selected transcripts which purport to constitute, in the opinion of the Agency, the only Watergate-related material contained on any tapes.

The January, 1973, destruction pertained only to recordings of room conversations. However, on Helms' instruction, his secretary destroyed his transcriptions of both telephone and room conversations.[7] *The evidence indicates that among those telephone transcriptions were conversations with the President, Haldeman, Ehrlichman, and other White House officials.*[8] Helms and [Director Helms' Secretary] have testified that such conversations were non-Watergate related.[9] Unfortunately, any means of corroboration is no longer available. We have examined summaries of logs made available by the CIA, but it is impossible to determine who was taped in many of the room conversations. In this regard, even the CIA's analysis does not provide this vital information.

---

at 23. Executive Session Testimony of [Office of Security Technician #2], February 6, 1974, at 53.

3. Executive Session Testimony of [Office of Security Technician #2], *supra* note 2, at 36. See also CIA memorandum for Director of Security, *supra* note 2.

4. Executive Session Testimony of [Office of Security Technician #1], *supra* note 2 at 10. Executive Session Testimony of [Office of Security Technician #2], *supra* note 2 at 36-37.

5. Executive Session Testimony of [Office of Security Technician #2], *supra* note 2 at 20.

6. CIA memorandum for Director of Security, *supra* note 2 at 4.

7. Executive Session Testimony of [Director Helms' Secretary], *supra* note 2 at 14, 17, 19. Executive Session Testimony of Richard Helms, March 8, 1974 (transcription not yet available).

8. Executive Session Testimony of [Director Helms' Secretary], *supra* note 2 at 22.

9. Executive Session Testimony of Helms, *supra* note 7; Executive Session Testimony of [Director Helms' Secretary], *supra* note 2 at 23.

There are several references to a "Mr. X." The CIA has not produced the actual logs for our examination. However, we were informed that there are "gaps" in the logs.

The circumstances surrounding the transcriptions of room and telephone conversations of former Deputy Director Cushman are bizarre to say the least. When Cushman testified before the Watergate Committee on August 2, 1973, he presented a transcription of the Cushman/Hunt conversation of July 22, 1971.[10] We recently discovered that there exists an original, more complete transcription; that the original transcription contained an insignificant but uncomplimentary reference to the President; and, that the original was available to the CIA at the time of the Committee's hearings in August of 1973. *In fact, the original transcript was not produced until February of this year, the day before Senator Baker was to listen to the Cushman/Hunt tape, per his request.*

The Cushman/Hunt conversation and one other were the only two room transcriptions saved by Cushman's secretary, [presently Director Colby's Secretary, hereinafter referred to as Cushman/Colby's Secretary], and his assistant [Executive Assistant to Deputy Director of CIA, hereinafter referred to as Exec. Asst. to DDCI], when Cushman's safe was cleaned out in December of 1971.[11] They claimed that they made a search for the original transcription shortly after the Watergate break-in but that it was not found, and therefore an abbreviated transcription was typed.[12] Therefore, we have a search by [Exec. Asst. to DDCI] shortly after the Watergate break-in in June of 1972 and another search in May of 1973, the original transcript not having been found until May of 1973.

In February of this year [Deputy Legislative Counsel] hand-delivered to Senator Baker a very significant document. It was the transcription of a portion of the Ehrlichman/Cushman telephone conversation. [Deputy Legislative Counsel] stated it had been recently discovered by [Exec. Asst. to DDCI].[13] *It was discovered during [Exec. Asst to DDCI's] third search for Watergate-related materials, and it was located in the same file as the Cushman/Hunt transcript.*[14]

The document is especially significant in that it quotes

10. Public Testimony of General Robert E. Cushman at 3291.
11. Executive Session Testimony of [Cushman/Colby Secretary], February 21, 1974.
12. Id. at 64; *see also* memorandum of [Exec. Asst. to DDCI], July 23, 1973, Supplemental CIA Materials, Volume IV.
13. *See* Ehrlichman/Cushman tape transcription, CIA memorandum "For All Employees" dated January 31, 1974, at Tab B.
14. Affidavit of [Exec. Asst. to DDCI], February 5, 1974, and Executive Session Testimony of [Exec. Asst. to DDCI], March 6, 1974 (transcription not yet available).

Ehrlichman as saying that Hunt was working for the President and that the CIA was to give Hunt "carte blanche." This, of course, substantiates the CIA's claim that Ehrlichman made the original call with regard to the CIA's assistance to Hunt. Surprisingly, we learned that [*Cushman/Colby Secretary*], *although she says she was told that Mr. Cushman did not have his calls monitored, did, in fact, monitor certain of his calls anyway, especially with people at the White House, without Cushman's knowledge.*[15] The Cushman/ Ehrlichman transcript was a result of the shorthand notes she took of a monitored call.[16]

There are two interesting aspects to this transcription. First, only the Ehrlichman portion of the conversation was transcribed, contrary to normal practice; [17] and secondly, Cushman does not recall any reference to the President or to "carte blanche." [18]

Hunt—TSD Support—Ellsberg Profile

The Committee has received much testimony over the past several months detailing the extensive support of Howard Hunt by CIA personnel with CIA materials and the CIA's role in the preparation of the psychological profiles of Daniel Ellsberg. Howard Hunt was involved in a wide variety of domestic undertakings with the use of CIA equipment and the assistance of CIA personnel, *e.g.*, the burglaries of Dr. Fielding's office and the DNC, the preparation of psychological profiles on Daniel Ellsberg and the investigation of the Chappaquidick incident. *In light of the facts and circumstances developed through the documents and conflicting testimony of CIA personnel adduced by this Committee, which are summarized below, the question arises as to whether the CIA had advance knowledge of the Fielding break-in.* The Fielding burglary was not made public until May of 1973.

While the CIA has previously belatedly acknowledged some of the technical support it provided to Hunt and Liddy prior to the Fielding break-in, the CIA has continually downplayed the extent of that technical support as well as the specific approval and detailed knowledge of such support by high level CIA officials.[1] The scenario of events culminating in the Fielding break-in caused a wealth of conflicting

15. Executive Session Testimony of [Cushman/Colby Secretary], *supra* note 11 at 12-13.
16. *Id.* at 17, 18.
17. *Id.* at 80-81.
18. Executive Session Testimony of General Robert E. Cushman, March 7, 1974 (transcription not yet available).
1. *See* affidavits of Cushman, [Exec. Asst. to DDCI], and [Deputy Chief, TSD], Original CIA Materials, Volume II, Tab D.

testimony among CIA officials as referred to hereinafter.

The CIA's assistance to Hunt began on July 22, 1971, when Hunt met with General Cushman, then Deputy Director of the CIA, in Cushman's office to request physical disguise and phony identification to effect a "one time operation, in and out." [2] This meeting was tape recorded by Cushman. Thereafter, pursuant to the specific approval of both Cushman and then Director of the CIA Richard Helms, a member of the CIA's Technical Services Division was assigned to provide Hunt with the assistance and materials he requested.[3] During the next thirty days, the CIA technical staff met with Hunt on four separate occasions. Most meetings were held at CIA "safe houses" (dwellings owned or leased by the CIA for clandestine meetings).[4] At those meetings Hunt was provided with the CIA equipment and assistance described in earlier Committee testimony, i. e., a wig, voice alteration devices, heel lift to cause a limp,[5] fake glasses, phony driver's licenses and identification cards, a Uher 5000 tape recorder disguised in a typewriter case, a camera hidden in a tobacco pouch, preliminary steps toward a phony New York telephone answering device, and the developing of the film of Hunt and Liddy's reconnaissance trip to Los Angeles to "case" Dr. Fielding's office.[6] This assistance was abruptly terminated on August 27, 1971—one week before the Fielding burglary of September 3, 1971.[7]

Recent testimony and documents have developed several matters of considerable import with regard to the assistance provided Hunt and Liddy. The technician who dealt with Hunt has testified that he received approval for each and every request of Hunt from his supervisory officials at the CIA.[8] He also testified that, contrary to earlier and other CIA testimony, Hunt informed him early in August that he

2. Partial tape transcript of July 22 meeting, Original CIA Materials, Volume II, Tab K, at 1; see also Cushman's affidavit, id., and complete unabridged tape transcript of July 22 meeting, CIA Supplemental Materials, Volume II, Tab 4.
3. See Executive Session Testimony of General Robert E. Cushman, March 7, 1974, at 10, 12; contra, Executive Session Testimony of Richard Helms, March 8, 1974, and Testimony of Richard Helms before the Senate Committee on Appropriations, May 16, 1973, at 195-196.
4. See Executive Session Testimony of [TSD Technician #1], February 5 and 6, 1974, at 3-25 (February 5 tr.), and Exhibit 1 to that testimony (notes of [TSD Technician #1] compiled contemporaneously with the support of Hunt) also found in CIA Supplemental Materials, Volume VII, Tab 8.
5. Staff interview with Howard Hunt, February 4, 1974.
6. Public Testimony of Richard Helms and General Robert E. Cushman, August 2, 1973; affidavits of [TSD Techniican #1, TSD Technician #2, Deputy Chief, TSD, and Exec. Asst. to DDCI], Original CIA Materials, Volume II, Tab D.
7. Id.
8. Executive Session Testimony of [TSD Technician #1], supra note 4 at 10 (February 6 tr.), at 57 (February 5 tr.).

would be introducing a second man (Liddy) to the technician for the provision of disguise and false identification.[9] CIA officials heretofore had claimed that Hunt introduced Liddy unannounced late in August and that this introduction had been one of the leading causes for the CIA's ultimate termination of its support for Hunt.[10]

Testimony and documents have also revealed, again contrary to the testimony of high CIA officials, that Hunt's request for a New York "backstopped" telephone (a telephone with a New York number which would in reality be answered by a Washington CIA switchboard) answering service was well on its way to completion.[11] A detailed memorandum of the TSD technician, dated August 27, 1971, reveals that the backstopped telephone request was about to be implemented.[12] This memorandum includes the actual relay number to be called. Previous CIA testimony had always been to the effect that this telephone request was so unreasonable that it was immediately disapproved and that it was also a leading cause of the ultimate termination of Hunt's support.[13]

Recent testimony also established that the CIA created a file on Hunt's activities entitled the "Mr. Edward" file. This file was maintained outside the normal CIA filing system, and this Committee's requests to obtain this file have not been granted, despite the fact that testimony has established that this file was turned over to Director Colby after the Watergate break-in.[14] Moreover, recent testimony also indicates that a "bigot list" (CIA term for treatment of

9. *Id.* at 55-57 (February 5 tr.); *see also* notes referred to in note 4, *supra.*
10. Affidavits of [Exec. Asst. to DDCI], [Deputy Chief, TSD], Cushman, *supra* note 1; memoranda [of Exec. Asst. to DDCI] dated August 23, 26, and 30. Original CIA Materials, Volume II, Tab K; *compare* Executive Session Testimony of [TSD Technician #1], *supra* note 4 at 55-56 (February 5 tr.) *with* Executive Session Testimony of [Deputy Chief, TSD], February 5, 1974, at 24.
11. Executive Session Testimony of [TSD Technician #1], *supra* note 4 at 8-10, 12 (February 6), and Exhibit 1 to [TSD Technician #1]'s testimony at 5, which details the steps taken by the CIA to implement Hunt's request.
12. *Id.*
13. *See* affidavits of [Exec. Asst. to DDCI], [Deputy Chief, TSD], Cushman, and memoranda of [Exec. Asst. to DDCI], *supra* note 10; Executive Session Testimony of Cushman. March 7, 1974, at 19-21. Moreover, Executive Session Testimony of Richard Helms, *supra* note 3, indicates that it was Hunt's request for a secretary which caused him to order the cut-off of support. This request, however, occurred on August 18 and was denied the same or next day. *see* Executive Session Testimony of [Exec. Assist. to DDCI], March 6, 1974 (transcription not presently available), *contra*, testimony of Richard Helms before the Senate Committee on Appropriations, *supra* note 3, at 197.
14. Executive Session Testimony of [Deputy Chief, TSD], February 5, 1974, at 14-15; Executive Session Testimony of [Chief, TSD], February 5, 1974, at 29-30.

especially sensitive case restricting access to a limited number of persons) was created for Hunt's activities.[15]

Testimony has indicated that the film developed for Hunt and Liddy was, in fact, of Dr. Fielding's office.[16] Not only was the film developed, however, but it was reviewed by CIA supervisory officials before it was returned to Hunt.[17] One CIA official who reviewed the film admitted that he found the photographs "intriguing" and recognized them to be of "southern California." [18] *He then ordered one of the photographs to be blown up. The blow-up revealed Dr. Fielding's name in the parking lot next to his office.*[19] Another CIA official has testified that he speculated that they were "casing" photographs.[20] Recent testimony has shown that *the CIA official who reviewed these photographs immedeiately reported their content to Cushman and his assistant in the office of the Deputy Director of the CIA.*[21] With a degree of incredulity, however, he denies telling his superiors that he blew up one of the photographs and that it revealed the name of Dr. Fielding.[22] Moreover, both Cushman and his assistant denied ever having been told about the content of the photographs by [Deputy Chief, TSD] or anyone else.[23] In any event, recent testimony shows that it was only after these photographs were developed and examined that the CIA technician dealing with Hunt was ordered to cut off all support for Hunt.[24] This decision was made by the Deputy Director of the CIA (Cushman) and/or the Director of the CIA (Helms).[25]

15. Executive Session Testimony of [TSD Technician #1], *supra* note 4, at 2-4 (February 6 tr.)
16. Executive Session Testimony of [Executive Officer to Director of Security], March 3, 1974 (transcription not presently available); Staff interview of Howard Hunt, *supra* note 5, wherein Hunt indicates that the film the CIA developed included shots of a "close-up of (Fielding's office) door, a close-up of the directory of (Fielding's) building, photographs of the ingress and egress of the parking lot . . ." as well as shots of the inside of Fielding's office, including the top of Fielding's desk.
17. Executive Session Testimony of [TSD Technician #1], *supra* note 4 at 20-24, 52-53 (February 5 tr.); Executive Session Testimony of [Deputy Chief, TSD], *supra* note 14 at 43-47.
18. Executive Session Testimony of [Deputy Chief, TSD], *supra* note 14 at 44.
19. *Id.* at 45-46.
20. Executive Session Testimony of [Chief, TSD], February 5, 1974, at 19-20.
21. Executive Session Testimony of [Deputy Chief, TSD], *supra*, note 14 at 47-49.
22. *Id.*
23. Executive Session Testimony of General Robert E. Cushman, March 7, 1974, at 22-23; Executive Session Testimony of [Exec. Asst. to DDCI], March 6, 1974 (transcription not presently available).
24. Executive Session Testimony of [TSD Technician #1], *supra* note 4, at 59-60, and Exhibit 1 to that testimony.
25. Executive Session Testimony of General E. Cushman, March 7, 1974, at 21-22, 16-20; Executive Session Testimony of Richard Helms, March 8, 1974, *contra* (transcription not presently available).

Finally, while previous public CIA testimony claimed that the CIA "had no contact whatsoever with Mr. Hunt subsequent to 31 August, 1971,"[26] recent testimony and secret documents indicate that Hunt had extensive contact with the CIA after that date. Not only did Hunt play a large role in the CIA's development of psychological profiles on Daniel Ellsberg (not completed until November of 1971), but he actually contacted the CIA's External Employment Assistance Branch (EEAB) and approached active CIA personnel regarding several operations, including, *e.g.*, Hunt's requests to the CIA for person(s) skilled in lockpicking, electronic sweeping, and entry operations.[27]

It is significant that during the same time period as the ongoing support of Hunt by the CIA, August of 1971, the CIA was also compiling a psychological profile on Daniel Ellsberg. Recent testimony has revealed that Hunt was deeply involved in that project as well.

The preparation of this profile was specifically approved by then Director Helms in late July of 1971.[28] The actual compiling of the profile was done by the CIA's medical

26. Lieutenant General Vernon A. Walters Memorandum for Record, July 28, 1972, Original CIA Materials, Volume I, Tab S.
27. Contacts after August 31, 1971, indicated in the Secret Supplemental CIA Materials, include the following:
a. Hunt was referred to [Former CIA employee] by [Chief, EEAB] of the CIA's EEAB, ([Chief, EEAB] retired on June 19, 1972) when Hunt requested a "retired lockpicker" and entry man in the time period of March-May, 1972. CIA Supplemental Materials, Volume I, Tab 4, Memorandum of June 19, 1973.
b. Hunt, in late 1971, requested some " 'security types' to check physical security and monitor telephones in Las Vegas," in connection with Hunt's work on the Hughes account with Mullen and Company. Hunt was referred by [Chief, EEAB] to an [Agency proprietary (name deleted at Agency request)] (CIA Supplemental Materials, Volume I, Tab 4)
c. Hunt contacted [deleted at Agency request] (an active CIA employee until November 10, 1972) sometime in late 1971 regarding a weekend entry operation.
d. Hunt contacted CIA employee [deleted at Agency request] in October of 1971 concerning certain *Indo-China War documents* (Original CIA Materials, Volume II, Tab D).
e. On December 8, 1971, Hunt requested and received a CIA computer name trace, by CIA employees, on a person who had allegedly formed the [deleted name of Latin American country at Agency request] National Independent Party in December of 1971 (Original CIA Materials, Volume II, Tab D).
f. The CIA acknowledges that the Deputy Director of Plans of the CIA did meet with Hunt on October 15, 1971 to discuss Mullen and Company problems.
28. Affidavit of [Deputy Director of Support, hereafter referred to as the DDS] and [Director of Medical Services Staff, hereinafter referred to as the DMSS] and [Chief of Psychiatric Staff on Medical Services Staff, hereinafter referred to as Chief Psychiatrist], Original CIA Materials, Volume I, Tab U; Volume II, Tab D.

services staff and, in particular, its chief psychiatrist.[29] Testimony has indicated that a meeting was held on August 12, 1971, in which both Howard Hunt and Gordon Liddy participated. They told the CIA psychiatrist that Ellsberg had been undergoing psychiatric analysis. Hunt and Liddy discussed witn him their desire to "try Ellsberg in public," render him "the object of pity as a broken man," and be able to refer to Ellberg's "Oedipal complex." [30] *At the ilose of the meeting, Hunt asked the psychiatrist not to reveal his presence in the profile discussions to anyone at the CIA, stating that he already had been in contact with General Cushman and was on good terms with Director Helms. The psychiatrist has testified recently that he was extremely concerned about Hunt's presence and remarks. He so reported this to his CIA superiors, both in memoranda and in a meeting on August 20, 1971. Access to the memoranda of both the psychiatrist and his superiors has been refused to this Committee.*[31]

The CIA psychiatrist also was given the name of Dr. Fielding as Ellsberg's psychiatrist and numerous FBI reports of interviews with Ellsberg's associates, as well as a memorandum of a reported telephone conversation between Ellsberg and another party.[32] And *recent testimony has revealed that it was reported back to the psychiatrist that Director Helms was advised of his concerns regarding Hunt's participation and comments.*[33] While Director Helms has denied that he was ever told that Hunt was involved in the CIA's Ellsberg profile project,[34] it is not without significance that the time period during which the CIA psychiatrist was briefing his superiors of his concerns regarding Hunt was circa August 20, 1971—a week prior to the developing of Hunt's film of "intriguing" photographs of medical offices in southern California which impressed at least one CIA official as "casing" photographs.[35]

With the aforementioned background, we are reminded that when the second profile on Ellsberg was completed (completion was delayed until November of 1971), Director Helms took pains to inform the White House that:

I do wish to underline the point that our involvement in

29. *Id.*
30. Executive Session Testimony of [Chief Psychiatrist], March 6, 1974 (transcription not presently available).
31. *Id.*, see also Colby letter refusing access, *infra.*
32. *Id.*
33. *Id.*
34. Executive Session Testimony of Richard Helms, *supra* note 3; Testimony of Richard Helms before the Senate Armed Services Committee, May 17, 1973, at 17.
35. See Executive Session Testimony of [Chief, TSD], *supra* note 20.

this matter should not be revealed in any context, formal or informal.[36]

In this recent testimony before this Committee, Director Helms stated that the above quoted language represented his concern only for the professional reputations of the CIA psychiatrists and *not* any concern over the possible illegality of the profile.[37] It should be noted, however, that in a memorandum from the psychiatrists' CIA supervisor to Helms in November of 1971, which accompanied the completed profile, their concern is expressed as follows:

> [DMSS] and [Chief Psychiatrist] . . . confirmed that their worries *did not . . . involve* professional ethics or credibility. Instead, they are concerned lest the Agency's involvement . . . become known and particularly that it might come to light during any proceeding. . . . We will be guided by your determination after you have had an opportunity to read the new paper. (Emphasis supplied.) [38]

The facts and circumstances related above, as derived from the recently curtailed investigation of this Committee, would appear to raise many unanswered questions as to the involvement of the CIA in matters outside its legislative parameters.

Hunt—Martinez—CIA

Director Helms, upon being questioned about Martinez, has consistently testified to little more than the fact that Eugenio Martinez was on a $100 per month retainer with the CIA as an informant on Cubans of interest to the Agency.[1] Our investigation has revealed relevant information concerning Martinez' CIA relationship, as set out below, not previously brought forward in testimony by CIA officials.

Because of Hunt's close relationship with Martinez at a time when Martinez was a paid CIA operative, *the basic question arises as to whether the CIA was aware of Hunt's activities early in 1972 when he was recruiting Cubans to assist in the Watergate break-in.*

Prior to assuming a retainer status in the summer of 1971, Martinez had been a full-salaried operative involved in

36. Memorandum from Richard Helms to David Young, November 9, 1971, Original CIA Materials, Volume II, Tab J.
37. Executive Session Testimony of Richard Helms, *supra* note 3.
38. Memorandum from [DDS], CIA Deputy Director of Support, to Richard Helms, Director of Central Intelligence, November 9, 1971, Original CIA Materials, Volume II, Tab J.
1. Senate Foreign Relations Committee Report of Richard Helms Testimony, February 7, 1973, at 24, 50; Senate Select Committee Transcript of Richard Helms Testimony, August 2, 1973, at 6733-6734, 6814-6815.

Agency [deleted at Agency request] endeavors.[2] In November of 1971, a month after his participation in the Fielding break-in, Martinez mentioned his contact with Hunt in an allegedly innocuous fashion to his case officer and the Miami Chief of Station.[3] There is also evidence that Martinez had mentioned Hunt even earlier to his case officer.[4] *In March of 1972, Martinez advised the Miami Chief of Station that Hunt was employed by the White House and asked the Chief of Station if he was sure that he had been apprised of all Agency activities in the Miami area.*[5] This concerned the Chief of Station who sent a letter to CIA headquarters requesting information on Hunt's White House status.[6] On March 27, 1972, the Chief of Station received a cryptic response at the direction of the Assistant Deputy Director of Plans advising the Chief of Station not to concern himself with the travels of Hunt in Miami, that Hunt was on domestic White House business of an unknown nature and that the Chief of Station should "cool it."[7] (It should be remembered that this was after the Agency provided Hunt with TSD support in July and August of 1971. It is not explained why Hunt, who had "used" the CIA, was not of more interest to the Agency, especially when he was contacting a current operative, Martinez.) The tone of this letter infuriated the Chief of Station and left him uneasy about the matter.[8] Accordingly, the Chief of Station requested that Martinez prepare in Spanish a report on the Hunt information provided the Chief of Station in March.[9] Martinez compiled a "cover story"[10] on April 5, 1972, after being

2. Executive Session Testimony of [Miami Chief of Station, hereinafter COS], February 7, 1974, at 5-9.
3. [Martinez' Case Officer (1971-1972), hereinafter referred to as Case Officer #1] Memorandum for the Record (excerpt), November 19, 1971, Agent: [Martinez' Code Name], found at Tab 1, CIA Supplemental Materials, Volume II; Executive Session Testimony of [COS], *supra* note 2, at 14-18.
4. [Case Officer #1] Memorandum for the Record (excerpt), *supra* note 3; Executive Session Testimony of [COS], *supra* note 2, at 13.
5. Executive Session Testimony of [COS], *supra* note 2, at 23-27.
6. *Id.* at 25-27; *See* [COS] Memorandum for Chief, [deleted at Agency request], March 17, 1972, Subject: Miscellaneous Information from [Martinez' Code Name], found at Tab 1, CIA Supplemental Materials, Volume II; [COS] [sensitive] letter, March 17, 1972, found at Tab 1, CIA Supplemental Materials, Volume II.
7. Executive Session Testimony of [COS], *supra* note 2, at 31-34; [Chief, Cuban Operations Branch, Western Hemisphere Division, hereinafter referred to as Chief, COB] letter to [COS], March 27, 1972, found at Tab 1, CIA Supplemental Materials, Volume II.
8. Executive Session Testimony of [COS], *supra* note 2, at 32, 80.
9. *Id.* at 33-34, 38-40; [Case Officer #1] Cable [deleted at Agency request], December 15, 1973, found at Tab 2, CIA Supplemental Materials, Volume II; Executive Session Testimony of Eugenio Martinez, December 10, 1973, at 45-47.
10. Executive Session Testimony of [COS], *supra* note 2, at 91; *see* Executive Session Testimony of Eugenio Martinez, *supra* note 9, at 11.

told by his case officer not to put anything in the report which might come back to haunt him.[11] The Spanish report, which did not contain any of the alarming innuendos suggested earlier by Martinez, was maintained in the Chief of Station's file until after the Watergate break-in.[12]

It is known that Martinez had two case officers during 1971 and 1972. There is conflicting evidence concerning the precise date of the spring, 1972 case officer change-over.[13] It is known that Martinez met with his last case officer on June 6, 1972, and at that time had at least two reporting requirements, i.e., maritime operation information and information pertaining to possible demonstrations at the Miami conventions,[14] contrary to earlier testimony by CIA officials.[15] The Agency has not afforded this Committee an unabridged examination of the case officer contact reports, despite requests for same.

The Agency has advised that Martinez' first case officer was on an "African safari" throughout June of 1972.[16] The second case officer has testified that the former case officer was in Miami on June 19, 1972.[17] The first case officer has been transferred to [Indochina] and was not made available for interview by our Committee. The second case officer stated in his interview that he was rushed to CIA headquarters the week following Watergate and told that he would be required to stay there until September for reasons related to his involvement with Martinez.[18] This case officer remains assigned to CIA headquarters.

On the morning of June 18, 1972, the Miami Chief of Station dispatched a cable to CIA headquarters regarding the activities of Martinez but deliberately omitting Martinez' prior reference to Hunt's activities.[19] On June 19, 1972, the Chief of Station received correspondence from CIA headquarters advising him to keep in better touch with his

11. Executive Session Testimony of Eugenio Martinez, *supra* note 9, at 53, 58-59. [Case Officer #1] Cable [deleted at Agency request], *supra* note 9.
12. Executive Session Testimony of [COS], *supra* note 2, at 33-34. *See also* Original Spanish Report and Translated Spanish Report, found at Tab 1, CIA Supplemental Materials, Volume I (attention to discrepancies).
13. Tab 2, CIA Supplemental Materials, Volume VII (indicating April 14, 1972 change-over); Tab 10. Original CIA Materials, Volume III (indicating a March, 1972 change-over); Executive Session Testimony of [COS], *supra* note 2, at 36 (indicating April 23-30, 1972 change-over).
14. Executive Session Testimony of [Case Officer #2], February 4, 1974, at 25-26, 41-42.
15. *Supra* note 1.
16. CIA Deputy Legislative Counsel showed this staff a printed itinerary for the first case officer which contained the referenced entry. Legislative Counsel has not made that itinerary a part of the supplemental materials furnished the staff.
17. Executive Session Testimony of [Case Officer #2], *supra* note 14, at 73.
18. *Id.* at 49-50.
19. *Id.* at 36-37, 78.

operatives in Miami.[20] This prompted the Chief of Station to forward a copy of the Martinez report in Spanish to headquarters.[21] The Chief of Station was confounded as to why he was not old to terminate the Martinez relationship if the CIA headquarters suspected the involvement of Hunt in political activities.[22] He later brought this matter up with the Assistant Deputy Director of Plans, who told him that the Agency was uneasy about Hunt's activities for the White House in "March or May" of 1972.[23] The Assistant Deputy Director of Plans testified that he assumed in March of 1972 that Hunt was involved in partisan political work for the White House and that this assumption formed the basis for his guidance to the Miami Chief of Station at that time.[24] He further testified that the Miami Chief of Station wanted to check on Hunt's activities domestically,[25] an allegation denied by the Chief of Station [26] and not reflected in any of the CIA correspondence made available to us.

Despite conflicting evidence from the FBI and the CIA,[27] it is known that the Agency received information on June 19, 1972, from an operative that Martinez' vehicle was at the Miami airport and contained compromising documents.[28] The Agency contacted the FBI with this information on June 21, 1972.[29] Our staff has yet to receive a satisfactory explanation regarding the aforementioned time lag and an accounting of Agency actiions during the interim.

Action Required

The following is a breakdown by area of interest of action desirable to complete the Watergate-related CIA investigation commenced by this staff.

MARTINEZ RELATIONSHIP

1. Interviews

20. [Chief, Western Hemisphere Division] "Dear Friend" letter, June 20, 1972, found at Tab 2, CIA Supplemental Materials, Volume II.
21. [COS] "Dear Friend" letter, June 20, 1972, found at Tab 2, CIA Supplemental Materials, Volume II; Executive Session Testimony of [COS], *supra* note 2, at 73-75.
22. Executive Session Testimony of [COS], *supra* note 2, at 80-82.
23. *Id.* at 82-83.
24. Executive Session Testimony of ADDP, February 28, 1974, transcript not presently available.
25. *Id.*
26. Executive Session Testimony of COS, *supra* note 2, at 84.
27. *Id.* at 62-65; Report of Interview of Agent Robert L. Wilson, dated January 11, 1974, at 4. A comparison reveals a discrepancy as to manner in which FBI was notified and raises questions concerning what the FBI found.
28. Executive Session Testimony of COS, *supra* note 2, at 58-60; Executive Session Testimony of Case Officer #2, *supra* note 14, at 15-17.
29. Report of Interview of Agent Robert L. Wilson, *supra* note 27, at 3

a. Chief, Western Hemisphere Division (1971-April, 1972).
b. Chief, Western Hemisphere Division (April, 1972-1973).
c. Chief, Cuban Operations Branch, Western Hemisphere Division (1971-1972).
d. Martinez' case officer (1971-March, April, 1972). Prior efforts to interview this individual have been frustrated by virtue of his present assignment in [Indochina].
e. Executive Assistant to the ADDP (1971-1973).
f. Executive Assistant to the DDP (1971-1973).

The aforegoing interviews are necessary in order to determine the extent of the CIA's knowledge of Hunt's activities.

g. Chief, Miami Office of Security (June, 1972).
h. Miami Chief of Station's informant with regard to Martinez' car.
i. Above informant's source with regard to Martinez's car.

These interviews are necessary to explain the time lag in giving notice to the FBI; to identify CIA actions (particularly the Miami Office of Security) regarding this information; and to determine the scope of information received by the Agency and transmitted to the FBI.

2. Documents
   a. All Martinez case officer contact reports (1971-July, 1972). We have repeatedly requested access to unabridged reports, but the Agency has made available only an abridged version of early reports. Access is necessary to determine the scope of Martinez' relationship in the relevant time frame and whether he provided any Watergate-related information to his case officer.
   b. All CIA correspondence re: Martinez car (cables, etc.). This information, although not previously requested per se, is critical to the documentation of Agency action on this issue and to resolve conflicting evidence supplied by the FBI.
   c. All reports or memoranda relating to the debriefing of Martinez' last case officer upon his return to Washington, D. C., after the Watergate break-in. This information has been previously requested but not provided to this staff.

MULLEN AND COMPANY RELATIONSHIP

1. Interviews
   a. Mullen and Company secretaries (1971-1972). This is needed to confirm or deny suspicions relevant to the indicated Agency/Bennett/Hughes link.
   b. Far East cover (June, 1972).

c. European cover.

The aforegoing interviews are necessary to a meaningful understanding of the "WH flap" and to gauge any relationship of same to the Watergate break-in.

    d. Chief, Central Cover Staff (1971-1972). This interview is necessary to clarify the "WH flap" and to ascertain the Agency's response to the Bennett information contained in the summer, 1972 memoranda.

2. Documents

Any and all reports of contacts between [Mullen and Company Case Officer] and Mullen, Bennett, Hunt and anyone else at Mullen and Company from April 30, 1970 to January 1, 1974, including but not limited to logs, records, or memoranda reflecting such contact or the content of that contact. This information was requested during the February 4, 1974 Executive Session of [Mullen and Company Case Officer] along with data reflecting changes in the procedure for maintaining and/or making reports of contacts outside the Agency.

TSD SUPPORT OF HUNT

1. Interviews
    a. [TSD Technician #3]—TSD technician who developed the photographs for Hunt and blew up a particular photograph for [Deputy Chief, TSD]. Determination needed as to what was done with blow-up and whether it was subsequently used for briefing others at CIA.
    b. [TSD Technician #2]—TSD technician who purchased the Uher 5000 tape recorder and equipped it for Hunt's purposes.
    c. [Executive Assistant to DDP]—Consulted during initial stages of TSD support and relayed the TSD requirement to the DDP.

2. Documents
    a. "Mr. Edward" file—The file containing all memoranda and other materials relating to the CIA's TSD support of Hunt. This file has been requested, but has not been produced, despite the fact that the file was given to Director Colby after the Watergate break-in.
    b. All memoranda prepared by [Executive Officer to Director of Security], or any other CIA employee, regarding the TSD support of Hunt, including but not limited to all internal memoranda concerning the TSD support which is not contained in the "Mr. Edward" file.

PSYCHOLOGICAL PROFILE OF DANIEL ELLSBERG

1. Interviews
    a. [DMSS]—Director of Medical Services who supervised

and participated in the preparation of both Ellsberg profiles.
  b. [DDS]—The immediate supervisor of the Medical Services staff who prepared the psychological profile and who served as liaison between Director Helms and the psychiatric staff.
  c. Executive Assistant to DDS—Knowledgeable with regard to the psychological profile.
2. Documents
  a. All information received by the CIA from the FBI or the White House which served as raw data for preparation of both psychological profiles. Testimony has etsablished that this data contained FBI reports of interviews with female associates of Ellsberg, as well as a report of a purported telephone conversation between Ellsberg and another party.[1] The data should establish the extent of the CIA's admitted knowledge of the name of Ellsberg's psychiatrist as well as the CIA's knowledge of the activities of Hunt.
  b. All documents, reports, or memoranda relating in any way to the psychological profiles, including but not limited to the internal memoranda prepared by [Chief Psychiatrist], [DMSS], and [DDS] regarding the two psychological profiles. Testimony has established that memoranda for the record were written detailing the concerns about Hunt. Director Helms has testified that he has no knowledge of same.
  c. The so-called "psychological profile file", presently located in the office of the Director of Medical Services, CIA, containing all materials regarding the preparation of the psychological profiles. Note: This file was previously requested, as well as the materials described in parts (a.) and (b.) above. By letter dated March 8, 1974, Director Colby indicated that he would release this information to the oversight committees only.

TAPES

1. Log maintained by the Office of Security with reference to known tapings of which transcripts are thought to be available. This has been previously requested, but not furnished.
2. All logs, memoranda, or notations reflecting communications into or out of the Office of Security for the time period from June 16, 1972 to June 22, 1972. This information has been requested but it is available to the Senate Armed Services Committee only. Such informa-

1. Executive Session Testimony of [Chief Psychiatrist], March 7, 1974, (transcription not presently available).

tion is critical to any determination as to the chronology of Watergate notification and related actions.

3. Access to the five inch reel of tape labeled, "McCord Incident/18-19 June 1972," which was found in the Office of Security on March 1, 1974. It is not known what is contained in this tape, but its importance is obvious.

MISCELLANEOUS

1. Access to the special Watergate file formerly maintained in the Office of Security. This file was requested as early as mid-January, 1974, and its existence at that time was denied by legislative liaison. Sworn testimony has since confirmed existence of such a file, now under control of the Inspector General.

2. Any and all CIA files relating to the activities of E. Howard Hunt. This was requested in January of 1974 and was ognired by the Agency. We are aware of at least an executive registry file in which information on Hunt was placed in 1971 and suggest that this would be a good starting point for compliance with this request.

3. Any and all CIA files relating to G. Gordon Liddy during the time frame of January, 1970, to the present. When this request was made in January of 1974, the staff was advised that CIA information on Liddy was limited to sensitive briefings, the subject matter of which was beyond the purview of this Committee.[2] Files relative to these briefings need to be examined, particularly in light of the time period of same, i.e., August and September, 1971.

4. Any and all CIA files pertaining to attorney [name deleted at Agency request] and/or his law firm from the period January 1971 to the present. While the CIA has confirmed that [attorney] is a former case officer and that [potentially significant information deleted at agency request] during the period of time that [attorney] served as counsel for the Committee to Re-Elect the President,[3] contact reports and memoranda must be reviewed in raw form before a determination can be made as to the impact of the aforementioned facts.

5. Office calendars for Director Helms, General Cushman, and the Deputy Director of Plans for the time frame from January of 1971 through June of 1973. These

2. *See* CIA's response to this inquiry regarding Liddy, Supplemental Materials, Volume II, Tab 13.

3. *See* CIA's response to this inquiry regarding [attorney], CIA Supplemental Materials, Volume II, Tab 14; Volume IV (CIA Memorandum, June 28, 1973).

calendars have been previously requested and are critical
to a thorough investigative analysis of knowledge available
to these respective officials at the critical times.
These calendars have not been made available to this
staff for review.

6. All records pertaining to Agency financing of Egil
   Krogh's activities, as evidenced by sworn testimony before
   this Committee. Also, interviews of superiors of [Secretary
   to Chief, CIA Narcotics Control Group].[4]

7. Interviews of [Chief, EEAB], (former outplacement director),
   [Agency employee], [Agency employee], [former
   Agency employee], [former Agency employee] and attorney
   [former Agency employee], all of whom were
   either in the employ or were former employees of the
   Agency at the time they discussed Hunt operation activities
   (including entry operations) during 1971 and
   1972.

8. A review of all CIA activities (regardless of nature or
   degree of support) in Mexico during the calendar year,
   1971-1972. This information, which is relevant to an
   objective assessment of CIA's post-Watergate posture
   and pre-Watergate potential involvement, has been requested
   (to an extent consistent with national security)
   since February 1, 1974.[5]

9. The "Pennington File," which was previously requested
   and made available only to the House Armed Services
   Oversight Committee. This file contains memoranda and
   other documents dealing with the activities of the CIA
   operative, Pennington, who was alleged to have participated
   in the burning of documents in the McCord
   home after the Watergate break-in. This file also contains
   data regarding the "domestic activities" of Pennington,
   and the CIA has made it known that there are "gaps"
   in this file during certain relevant time periods.

10. At the conclusion of his Executive Session on Friday,
    March 8, 1974, Ambassador Helms testified concerning
    an individual in a peculiar position to know the activities
    of both the Agency and the FBI. While Helms knew of
    no Watergate information in this individual's possession,
    other evidence suggests the contrary. Consideration should
    be given to interviewing this individual who has already
    commenced preparation of a Watergate-related memorandum
    in response to a previous request by the staff.[6]

4. See Executive Session Testimony of [Secretary to Chief, CIA Narcotics
Control Group], March 2, 1974, (transcription not presently available).
5. The CIA, through its legislative liaison, has confirmed that Mexico is
an "important country" to the CIA, but has refused to provide any other
information regarding CIA Mexican activities during the 1971-72 time period.
6. See CIA Supplemental Material, Volume II, Tab 18.

11. Michael Mastrovito of the Secret Service should be interviewed concerning his Agency communications on June 17, 1972. Agency documents indicate that Mastrovito agreed to downplay McCord's Agency employment; that Mastrovito was being pressured for information by a Democratic state chairman; and that Mastrovito was advised by the CIA that the Agency was concerned with McCord's emotional stability prior to his retirement.[7]

7. *See* CIA cable traffic shortly after the Watergate break-in, CIA Supplemental Material, Volume VI.

INDEX

765